MEANING IN MIND
Fodor and His Critics

B

PHILOSOPHERS AND THEIR CRITICS

General Editor: *Ernest Lepore*

Philosophy is an interactive enterprise. Much of it is carried out in dialogue as theories and ideas are presented and subsequently refined in the crucible of close scrutiny. The purpose of this series is to reconstruct this vital interplay among thinkers. Each book consists of a contemporary assessment of an important living philosopher's work. A collection of essays written by an interdisciplinary group of critics addressing the substantial theses of the philosopher's corpus opens each volume. In the last section the philosopher responds to his critics, clarifies crucial points of the discussion, or updates his or her doctrines.

MEANING IN MIND
Fodor and his Critics

Edited by
Barry Loewer and Georges Rey

BLACKWELL
Oxford UK & Cambridge MA

First published 1991
First published in paperback 1993

Blackwell Publishers
238 Main Street, Suite 501
Cambridge, Massachusetts 02142, USA
108 Cowley Road, Oxford, OX4 IJF, UK

Library of Congress Cataloging in Publication Data
Meaning in mind: Fodor and his critics/edited by Barry Loewer and Georges
Rey.
p.   cm.
Includes bibliographical references and index.
ISBN 0-631-17103-7 – ISBN 0-631-187014 (pbk.)
1. Fodor, Jerry A.   2. Philosophy of mind--History--20th century.   3. Content
(Psychology)--History--20th century.   4. Semantics (Philosophy)--History--20th
century.   5. Intentionality (Philosophy)--History--20th century.   I. Loewer, Barry.
II. Rey, Georges.
B945.F634M4   1991
128'.2'092--dc20   90-46105
                                                                                           CIP

British Library Cataloguing in Publication Data
A CIP catalogue record for this book is available from the British Library.

Typeset in Plantin on 9.5/11pt
by Times Graphics, Singapore
Printed in Great Britain by T.J. Press Ltd, Padstow, Cornwall

To Jerry Fodor, without whom

Jerry Fodor and his Granny

Contents

Contributors

LOUISE ANTONY is an Associate Professor of Philosophy at North Carolina State University at Raleigh. She is the author of articles in action theory and philosophy of language, and editor (with Charlotte Witt) of *Feminism and Reason.*

LYNNE RUDDER BAKER is a Professor of Philosophy at Middlebury College and at the University of Massachusetts at Amherst. She is the author of *Saving Belief* and articles in the philosophy of psychology.

NED BLOCK is a Professor of Philosophy at the Massachusetts Institute of Technology. He is the editor of *Readings in the Philosophy of Psychology* (two volumes) and of *Imagery,* as well as the author of articles in the philosophy of mind and psychology.

PAUL A. BOGHOSSIAN is an Associate Professor of Philosophy at the University of Michigan at Ann Arbor. He is the author of articles in the metaphysics and epistemology of mind and language.

DANIEL C. DENNETT is a Professor of Philosophy and director of the Center for Cognitive Studies at Tufts University. Among his publications are *Content and Consciousness, Brainstorms, Elbow Room,* and *The Intentional Stance,* and (with Douglas Hofstadter) *The Mind's I.*

MICHAEL DEVITT is a Professor of Philosophy at the University of Maryland at College Park. He is the author of articles in the philosophy of language, and of *Designation, Realism and Truth,* and (with Kim Sterelny) *Language and Reality.*

DAVID ISRAEL is a research scientist at SRI International and the Center for the Study of Language and Information at Stanford University. He has written articles on philosophical issues in artificial intelligence.

JOSEPH LEVINE is an Associate Professor of Philosophy at North Carolina State University at Raleigh. He is the author of articles in the philosophy of mind.

BRIAN LOAR is a Professor of Philosophy at the University of Southern California. He is the author of *Mind and Meaning* and of articles in the philosophy of mind and language.

BARRY LOEWER is a Professor of Philosophy at Rutgers University. He is an author of articles in the philosophy of science and philosophy of psychology.

ROBERT J. MATTHEWS is a Professor of Philosophy at Rutgers University. He has published articles in the philosophy of psychology and in theoretical psycholinguistics.

RUTH GARRETT MILLIKAN is a Professor of Philosophy at the University of Connecticut at Storrs. She is the author of *Language, Thought and Other Biological Categories.*

JOHN PERRY is a Professor of Philosophy at Stanford University. He is the author of articles in the philosophy of mind and the philosophy of language, as well as of (with Jon Barwise) *Situations and Attitudes.*

GEORGES REY is an Associate Professor of Philosophy at the University of Maryland at College Park. He is the author of articles in the philosophy of mind and moral psychology.

STEPHEN SCHIFFER is a Professor of Philosophy at the Graduate Center of the City University of New York. He is the author of *Meaning, Remnants of Meaning,* and of articles in the philosophy of language and mind.

PAUL SMOLENSKY is an Associate Professor of Computer Science at the University of Colorado at Boulder. He is the author of articles on connectionism and other techniques in artificial intelligence.

ROBERT STALNAKER is a Professor of Philosophy at the Massachusetts Institute of Technology. He has published articles in philosophy of language, and modal logic, and is the author of *Inquiry.*

STEPHEN P. STICH is a Professor of Philosophy at Rutgers University. He has written articles in the philosophy of language and the philosophy of psychology, and is the author of *From Folk Psychology to Cognitive Science,* and of *The Fragmentation of Reason.*

Editors' Introduction

In a tribute to Jerry Fodor some years ago,[1] Daniel Dennett observed that

> most philosophers are like old beds: you jump on them and sink deep into qualifications, revisions, addenda. But Fodor is like a trampoline: you jump on him and he springs back, presenting claims twice as trenchant and outrageous. If some of us can see further, it's from jumping on Jerry.

Leaving open the question of just who is seeing further, it was in part with this observation in mind that the present volume was conceived. It contains 14 contributions by philosophers and cognitive scientists who jump up and down on one or another of Fodor's "outrageous" claims.[2] His replies exhibit his usual resilience. The exchanges are, however, but brief episodes in various debates that have been raging and will doubtless persist for decades. In this introduction we want to indicate something of the content and context of these debates as well as some of the rich and systematic structure of Fodor's views.

Even in the eyes of many of his critics, Fodor is widely regarded as the most important philosopher of psychology of his generation. With Noam Chomsky at MIT in the 1960s he mounted a strenuous attack on the behaviorism that then dominated psychology and most philosophy of mind, and, since then, he has articulated and defended in considerable richness and detail a computational theory of intentional causation that is central to the emerging cognitive sciences. This theory provides a framework both for the resolution of many traditional problems in the philosophy of mind and language, and for actual psychological research and experimentation, some of which Fodor has himself also pursued in the areas of modularity and natural language processing.[3] Although there is certainly for Fodor no real distinction between psychology and its philosophy, in order to keep the present volume within manageable bounds, we have restricted it primarily to the more philosophical topics.

I Fodor's Commitments

Fodor's central commitment in the philosophy of psychology is to *the primacy of nomic empirical explanation*: questions about the nature of mental phenomena are to be addressed primarily from the point of view of an empirical scientific psychology. The more traditional concerns of philosophy of mind with *a priori* epistemology and metaphysics Fodor regards as secondary. Questions like "What is a belief or a desire?" or "What is the relation between a belief and a neural state?" or "Are there propositions as objects of belief?" are not to be settled in the first instance by analysis of concepts or of the ordinary use of words, but by determining precisely what the best explanatory theories in psychology require.[4] Fodor does, however, take explanation in psychology to be committed, as a matter of empirical fact, to a number of fairly strong theses. These are (a) physicalism, (b) intentional[5] realism, and (c) the computational/representational theory of thought. We will consider each in turn.

Physicalism

Physicalism is the view that all genuine phenomena (properties, events, states, processes, laws, causal relations) supervene on physical phenomena.[6] Fodor's version of this doctrine involves three basic commitments: (1) all events (and objects) are identical to or composed of physical events, (2) for every exemplified property there are physical conditions which are sufficient and explanatory of the exemplification of that property, (3) all basic laws are laws of physics. There is always a reasonable worry here about just what consitutes the "physical": the phenomena cited in *present* physics? Some as yet unspecified future, ideal physics? We think the most reasonable way to understand the commitment here is simply as a requirement that the laws and other truths of any special science supervene in an explanatory way upon the laws of the most general theory of the world, whatever it turns out to be – adding that, as a matter of fact, physics seems to present the best candidate for that theory that anyone has yet conceived. So understood, physicalism in effect comes to the plausible claim that the laws of a special science like psychology are not to be taken as ultimate, but need in turn to be shown to depend upon underlying physical laws. As Fodor (1987d:97) puts it,

> [when] the physicists ... complete the catalogue ... of the ultimate irreducible properties of things, ... the likes of *spin*, *charm*, and *charge*, will perhaps appear on [it], but *aboutness* surely won't; intentionality simply doesn't go that deep.

Despite its vagueness, a commitment to physicalism has proven extremely fruitful in providing an explanatory strategy in the special sciences. Properties introduced in a special science like biology are constrained by the existence of more basic, ultimately physical properties in terms of which their exemplifications can be explained. Early geneticists, for example, were constrained by a presumption that there existed more basic biological properties and entities in terms of which a genotype would be explained, which presumption led to the discovery of DNA. Moreover, the laws introduced in a special science are constrained by the existence of more basic physical processes that implement such laws. Thus physicalists are skeptical of telepathy insofar as they have no reason to suppose that there are physical processes capable of implementing alleged telepathic phenomena.

Notoriously, however, psychology has had trouble complying with these constraints. Such properties as rationality, intentionality, and consciousness, and the processes involving them, have persistently resisted incorporation into physical theory. Part of Fodor's aim is to provide physicalistically acceptable accounts of at least the first two of these properties, and particularly of the associated process of *thought*.

Fodor's version of physicalism is, however, considerably weaker than many traditional versions. In particular, it is non-reductive: there is no requirement that there be bi-conditional bridge laws linking the phenomena of some special science to the underlying phenomena of physics. Fodor views "special" sciences in general as searching for causal explanatory laws at a level appropriate to their subject matter, developing relatively autonomously from deeper theories whose regularities they may cross-classify.[7] In the case at hand psychology may classify events as belonging to the same psychological type that differ in their neurophysiological properties, and neurophysiology might classify events belonging to the same neurological type that differ in their psychological properties. One reason to suppose this to be true, originally emphasized by Putnam (1960) in his discussion of computers, is the "multi-realizability" of a program by an indefinite variety of physical processes: programs and other abstract structures defined in terms of functional roles may be "realized" in an indefinite variety of ways by different physical arrangements.[8] If this is true, then it is extremely implausible that one would learn a great deal in detail about *the mind* from a neurological study of *the brain*, any more than one would learn very much about an ingenious computer program from a study of the electrical circuitry of the computer that might run it, or much about Shakespeare's plays by studying the chemical composition of the ink in which they were written.[9]

A second way in which Fodor's physicalism differs from more traditional versions is in his recognition of the ineliminable role of *ceteris paribus* clauses in specifying the laws of the special sciences. Fodor doesn't regard such clauses as short for some description of appropriate boundary conditions that will be spelled out once the science matures. Rather, they are a way of indicating that apparent exceptions to the law are to be explained by interference from other quarters that may not be (and usually are not) specifiable within the terms of the law itself.[10] A *ceteris paribus* qualified law is thus not vacuous, even though the theorist may not, even in principle, be able to specifiy explicitly the conditions under which the law is true.[11]

In view of these differences between Fodor's and the traditional versions of physicalism, we will sometimes refer to Fodor's view as "naturalism," and to the problem of showing how a mental phenomenon explanatorily supervenes on (without being strictly reducible to) physics, as the problem of "naturalizing" that phenomenon.

Scientific Intentional Realism

Belief in physicalism generally is of piece with a rejection of Cartesian dualism; and, because dualism has been traditionally associated with any realistic theory of the mind, this rejection has led many philosophers to view such theories with suspicion. Thus, Ryle (1949) railed against "the ghost in the machine," Wittgenstein (1953:§308) against believing in some "yet uncomprehended process in [a] yet unexplored medium," and Quine (1960) argued for an "indeterminacy of translation," for relegating mental talk to a "second-grade status," a "dramatic idiom" applied with "charity," but lacking any serious factual or scientific status.[12] This tradition persists more recently in the instrumentalist proposals of

Dennett's (1971, 1987) "intentional stance," and the eliminativist proposals of Rorty (1979), P. M. Churchland (1981), P. S. Churchland (1986), and Stich (1983).

Fodor stands squarely against this tradition. He insists not only upon *intentional realism* – the view that there really are propositional attitude states with genuine intentional properties that are causally implicated in the production of behavior – but upon *scientific* intentional realism – or the further thesis that a scientifically adequate psychology will contain laws that quantify over intentional phenomena in intentional terms. Full-fledged beliefs and desires (or states very like them) are to figure in the best explanation of human and much higher animal behavior.

Fodor is particularly impressed by the difficulty of accounting for the sensitivity of human beings to indefinitely many non-local, non-physical properties: not only, as Chomsky (1965, 1968) has emphasized, to highly *abstract* grammatical properties, like being a morpheme, a noun phrase, or a grammatical sentence; but also to *arbitrary non-physical* or *non-local* properties, such as being a Rembrandt portrait, being granny's favorite wine glass, being a crumpled shirt, being a survivor of the battle of Waterloo, being a collapsing star. These sensitivities are particularly impressive given that they seem to be *productive* and *systematic*: people seem capable of discriminating a potentially infinite class of distinct stimuli of increasing logical complexity (productivity); and anyone capable of discriminating one logical form is capable of discriminating logical permutations of it: e.g., one can discriminate that aRb iff one can discriminate that bRa; if one can discriminate something of the form "if p then q" then one can discriminate "if q then p" (systematicity).[13] It is difficult to see how any physical mechanism could be sensitive in these ways to such an extraordinary *range* of arbitrary properties of the world without exploiting internal processes of logical combination, inference, and hypothesis confirmation that essentially involve intentional properties.

A good deal of Fodor's work has been devoted to showing that no non-mentalistic account – i.e., no account that doesn't assume intentional realism – can explain these phenomena. Thus he has argued at length that purely physicalist, behaviorist, Gibsonian, syntactic, and eliminative connectionist accounts of behavior are either vacuous or empirically inadequate.[14] He argues that the only theory that stands a chance of succeeding is one that posits mental states like the familiar "propositional attitudes" with which the folk routinely explain each other's behavior, the loose theory that has come to be called "folk psychology." Scientific intentional realism, then, is simply a way of taking folk psychology seriously as the beginnings of a serious scientific psychology.[15]

Not that the folk are always right about the mind. Indeed, many of the specific terms they employ – "learning," "memory," perhaps even "belief" and "desire" – may well turn out to be theoretically inadequate.[16] Fodor only presumes that, whatever the particular kinds of states invoked by an ultimate psychology, they will display certain familiar and troublesome properties: viz., as some or other species of propositional attitude, they will be intentional, or, more generally, semantically valuable (referential; capable of being true or false); as parts of a systematic, occasionally rational and potentially infinite system of representation, they need to be logically structured; and, as ultimately explanatory of action, they need to be causally efficacious. Indeed, they need to be causally efficacious by virtue of their logical structure; e.g., it is only because the thought [that A seems to be the best way to get B] has *that* structure that it causally combines with the agent's desire to get B and so produces performance of action A; B forms the crucial link between the two thoughts. One of the chief problems Fodor addresses is the identification of states that could have all these properties.

Fodor does remain agnostic about one set of states that are also of great importance to the folk, and that have been the object of traditional philosophical discussion: the so-called "qualitative states" – states of feelings, sensations, consciousness – about which one can wonder "what it's like." His interest is explanation, not introspection, and, at least since Freud, it has been an open possibility that a great many mental states could be causally explanatory without being introspectible. At any rate, Fodor makes no assumption that the mental states defined by their roles in the above framework are conscious, and for the most part does not address the problems that conscious states raise.[17]

It is worth noting that Fodor's intentional realism is of a piece with his realism about science generally.[18] He takes a realist stance not only towards theoretical entities postulated by most scientific theories, but also towards properties and laws even of the special sciences (thus, "being a bacterium" and "being a metabolic system" express real properties that enter into biological laws, although presumably "being a bacterium or a metabolic system" does not). These entities, properties and laws obtain independently of us, and the only chance we have of learning about them, in either the natural or the social and psychological sciences, is by exploiting standard scientific methodology.

The Computational/Representational Theory of Thought (CRTT)

Once these background issues of physicalism and intentional realism are settled, there is the question of how they can both be true. The question arises because it has seemed to many philosophers that scientific intentional realism is incompatible with physicalism. Specifically, one may worry whether propositional attitudes can be physicalistically explicated and whether the putative laws of intentional psychology are physicalistically implementable. The former worry arises because propositional attitudes possess features like *intentionality* that are resistent to physical explication. The second worry arises because putative psychological laws apparently relate to intentional states in ways that correlate with their *rational* (e.g., logical, evidential) relations and many philosophers (e.g., Descartes (1637/1973)) have found it hard to understand how any natural processes can do that.

Fodor's answer to these worries involves three parts: the first is a thesis about the nature of propositional attitudes: "the Representational Theory of Thought" (RTT); the second is a thesis about the nature of mental processes: "the Computational Theory of Thought" (CTT); and the third is a thesis about the naturalistic basis of intentionality: "the Asymmetric Dependency Theory of Meaning." We will discuss the first two theories in this section, returning to the third in the context of theories of meaning generally in section III.

We observed that Fodor's argument for intentional realism turned on the need to postulate semantically valuable, logically structured, causally efficacious states in order to explain human behavior. What sorts of physical states might these be?

Fodor argues that the only candidates available for the first two properties are semantically valuable *sentences*. He thus proposes (RTT), according to which intentional states involve relations to sentential representations in what he calls "a language of thought," a special, relatively unambiguous formal language often referred to as "Mentalese."[19] Different propositional attitudes involve different relations to sentences in this language. Thus, to believe or desire that one owns a crumpled shirt is to bear the *believe* or *desire* relation to a Mentalese sentence which means that one owns a crumpled shirt.[20] And the semantic properties of beliefs, desires, and other intentional states are inherited from the semantic properties of their constituent Mentalese expressions: an agent's belief that one owns a crumpled shirt is *about* shirts because she's appropriately related to a symbol, e.g. "Shirt," that's about shirts.

Among other virtues, (RTT) promises an illuminating account of the so-called "Frege puzzles," or the notorious "fine-grainedness" of the attitudes: believing Sam Clemens is bald is different from believing that Mark Twain is; thinking London is beautiful is different from thinking Londres is; wondering whether a fortnight is two weeks is different from wondering whether a fortnight is a fortnight; thinking that 2 + 2 = 4 is different from thinking that 3 + 3 = 6 or that arithmetic is incomplete.[21] If belief is conceived of as a *dyadic* relation between a thinker and a proposition, then, on most of the current theories of propositions (e.g., as functions from possible worlds to truth values, or structured entities composed of individuals and properties), the property of believing that Sam Clemens is bald is identical to the property of believing that Mark Twain is bald. (RTT) offers the possibility of conceiving of belief as (at least) a *triadic* relation of a thinker, a proposition, and a Mentalese sentence. Thus, (RTT), while still allowing for attitudes classified by propositions, also permits classifying them by the different representations with which an agent expresses them (Fodor, 1978d, 1990a).

Finally, of course, the productivity and systematicity of thought can be explained by the productivity and systematicity of Mentalese: if a mental agent has a propositional attitude by virtue of standing in a certain relation to sentences in a language of thought, then it is plausible to assume that that relation provides a basis for the agent's command of a potential infinitude of expressions in that language, and for the ability to permute the expressions in standard logical ways.

Indeed, to a very first approximation, Mentalese might be thought of as a logical language of the sort introduced in symbolic logic texts for the purpose of actually systematizing the potential infinity of possible sentences and theorems.[22] Ordinarily, this language is manipulated by people consciously following explicit rules that are defined over the sentences' shapes (or "form"). However, these rules could be *obeyed* not by virtue of someone representing and following them, but as a result of the causal organization of the brain, much in the way a computer can obey rules by virtue of the causal organization of its hardware.[23]

This last analogy is no mere metaphor. Recall that an important problem for intentional realism is to offer an account of how intentional states can be *causally related* to each other, to the world, and to behavior in ways that are sensitive to their intentional content. Cartesian dualists simply postulate special causal powers of intentional states that are not derivable from an underlying physical mechanism, a postulation that would, of course, be incompatible with physicalism. In Fodor's view, the crucial step towards the solution of this problem was made by Alan

Turing. He proposed a systematic conception of computation (a "Turing Machine") whereby any rational computation could be defined by simple operations on syntactically structured representations.[24] Just as addition can be characterized in terms of computational operations defined over numerals, valid (truth preserving) operations can be characterized in terms of computations defined over sentences. Moreover, as the modern computer industry reveals, Turing computations can be implemented on actual, physical machines. The hypothesis that intentional mental processes are physically implemented computations over representations is called "the computational theory of thought" (CTT).

Fodor uses (CTT) to supplement (RTT), identifying the *propositional* attitude relations (believes, desires, etc.) presupposed in (RTT) with the *computational* relations afforded by (CTT). Different propositional attitude relations correspond to different computational relations. For example, to believe that p is for a sentence of Mentalese that means [p] to be accessible to *one* set of computations, where to desire, to hope, to expect that p is for the same sentence (with that meaning) to be accessible to *other* sets of them. It is useful (but not essential) to think of such relations as involving the presence of representations in particular *addresses* that are accessible to some and not other operations. Hence one reads of sentences being stored in a "belief box," or a "volition box," all of which, understood literally, is patent nonsense in the case of the brain, but provides a graphic way of discussing what are otherwise very abstract computational relations.[25]

(CRTT) is also intended to provide an account of how intentional laws are implemented at a more basic level. For example, suppose it were an intentional law that, within a certain period of time, if a person notices that p and notices that if p then q, then *ceteris paribus* she will notice that q. According to (CRTT), this law would be implemented by computations that actually derive Mentalese correlates of "q" from correlates of "p" and "if p then q," using standard computational procedures. Similar accounts would presumably be available for induction, abduction, and practical reasoning, exploiting the resources of formal theories of inductive logic, statistics, and decision theory (Fodor, 1975a:28–33).

A very rough version of (CRTT) might apply to human beings as follows: there are sensory modules (e.g., visual and auditory systems) that transduce ambient energy forms into electrical signals that in turn produce structured sentences as input to a central cognitive system (perception). This central system selects certain sentences from a pre-established ("innate") set, tests their deductive consequences against this input for a "best fit," and produces as output those sentences that pass that test above threshold (belief). These sentences in turn may be the input to a decision making system in which – on the basis of that input, pre-established preferences, and pre-established utility functions – a course of action is determined, i.e. a basic act-description is selected (intention). Finally, the selection of a basic act-description causes a basic act satisfying that description to be performed (action).

II Relevant and Irrelevant Objections

Given misunderstandings of Fodor's claims that are abroad, it is important to be clear about what (CRTT) is *not* committed to, and the kinds of arguments Fodor takes to be germane to his views.

(1)   Fodor's (1975a, 1987d) main argument for (CRTT) is that it is presupposed by the best explanations currently available in psychology of such phenomena as decision making, concept learning, perception, and the productivity and systematicity of language. (CRTT) is not intended to be a necessary truth, or one knowable *a priori*; nor is it meant to be establishable by introspection or reflection on ordinary ascriptions of propositional attitudes. It is most decidedly *not* committed to any claims about the character of human phenomenology, which may well seem (as to many of us it does seem) not the least bit sentential or propositional. As should be clear from Fodor's (1975a:174–94) discussion of "mental imagery," even the most intense eidetic imagery and visual hallucination are compatible with (CRTT). (CRTT) will stand or fall only by careful consideration of its explanatory power, a consideration that is only indirectly touched by *a priori* or introspective reflections.

It may well turn out that there is a better explanation. Dennett (1987), Cummins (1986, 1989) and Matthews (1988 and in his contribution) challenge (CRTT) directly, claiming that psychology does not require explicit representations of content. Schiffer (1987a and in his contribution) tries to show how productivity and systematicity could be otherwise explained. And Smolensky (1988a and in his contribution) argues that recent "connectionist" models in computer science provide such a better theory of the mind, one that is not susceptible to the practical intractabilities and "hard constraints" of classical Von Neumann models like Fodor's.

(2)   As something of an historical accident: Fodor presented the (CRTT) hypothesis in the same book in which he also defended a highly controversial thesis about *the innateness of all concepts*. That thesis originally stirred more controversy than did (CRTT) itself, much of which was addressed in Fodor (1981c). But that thesis is independent of (CRTT), depending as it crucially does upon further claims about the nature of concepts, definitions, and learning.[26] So arguments against nativism in no way tell against (CRTT). This, however, is not an issue that any of the contributors below addresses.

(3)   Fodor's proposal bears only a very indirect relation to most current work in artificial intelligence, almost none of which ever appears in his discussions. This is largely because much of the existing work in artificial intelligence, partly under the influence of the behavioristic "Turing Test,"[27] is aimed at replicating intelligent *behavior*. Such replication is neither necessary nor sufficient for a computational understanding of the mind.[28] As discussed above, (CRTT), as a species of functionalism, is concerned with the characterization of *sub-systems* of the mind in considerable abstraction from actual behavior. For Fodor, the right way to produce artificial intelligence would be, first, to construct theories about human cognitive *competencies* – in perception, scientific reasoning, decision making, language comprehension, and production. Only then should an attempt be made to integrate these systems into a system that might conceivably behave with anything like the sophistication of human beings in a natural environment.[29]

(4)   It could seem that, since (CRTT) claims that casual connections between intentional states are implemented by purely formal computational processes, there is no room within (CRTT) for genuine intentional causation. Fodor, however, thinks that on a proper understanding of causation, both intentional and computational causal claims are compatible. In Fodor (1989b), he defines a

property P as being causally relevant in a particular causal transaction, c causing e, just in case c is P and e is Q, and there is a law of the form "*ceteris paribus*, Ps cause Qs" (and *ceteris* are indeed *paribus*). The causal relevance of intentional properties depends, therefore, merely on there being intentional causal laws. And, of course, Fodor thinks that there are such laws. But this is compatible with there *also* being laws of computation. Indeed, by (CRTT), when a pair of events instantiate an intentional law then they also instantiate a computational one – but possibly a *different* one for each *different* instantiation. Even though the mechanisms are computational, one needs the *intentional* law to capture the generality of many different computations subserving one intentional function, just as one needs *computational* laws to capture the generality of many different *physical* states subserving one computational function. In this way Fodor aims to "have it both ways," maintaining both that intentional properties are causally relevant and that computational psychology provides the underlying account of how intentional laws are implemented. Whether or not this is a viable position is discussed in the papers by Devitt and Stich. We will return in a moment to the implications it has for a theory of meaning.

(5) Some philosophers seem to think that Fodor presents (CRTT) as a theory of meaning.[30] It is true that Fodor expects that the meanings of public language sentences (as of other public representations) will be accounted for along lines suggested by Grice (1957), in terms of their expressions of propositional attitudes, which involve Mentalese sentences. Thus, for example, the meaning of the French "Les ormes sont arbres" is presumably inherited from the meaning of some Mentalese sentence. In this way Mentalese has a role to play in a theory of meaning for non-mental representations. But Fodor clearly does *not* think that this sort of story would suffice for the meaning of the mental representations themselves. Indeed, as will become apparent in the next section, in the 15 years since the publication of *The Language of Thought*, Fodor has proposed several theories addressed to what he takes to be the serious problem of determining the content of Mentalese expressions. The issues involved are complicated, since Fodor has also been struggling with the issue of exactly what role the meanings of Mentalese sentences play in psychological explanations and in psychological causation. We will sort through some of these issues in the next section.

(6) Although (CRTT) is not presented as a theory of meaning, Fodor does think it has important implications for the theory of meaning for Mentalese, a result of a certain tension between the component theses (RTT) and (CTT). In keeping with (CTT), Fodor (1981) proposes a "methodological solipsism" as a "research strategy in cognitive psychology." He takes this to be a consequence of what he calls a "formality condition" that must be observed in psychological explanation: mental states have their efficacy as a consequence of the formal character of their tokens. At the same time, in keeping with (RTT), intentional properties of mental representations are essential to their role in causal explanation. Consequently, intentional properties averted to in psychological explanation must supervene on formal properties. But he has also argued that ordinary content properties ("broad content" properties) do *not* so supervene. It seems to follow that intentional psychology requires a notion of "narrow content" that supervenes on formal and/or computational properties. Whether

he can in this way, too, "have it both ways," maintaining both a formality condition and a *narrow content psychology* is discussed by Devitt, Stich, and Perry and Israel in their contributions, which the reader should consult for the multitude of distinctions – between "formality," "syntax," and various construals of "narrow content" (to some of which we'll return below – that may be important here.

Indeed, the theory of meaning for Mentalese has become the central issue over which Fodor and his leading critics have been arguing heatedly for at least the last six years. For this reason, it is the main topic of the present volume. In the remainder of this introduction, we will attempt to sketch some of the background and presuppositions to that specific debate.

III   Theories of Meaning

The Austrian philosopher Franz Brentano (1838–1917) is widely credited with having raised a problem with which twentieth-century philosophy has been grappling ever since: how can the fact that a propositional attitude and/or representation is *about* something be explained in terms of natural science? If propositional attitudes are relations to semantically evaluable Mentalese sentences, then, as a physicalist, Fodor must find a way of naturalizing the semantics of Mentalese. Some philosophers are skeptical that this is possible, and this has led some of them (e.g., Quine (1960); Paul Churchland (1981)) to conclude that there are no semantic properties at all, and others to draw the more cautious conclusion that intentional properties simply do not appear in scientific laws. The least that one might say is that without a naturalistic account of intentionality we would be left with an explanatory deficit. We wouldn't know how intentionality is the result of more basic naturalistic processes in the way that we know, for example, how photo-synthesis emerges from simpler chemical processes. Since Fodor thinks that there are intentional properties and that they figure in laws, he has accepted the challenge of the intentional skeptic to provide naturalistic sufficient conditions for Mentalese semantics.

Intentions

A natural answer to the question how it is that a natural language symbol has content is that it does so by virtue of the intentions of its users. This answer was developed in some ingenious detail by Grice (1957), Lewis (1969), and Stephen Schiffer (1972). But whatever may be the case for public languages, this cannot be an adequate account for Mentalese. Mentalese is not a natural "public" language, used by intentional agents to communicate with one another.[31] Moreover, even if it were, Grice's theory cannot provide a satisfactory naturalization since it derives the intentionality of some representations from the intentionality of further propositional attitudes whose intentionality is left unexplained.

Someone might think that the grounding of meanings in intentions is essential to a computational model, since computers have semantics only by virtue of the intentions of their users. In terms of Haugeland's (1981) distinction between "original" and "derived" intentionality, one might insist that the intentionality of computers can only be derived. But, of course, anyone who subscribes to (CRTT) and takes human intentionality to be original would find this argument question-begging, so we won't pursue it here.[32]

Alternatively, one could try to regard all intentionality as derived. This would seem to be the force of Dennett's (1970, 1987) influential view that the propositional attitudes of a person (or other object) are entirely relative to the stance of an interpreter, which would seem to entail that a person has a propositional attitude iff an interpreter can successfully attribute that attitude to her (where success might be measured, for example, in terms of accuracy of prediction and systematization of behavior). Aside from the implausibility of relativizing propositional attitudes to interpreters (does Bush have one belief relative to Reagan and a different one relative to Quayle?), this proposal cannot be an adequate solution to the naturalization problem for much the same reason that Grice's cannot. An interpreter's taking a stance and attributing an attitude from that stance are, after all, themselves intentional attitudes. Perhaps for this reason, advocates of this view are frequently taken to be attempting not to naturalize intentionality but to demote it to a second-grade status (as in Quine (1960) and Dennett (1971)). Insofar as one is an intentional realist, not all intentionality can be derived, and so we need to look elsewhere for an account of intentionality grounded in naturalistic processes.

Internalist semantics

If the semantics of thought is not dependent upon the intentions of an external agent, a natural place to look for original intentionality is within the mind or brain itself. A number of proposals for such an internalist semantics have been made.

(a) *Images*

Historically, an appealing idea has been that mental representations are images.[33] The idea is that imagistic representation is somehow unproblematic: an image represents what it resembles. Thus a green triangle image is supposed to represent a green triangle because it resembles one. As appealing as this idea has been, it is obvious that it won't get us very far with the naturalization project. No one expects to find entities that are actually triangular and green in the brains of people who think about green triangles. Perhaps talk of resemblance is just a way of talking about a mapping from the neural features of events to real-world properties, but then the naturalization problem is the problem of specifying why one mapping rather than another provides the correct interpretation. In any case, even if some mental representations can be usefully thought of as images, it is extremely implausible that *all* (or even a significant proportion of) Mentalese representations can be. So far as anyone has ever proposed, images don't combine to produce *logically complex* images: what image represents that there are *no* green triangles, or that if someone loves everyone then everyone is loved by someone? Sentences seem to be the only physically realizable objects that have this expressive potential.[34]

(b) Conceptual Role

One kind of proposal that naturally emerges both from functionalist accounts of mental states and from Wittgenstein's (1953) dictum "the meaning of a word is its use" is that the meaning of a Mentalese expression is determined by its conceptual role.[35] There are various versions of "conceptual role semantics" in the field (e.g., Field (1978), Loar (1981), LePore and Loewer (1987), Block (1986)). The version that Fodor discusses characterizes an expression's conceptual role in terms of the totality of its evidentiary and other logical connections to other expressions. Fodor calls these connections "epistemic liaisons." The notion of an epistemic liaison must, of course, be spelled out naturalistically, presumably in terms of causal relations.

Conceptual role theories are most plausible for the logical connectives. For example, a certain expression "#" means "and" in virtue of the fact that thinking "P#Q" tends to cause thinking P and thinking Q, which in turn tends to cause thinking "P#Q". But no one has actually constructed an adequate conceptual role theory that specifies exactly how conceptual role in general determines meaning in a way that is applicable across different individuals. Fodor is skeptical that any such account is possible.[36] Indeed, he thinks that a conceptual role theory is actually at odds with scientific intentional realism. His reason for the latter stems from the *holism* of epistemic liaisons, and so of conceptual role: as Quine (1953:41) emphasized in his compelling remarks about confirmation, the epistemic liaisons of any expression are potentially entangled in the liaisons of every other in such a way that our beliefs about the world "confront the tribunal of sense experience not individually but only as a corporate body." In Fodor's view this holism leads to a dilemma. Either every difference in conceptual role makes for a difference of meaning, or only certain ones do. If the former, then it would be a cosmic coincidence if two people ever shared a concept, and serious generalization in psychology would be impossible: there would be no generalizations of the sort "If anyone thinks/desires Fa, then . . ." which apply to more than a single individual. This, in Fodor's view, is tantamount to the defeat of intentional realism.[37]

If only certain differences in conceptual role make a difference to meaning, then two individuals could share a concept while differing in their other beliefs. However, so distinguishing some subset of the totality of a term's liaisons would, according to Fodor, entail an analytic-synthetic distinction, a distinction widely thought to have been discredited by Quine (1953, 1956b).[38] There seems to be no non-circular way to draw the distinction, and – a problem of particular significance for psychology – people who, we have every reason to suppose, *possess* a concept seem nevertheless capable of entertaining arbitrary beliefs involving it. With a little imagination, it seems always possible to construct a story whereby someone (particularly a philosopher) arrives at an arbitrary belief, or breaks an arbitrary epistemic liaison, by having a sufficiently bizarre theory about the world. Thus, some creationists seem to be denying that humans are animals, some nominalists that numbers are abstract, and some idealists that tables are material objects.[39] For most concepts there would seem to be no epistemic liaison so secure that someone couldn't break it and yet still be competent with the concept.

Still another problem with any internalist theory emerges from considerations about the apparent context dependency of meaning. In a series of highly influential papers in the 1970s, Kripke (1972/1980), Putnam (1975a), and Burge (1979) drew attention to the ways in which the meanings of many terms in natural language depend crucially upon the environment of the speaker. Putnam imagined that far away in some other solar system there was a planet, "Twin-Earth," that was identical in every "intrinsic" respect to the earth, except that wherever on the earth there was H_2O, on Twin-Earth there was a very different chemical compound, XYZ, which, however, had all the same superficial characteristics of H_2O (i.e., it was odorless, tasteless, transparent, filled the seas and drinking glasses, etc.). He argued that, according to present usage of English, there was no *water* on Twin-Earth, only a compound that resembled it. If so, then there are some surprising consequences for a theory of meaning. Consider some Earthling adult, Sophie, who knows no chemical theory, and her "twin," Twin-Sophie, on Twin-Earth: we can imagine them to be molecule-for-molecule duplicates of each other.[40] Certainly, there would seem to be no "internal" psychological differences between them. And yet, if XYZ is not genuine water, then Sophie and Twin-Sophie are not referring to the same substance when they use the word "water." If meaning is what determines extension, then, as Putnam (1975a:227) pithily put it, "cut the pie any way you like, 'meanings' just ain't in the *head*."

Whatever one's views of Putnam's cases, still a further problem can be raised in terms of a general question for any theory that takes thought to be formal symbol manipulation: according to the Löwenheim-Skolem theorem it's always possible to provide incompatible interpretations of a formal theory on which all its theorems remain *true*. If, moreover, we relax this latter constraint, there are obviously even further possible interpretations. Now, it's not clear that programming a computer to manipulate formally specified symbols provides any serious constraints. Indeed, a computer could use "the same program" one day to play chess, the next to fight a war.[41] It would seem that something *external* to the language, program, and computer must determine the meaning of at least some terms in any language.[42]

External Relational Theories: Wide Content

In view of these difficulties with internalist accounts of meaning, many philosophers have turned to relations the mind/brain bears to its environment. At least three main types of such "externalist" theories have been proposed: those that appeal to actual historical causal chains, those that appeal to "teleofunctional" roles, and those that appeal to various sorts of causal covariation. We will examine each of them in turn.

(a) Historical ("Actual") Causal Theories

The critics of internalist semantics proposed an alternative "picture" of reference whereby the reference of a token term is determined by the causal relations it bears to other tokens and ultimately to individuals or kinds.[43] An early effort to account for this aspect of meaning involved considering actual causal chains linking a speaker's use of a particular word to users of that word to dub the thing (object, substance, kind) to which the speaker thereby refers. Kripke (1972/1980) vividly argued for such an account of proper names and for natural kind terms: thus, suppose H_2O was originally dubbed "water" and that a chain of speakers heard, remembered, and themselves used the same word to refer to what previous speakers in the chain referred to, all the way down to the present. In this case, Kripke argued, it refers to that substance even in the case of a speaker who knows no chemical theory. Our Earthling English speaker thereby refers to H_2O, while her twin refers to XYZ.

Although many philosophers are persuaded that actual causal histories have some role to play in a theory of reference, it is widely recognized that such histories are not in themselves sufficient for a naturalistic theory, since at every stage of such causal chains there are events (such as *ostensions, dubbings, communications, understandings*) that require intentional characterization.[44] For example, it requires that the original dubber had one thing rather than another in mind on the occasion of the dubbing. What in a person's brain determined that it was the *ducks*, and not *birds* or *animals* or just *that particular duck*, or one of its *feathers* that got dubbed? They all, after all, are equally in the path described by the dubber's ostending finger.

Historical causal theories took *proper names* as their prime examples, extending the treatment to *natural kind* and to some artifactual *terms*. The problems just raised seem to require, however, a more general account of the meaning of *predicates* generally.

(b) Teleofunctional Role Theories[45]

Millikan (1984) and Papineau (1987) have (independently) proposed a general account of meaning based upon the role mental states play in a biological account of the evolution and life of an organism. On this view, beliefs (and other intentional states) possess certain information-carrying functions, even if there are no conditions under which they actually carry out such functions. These functions, determined by natural selection, fix the belief's intentional content. Thus, a frog's tokening "F" whenever a black speck crosses its retinal field should be interpreted as meaning [fly], since it is *flies* that are responsible for the survival of frogs (cf. Lettvin, Maturana, McCulloch, and Pitts (1951)).

Fodor is convinced that all such teleofunctional approaches suffer from some general problems: "Panglossianism"[46] with regard to natural selection, and an unusually crude extensionalism; selectional processes cannot distinguish between a representation S's having the content that x is F and its having the content x is G, where Fs and Gs lawfully covary. Thus, if frogs have evolved in environments in which the properties of being a fly and being a moving black speck lawfully covary, then, according to Fodor, selection does not determine whether the frog's representation "@#$" was selected to represent flies or to represent little black specks, or both, or something else which covaries with both (see Fodor's reply to Millikan below).

(c) Covariational ("counterfactual") Causal Theories

Returning to the historical causal theory, a natural answer to the question of what a dubber dubbed might be: whatever kind of thing she would *discriminate* as that thing; that is, whatever she would apply the thing to, as opposed to everything she wouldn't. Along these lines, a number of philosophers have considered ways in which states involving token expressions might have, in addition to *actual* causal histories, certain *counterfactual* dispositional properties to covary with certain events or properties in the world. The suggestion has its origin in the "natural sign" theories of Pierce (1931) and Morris (1946) in the 1930s in America, and was incorporated into behavioristic theories of meaning such as one finds in Skinner (1957) and Quine (1960). Of course, the versions of the theory that interest us here will be ones that take this behavioristic proposal "inside," permitting internal functional states to be one of the covariants. The idea essential to this approach is that intentional meaning is treated as a species of "information," or so-called "natural" meaning, the kind of meaning that is said to obtain between dark clouds and rain, red spots and measles, expansions of mercury in a thermometer and ambient temperature.[47] One event naturally means another if there is a causal law connecting them, or, to put it in Dretske's (1981) terms, the one event carries "information" about the other. A sentence, on this view, means what it carries information about.

So stated, the view is open to several immediate objections. Any such naturalistic theory needs to say what's *special* about meaning. As Antony and Levine emphasize in their discussion below, buying meaning too cheaply from nature runs the risk of "pan-semanticism": almost everything would mean something, since almost everything is reliably caused by something. So there must be some further condition. In particular, *most* tokenings of sentences (whether in English or Mentalese) are produced in the *absence* of the conditions that they nevertheless mean: "That's a horse" can be uttered on a dark night in the presence of a cow, or just idly in the presence of anything. Fodor (1987d) calls these latter usages "wild," and the property whereby tokens of symbols means things that aren't on occasion their actual cause, "robustness."

The problem for any covariational theory is to account for robustness. In doing so it needs to solve what Fodor calls the "disjunction" problem: given that among the causes of a symbol's tokenings, there are meaning-forming and wild causes, what distinguishes them? In particular, what makes it true that some symbol 'F' means [horse] and not [horse or cow on a dark night], or [horse or cow on a dark night or w_2 or w_3 or ...] (where each w_i is one of the purportedly "wild" causes)?[48] Several proposals have been advanced for handling the disjunction problem. They have in common trying to constrain the occasions on which the nomic connection is meaning-forming.

Teleological Theories. A natural suggestion regarding meaning-forming conditions is that they are in some sense "optimal" conditions,[49] conditions that obtain when nothing is interfering with the belief formation system, and it is functioning as it was "designed to." Fodor (1987d) calls such theories "teleological"[50] and he himself proposed a version of such theory in the widely circulated *paper* called "Psychosemantics" (Fodor (1990)), to be distinguished from the *book* – Fodor (1987d) – of the same title in which he *rejects* any such theory. The attraction of such a theory lies in its capturing the idea that two individuals *meaning* the same thing by some symbol consists in their agreeing about what it would apply to, were *everything else* about the world to be known. Their disagreements are to be explained as due to their limited epistemic positions and reasoning capacities, which interfere with their being as omniscient as the right conditions for agreement would require.

Although Fodor nowhere suggests such theories are false, he does think they are subject to a number of difficulties, the chief one consisting of the circularity that seems unavoidable in specifying the optimal conditions: it would appear that those conditions cannot be specified without employing the very intentional idiom the theory is supposed to explain (see Fodor (1987d:104–6), and Loewer (1987)). For example, it is difficult to see how to rule out the interference of other intentional states – e.g. the aforementioned "bizarre" theories that are the bane of conceptual role accounts – or the cooperation of certain intentional states, such as "attending," "thinking of," "wanting to get things right," or merely the effects of "ignorance."

In order to avoid these problems Fodor (1987d, 1990) went on to propose another kind of covariation in what has come to be known as the "asymmetric dependency" theory. Although it makes no explicit appeal to ideal epistemic conditions, much of its motivation can be appreciated by thinking of the ideal covariational theory in the background.

The Asymmetric Dependency Theory. According to the ideal covariational theory, under epistemically ideal conditions, tokenings of a predicate covary with the property it expresses. But, of course, tokens of it may also be produced by many properties it doesn't express: tokens might be produced by things erroneously taken to have the property, by things associated with the property, by mere thoughts about the property, etc. Now, one way to understand the asymmetric dependency theory is first to notice that, plausibly, *all these latter cases depend upon the ideal case, but not vice versa*: the wild tokenings depend upon the ideal ones, but the ideal ones don't depend upon the wild ones (getting things wrong depends upon getting things right in a way that getting things right doesn't depend upon getting things wrong). Thus, the property HORSE causes "cow" because some horses (for example, those at the far end of the meadow) look like cows and, under ideal conditions, COW causes "cow." MILK causes "cow" because seeing some milk causes one to think "milk," and this reminds one of where milk comes from, which, under ideal conditions, would be the sort of thing that causes "cow" tokenings.

So formulated, of course, the account still mentions ideal conditions, and these Fodor has conceded cannot be specified non-circularly. His further interesting suggestion is, however, that mention of the ideal conditions here is entirely inessential: *the structure of asymmetric causal dependency alone, abstracted from any specific conditions or causal chains, will do all the required work!*

To simplify the discussion, let's define a predicate, "x is locked onto y," to capture this asymmetric causal structure:

A symbol 'S' is *locked onto* property F just in case:

(i) there is a law that instances of F cause tokenings of 'S';
(ii) tokenings of 'S' are robust: i.e. are sometimes caused by instances of a property G other than F;
(iii) when Gs (other than Fs) cause tokenings of 'S' then their doing so asymmetrically depends on (i), i.e. on the law that Fs cause 'S's.

where X's causing Ys "asymmetrically depends" on a law, L, iff X's causing Y wouldn't hold but that L does, but not *vice versa*.[51] Fodor's thesis then is that:

(M) *if* 'S' is locked onto F, *then* 'S' expresses F.

Thus, a predicate 'C' expresses cow if (a) it were a law that the property[52] cow causes 'C' tokenings, and (b) other causal relations between properties (e.g., HORSE, MILK etc.) and 'C' tokenings asymmetrically depend upon this law. To be sure, it's a *ceteris paribus* law – but a law of the sort one expects to find in any macro-science (see section I above). Now, of course, there will also be cases, like that of a cow seen on a dark night, that also cause tokenings of 'C'. But presumably it is in the nature of the world which of these causings depend upon which. If cow-caused 'C's and horse-caused 'C's – but no other-caused 'C's – are nomologically *dependent* upon one another, then 'C' means [horse or cow]; if they are nomologically *independent* of one another, then 'C' is ambiguous between [horse] and [cow]. On the other hand, if the cow-caused ones depend upon the horse-caused ones, then it means HORSE; the cow-caused ones are "wild." The wild cases depend upon the meaning-forming cases, but the meaning-forming cases do not depend upon the wild ones.[53]

A useful analogy might be made with the phenomenon of imprinting:[54] goslings are evidently born with a disposition to become bonded to the first animal they encounter. But this disposition causes goslings to imprint on different animals in different niches. Moreover, once the imprinting occurs, mis-identifications of an animal as the imprintee depend upon the (original) correct identifications, but not vice versa. One can imagine there being a variety of different imprinting mechanisms in an animal: one for its prime caretaker, another for its home, another for certain foods, and so forth. In a way, concepts, on the present proposal, can be regarded as an elaborate expansion of such imprinting dispositions.

Note that, in keeping with Fodor's more modest moments (e.g., Fodor, 1987d:124), we have confined the asymmetric dependency thesis to supplying only a *sufficient*, not a necessary physicalistic condition for predicate expression. He believes this is all that he is required to do, given his merely "supervenient" physicalism discussed in section I above. Fodor feels that, if there are no counterexamples to (M), then he has done all that he needs to do to show that, contrary to dualism, certain physical arrangements are sufficient for intentionality.

In their contributions below, Baker and Boghossian challenge this claim, Baker raising a number of classes of counterexamples, and Boghossian criticizing it for what he takes to be its commitment to verificationism. Antony and Levine worry that such a theory is incompatible with the original criticisms Fodor made of the work of Skinner and Gibson, to the effect that there aren't laws relating an agent's states to arbitrary properties of the environment.[55]

The asymmetric dependency theory does seem to accord well with the original externalist intuitions urged by Putnam. It seems to have the consequence that Sophie's and Twin-Sophie's Mentalese tokens of "water" refer to different properties. Sophie's tokens get locked onto H_2O while her twin's get locked onto XYZ. Although for both there are nomological connections between H_2O and "water" and XYZ and "water," the dependency relations are reversed. Sophie's XYZ-"water" connections depend on her H_2O-"water" connections since, if the former were broken (e.g., Sophie discovers how to detect XYZ) the latter would remain intact but not vice versa. The situation is reversed for Twin-Sophie.

However, for all its success in dealing with such externalist intuitions, it is hard to resist the older intuitions that there is *something* semantic "in the head." Isn't there some important "narrow" sense of content in which Sophie and Twin-Sophie have the very same thoughts, thoughts with the very same content? Wouldn't the same intentional explanations be at some important level true of each of them? Both, for example, would think that what rained from heaven also filled the seas, would reach for what they each called "water" when they were thirsty, and would have the same illusions "as of water" on the hot road ahead.[56] Doesn't psychology need a notion of narrow content to capture such generalizations?

What Remains in the Head: Narrow Content

Philosophers have disagreed over whether intentional psychology requires a notion of narrow content, over whether there is a viable notion of narrow content, and, if there is a notion, how to characterize it. Most of the original proponents of "wide" content – Putnam (1975a, 1988), Burge (1979, 1986) – think that that notion is the only viable notion of content at all. Burge (1986), in particular, has argued that psychological explanations, such as Marr's (1982) theory of vision, actually presuppose wide content. We cannot enter this debate here – the issue is a complicated one in the philosophy of science, involving requirements on causal laws and causal explanation (Burge (in preparation) and Fodor (in press-d)). We will simply discuss Fodor's most recent views on narrow content.[57]

Fodor joins a number of others – e.g., Loar (1981), Block (1986) – in thinking that some notion of narrow content can be, and must be preserved for purposes of psychological explanation. Block (1986) defends a conceptual role account, and Loar in his contribution below, for example, urges a notion of narrow content that is based mostly in first-person judgments of similarity and "fit." As is evident in his reply to Loar, Fodor has a variety of disagreements with these proposals, and has recently settled on the following in their stead: *the narrow content of a*

Mentalese expression is a function (in the set theoretic sense) that maps a context onto a broad content.[58] For example, the narrow content of Sophie and Twin-Sophie's "water" is the function that maps Sophie's context onto H_2O and her twin's context onto XYZ. When Sophie utters "water is wet," she thereby expresses the content [H_2O is wet], while when Twin-Sophie utters it she expresses the content [XYZ is wet]. Two symbols have the same narrow content just in case they serve to compute the same such function: it is this that is shared by Sophie and her twin.

An important feature of such an abstract notion of narrow content is its surprising, but perhaps entirely apt indifference to the *way* in which the function is computed. Not only Sophie and her twin, but two people with very different ways of thinking could still share the same narrow content, so long as those different ways resulted in locking a symbol onto the same property in the same context. Moreover, some – maybe all – of the ways may involve holistic procedures that are both "Quinian" (computed over the totality of a belief set) and "isotropic" (every belief potentially sensitive to every other), in the way that Fodor (1983) allows that human confirmation may turn out to be. But while this holism may be a property of the *means* of computing a narrow content function it is not thereby a property of the *function itself. Pace* Quine (1969, 1970) *epistemic* holism need not bring *semantic* holism in its train.

Moreover, Fodor's proposal affords a way of dealing with a problem that vexed most causal accounts of specifying what counts as a "context": a context is any circumstance in which a locking pattern constitutive of wide content obtains. Narrow content is that state of an organism that brings about such locking. Thus, if Putnam's intuitions are to be believed, the earth is such a context in which 'water' is locked onto water, and Twin-earth is one where it is locked onto XYZ. What Sophie and her twin share is a state disposing their symbols to become so locked.

To return to the analogy with imprinting, what counts as a niche in which a gosling imprints can only be determined by observing just when goslings imprint upon one or more (i.e., a disjunction of) different animals. Although it is a mechanism that probably can be identified only in a niche, it is presumably a feature shared by the goslings across niches. And (to anticipate some of Fodor's reply to Block) the details of the mechanism might vary from gosling to gosling. Thus, just as there are presumably different internal mechanisms for each kind of imprinting to which a gosling is disposed, so too are there different internal mechanisms for each narrow concept a human being is able to grasp, all the mechanisms for a given concept simply sharing the property of getting the agent to lock on to a certain property given a certain context.[59]

If there is an air of circularity about this account, perhaps it arises from the expectation raised by the phrase "in the head," that there must be some characterization of narrow content that refers only to phenomena inside the head. But this would be a mistake. Narrow content might be characterizable only by terms that refer to phenomena *outside* the head even though it is a feature that supervenes entirely on features *inside* it. The situation may be rather like that of the property *being poisonous*, which is identifiable *only* by citing the relation of a substance to normal human beings. Poisonous things may have nothing else in common besides this disposition,[60] and so be *identified* only by these counterfactual relations. But this disposition is presumably a property that supervenes entirely on the intrinsic properties of the substance, whatever they may be (e.g., human beings might cease to exist, but still arsenic would be poisonous). Similarly, the notion of narrow content may be a perfectly clear and useful notion even if the search for some *internal characterization* of it is in vain. It may, for example, enter into such psychological generalizations as: "Reflection of light on a hot road produces a narrow-[water] illusion": i.e., an illusion involving a narrow concept that on earth maps the agent to the broad content [water] and on Twin-Earth to [twater].

The extent to which psychological explanations of the latter sort could be sustained by so spare a notion of narrow content is explored by Stalnaker and Block in their frankly skeptical essays. Stalnaker argues that merely defining such a function in no way insures a substantive notion of narrow content, and that it's unclear what substantive notion of content Fodor may have in mind. Block argues that a number of natural candidates for narrow content – e.g., descriptive content – cannot serve that role without either collapsing to mere syntax, or falling afoul of the holism that Fodor is anxious to avoid.

It is worth noticing that, if Fodor is to secure a viable notion of narrow content for psychology, he needs to show that it will apply to more than Twin-Earth examples, since these are examples in which presumably the *whole* of the two agents' narrow states coincide. These cases are therefore compatible with narrow content depending upon the whole of the computational organization of the brain, precisely as the conceptual role theorist is inclined to claim. If narrow content is to play a role in actual psychological laws, then, as Block notes, by Fodor's own lights it had better be a more general notion than that. But it's not at all clear what such a notion might be, or how it could be specified without falling afoul of the opposite horn of Quine's dilemma, presupposing a principled analytic/synthetic distinction.[61] Fodor takes on this problem in his reply to Block, making a novel suggestion that will undoubtedly be the subject of a great many further debates that we mercifully will not try to anticipate here.

Stating the whole of Fodor's theory succinctly, we might put it this way: propositional attitudes are computational relations to symbols encoded in the brain, whose broad content is determined by the properties onto which they lock and whose narrow content consists in a disposition to so lock. Psychology consists in stating laws about such dispositions, laws that are true by virtue of underlying, ultimately physical mechanisms that implement the computations performed on the symbols to which those dispositions are attached. It is this theory that is the object of dispute in the essays that follow.[62]

Barry Loewer
Georges Rey

NOTES

1   At the end of the 1971 Cognitive Science Summer Institute at the University of Washington, Seattle, in which Fodor and others presented the then recently developing framework of cognitive science.

2   Thus this volume is in no way a "Festschrift." It is entirely accidental that anyone has been included who would regard themselves as particularly sympathetic to Fodor's work. The intention (about which Fodor has expressed some mixed feelings) was to present Fodor with his severest critics, and then with an opportunity to respond.

3   Some indication of the breadth of Fodor's involvement in both philosophy and experimental cognitive psychology is afforded by the bibliography of his work that we include at the end of the present volume. Useful discussion of some of the empirical work that will not be treated here can be found, regarding modularity, in Garfield (1987) and regarding lexical decomposition, in Gergely and Bever (1986).

4   In this way, he clearly could be regarded as sympathetic to Quine's (1969) program of "naturalized epistemology," even if he is not sympathetic to Quine's (oddly *a prioristic*) commitment to a purely behavioristic psychology.

5   A word about this vexed term. As it is used in the present discussions, "inten*t*ional(-ity)" – with a 't' in the middle – refers to the phenomenon whereby some things (e.g., words, thoughts) are *about* other things, whereby, for example, 'cat' is about cats. "Inten*s*ional(-ity)" – with an 's' in the middle – refers to a logical phenomenon exhibited by a wide variety of linguistic contexts in which certain standard "extensional" logical principles (e.g., Leibniz's Law) appear to break down. Talk about modal, deontic, nomological, and, indeed, inten*t*ional phenomena is widely thought to be inten*s*ional: thus, for example, the belief that Sam writes well, *about* Sam Clemens, is different from the belief that Mark does, even though Mark = Sam. For important discussions see Quine (1956a) and Kaplan (1969).

6   One set of phenomena, A, supervenes on another, B, iff two objects can't differ with respect to A without differing with respect to B. For example, pains supervene on brains insofar as two people couldn't differ with respect to pain without differing with respect to their brains. See Kim (1984) and Teller (1984) for richer discussion than is possible here.

7   See Fodor (1974), and the related discussion of the "token" identity theory, first propounded in Nagel (1965), and Taylor (1967) and discussed at length in Davidson (1970). For dissenting discussion of this issue, see Richardson (1979), Enc (1983), and P.S. Churchland (1986:357–358).

8   This has the consequence that one could make a mind out of practically anything. This is attractive if one thinks about the possibility of other forms (mechanical, extra-terrestrial) of mental life, or of how one's own brain might, neuron by neuron, be replaced by sturdier stuff. It is disquieting insofar as it seems to entail that the right arrangement of the billion people of China might have a mind (Block, 1980). Fodor nowhere addresses this issue. For a discussion compatible with Fodor's views, one which nicely brings out the pervasiveness of functional description at many levels of science, see Lycan (1981).

9   This analogy could be, and sometimes is, exaggerated. Certainly many psychological phenomena – amnesia, emotional reactions, the effects of drugs – have at least partly physiological explanations. The point is that there are important classes of psychological phenomena that, for the standard functional reasons, clearly do not. Excellent examples are afforded by any of the rules of grammar postulated by linguists, or by accounts of practical reasoning that might be advanced by decision theorists. How would *physiology* conceivably explain why certain strings of words are grammatical and others not; or why (and whether) people discount later for nearer benefits?

10 That is, for Fodor the "heteronomous" character that Davidson (1970) observes in regard to psychological laws is a trait of laws in special sciences in general. See also Cartwright (1983) for reasons to think that *ceteris paribus* clauses may be ineliminable from basic physics as well.

11 The reader is urged to bear this feature of laws particularly clearly in mind in

considering Fodor's heavy use of nomic connections in his discussion of his "asymmetric dependence" theory of intentionality in *Psychosemantics* and *Theory of Content*. See section III below and Fodor's replies to Baker and Boghossian.

12   Most of these latter phrases, and especially the denigrating attitude, are from Quine (1960:221); but see also Putnam (1988). Dennett (1971, 1987) introduced what he calls "the intentional stance." Although he often disavows non-realism about the mental, Dennett's dominant opinion seems to be that this stance is at best predictively useful, but does not play the same genuinely explanatory role of various non-intentional (e.g., physical) stances. Davidson (1980) adopts many of Quine's ways of describing the practice of radical translation and interpretation, while seeming to resist an anti-realist interpretation (see Antony (1989) for useful discussion).

13   See Fodor, Bever, and Garrett (1974a:ch. 1) for a discussion of productivity (also called "creativity" in e.g., Chomsky, 1968). Considerations of "systematicity" were introduced in Fodor (1987d:147ff) in reaction to skepticism about productivity.

14   We can't possibly review the arguments here. For arguments against behaviorism, see Chihara and Fodor (1965f) and Fodor (1968d). Much of Fodor's critique of behaviorism presupposes a familiarity with the experimental literature usefully reviewed in e.g., Gleitman (1986), as well as with Chomsky's (1959) review of Skinner (1957). For arguments against Gibsonian "Ecological Realism," see Fodor and Pylyshyn (1981). Arguments against the purely syntactic theory can be found in Fodor (1987a:161–163) and against eliminativist-connectionism in Fodor and Pylyshyn (1988) and Fodor and McLaughlin (1990). (Against mere "implementationist" connectionism, Fodor has no particular quarrel.) Further discussion in regard to these latter two programs is also raised below in his replies to Devitt, Matthews, Smolensky, and Stich.

15   The character of "folk psychology" as a theory – indeed, whether it is a theory at all – is discussed at some length in Stich (1983) and P. M. Churchland (1984), and disputed by Schiffer (1987:29–31).

16   See Stich (1983:chs 10–11) and P. S. Churchland (1986:ch. 9) for worries of this sort. One way in which Fodor is quite prepared to find scientific psychology diverging from folk views is in its commitment to "narrow" as opposed to "wide" content; see section III below.

17   For discussion of the reality and importance of unconscious mentation, see Chomsky (1968:ch. 2), Nisbett and Wilson (1977), Lyons (1986), Horgan and Woodward (1985), and Rey (1989). For discussions of consciousness and qualitative states that are related to Fodor's general approach, see Block (1978), Shoemaker (1984), White (1982), Lycan (1981), and Rey (1988b). See also Searle (in press) and commentaries included thereafter for recent discussion of the separability of consciousness from cognition.

18   Thus, to take an issue slightly tangential to the issues discussed in this volume, Fodor (1983, 1985a, 1989a, and in preparation-a), has devoted considerable attention to the development of a modularity thesis about the mind, which he argues (1984b, 1988b) affords a psychologically sound basis for the traditional observation/theoretic distinction, and so for claims of objectivity in science, *pace* Kuhn (1962) and Goodman (1978).

19   Harman (1972) proposed a similar hypothesis to Fodor's, but has insisted that it be largely the agent's natural language. Aside from the fact that (as Harman recognizes) this hypothesis requires supplementation for the case of infants and animals, there are problems about lexical ambiguity that are arguably an *advantage* to natural languages but, as stressed in Fodor (1981c), are an obvious disadvantage to computational ones (cf. Barwise and Perry (1983)). On the other hand, there is the nice point raised by Putnam (in conversation) regarding whether Lincoln really did have a determinate thought in mind when he said "You can fool some of the people all of the time . . . "

For other anticipations of (RTT) see Carnap (1937:248), Sellars (1956), and even Quine (1960:sect. 44).

20   Dennett (1978a:104) notes that this account couldn't possibly be true for every ordinarily ascribed belief, e.g., that zebras don't wear overcoats. Presumably, many ordinary ascriptions allow for what the agent *would* think (i.e., for Fodor, what she would compute) if asked.

21   For discussion of these various cases, see Church (1946), Mates (1951), Burge (1978), Stalnaker (1984), Kripke (1979), Bealer (1982). For independent argument that something like a language of thought is required for these problems see Salmon (1986:121-3), and also, in a different vein, Perry (1979).

22   However, there need be no commitment here to the rules of psychology cleaving to only *valid* rules of inference, in the way that Newell and Simon (1981) complain have overly constrained purely logic-oriented approaches to AI. Similarly, there is no commitment to people actually performing well on standard logic problems in the way that Johnson-Laird (1983) finds that they don't. The role of logic here is as a *medium of expression*, whether of thoughts or of "mental models," and of syntactically defined operations on those expressions, *not* as a system specifically for deductive theorem proving.

23   This is probably as good a place as any also to address the chestnut of "the Homunculi regress," whether a language of thought view presupposes homunculi that can read and interpret the language (see Ryle (1949), Wittgenstein (1953), and Dennett (1978c:ch.3)). The short answer is no. What the theory of computers has taught us is that complex computational processes – such as operations upon symbols in a language – can be broken down into simple operations that are so stupid that (it's obvious that) a machine can execute them (see Fodor (1975:73) and Dennett (1978c:80-1)).

24   This, of course, depends upon the Church–Turing thesis that any intuitively computable function is computable by a Turing machine. See Fodor's reply to Dennett below for his reference to Turing, Chomsky, and Freud as having the few really good ideas in cognitive science. Expanding a little on Fodor's pantheon, we might add Frege and Hilbert as essential contributors to the conception that flowered fully in the work of Turing.

25   Similarly, talk of "sentences" in the brain mustn't be taken on the model of sentences as they are inscribed on pages of books. One natural objection to the proposal – "*Sentences* in the head??!" – is due to an overly concrete conception people often have of sentences. Sentences, it must be remembered, are highly abstract objects that can be entokened in an endless variety of ways: as waveforms (in speech), as sequences of dots and dashes (Morse code), as sequences of electrically-charged particles (on recording tape). It is presumably in something like the latter form that sentences would be entokened in the head (see Stich (1983:35-8) for excellent expansion of this point). Indeed, (CRTT) is best viewed as simply the claim that the brain has logically structured, causally efficacious states. Surely, *that* isn't *patently* absurd.

26   Roughly, Fodor argues that since (1) learning is hypothesis confirmation, and (2) there are no serious "decompositions" of any substantial concepts into sensory ones, all concepts must be innate. A proponent of (CRTT) might deny either of these premises and/or the validity of the argument. Thus, *pace* P. S. Churchland (1986:389), it is not enough to argue against (CRTT) that the postulation of concepts as innate is "sufficiently unacceptable to be a *reductio* of the Mentalese hypothesis." For more recent discussion of the innateness issue, see Samet (in preparation). An interesting point of intersection between this view and the theory of meaning is discussed further in fn. 59 below.

27   Interest in Turing machines in no way commits someone to acceptance of the "Turing test" of intelligence – that x is intelligent iff x's teletype responses are indistinguishable

from a normal human being's. This is an exceptionally narrow behavioristic test that would be anathema to any self-respecting functionalist. (This is one of the several unnecessary claims with which Searle (1980, 1984) burdens approaches like Fodor's; see Rey (1986) for discussion.)

28   Dreyfus (1972) and Dreyfus and Dreyfus (1986) rightly chastise many computer scientists for making exaggerated claims about their programs, which are generally suitable only for what from a normal human point of view are extremely artificial environments in which the problems are artificially standardized. Dreyfus and Dreyfus think that these problems for programming intelligence constitute in principle arguments against the success of *any* computational/representational (or so-called "classical") program. These problems, however, show no such thing, any more than the failure of a physicist to mimic the motion of a leaf in the wind tells against the truth of proposed physical laws. See Fodor's reply to Dennett below.

29   It is worth noting a point about which Fodor and the Dreyfus brothers may agree: that there may never be an adequate theory of the central processor. Fodor (1983:ch 4) argues that it may simply be too holistic – in particular, too "Quinian" (confirmation is defined over the whole of one's beliefs) and "isotropic" (confirmation of any one belief is potentially sensitive to confirmation of any other). This, however, doesn't argue against (CRTT) *per se* but only against a successful psychology of confirmation. It certainly doesn't rule out (CRTT)-style theories of sensory and language processing, which Fodor argues to be sufficiently "encapsulated" to be immune from these problems.

30   See, e.g., Putnam (1988:21,40–1). Jackendoff (1987:129–33, 1989:73) comes perilously close to actually endorsing a theory of this sort. Searle (1980) seems to require that intentionality be "intrinsic" as a requirement on any satisfactory theory of thought, and rejects computational theories accordingly. Some confusion in this regard can be generated by equating "original" with "intrinsic" intentionality (see Haugeland 1981:32–3 and Dennett 1987:288ff for useful discussion). As we will use the terms, the "original" intentionality normally ascribed to mental states is to be distinguished from the "derived" intentionality of, e.g., sentences in books; "intrinsic" intentionality is the intentionality that would attach to a symbol independently of its relations to the world. See also Fodor's reply to Perry and Israel below, and his complaints there of being misunderstood in Barwise (1986).

31   This is not to say that it is in the least a "private" language of the sort deplored by Wittgenstein and his followers. Fodor's (1975) facetious suggestions to one side, Wittgenstein was presumably concerned with a language whose expressions referred to entities such as "sense-data" knowable only by the user/introspector. There is no suggestion that Mentalese is remotely any such language.

32   In his famous "Chinese Room" example, Searle (1980) argues that no computational theory could be relevant to intentionality, but for fallacious reasons; see, e.g., Fodor's (1980d) reply to him, as well as Rey (1986) for criticisms along the lines of the present discussion.

33   Aristotle and Locke both seem to have had versions of imagistic views. See Cummins (1989) for useful discussion.

34   For further discussion of a limited role images may play in thought, see, e.g., Kosslyn (1980), Rey (1980a), Pylyshyn (1981), and Block (1981). See also Millikan's contribution below, and Fodor's reply.

35   There are also "long-armed" conceptual role theories which include an expression's epistemic relations to distal stimuli in an expression's conceptual role; see Harman (1982) and Block (1986). We ignore this possibility here as it is not germane to Fodor's discussion.

36   Thus, Grice and Strawson (1956) and Field (1977) propose a confirmation theory of

meaning, but one that, as Field readily acknowledges, is not applicable intersubjectively. Remembering the decompositional proposals notoriously advanced in Fodor and Katz (1963a), one may think that Fodor endorses a conceptual role account. However, he has not only long repudiated those views, but has mounted considerable experimental arguments against them in Fodor, Fodor, and Garrett (1975), and Fodor, Garrett, Walker, and Parkes (1980). See also Fodor and Pylyshyn (1981b) and Fodor (1987d:ch. 3).

37 Indeed, a thorough-going conceptual role semantics arguably imperils claims of objectivity and realism in general, as in Kuhn (1962). Fodor (1984b, 1988b) discusses the relation of conceptual role semantics to the observation/theoretic distinction and the grounds of objectivity generally; cf. fn. 18 above.

38 Although Fodor says that he follows Quine in rejecting the analytic/synthetic distinction, his own theory of meaning is committed to the possibility of sentences which are "true in virtue of meaning" and therefore analytic. Indeed, any theory that accepts that there is a definite matter of fact about what an expression means is committed to the possibility of sentences like "All and only Fs are G" being analytic since it may turn out that as a matter of definite fact "F" and "G" possess the same meaning (although not any theory is committed thereby to the analytic being a priori). Of course, it may be that for some reason there are no Mentalese sentences of this sort, but the conceptual role theoriest could equally say that for some reason or other there are no Mentalese sentences that are true in virtue of their conceptual roles.

39 Fodor (1987d:125) cites the example of Berkeley who thought chairs were *ideas*: "Which are we to say he lacked, the concept MENTAL or the concept CHAIR?" Burge (1978) also explores ways in which it seems reasonable to suppose people could make errors about analyticities: e.g., mistakenly thinking a fortnight is ten days. See also other references in fn. 21 above.

40 Barring differences in H_2O and XYZ. This was an unfortunate artifact of Putnam's original example. There are many other, less far-fetched, but also less well-known examples in Burge (1979) and in Stich (1983).

41 See Rey (1980b), Fodor and Pylystin (1981b:207), Stich (1983:108), and Baker (1987a:57) for discussion. It is this fact that exercises Searle (1980, 1984) in his rejection of computational theories. As should be clear from the discussion that follows, this is hardly an issue that computationalists must despair of addressing.

42 Devitt, in his comments below, emphasizes the non-syntactic character of inputs and outputs as a possible source of semantic constraints.

43 See Kripke (1972) and Devitt (1981) for developments of this view. Boghossian presupposes and discusses it at some length in his contribution. Fodor (in press-f) includes a clause about actual chains in the latest version of his own semantic theory. For simplicity here, we include Burge's (1979) emphasis upon the social context of the agent as a species of historical causal chains.

44 Kripke (1972) was under no illusion here, not even regarding the "alternative picture" he drew as a "theory" at all. Much of the problem here comes to the "qua" problem raised by one of the historical theory's most ardent defenders, Devitt (1981), and by Devitt and Sterelny (1987:sect 4.4).

45 Millikan's "teleofunctional" theories are to be distinguished from the kinds of theories Fodor (1987d) calls "teleological," to be discussed in due course. The crucial difference between them is that the former, but not the latter, are committed to claims about some form of covariation.

46 This is the view that nature always selects for optimal characteristics. See Gould and Lewontin (1979) for discussion of this issue and, for nevertheless a defense of this approach in biology, Dennett (1987:ch. 7).

47 Grice (1957) distinguished "natural" "meaning-n" from "non-natural" "meaning-

nn." Covariational views in general attempt to construct the latter as a species of the former. See also Stampe (1977) for a rich suggestion along these lines.

48   Kripke (1982) discusses virtually the same problem in his explication of Wittgenstein's worries about rule-following. What makes it true, he asks in regard to a case in which someone has "added" 57 and 63 and obtained 5, that the person is making an "error" in *addition* as opposed to computing a different function, "quaddition" which is identical to addition except for the case of 57 and 63? Note that disjunctive concepts need not be at all unnatural: [human] might well be understood to be [male-human or female-human]; [US Citizen] as [native born or naturalized].

49   Boghossian in his paper calls such situations "type 1," and argues that even Fodor's later theory is committed to the existence of such situations. We ignore as implausible for purposes here readings of "optimal" as "normal," as in Stalnaker (1984).

50   Since many of them originated with Fred Dretske and Dennis Stampe at the University of Wisconsin, Fodor also calls this set of views "Wisconsin Style Semantics." For further discussion and criticism of Wisconsin semantics see Loewer (1987).

51   As emphasized in Fodor (1987d:109), the dependence here is intended to be *synchronic*, not *diachronic*. An example of the sort of dependence Fodor has in mind is afforded by the behavior of sail boats: their moving into the wind depends upon Bernoulli's Principle, but that principle doesn't depend upon sail boats moving into the wind (since the effect will only be achieved given certain properties of wind, etc.). Fodor (in press-f) does provide a further, "actual causal" diachronic clause, as one way of dealing with Twin-Earth examples. For simplicity, we ignore it here.

52   Fodor (1989b) regards the relata of laws to be *properties*, not individual things: thus, it's not the *horses* but *the property of being a horse* that is the relevant cause of a tokening of "F". For brevity, we will assume and omit this proviso throughout the discussion below, although we will refer to properties by writing the terms for them in uppercase (e.g., 'cow'). In being couched in terms of properties this account has certain further attractive features: (i) it allows covariation to be more selective than it might be of objects, and it affords a way of accounting for the meanings even of predicates that express uninstantiated properties, such as [unicorn]. On any reasonable account of laws there can be a law linking UNICORN to "unicorn" even if there are no unicorns.

53   Fodor's presentation of this theory has evolved from his initial presentation in (1987d), in which he is concerned largely to account for error, to (1990) in which the theory is presented as a theory of "wildness" in general. The latter account also replaces claims about *causation* with claims about *nomic connection* and deletes what turned out to be a superfluous account of sufficiency for correct applications.

54   This analogy arose in discussion with Michael Slote. It has the defect, which the reader should ignore, of making dependencies seem *diachronic*, whereas Fodor intends his to be read *synchronically*; cf. fn. 51 above.

55   Straying from the bounds of an introduction, the present editors can't resist wondering about the possibility of "irrelevant" lockings: thus, tokenings of a symbol that is *cognitively* locked on to cow might be "accidentally," non-cognitively locked on to any number of other purely physical causes: e.g. chemicals, neurosurgical pokings, cosmic rays. These latter would not seem to be even remotely semantically related to the symbol: they do not give rise to any meaning intuitions, and, more importantly, would not seem to figure in any *psychological* laws (cf. Block contribution below). And then there also seem to be association-caused tokenings (e.g., 'salt' with 'pepper') that might well persist in a language module even where the meaning-caused ones were broken, but are also presumably not to be included in the original symbol's meaning ('salt' doesn't mean PEPPER despite pepper continuing to elicit it in someone for whom SALT no longer does).

56   It actually is quite difficult to state this point clearly, since for every "narrow" behavior ("reaching for what we each call 'water' ") the internalist can argue is shared by twins, the externalist can cite a "wide" behavior that isn't (I reach for water where he reaches for XYZ). This is the topic of an extended exchange between Burge (1986, and in preparation) and Fodor (1987d:ch. 2 and in press-d) into the intricacies of which there is not space to enter here.

57   Fodor has made a number of earlier proposals that we won't discuss. Thus, Fodor (1980c) proposes that narrow content is *de dicto* content; and in an unpublished MS, "Narrow Content and Meaning Holism," that it is constructed out of observation expressions. For discussion of some of these views see LePore and Loewer (1986).

58   Fodor models his treatment of narrow content on a treatment of indexicals and demonstratives developed by David Kaplan (1979a, b; 1989). As Fodor acknowledges, Stephen White (1982) independently made a similar proposal.

59   On this account of narrow concepts, it is easy to see Fodor's (1975, 1979a) attraction to the claim that all (narrow) concepts are innate: Mentalese may be controlled by brain mechanisms that heavily constrain the set of properties to which a given mental symbol can attach. These mechanisms cause those symbols to lock onto some properties in one context and other properties in others; but not onto just any property in any context. Mentalese in this way is different from a natural language, which, controlled only by convention, permits a predicate to attach to any property whatsoever, a feature much exploited by Block in his discussion below.

60   Contrary to Quine (1969: ch. 5), who supposes that a dispositional term is merely a way of identifying an underlying natural kind.

61   Thus, for example, Fodor (1987d:93–5) commits himself to claiming that "learning what *anything* really is changes one's narrow concept of that thing." So it would appear that 'water is H_2O' would be analytic, at least for a chemist, whose narrow concept would be different from that of a layperson. But perhaps the analytic/synthetic distinction arising with respect to narrow contents is not as problematic as when it applies to wide. In his contribution Block argues, however, that even if an analytic/synthetic distinction could be drawn, it would be insufficient for the purposes of narrow content.

62   We are indebted to Kati Balog, Ned Block, Luca Bonatti, Mark Defenbaugh, Michael Devitt, Frances Egan, Jerry Fodor, Terry Mackey, Patricia Ross, and Michael Slote for helpful comments on drafts of this introduction.

1

The Nomic and the Robust

LOUISE ANTONY AND JOSEPH LEVINE

Faced as we now are with the prospect of criticizing a philosopher as insightful, lucid, and imaginative as the subject of this volume, whom we like and respect as much as we do, we want to make our intentions clear. It would be all too easy to dwell on his enormous achievements, his profound impact on the field, etc. So (borrowing a phrase from one of our ancestors who found himself in a similarly delicate situation), we want you to know that we come to bury Fodor, not to praise him.

The Problem

Most of Fodor's work has been concerned with the development and defense of the view known as the Representational Theory of Mind (RTM). In his hands, RTM proposes to treat mental states as functional states of the organism's nervous system (or of the organism's brain, or of the whole organism – that doesn't matter for present purposes). These functional states have causal powers, which they inherit from the physical properties of the stuff that realizes them, but also "semantic powers," which they possess in virtue of being *representational* states. It's this insistence on the intentionality of computational states that makes RTM distinctive among functionalist views. Fodor thinks it's the goal of vindicating folk psychology that requires the attribution of content to computational states. If we didn't feel sure – pretheoretically – that actions are typically caused by mental states and caused by them *in virtue of the contents* of those mental states, then we might be able to make do with something considerably less ambitious than a *representational* theory of mind.

But anyone who sees RTM, as Fodor does, as part of the empirical study of the mind, has to confront two problems. First, there's the problem of naturalization: the relation of representation, hypothesized to hold between mental states and things in the world, must be shown to be a species of natural relation. Intentionality can be original, but not primitive. Secondly, representationalists must defend (what we might call) intentional realism: the thesis that there is an objective difference between those systems whose behavioral responses can be mediated by representational states – intentional systems – and other systems. Possession of the capacity to represent must be shown to entail a distinctive set of causal powers.

1

Fodor has been especially hard at work at the first of these projects, though he has tackled the other one in connection with his and Pylyshyn's work on Gibson (see Fodor [1986b] and Fodor and Pylyshyn [1981b]). Interestingly, as Fodor's own work shows, these two projects, despite their common origins in the commitment to an empirically respectable RTM, push in diametrically opposed directions. While the naturalization project works on the idea that, when all is said and done, the mind is just part of nature after all, the intentional realism project is fueled by the intuition that there really is something special about minds, that they are, when all is said and done, quite *different* from other natural things in their ability to represent.

Fodor's own work has brought this tension[1] to a head. Let's first consider his most recent efforts toward the naturalization of representation (Fodor, 1987d; in press-f). Fodor's aim is to display representation as a species of causal connection, by exploiting the fact that reliable nomic relations are *ipso facto* information-bearing relations. A symbol's power to represent is supposed to derive somehow from the existence of a nomic relation between some property of the environmental causes of that symbol, and a property of the responding organism, yielding a disposition on the part of the organism to respond selectively (i.e., to produce the symbol) to stimuli with that property.[2]

But while this view makes representation *depend* upon information-bearing, Fodor has good reasons – stemming from his commitment to intentional realism – for not allowing representation to be simply *reduced* to information-bearing. There's information wherever there's causation. If there's also representation wherever there's information, then representation is everywhere: "*pansemanticism*." Smoke is reliably caused by fire, and thus bears information about fire, but if that's enough to make smoke *mean* or *stand for* fire, there would be no principled basis for distinguishing "intentional systems" from any other sort of system. The intentional system's capacity for representation would amount to no more than the fact that its own states covary lawfully with states of its environment, and references to mental representation in explanations of behavior would be nothing more than just-so stories.

Of course, this is precisely what some psychologists and philosophers believe to be the case. Consider the dispute in psychology over the role of representation in perception. According to standard computational accounts (e.g., Gregory, 1970; Marr, 1982), perception is largely an inferential process that takes patterns of proximal stimuli as data and delivers perceptual judgments concerning distal objects as conclusions. Fodor took this as grist for his representational mill in *The Language of Thought*, where he argued that such a model presupposes the existence of a representational medium in which the data and hypotheses are couched, plus computational processes defined over such representations.

But J. J. Gibson (1979) and his followers (e.g., Turvey *et al.*, 1981) have challenged this computational model of perception. On their view, perception is not an inferential process, but rather a matter of "picking up" or "detecting" environmental information, of "resonating to higher-order invariants." According to the Gibsonians, there is no need for inference because the information present in the percept is already completely present in the stimulus.

The relationship between percept and stimulus is thus, for Gibson *et al.*, no different, no less "natural," than the relationship between the pH of a solution and the color of a piece of litmus paper. If this view of perception is correct, however, it would raise a serious threat to intentional realism. It would mean that there would be no need for appeal to representations to explain an organism's responses to its perceived environment, and no difference in kind between the response of a person to the sight of a speeding car, and the "response" of a thermostat to a drop in temperature.

A different, but equally serious challenge to intentional realism, comes from Dan Dennett, who has nothing against computational models *per se*. He has always held that the appellation "intentional" indicates only a way of looking at a system, rather than an objective property some systems possess and some lack. The question, according to him, is not whether a creature really does embody an intentional system, but whether or not it is fruitful or efficient for us to adopt the "intentional stance" when dealing with it.

In his review of *The Language of Thought*, Dennett (1981c) contends that one of Fodor's chief arguments for the attribution of representational mechanisms to human beings is the fact that we display *adaptive* behavior. Possession of such mechanisms is supposed to explain our ability to produce appropriate responses to changes in our circumstances. However, Dennett argues, we can find adaptive behavior all the way down the phylogenetic chain, from bats that track moths, to fish that keep themselves at certain water depths, to single-celled organisms that avoid too much light. Dennett then throws down the gauntlet to Fodor: show that there's not just a slippery slope, with respect to intentionality, all the way from us down to paramecia; that we couldn't, with equal warrant, attribute intentionality to the latter as to the former.

Fodor accepts the challenge. He can answer Dennett, he contends, if he can specify a property P such that (a) some things (like us) have P and some things (like paramecia and thermostats) lack P, and (b) the possession of P is what warrants the attribution of the capacity for mental representation to some things but not to other things. The property that fills the bill, Fodor argues, is the ability to respond selectively to *anomic properties*:

> ... a system is intentional if it can respond selectively to a stimulus properly even though no law connects the property it responds to and the selective property of its response.
>
> (1986b:14)

It's important to note that the characterization of P rests heavily on a prior intuitive division among properties, between those that are *nomic* and those that are not. Intuitively, basic physical and chemical properties, like having such and such a mass, or having a valence of 1, fall into the nomic category, while properties like being 30 feet to the left of the Eiffel Tower, or having spiral rather than ring binding, are anomic. The difference between the first set and the second, Fodor alleges, is that those in the first set, but not the second, are capable of entering into lawful relations:

> ... if a property is such that objects fall under laws in virtue of possessing it, then that property is *ipso facto nomic*. All and only nomic properties enter into lawful relations; and, since not all properties enter into lawful relations, not all properties are *nomic*.
>
> (1986b:11)

If the nomic/anomic distinction can be maintained, then appeal to the property P also provides Fodor with a crisp critique of the Gibsonian model: "resonance" is, by hypothesis, simply the lawful covariation between some environmental property and some aspect of the perceptual response. Gibsonians even speak of their own work in terms of the discovery of "ecological law." That entails that every *perceivable* property must be a nomic property.

But what are the Gibsonians going to do with the fact that we can perceive, and respond selectively to, things like crumpled shirts? Either they must insist that being a crumpled shirt is a nomic property, the sort that enters into laws, or they must claim that there is some other, presumably "higher-order," nomic property possessed by crumpled shirts, resonance to which accounts for our ability to respond selectively to them. But neither alternative, Fodor argues, is plausible. If any property is anomic, he contends, being a crumpled shirt is. And there's no reason to think, either, that there can be found an appropriate higher-order invariant that corresponds to being a crumpled shirt, because it seems highly unlikely that there is any nomologically principled way of capturing the multifarious ways in which crumpled shirts might present themselves to us.

On the other hand, Fodor points out, RTM is tailor-made for explaining how intentional systems can manage to respond selectively to anomic properties – they do it by constructing representations of them.

> When the stimulus property in a primal scene is non-nomic, what connects S's being O with A's response coming to be C is that O is a property which A represents S as *having* . . .
>
> (1986b:18–19)

In short, RTM attempts to answer the question how S's being O can account for A's behavior coming to be C (When O is anomic), and it does so by introducing a *semantic* connection into the causal chain (1986b:20–1).

But by now it should be obvious that this particular line puts the defense of intentional realism directly at odds with the naturalization project. Recall that the naturalization project requires that there *be* nomic relations between mental states and their contents (in order that the representation relation turns out to be a species of some natural relation). But Fodor has here pinned that defense of intentional realism on there *not* being any nomic relations between mental states and their contents.

In order to appreciate the full extent of this difficulty for Fodor, we need to look at the situation in a bit more detail. As things stand, there is no formal contradiction. In the first place, the naturalization project requires only naturalistic *sufficient* conditions for a mental state's having content – it leaves open the possibility that content could be determined in other ways as well. And in the second place, Fodor never says that genuinely intentional systems must be *incapable* of representing nomic properties, only that they be *capable* of representing *anomic* ones. It might thus appear that Fodor has the following easy way out: he could say that satisfaction of the (to-be-specified) naturalistic conditions for representation is enough to make a system *representational*, but that to be fully *intentional* it must be capable of representing and responding to anomic properties. What makes our internal states representational in the first instance, would therefore be different from what makes us as systems genuinely intentional.

So let's consider, for a moment, the possibility of a two-level analysis of representation: we would have, at the first level, "primitive" or "original" representation, which obeys the constraints of naturalism, and at the second level, some kind of "derived" representation, which permits representation of anomic properties. Some mental representations would get their contents by virtue of some lawful covariance between instantiations of some environmental property and the relevant mental state, while other mental representations, like our representation of "crumpled shirt," would get their contents in some other way.

But while this logical space exists, Fodor is not going to want to occupy it, for a number of reasons: first, the proposal is not really in the spirit of Fodor's response to the slippery slope problem. Although he never explicitly asserts that the only systems with representational capacities are the genuinely intentional ones, there are strong suggestions that this is what he has in mind. He does say, for example, that the ability to respond selectively to non-projectible properties is the best evidence one could have for attributing mental representations to a system:

> *any* system that can respond selectively to non-nomic properties is, intuitively speaking, a plausible candidate for the ascription of mental representations; and any system that can't, isn't
>
> (1986b:14)

On the current proposal, a system could theoretically satisfy the conditions on original representation without displaying the additional feature of selective response to non-projectible properties. Such a possibility just doesn't fit with Fodor's idea that mental representations exist in order to *permit* a system to respond selectively to other than nomic properties:

> ... selective response to non-nomic properties is, on the present view, the great evolutionary problem that mental representation was invented to solve. And the solution of that problem was perhaps *the* crucial achievement in the phylogeny of cognition.
>
> (1986b:19)[3]

Second, taking this tack would disallow the possibility of primitive representation of non-projectible properties, like being a crumpled shirt. Fodor would be extremely reluctant to saddle himself with this constraint. To begin with, he generally tries to avoid making his semantic theories rest on substantive claims about the organization of Mentalese. But more significantly, he is constitutionally indisposed toward definition, and is willing to allow what some people think is a shocking amount of nativism in order to avoid it (see Fodor, 1975a, 1981d:essay 10, and Fodor *et al.*, 1980e.). He is thus quite concerned to allow wide latitude in what can be primitively represented. And indeed, while it's not utterly implausible that our representation of "crumpled shirt" is complex, defined in terms of "crumpled" and "shirt," what about "crumpled" and "shirt"? Or "virtue," or "person," or a host of terms not readily definable in terms of either conceptual or sensory primitives?

But the final and most serious problem with this proposal is one that highlights the fundamental difficulty in Fodor's appeal to a distinction between nomic and anomic properties in a defense of intentional realism. On the first formulation of Fodor's criterion of intentionality, everything depends on there being anomic properties for the system to represent. That suggests that it's not enough to show that representations of properties like "crumpled shirt" *could* get their contents without entering into lawlike relations with instantiations of those properties – "crumpled shirt" must be *guaranteed* anomic. But in order to ensure the anomicity of such properties, it would be necessary to show that these properties *could never* enter into lawful relationships, and how could one show such a thing as that? Fodor anticipates this objection, and in an important footnote, qualifies the criterion of intentionality:

> Even on [the assumption that the property of being a left shoe *is* nomic], however, it counts for our having mental representations that we can respond selectively to left shoes. This is because, though there is a law in which the property of being a left shoe is ineliminably involved, this law does not subsume *our* transactions with left shoes; specifically, it doesn't enter into the explanation of our ability to respond selectively to *left shoes*. This suggests a revised, less concessive version of the main principle: a system is intentional if it can respond selectively to a stimulus property even though no law connects the property it responds to and the selective property of its response.
>
> (1986b:14)

This emendation has much to recommend it – for one thing, it frees Fodor from the necessity of giving criteria for the nomicity of properties. Also, it represents a finer articulation of the intuition that underlies the position, viz., that it's not so much the *kind* of properties a thing can respond to, but the *way* in which the response is achieved. There are, after all, many nomic properties to which human beings can selectively respond, but only by massively cognitively mediated processes. We can respond to the property "having a temperature of precisely 180°F" but not in the same way as the thermometer we must rely on to do it.

But at the same time, the new criterion makes the conflict with the naturalization project unavoidable for Fodor. For now we must ask what it means for a property to be connected *lawfully* to a mental representation. We've already seen that Fodor is willing to count as nomic any property that figures in natural law. But now, what is a natural law? Specifically, if we were to find a true counterfactual-supporting generalization describing the relationship between the instantiations of some property, and some aspect of the organism's response, would that be enough to say that the relationship was *lawful*? Fodor's recent work on the nomic legitimacy of "hedged" laws, like the laws of psychology, strongly indicates that his answer is yes (see Fodor, 1989b). It then becomes all too likely that *any* property can become nomically related to some mental state.

The very language of the "paramecium" paper lays the trap. To possess property P, an organism must be able to respond *selectively* to some non-projectible property, say, O. That suggests that there must be some true, counterfactual-supporting generalizations relating O to some property of the organism's response. That's enough, on Fodor's current view of laws, to make O nomic, and hence projectible. But we can go even further. We can easily imagine someone's developing a phobic response to, say, crumpled shirts, so that whenever this person senses the presence of a crumpled shirt, she suffers an anxiety attack, complete with cold sweat, hyperventilation, vertigo, etc. In such a case, it's undeniable that there's a lawful relation between the property of being a crumpled shirt and the property of having an anxiety attack: the onset of the attack is strongly predictable from the presentation of a crumpled shirt, and it is clearly in virtue of the thing's being a crumpled shirt that it provokes the anxiety.[4]

So the upshot is that there's really no way to prevent a prima-facie anomic property from "becoming" nomic by means of entering into a lawful relationship with the internal states of some representational system. Here's the irony – it's the representational relation itself that makes possible lawlike relationships involving such properties as being a crumpled shirt. Fodor is right in thinking that no thermostat can respond to being a crumpled shirt and that we can, but the difference can't lie in our response's being anomalous. It's true that in the thermostat's case, the lawful connections between its states and the temperature of its environment are not dependent upon the thermometer's representations of the temperature – but obviously it would be circular to cite *this* difference in this context.

Once we realize that what's at issue is not the nature of the property to which we respond, but rather the nomic character of the interaction, we see that this particular defense of intentional realism is bound to conflict with the naturalization project. Any naturalistic theory of representation is going to demand that we *do* respond nomically to instantiations of the properties that we are capable of representing.

The Solution?

A brief recap: Fodor has signed on to at least two projects: (1) show how the relation "means that" can be a species of some naturalistic relation, and (2) show there to be a fact of the matter as to which things are and which things are not intentional systems. As Fodor has handled them, the first project requires that mental representations be shown to covary lawfully with their intentional objects, and the second requires that mental representations *not* covary lawfully with their intentional objects.

This tension, we claimed, was symptomatic of a deeper tension in the wider project of developing an empirical theory of the mind. This project, by its nature, presents conflicting demands. On the one hand, if the mind is to be studied empirically, it and all its properties must be shown to be part of nature, requiring for their explication nothing but the normal non-intentional tools of empirical science. On the other hand, if it's really *the mind* we're studying – that is, if we're not going to handle the naturalization project via eliminativism or conventionalism – then we have to show how mentality is special, distinct from the rest of nature. We've examined in detail one way this tension appears in Fodor's work, but there's yet another manifestation to consider, and this one may contain the germ of its own resolution.

One of the best arguments for the existence of genuine intentionality, and for specific intentionalist treatments of perceptual and cognitive processes, is the possibility of error by *mis*-representation. From optical illusions to false premises, errors provide the best evidence for the existence of some mechanism for "seeing-as," for a level of representation mediating between the stimulus and the response. At the same time, however, the possibility of misrepresentation provides the sharpest challenge to any attempt to naturalize semantic relations. Crude information-theoretic accounts of meaning founder on the fact that representations can be caused by, and thus carry information about, things that are not part of what is intuitively their meanings: if cat-thoughts are sometimes occasioned by Pekinese dogs, then what makes the cat-thought a thought about *cats*, rather than about *cats-or-dogs?* And if it is a cat-or-dog thought, how is it possible to *mistakenly* think of a Pekinese that it's a cat?

To say that Fodor is aware of this latter point would be, to understate the matter, an understatement. He is the one chiefly responsible for pointing out that the possibility of error, and the resulting "disjunction problem" (exemplified above), is only one aspect of the general phenomenon of *robustness* – the fact that representations, by their nature, can have an unlimited variety of causes, and still manage to mean something nonetheless.

> If one is sympathetic to the Skinner–Dretske tradition, the trick in constructing such a theory is to explain how the meaning of a symbol can be insensitive to the heterogeneity of the (actual and possible) causes of its tokens even though, on the one hand, meaning is supposed somehow to reduce to information and, on the other hand, information varies with etiology.
>
> (in press-f:37)

The robustness of genuine representations thus entails not only the possibility that they may on occasion, misrepresent, but that they display a certain "detachedness" from their contents, that is, that they can occur without their contents being around to occasion them.

The paradigm of detachedness seems to be provided by purely conventional relationships – like the relationship between an expression of natural language and its extension, or the relationship between a red light and the imperative to stop. Such relations as these contrast markedly with those relationships that betoken tight causal control – smoke and fire, mercury levels and temperature. (This is essentially Grice's (1957) distinction between "non-natural" and "natural" meaning.[5])

The problem for Fodor, and for anyone who would naturalize original intentionality, is to show how a representation can be natural, while still displaying the detachedness characteristic of non-natural meaning. This is vexing because the detachedness of non-natural representations is the result of there being *no* natural relationship underlying the meaning relation. Red lights mean "stop" because of a deliberate decision someone once made to use them for that purpose. "Red" means red because of the existence of a social practice involving the tacit and explicit intentions of the members of the English-speaking community. In neither case was there an *antecedent* causal connection grounding the relationship between the sign or symbol and its meaning.

This is not to say that no causal relationships exist – surely there's a causal connection between my stopping and the light's being red, and between my saying that it's red, and its being red. The point is that such causal relationships come into existence as a result of the *meaning relationship*, rather than the other way around. So the paradigms of detachedness get that property via intentionality. Obviously the explanation of the detachedness of *originally* intentional states must be different.

But now here's the ray of hope – the robustness of genuine representation is what prevents us from simply assimilating representation to causal covariance. We thus have reason independent of the intentional realism project for distinguishing between us and thermometers. *If*, therefore, we could find some non-intentional account of the detachedness of mental representations, such an account would necessarily yield a *kind* of nomic relation different from the relation between thermometers and temperature. In other words, *if* we can solve the problem of robustness in the context of the naturalization project, we might just get a defense of intentional realism for free. We now want to argue that Fodor's current theory of content may fill the bill.

In (1987d) and (in press-f), Fodor has proposed the following, which we'll call the Robust Asymmetric Dependence Condition (RADC), as a sufficient condition for representation:

Tokens of type S represent Ps if:

(i)   Ps cause S-tokenings, and do so in virtue of being Ps; that is, there is a nomic relation between the property of being an S-token and the property of being a P.

(ii)   some non-Ps cause S-tokenings.

(iii)   for any $X \neq P$, if X's cause S-tokenings and do so in virtue of being X's, the nomic relationship between S-tokenings and the property of being an X is asymmetrically dependent on the nomic relation between the property of being an S-tokening and the property of being a P.

Condition (i) establishes the basic causal/informational relation on which the representational relation is built. It answers the demands of the naturalization project, embodying what's right in the Skinnerian–Gibsonian idea that meaning is a matter of selective response to environmental variables.

Condition (ii) captures the respect in which representational relations *differ* from purely informational relations, as required by intentional realism. It asserts that S-tokenings are detachable from instantiations of (what Skinner would call) their "controlling" properties. Representation arises out of information precisely when the information-bearing structure declares its independence from the property it expresses.

Condition (iii) mitigates the potential conflict between (i) and (ii), by explaining what *kind* of nomic dependence there could be that allows for both (i) and (ii) to be satisfied. Given a variety of properties bearing a nomic relation to S-tokenings, condition (iii) tells us what privileges the property of being P over the others, making it the case that S-tokens represent Ps rather than any of their other causes.

What we now propose is that robust nomic dependence can do the job that anomic dependence was originally employed to do, and that it unites the project of naturalization and the project of intentional realism in a principled way.

Let's look at the slippery slope problem again. Fodor originally proposed to solve the problem by finding a property that things like us have, and things like paramecia lack, and which is plausibly explained by our possessing the capacity to represent. His candidate was the ability to respond selectively to anomic properties, or, more precisely, to respond *anomically* to stimulus properties. We've argued that the terms of the naturalization project puts this proposal out of bounds. Still, there does seem to be a feature of the paramecium's mode of response that distinguishes it from us.

Suppose that I say "My, what a crumpled shirt you're wearing today" in response to seeing your crumpled shirt. The property of being *crumpled* enters into the explanation of my behavior, and does so in virtue of its nomic relation with some property of my internal state. Up to this point, the paramecium is no different: when light of a certain intensity hits the paramecium, it moves, and its doing so is explained (in part) by the nomic relation between an internal state of the paramecium and the light intensity. But there the similarity ends – there is an important difference between the *kind* of nomic relation that holds, on the one hand, between my internal state and the property of being crumpled, and, on the other, the paramecium's internal state and the light intensity. The former relation, while nomic, is *robust*; i.e., it is a dependence that satisfies RADC. The latter dependence does not satisfy RADC.[6] Hence, we are justified in saying that the relation between the property of being crumpled and the selective property of my response is mediated by a representational state, whereas this is not the case with the relation between light intensity and the movement of the paramecium.

On the current proposal, the crucial difference between us and the paramecium does not depend on an objective difference in the kinds of properties to which we can selectively respond, but instead on a difference in *the way* we can respond. We can do it robustly (i.e., via a robust asymmetric dependence); they can't. Viewed in this way, the response to the slippery slope objection is of a piece with the intuition that what makes a creature capable of honest-to-God representation is a capability for misrepresentation. While it would have merely begged the question to just say that what distinguishes us from paramecia is our ability to misrepresent, to get it wrong, once we have the RADC account we can point in a non-question-begging manner to a difference in the way we are related to the properties on which our internal states nomically depend and the way paramecia are related to the properties on which their internal states nomically depend. That this difference should line up with the original intuition that our thoughts can get it wrong, or, more generally, be almost indefinitely detached from the properties that endow them with their content, is precisely what a defense of the intentional realism project should yield.

But, given all that, we think that perhaps there still is a way of reconstructing Fodor's original distinction between nomic and anomic properties, vindicating the intuition that there is really an important difference between properties like *having candlepower of 50* and properties like *being crumpled*. One manifestation of the difference seems to be the following: whereas you can get a device to respond to light intensity by merely having it instantiate a natural law, the only way to get a device to respond to being crumpled is to endow it with the ability to *represent* crumpledness. As some would put it, you can *transduce* light intensity but not crumpledness.

Fodor rejected transducibility as the basis of his distinction among properties, not because he thought it yielded the wrong criterion, but because he thought that the notion of transduction was parasitic on the notion of nomicity.

... as far as I can see, the only difference between a transducer and anything else that responds selectively to proximal stimulation is that transducers are devices whose outputs, taken under their computationally relevant descriptions, are lawfully related to corresponding properties of their inputs; in short, the point about transducers is that they respond selectively only to nomic properties.

(1986b:21)

But he agrees that the right kind of characterization of transduction would be well worth having: "If there were a way of defining 'transducer' independently of notions like nomicity, I would jump at it" (1986b:21–2).

We think we've got one, courtesy of the Robust Asymmetric Dependence Condition. The basic idea is that transducers are devices that detect without representing. A transducible property, therefore, is one for which a transducer could be built, a property which can be detected by a non-representational device. The RADC gives us a kind of nomic relation that is sufficient for representation, and hence a non-question-begging way of distinguishing systems that detect via representation from those that detect by exploiting some other kind of natural connection. Thus:

A property is *transducible* if at least some of its nomic relations with other properties fail to meet the RADC. A property is *non-transducible* if the only nomic relations with other properties into which it enters are relations that satisfy the RADC.

We can then say that a system is genuinely intentional iff it can respond selectively to *non-transducible* properties.

Our criterion connects non-transducibility to the capacity to represent in a desirable way. It implies something about the kind of system needed to detect certain kinds of properties: if you want to construct a device that can respond selectively to being crumpled, it's going to be a device which is *ipso facto* liable to error, and one which does not need crumpled things around in order to go into a crumpled-related state. Clearly this criterion is not meant as a replacement for the RADC criterion, since the proposed definition of "transducible" depends on the RADC. We offer it only as a way of vindicating the intuition that there's a real difference, of the sort Fodor was bruiting, between properties like crumpledness and others. We still maintain that the fundamental difference between representational systems and non-representational systems is to be found in the *kind* of nomic relationships into which the systems can enter. Thus, the defense of intentional realism need not depend upon the distinction between transducible and non-transducible properties, even if the distinction can be made. Even if it should turn out that every property – even crumpledness – is tranducible by our criterion, there will still be an objective difference between detection *by transduction* and detection *by representation* upon which to ground the difference between non-intentional and intentional systems.

We've argued, then, that an appeal to robustness obviates the problematic appeal to nomicity in Fodor's handling of intentional realism. But hang on to your shirts (crumpled or otherwise). There's yet another problem for representationalism that Fodor proposes to solve by appeal to an intuitive conception of the nomic which we don't think robustness is going to be able to handle.

Another Problem

A naturalistic theory of representation must not only show how it's possible for a mental state to have content – it must also assign to mental states the right sorts of contents. Specifically, it must give an account of how our mental states can refer to things in our external environment; it must not entail that all we can think about is our own internal states. This constraint is coordinate with the need to preserve the possibility of misrepresentation. If I am thinking of a Pekinese dog, "that's a cat," I'm wrong; but if I'm thinking simply "there's a kitty-appearance for you," I'm right. Since one of the chief arguments for representationalism is the possibility it affords for explaining seemingly odd or irrational behavior as the product of false beliefs, RTM clearly needs an account of content that doesn't make all our thoughts into sense data reports.

Enter the *proximal stimulus problem.* There are two ways in which this problem may arise for Fodor's theory of content. The first is via causal chains. Consider a causal chain of the form A $-->$ B $-->$ C. In such a sequence of events, it appears that the causal connection between A and C is asymmetrically dependent upon the causal connection between B and C, since A wouldn't cause C but for the fact that B does. Does C therefore *mean* B? The proximal stimulus problem appears as a special case: let A be a horse, B a pattern of retinal irradiation, and C a mental representation (call it 'H'), the content of which is in question. Does H stand for the retinal stimulation, in virtue of the nomic dependence of the horse $-->$ H connection on the connection between the retinal pattern and H?

Fodor discusses the general causal chain problem in *A Theory of Content and other Essays* (in press-f:61) where he points out that not all cases of asymmetric dependency are cases of *robust* asymmetric dependency. The mere existence of a causal chain is thus not enough to engender representation: there must be, in addition (as RADC requires), non-B-caused Cs (note that all A-caused Cs are, by hypothesis, B-caused Cs) such that the nomic relation between the non-Bs and the Cs is asymmetrically dependent upon the B-caused Cs. This is enough to answer this version of the proximal stimulus problem: the mere fact that a horse requires the mediation of some proximal stimulus in order to cause H-tokens is not enough to make H refer to that stimulus rather than to the horse.[7]

But the proximal stimulus problem recurs in more virulent form when we reflect on the facts about robustness. (This will take a little work.) Horses are good at causing H-tokens, we may suppose. But so are cows-on-dark-nights. The RADC is designed to block the conclusion that H-tokens have, by virtue of this fact, an extension that includes both horses and cows, or even horses and cows-on-dark-nights. But suppose someone argues in the following way: "if cows-on-dark-nights can cause H-tokens, it must be because of some property they share with horses – presumably some property of their visual appearance. It's plausible, for instance, that horses and cows-on-dark-nights both project the same patterns of light onto the retinas of normal observers. Call such a pattern P1.

Then the following seems to be true. Horses cause P1, which causes H, and cows-on-dark-nights cause P1, which causes H. Why not say that H refers to instantiations of P1, rather than to horses?"

No problem. The RADC, together with plausible assumptions about the way horses cause horse-tokenings, will rule out such a conclusion. H cannot mean P1, by the RADC, unless there are at least some non-P1-caused H-tokenings. But if there are non-P1-caused H-tokenings, they are likely to be caused by other sorts of *horse-caused* proximal stimulations: the sound of a horse whinnying, for example.[8] In that case, there will be no dependency, asymmetric or otherwise, of horse-caused H-tokenings on P1-caused H-tokenings.[9] Indeed, given the enormous variety of ways in which horses can cause H-tokenings, it's far more likely that the P1 --> H connection is asymmetrically dependent upon the horse --> H connection – that the ability of P1's to cause H's depends upon the fact that horses cause H's.

OK. The moral here is that distal stimuli are not generally dependent upon any particular mode of proximal stimulation to cause tokenings of the relevant mental state. Thus, there will never be a particular kind of proximal stimulus onto which all the distal stimuli converge. But now consider the "super proximal stimulus" – the open (and possibly infinite) disjunction of *all* the different ways by which horses (and for that matter, cows-on-dark-nights or anything else that we can mistake for a horse) cause H-tokenings: (Pi v Pii v Piii v . . .). (We'll abbreviate this as 'P(INF)'.) It would seem that for any given distal cause, X, of H-tokenings, X's ability to cause Hs is going to depend upon P(INF)'s ability to cause Hs. All distal causes of H-tokenings, it appears, must do their causing through P(INF).

Here's the problem. We originally thought that the robustness clause would once again save the day. That is, we reasoned, if it's true that P(INF) *really* includes all the different proximal stimulations that could prompt H-tokenings (and hence all the different sensory presentations a horse could make), then the P(INF) --> H connection would not be *robust*. But alas, we were forgetting about an essential aspect of robustness – *detachedness*. H-tokenings can occur in the absence of any particular distal stimulation; they can be triggered by one's own thoughts. But such causes of H-tokens as idle thoughts of dogfood are not going to be included in P(INF), since they are not proximal sensory stimulations.

This is big trouble, in our view. Fodor (in press-b) designed the RADC to cover not only cases of misrepresentation, but what he calls "non-labelling uses" of mental representations, uses that include our idly thinking of horses when none are present. An H-token can mean *horse* despite its being detachable from horses *if* the RADC is satisfied, that is, if the non-horse-caused H-tokenings depend upon the horse-caused H-tokenings. But any candidate for the mental representation of horse that meets this condition is unfortunately going to meet the following condition: non-P(INF)-caused H-tokenings are asymmetrically dependent upon P(INF)-caused H-tokenings, because horses have to effect H-tokenings *through* P(INF)s. It looks like we have prima facie reason to say that H-tokens mean P(INF).

Fodor doesn't worry about this problem, because his strategy for dealing with the proximal stimulus problem doesn't go through the RADC at all. Fodor rules out such properties as P(INF) on the grounds that they are *anomic*:

So barring appeals to *open* disjunctions, it seems likely that there is just no way to specify an array of proximal stimulations upon which the dependence of cow-thoughts upon cows is asymmetrically dependent. And here's where I quit.

Then he continues:

... The idea would be that, on the one hand, content depends on *nomic* relations among properties and, on the other, nothing falls under a law by satisfying an *open* disjunction (open disjunctions aren't projectible).

(in press-f:54)

This appeal to a nomic/anomic distinction taps a slightly different intuition than the earlier appeal. Here the idea is that no *unprincipled* disjunction could represent a property that figures in a natural law. While we acknowledge the pull of this intuition, we foresee significant difficulties in working it out.

First of all, remember that on the liberal view of natural law, properties like being crumpled, which are implicated in true, counterfactual-supporting generalizations, are going to get counted as nomic. (They're not *transducible* on our account, but transducibility can't be what's at issue here, since we're talking about candidates for the meanings of mental representations, and those can't be limited to transducible properties.) So we need a way of characterizing the nomic so as to disallow properties like P(INF), *without* disallowing properties like being *crumpled*.

Well, what Fodor says he objects to in a property like P(INF) is that it is an "open disjunction." "Crumpled," of course, is a logically simple predicate. But surely the fact that we have a lexical primitive to express a given property should be neither necessary nor sufficient for making the property *nomic*: on the one hand, there may be many clearly nomic properties for which no one has bothered to invent a lexically primitive expression; and on the other hand, we *can* invent such expressions for any crazy, cooked-up property we like. We could, after all, have denoted the set of proximal stimulations that cause H-tokenings by means of some simple, connotative expression like "horselike."

The deep issue raised by this rejection of "open disjunctions" is this. As we understand Fodor's metaphysics, both properties and the nomic relationships among them are objective – their existence and nature are supposed to be language-independent. But "disjunction" is a *formal* notion, applicable primarily to modes of expression. *Predicates* can clearly be disjunctive or not, but it's quite unclear what it would be for a *property* to be disjunctive. It's simply not to the point to say, as Fodor does, that "nothing falls under a law by satisfying an *open* disjunction ..." (emphasis original), or that "open disjunctions aren't projectible," if, as Fodor also seems to hold, laws are not formal objects.

What's needed at the very least is some principle for dividing properties into simple and complex, without simply collapsing property structure and predicate structure. The structure of predicates in natural language has clear relevance to the issue of taxonomizing underlying mental states – though even here, as Fodor has pointed out repeatedly, one can't be too quick to read mental structure off linguistic structure.[10] But as the argument above shows, the logical form of a predicate can hardly be a guide to the nomicity of the property it expresses.

But maybe the logical structure issue is a red herring. After all, it does seem that Fodor's real objection to properties like P(INF) lies more in their "openness" than in their disjunctiveness. The property P(INF), whether we express it that way, or via the lexically simple neologism "horselike," appears to be *unprincipled* – there are no rules or constraints for determining what falls within its extension. Anything goes.

Again, we're sympathetic. But since at least one of us thinks that Wittgenstein wasn't a complete dope, we have to express some pessimism about getting the right kind of payoff from a criterion of nomicity built on the idea of "principledness." Again, consider the predicate "crumpled." Isn't such a predicate as this, on the one hand, just shorthand for an unprincipled assortment of fabric conditions? And on the other hand, don't we seem perfectly well able to project it nonetheless? The situation is the same for a large number of predicates that express artifact kinds – "table," "flour" – oh, what the hell – "*game.*" That is, we can't get very serious definitions, but we do OK with them despite that fact. On the other hand, we must also say that we continue to feel a difference between a property like *being horselike* and one like being a *horse*, and we fervently hope that Fodor or someone else can explain what that difference is. (Goodman's "it's-just-what-we-do" response won't be adequate here, since we need a notion of nomicity *independent* of human practice in order to solve the proximal stimulus problem in the context of the naturalization project.) Still, we conclude that Fodor's appeal to nomicity in the context of the proximal stimulus problem is unsatisfactory, and that he needs either a fuller account of projectibility or a different strategy altogether.

We began our discussion by noting a tension between the goals of naturalizing intentionality and exhibiting it as distinctive of (what we pretheoretically take to be) minds. We argued that Fodor's latest treatment of the naturalization problem produces a conception of the origins of intentionality – the RADC – that itself relieves this tension. Whether or not Fodor's current theory can serve the purposes for which it was designed is, of course, a matter of great controversy, and in the last section, we've added a little fuel to the fire. Still, we're prepared to go on if Fodor is – the fact that his solution to the robustness problem should also reinforce the intentional realist project seems to us to provide independent motivation for working out the problems that remain.

NOTES

1 "Tension" is, of course, polite for "contradiction."

2 In this, Fodor locates himself within the *semantic* tradition of Skinner (1957), according to whom a symbol's meaning is determined by the range of discriminative stimuli that "control" the production of the symbol. For views that are more purely information-theoretic than Fodor's, see Dretske (1981) and Stampe (1977).

3 In a note, Fodor adds a significant qualification to this claim. We discuss the import of this note below.

4 These sorts of connections can display an impressive degree of cognitive mediation. One of us, an arachnophobe, has been known to calmly count the legs of a beast on the wall before running screaming from the room.

5 Grice (1957:41) contends that not all non-natural meanings are purely conventional and cites "certain gestures" as cases in point. Still, he does allow that his distinction between natural and non-natural meaning is "what people are getting at when they

display an interest in a distinction between 'natural' and 'conventional' signs." And, for what's it's worth, it's not clear that those gestures that are not "conventional in any ordinary sense," which are not, for example, culture-relative, ought really to be counted as cases of non-natural meaning.

6   Note that satisfying RADC means more than having multifarious causes. It also means that one among the multifarious causes is privileged in that all the rest asymmetrically depend on it. So one doesn't say that the dependence of the paramecium's internal state on the light intensity satisfies robustness just because it can be induced in other ways; those other ways must also be asymmetrically dependent on the relation between light intensity and the internal state. Presumably this is not the case.

7   Actually, we don't need to go even this far to eliminate the proximal stimulus problem as stated.

8   Nothing depends here on switching sensory modalities – it just makes exposition easier to do so.

9   Dretske (1981) proposes a solution to the proximal stimulus problem along these lines.

10   Most pertinently, see the discussion of alleged transducers in "Paramecia," and the discussion of Lynne Rudder Baker's robot–cat example in Fodor (in press-f:50).

2

Has Content Been Naturalized?

LYNNE RUDDER BAKER

The Representational Theory of the Mind (RTM) has been forcefully and subtly developed by Jerry A. Fodor. According to the RTM, psychological states that explain behavior involve tokenings of mental representations. Since the RTM is distinguished from other approaches by its appeal to the meaning or "content" of mental representations, a question immediately arises: by virtue of what does a mental representation express or represent an environmental property like *cow* or *shoe*?

This question asks for a general account of the semantics of mental representation. Fodor places two conditions on the requisite theory: it must be *physicalistic* (that is, it must be couched in nonsemantic and nonintentional terms, free of expressions like "refers to" or "denotes" or "means that"), and it must be *atomistic* (that is, it must allow that the thinker can have a single intentional state without having any others). What is wanted, then, is a reductive theory that "naturalizes" content by specifying sufficient conditions, in physicalistic and atomistic terms, for a mental symbol to represent or express a certain property.

The Reduction

The naturalistic relation that carries the weight of the reduction of representation is causation. The aim is to show how representational properties (e.g., the property of representing *cat*) can be understood in terms of wide causal properties (e.g., the property of being caused by *cat* instantiations, or, for short, by cats). Fodor understands representation in terms of nomic relations between instances of the property (cats, say) and mental tokens of a given type.

The basic idea is that tokens of a certain type represent those properties whose instantiations produce them. The difficulty with this simple formulations is that tokens of any given type may have countless different kinds of causes. Fodor calls this phenomenon the "robustness" of thought. A thought of a cat may be produced, for instance, not only by an instantiation of a cat, but also by an instantiation of a shoe that you mistake for a cat, or by some preceding thought of tigers, say, when there are not any cats around. Yet, we do not want to say that your token represents some disjunctive property, *cat-or-shoe-or-preceding thought-or-...*, and so on. We need sufficient conditions that allow your thought to represent a cat and that rule out the disjunctive property.

17

To avoid this problem, which Fodor sometimes calls "the disjunction problem,"[1] he formulates a notion of asymmetric dependence. Roughly, no matter what the actual cause of your token, it represents the property *cat* if non-cat-caused tokens of that type are "asymmetrically dependent" on cat-caused tokens of that type — if, that is, noncats would not cause tokens of that type unless cats did, but cats would still cause tokens of that type even if noncats did not. Asymmetric dependence, officially, is this:[2]

> (AD) The law C '--> D' is asymmetrically dependent on the law 'A --> B' (where A, B, C, D are properties) iff the A/B connection can not be broken without breaking the C/D connection; but the C/D connection can be broken without breaking the A/B connection.

The asymmetric dependence of 'C --> D' on 'A --> B' is to be determined by answering the question — In the nearest possible world in which the A/B connection is broken, is the C/D connection thereby broken? – in the affirmative, and by answering the question – In the nearest possible world in which the C/D connection is broken, is the A/B connection thereby broken – in the negative.

Combining the idea of asymmetric dependence with that of nomic relations, we have Fodor's reduction, (R):

> (R) A token of some nonsemantic type T represents a property P if
> (i) instances of P cause (or are nomically related to) tokens of T, and
> (ii) any tokens of T that are caused by instances of non-P are asymmetrically dependent on tokens of T that are caused by instances of P.[3,4]

Clause (i) of (R) marks this view as a variety of information-based semantics, and Clause (ii) of (R) aims to solve the disjunction problem. As Fodor illustrates, "'Cow' means *cow* and not *cat*, or *cat-or-cow*, because there being cat-caused 'cow'-tokens depends on there being cow-caused 'cow'-tokens, but not the other way around."[5] Or, again, "[W]hat the story about asymmetric dependence comes down to is that 'cow' means *cow* because (i) there is a nomic relation between the property of being a cow and the property of being a cause of 'cow'-tokens; and (ii) if there are nomic relations between other properties and the property of being a cause of 'cow'-tokens, then the latter nomic relations depend upon the former" (TC, 40). (R), I think, captures these conditions.

I shall discuss two major tests of this account of representation: first, how it handles representation of uninstantiated properties, and second, how it solves the disjunction problem. Then, I shall raise a general theoretical problem for the reduction – a problem of specifying which relations are semantically relevant. Before turning to these issues, however, we must look again at (R). For I believe that Fodor vacillates in his interpretation of (R).

Interpretations of (R)

The first clause of (R) is open to different interpretations: Does it require that instances of P *actually cause T-tokens*, or that instances of P *would cause T-tokens but for accidental circumstances* (i.e., P is locally instantiated, and it does not matter whether or not P has caused T-tokens), or only that instances of P *would cause T-tokens if the property P were instantiated* (i.e., it does not matter whether P is locally instantiated or not)? These distinctions lead to three different versions of (R). Call them the "actual-history" version, the "local-instantiation" version, and the "pure-informational" version, respectively.[6]

(AH) A token of nonsemantic type T means X if:
    (1) "Xs cause T-tokens" is a law;
    (2) For all Y (not = X), if "Ys cause T-tokens" is a law, then *Ys cause T-tokens* is asymmetrically dependent on *Xs cause T-tokens*;
    (3) Some T-tokens are actually caused by Xs.

(LI) A token of nonsemantic type T means X if:
    (1) "Xs cause T-tokens" is a law;
    (2) For all Y (not = X), if "Ys cause T-tokens" is a law, then *Ys cause T-tokens* is asymmetrically dependent on *Xs cause T-tokens*;
    (3) The property X is locally instantiated.

(PI) A token of nonsemantic type T means X if:
    (1) "Xs cause T-tokens" is a law;
    (2) For all Y (not = X), if "Ys cause T-tokens" is a law, then *Ys cause T-tokens* is asymmetrically dependent on *Xs cause T-tokens*.

Fodor's official view is the pure-informational version. This line is in accord with his sustained emphasis on nomic relations between properties (which hold whether the properties are instantiated or not), as opposed to actual causal interactions among individuals. However, as we shall see, it is the local-instantiation version to which Fodor actually appeals (except when he is considering unicorns). Although he formulates the actual-history version as a possible alternative,[7] he does not actually endorse it. And he does not distinguish the local-instantiation version from the others at all. Now, turn to the test cases.

Uninstantiated Properties: The Unicorn Case

We can represent uninstantiated properties like *unicorn*; and assuming it to be nomically possible that there be unicorns, we may represent unicorns by means of primitive symbols. (If you disagree, select any other uninstantiated property that might have been instantiated.) The asymmetric dependence view should allow that certain tokens represent unicorns.

Fodor has explicitly applied his view to the unicorn case. Clearly, neither the actual-history version nor the local-instantiation version permits a primitive symbol of Mentalese to mean *unicorn*. So, if Fodor's view is to allow primitive symbols to represent uninstantiated properties, the view (as Fodor prefers) must be given the pure-informational interpretation.

Does the pure-informational version allow a person S's U-tokens (internal tokens of some nonsemantic type U) to represent *unicorn*? The first clause of the reduction sails through fine: there is a nomic relation between unicorns and S's U-tokens, because, as Fodor says, if S were in a world in which there are unicorns, they would cause S's U-tokens.

But now consider: there is as much a nomic relation between S's U-tokens and shunicorns – where a shunicorn is a unicorn look-alike that is really a small zebra with a horn in the middle of the forehead – as there is between S's U-tokens and unicorns. The description of shunicorns is merely a heuristic device; 'shunicorn' is as primitive a term as 'unicorn.' The fact that 'unicorn' is an English word, but 'shunicorn' is not, is strictly irrelevant to the case.[8] If either unicorns or shunicorns could have been instantiated in our world, then *both* could have been.

Since shunicorns are instances of non-unicorns, the asymmetric dependence condition comes into play. The asymmetric dependence condition should allow misrepresentation of a shunicorn as a unicorn, but it does not: Since we have no basis on which to distinguish the relative distances of worlds in which there are shunicorns and worlds in which there are unicorns from the actual world, we should treat them as equidistant from our world. Similarly, worlds in which a person's shunicorn/U connection is broken, but her unicorn/U connection remains intact are the same distance from the actual world as worlds in which her unicorn/U connection is broken, but her shunicorn/U connection remains intact. At least, we have no principled way to distinguish the two.

The fact that worlds in which unicorns cause U-tokens, but shunicorns don't, seem equidistant from us as worlds in which shunicorns cause U-tokens, but unicorns don't, suggests a general dilemma concerning uninstantiated properties: either the required asymmetric dependence is missing and the pure-informational version (along with the other versions) fails to account for primitive tokens that represent uninstantiated properties at all, or there is "too much" asymmetric dependence and we get the contradiction of mutual asymmetric dependence (or a new disjunction problem).

Here is the first alternative. As long as neither *unicorn* nor *shunicorn* is instantiated in the actual world, we have no basis for the needed asymmetric dependence: the nomic relation between *shunicorn* and S's U-tokens is not asymmetrically dependent on the nomic relation between *unicorn* and S's U-tokens. In this case, none of the three versions of (R) can account for S's U-tokens representing *unicorn*, and similarly for any other uninstantiated property.

Here is the other alternative. If we accept Fodor's gloss on asymmetric dependence, we get a contradiction. Fodor has explained that "it can be true that the property of being a unicorn is nomologically linked with the property of being a cause of 'unicorn'-tokens *even if there aren't any unicorns.*" He continues:

> Maybe this cashes out into something like "there wouldn't be nonunicorn-caused 'unicorn' tokens but that unicorns would cause 'unicorn' tokens if there were any unicorns." And maybe that cashes out into something like this: there are non-unicorn-caused 'unicorn' tokens only in nearby worlds in which there are unicorn-caused 'unicorn' tokens. But [he adds]... I am not an enthusiast for such translations.
>
> (*TC*, 46)

If we took this seriously – though the qualification at the end suggests that we don't have to – we would say, by parity of reasoning, that there are shunicorn-caused U-tokens only in nearby worlds in which there are unicorn-caused U-tokens. But as Fodor says, there are uniocrn-caused U-tokens only in equally nearby worlds in which there are shunicorn-caused U-tokens. So, we get a contradiction: shunicorn-caused U-tokens, if there were any, would be asymmetrically dependent on unicorn-caused U-tokens AND unicorn-caused U-tokens, if there were any, would be asymmetrically dependent on shunicorn-caused U-tokens. (The contradiction could be avoided by taking S's U-tokens to represent *unicorn-or-shunicorn*; but this is just the disjunction problem again.)

Since Fodor backs away from his gloss by saying, "I am not an enthusiast for such translations," I am not charging him with a contradiction here. But I do believe that he is on the horns of a dilemma: if the asymmetric dependence condition is satisfied by *unicorn*, then it is equally satisfied by *shunicorn*, and we get contradiction or disjunction – and a straightforward counterexample to the analysis. (Both conditions would be satisfied, but, because of contradiction or disjunction, we can not conclude that S's token represents *unicorn*.) On the other hand, if the asymmetric dependence condition is not satisfied, the reduction cannot handle uninstantiated properties generally, and we are left with a serious gap. Either way, the reduction fails for unicorns.

Of course, there is an obvious way to avoid the problem: Treat 'unicorn' not as a primitive but as a defined term. Treating 'unicorn' as a nonprimitive term would seem reasonable enough, but it would put an unreasonable constraint on the naturalization project. For it would require that the primitive terms represent only instantiated properties.

Such a restriction of the theory to instantiated properties may be described in either of two ways: it makes instantiation of the relevant properties a necessary condition for asymmetric dependence; alternatively, it abandons the pure-informational version for the local-instantiation version (or perhaps the actual history version). Neither description, I think, would be welcome to Fodor. For both tie the theory to what actually exists, as opposed to nomic relations among properties.

But there seems to be a more serious problem. It is implausible to suppose that whether or not a symbol is (semantically) primitive depends on whether or not the property it represents is instantiated. Let me give three examples of the implausibility.

(a) Consider your Doppelganger in a world that has unicorns. Your Doppelganger has never seen a unicorn but has read about unicorns and has seen pictures of them – just exactly as you have. On the current suggestion, your Doppelganger's symbol that represents *unicorn* may be (semantically) primitive, but yours must be an abbreviation of symbols that represent instantiated properties. Prima facie, it would be at least odd for there to be two individuals who have been molecular duplicates all their lives, who have the same *wide* causal histories, and who have mental symbols that represent the same property, but one of whose symbols is semantically primitive and the other not.[9]

Moreover, on the Fodorian assumption that syntax is "in the head," you and your Doppelganger must have the same syntactically primitive predicates. Thus, if Fodor's view allows you and your Doppelganger to differ in your semantically primitive predicates, the view severs the connection between syntax and semantics. And Fodor would be mistaken in saying that his view explicates "the semantical relation between a *syntactically* primitive predicate and the property it expresses" (*TC*, 70; my emphasis).

(b)   Consider a would-be natural kind, a property that was widely but mistakenly thought by experts to be instantiated – say, *phlogiston*. On the current suggestion that "concepts that express uninstantiated properties are *ipso facto* constructions out of concepts that express instantiated properties" (*TC*, 67), the concept that expresses *phlogiston* is *ipso facto* a construction out of concepts that express instantiated properties. What might those constituent concepts be? The supposition that the concept that expresses *phlogiston* is "a construction out of concepts that express instantiated properties" does not seem to capture what scientists intended when they postulated phlogiston as a natural kind to explain combustion; nor does it seem to capture what *we* mean when we say that eighteenth-century scientists incorrectly postulated phlogiston.

(c)   Consider symbols that represent artifacts. There was a time when, say, *shoe* was uninstantiated. On the requirement that only instantiated properties can be expressed by primitive symbols, it would seem that the symbol for *shoe* (or for any other artifact) could not be primitive – at least before the advent of shoes. And it seems unlikely that, at the first shoe instantiation, the derived symbol for *shoe* was transformed into a primitive symbol. By like reasoning, no symbol that represented an artifact could be primitive.

Thus, I do not think that representation of uninstantiated properties has been handled satisfactorily. Uninstantiated properties do not seem expressible by primitive symbols, and the alternative view that they are expressible by nonprimitive symbols has the implausible consequences canvassed in (a)–(c).

The Disjunction Problem: Cats/Robot-Cats

Suppose that young Sally – let us keep her isolated from spoken language for a while – lives in an environment populated not only with ordinary cats, but with an equal number of robot-cats. The robot-cats are distinguishable from the cats by knowledgeable people (though not by Sally).[10] Sally has seen 1,001 robot-cats, each of which has produced in her a token of nonsemantic type F, and she has never tokened F under any other circumstances. Then, one day, she sees for the first time a cat, which also produces in her a token of type F. Until the cat-caused F-token in question, Sally has never seen or otherwise been exposed to cats, and, of course, we are making no assumptions about what she has been told. (In intentional terms, Sally at this point can not distinguish robot-cats from cats.) What does the cat-caused F-token represent?

There are three candidates. (i) The cat-caused F-token correctly represents a cat, and the other F-tokens have misrepresented robots as cats all along; (ii) the cat-caused F-token misrepresents a cat as a robot; (iii) the cat-caused F-token correctly represents the cat as a cat-or–robot-cat. Fodor opts for the third answer. Let us see why.

(i)   Suppose that the cat-caused F-token correctly represents a cat, and that the other F-tokens have misrepresented robot-cats as cats all along. This option is not plausible on the asymmetric dependence view. For it would describe all the robot-cat-caused F-tokens as asymmetrically dependent on the cat-caused F-tokens. But if there is any asymmetric dependence, it is the other way around: The cat/F connection would be asymmetrically dependent on the robot-cat/F connection.

(ii) Suppose that the cat-caused F-token represents *robot-cat*, and thus misrepresents the cat as a robot-cat. But this option ignores the relevant counterfactuals. If Sally had encountered cats, they would have caused F-tokens. It is only an accident that she encountered only robot-cats, and Fodor says that "the *semantically relevant* samples include not just the ones that *were* encountered, but also the ones that would have been encountered but for an accident."[11] Notice that this response implicitly appeals, not to the pure-informational version but to the local-instantiation version. Thus, instead of saying that the cat-caused F-token represents *robot-cat*, Fodor (*TC*; 49) takes the third option.

(iii) Suppose that the cat-caused F-token represents *robot-cat-or-cat*.[12] Fodor points out

> It is OK for some predicates to be disjunctive as long as not all of them are. One can perfectly consistently hold, on the one hand, that "cat" means *robot or cat* when it's *accidental* that you learned it just from robot-cats; while denying, on the other hand, that it would mean *cat or robot* if you had learned it in a world where all you *could* have learned it from were robot-cats (e.g., because there aren't any cats around).
>
> (*TC*, 49)

First, notice that this just abandons the pure-informational version in favor of the local-instantiation version of the reduction. It is obvious that the local-instantiation version precludes Fodor's favored approach to unicorns.

Second, of course, it is "OK for some predicates to be disjunctive as long as not all of them are." But the cat/robot case is generalizable. For example, suppose that Sally has also seen 1,001 mules, each of which has produced in her an M-token; then one day, for the first time, she sees a horse, which also produces in Sally an M-token. By parity of reasoning, we should say that Sally's first M-token represents *mule-or-horse*. The same story could be told about (almost?) any symbol.[13]

For these reasons, the disjunctive option (iii) seems a risky resting place for Fodor. But let us press on. Let's call the story up to this point 'scene 1.' When we leave scene 1, Sally can not misrepresent a cat as a robot-cat, because her F-tokens represent some disjunctive property *cat-or-robot-cat-[or perhaps something else]*.

On to scene 2. Even though robot-cats and cats and perhaps other things initially are in the extension of F-tokens, surely it must be possible at some stage for Sally to misrepresent a cat as a robot-cat. Perhaps, over time, Sally sees lots of cats as well as robot-cats, and observing them closely, comes to respond to cats and robot-cats differently. No longer do cats and robot-cats indiscriminately cause F-tokens, but now cats and robot-cats cause tokens of different types.

Then, one day, Sally sees a cat, which, under the circumstances that day, she misrepresents as a robot-cat. There are three points to notice.

1 The first point concerns the impossibility of error in scene 1. Suppose that from her vantage point in scene 2, Sally thinks back to the time when she saw her first cat (scene 1) and thinks, I mistook that cat for a robot-cat. But if in scene 1, her cat-caused token represented, not *robot-cat*, but *cat-or-robot-cat*, as Fodor has

claimed, then there was no mistake to be made. Sally's mistake is to think that she made a mistake.

Fodor replies by offering an "easy answer" and an "interesting answer." The easy answer is that "her indiscriminate application of the same term to both cat and robot-cat was a symptom of her failure to distinguish between them. Not distinguishing between [them] was a serious mistake (by [Sally's] current lights)" (*TC*: 50). But this reply is not really to the point.

The point is that, in scene 1, the inclusion of both cats and robots in the extension of Sally's F-tokens is not correctly described as a failure or a mistake at all. For anyone who, like Fodor, endorses the disjunctive option (iii), the difference between scene 1 and scene 2 is that Sally's cat-caused tokens represent different properties – *cat-or-robot-cat* in scene 1 and *cat* in scene 2. The fact that, in scene 2, Sally knows the difference between cats and robot-cats does not make the cat-caused tokening of F in scene 1 a misrepresentation, when in scene 1, Sally's F-tokens represented *cat-or-robot-cat*.

What Fodor calls "the interesting answer" requires distinguishing between what is in the extension of the symbol (cats and robot-cats) and what concept a person uses the symbol to express. Fodor describes Sally as having made a mistake, which he describes by saying that "she took it that the robots that she called 'cats' had a certain non-disjunctive property which they shared with everything else in the set (cats U robots). By her present lights, by contrast, *there is no such property*" (*TC*, 50).

Perhaps, in scene 2, when Sally thinks back to her days of not distinguishing between cats and robot-cats, she is using a symbol to express a certain property; but in scene 1, there is no question of her *using* a symbol to express a property, nor of her *intending to apply* a symbol in a certain way. In scene 1, we are trying to establish what property the primitive symbol represents – solely on the basis of causal relations and asymmetric dependence. Moreover, Fodor's atomism requires that it be possible for Sally to be capable of being in a single intentional state, without attributing to her any other intentional states, such as an intention to use a symbol in one way rather than another.[14,15]

It seems inconsistent to say both that the "first 'cat' token means *cat or robot* and is thus true of the cat that it's applied to" (*TC*, 49) AND that its tokening involves a mistake. So, the first point – that Sally's thought in scene 2 that she had mistaken a cat for a robot-cat (in scene 1) was itself a mistake, on Fodor's view – still stands. And this leads to the second point:

2 The second point is that the asymmetric dependence account leaves a large hole. How do we describe, in nonintentional and nonsematic terms, the change from scene 1 (with no misrepresentation) to scene 2 (with misrepresentation of a cat as a robot-cat). To answer in terms of Sally's ability to distinguish cats from robot-cats does not suffice.

If she is presented with two robot-cats and a cat, Sally can discriminate in the sense of classifying the robot-cats as more like each other than either is like a cat. But *this* ability can not be the relevant difference between scene 1 and scene 2, for three reasons. First, it is an ability that Sally has in scene 1, as well as in scene 2. Secondly, the ability to distinguish between robot-cats and cats does not suffice for the difference anyway. If Sally is presented with two chihuahuas and a Doberman pincher, she can distinguish in the sense of classifying the chihuahuas as more like each other than either is like the Doberman; but the three are all dogs for all that. And if she is presented with two small cats and a large cat, Sally can classify the two small cats as more like each other than either is to the large cat, but that does not count against their all being cats. Thus, the ability to distinguish (put as nonintentionally as I can put it) does not account for the difference between scene 1 and scene 2.

A direct appeal to asymmetric dependence does not explain the change from scene 1 to scene 2, because the same question re-arises: how do we get from the absence of asymmetric dependence in scene 1 to its presence in scene 2? In scene 1, the law '*cat* --> F' was not asymmetrically dependent on the law '*robot-cat* --> F' since cats and robot-cats were both in the extension of F-tokens. But if asymmetric dependence is supposed to account for misrepresentation, and if Sally can *ever* misrepresent a cat as a robot-cat (and surely she can in scene 2), then we need an account of how '*cat* --> F' comes to be asymmetrically dependent on '*robot-cat* --> F' for Sally.

3 The third point is that the distinction between scene 1 and scene 2 bears an uncanny resemblance to the distinction on which Fodor has argued that teleological theories of content rest, and against which Fodor has argued. The distinction to which teleological theories seem committed is a distinction between type 1 situations and type 2 situations. In type 1 situations, "if Ps cause S-tokens, then S means P (and if P is disjunctive, then so be it)" (*TC*, 13). In type 2 situations, S-tokens may be caused by nonPs, and they still mean P. Misrepresentation, according to these theories, is possible only in type 2 situations – just as, in the story of Sally, her tokens could misrepresent a cat as a robot-cat only in scene 2.

One difference between Fodor's theory and teleological theories is this: according to teleological theories, in type 1 situations, which are "normal" or "optimal," only the property in the extension of T causes T-tokens. But since Fodor does not want to appeal to normal conditions it seems that for him, in type 1 situations (as in scene 1), any property that, but for an accident, would have caused T-tokens must be included in the extension of T.[16]

If scenes 1 and 2 of Sally's story correspond to type 1 and type 2 situations of teleological theories of content, then Fodor is saddled with the same problems that he has detected in the teleological theories of content.

For these three reasons, I conclude that Fodor's reduction has not given an adequate account of the cat/robot-cat case.

Semantically Relevant Relations

With respect both to the unicorn case and to the cat/robot case, we have seen the persistent threat of the disjunction problem. Fodor's solution to that problem lies in the requirement of asymmetric dependence. In order to make the crucial asymmetric dependence relation work in the required way, however, Fodor must restrict its application to semantically relevant relations. He says, "If there's going to be a causal theory of content, there has to be some way of picking out *semantically relevant* causal relations from all the other kinds of causal relations that the tokens of a symbol can enter into."[17] He does this by adding a condition to the reduction: robustness.

In this section, I shall first show why robustness, or some other requirement that restricts the asymmetric dependence condition, is needed; then, I shall show why it is unavailable on a physicalistic account.

Fodor appeals to robustness to block counterexamples to his reduction.[18] Suppose that 'A --> B' is a law and 'B --> C' is a law. Then the law 'A --> C' is asymmetrically dependent on the law 'B --> C.' "Since causal chains give rise to a species of asymmetrical dependence, and since every event belongs to some causal chain or other, how are we to avoid concluding that everything means something? Pansemanticism gone mad." The solution is that "content requires not just causal dependence but robustness too." In the causal chain example, all A-caused Cs are also B-caused, and conversely. "So the asymmetric dependence of 'A --> C' on 'B --> C' doesn't satisfy the conditions on robustness; so it's not sematically relevant" (*TC*: 62).

Let me try to make more vivid the need for a condition (like robustness) in addition to the nomic-relations condition and the asymmetric dependence condition as originally stated. (The differences among the three versions of the reduction are irrelevant to the present point.) Suppose that it is a law that A --> T and it is a law that C --> T, where A and C are properties, and T is a nonsemantic type of mental token, and the law 'C --> T' is asymmetrically dependent on the law 'A --> T'. Construe asymmetric dependence as Fodor originally defines it: the A/T connection can not be broken without breaking the C/T connection, but the C/T connection can be broken without breaking the A/T connection. Does it follow, as it should from the account, that A is in the extension of T? No. Without some further restriction, it does not even follow that T has content.

Suppose that being at the top of a long escalator causes in Jones feelings of panic, and suppose that being at great heights out in the open causes Jones feelings of panic; and suppose that the escalator/panic connection is asymmetrically dependent on the open-heights/panic connection. Then, the two (original) conditions of nomic relations and asymmetric dependence are satisfied. Yet I do not think that we should say that the feelings of panic represent open heights; indeed, I do not think that the feelings of panic have any intentional object.

Fodor, I believe, would try to block this counterexample by appeal to robustness: the escalator-caused panic is an instance of open-heights-caused panic; hence, all such feelings of panic are nomically related to open heights. If so, there are no non-open-height-caused feelings of panic, but robustness (deployed as a requirement) demands that Ts represent As only if nonAs can cause Ts. So, "if we stipulate that asymmetric dependence engenders content only if it produces robustness," the counterexample may be claimed to fail on the grounds that the asymmetric dependence does not produce robustness.[19]

Originally, robustness is described as a pretheoretical fact about meaning with which the asymmetric dependence condition is claimed to be compatible: "satisfaction of the asymmetric dependence condition is compatible with any amount of heterogeneity in the causal history of 'cow' tokens" (*TC*: 38). But by the end of "A Theory of Content," robustness is deployed, as in the above example, not as an observation about meaning, but as a requirement on the theory: " 'X' means X only if you can have X-tokens that aren't caused by Xs" (*TC*: 71).

It is one thing to say that asymmetric dependence is compatible with causal heterogeneity, another to say that it produces content only when there is causal heterogeneity. Without robustness as a *restriction* on the asymmetric dependence condition, rather than an interesting fact with which asymmetric dependence is compatible, the theory is subject to counterexamples. But if robustness is taken to be a requirement on the theory (rather than a pretheoretical fact about meaning), and if the theory is to be physicalistic, then robustness must be construed nonsemantically and nonintentionally. Can it be?

As Fodor introduces the idea of robustness, he describes it as an unreduced semantic fact: " 'cow' tokens get caused in *all sorts* of ways, and they all mean *cow* for all that" (*TC*: 37). This formulation requires that the tokens at issue are typed semantically (as 'cow'-tokens, not as #cˆoˆwˆ#-tokens).[20] Since the point of the theory is to provide a physicalistic reduction, it can not be a condition on the reduction that the relevant tokens *already* be typed semantically, on pain of circularity. Can robustness be construed nonsemantically, in a way that would allow it to be a requirement of a physicalistic theory?

If so, then the robustness requirement must type X-tokens *nonsemantically*. But in that case, the robustness requirement is no requirement at all. It rules out nothing. For example, a token of nonsemantic type C, which is usually caused by cows, say, may be produced by an electrical probe. In that case, tokens of that nonsemantic type can be caused by noncows, and they pass the robustness requirement. Since, presumably, tokens of (almost?) any nonsemantic type can be produced by appropriate electrical probes in the brain, as well as by instances of distal properties, tokens typed nonsemantically are always robust.

Indeed, it is less than clear that a nonsemantic construal can do justice to the original intuition behind the idea of robustness. If we take robustness to require that X-tokens can be caused by non-Xs and if we take X-tokens to be a nonsemantic typing (by shape, say), then we get some formulation bordering on the ridiculous: S-shaped-tokens can be caused by non-S-shapes. Thus, as a nonsemantically specified requirement, robustness does not provide the needed restriction on asymmetric dependence. But as an unreduced semantically specified requirement, robustness robs the theory of its physicalistic credentials.

The point that I am trying to make here is subtle. There is no problem with taking robustness to be a semantic fact with which the asymmetric dependence condition is compatible. The difficulty arises in taking robustness to be a part of the theory, a way to rule out irrelevant cases of asymmetric dependence. If robustness (as an unreduced semantic notion) is a condition on asymmetric dependence, then it is not the case that "you can say what asymmetric dependence is without resort to intentional or semantic idiom" (*TC*: 38). And Fodor's suggestion that "intentionality equals information plus robustness" (*TC*: 71) fails to meet the demands of physicalism.

So, robustness can not serve to restrict the asymmetric dependence relations to the semantically relevant ones. If construed semantically, it is question-begging; if construed nonsemantically, it does not rule out semantically irrelevant relations. Indeed, no requirement can rule out semantically irrelevant relations unless it can give a *nonsemantic specification of which relations are semantically relevant*. For my part, I doubt that nonsemantic specification of semantic relevance will ever be produced.

Let me venture a diagnosis of what has happened. I think that there has been a conflation of two distinct questions, one of which identifies mental tokens nonsemantically, and the other of which identifies mental tokens semantically, and that this conflation has allowed robustness to slip into the account, unnoticed, as a semantic idea:

(a) Given that token t is a T_n-token (i.e., has a certain nonsemantic narrow property), what determines its extension?

(b) Given that token t is a 'cat'-token (i.e., has the wide property of representing *cat*), how can it have any one of an indefinite number of causes and still represent *cat*?

(a)   asks for a solution to the disjunction problem; (b) asks for an account of robustness. The conflation can be seen when Fodor says, "Solving the disjunction problem and making clear how a symbol's meaning could be so insensitive to variability in the causes of its tokenings are really two ways of describing the same undertaking" (*TC*: 37).

The disjunction problem, which makes (a) difficult to answer, arises in the determination of the extension of a nonsemantically identified symbol; the robustness problem arises only *after* the mental token is typed semantically, only after the extension has been established. Again, the robustness problem is to account for the fact that tokens with a variety of causes can represent the same property – a problem that does not arise until the tokens are typed semantically. Therefore, appeal to robustness can not solve the disjunction problem.

Indeed, no answer to (b) produces an answer to the logically prior (a). To see that (a) is the relevant question, ask: What are the *relata* of the nomic relation to which representation of a cat, say, is to be reduced? How do we complete the statement: "It is a law that cats cause Xs," where Xs are tokens of a certain type? Is it that cats are nomically related to

(i) tokens of a type that represents cats?
(ii) tokens of a type lawfully caused by cats?
(iii) tokens of some narrow type T_n?

To say, as the first option has it, "It is a law that cats cause tokens of a type that represents cats" would be, at best, an intermediate step. For there is no reduction if the property nomically related to cats is that of representing cats. The property of representing cats is itself a semantic property. To say, as the second option has it, "It is a law that cats cause tokens of a type lawfully caused by cats" is obviously trivial. By contrast, the third option would yield, "It is a law that cats cause tokens of type T_n"; clearly, only this latter would yield an informative reduction. Only question (a) asks for an answer in terms of tokens typed nonsemantically. If the theory is to be physicalistic, it must answer (a).

Conclusion

Fodor has emphasized that he is only giving sufficient conditions for a mental token to represent a property. His claim is that if the counterfactuals that he stipulates were true, then a token would mean so-and-so (*TC*: 42). Even considered apart from the difficulties that I have raised here, this claim is doubly difficult to evaluate: first, it piles counterfactuals on counterfactuals in ways that are not intuitively obvious; and second, there are no clear examples in which the allegedly sufficient conditions do hold. (My intuitions, at least, boggle at comparing nomologically impossible worlds, as the asymmetric dependence condition requires.)[21]

Nevertheless, let me conclude by venturing an outright counterexample (one that does not raise problems of disjunction or robustness) to Fodor's allegedly sufficient conditions for representing a property. Suppose that it is a law that tomatoes cause A-tokens, and that it is a law that apples cause A-tokens, and that the "tomato" law is asymmetrically dependent on the "apple" law. Then, both the conditions of the reduction are satisfied, and by reasoning exactly like that in the cow/cat case, Fodor should say that A-tokens represent *apple*.[22] But suppose that the "apple" law and the "tomato" law are both asymmetrically dependent on the law that fruit causes A-tokens, and that apples are closer to a paradigm of fruit than are tomatoes.[23] In this case, we should say that A-tokens represent *fruit*, not *apple*. That is, even if it is a law that apples cause A-tokens and tomatoes would not cause A-tokens unless apples did, it does not follow that the apple-caused token represents *apple*.

Whether this toss-away counterexample succeeds or not, let me sum up what I hope to have shown: the disjunction problem, first identified by Fodor himself, is both deep and pervasive, and the account of representation in terms of asymmetric dependence has not solved it.

Along the way, I have argued for the following: (i) Fodor vacillates between two interpretations of the reduction – the pure-informational version (when he considers unicorns) and the local-instantiation version (when he considers cats and robots); (ii) none of the versions of Fodor's view can adequately handle representation of uninstantiated properties generally; (iii) none of the possible options in the cat/robot case is adequate; (iv) Fodor's view collapses into the kind of two-types-of-situation view characteristic of the teleological theories that he criticizes.

In the face of these problems, I conclude that the claim that mental representation has been naturalized has not – or at least not yet – been sustained.[24]

NOTES

1 As we shall see, there really are two distinct problems here – the disjunction problem

and the problem that Fodor (1987d) calls the problem of "robustness" – that are not clearly distinguished. See section "Semantically Relevant Relations."

2   Fodor (unpublished-c) relativizes his account to persons. In that case, we could say that an Earthian's XYZ-caused W-tokens (if there were any) would be asymmetrically dependent on her H_2O-caused W-tokens; and a Twin's H_2O-caused W-tokens (if there were any) would be asymmetrically dependent on her XYZ-caused W-tokens. Since this seems to yield a peculiar idea of what a law of nature is, and since none of my present points turns on relativizing the view or not, I shall ignore the relativization (which seems to me implausible anyway).

3   This is a paraphrase from Fodor's *A Theory of Content* (1990b). Hereafter, I shall abbreviate the title by *TC* and put citations in the text. I wish to thank Fodor for making this important paper, as well as the July 1988 draft, available to me.

4   Officially, asymmetric dependence is a relation between laws, but I shall follow Fodor and speak of Q-caused T-tokens as being asymmetrically dependent on P-caused T-tokens when there are laws "Q --> T" and "P --> T" such that the former is asymmetrically dependent on the latter.

5   *TC*, 29. For purposes of reduction, I shall identify the relevant mental tokens nonsemantically. Fodor recognizes the necessity of nonsemantic and nonintentional specification of the tokens whose interpretations are at issue, but he prefers to speak of "cat-caused 'cow'-tokens," instead of, say, "cat-caused C-tokens," where C is a nonsemantic type. (I try to use the expression "'cow'-tokens" consistently to pick out a semantic type, the type of tokens that represent *cow*.) I believe that Fodor's (1987d) equivocal use of expressions like "'cow'-tokens" – sometimes as a semantic specification and sometimes as a nonsemantic specification – has obscured the difference between the disjunction problem and the robustness problem. See the section "Semantically Relevant Relations."

6   The term "pure-informational" is Fodor's.

7   Fodor formulates the actual-history version "if only as an exercise" (*TC*, 63), in order to show how the asymmetric dependence view can avoid the kind of verificationism that attends the treatment of Twin-Earth cases by the pure-informational view.

8   Since spoken languages like English stand as much (or as little) in need of naturalization as thought, no facts about the semantics of natural language can help in naturalizing mental representation (unless one has an independent account that naturalizes English). On Fodor's view, the semantics of spoken language derive from the semantics of mental representation. So, specification of the semantics of primitive mental symbols must not appeal to the fact that such-and-such is a word in English, nor even to the fact (if it is one) that a thinker is a speaker of a public language.

9   On the actual-history version, as opposed to the local-instantiation version, a causal theorist could respond that "unicorn" could not be semantically primitive for my Doppelganger any more than it could be for me since neither of us has had any causal interactions with unicorns. I thank Gabriel Segal for pointing this out to me.

10 This case was originally in Baker, 1989. Fodor's response is in *TC*, pp. 48–50. I am tightening up the example here in two ways: I am making it explicit that what property the F-token represents must be determined by facts free of assumptions about spoken language; and I am making it explicit that the robots look like a species of cats that knowledgeable people can distinguish from real cats. In the earlier version, this latter point was implicit since Sally herself later comes to know that the robot-cats are not cats.

11 *TC*, 50; draft of July 1988. Fodor makes the same point, but less clearly, I think, in the March 1989 draft.

12 Fodor also says that the cat/robot case is underdescribed, because I do not say whether or not Sally has a standing intention to use 'cat' as a kind term (*TC*, 60). But attribution

of any such intentions at this point would be way ahead of the game. The issue here is not how a thinker uses (or intends to use) a symbol, but how we theorists are to interpret it (without assuming that the thinker knows a spoken language). At this fundamental level, the interpretation of primitive Mentalese symbols must be understood solely in terms of causal relations and asymmetric dependence.

13 Moreover, the disjunctive option (iii) seems to compromise robustness. As we shall see in the next section, the matter of robustness is not straightforward. To see that there are two formulations of robustness, compare *TC*, 68 with *TC*, 62.

14 I am not assuming that Sally has any intentions about natural kinds. (I think it empirically unlikely that children distinguish natural kind terms in Mentalese or in spoken language from others. In learning *any* new term, the learner has the intention of "going on in the same way" – whether the new term is 'robot-cat', 'basket,' 'break,' 'promise,' or anything else.) Also, it seems unlikely that Sally was capable of distinguishing disjunctive from non-disjunctive properties in scene 1. If we must impute to a thinker sophisticated cognitive maneuvering in order to interpret Mentalese primitives, then it seems unlikely that the naturalization project will ever get off the ground.

15 Throughout his account, and especially when dealing with Twin-earth cases, Fodor attributes to the thinker settled policies or intentions to apply a term in a certain way. His reason for thinking that such attribution is not question-begging has two parts: First, what matters is the truth of certain counterfactuals – e.g., that in a world where there are both water and XYZ and they are distinguishable, an Earthian's tw-tokens would track H_2O and a Twin-Earthian's Tw-tokens would track XYZ – and it is the intentions that make the relevant counterfactuals true. Second, "semantical relations hold in virtue of counterfactuals which can be specified naturalistically by quantifying over (e.g., intentional) mechanisms in virtue of whose operations the counterfactuals hold." (See Fodor (unpublished-c), comments on my APA paper, "What is a Mental Representation?", 9 (Baker 1988).

But the question is this: if you, the theorist, do not have access to the content of the intentions, how do you know over which mechanisms to quantify? But if you do have access to the content of the relevant intentions, then you must assume that there is a naturalistic account of that content. But you can not make such an assumption in the context of *offering* a naturalistic account, on pain of circularity.

16 As Fodor puts it in the July 1988 draft: "the extension of S's term T includes things of type X whenever (i) no Xs have been encountered by S, (ii) if S had encountered Xs, S would have tokened T; and (iii) S's failure to encounter Xs was fortuitious" (*TC*: 50; July 1988).

17 *TC*: 38; emphasis his. I think that the expression "tokens of a symbol" in this quotation displays the equivocation that I shall identify below, cf. note 20.

18 I believe that there are some typographical errors in Fodor's statement of the example in the draft of the text that I have.

19 At any rate, as we have just seen, Fodor responds to other putative counterexamples in this way. Put aside for a moment suspicion that the story *does* satisfy the robustness requirement: if you trick the subject into thinking that he is at a great open height, but he is not, his same feelings of panic are caused by non-open-heights. As we shall see, robustness cannot do the job assigned to it anyway.

20 This use of " 'cow' token," thought crucial for the point about robustness, violates Fodor's reply to Block's objection. (See *TC*: 56–8.) From *Psychosemantics* on, there is an ambiguity in Fodor's use of expressions like " 'cat'-token" or " 'A'-token," expressions employing single quotes. Sometimes he takes 'cat'-tokens as being typed by what they represent – as when he speaks of 'red'-tokens as tokens that represent red. But when he first entertains the disjunction problem, he considers whether 'A'-tokens

represent As and misrepresent Bs or represent the disjunctive property (A or B) (Fodor, 1987d: 101). In this latter usage, 'A'-tokens are not typed by what they represent.

21   Also, the conception of law in play here needs a good deal of spelling out.

22   This description of the apple case parallels Fodor's description of the cow/cat case. However, I am not confident that Fodor's two conditions can *ever* be applied nonquestion-beggingly. It seems to me at least arguable that our calling (in public language) apples and tomatoes both fruit is the reason that apples and tomatoes both cause 'fruit'-tokens (if they do), and not the other way around.

23   The assumption that apples are closer to being a paradigm of fruit that are tomatoes is needed to make the counterfactuals work out right: The tomato/A connection is asymmetrically dependent on the apple/A connection in that tomatoes wouldn't cause 'fruit' tokens if apples didn't. The apple/A connection is asymmetrically dependent on the fruit/A connection in that apples wouldn't cause 'fruit' tokens if fruit generally didn't.

24   I read earlier versions of this paper to helpfully critical audiences at Brandeis University, Duke University, the University of Nebraska (Lincoln), and SUNY at Buffalo, as well as at the 1988 Eastern Division meeting of the American Philosophical Association, where Jerry Fodor responded. I especially want to thank Gabriel Segal for commenting on a penultimate draft. Work on this paper has been generously supported by the Woodrow Wilson International Center for Scholars and by Middlebury College.

3

What Narrow Content is Not

NED BLOCK

Jerry Fodor has set the main agenda for contemporary philosophy of mind. This paper is about one of the many current controversies for which Fodor is responsible, the debate about narrow content.[1]

Having been convinced by the arguments of Putnam (1975a) and Burge (1979) that one kind of content is not "in the head," Fodor (1980c) responded by developing a view of another kind of content that is in the head, and also serves psychological explanation and psychological law: narrow content. Narrow content is "in the head" in the sense that it supervenes on properties of the body that are non-intentional and do not involve relations to things outside the body. For example, it is shared by me and my twin on Putnam's (1975) Twin-Earth (which is identical to Earth except that the stuff that looks like water is actually something else) when we both think the thought that we would express with "Water puts out fires." Over the years, Fodor has tried out a number of ways of explicating narrow content. This paper is about his current view of the matter, that narrow content is a function from contexts to truth conditions. Appearances to the contrary, this paper is not intended as a critique of the function theory (or, as I shall call it, in order to distinguish it from functional*ism* as a theory of narrow content, the Mapping Theory). What I will be arguing is that the Mapping Theory does not fit together with Fodor's view of psychological explanation, and his opposition to holism. I reserve judgment on the issue of whether there is a viable holistic version of the Mapping Theory that is relevant to a type of psychological explanation different from the one Fodor favors.

I will begin with a discussion of problems of formulation of the mapping theory. I will argue that on one version of the theory, narrow content collapses into syntax, a result that renders it too coarse-grained to be usable for psychological explanation. On another version, narrow contents are shared only by functional and/or physical twins; hence you and I share no narrow contents. Fodor is committed to rejecting these narrow contents as lacking the kind of generality required for psychological explanation and psychological law. This part of the paper presents the basic problem for the Mapping Theory. I then go on to suggest my own version of the mapping theory, one that is motivated by the concerns I raise. It leads to a dilemma much like the basic one just mentioned: On one approach to reference, large numbers of psychologically different items would turn out to have the same narrow content, contrary to the needs of psychological

33

explanation. On the only reasonable alternative approach to reference, narrow content is holistic (in a sense to be defined later), and hence narrow contents are never shared by real people. I go on to argue that holism of narrow content is unavoidable. The basic concern of the paper is with psychological explanation, and the main problem with the mapping theory is that it cannot serve psychological explanation, on Fodor's conception of it.

Character

If you and I both say "My pants are now on fire," we express contents (truth conditions) that are importantly different. What you say is true just in case *your* pants are on fire; what I say is true just in case *my* pants are on fire. Nonetheless, there is also an important semantic commonality. One way of seeing the commonality is to note that both utterances determine the same mapping from contexts of utterance to truth conditions. This mapping maps the utterer and the time of utterance into the proposition that is true just in case the utterer's pants are on fire at the time of utterance. Let us call this mapping the character of the utterance.[2]

Character is relevant to psychological explanation in a way that content is not. Suppose you and I think thoughts with the same character, thoughts that we both would express with "My pants are on fire," and as a result, we jump into a nearby pool. The common character of our thoughts would seem to be part of the explanation of the commonality in our behaviors. By contrast, if we both had thoughts with the same content, the content that I express with "My pants are on fire," we would have done quite different things: I jump in the pool, but you don't jump – you push me in (Perry, 1977).

White (1982) and Fodor (1985c, 1987d) have articulated versions of the view that character provides a model for thinking about narrow content. The most straightforward application of the model of character to narrow content is that the narrow content of the thought expressed by my utterance of "Water puts out fires" is the mapping from contexts (actual and possible) of acquisition of my words to the contents (truth conditions) of the thoughts that would be expressed by the utterance of those words in those contexts. Had I grown up on Twin-Earth, the thought I would express by "Water puts out fires" would have been true just in case twater (twin water) puts out fires; had my twin grown up on Earth, his thought would have been true just in case water puts out fires. It is this sort of theory of narrow content that I will be examining in this paper.

Narrow content contrasts with "wide content." I will follow Fodor in understanding "wide content" to mean truth conditions.[3] The need for narrow content arises, on Fodor's view, because it is narrow content rather than wide content that serves psychological explanation and the important kind of psychological law (Fodor, 1987d: chapters 1 and 2). If my twin on twin earth and I both infer from "It's water" to "It's just what we need for making coffee," then we are subsumed under the same laws of content, and the same psychological explanation is to be given of what we do, despite our differing wide contents.

For the purposes of discussing Fodor's theory of narrow content, I propose to adopt a version of Fodor's famous "language of thought" theory. According to this account, having the thought that grass grows is being in a certain computational relation to a formula in the head that means that grass grows. (Hence the slogan: believing that grass grows is having a formula that means that grass grows in the belief box.)

However, I will also adopt a viewpoint that may be different from Fodor's – that part of our language of thought is English. (Our language of thought might also include other types of linguistic structures, and also non-linguistic representations such as images.) I will tend to ignore respects in which the contents of what we say cannot be taken straightforwardly to be contents of what we think. For example, one can refer to Rabinovitch on the basis of having heard his name come up in conversation without having any conception of him, but perhaps one cannot on this basis think about him. (See Evans, 1982:400, and Devitt, 1985, for an opposed view.) I don't think that anyone knows whether or not we actually think in our external language. Nonetheless, I see no problem in assuming that we do, because there is no doubt that thinking in one's external language is *possible* for persons who are otherwise much like us, and a theory of narrow content that would not apply to such persons would not be of much interest.

What is the Mapping Theory?

The Mapping Theory says that narrow content is a mapping from a range of contexts to a range of truth conditions (wide contents). What is the notion of context used here? Note that whatever this context is, it must *include* context of acquisition of the relevant bits of language. Suppose that I travel by spaceship to Twin-Earth, crash-landing in one of their "oceans." Unaware of the composition of the liquid that surrounds me, I radio home, "Surrounded by water." My message is false, however, since the stuff I am surrounded by is not water. (Fodor relies on this view of the grounding of reference at home at a number of points. See, for example, 1987:36.) I speak English, not twin English, and so my word 'water' is grounded in the "dominant causal source" (in Evans's terminology) of my word at home. In Harman's (1982) terminology, the "normal context" for my use of 'water' is the home context. Of course, if I stay on Twin-Earth for many years, my word 'water' will switch its reference to twater, as the dominant causal source of my word shifts. (See Evans, 1977; Devitt, 1981.)

What holds for reference also holds for a variety of other causal notions. Suppose I have a Zsa Zsa Gabor recognitional capacity. I am drugged and transported to Twin-Earth, where, thinking I am still at home, I see twin-Zsa Zsa and mis-recognize her as Zsa Zsa. At first, my recognitional capacity misfires, but after enough time has passed, it becomes a twin-Zsa Zsa recognitional capacity.

At this point, I must confess that Fodor does not actually *say* that the contexts that are the inputs to the mapping theory's mappings must include context of acquisition.[4] His current view, as I understand it, is that the issue of what the contexts are is to be settled by his causal-informational view of wide content: roughly, the contexts are to be individuated by their covariation in the appropriate way (as specified by Fodor's asymmetric counterfactual analysis) with certain uses of mental language. My reason for assuming that his contexts include contexts of acquisition is the one given in the two preceding paragraphs. Any viable version of the Mapping Theory must assume that the input contexts include context of acquisition. Lynne Rudder Baker's (1987b) criticism of Fodor would be correct if he were committed to taking 'context' as context of utterance rather than as including context of acquisition.

Critics of narrow content (notably, Burge – see his 1986, for example) have emphasized that the proponent of narrow content must say what it is. A great advantage of the Mapping Theory's narrow contents, a proponent might say, is that they are well defined. The narrow content of my utterance could be defined as the partial function whose arguments are possible environments of the utterance, including the contexts in which the words used are acquired, and whose values are the truth conditions (wide contents) that my utterance of those words (or sounds) would have in that environment (see the paper by Stalnaker in this volume). The function is partial because not every environment will be one in which the utterance *has* a content. As will become clear shortly, this definition of narrow content is far less clear than might appear at first glance.

How are we to judge the Mapping Theory's proposal? Here are some obvious desiderata.

1   Narrow content should be narrow, i.e., individualistic. It should supervene on nonintentional nonrelational properties of the body.
2   Narrow content should be relevant to psychological explanation, where by explanation, I mean causal explanation. This is how the notion of narrow content has generally been understood, both by its proponents and opponents. (See Fodor, 1987d Loar, 1987a and Pettit and McDowell, 1986.) But there is no point in arguing about the use of what is after all a technical term. This paper simply assumes that the rationale for narrow content is (causal) psychological explanation. Actually, I will be assuming a bit more. Fodor emphasizes the role of narrow content in psychological laws, and it is part of his view of psychological law that the narrow contents appealed to must be ones that are general. Holistic contents that are shared only by functional or physical duplicates will not do.
3   Narrow content should be a kind of content.

What makes the Mapping Theory's candidate look promising is that it seems to have some chance of satisfying all of these desiderata. First, when we consider what it is about a person and his use of a word that determines his mapping from context to contents for that word, we abstract away from the person's actual environment, considering various possible environments that he might have had. Hence, whatever it is that determines the mapping would seem to be what is shared by the person in all those environments, hence individualistic. My word 'water' maps onto water, given the context in which I learned it. And were I to have acquired language on Twin-Earth, my word 'water' (or the sound made by that word) would map onto twater. (The point of the "or the sound made by that word" is that a plausible criterion of identity of words requires that for x and y to be the same word, they must be a product of the same language community. Having mentioned this qualification, I will leave it out in what follows.) Whatever it is about me that makes this the case, the same holds for my twin, since he is as much like me as you please.

Second, being modeled on character, the Mapping Theory's candidate will presumably inherit character's success with psychological explanation. (Recall the point from Perry, 1977, mentioned earlier.) Third, we have the issue of whether the Mapping Theory's mappings are really contents? Some views have it that what makes something a content is that it represents the world as being a certain way, and so narrow content, being representative only *relative to contexts*, could not be content. If a clear version of the mapping theory satisfies the other desiderata, those who insist that only unrelativized representers are contents will be seen as making a merely verbal point.

The Problem of the Collapse of Narrow Content into Syntax

I said that the narrow content of my utterance is the partial function whose input is one of a variety of possible contexts, including context of acquisition, and whose output is the truth conditions that my utterance of those sounds would have in that context.

It is time to get clearer about what function we are talking about. Suppose I say, "Mud makes a good shampoo." The inputs to the function are various non-actual contexts in which I utter these words, and the outputs are the truth conditions that the utterance would have in that context. But this formula doesn't really tell us what the function is. For it doesn't tell us exactly what my relation to the input contexts in supposed to be. Am I to be thought of as somehow *appearing* in these environments as an adult? Or do I grow up in them? Let us go for the latter understanding. The Mapping Theory, on this understanding of it, says that *the narrow content of my utterance of "Mud makes a good shampoo" is the mapping whose inputs are a variety of contexts – possible worlds – in which I am raised and learn language, and whose outputs are the truth conditions of my utterances of these words as an adult raised in those contexts.* Now we have a version of the Mapping Theory that is sufficiently precise to be evaluated.

The reader should note a very strange fact about this mapping: it has virtually nothing to do with features of the mind of the speaker in the actual world. For what I will mean by uttering "Mud makes a good shampoo" in various contexts of acquisition will depend *entirely on my upbringing in the physical and social world of the contexts* in which I acquire language. In one context, I will mean that Dwight D. Eisenhower is a duck, and in another that the agony has abated somewhat, depending on the facts about my social and physical embedding. All that its being *me* contributes to the mapping is whatever capacities and limitations are a product of my genes, most notably the capacity to learn the language and to make the right kinds of noises. It is certainly hard to see how the mapping for my utterance of "Mud makes a good shampoo" could index anything in my head that could be used in a psychological explanation of my washing my hair with mud. Consider the fact that in some context of acquisition I would use "Mud makes a good shampoo" to mean that Eisenhower is a duck – is this fact (or property of me) causally relevant to my washing my hair with mud? The only relevant things that I share with my possible selves in these other worlds in which these same sounds are uttered are the sounds of "Mud makes a good shampoo" themselves, and, of course, that these sounds are meaningful and part of a larger language.

Let us ask what the difference is between this version of the Mapping Theory's narrow contents for two different utterances, utterances of "Mud makes a good shampoo" and "Eisenhower is a duck." Each narrow content is a set of pairs of contexts and the contents acquired in those contexts. What constant difference will there be between (a) my states of mind in worlds in which "Mud makes a good shampoo" is acquired, and (b) my states of mind in worlds in which "Eisenhower is a duck" is acquired? Of course, in many worlds both will be acquired, but the only constant difference between (a) and (b) will be the difference in the "syntactic shapes" of the sounds themselves, and whatever is required by these differences. There will be no constant difference in anything about my states of mind that would intuitively or pre-theoretically count as semantic, since what both of these noises will mean will depend entirely on the physical and social embedding in the context of acquisition. If we are to take these mappings to represent anything at all, this fact about the difference between the two mappings would suggest that the mappings could be taken to represent the "syntactic shapes" of the utterances, not any kind of content.[5]

The conclusion I just reached – that *Mapping Theory narrow content collapses into syntax* – depends on all sorts of decisions made on the way. I specified the mapping from contexts of acquisition to truth conditions for a given utterance type by saying that the truth conditions are the ones an utterance of that type by me would have if I had grown up in that context.

Perhaps I should have spoken instead of the truth condition my utterance type would have if I simply "appeared" in that context as an adult, and produced an utterance of the type in question. No doubt this suggestion will seem bizarre, but the reader must realize what a *terrible problem* it is to figure out what the Mapping Theory is supposed to be. If you don't believe me, *you* try to give a specification of the mapping that is both precise enough to be evaluated and doesn't obviously yield narrow contents that are unacceptable for psychological explanation.

Let us continue with the suggestion of the last paragraph: the mapping is the one whose input is contexts in which I appear more or less as I am, producing an utterance of the type in question, and the output is the truth conditions that that utterance would have. This specification of the mapping raises many familiar problems about the obscurity of counterfactuals. (Of course, the previous specification of the mapping raised the same issues, but I didn't mention them.) What are we supposed to think about the physics of a world in which someone (me, of all people) can appear on a street corner out of thin air? Also, what are we to say about worlds whose description is actually incompatible with such an appearance? Treating the suggestion charitably, let us ignore the physics problem and take advantage of the fact that the narrow content mapping is a partial function. Contexts in which my appearing on a street corner saying "Mud makes a good shampoo" is impossible are contexts for which this mapping is simply not defined. So the inputs to the mapping are contexts where I appear and say "Mud makes a good shampoo," and the outputs are the truth conditions this utterance would then have. But what truth conditions would it have? These haven't been specified by what has been laid down. Well, suppose that I mean by the utterance what I mean by it in the actual world. I am afraid that I have just specified a very dull mapping, namely the mapping from a variety of contexts to the single truth condition that "Mud makes a good shampoo" actually has – namely, that it is true just in case mud makes a good shampoo. This mapping fails to be narrow, for it wouldn't be shared by me and a twin on a Twin-Earth in which what they call 'mud' is ZYX.

So perhaps we should imagine, not that I appear in each context, making my utterance immediately, but rather that I stay long enough to absorb the local language. But now we are back to the first interpretation, the one on which narrow content collapsed into syntax. For me to stay long enough to acquire the language is to allow my states of mind on uttering "Mud makes a good shampoo" to change arbitrarily, depending on the physical and social situation. And as before, what I mean by that utterance in that context will depend mainly on my embedding in that context.

Well, what is so bad about narrow content collapsing into syntax anyway? The problem is that syntactic narrow contents are far too coarse-grained to serve psychological explanation. Syntactically identical objects can play very different functional roles, and be associated with very different recognitional capacities. If my utterance means that mud makes a good shampoo, the thought behind it may lead to a dirty bathtub, whereas if the utterance means that cleanliness is next to godliness, especially when it comes to bathtubs, the thought behind the utterance may have the opposite effect.[6]

What has gone wrong? I have been specifying the mapping-theoretic narrow content for my utterance of "Mud makes a good shampoo" by talking about what I would mean in each context in which I make this type of utterance. But the appeal to its being *me* has been of no consequence. I start out the same in each world, but what I am like as an adult depends on the features of the world. Intuitively, what we would like is for the mapping to *hold narrow content constant*, that is, to be a mapping in which the same narrow content as in the actual world is associated with the utterance in each context of acquisition. Of course, we can't just *say* that the narrow content should be held constant, since that would render the mapping theory vacuous. The fervent hope of the mapping theorist is to find some condition that has the *effect* of forcing the narrow contents in each context to be the same as in the actual world without actually stipulating this directly. His task is to find a restriction on the input contexts that has this effect without itself presupposing the notion of narrow content. The tragedy of the Mapping Theory is that no one has ever made a non-holistic proposal that begins to do this job. I will repeat this claim at the end of the paper. By the time you have gotten that far, I hope that you will be doubtful that there is any way of doing it.

Here is a try: let the mapping for the narrow content of my utterance of "Mud makes a good shampoo" map each input context into the truth conditions that an utterance of this type would have in each world in which the utterer grows up and acquires the language of that world *so long as the utterer ends up being a functional and/or physical duplicate of me at the time of utterance.*[7] In contexts in which the utterer is not a physical and/or functional duplicate of me at the time of utterance, the mapping is underfined. Think of physical and/or functional constitution as providing a kind of *filter* on the mapping theory's contexts: if the contexts are not ones in which the utterer is a duplicate of me, then they don't count. The idea here is to guarantee holding narrow content constant by holding constant everything that could possibly be relevant to it.

There are a number of problems with this suggestion, but I will mention only one. Physical and/or functional sameness is certainly a sufficient condition for sameness of narrow content, but to make it a necessary condition too is to adopt a notion of narrow content that cannot play the kind of role in psychological explanation that Fodor envisions. As I mentioned earlier, Fodor wants the narrow contents used in psychological laws to be general enough to be shared by real people. (See Fodor, 1987d: chapter 1, for an idea of the degree of generality that Fodor expects for psychological laws.) Narrow contents that are shared only by physical and/or functional duplicates will not be sufficiently general. If I say "damn" when you say "darn", we are physically and functionally different, at least on one way of individuating functional states (Block and Fodor, 1972b), and so the narrow contents that explain what I do won't explain what you do. Of course a fine-grained account can be thickened, but it is one thing to say this and another to do it. Talk of "near duplicates" or functional organizations that are "close enough" (White, op. cit.) does not tell us how to do this thickening.

It is often said that there are many levels of "grain" of functional organization (Lycan, 1987). An obvious approach to the thickening just mentioned would be to develop a notion of functional equivalence that ignores functional differences that don't make a difference to psychological explanation. Thus, the narrow content of "mud" might include causal relations to a certain recognitional capacity; to inferences involving the narrow contents of "dirt" and "water"; to the desire to avoid certain kinds of interactions with it, and so on. This sort of functionalist approach has a promising sound to it, but it has to be said that there has been little progress beyond this promising sound. For example, no one has provided a convincing reason for including some inferences and excluding others. Further, though one might hold *both* functionalism and the Mapping Theory (there being no incompatibility) the Mapping Theory would lose its luster if it depended on the development of *another* theory of narrow content. Finally, Fodor hates functionalism, so he would not want to pursue this line (1987d: chapter 3).

Let us say that narrow content is holistic if there is no principled difference between one's "dictionary" entry for a word, and one's "encyclopedia" entry, and, further, there is no way of individuating the narrow content of a word on the basis of any subset of the dictionary/encyclopedia entries. If there is any difference in dictionary/encyclopedia entries between two words, then the words have different narrow contents. For example, if I say, "Water is more greenish than bluish," and you say, "Water is more bluish than greenish," then we have different narrow contents for "water."[8]

If one is willing to accept holistic narrow contents, then our current versions of functionalism are more plausible, and it becomes more reasonable to let the success of the mapping theory depend on functionalism. If narrow contents are holistic, psychological laws could not have the generality that Fodor envisions, and further, narrow contents are not much like the contents that we ordinarily appeal to in common sense psychological explanation. We commonly suppose that many people share the same contents – e.g., believing that water is heavier than air. Of course, Fodor rejects this whole package – holism, functionalism, less general laws, and revisionism about narrow content. My own view – to be argued for later in this paper – is that narrow content, if it exists at all, is inevitably holistic. The conception of psychological law that goes with this view is one on which in the real world we can expect no two cases to be subsumed by the same law of content. Laws of content, on this conception of them, will be nothing like "People get angry at those who they think have insulted them." I cannot defend this idea here, but let me say a few words so as to make it seem less than totally bizarre. Think of the kind of explanation we might give of the output of a computer, given its current state. Its current state might be specified by the state of its central processor, plus the contents of each register and each disk entry. This is a configuration which – even for a computer of the complexity of the common PC – is unlikely to be repeated again in any other computer. Nonetheless, there are straightforward principles for explaining what the computer does on the basis of these facts about it. Thus we have an example of how explanation of behavior might appeal to highly idiosyncratic configurations, yet be perfectly scientific.

There is one general type of proposal for what the mapping is that I have not yet discussed. The narrow content of my utterance of 'water' is given by the mapping that maps each input context into the local colorless odorless liquid found in rivers and streams (or rather the satisfaction condition that holds just in case the word refers to the local colorless . . .) in that context. But this can't be right – for what if the word 'water' is used in that context to mean, say, 'if,' and is not used to refer to the local colorless odorless liquid? So let's reformulate: the narrow content of my utterance of 'water' is given by the mapping that maps each input context in which 'water' is used to pick out the local colorless odorless liquid onto the local colorless odorless liquid (or rather the corresponding satisfaction condition). Contexts for which 'water' is not so used are ones for which the mapping is undefined, that is, contexts in which 'water' does not denote the local colorless odorless liquid are "filtered out." But this idea isn't quite right either, for in some of these contexts, people might use the word "water" to pick out the local colorless odorless liquid without even having the concept of colorless, odorless, or liquid. They might pick out the stuff via some other properties (even properties of which we have no conception) that are coextensive with being a colorless, odorless, liquid. For example, they might use highly sophisticated scientific concepts having to do with light transmission properties, and molecular structure of which we have no conception, while they themselves have sensory systems and recognitional capacities that are so different from the ones humans have that they don't have any concept of color or odor. Indeed, if they parse nature differently from the way we do, they needn't have the concept of a liquid either. This would ruin the proposal, because people could fit it without having anything that would answer to the narrow content of our utterances of 'water.' Recall that intuitively, we are trying to guarantee that each utterer of "water" in each input context has the same narrow content that we have, so for the reason just mentioned, the proposal at hand does not have the right effect.

A natural way of dealing with this difficulty is simply to require that the word "water" be used in each context with the same *wide conception* (in the sense of set of beliefs) that is associated with it in the actual world. This is, the mapping is the one that takes input contexts in which "water" is associated with the conception of being the local colorless odorless thirst-quenching liquid and maps them onto the obvious satisfaction condition. Input contexts in which the wide content condition is not met are ones for which the mapping is undefined.

But once this proposal is made, it is immediately obvious that it too is doomed. The problem is this: as I have emphasized, what we intuitively want from a narrow content mapping is that it be one in which 'water' is used in each context with the same *narrow content* with which it used in the actual world. Of course, we can't require this explicitly, and so we must try via some other means to ensure it. The means chosen in the proposal at hand is to require that 'water' be used in each context with the same beliefs about it (that is, beliefs with the same wide content) as in the actual world. There are a number of problems with this proposal, but the killer is that by requiring the same wide conception, we make what is supposed to be a narrow content *non-narrow*. One easy way to see this is to note that there could be a physical and/or functional duplicate of me who does not share my wide 'water' conception. Of course, being a duplicate of me, he will have to share my 'water'-*description* – colorless, odorless, thirst-quenching, liquid found in rivers and lakes.' But he can live in a world in which, because of differences in his language community and his physical environment, none of the words in the description have the same meaning for him that they have for me. Indeed, he needn't even *have* the concepts of colorlessness, odorlessness, liquid, etc. For example, he might live in a Burgean language community which possesses concepts rather like our concepts of colorlessness, odorlessness, liquid, etc., but not those very concepts. Or, to use an example from White (op.cit.), he may use 'liquid' to pick out a slippery granular solid that has the superficial appearance of a liquid. The upshot is that, being my twin, he must share my narrow contents, but according to the present mapping theory proposal, he does not, so the present mapping theory proposal will not do.

The proposal just considered and rejected is in my experience a very commonly held version of the mapping theory. For this reason, and because it is an attractive proposal from the point of view of psychological explanation, I will have more to say about it later.

Where are we? Mapping theory proposals often seem to engender a *cognitive illusion* to the effect that we know *what the proposed mapping is.* I'm not sure what the source of this illusion is. Perhaps it is the idea that since we have a few examples – Earth/water, Twin-Earth/twin-water – we can simply continue the series. But how is the series to be continued? If we allow just any old world in which the word 'water' is learned, then as I pointed out, 'water' can mean anything at all, and narrow content reduces to syntax. If we confine inputs to contexts in which the speaker is a functional and/or physical duplicate of me, we get narrow contents that are far too un-general for Fodor. If we require the contexts to be ones in which the utterer shares our wide conceptions, we make the putatively narrow contents non-narrow, as just explained. It is because of this cognitive illusion that I insist on a formulation of the mapping theory that is precise enough for us to know what contexts are being mapped onto what contents. Every formulation that I have tried out has failed. The first formulation was this: the narrow content of my utterance is the mapping whose inputs are contexts in which I acquire language and make the utterance, and whose outputs are the contents that the utterance would have in those contexts. As I pointed out, the contexts *alone* do the major work in determining the contents; the only thing that the learner shares in all the contexts is the syntactic object uttered, and so narrow content collapses into syntax. Another formulation introduced the "filtering" idea: the narrow content of my utterance is the mapping from contexts in which I acquire language and end up with the same functional state as in the actual world to the contents that the utterance would have. Contexts in which I do not achieve the same functional state as the one that I have in the actual world at the time of utterance are "filtered" out; that is, the mapping is not defined for those inputs.

This functionalist proposal divides into two, depending on what is meant by "same functional state." One option is to try for a notion of sameness of functional state for which, for example, the functional state connected with "mud" is shared by all who have a common recognitional capacity and normal widespread mud-beliefs. The main problems that I raised for this approach were (a) that functionalism has not progressed beyond its promising "sound", (b) that the Mapping Theory of narrow content would not be so attractive if it depended on a *different* theory of narrow content, and (c) that Fodor is committed to rejecting this sort of functionalist proposal. Another functionalist option would be to go for fine-grained functional sameness of the familiar holistic sort that precludes *real* cases of functional sameness. The resulting narrow contents, as I pointed out, would be too un-general for Fodor's view of psychological explanation.

I am belaboring the point about precision because I fear that the forest will be obscured by the trees. One can read one ill-fated proposal after another without really taking in the fact that no one has given us a glimmer of an idea of how to construct a mapping that will yield non-holistic narrow contents that are of any use for psychological explanation. My conclusion is that the burden of proof is on Fodor to actually *formulate* a version of the Mapping Theory that avoids the problems I have been describing.

The reader should note that the reasoning of this section does presuppose that external language can be part of internal language, and that not all elements of internal language need have an innate functional role or innate links to perceptual recognitional routines. Suppose for example, that the innate Mentalese term for 'elephant' is '*.' If '*' is hard-wired to the neurological basis of the look of an elephant, then arguably it won't be true that '*' might mean *water* in a counterfactual language learning environment. Perhaps human psychology is such that '*' can only be used as a term for something that looks like an elephant. So, the objection might go, innate factors such as the one mentioned constrain what words can be mapped onto what things, thereby preventing narrow content from collapsing into syntax – without opening the floodgates to holism.

Unfortunately for the defender of the mapping theory, the use of this objection is suicidal, for it leads to a version of the Mapping Theory that is actually *incoherent*. I am fond of the objection because it allows me to reveal a deep tension in the Mapping Theory, one that creates grave difficulty for it even if the mapping theorist abandons the incoherent version of the view. Following my own advice, I must be clear about the version of the Mapping Theory under discussion. In order for the innateness objection to get to first base, the mapping theorist must be working with a Mapping Theory something like this: the narrow content of my utterance of "elephant" is the mapping whose inputs are possible worlds in which I have whatever innate connections to perceptual routines or innate functional roles that I have in the actual world, and whose outputs are the satisfaction conditions for the utterance of 'elephant.' Input contexts in which I lack these innate connections are "filtered out" – they are regarded as inputs for which the mapping is undefined.

I claim that this version of the Mapping Theory is incoherent. To see the incoherence, let us assume that the objector is right about the actual innate links between internal terms and functional roles or perceptual recognition routines. Note that it is nonetheless possible for there to be beings who have a cognitive organization very much like ours as adults, but who have a different course of development, because they lack these innate links (perhaps different innate links or none at all constrain their development). Indeed, perhaps the success of cognitive science will allow us to build creatures whose information processing is just like ours as adults, but whose external language is just the same as their internal language, and who have very different hard-wired functional roles – or none at all. Because their information processing is just like us as adults, we must give the same narrow content explanations of what they do and think as we give for ourselves.

Beings who are just like us as adults must share all adult narrow contents with us, no matter how different they were when they were born. For it they are as like us in adulthood as you please, by the condition that narrow content is narrow (supervenes on non-intentional, non-relational features of the body), these "twins" must have the same narrow contents as we do. But the Mapping Theory that we are considering says that their narrow contents are different from ours because they lack – and we have – certain innate connections. So this Mapping Theory runs afoul of a basic feature of narrow content – namely that it be narrow.

The argument I have just given assumed that innate information can be lost in the course of development. That is why beings who are as alike as you care to imagine as adults can nonetheless be different in childhood. Perhaps the most vivid example of this sort is the loss of the ability to acquire a native accent at puberty. One of my grandmothers arrived in this country at 11, and she speaks perfect English; the other arrived at 15, and had a thick accent all her life. The ability to master the syntax of a language also undergoes a sharp decline at puberty (Newport, forthcoming). Of course, the genetic linguistic information stored in each of our cells remains, though not in a usable form . (However, one can imagine beings for whom not even this is true.)

Here is another way of seeing the problem with the innateness objection. Consider the Davidsonian swampman, a molecule-for-molecule duplicate of you who has just come together from molecules in the swamp. All of the swampman's internal connections are "innate." Does that make a difference to his mappings? If so, the swampman's narrow contents are not the same as yours. But since he is your twin, his narrow contents *must* be the same as yours.

It is not very hard to see what has gone wrong. The Mapping Theory's narrow contents are subject to two forces. On the one hand, like any narrow contents, they must be narrow. Twins must share them. This focuses narrow content on the here and now. But the Mapping Theory has another commitment that focuses not on the here and now but on history (actual and possible) instead: the commitment to individuating narrow content in terms of what would be acquired in various environments. Of course the literal incoherence just mentioned can easily be avoided. All the mapping theorist has to do is to make his mappings independent of what is innate. The incoherent version that I have been criticizing filters out input contexts in which speakers do not share our innate constitutions, regarding those contexts as ones for which the mapping is undefined. This filter is the source of the incoherence, but it can be omitted, leaving us where we were before the innateness objection was introduced.

The discussion of the innateness objection reveals a deep tension in the Mapping Theory. The purpose of narrow content is to serve causal explanation. The immediate causal explanation of adult thought and behavior (the "triggering" cause) is independent of origins. That is, it must be the same for all "twins," including the swampman. Thus the individuative concern of narrow contents for causal explanation are independent of origin. But the Mapping Theory's narrow contents are individuated on the basis of acquisition of language. What reason is there to suppose that these two quite different individuative concerns will coincide?

Objection: "Can't the real point behind the innateness objection be preserved by changing the objection slightly? Instead of constraining the mappings by innate connections between words and recognitional capacities, let us constrain the mappings by connections between words and recognitional capacities in adulthood. There are all sorts of "laws of thought" that link our 'mud' to recognitional capacities, related visual images, disgust reactions if we find stuff that fits the recognitional stereotype (something that looks like mud) in our food, and so on. The input contexts for the narrow content of "mud" are those in which language learners *end up* with these "laws of thought," regardless of what is innate. Your reply to the objection depended on these "laws of thought" being innate, so it is disarmed if the mapping theory does not assume this."

I think this objection has a plausible sound to it, and I acknowledged that fact *when I discussed the view earlier* (twice). The view presupposed by the objection is none other than our old friend, functionalism. The proposal is that we hold certain functional states constant – environments in which they are not attained are to be regarded as input contexts for which the mapping is not defined. I will repeat my response. First, the Mapping Theory loses its luster when it is seen to depend on another theory of narrow content. This is not to say that the Mapping Theory is false, but only that once we have a functionalist theory of narrow content, it remains to be seen what would be the additional value of adopting the Mapping Theory too. Second, Fodor is a diehard opponent of the functionalist approach, so this objection is of no use to him. Finally, despite its promising sound, the functionalist approach has so far not advanced much beyond the sound.

At the end of the innateness discussion, I mentioned a deep tension in the Mapping Theory between the individuative demands of psychological explanation in the here and now, and the more historical individuative demands having to do with acquisition and reference. I will now explore this point with respect to the model for the Mapping Theory's approach to narrow content, character itself.

Character Again

You will recall that the character of an utterance is the mapping from contexts of utterance to the truth conditions an utterance of that type would have in those contexts. Consider the context in which I now make up and decide to speak for a short time a variant of English in which 'I' means *Chicago*. Does the character of 'I' map my current utterance of 'I' onto Chicago? To answer, we must make a decision about what we are going to mean by 'character.' However, we have already made the decision in supposing that the character of 'I' is captured by the rule that 'I' refers to the speaker. Thus, when we speak of the character of 'I' as a mapping from contexts to contents, we tacitly assume a condition on the context of utterance that restricts it to utterances of 'I' that have their *normal linguistic meaning* in English. The character of 'I' is not defined for other utterances of 'I.' (Character is a partial function.) But if we can get away with this for character, why can't we use the same trick to avoid our problems in specifying the narrow content mapping? Why can't we just say that the narrow content mapping is not defined for input contexts in which the relevant word doesn't have its normal *narrow content*? Sure, this would be circular, but if the circularity doesn't matter in the one case, why should it matter in the other?

One answer is that while the notion of the normal linguistic meaning of 'I' is not likely to be a *mirage*, we can hardly say this for narrow content. So the circularity of using the meaning of 'I' to capture the character of 'I' (which is really just the meaning of 'I') is not so bad as using the notion of narrow content to characterize narrow content itself. More importantly, for character, we can go a long way – maybe all the way – towards specifying the function *extensionally*. We can say that character maps 'I' to the speaker, 'now' to the time of utterance, 'here' to the place of utterance, 'this' to the contextually indicated thing, and so on, for the rather small class of words whose content is determined by context of utterance in this way. We wouldn't know how to start doing this for the narrow content mappings, as I argued earlier.

Let me now shift to a second comparison between Mapping Theory narrow content and character. Note that in talking of giving causal explanations of behavior in terms of character, we are really using set-theoretic constructs to classify states of mind. That is, when we explain behavior in terms of character, what we are really doing is explaining behavior in terms of mental states individuated in terms of character. And of course the same would hold for narrow content thought of in mapping-theoretic terms.

But once this point is raised, it is natural to wonder whether the way of individuating mental states appropriate to determining reference is the *same* as the way of individuating mental states appropriate to psychological explanation. Consider the concept that each of us has of himself that no one else can have, the way we all have of thinking of ourselves that is different from the ways others can think of us, the 'I-conception.' The question I wish to ask is this: does the I-conception outrun the character of 'I'? If the I-conception involves dispositions to intend to behave in certain ways, given certain beliefs, then it would seem that it has properties that are not captured by the function from 'I' to the utterer.

Peacocke (1981) makes a case that, generally, demonstrative conceptions ("modes of presentation") may have a variety of "constitutive" connections with a variety of mental states. For example, he points out that it is plausible that it is constitutive of the now-conception that anyone who has an intention of the form 'I do it now' at t tries to do it at t, other things equal. This feature of the now-conception would seem to outrun the character of 'now,' the mapping from utterance to time of utterance.

I don't feel very confident about any of this. (Perhaps the resolution of the issue hinges on whether it is possible for psychologically different demonstratives to have the same character.) But I hope that the points of the last two paragraphs succeed in putting the burden of proof on anyone who claims that demonstrative conceptions of 'I,' 'now,' etc., *obviously* coincide with their character.

And that is enough for the point I wish to make about the Mapping Theory of narrow content. The proponent of this theory is committed to the claim that the causal-explanatory individuation of the mental coincides with (or at any rate, does not outrun) the individuation appropriate to the mapping from contexts of acquisition to contents. As the consideration of character shows, this cannot simply be assumed to be true.

This point leads to a closely related challenge. Could our I-conceptions be different from one another while nonetheless doing the job of an I-conception of mapping 'I' onto the speaker? If so, then why couldn't I-conceptions with the same character be explanatorily different? Whether or not this problem affects character, it does seem obvious that it affect the Mapping Theory's narrow contents.

Let me explain. As Fodor has observed, there are many ways in which a person's tokens of 'dog' can succeed in bearing the reference relation to dogs. In one person, one bit of internal goings on may mediate the connection, in another person, another bit of internal goings on may mediate the connection. Different people can equally well use 'dog' to refer to dogs, even though they have quite different beliefs about them, different recognitional capacities, different functional roles for 'dog,' etc. (One person's connection with dogs may be limited to glimpsing dachshunds in the arms of ladies with fur coats, another person's may be limited to seeing wild mastiffs kill sheep, another person's may be limited to eating dog meat.) Different people can equally well use 'dog' to refer to dogs even though their internal goings on with respect to dog have little in common. What mediates references for a single word can be wildly disjunctive.

However, such wildly disjunctive internal processes are a big problem for a 'dog'-conception aimed at psychological explanation. (By 'conception,' I just mean a set of beliefs.) If we want to explain what people do on the basis of the conceptions they attach to 'dog,' there had better be some commonality to these conceptions – at least if we share Fodor's picture of psychological explanation based on laws of contents that many people share. In short, typing the mental by what mediates reference promotes disjunction, whereas the demands of Fodorian laws of content require some measure of uniformity. The demands of the two ways of typing what is in the head pull in opposite directions.

Don't get me wrong. I am not saying that this point is the death of the Mapping Theory of narrow content. After all, one could use the demands of psychological explanation to tame the wild disjunctions. One could simple type elements in the disjunctions according to their role in explanation. But if one is going to use the demands of psychological explanation to regiment the disjunctions, why bother with the Mapping Theory to begin with? One might as well just go at the task of typing what is in the head in accordance with the needs of psychological explanation without the distraction of starting with what mediates reference.

Another response to this problem would be to take each disjunct in the wild disjunction as a distinct entity for the purposes of psychological explanation. If someone's 'dog'–dog relation is mediated mainly by his experience with his pet, we simply count that as a distinct state – for the purposes of psychological explanation – from someone whose 'dog'–dog relation is mediated by sheep-herding. In other words, the shepherd has a different narrow concept of dog from the pet-owner. I consider this line of thought a live option, but for Fodor to accept it would be to give in on the issues of generality of psychological law and psychological explanation that I have been brandishing (and will continue to do so below) as one horn of his dilemma.

This concludes the main argument of this paper. Nothing important to my argument will be lost if the reader skips the next four sections, moving instead to the last two, "Fodor's View of Change of Narrow Content" and "Holism Again" (in which I argue that narrow contents can not avoid being holistic). Indeed, on reading over the galleys of this paper, I am inclined to *invite* the reader to skip these intervening sections. In these sections, I am going to discuss further the proposal mentioned above in which wide conceptions are held constant. Though the resulting "narrow" contents are non-narrow (as I pointed out), still this deficiency can be isolated and ignored for the purpose of seeing how problems related to the ones I have discussed so far come up in the context of a different proposal. My main aim in the remainder of the paper is to motivate holism of narrow content. First I will argue that the version of the Mapping Theory in which wide conceptions are held constant – which is the version of the Mapping Theory best suited to psychological explanation – leads to holism. Then I will give an argument for holism of narrow content that is independent of the Mapping Theory. I do want to emphasize that the points against the Mapping Theory that are to come are more speculative than the ones that I have discussed so far, and their relevance is far less direct.

Conceptions

An obvious direction in which to look for an acceptable version of the Mapping Theory is to frame the Mapping Theory's mappings so as to individuate the mental as appropriate for psychological explanation. But how is this to be done? There are many aspects of the mental that are important to psychological explanation that one might look to: recognitional capacities, functional roles of mental representations, and wide contents themselves. I've tried out various functional role approaches earlier in the paper without success. Recognitional capacities are important for some concepts, but for others (e.g., bachelor) we don't even have recognitional capacities, and we do want a theory of narrow content that applies to all concepts.

What I will now explore is the use of wide contents in specifying mappings mentioned earlier. You will recall that the idea is this: let the mapping that captures the narrow content of my utterance of 'water' be the mapping whose input contexts contain utterers of 'water' *who share my 'water'-beliefs*, and whose output is the satisfaction conditions for 'water' in those contexts. The mapping is not defined for input contexts in which utterers of 'water' do not share my 'water' beliefs. One's 'water'-beliefs are beliefs about what one uses 'water' to refer to, excluding the belief that one uses 'water' to refer to water. Thus since my twin on Twin-Earth and I agree that what we call 'water' is colorless, odorless, thirst-quenching, etc., we share the same 'water'-beliefs. Let's call this proposal the wide conception mapping.

The rationale for the wide conception mapping is that wide contents are important to psychological explanation. I conceive of sharks as voracious, sometimes man-eating, carnivores that swim and feed best in open water. When I see sharks while swimming, I flee. I conceive of frogs as timorous, harmless creatures. Being a curious fellow, when I see frogs in the water, I go in for a closer look. The difference in my conceptions of frogs and sharks is part of the explanation of my behavior.

The reader may feel that the wide conception proposal is ill-advised on the following ground. If I have a thought that I would express with "These sharks are voracious carnivores that stay in open water," then I'll head for the rocks – but I would have headed for the rocks even if I had had a thought that I would express with "These frogs are voracious carnivores that stay in open water." So, the objection might go, it isn't my conception of sharks (as opposed to frogs) that explains why I flee rather than linger. Rather, it is the properties that I believe these animals have that count. According to this objection, the aspect of my thought that counts is given by "These ——s are voracious carnivores that stay in open water." And it doesn't matter what I fill the blank with.

This objection involves a misunderstanding. I am not *making* any distinction between one's conception of a shark and the properties one believes that sharks have. It is true that if I believed that frogs were voracious carnivores, then I would flee from what I took to be frogs, but it would then be my conception of frogs – in my sense of the term – that explained my fleeing.

In talking about our conceptions of things, I am not making a distinction between the entries in our dictionaries as opposed to our encyclopedias. My reason is not skepticism about the analytic/synthetic distinction, but rather that I don't see how any plausibly analytic part of our conceptions of things can be of much use in psychological explanation. I am willing to accept the claim – at least for current purposes – that 'dogs are animals' is analytic, but *that* isn't going to distinguish 'dog' from 'cat.' It is part of our conceptions of dogs and cats that dogs bark and cats meow, and this is the sort of aspect of conception that comes into the explanation of behavior. But I don't see any interesting connection between 'dog' and 'bark' that is plausibly analytic. Indeed, I don't know of any plausibly analytic truth that distinguishes dogs from cats – other than 'dogs are canine' and 'cats are feline.' (Katz, 1972, takes 'canine' and 'feline' to be primitives). But if caninity entails barking, then 'dogs are canine' won't be analytic. If caninity does *not* entail barking, then caninity isn't distinguished from felinity by analytic truths.

Many are tempted by the idea that narrow concepts *are* wide conceptions. (Talk of narrow concepts is a way of talking about narrow contents of subsentential elements. According to the Mapping Theory, narrow concepts are mappings from contexts to satisfaction conditions, as distinct from the mappings from contexts to truth conditions with which the Mapping Theory identifies the narrow contents of whole sentences.) Indeed, Fodor once suggested this view (Fodor, 1982). Suppose, yielding to this temptation, one defines 'water' as the colorless, tasteless, odorless, thirst-quenching liquid found in lakes and rivers around here. (This is what White (op.cit.,) calls the indexical-description theory.) The trouble with this theory is the one remarked on earlier: it makes "narrow contents" non-narrow, for the words used in the definition are themselves subject to Putnam and Burge "Twin-Earth" arguments. (See Burge, 1982, and White, op.cit.) Recall White's example of a Twin-Earth on which the stuff that looks like water is not a liquid at all, but rather a slippery granular solid. You can't define the narrow content of 'water' as 'colorless . . . liquid,' because it makes narrow contents a species of wide contents. 'Liquid' picks out one thing on earth, another thing on this Twin-Earth. And the point that Burge makes about 'arthritis' could be applied to 'colorless,' 'tasteless,' 'odorless,' and 'thirst-quenching.' If the narrow content of 'water' is a conception, it must be a *narrow* conception. But how can we specify a narrow conception? Perceptual-recognitional concepts won't do, because so many words that presumably have narrow contents don't have corresponding perceptual-recognitional concepts (e.g., 'cousin,' 'married,' and 'entropy'). And for this and other reasons, phenomenal concepts won't do either.

So there is certainly reason to consider the wide conception proposal. The resulting narrow contents would be specified by using wide contents, but that all by itself is not enough to make them wide contents. After all, if Mapping Theory narrow contents are simply listed as sets of ordered pairs of contexts and truth conditions, then wide contents (i.e., truth conditions) will be used to specify narrow contents – without making them non-narrow. If we hold wide conceptions constant, this may be seen as a way of generating narrow contents that are appropriately narrowed conceptions.

Of course, this move does not succeed in appropriately narrowing conceptions, for reasons that have now been mentioned twice, but that I will briefly mention again so as to avoid any misunderstanding. Recall what the wide conception proposal is. My narrow content of 'water' is to be identified with a mapping from contexts in which utterers of 'water' believe it to be the local colorless, odorless, thirst-quenching liquid, onto the satisfaction condition that something is the referent of 'water' just in case it is the local colorless, odorless, thirst-quenching liquid. The problem with this proposal is that I can have a molecule-for-molecule twin who doesn't even have the concepts of colorlessness, odorlessness, liquidity, etc. For example my twin on a Twin-Earth where 'water' picks out a slippery granular solid and on which there are no true liquids won't have the concept of a liquid. In order for the proposal's "narrow" contents to be narrow, this twin must share them. But he doesn't, so the proposal's contents are not narrow.

Having mentioned this problem I propose to ignore it. I can safely do so in thinking about the narrow content of 'water' if I don't consider contexts in which people fail to associate 'water' with the wide content of being a colorless, odorless, thirst-quenching liquid. Restricting the discussion to contexts of acquisition that don't reveal the non-narrowness of this putative narrow content will allow us to examine it to see if it has other interesting difficulties. My reason for proceeding in this way is this: most of the Mapping Theory proposals that I have run through in this paper have run into trouble with psychological explanation. The present proposal does better in this respect than any others that I can think of, and though its putative narrow contents aren't really narrow, I won't exploit this fact. My main aim is to show that this version of the mapping theory leads to holism.

To avoid misunderstanding, let me say what I am not doing. First, I am not endorsing the wide conception proposal. Second, the wide conception proposal is not the view that narrow contents *are* wide conceptions (or functional roles). Rather, the view is genuinely a version of the Mapping Theory, but one that attempts to capture within mapping-theoretic terms as much as possible of the idea that narrow contents are conceptions. Third, I am not actually going to hold constant *all* my beliefs about, say, water. I know a lot more about water than that it is a colorless, odorless, drinkable liquid. I'm going to pick a subset of my water-beliefs that are likely to be widely shared. I'm not making any covert appeal to analyticity or essentialism. I'm just making a pragmatic decision geared towards coming up with a version of narrow content aimed at psychological explanation.

I intend to present Fodor with a dilemma. One horn is this: on one way of looking at reference, 'frog' and 'shark' don't differ (except syntactically) in Mapping Theory narrow content. Conceptions don't figure at all, and that is not acceptable for narrow content, since narrow content is geared to psychological explanation. The alternative horn is that another – more plausible – view of reference leads us to holism. On this view of reference, all (or anyway, unacceptably many) differences in conception make for differences in narrow content. I think Fodor will find the first horn unacceptable (at least, if he doesn't, I hope he will say why); also, Fodor has vehemently rejected holism, and so he should reject the second horn as well.

In what follows, I will be taking the wide conception version of the Mapping Theory as the target.

Holism and the Wide Conception Theory

Fodor hates holism and firmly rejects holistic conceptions of narrow content. (It is chiefly on this ground that he rejects functionalist approaches to narrow content. See Fodor, 1987d: chapter 3.)

One objection to holism mentioned by Fodor is that if you assert and I deny "water is more bluish than greenish," then it is not the very same narrow content that you assert and I deny, since we do not use 'water' to express the same narrow content. Thus holism may be said to be incompatible with our ordinary conception of disagreement. Further, holism makes some psychological explanations hard to formulate. Suppose that you reject one of your beliefs *because* you find that it leads to a contradiction. If holism is true, we cannot explain your change of mind as I just did in the last sentence. For the narrow content that you rejected at the end is not the same as the one that you started out with.

Fodor wants a notion of narrow content that is close to our common sense idea of content, and hence considerations of the sort just mentioned lead him to pessimism about the chances of survival of a theory of narrow content which turns out to be holistic. By contrast, I am a revisionist about narrow content: I think it is a notion that *derives* from common sense explanatory practice, but that has moved some distance away from it (and will move ever further, if it becomes part of a genuine scientific inquiry), and so I do not find holism an overwhelmingly negative portent. But I don't propose to go into the issue of revisionism in this paper.

Let us begin our examination of the wide conception version of the Mapping Theory by temporarily assuming a crude description theory of reference. One has a set of beliefs connected with any referring term, and the term picks out whatever best satisfies those beliefs, if anything. If no unique thing satisfies them minimally, then there is no referent. Now it is clear that this theory of reference, together with this version of the Mapping Theory of narrow content, makes narrow content holistic. Consider Bert and Ernie, both of whom have commonplace *de dicto* panda beliefs except that Bert thinks pandas' ears are slightly shorter than Ernie does. Now consider a "Twin-Earth" which contains a counterpart of Bert whose 'panda'-conception is the same as Bert's, and a corresponding counterpart of Ernie. Suppose further that in the Twin-Earth language, 'panda' is ambiguous. There are two species of black and white furry bamboo-eaters from China, a longer-ear species that is a type of racoon, and a shorter-ear species that is a type of bear. Thus twin-Bert's 'panda' picks out the bear, whereas twin-Ernie's 'panda' picks out the raccoon. (And their *de dicto* "panda" contents concern different animals in the same way.)

What this shows is that the mappings that give the narrow content of 'panda' for the real Bert and Ernie are such that there is an input context for which they yield different outputs, and this shows that Bert's 'panda' mapping is different from Ernie's. (If f_1 is the same function as f_2, it yields the same output for every input. Finding even a single input for which f_1 yields a different output from f_2 demonstrates that they are different functions.) Further, the example yields a recipe: you give me a belief difference between Bert and Ernie, and I'll give you a possible world in which that very difference makes a difference in what they refer to.

Recall that the wide conception version of the Mapping Theory that is under discussion holds constant sets of properties associated with 'panda' as well as the physical shape 'panda' itself. The point just made is that if we consider all the possible contexts which contain someone who is like Bert in the set of properties he associates with 'panda,' and someone who is like Ernie in the set of properties he associates with 'panda,' the two sets will pick out different animals in at least one context.

Of course, the description theory of reference that I just employed is certainly wrong, so I haven't yet raised any problem for the current version of the Mapping Theory. I have brought up holism at this point by way of framing the dilemma I am posing for Fodor. I am about to consider a very different approach to reference from the description theory just mentioned, namely the approach according to which certain terms – e.g., natural kind terms – have no descriptive senses at all. On such theories, I will argue, there are large classes of words that have the same mapping theory narrow contents despite very different roles in psychological explanation. For example, words like 'shark' and 'frog' have the same narrow content (modulo syntactic differences), and thus narrow content has an overly coarse grain. After presenting this horn of the dilemma, I will argue that a different but also plausible account of reference has the same effect on the Mapping Theory as the crude description theory just mentioned, and thus the holism problem discussed just now reappears. My strategy, then, is to suggest two approaches to reference (both distinct from the crude description theory), one of which leads to the coarse-grain horn of the dilemma, the other of which leads to the holism horn.

Causal and Social Embedding

Why is the crude description theory wrong? As everyone knows, the things a person's words refer to have a good deal to do with his causal embedding in the world of things and substances, and also his allegiance to a language community, involving a commitment to accepting certain practices of the language community as correct, and thus deferring to them. We might speak of all this as the speaker's causal and social embedding in the world.[9]

Given my actual context of acquisition, my word 'tiger', together with the associated conception – dangerous yellowy striped silent stalker – is mapped onto tigers. But it is not hard to imagine a context in which my causal and social embedding is such that my word 'tiger' together with the same conception would have been mapped onto any one of a vast variety of other things – not bricks, perhaps, but surely any one of a vast variety of living things. Consider a counterfactual language community in which a variant of English is spoken in which the word 'tiger' means panda, that is, they actually use the word 'tiger' to refer to the bamboo munchers, saying such things as "Tigers are endangered vegetarians, and we hope the Chinese will send us another one so that we can try to raise them in captivity." It is not hard to imagine a story in which my experience in this counterfactual community has been such as to mislead me as to the properties of the things that the community calls by the name 'tiger,' so I say (as in the actual world) "Tigers are man-eating cats." One can add details that involve my learning the word "tiger" when exposed to glimpses of pandas (you know how elusive they are) in atmospheric conditions that make them seem yellowy and catlike to me. The end result is that in this counterfactual circumstance, I think that pandas are yellowy carnivores called 'tigers.' If this seems impossible to you, note that it is just a version of the Kripkian point – transferred from names to natural kind terms – that Moses might have been an itinerant Egyptian fig merchant named 'Abdul' who spread stories about himself (including that his name was really 'Moses'). Thus we can imagine circumstances in which someone has good reason to believe falsely that Moses was an itinerant fig merchant who spread stories about himself. (See Salmon (op. cit.) for references, and for a distinction among epistemological, modal and semantic forms of the argument.)

The picture of reference that I am assuming is one according to which something is the referent of my use of a word if it is causally connected to my word in the right way, and if my use is derived (in the right way) from a language community that uses the word to refer to that thing. The 'tiger' example indicates just one of many ways in which these conditions are compatible with a wide variety of very mistaken beliefs about the thing referred to. With terms that are more theoretical than 'tiger' – e.g., 'molecule,' the entire language community can have false beliefs about the referent of the term without any perceptual hanky-panky of the sort described above. Beliefs are often involved in the causal relations to the referents, but if the causal relations – direct ones, and ones mediated by the linguistic community – are in place, then we can imagine a variety of changes in a person's beliefs that would leave reference as it is.

In the context described above, my word 'tiger', together with my conception of dangerous yellow striped silent stalkers, would be mapped onto pandas. And, as I said, similar stories could be told about how my word 'tiger' together with my actual conception would be mapped onto a vast variety of different types of things. This point is just a more moderate version of the point I started out with about the collapse of narrow content into syntax. There, the point was that 'tiger' could be mapped onto any satisfaction conditions at all – in some language, it could mean *and*. Here we have added the restriction that the speaker associate some such wide content with 'tiger' as *yellowy striped silent stalker*. It does seem inconceivable that someone might associate this content with 'tiger', yet nonetheless mean *and* by it, but it does not seem inconceivable that, because of his social and physical embedding, he might mean *panda* by it. Just how convincing you find this point will depend on the details of your view of reference. I suspect that on any view of reference that takes the Burge and Kripke–Putnam points seriously, some such example could be constructed. But I won't try to go into more detail, since the horn of the dilemma that I take most seriously is yet to come.

Now there is no need for us to decide exactly how vast the variety of satisfaction conditions that someone who shares the wide conception we associate with 'tiger' could have. What I have just said is enough to set the burden of proof on anyone who claims that the difference between one's tiger conception and one's panda conception has much to do with determining that one's 'tiger' applies to tigers, whereas one's 'panda' applies to pandas. The mechanisms by which contexts map words onto things are a matter of embedding in the world and in the language community. Conceptions provide some constraints, but they fail to distinguish among a wide variety of values. On this version of the Mapping Theory, narrow content does not reduce to syntax. Nonetheless, the only difference among the narrow contents of large classes of words, e.g., animal names, will be syntactic differences.

The upshot is that the narrow contents specified by these mappings seem unsuitable for psychological explanation because they are too coarse grained. To repeat the point made earlier: If I think there is a loose tiger around the corner, I flee. If I think there is a loose panda around the corner, I go for my camera. The difference between these conceptions is important to psychological explanation and prediction. If this version of the Mapping Theory's narrow contents leaves them out, yielding the same narrow content for 'tiger' as for 'panda', so much the worse for them.

Holism and Conception

There is an important gap in the argument just sketched. Even if conception makes little or no difference in contexts of acquisition like the ones I mentioned, that doesn't show that there are no other *types* of contexts in which conceptions *do* play a crucial a role in determining reference. Indeed, there is an obvious candidate for such a type of context. What I will now do is to explore this suggestion. If it is right, it can be used to defeat the argument that I just gave to the effect that the wide conception version of the Mapping Theory must give the same narrow content to 'tiger' as to 'panda' (that is, the same narrow content modulo syntax). However, as I shall argue, if this suggestion does defeat the argument just given, it does so only at the cost of introducing a degree of holism that Fodor will find unacceptable.

On the argument of the last section, Mapping Theory narrow contents are too coarse, but if the argument of this section is right, then they are too fine (for Fodor, that is; I am not so uncomfortable with holism). I am going to adopt the pretense that the points about reference to be made in this section are part of a theory of reference distinct from the approach discussed in the last section. So my line is that on the old theory of reference, Mapping Theory narrow contents are too coarse, while on the new theory of reference they are too fine for Fodor.

The approach to reference discussed in the last section (the view that what we refer to is a matter of our embedding in the physical world and our language community) says that conceptions do not determine reference. The word 'tiger' does not apply to tigers in virtue of their fitting our conception of a tiger – indeed, tigers could be discovered to fail wildly to fit our conception of a tiger. However, on the approach to reference to be brought in here, conceptions are semantically connected with terms in a different way, playing a determining role in the acquisition of the reference of a term. Indeed, it is obvious that conceptions sometimes do play some role in our acquisitions of words. Wondering what 'tiger' means, a child may be told that a tiger is the type of striped carnivore that ate Grandpa. In this case, the child's word gains its reference in a complex way that involves conception together with "borrowing" the reference from the speaker and from the larger language community.

However, there are also pure cases in which the reference is fixed entirely by description, without any borrowing. The cases that I have in mind are those in which a word is *introduced* into the language via a description. I think the word 'neutrino' was introduced into the language via a description of the sort 'the massless particle responsible for such and such phenomena.' This was enough to fix the reference of the word – after which the semantic significance of the description was exhausted. Satisfying the original conception of a neutrino isn't what makes it the case that 'neutrino' applies to a given kind of thing, but nonetheless that conception of a neutrino is what *originally* fixed the reference to a kind.

The crucial distinction between the old and the new approaches to reference is that the old approach has a notion of reference determination, whereas the new one has both this notion and a notion of reference fixing. (To repeat: the old view is an artifice; no actual theorist that I know of rejects reference fixing.)

There are many different types of reference fixing situations. Consider the following two types of cases. In one case, the term doesn't pick out anything unless there is a unique satisfier of the description. In the other case, the term can pick something out even if the description is false of it, so long as the description is *believed* to apply to it. The latter case would normally involve some sort of causal relation between the thing named and the namer. I suspect that the difference depends on the intentions of those who introduce the word, and that many real cases may be indeterminate as between these possibilities. (A third possibility that I wish to exclude here is that in which the term is merely an abbreviation for the description.) For reasons that I will explain, I want to concentrate on the first possibility – the pure description case, in which the new word picks out the unique satisfier of the definition, or else nothing at all. I want to focus on this case, even if it is relatively rare, and even if 'neutrino' isn't really an example of it.

Reference fixing of this pure descriptional sort may be usable to save the current version of the Mapping Theory from the problem of overly coarse-grained narrow contents. The key idea is this: even if it is rare for a word to be introduced into the language via a reference fixing definition, still any word *might* have been introduced in this way. There is a possible world in which tigers exist, but no one has seen them and there is no word for them. Sherlock Holmes goes to the jungle to investigate reports of terrible murders in which the victims are savagely torn apart. He consults evolutionists, thinks about what sort of animal would be camouflaged in the jungle, and postulates a large carnivorous striped cat which he calls a "tiger." The reference of the word in that language community is therefore fixed to the reference of his description. His intention is to pick out the unique species satisfying his description; if there is no unique satisfier, he intends his reference to fail. The kind of case I have in mind may be most unusual, but it is the one I intend to exploit.

Here is how this idea might be able to save the version of the Mapping Theory currently under discussion from the problem of the last section. In the last section, I argued that conceptions play only a constraining role in mappings from context to contents, and thus that items that fall within the same sets of constraints, words like 'tiger' and 'panda,' will have the same Mapping Theory narrow content. But for any word whose reference is *actually* fixed by social and physical embedding, that word might have been introduced via a reference fixing description of the sort envisioned above for 'tiger' in which the conception picked out the item to which the term became fixed. And that *possibility* is enough to distinguish the Mapping Theory narrow content of 'tiger' and 'panda.' For in many contexts, a description that would fix the reference of a word to tigers will not be suitable to fix the reference of a word to pandas.

Consider the set of contexts of acquisition in which people have roughly our conceptions of tigers and of pandas and use 'tiger' to refer to tigers and 'panda' to refer to pandas. In many of these possible contexts, the referents of these words will be a matter of embedding in the physical world and the language community, and the different conceptions will make no difference at all. But there will be other possible contexts in which 'tiger' and 'panda' did not exist in the language until people introduced the terms on the basis of reference-fixing definitions as in the Sherlock Holmes story (reference-fixing definitions that were intended to pick out nothing if there is no unique satisfier of the definition). In these possible contexts of acquisition, the difference in conception makes a difference as to the referent that is fixed. For example, there is a possible context in which Sherlock coins *both* 'tiger' and 'panda,' correctly describing both animals. The difference in descriptions is responsible for the difference in what animal the word is fixed to. All it takes to make one function distinct from another is one argument (input) for which there are different values (outputs), and since I have just described such a case – the input being the world in which Sherlock coins both words, and the different outputs being the different referents for the two words – it follows that the Mapping Theory narrow content for 'tiger' differs from that for 'panda.' And the difference is determined by the difference in conception.

Note that what I am allowing is that the reference of the word 'tiger' could be fixed in one context of acquisition by a baptismal event and in another by a reference fixing description. On the version of the Mapping Theory I am assuming (the wide conception version), it is required that the language learner who has acquired 'tiger' have a conception of the reference of 'tiger' as a yellowy striped carnivorous cat-like mammal. But there are many ways in which the learner can end up with this conception. One way is to have it foisted upon one by the language community. Another is to make it up oneself, using it to fix the reference to something in the world. In the first context, the conception plays no role in fixing reference, but in the second it does, for in the second, the word 'tiger' applies to whatever satisfies the reference-fixing description.

As I warned, however, this line of thought saves the Mapping Theory's narrow contents from overly coarse grain only by plunging them into a grain too fine for Fodor. Indeed, the Bert/Ernie argument I gave earlier for holism, the one that assumed a crude description theory, comes back into play. For the role I am now envisioning for descriptions in *fixing* reference has the same effect on the Mapping Theory's narrow contents as the role I envisioned earlier for descriptions in *determining* reference in the crude description theory of reference. (What is the distinction between determining and fixing reference? A description determines reference if it applies to something just in case it satisfies the description – in counterfactual circumstances, as well as here and now. For a description to fix reference, by contrast, the referent must satisfy the description in the actual world at the moment of fixing, but need not satisfy it under counterfactual conditions or at other times. I can say "I hereby designate the man with the red toupee 'Bruno,' " yet wonder what Bruno would have been like even if he'd never had a red toupee.)

Here is how the analog of the Bert/Ernie argument given earlier applies. For any given word, say 'tiger,' there will be possible contexts of acquisition in which the word is coined by more than one person. And among these possible words will be some in which different coiners have somewhat different conceptions in mind. Consider a difference of the sort that no doubt exists among ordinary users of 'tiger' in English. Perhaps some of us think that tigers are more orange than black, and others think that tigers are more black than orange, or perhaps there are differences of opinion on how long tigers' tails are. For any such difference, there will be possible contexts of acquisition (nothing in these stories shows any sign of conflict with laws of nature) in which the difference makes a difference to which of two distinct species of creature is picked out. For example, there is a possible context in which there are two different species of cat-like silent stalkers, one that is more orange than black, and another that is more black than orange. If the intentions of the introducers of 'tiger' are such that their term is fixed to the unique satisfier of their conception (as will be the case in some of these possible contexts, possibilities – even nomological possibilities – being so plentiful), then our 'tiger' coiners will fix their words to two different species according to their difference in conception. All it takes for f_1 to be different from f_2 is for there to be a single input context in which f_1 yields a different output from f_2. Thus, every single small difference in conception yields a different Mapping Theory narrow content, and we have holism of just the sort scouted earlier in the Bert/Ernie discussion.

Of course, not every difference in word-coiners' beliefs *need* be part of their reference-fixing definitions. So there are possible contexts in which we have two people who differ as mentioned above on the exact colors they associate with 'tiger,' but in which they do not include anything so precise in their reference-fixing definitions. My point, however, is that there are also possible contexts in which the coiners of the words *do* include 'more black than orange' and 'more orange than black' in their reference-fixing definitions, and in which there are also two different types of creatures answering to the two different descriptions. Thus any difference in description will make a referential difference in *some* possible context, and so any difference in description makes for a difference in narrow content on the Mapping Theory view of it. So the version of the Mapping Theory I am discussing is committed to holism.

This concludes my discussion of the wide conception version of the Mapping Theory. The main argument of the paper, as you will recall, was not concerned with this version of the Mapping Theory, which as I emphasized is in any case wrong, yielding non-narrow "narrow" contents. I have now completed most of what I want to say about the Mapping Theory. In the next section, I will make two brief remarks concerning Fodor's discussion of change of narrow content. Then I will turn to an argument that if there are narrow contents, then they are holistic.

Fodor's View of Change of Narrow Content

Let us examine Fodor's defense of the idea that learning that water is H_2O changes one's narrow concept of water.

> ... learning that water is H_2O changes one's narrow concept of water. Why? Well, consider somebody who learns that water is H_2O and thus comes to distinguish between water and XYZ ... This person has *no* concept which denotes water in my context and water2 [twater – NB] in my Twin's, for the narrow WATER concept that he applied to H_2O he ipso facto witholds from XYZ and vice versa. So he's not the same function from contexts to truth conditions that my Twin and I are. So learning what water really is has changed his narrow concept of water. Mutatis mutandis: Learning what *anything* really is changes one's narrow concept of that thing.
>
> (Fodor, 1987d:94–95)

The case Fodor mentions is underdescribed, but what he seems to have in mind is that someone who believes that water is H_2O will refuse to apply 'water' to a known sample of XYZ. But doesn't this reasoning apply equally well to *any* property? If I believe that all water is F, and I come upon a known non-F liquid, won't I then believe that it is not water? Of course if I am not *sure* that all water is F (perhaps I convince myself that although some samples of water are F, others might not be), then I shouldn't preclude the possibility that the new liquid is water. But the same will hold for F = H_2O, i.e., if I'm not sure that all water is H_2O.

There is another peculiar feature of Fodor's line of argument. Suppose a very scientifically ignorant but otherwise normal person refuses to drink water on being told it is H_2O. "Nothing could be water if it has hydrogen in it, since that's for bombs?" he exclaims. Nonetheless, his concept of water and his word 'water' pick out H_2O; it is what he has been in contact with under the name 'water' all his life and what his fellows in the language community also pick out with the word 'water.' Even when he insists that water is not H_2O, the word 'water' he uses in so insisting *picks out* H_2O. Similarly, if Fodor's man who believes that water is H_2O has spent all his life in contact with XYZ under the name 'water,' and if his linguistic fellows all pick out XYZ via 'water,' that is what he picks out with his 'water' too. Even if he insists that water is H_2O and not XYZ, the word 'water' he uses in so insisting picks out XYZ. In short, people do not have the kind of control over what their words refer to that Fodor seems to suppose that they have. If their words have acquired a reference from their social and physical embedding, they have that reference, whatever the person's views about what things really are.

Of course, the man in Fodor's example can say "I hereby stipulate that 'water' as I use it refers only to H_2O." Anyone can decide to use a word a new way. My point is that if he does not decide on a new use, if he uses the word as he acquired it, then what he picks out is determined by his embedding in the physical and socio-linguistic world in which he learned it, not by his beliefs about what "water" really is. For this reason, an aspect of Fodor's example may mislead the reader. The contexts in question in the Mapping Theory, you will recall, include contexts of acquisition (and maintenance). It would be easy for the reader of Fodor's argument to think the issue is this: if a person who believes that water is H_2O arrives on Twin-Earth, would he use 'water' to refer to XYZ? But thinking of it this way focuses attention away from where and in what context the person has *acquired and used* the word 'water,' and this is what normally determines references, as I mentioned at the beginning of the paper. If someone acquired and used the word 'water' in a place where the local wet stuff is XYZ, and where he is a part of a language community that uses 'water' to refer to XYZ, then he will also use 'water' to refer to XYZ.[10]

Holism Again

My argumentative strategy in this paper has been to present Fodor with alternatives that lead either to holism or to excessively coarse-grained narrow contents, or to non-narrow contents. I now propose to put more of my cards on the table, arguing that narrow contents, if such there be, must be holistic, and hence that any theory of narrow content that precludes holism must be wrong. My argument will be independent of the Mapping Theory; it is intended to apply to narrow content, however it is understood. But there are implications for the Mapping Theory. One could conclude that some holistic version of the Mapping Theory is right; or if one is impressed by the objections to holism, one could conclude that there are no narrow contents. My argument will be based on an example of Putnam's (1983), one that Fodor quotes and discusses, but my argument will be different in a crucial respect from Putnam's.

The argument depends on two assumptions about narrow content that I have been using throughout the paper. These are not so much facts as stipulations, stipulations, though, that depend on the purposes that narrow content is supposed to serve. I'll repeat them to make clear which of the assumptions I've been making come into the argument of this section.

1 Narrow content is narrow, i.e., it supervenes on nonrelational (that is, non-external-relational) physical properties of the body. Duplicate twins of the sort that populate the recent literature have all the same narrow contents.

2 The narrow concept that you or I are likely to have of water is different from the one (or ones) that you or I are likely to have of vodka; narrow concepts of aluminum are normally different from those of silver, narrow concepts of koala bear are likely to be different from tiger, and so on. The reason for this is just the one that I have appealed to repeatedly in rejecting coarse-grained narrow contents. If, say, all animal words have the same narrow content, what good is narrow content for psychological explanation? We want to appeal to the difference in my narrow concepts of tiger and koala to explain why I run away when I think there is a loose tiger about, whereas I stick around with my camera when I think there is a loose koala about.

I mean the second assumption to apply interpersonally as well as intrapersonally. I want to say that *your* narrow concept of koala bear differs from *my* narrow concept of tiger, because I want to appeal to this difference to explain why you get your camera on hearing that there is a koala about whereas I run away when hearing that there is a tiger about.

On to Ruritania: Barry and Bruce are 10-year-old twins who were adopted at birth into different homes in North and South Ruritania, where they each observe adults drinking a liquid called 'grug' that causes the drinkers to act silly. Northern "grug" is Scotch whisky, southern "grug" is beer. Though there are many differences between Scotch and beer to be sure, none of these differences has *as a matter of fact* differentially impinged on Barry and Bruce. The adults drink out of opaque plastic mugs, and Barry and Bruce don't pay much attention to the pouring and drinking of the "grug." All that Barry and Bruce know about their respective "grugs" is that they are roughly earth toned liquids that make the adults drunk. Since there are no relevant differences between Barry and Bruce "inside the head" with respect to 'grug,' that is, since they are as similar in non-relational physical properties as you like, the first of our assumptions comes into play: Barry and Bruce have the same narrow contents for 'grug.'[11]

Next stage: the Peace Corps sends volunteers into Ruritania, and Bruce and Barry each get an American volunteer teaching them American English, and at the same time they hit adolescence, becoming more curious about the adult world. Bruce learns four facts about what he calls 'grug':

1 It is called 'beer' in American English;
2 It comes in containers much like those of soda bottles and cans;
3 It takes a fair number of glasses before the drinker is stinking drunk;
4 The drinkers make many trips to the toilet.

At the same time, Barry learns four facts about what he calls 'grug':

1 It is called 'Scotch" in English;
2 It comes in bottles rather like wine bottles;
3 It is expensive;
4 Anyone who drinks more than a whole glass of the stuff gets sick as a dog.

At this stage, our second assumption comes into play. Bruce's wide concept of "grug" is as different from Barry's as are most people's wide concepts of beer and Scotch, and hence their 'grug's have different narrow contents. The narrow contents were the same at stage one, but different at stage two, so at least one narrow content has changed, and for reasons of symmetry we must conclude that both have changed. But what has happened in between stages one and two? Only that they have learned a few ordinary facts of the sort one is always learning and forgetting, including a translation into another language. The conclusion of the argument is that perfectly ordinary run-of-the-mill changes of belief can change narrow content.

A further conclusion is that our narrow contents are always changing. There are many things about which we know little, and about which we learn more, and sooner or later, we all come to know less than we once did.

Note that my argument depends only on the assumptions mentioned, and not on any *theory* of what narrow contents actually are. I have not supposed that they are functional roles or sets of notional worlds or mappings or anything else.

Note also that it is not plausible that Bruce and Barry have learned either scientific definitions or ordinary language analytic definitions of 'beer' or 'Scotch.' Bruce knows a fair bit about the social and biological role of beer, but he does not know that it is brewed and fermented from cereal, that hops are used in its manufacture, that it contains 3–6 per cent alcohol, or what it tastes like. Someone who did know these things but not what Bruce knows would also have an at least moderately rich conception of beer, but would be more plausibly described as knowing some sort of definition.

I have designed what Barry and Bruce know at stage two to be typical of the eccentric grab-bag of features that characterize our knowledge of things, the knowledge that helps to explain what we do.

The upshot is not quite holism, but it is close enough for Fodor to be committed to rejecting it.

Fodor may be construing Putnam's argument as, in effect, a slippery slope fallacy.[12] Putnam asks of Oscar and Elmer (who play the role in his example that Bruce and Barry play in mine) "... *when do they come to differ in content?*" After the learning "... they certainly will not have the same conception of grug ...

[but] ... this change is continuous" (Putnam, 1983:144–6; as quoted in Fodor, 1987d:94). Fodor's response is: why should this pose a problem for the mapping theory? All that is required of the Mapping Theory's narrow contents is that they change as narrow content does. (If there is no sharp change in narrow content, then there should be no sharp change in the mapping.) "Putnam provides no reason to suppose that its [the question of when the mapping changes] application in the Oscar/Elmer case is of any special theoretical interest" (Fodor, 1987d:94). I hope that the theoretical interest is clear from my rendition: if everyday changes in belief change narrow content, then narrow content is revealed to be heavily holistic.

The main argument of this paper came in the first half of it. There I argued that the Mapping Theory's persuasive power is a kind a cognitive illusion: when you try to be precise about just what the mapping is, you come up empty-handed. My argument was not of the form: these are the only ways of formulating the mapping theory and they don't work. I also argued that one would not expect the Mapping Theory to work. The intuitive idea of the Mapping Theory is that one can identify the narrow content of 'water' with the set of pairs whose first members are contexts in which 'water' is acquired and uttered *with the same narrow content that it has in the actual world*, and whose second members are the resulting contents. The trick is to specify the mappings so as to ensure that 'water' has its normal narrow content without rendering the theory vacuous by actually using the unanalyzed concept of narrow content itself. The problem with the Mapping Theory is that no decent, non-holistic idea of how to do this has ever been offered. Fodor's special spin on the problem is to think of it in terms of his causal-informational approach to wide content. But Fodor's approach shows no sign of helping with the basic problem. For the individuative demands of causal covariation between words and the world are in tension with the individuative demands of psychological explanation. The former require a vast disjunction of intervening states of mind whose only constraint is that they mediate the causal covariation; the latter requires enough unity to be of use in psychological explanation.

The argument just summarized constitutes the main point of the paper. In the second half, I tried out a more speculative approach. I adopted an admittedly defective version of the Mapping Theory in which wide conceptions of things are held constant. I picked this version because it was the best version of the Mapping Theory I could think of from the point of view of psychological explanation, and I could easily avoid the kind of case that causes problems for it. My purpose in discussing it was to show how it leads to holism, the point being to suggest that any version of the Mapping Theory with anything going for it might end up holistic. I then gave an independent argument for holism of narrow content.

NOTES

1   Because I was late in revising this paper, Fodor wrote a reply to an earlier version, which he sent me as I was finishing this draft. I haven't changed my line of argument, but the paper has profited very much from the opportunity to clarify my argument in response to Fodor's objections. I am also indebted to Martin Davies, Michael Devitt,

Paul Horwich, Brian Loar, Georges Rey, Mark Sainsbury, Robert Stalnaker and Stephen White for helpful comments on an earlier draft; to the Birkbeck College philosophy faculty discussion group to which an earlier draft was presented; and to Stalnaker (1989, 1990). I am grateful for support to the American Council of Learned Societies and the National Science Foundation (DIR88 12559).
2   I am deviating slightly from Kaplan's (1979a) terminology in which character is represented by (not identical to) a function from contexts of utterance to contents. Contents are themselves represented by functions from contexts of evaluation to truth values.
3   There is a familiar ambiguity between what one might call Fregean truth conditions and Russelian truth conditions. "I see the morning star," and "I see the evening star" have the same Russelian truth conditions, but different Fregean truth conditions. The difference won't matter to anything I say in this paper.
4   Though it is clear that he does not take the contexts to be contexts of utterance either. See fn. 12, p. 159 of Fodor (1987d).
5   By 'syntax' I mean the aspects of the spoken or written bits of language that are relevant to their form class, i.e., what types of sounds, or letters, words, phrases, and so on that they fall under. This is not the linguist's notion, in which noun phrase and the like are syntactic categories. See Block (1990) for a discussion of syntax in this sense.
6   I have been saying that if we hold only the physical shape of the utterance constant we get overly coarse-grained contents, but the contents we get might also be overly fine-grained. Suppose I use 'bachelor' so as to mean the same as 'never married man.' Still, in other possible worlds with different learning environments, these expressions could pick out different (even non-overlapping) extensions. (For example, 'bachelor' could mean politician, and 'never married man' could mean utterly incorruptible man.) Indeed, any two linguistic expressions that are actually synonomous, if such there be, will differ in extension in *some* learning environment, and thus there can be no synonomy of narrow contents. (I am indebted to Bob Stalnaker here.) If one is holding functional organization constant across possible environments, then one would hold constant any disposition to use two words interchangeably, and that would result in synonomies. But, as I argue in the next few paragraphs, holding functional organization constant results in narrow contents with insufficient generality for the kind of psychological explanation and psychological law that Fodor wants for narrow contents.

    I don't think that the fact that narrow synonomy is precluded is a major problem for the mapping theory, since it is not all clear whether there *should* be narrow content synonomies. Loar (op. cit.) in effect argues against such synonomies.
7   White (op.cit.) suggests limiting the Mapping Theory to duplicates in order to deal with a variant of the 'any word could mean anything' problem. Loar, (1987a:fn. 6), also notes the 'any word could mean anything' problem. I noticed their remarks only after I had written a draft of this paper, though in the case of White's comment, I had actually read it without taking it in.
8   This "*word* holism" is to be contrasted with the "sentence holism" that is Fodor's official target, according to one version of which, two sentences have the same narrow contents if and only if they have the same conditional probability relative to every sentence, and every sentence has the same conditional probability relative to both of them. The two doctrines are clearly different, though in my opinion, sentence holism entails word holism, and word holism entails a limited sentence holism. Fodor is not very concerned with the specific formulation of holism, so I will not go into the matter further. Incidentally, the view that Putnam (1988) calls "meaning holism" is something like the opposite of holism in the sense in which Fodor and I use the term. Putnam means that meanings retain their identities through change in conception. Thus the Greek word for water means the same as ours despite the fact that they

thought of water as one of the four basic elements (the others being earth, air, and fire), and we think of it as a compound of elements. Putnam tells me that he follows Dummett in using 'holism' in this way, and that the oddity of the definition is what you get when you let an opponent of a doctrine coin its name.

9   See Burge (1979) on both causal and social embedding; see Salmon (1989) for a review of the direct reference point of view, and see Devitt (1989a) for a causal theory in which the internal parts of the causal chains serve as narrow contents.

10   Stalnaker (this volume) and I have independently made related (but non-identical) criticisms of Fodor on this point.

11   Incidentally, this version of the story shows how proponents of the Putnam–Burge sort of line on Twin-Earth ought to deal with criticisms (Kuhn, 1989) to the effect that the water/XYZ story assumes a physical impossibility, namely, that there could be another liquid just like water in observable respects. All that is required for the point of Twin-Earth examples is that the people in the story don't notice anything that distinguishes the two substances.

12   This is not an unfair construal, though Putnam tells me he had my interpretation in mind.

4

Naturalizing Content

PAUL A. BOGHOSSIAN

Introduction

The conviction that intentional realism requires intentional reductionism has the philosophy of mind in its grip. Thus, Jerry Fodor:

> I suppose that sooner or later the physicists will complete the catalogue they've been compiling of the ultimate and irreducible properties of things. When they do, the likes of *spin, charm,* and *charge* will perhaps appear on their list. But *aboutness* surely won't; intentionality simply doesn't go that deep. It's hard to see, in face of this consideration, how one can be a Realist about intentionality without also being, to some extent or other, a Reductionist. If the semantic and the intentional are real properties of things, it must be in virtue of their identity with (or maybe their supervenience on?) properties that are themselves *neither* intentional *nor* semantic. If aboutness is real, it must be really something else.[1]

It is worth noting – if only because it so seldom is nowadays – that this rationale for the naturalistic conviction begs a question that doesn't obviously deserve to be begged. Why, indeed, must we think that no property can be real unless it is identical with, or supervenient upon, the properties that appear in the catalogues provided by physics? There is, I think, no *obvious* answer.

For one thing, *identity* of intentional properties with physical properties would appear to be out of the question. Not only does nothing seem to be identical to anything else, but there are several, to all appearances decisive, reasons why the intentional in particular is not identical to the physical in particular. If the naturalistic conviction is to have any face plausibility whatever, then, it must be formulated as a supervenience claim. And what the naturalist needs is an argument why, in general, it is a condition on a property's being real that it supervene on the properties recognized by physics. There are, to be sure, specific local areas in which some sort of supervenience thesis seems correct. For example, mere reflection on the *concept* of a moral property reveals that moral properties weakly supervene on non-moral properties: someone isn't so much as competent with moral concepts, if he treats non-evaluatively equivalent cases differently from a moral point of view. But this sort of deliverance – which, it is worth emphasizing, is in any case only of a *weak* supervenience thesis – does not appear to be forthcoming in general.[2] It is simply not true that mere reflection on the concept of an arbitrary property discloses that property's supervenience – however weak – on the physical. In particular mere reflection on the concept of an intentional property doesn't.

If any of this is right, we are owed an explanation why we ought to believe in the supervenience thesis.[3] Let us pretend, however, and for the sake of argument, that we have been given one. Now, Fodor seems to believe that his commitment to the supervenience thesis requires him to provide

> a *naturalized* theory of meaning; a theory that articulates, in non-semantic and non-intentional terms, sufficient conditions for one bit of the world to *be about* (to express, represent, or be true of) another bit[4].

It will prove useful to pause a while here to reflect on the connection: how, precisely, does commitment to the supervenience thesis imply a commitment to a naturalized theory of meaning in Fodor's sense?

The answer is that a naturalized theory of meaning is needed – as I should like to put it – to render the supervenience thesis intelligible. In its absence, a supervenience thesis linking the intentional and the physical must be regarded as hopelessly mysterious and cannot be accepted. I shall explain.

A set of properties A supervenes on another set B just in case no two things can differ in their A-properties without differing in their B-properties. It follows that if A supervenes on B, then for every property P in the supervenience set A, there exists a property Q in the subvenient set B, which is a sufficient condition for it.[5] The relation of supervenience implies, in other words, that there are necessary connections between the properties that it relates. In particular, if intentional properties supervene on physical properties, then every intentional property has a physical property that necessitates it.

Now, we may appreciate the role of a naturalized theory of meaning by observing that, in the absence of further comment, a relation of supervenience between sets of distinct and highly disparate properties is puzzling. How could there be a set of necessary connections between such properties as being a certain configuration of molecules and believing that *Lully was a better composer than Purcell,* given the admittedly highly divergent characters of the properties involved? We are entitled to be mystified.

It is the point of a naturalized theory of meaning to help remove this mystification. By supplying a property that is both *incontestably physicalistic* and *recognizably sufficient for the instantiation of an intentional property,* a naturalized theory of meaning seeks to render intelligible the existence of necessary connections between the physical and the intentional and, thereby, the existence of a supervenience relation between them. It attempts to purchase a right to believe in the supervenience thesis.

So, a naturalized theory of meaning is what you need, if the naturalistic conviction has you in its grip. In this paper, however, I want to argue that, the naturalistic conviction notwithstanding, a naturalized theory of meaning is precisely what you are not likely to get. Not, at any rate, if what you mean by a naturalized theory of meaning is an information-theoretic semantics.[6]

Informational Theories of Meaning and Type 1 Situations

The Basic Formula

Let's assume, for ease of exposition, that we think in a 'language of thought': having the concept *cow* involves having a mental symbol – "cow" as it may be – which means *cow*. Now, an informational theory of meaning is the idea that the meaning of such a mental symbol is determined by the information it carries. The root idea – and the basis for all further refinements – is supplied by the following *basic formula*:

> S-events (e.g. the tokenings of symbols) express the property P, if (it's a law that) Ps cause S-events.[7]

The prospects for such a theory depend entirely on whether this basic formula can be converted, via the imposition of appropriate non-semantic and non-intentional constraints, into a plausible theory of meaning.

Why does the basic formula need to be modified at all? Consider some mental symbol S and suppose it means *horse*. Now we all make mistakes: we are all prone, when conditions are sufficiently unfavorable, to misidentifying items that we are presented with. So it can happen that, when presented with a deceptively horsey looking cow, I misclassify it as a horse: I believe *falsely* of some cow that it is a horse. But that is just to say that, on a given occasion, it is the property of being a cow that is nomically sufficient to cause a tokening of a symbol which means *horse*.

The basic formula, however, can make no sense of this. For according to it, a symbol expresses whatever property is nomically sufficient to cause its tokening; it follows, therefore, that since tokenings of S are also being caused by cows, S cannot simply mean *horse*, but must mean *cow or horse*. In other words, what intuitively seemed to be a case of a non-disjunctive symbol being applied falsely to something not in its extension, the basic formula would have us describe as a case of a disjunctive symbol being applied correctly to something in its extension.

In general, then, since applying a symbol falsely involves applying it to something not in its extension and since, according to the basic formula, every property that can cause the tokening of a symbol is, *ipso facto*, in the extension of that symbol, the basic formula can make no sense of error.

Errors, however, aren't the only way in which a symbol might get caused by something that isn't in its extension. The thought that cows are mammals might get caused by the thought that platypi aren't; this would be a non-erroneous tokening of the expression "cow" yet, nevertheless, not a tokening of the expression that is caused by the property it expresses. Here again, and for much the same reason as before, the basic formula yields the wrong result: it has "cow" meaning *cow or platypus-thought*, whereas "cow" means *cow* and no more.

In sum: Because under ordinary circumstances it is possible for a symbol to be caused by something that it does not express – either through error or through its occurrence in a sequence of non-labelling thoughts – the basic formula appears bound to deliver the wrong verdicts about the meaning of practically every expression in the language. Following tradition, we may call this the *disjunction problem*.[8]

It is a condition of adequacy on a causal theory of meaning that it solve this problem. Solving it requires selecting, from among all the laws that govern the tokening of a symbol S, that law which is *meaning-determining*: a property M, specifiable without the use of semantic or intentional materials, must be defined so that: possession of M by a nomic cause of a tokening of S is necessary and sufficient for that cause to be in the extension of S.[9]

Those causes of S not possessing M would then not count as in the extension of S and would be free, therefore, to cause tokenings of S that are false.

Meaning-Determining Causal Laws and Type 1 Situations

Suppose that both P and Q are nomic causes of tokenings of S. And suppose that S means P. The causal theorist must somehow select the P $-->$ S law as the one that fixes S's meaning. He must specify a property M that is possessed only by the P $-->$ S relation. How is this trick to be turned? As Fodor notes, the standard attempts to turn it exhibit a common feature: they attempt to select the P $-->$ S law by defining a *situation* in which only Ps can cause tokenings of S. In other words, their common strategy is to attempt to define a situation in which only the referent of a symbol can cause its tokening; they then proceed to identify the fact that the symbol expresses a given property with the fact that it is that property that is solely responsible for causing tokenings of the symbol under that sort of situation. Let us call a situation in which nothing but the referent of a symbol can cause its tokening, a situation of type 1; and let us call theories that specify meaning in terms of such situations, type 1 theories.

Teleological Type 1 Theories

The literature contains a number of proposals concerning the identity of situations of type 1, of which the most influential is the *teleological* proposal. The idea here is that there is a set of Normal conditions, specified by evolutionary biology – hence, one presumes, naturalistically – under which our cognitive mechanisms are functioning just as they are supposed to. The teleological proposal is that we equate type 1 situations – situations under which nothing but the referent of a symbol can cause its tokening – with Normal conditions so specified.

Its prima facie appeal notwithstanding, the teleological proposal suffers from a number of severe problems, some of which are outlined very effectively by Fodor.[10] First, it rests on an incredible conception of evolutionary selection assuming, for instance, that cognitive mechanisms are never selected for the purpose of hiding, rather than tracking, the truth. Second, it does not really solve the disjunction problem because facts about teleological function go soft at precisely the point at which the disjunction problem arises. And, finally, the root idea upon which the teleological proposal depends – the assumption that "when things go right" S will be tokened only in application to its referent – seems simply wrong. As Fodor observes, a glaring counterexample is provided by the humdrum phenomenon of one thought causing another. In the course of musing about horses I might be led to muse about cows. This would be a case of a horse-thought causing a cow-thought, hence, not a case of a cow-thought being caused by its referent. But also, surely, not a case where anything has gone wrong from a teleological point of view. The point is that, even if evolutionary biology could help define a set of conditions which abstract from sources of *error*, it is hardly likely to help define a set of conditions which abstract from *thinking*. It is hardly likely, therefore, to deliver what a type 1 theory of meaning needs: a nonintentionally, nonsemantically specified situation in which only the referent of a symbol can cause its tokening.

Fodor's Theory: Assymmetric Dependence

Now, all this is, I think, pretty much decisive against teleological versions of type 1 theories. In fact, however, Fodor disapproves not merely of *teleological* versions of type 1 theories, but of *any* type 1 causal theory of meaning. He says:

> what's *really* wrong with teleological theories of content . . . is the idea that [in a certain kind of circumstance] the tokens of a symbol can have only one kind of cause – viz. the kind of cause that fixes meaning. . . . But surely this underestimates . . . the *robustness* of meaning: In actual fact, "cow" tokens get caused in *all sorts* of ways, and they all mean *cow* for all of that . . . If there's really going to be a causal theory of content, there has to be some way of picking out *semantically relevant* causal relations from all the other kinds of causal relations that the tokens of a symbol enter into. *And we'd better not do this by idealizing to contexts of etiological homogeneity.* [Final emphasis mine.][11]

And he commends his own view (to which we will come below)

> for having the desirable property of not assuming that there are such things as type 1 situations; in particular, it doesn't assume the possibility of specifying – naturalistically and otherwise non question beggingly – circumstances in which it's semantically necessary that only cows cause "cows."[12]

Well, how are we to naturalistically specify a symbol's meaning-determining causal relations without "assuming that there are such things as type 1 situations." The crux of Fodor's proposal is neatly summed up in the following passage:

> Cows cause "cow" tokens, and (let's suppose) cats cause "cow" tokens. But "cow" means *cow* and not *cat* or *cow or cat* because it's being a law that *cats cause "cow" tokens depends on it's being a law that cows cause "cow" tokens, but not the other way around.* "Cow" means *cow* because, as I shall henceforth put it, non cow-caused "cow" tokens are *assymmetrically dependent upon* cow-caused "cow" tokens.[13]

How, precisely, is this to be understood? It's not, I'm afraid, all that easy to say.

The trouble stems, on the one hand, from Fodor's insistence that the theory is best understood directly in terms of the nomic concepts in which it's couched; and, on the other, from the conspicuous absence of any account of those concepts. Fodor bemoans counterfactual analyses of law and possible worlds analyses of counterfactuals, castigating them as exemplifying the "sort of reductive move that is always blowing up in philosophers' faces." It is hard, in view of the less than spectacular achievements of the analytic enterprise, not to sympathize with this. But the fact remains that we need *some* handle on how the theory is to be understood and those accounts, warts and all, are the best we've got at the present time. Having acknowledged Fodor's reservations, then, I propose henceforth to ignore them. I shall expound his theory in terms of the language of counterfactuals and possibilia of which he disapproves. In proceeding in this fashion, I am emboldened by the fact that, although I may be flouting Fodor's ideology, I am not flouting his actual practice:

> Having gotten all that off my chest, I shall join the crowd and talk counterfactuals from time to time, *faute de mieux*. And since it's widely supposed that talk about counterfactuals itself translates into talk about possibilia, I shall sometimes equate "there is a nomic dependence between the property of being a Y and the property of being a cause of Xs" with "Ys cause Xs in all (nearby? see below) nomologically possible worlds."[14]

What, then, is the proposed sufficient condition for S's meaning P? A first counterfactual approximation would have it that S means P if it satisfies the following condition. If P ceases being capable of causing S tokens, then every other cause of S is rendered similarly impotent; but not the other way around: any non-P could cease being capable of causing S tokens without this affecting P's ability to do so.

It may strike you, right off the bat, that this suggestion couldn't be right because it would have us thinking not about, say, cows but about their proximal projections. For it's presumably true that no cow would cause a "cow" token except as it produces some proximal projection. And it's plausible, moreover, that such proximal stimuli would be sufficient to cause "cow" tokens even if they weren't produced by cows. If all this is true, then it would appear that the cow-prompted "cow" tokens are asymmetrically dependent on the disjunction of proximal cow projections, and hence, on the terms of the theory on offer, that "cow" means not *cow* but that inner disjunction instead.

Fodor, however, won't admit any of this and for reasons to which we shall have occasion to return:

> It might still be said, however, that the dependence of cow thoughts on asymmetrically dependent on their dependence on *disjunctions* of proximal cow projections; distal cows wouldn't evoke COW tokens but that they project proximal whiffs or glimpses or snaps or crackles OR. . . . well, OR what? Since, after all, cow spotting can be mediated by theory to any extent you like; the barest whiff or glimpse of cow can do the job for an observer who is suitably attuned . . . To the extent that this is so, just about *any* proximal display might mediate the relation between cows and cow-thoughts for some cow-thinker on some or other cow-spotting occasion . . . So barring appeals to open disjunctions, it seems likely that there is just no way to specify an array of proximal stimulations upon which the dependence of cow-thoughts on cows is asymmetrically dependent.[15]

The bruited objection is no good, Fodor says, because it ignores the holistic and open-ended character of belief fixation. Since just about any theory can mediate the fixation of beliefs about cows, just about any proximal stimulation can cause a "cow" token; and open disjunctions of properties are not eligible to serve as the referents of our primitive expressions.

Now, there is room for doubting the effectiveness of this rejoinder, but I propose for the time being to accept it. The effect is to restrict the referents of our predicates to their *distal* causes; and so, on Fodor's view, S means P, if P is the distal cause of S tokens on which all the other distal causes of S tokens depend. Henceforth, let it be so understood.

Another prima facie difficulty with the theory will help specify it further. So far we have it "cow" has cows it its extension but not cats, because if the cow $-->$ "cow" connection were to break, then so would the cat $-->$ "cow" connection, but not vice versa. Put in the language of possibilia, this seems best interpreted as suggesting that "cow" has cows in its extension and not cats, provided that, although there are worlds in which *cow* can cause a "cow" token but *cat* can't, there are no worlds in which *cat* can cause a "cow" token, but *cow* can't.

This, however, can't be precisely what's meant. The point is, of course, that even by the theory's own lights, there have to be *some* worlds in which the property of being a cat can cause "cow" tokens even if the property of being a cow can't, for there presumably are some worlds in which "cow" means *cat*. A more accurate statement of the theory, then, would have it that what's required

is not that cows cause "cow"s in *every* nomologically possible world where Xs cause "cow"s. Rather, what's required is just that there be a world W such that (i) in W, cows cause "cow"s and non-cows don't; and (ii) W is nearer to our world than any in which some non-cows cause "cow"s and no cows do.[16]

Asymmetric Dependence and Type 1 Situations

A really plausible theory of content, Fodor says, would not be a type 1 theory: it would not commit itself to the existence of naturalistically specifiable circumstances in which a symbol can get caused only by its referent. As we shall see later on, there is much to be said in favor of this claim.

The trouble is, however, that in all essential respects Fodor's own theory would appear to be a type 1 theory and, hence, itself vulnerable to the attendant problems. Let me explain.

A traditional type 1 theory has it that S means P because, in a favored naturalistically specified circumstance C, only P can cause S tokens. In such theories, then, the meaning of a symbol is specified directly in terms of *the causes that tokenings of that symbol may have in a certain type of situation*. Now, admittedly, Fodor's theory does not look like that. On his view, the meaning-determining cause is picked out not in terms of its relation to certain kinds of situation, but in terms of its relation to the symbol's other causes: that cause on which the other causes of the symbol asymmetrically depend, is the symbol's meaning. I propose to argue, however, that on the most favorable understanding of the theory on offer, if symbol S possesses asymmetric dependence base P, then there exists a world in which *only* P can serve as a cause of tokenings of S. I propose to argue, in other words, that even Fodor's theory is a type 1 theory, because even asymmetric dependence implies the existence of type 1 situations for symbols.

Suppose that among S's causes are properties P and Q. Now, clearly, a distribution of nearby worlds according to which there are some worlds in which S has only P as a cause, but no worlds in which it has only some non-Ps as a cause, would be *sufficient* to ground P's status as S's asymmetric dependence base; the question is whether such a distribution is *necessary*. Well, what *other* distribution of worlds would also ground the fact in question? The only remotely plausible suggestion is that a distribution of nearby worlds which contains worlds in which both P and Q can cause S tokens, and worlds in which both P and R can, but no world in which only P can and no world in which only non-Ps can, would equally suffice to certify P's status as S's asymmetric dependence base.

And even *it* doesn't work. For there is nothing to distinguish the envisaged distribution from one in which the real asymmetric dependence base for S's causal relations is not P but, rather,

(P & R)v(P & Q).

Without a world in which only Ps can cause S, the most we would be entitled to claim is that it seems impossible to break any particular non-P causal relation without enforcing at least one of the others (in combination with P). And this falls far short of saying that it is precisely the P $-->$ S connection that cannot be broken without breaking all the others.

Now, it might be objected that we are not *guaranteed* that (P & R)v(P & Q) will be a candidate asymmetric dependence base for S whenever P is. That is true, but irrelevant. It is true because there is, in general, no guarantee that whenever P $-->$ S is a law and R $-->$ S is a law that (P & R)v(P & Q) $-->$ S will be a law also. It is irrelevant because the point at issue requires only that there be at least *one* case in which (P & R)v(P & Q) $-->$ S is a law and, hence, (P & R)v(P & Q) a candidate asymmetric dependence base for S. Since Fodor's theory says that it is a *sufficient* condition of S's meaning X that X be S's asymmetric dependence base, any case in which S has both P and (P & R)v(P & Q) as candidate asymmetric dependence bases will be a case in which his theory yields either the wrong result or an indeterminiate one. Hence, any such case would constitute a straightforward counterexample to his theory. So, as I have said, all that's required is that there be at least one case in which (P & R)v(P & Q) $-->$ S is a law whenever P $-->$ S is and R $-->$ S is; and it seems pretty obvious that there will be plenty of such cases.

To be sure to have eliminated this entire class of counterexamples, then, Fodor's theory must be read as follows: S means whatever properties are possible causes of S tokens in the closest world with the smallest subset of S-token causes in the actual world. Or, in the case of an expression with a *single* property P as referent, S means P if P is the sole cause of S tokens in the closest single-cause world. Or, to put this yet another way: Fodor's theory is a type 1 theory where the type 1 situation for S is specified as being: the closest world in which S can get tokened by only one sort of cause.

Now, Fodor has admitted that asymmetric dependence implies a commitment to the existence of circumstances in which a symbol can get caused only by its referent. But he has denied that this commits him to the sorts of situation envisaged by traditional type 1 theories.

> ... real type 1 theories say that situations in which only Xs cause Ss are nomologically possible. Whereas my theory says only that the dependence of Ss on Xs is nomically dependent on their dependence on Xs. If you spell this out in terms of possible worlds, then what you get is that worlds in which Xs cause Ss but nonXs don't, are closer, ceteris paribus, than worlds in which nonXs cause Ss but Xs don't. But, notice, ALL THE WORLDS THAT FIGURE IN THIS RELATION ARE,

BY ASSUMPTION, NOMOLOGICALLY IMPOSSIBLE. In particular, even the nearest of these worlds breaks the connection between nonXs and Ss, and that connection is, by assumption lawlike. . . . So, the difference between my story and a true type 1 story is that true type 1 stories hold that type 1 situations are nomologically possible; and my story doesn't.[17]

I must admit to being somewhat confused by this response, but for reasons that will detain us too long to look into. So I wish simply to grant the point: traditional type 1 situations are conceived as nomologically possible, whereas Fodor's type 1 situations aren't.[18] This particular difference won't matter to anything that's to follow.

For what follows is a set of objections to theories that are based on the existence of type 1 situations, regardless of their nomological status. I shall argue for two main claims. First, that there couldn't be naturalistically specifiable circumstances under which nothing but the referent of a symbol can cause its tokening. And, second, that even if there were such conditions, we could never be in a position to *certify* that there were. I'll end by returning to Fodor's theory and showing explicitly that it does not provide a convincing naturalistic sufficient condition for meaning.

Could there be Naturalistic Conditions of Type 1? – Verificationism and Natural Kind Terms

Causal Theories and Verificationism

I propose to begin by arguing that any attempt at specifying a type 1 situation for a symbol S, however refined, is bound to fail: *any* specified situation will contain possible causes of S tokens not in the extension of S.

The reason is painfully obvious: any situation in which X is a possible cause of my S-tokens is also a situation in which any other property Y, indistinguishable from X in all physically possible circumstances accessible to me, is *also* a possible cause of my S-tokens. Since there are no physically possible circumstances accessible to me in which X and Y can be told apart, any circumstance in which X can cause my S tokens is also a circumstance in which Y can. It follows, therefore, that on a type 1 theory, if S has X in its extension, then it also has all these other "X-equivalent" properties equally in its extension. But is this plausible? Is it really true that my having a symbol that means X but not Y depends on my being able to tell Xs and Ys apart? After all, it surely doesn't follow from the fact that Xs and Ys can only be told apart in worlds that are too far for *me* to get to, that being X and being Y are the same property. But, then if the difference between being X and being Y is real, then so too, presumably, is the difference between being X and being (X or Y). And if this difference is real, then why shouldn't we be able to think in ways that respect that difference?[19]

Natural Kind Terms

It will prove useful to present a concrete case of an expression that has X in its extension, but not all its X-equivalent cousins.

I have chosen to focus on natural kind expressions. The choice is particularly apt, for three reasons. First, because natural kind terms are of incontestable importance. Second, because there is the fairly widespread conviction that recent philosophy of language has made significant progress in understanding their *intuitive semantics*. One of the many difficulties that bedevil discussion of the naturalization of semantic properties is the absence, in a significant range of cases, of an intuitively correct semantics to naturalize: we simply don't know what extensions to assign to various expressions under various counterfactual circumstances, and, hence, don't know whether particular naturalistic proposals capture those extensions correctly. Through the recent work of Kripke and Putnam, however, we have in hand the rough contours of a convincing and widely accepted description of the semantic functioning of natural kind expressions; and so a meaningful test becomes possible. Finally, and perhaps most importantly; because causal theorists themselves invariably illustrate their theories with the use of natural kind expressions. It is widely supposed by the proponents of such theories, that causal theories are at their strongest in application to natural kind expressions. It is easy to explain why. The point is that it is part of the moral of the Kripke/Putnam story about natural kind expressions, that they have an intuitively *externalist*, indeed *causal*, semantics: according to such views, it is true independently of any attachment to informational theories of meaning, that causal relations play an important part in fixing the reference of natural kind expressions. So what better candidate for naturalization via a causal theory than a natural kind expression?

In fact, I wish to argue, just the opposite is true; the semantics of such terms, properly understood, resist naturalization by a causal theory.

We need to start off with an account of their intuitive semantics. What, in rough outline, is the Kripke/Putnam account of the reference of such terms as "water," "cow," or "gold"? The essentials are neatly summarized in the following passage from Kripke. A natural kind concept, says Kripke, is the concept of

> *that kind of thing*, where the kind can be identified by paradigmatic instances. It is not something picked out by any qualitative dictionary definition . . .[20] The same observations hold for such a general term as 'gold.' If we imagine a hypothetical (admittedly somewhat artificial) baptism of the substance, we must imagine it picked out as by some such 'definition' as, 'Gold is the substance instantiated by the items over there, or at any rate, by almost all of them' . . . terms for natural kinds (e.g., animal, vegetable, and chemical kinds) get their reference fixed in this way; the substance is defined as the kind instantiated by (almost all of) a given sample.[21]

According to this plausible proposal, then, a natural kind expression S functions *as if* it had been introduced via a reference-fixing description of the following form: S names the naturally delineated kind exemplified by all, or most, of certain local exemplars.[22] Several aspects deserve comment.

First, there is the commitment that the expression name a naturally occurring kind, hence that some sort of basic naturally explanatory property unite all the things that are correctly said to fall in its extension.[23]

Which kind? The kind exemplified by all, or better *most*, of certain local samples. Not simply "all," for we need to allow for impurities in the local samples. "Gold" refers to the substance with atomic number 89, even though not *everything* in the local samples has that atomic number: some of the samples are iron pyrites.

Finally, what if there is no dominant natural kind in the local samples? If investigation uncovers that there is no single hidden structure uniting the local samples, but that there are two (or so) well-defined such structures, then there appears to be a temptation to say that the expression has both of those structures in its extension. Thus, "jade," for example, applies to two minerals, jadeite and nephrite, which are chemically quite different. But if it turns out that nothing but a messy motley of basic properties unites the local samples, then the correct conclusion would appear to be that the term fails to refer: there simply is no naturally delineated kind for the term to refer to.

Does an information-theoretic semantics correctly capture these intuitive results? I shall argue that it does not, and could not.

Causal Theories and Natural Kind Terms

Consider "water." "Water" functions so as to name all and only the stuff bearing the same-liquid relation to all, or most, of such-and-so local samples. As it happens, that stuff is H_2O; so "water" refers to H_2O. It has all and only H_2O molecules in its extension. It does not have such possible substances as XYZ in its extension because XYZ is not of the same kind as H_2O, even though an ordinary speaker exposed to XYZ would call it "water."

Now, XYZ does not provide a straightforward counterexample to a type 1 informational theory of meaning, because it is part of the standard story about XYZ that there are physically accessible circumstances under which XYZ is distinguishable from H_2O. So there presumably are worlds where you would call H_2O "water" but not XYZ – namely, in those worlds where you could tell them apart.

But consider a substance – ABC – which is just like XYZ in being kind-distinct from H_2O, but yet which is distinguishable from H_2O only in circumstances that are physically inaccessible to humans. Let's suppose that this is because ABC would exhibit its distinctive characteristics only in gravitational fields of such intensity – characteristic of the interior of black holes – that nothing as complex as a human body could survive in them long enough to perform even the fleetest measurement; we needn't be too fussy about the physical details. ABC exists in abundance on Pluto, and hence is a potential, even if not actual, cause of "water" tokens.

Is such a substance coherently imaginable? Well, is there anything in physics that precludes the possibility of kind-distinct molecules that behave in precisely the same ways *in all circumstances physically accessible to human beings?* I know of no theorem of physics that precludes this. Which is not, if you think about it, all that surprising. For, remember, what's at issue is not the possibility of kind-distinct molecules that behave in exactly the same way in *all* physically possible worlds, but only the possibility of kind-distinct molecules that behave in exactly the same ways in all the physically possible worlds *that we can get to*, which is a rather different matter. And so physics couldn't preclude the possibility of such substances, because physics doesn't taxonomize molecules with reference to our biological and medical limitations. So far as I can tell, then, there is absolutely no reason to believe that two molecules *couldn't* differ in respect of the sorts of property that make for a difference in kind, if they are distinguishable only in situations that are inaccessible to human beings.

Yet standard intuition would have it, I submit, that ABC is no more in the extension of "water" than XYZ is. "Water" is, as we have said, a natural kind term; it either denotes the non-disjunctive property exemplified by most paradigm local samples, or it denotes nothing. This kind, as it happens, is H_2O, not XYZ or ABC. Yet pure informational theories cannot respect this result. Since such theories equate what a term means with what could cause their tokening under a certain sort of physically accessible circumstance, and since there is no physically accessible circumstance under which H_2O could but ABC couldn't cause a tokening of "water," pure informational theories have to conclude – contrary to intuition – that both H_2O and ABC are in the extension of "water."

The problem, of course, is general. Provided only that it is consistent with the laws of physics that there could have been substances, kind-distinct from the ones that are actual, but which would manifest their distinctive features only in circumstances that are inaccessible to humans, it will follow, on a pure informational theory, that all our 'natural kind terms' have wildly disjunctive extensions, and hence are not really natural kind terms after all. And I would be very surprised if it weren't consistent with physics that there could be such substances.[24]

The Actual History Condition

Now, as I have already indicated, Fodor has expressed considerable sympathy with this sort of worry. Indeed, he has gone so far as to propose a modification to his own pure informational theory in an attempt to meet it.[25]

> [Pure informational] theories distinguish between concepts only if their tokenings are controlled by different laws. Hence only if different counterfactuals are true of their tokenings Hence only if there are (possible) circumstances in which one concept would be caused to be tokened and the other would not . . . That is how you get from informational semantics to verificationism . . . Correspondingly, the way you avoid the verificationism is: You relax the demand that semantic relations be construed solely by reference to subjunctive conditionals; you let the actual histories of tokenings count too.[26]

Fodor's idea is to block the objectionable verificationist consequences of a pure informational theory by adding an 'actual history' condition: it is now to be required not merely that it be a law that Xs cause S-tokenings, if S is to mean X; it is further required that some S-tokenings *actually* be caused by Xs. And this would appear to rule out the sort of case we have just been contemplating: since it is true by assumption that ABC is only a *potential* cause of "water" tokens, it couldn't actually have caused any tokenings of "water," and, hence, doesn't satisfy the actual history condition. It is, therefore, ineligible to be in the extension of "water," just as intuition requires. So everything would appear to be OK.

Unfortunately, matters are not quite so simple. For one thing, the actual history condition is purchased at a terrible cost. For another, it doesn't ultimately help with the problem about verificationism. And, finally, even if we ignored the issue about verificationism, it still doesn't yield the right meaning ascriptions. All that, in any case, is what I propose to argue next.

It is one of the virtues of a pure informational theory that it can treat "unicorn" in just the way it treats every other syntactically primitive symbol. Since, according to such theories, all that semantic relations care about are nomic connections between properties, and since there can be nomic connections between uninstantiated properties, such theories would appear well-poised to explain – or at least not precluded from explaining – how it is possible for us to represent unicorns, even though there are actually no unicorns. And this seems highly desirable because, on the face of it anyway, there would appear to be no deep connection between being a primitive concept and being instantiated; there seems no reason to believe that every concept that has an empty extension in the *actual* world will turn out to be *complex*.

The actual history condition, however, incurs that implausible commitment. Since it requires that an instance of some property actually have caused a tokening of a symbol that has it in its extension, it must hold that all uninstantiated concepts are, appearances to the contrary notwithstanding, complex. But just what is the (non-question-begging) argument which shows that you couldn't get a primitive concept that was uninstantiated?

The second difficulty with the actual history condition is that it doesn't really help with the problem about verificationism.

Partly for heuristic reasons, I stipulated that ABC was to be found only on Pluto, and not on Earth. But this is, I think, completely inessential to the point it is meant to illustrate. The basic intuition behind the anti-verificationist objection, to repeat, is that there is no reason whatever – intuitive or otherwise – to believe that having a word S that means X but not Y depends on being able, in principle, to tell Xs apart from Ys. If the difference between being X and being (X or Y) is real, why shouldn't we be able to think in ways that respect that difference? But there is absolutely nothing in this intuition which depends on Y's being *remote*. The intuition persists even on the supposition that both of the substances in question are involved in the actual causal history of S-tokenings. Fodor says:

> The mixed theory is itself just a soupçon verificationist, but only in a way that might surely be considered untendentious. We used to have to say that "X"'s meaning X requires the nomological possibility of distinguishing X from any property that would cause "X"'s *if it were instantiated* . . . Now all we require is that it be possible to distinguish X from any property that is *actually* instantiated in the causal history of "X"'s.[27]

But I don't see that this is any less tendentious than the verificationism entrained by the original pure version. To be sure, the present proposal cuts down on the number of properties that must be distinguishable, if they are to be ineligible to count as in the extension of the term in question. But the end result is no more plausible: the theory continues to deliver verdicts that are at odds with the intuitive semantics of natural kind terms.

We may illustrate this by describing a situation in which ABC is instanced locally. Trace quantities of it, let us suppose, exist in our lakes and rivers and in the atmosphere. It is sometimes, even if rarely, the cause of "water" tokenings. It remains, as before, however, indistinguishable from H_2O in any circumstance accessible to humans. Thus, there is no possible circumstance under which H_2O can cause "water" tokens and ABC can't.

Standard intuition would have it, I submit, that ABC is still not in the extension of "water." ABC remains a different *kind* of stuff from H_2O; and the intuitive semantics of "water" is such that, if it denotes anything at all, it denotes the kind exemplified by most of the paradigmatic local samples. ABC, however, is not exemplified by most of the local samples; by stipulation, it exists only in trace quantities. It stands to water like iron pyrites stand to gold: it is an impurity. Hence, it does not count as within the extension of "water."

Still, this is a judgment that the mixed theory cannot respect. ABC is an occasional cause of "water" tokens, so it satisfies the actual history condition. Since it is not physically distinguishable from H_2O, there is no physically possible circumstance in which H_2O can and ABC can't cause tokenings of "water." So, contrary to intuition, it counts as in the extension of "water."

In sum: an informational theory of meaning is necessarily verificationist and the implausibility of this verificationism can be vividly illustrated through the consideration of expressions – like natural kind terms – which intuitively possess non-disjunctive extensions but which are assigned wildly disjunctive extensions by such theories.[28]

Could you Recognize Naturalistic Conditions of Type 1?

I have been arguing that it won't prove possible to naturalistically specify a situation of type 1 because, even if you could naturalistically specify a situation in which all *verifiable* sources of error had been removed, you couldn't, in the nature of things, specify a situation in which all *unverifiable* sources of error had been removed. But since unverifiability doesn't correctness make, the most refined attempt at a naturalistic specification of a type 1 situation is bound to fail.

I now want to argue that, even if, *per impossibile*, there were naturalistic situations of type 1, we could never be in a position to recognize that there were. If, by a stroke of vastly implausible luck, we were to stumble onto a specification of such a condition, we could never be entitled to conclude that we had. If this is true, then there can be no point in attempting to develop such theories.

Type 1 Conditions and Belief Holism

The single most impressive reason for being skeptical about the existence of situations in which only the referent of a symbol can cause its tokening has to do with what we may call the *holistic character of belief fixation*.[29] I shall explain.

Under normal circumstances, belief fixation is mediated by background theory – what contents a thinker is prepared to judge depends upon what other contents he is prepared to judge.[30] And this dependence is again typically, arbitrarily robust: just about any stimulus can cause just about any belief, given a suitably mediating set of background assumptions.

So, for example, suppose you think, in response to some stimulus or other, "Lo, a magpie." Need there really be a magpie in respect of which this is thought? Of course not. It could be that you saw a currawong, but believing there to be no currawongs in Australia, and believing this to be Australia, you concluded it was a magpie. Or perhaps you heard a currawong call and you believe that that is just what magpies sound like. Or then, again, perhaps you believe that whatever the Pope says goes and the Pope says that this presented currawong is a magpie. Or . . . The point is that magpie beliefs can be mediated by theory to any extent you care to imagine. The thought that something is a magpie can get triggered by a currawong in any of an *indefinite* number of ways, corresponding to the potentially indefinite number of background beliefs which could mediate the transition.

We have had occasion to remark on this doctrine before and to note its importance for Fodor's purposes. The point surfaces, as we saw, in the course of showing that it doesn't follow from the asymmetric dependence story about meaning that the intentional content of "cow" is not *cow*, but rather some disjunction of proximal cow projections. Just about any cow-projection can cause a cow-thought, Fodor argues, since just about any theory can mediate the fixation of beliefs about cows. That is why cow-projections are not eligible to serve as the referents of our expressions. But by the same token, just about any *non-cow* can cause a cow-thought too, if just about any theory can mediate the fixation of beliefs about cows. Indeed, it follows, and is in any case independently plausible, that just about any property can cause just about *any* thought, given a suitable set of background assumptions.

But now we are in a position to see why the existence of naturalistically specifiable situations of type 1 should appear so wild. A type 1 situation is, by definition, a situation in which, if the concept *magpie* gets tokened, then it's nomologically necessary that that tokening was caused by a magpie. Specifying a situation of type 1 naturalistically will involve, therefore, specifying a situation, in non-semantic and non-intentional terms, in which one can think "Lo, a magpie" only in application to magpies.

But the point about the holistic character of belief fixation suggests that *anything* can cause the thought "Lo, a magpie" in just about *any* type of situation provided only that the appropriate background beliefs are present. And, as I have argued, these background beliefs could be just about anything. Consequently, specifying a situation in which no non-magpie can cause the thought "Lo, a magpie" involves, at a minimum, specifying a situation that ensures the absence of all the beliefs which could potentially mediate the transition from non-magpies to magpies. Since, however, there looks to be a potential infinity of such mediating background clusters of belief, a non-semantically specified situation of type 1 would consist in the specification of a situation in which it has somehow been non-semantically guaranteed that none of this potential infinity of background clusters of belief is present. And it appears utterly incredible that there should be such a specification.

The impact of this observation on various *particular* proposals is transparent. For example, the observation that type 1 conditions must exclude a potentially indefinite array of frustrating background beliefs provides us with one more way of saying what is wrong with a teleological causal theory: it is simply not plausible to suppose that our cognitive mechanisms' functioning as they are supposed to is sufficient to ensure the absence of any untoward background theory. Hence, it is not plausible to claim, as a teleological theory does, that when they are so functioning, it will prove impossible to think "Lo, a magpie," except in application to magpies. But does the observation provide us with a more general reason for doubting the feasibility of a type 1 style causal theory of meaning? I think it does.

Suppose you come up with a naturalistic specification of some situation C, which you conjecture to be a type 1 condition: under C, nothing but the referents of symbols can cause their tokenings. Could you show that your conjecture was in fact true? I want to argue that you could never non-question-beggingly certify that C is a condition of the required kind, even if it is one.

The worry that needs allaying is that the specified condition is consistent with the presence of background beliefs which would frustrate the covariation between symbol tokenings and their referents – magpie beliefs and magpies, as it may be. Putting this worry to rest requires showing that the situation's being C is enough to ensure the truth of the following open conjunction:

$$(*) \quad \text{-Bel}_1 \ \& \ \text{-Bel}_2 \ \& \ \text{-Bel}_3 \ \& \ \ldots$$

where the Bel_i stand for the various clusters of background beliefs which could potentially frustrate the connection between being a magpie and the tokening of an expression which refers to it. Well, could C ever be recognized as sufficient for the truth of (*)?

Recognizing that a particular naturalistic condition ensures the absence of a set of beliefs, requires possession of naturalistic *necessary* conditions for those beliefs; we need to be able to tell that nothing in the naturalistic condition in question adds up to one of the beliefs in question. Now, we may, for present purposes, assume that we possess naturalistic necessary conditions for something's being a *belief*. But possession of naturalistic necessary conditions for being the *belief that p* requires possession of naturalistic necessary conditions for something's *meaning p*.

Now, suppose that the envisaged C condition is in fact a type 1 condition for *magpie*. Under the terms of this assumption, there would be naturalistic *sufficient* conditions for meaning: type 1 causal theories of meaning, remember, are advertised as providing no more than sufficient conditions for meaning. However, what's needed to certify that C is a type 1 condition for *magpie* is a certification that it is sufficient for the truth of (*); and what's needed to certify that it is sufficient for the truth of (*) is a set of naturalistic *necessary* conditions for meaning. So, we can't certify that C is a type 1 condition for *magpie*, even on the assumption that it is one. So, we can't certify that it is one.

Suppose, however, that the causal theorist sheds his modesty and promotes his theory as providing both necessary and sufficient conditions for meaning. As before, we have a specification of C, but now it is a clause in a *necessary and sufficient* condition for S meaning M. Could we now certify that C is a type 1 condition for *magpie*, on the assumption that it is one?

Well, on the assumption that it is one, there would be a set of necessary and sufficient conditions for an expression's expressing a certain property. Unfortunately, even so, we would still not be in a position to certify that C is a type 1 condition. The trouble is that proposition (*) is not finitely stateable: there is no finite way to state what beliefs the causal theorist must exclude before he may be assured of the desired concomitance of magpie beliefs and magpies. Literally any belief can frustrate the desired connection. So, there is no way to certify that C is sufficient for the truth of (*), even granted a set of naturalistic necessary and sufficient conditions for meaning. So, there is no way to certify that C is a type 1 condition for *magpie*.

If these considerations are correct, then there can be no point in constructing type 1 naturalistic theories of meaning. Even if, *per impossibile*, we were somehow to stumble onto such a theory, we could never convince ourselves that we had. For perfectly general reasons, we could never non-question-beggingly certify that a particular naturalistic condition was in fact a type 1 situation.

Asymmetric Dependence Revisited

If any of this is true, then Fodor's asymmetric dependence proposal could not constitute a convincing naturalistic sufficient condition for meaning. For as we have seen, Fodor's theory is a type 1 theory in disguise: to say that P is an asymmetric dependence base for S is simply to say that P is the sole cause of S tokens in the closest world where S has a single cause. And so, since it is the burden of the preceding considerations that there can be no convincing naturalistic specification of a type 1 situation, either Fodor's criterion yields the wrong meaning ascriptions, or it is not naturalistic in character.

Nevertheless, since arguments at this level of generality can seem disengaged from their targets, and since it may in any event prove independently edifying, I now propose to run through the relevant dialectic with explicit reference to the details of Fodor's particular proposal. I propose to show directly, in other words, that Fodor's asymmetric dependence condition for S's meaning P is either not naturalistic, or not sufficient for S's meaning P.

Let's go back to H_2O and XYZ. As before, "water" is undoubtedly a natural kind term, so it has H_2O in its extension but not XYZ; and, as before, it is true by stipulation that both H_2O and XYZ are nomically sufficient to cause tokenings of "water." What makes it true, according to Fodor, that "water" means H_2O and not XYZ, is that the closest world in which "water" tokens can get caused by one and not the other of these properties, is a world in which it is H_2O that can do the causing, and not XYZ.

But *closer* with respect to what? Clearly, everything depends on whether the relevant similarity relation can be specified non-question-beggingly – without the benefit of sidelong looks at the meanings of the expressions in question. What the success of Fodor's theory depends on, in other words, is that when nearness of worlds is judged from a purely non-semantic and non-intentional – for our purposes, therefore, from a purely physical – point of view, the H_2O-only world always turns out to be closer than the XYZ-only world. Will this be true?

Now, Fodor thinks that the results are bound to turn out as desired because:

... to get to a world where we can [infallibly] tell XYZ from H_2O, you have to either change us (provide us with instruments of observation we don't now have, for example) or change H_2O/XYZ (make their molecular structure visible to the naked eye, for example) or do both. But now, having gotten to such a world, if you want to also make it the case that our "water" tokens track XYZ rather than H_2O (or XYZ and H_2O) you would also have to change something about us which corresponds to the disposition which, I take it, everybody agrees underlies our use of "water" in THIS world, viz., our disposition to use "water" only of things that bear the same kind relation to our local samples.

So you'd have to change more things to get to a world where XYZ is distinguishable from H_2O and our use of "water" tracks XYZ than you would to get to a world where XYZ is distinguishable from H_2O and our use of "water" tracks H_2O ... of course, this extra thing that you'd have to change IS an intention to use "water" as a kind term; and that intention may or may not be a physical state (depending on whether physicalism is true of our intentions).[31]

To get from our world to an XYZ-only world, argues Fodor, you have to make H_2O infallibly distinguishable from XYZ *and* you have to change whatever intentional facts ground the fact that in this world "water" means H_2O; whereas, to get to an H_2O-only world, you have only to make XYZ infallibly distinguishable from H_2O. Hence, any XYZ-only world is bound to be further than any H_2O-only world.

To begin to get a sense for what's wrong with this argument we may start with the observation that the purely physical changes involved need not be on a par. From a purely physical standpoint, it may be much easier to get to a world where you will apply "water" only to XYZ, if you want to, than to get to a world where you will apply "water" only to H_2O, if you want to. This ought to be obvious. To bring it about that H_2O never gets confused for XYZ (or anything else for that matter), you only have to bring it about that H_2O has some unique distinguishing and infallibly detectable property; you don't also have to bring it about that XYZ is never confused for anything else. Vice versa for bringing it about that XYZ is never confused for H_2O. But bringing it about that some substance has some unique infallibly detectable property is a function not only of our detecting capacities but of the substance's chemistry as well. And so, it seems inevitable that it will be easier to render some substances infallibly detectable than others.

Imagine, in fact, that the chemistry of XYZ is such that, by the merest alteration of some tissue in our nostrils, we are able to *smell* its presence wherever it may be. In a world with the contemplated nasal alteration, XYZ is uniquely and infallibly detectable by the foul scent it gives off. In that world, then, there is no problem ensuring that "water" gets applied only to XYZ (if that's what you want to do): all you have to do is ensure that it gets applied only to substances that give off the distinctive scent. It doesn't follow, of course, that this foul-smelling world is equally optimal for the infallible detection of H_2O – H_2O need give off no distinctive scent of its own in this world, and may remain confusable with substances other than XYZ. Nor does it follow that it will be *equally* easy to get to a world in which H_2O is in like manner infallibly detectable: H_2O's chemistry may not allow for that. Getting to a world in which you apply "water" only to H_2O, if you want to, may involve making many more changes in us and our surroundings than it took getting to the foul-smelling XYZ world.

Suppose in fact that that's precisely the way things are. To get, then, from our world – in which "water" means H_2O – to a world in which "water" gets applied only to H_2O, you have to make a big physical change; to get to a world in which it gets applied only to XYZ, you have to make a small physical change and a small intentional change. Now: which world is closer to ours?

Well, if the distance measured were specified as follows, the answer would be clear: all physical changes are on a par, and every intentional change counts for as much as every physical change. But, of course, this specification would be entirely question-begging in the present context. It is not allowed to specify the similarity relation in intentional terms. And yet, on the other hand, I don't see that any other specification will yield anything like the desired results.

Fodor says:

> ... of course, this extra thing that you'd have to change IS an intention to use "water" as a kind term; and that intention may or may not be a physical state (depending on whether physicalism is true of our intentions). But you don't ... have to MENTION its being an intention to say what I just did say ... viz., that you have to change more things to get to worlds where H_2O is distinguishable from XYZ AND our "water" tokens track XYZ ... than you have to change to get to a world where H_2O is distinguishable from XYZ and our "water" tokens track just H_2O. So it doesn't look to me as though the required notion of distance is question-begging.[32]

This argument depends on the claim that getting to a world in which H_2O is infallibly detectable involves exactly as much (or as little) as getting to a world in which XYZ is. Thus, the detecting changes drop out, leaving the intentional change to settle the matter. But as I have just argued, there is absolutely no reason to believe this.

If we correct for the false assumption, it is perfectly plain, I think, that there will be no non-question-begging way of getting the H_2O-only world to come out closer than the XYZ-only world. Judged from a purely physical standpoint, the XYZ-only world may well come out closer. And no other standpoint is acceptable in the present context. Hence, Fodor's theory is either false, or it's not naturalistic.

NOTES

I want to express a special debt of gratitude to Jerry Fodor for sharing and discussing his work with me over several years. For much helpful discussion I am also grateful to Barry Loewer, Stephen Schiffer, Steve Yablo, David Velleman, Larry Sklar, Allan Gibbard, Jennifer Church and Jaegwon Kim.

1   *Psychosemantics*, 1987, MIT Press, p. 97.
2   A set of properties A *weakly* supervenes on a set B, if no two objects in a given world could differ in their A properties without differing in their B properties. On the other hand, a set of properties A *strongly* supervenes on set B, if no two objects drawn from any two worlds could differ in their A properties without differing in their B properties.
3   I think, actually, that considerations based upon the problem of mental causation may provide such an explanation; but here is not the place to go into why. For useful discussion see Stephen Yablo, "Mental causation," (forthcoming) and Brian P. McLaughlin, "Type epiphenomenalism, type dualism, and the causal priority of the physical," in *Philosophical Perspectives* 3, Ridgeview, 1989.
4   *Psychosemantics*, p. 98.
5   See Jaegwon Kim, "Concepts of supervenience," *Philosophy and Phenomenological Research*, 1984.

6   Which is not, perhaps, as big an "if" as it may at first appear. For I am inclined to believe that if there is to be a naturalized theory of meaning at all, it is likely to be a causal theory: i.e., it is likely to attempt to reconstruct the relation between a predicate and the property it expresses in terms of the *causal* relations between that predicate and that property. (What *other* sort of possible naturalistic relation between a predicate and a property looks even remotely semantically relevant?) Furthermore, any such theory is likely to be framed, not just in terms of the *actual*, but in terms of the *counterfactual*, causal relations that may obtain between a predicate and a property. In contrast with the case of the reference of proper names – where actual causal history seems paramount – it seems wrong to ignore counterfactuals in determining the meaning of predicates. But a causal theory of meaning couched in terms of truths about a symbol's counterfactual causal history is precisely what an information-theoretic semantics is all about.

7   For theories based on this basic formula see Fred Dretske, *Knowledge and the Flow of Information*, MIT Press, 1981; Dennis Stampe, "Towards a causal theory of linguistic representation," in French, Uehling, and Wettstein (eds), vol. 2, *Midwest Studies in Philosophy*, University of Minnesota Press, 1977; R. Stalnaker, *Inquiry*, MIT Press, 1984, Jerry Fodor, op. cit., and "A Theory of Content," Parts I and II, (in press-f) (henceforth *TOC*). It is with this latter piece that the present paper is most concerned.

   In the interests of presenting the strongest possible version of a causal theory, I am going to suppress many qualms and follow Fodor in two important respects. First, I am going to allow that we can talk about genuine (obviously *ceteris paribus*) laws here – despite the fact that what's in question are such "laws" as that presidents cause "president" tokens and that sopranos cause "soprano" tokens. And, second, I will allow that "it's bedrock that the world contains properties and their nomic relations" (p. 41 of *TOC*), so that it counts as a perfectly objective matter what properties are causally responsible for what effects.

   Notice by the way, that it can be a law that Ps cause S-events, even if there are no Ps: all that's required is that Ps would cause S-events, if there were any.

8   Causal theories of meaning face, I believe, another serious problem, that of accounting for the *normative* character of the notion of meaning. For a discussion of this point see my "The rule-following considerations," *Mind*, October 1989.

9   Strictly speaking, of course, it is instances of a property, rather than the property itself, that are said to be in extensions. To avoid prolixity, however, I shall continue to talk of properties as being in extensions; it is hardly likely to cause confusion.

   It is sometimes suggested that it would be enough if possession of M were *sufficient* for being in the extension of S. But that is not right. If only sufficiency were required, we would not know S's meaning simply as a result of a definition of M. For although we would know what properties were definitely in the extension of S, we would not know if we had them all. Thus, a definition of M would not even constitute a sufficient condition for a symbol possessing a given meaning, which is the very least required from a (naturalistic) theory meaning.

10   In *TOC*, Part I.

11   ibid., p. 38 (of the typescript).

12   ibid., p. 39.

13   ibid., p. 39.

14   ibid., p. 43.

15   ibid., p. 56.

16   ibid., p. 59.

17   This is cited from Fodor's reply to a talk I gave on asymmetric dependence at the Eastern Division of the APA in Washington D.C. in December 1988. I shall refer to this reply henceforth as "D.C. Notes." The passage is from p. 9.

18 Of course, both types of situation are *physically* possible – that is, possible relative to the laws of physics, even if not possible relative to the laws of psychology – which is all that will matter to the discussion that follows.

19 cf. *TOC*, p. 65.

20 Saul Kripke, *Naming and Necessity*, p. 122.

21 ibid., pp. 135–6.

22 I stress the "as if." What we are after here is a description of the intuitive semantics of natural kind expressions, not a theory of the facts in virtue of which they come to have those semantics. What we need to know is what the intuitively correct assignments would be under a variety of counterfactual circumstances, so that we can assess theories that purport to capture those assignments; we don't also need to commit ourselves to a conception of the mechanisms by which they come to have those assignments. I emphasize this because causal theories are restricted to primitive symbols, which for our purposes means "syntactically primitive symbols that are not introduced by definitions." And so, I wish to emphasize that accepting the Kripke/Putnam account of the functioning of natural kind expressions does not imply that these expressions had to have been introduced by definitions. (As Kripke himself notes, the idea of such introductory baptisms is in any case artificial.)

23 What counts as a basic explanatory property? That's a good question to which I have no decisive answer. Information-theoretic semantics is in any event committed to hyperrealism about which properties are suitable for entering into nomic relations; it is enough for our purposes if we say that the basic explanatory properties will be some proper subset of these.

24 In the interests of keeping matters as simple as possible, I have described the case directly in terms of molecules; but it is probably more intuitive to do it first at the level of elementary particles and then work up to the molecular level.

Thus, consider "T." "T" is a name for a certain kind of elementary particle characterized by a particular array of fundamental features – charge, mass, baryon number, charm, what-have-you. It has been frequently observed and its fundamental features have been accurately recorded. It is often the cause of "T" tokens. Now, suppose that there is a physically possible particle T* that, although possessing some fundamental features distinct from T – and, hence, although constituting a different kind of particle than T, according to the basic principles of elementary particle taxonomy – nevertheless would behave just like T in all circumstances accessible to humans, or to appropriate idealizations thereof.

Now, standard intuition would have it, I submit, that T* is not in the extension of "T." "T" is a term in a basic science; it is intended to denote a natural kind: the kind defined by the non-disjunctive property exemplified by paradigm local samples. This kind, as it happens, is T. T* is not of the same kind as T. That much can be incontrovertibly clear: simply let T and T* possess different values for the basic parameters in terms of which physics taxonomizes elementary particles. So T* cannot count as within the extension of "T" and, hence, the use of "T" in application to T* is false.

If there can be kind-distinct *particles* that are indistinguishable, it seems overwhelmingly plausible that there could be kind-distinct *molecules* that are indistinguishable. Not to say that this is an automatic inference. But what with molecules being individuated partly in terms of the atoms that constitute them, and what with atoms being individuated partly in terms of the particles that constitute them, it would be very surprising, to say the least, if it were simply inconsistent with physics that there should be kind-distinct molecules between which no humanly possible experiment could distinguish.

25 I first expressed this objection in the APA paper. The modification found its way into

later drafts of *TOC*.

26   *TOC*, p. 66.

27   ibid., p. 68.

28   That's one side of the coin; the other side is that such theories would assign disjunctive extensions to expressions even when the correct result is that they have *no* extensions, because they fail to refer.

Thus, it would appear to follow from the account of natural kind expressions that we have been working with, that if there were no natural kind uniting the local paradigm samples used to fix the referent of S – if, for example, the only thing the chosen exemplars had in common was a messy motley of basic properties – that S would fail to refer. But informational theories cannot respect this result.

Again, the easiest way to see this is by emphasizing the verificationism entrained by such theories. Just imagine that the samples used to fix the extension of "water" contain a myriad distinct but indistinguishable substances. Then, all those substances will be in the extension of the term "water," even though the intuitive result is that none should be. (A myriad kind-distinct but humanly indistinguishable water-like substances may seem far-fetched; but that's no objection to its use in the present context.)

29   A version of this argument was first given in my *Essays on Meaning and Belief* (Princeton Ph.D., 1986).

30   Note that this is *psychological* holism, not the controversial doctrine of semantic holism. Fodor, for example, rejects the latter; but, as we have seen, it is very important for his purposes that he accept the former.

31   D.C. Notes, p. 10.

32   ibid.

5

Granny's Campaign for Safe Science

DANIEL C. DENNETT

What is the thread tying together all of Jerry Fodor's vigorous and influential campaigns over the years? Consider the diversity of his *bêtes noires*. In "Operationalism and ordinary language," (1965) it was Wittgenstein and the "no private language" gang; in *Psychological Explanation* (1968d) and *The Language of Thought* (1975a), it was Ryle, Skinner and other behaviorists; in "Tom Swift and his procedural grandmother" (1978b, reprinted in 1981) it was AI in general and procedural semantics in particular; in "Three cheers for propositional attitudes" (1978c, reprinted with revisions in 1981) it was me and my "irrealist" way with stances; in "Methodological solipsism considered as a research strategy in cognitive science" (1980c, reprinted in 1981) it was the brand of "naturalism" that claimed that psychology had to traffic in meanings that were not inside the head; in *The Modularity of Mind* (1983) it was Bruner and the other New Look psychologists who infected perception with thought, but also, in the shocking punch line of the last chapter, AI again; in *Psychosemantics* (1987d) it was the meaning holists and those who would ground their naturalistic appeal to teleological formulations in what Fodor elsewhere has called "vulgar Darwinism" (these villains take another drubbing in his forthcoming "A Theory of Content" (in press-f); and in "Connectionism and cognitive architecture: a critical analysis", (Fodor and Pylyshyn, 1988a) it is the connectionists and their many friends.

What do these various heresies have in common? From Fodor's point of view, two things, obviously: (1) they are all wrong, wrong, wrong! and (2) they are endorsed by people who are otherwise quite decent company. That would be thread enough to tie Fodor's targets together if he were right, but as one who finds more than a morsel of truth in each of the derided doctrines, I must seek elsewhere for a uniting principle, and I think I have found it: they are all doctrines that make Fodor's Granny exclaim "Well I never!" and lurch alarmingly in her rocker. The cat is out of the bag. Jerry Fodor is a Granny's boy, a romantic conservative whose slogan might well be "What is good enough for Granny is good enough for science."

Now I don't know Jerry's real Granny from Marlene Dietrich, but his notional Granny, of whom we have all heard, believes in beliefs, in thoughts, in the genuine, intrinsic content of mental states.[1] In short, Granny believes in minds and mental events with all her heart and soul. And Jerry has eagerly sought to defend her: contrary to certain sophisticated opinions, Science does not suggest that she is wrong; we can have Granny and Science too! Cognitive Science is – had better be – the vindication of Granny in spades.

Clever boy that he is, Fodor has seen the futility of other heroic defenses of Granny against the insidious march of Science: the crypto-dualisms of Elizabeth Anscombe, John Searle, Thomas Nagel, and Charles Taylor, for instance. He, like Noam Chomsky[2], has had a subtler game plan: saving Granny's Cartesianism by outsciencing Science, by turning Granny's cherished views into redoubtable science itself: Cognitive Science. He is happy to call himself a mentalist, but he's the "thoroughly modern mentalist."

As he says in *The Languate of Thought:*

> Contemporary cognitive psychology is . . . by and large conservative in its approach to the commonsense tradition. . . . Cognitive psychologists accept, that is, what the behaviorists were most determined to reject: the *facticity* of ascription of propositional attitudes to organisms and the consequent necessity of explaining how organisms come to have the attitudes to propositions they do.
>
> What is *un*traditional about the movement . . . is the account of propositional attitudes that it proposes: . . . having a propositional attitude is being in some *computational* relation to an internal representation.
>
> (p. 198.)

As a bit of sociology of science, this is egregiously tendentious; and ever since, Fodor has been hard pressed to insist that you can't be a *proper* cognitive scientist unless you accept the "facticity" of propositional attitudes. This comes out most clearly, perhaps, in his recent broadside against the connectionists, who are, by his lights, enemies of cognitive science precisely because they don't accept the facticity of the "classical" mental types and processes.

Fodor is justly renowned as a philosophical champion of cognitive science, but if you look closely you will note that he is its champion only so long as it hews to the traditional line. Any breaking ranks on facticity earns an immediate reprimand from him. If he has to choose between Granny and science, he has made it clear that he'll choose Granny, and in several recent publications (see especially Fodor, 1985b), he has been candid in acknowledging the contortions he is willing to submit himself to in order to hold the faith.

Now that I have discovered the secret thread, I will use it to conduct a tour of recent history, following its winding path through labyrinths of controversy.

In one of the most often-quoted passages in contemporary philosophy, Quine declared a watershed:

> One may accept the Brentano thesis either as showing the indispensability of intentional idioms and the importance of an autonomous science of intention, or as showing the baselessness of intentional idioms and the emptiness of a science of intention. My attitude, unlike Brentano's, is the second.
>
> (1960:221)

There has been a growing consensus in philosophy of mind since then (for some details, see Dennett, 1987) that, one way or another, one must accept Quine's message and opt for one of the two choices: championing a *non*-physicalistic, *non*-naturalistic "autonomous science of intention" (something akin to Cartesian dualism), or siding with the natural sciences at the cost of taking propositional attitudes less than entirely seriously. Fodor has always thought otherwise. He has tried to show that you can have what he calls intentional realism (taking Brentano's intentionality entirely seriously) *and* make it live with the rest of physical science: scientific mentalism, in short. This is a delicate balancing act indeed, and if cognitive science is to fulfill this role, it must be carefully protected from variations that slide off either into anti-scientific mentalism (dualism, and other bizarre doctrines such as Searle's) or into scientific anti-mentalism (eliminative materialism, behaviorism, instrumentalism, etc.).

Fodor has reveled in his iconoclasm: in Fodor (in press-f) he puts it this way: "it counts as conventional wisdom in philosophy that (i) the intentional/semantic predicates form a closed circle and (ii) intentional states are intrinsically holistic." The conjunction of these theses he sees as fatal to "naturalism," and he importunes us to "become cautious about taking intentional irrealism for granted; more cautious, at a minimum, than has been the philosophical fashion for the last fifty years or so." – a rough doubling of the actual time span, but perhaps that is the way it has seemed to Jerry, as he has cast about for a stable version of realism.

In Fodor (1968d) he resolutely turned his back on Quine, Ryle, and Wittgenstein and began sketching an account of mental events as *inner processes*, distinguished or identified by their functional properties. It looked, and was supposed to look, like quite a radical alternative. It appeared to be a way of undercutting what seemed at the time to be a stifling Behaviorist dogma: *what goes on inside doesn't settle anything.* One way of understanding the limits that Fodor imposes on his own theorizing (and that of anyone else who will listen) is that it must come out in the end that *something* about what is going on inside the head must trump the "behaviorists" *criteria*, their *principles of charity*, their *procedural semantics*, their *skepticism about meanings*. That is what it means for content to be Real.

Here is how Fodor put it at the time:

> To qualify as a behaviorist in the broad sense of that term that I shall employ, one need only believe that the following proposition expresses a necessary truth: For each mental predicate that can be employed in a psychological explanation, there must be at least one description of behavior to which it bears a logical connection.
>
> (Fodor, 1968d:51)

A mentalist is simply anyone who denies this (Fodor, 1968d:51), and ever since then Fodor has been seeing to it that he, and others, resist the siren song of this proposition. In his first book we get his discussions of function that make him one of the original functionalists – and it is easy to overlook the fact that nowhere does he tie the *content* of mental states to their functions, though some passages certainly seem to permit it. He says:

> The functional character of a machine state is determined by its total role in the machine's computational processes as well as by its relation to machine behavior in the narrow sense of machine output.
>
> (Fodor, 1968d:143)

Hence holism is true of *functional* attributions, but he doesn't explicitly relate the content of a state to its functional character. He does, however, go on to say:

> It is a question of fact, and not of how we should decide to talk about the facts, whether, or to what extent, a given kind of organic behavior is the consequence of

psychological processes that are functionally equivalent to some machine processes
... In the present case, we demonstrate functional equivalence between machine and
organic processes by determining that the psychological theory realized by the
machine's program provides an adequate and simple account of the organism's
behavior.

(Fodor, 1968d:149

If "demonstrating functional equivalence" is to be the touchstone of a *psycho-logical* theory, as this passage suggests, one would suppose that "content equivalence" would go along with it, but Fodor refrained from explicitly making this step, unlike such functionalists as Sellars and me, and only recently has he explicitly rejected this step (in Fodor, 1987d). There are two brands of functionalism, he says, and he endorses – has always endorsed, apparently – only the weaker version:

> ... all you need is the claim that *being a belief* is a matter of having the right connections to inputs, outputs, and other mental states. What you *don't* need – and what the philosophical motivations for Psychofunctionalism therefore do not underwrite – is the much stronger claim that being the belief *that p*, being a belief that has a certain *content* is a matter of having the right connections to inputs, outputs, and other mental states.

(Fodor, 1987d:69)

So Fodor's functionalism is eviscerated; he disagrees with those of us, from Sellars to the present, who in one way or another take "functional role semantics" to be the chief beauty of functionalism. I had argued (in Dennett, 1969) that content was a function of function, and this, it turns out, is the chief point Fodor and I have covertly disagreed about ever since. For Fodor, content is not a function of function after all. Or at any rate, it is not *much* of a function of function – for he does grant that functional role "is a marginal – a not very important – determinant of meaning" (Fodor, 1987d:72).

What, then, is content a function of? This has been the nagging problem for Fodor. At one point, during the early days of the Language of Thought, his friend and collaborator Zenon Pylyshyn could jokingly remind us of the lady who said that the earth rested on the back of an elephant who stood on a turtle, and when asked what the turtle stood on, replied "It's turtles – all the way down!" For Jerry, said Zenon, "it's syntax – all the way down!" That, we can presume, was not to be taken entirely seriously, but then what did Jerry himself say content was a function of? He didn't say. He did, however, have a lot to say about what wouldn't work: procedural semantics.

Fodor's first broadside against AI, in Fodor (1978b) set the tone and method for his later attacks: a priori "refutations" of what might charitably be called rational reconstructions or idealizations of the actual claims of his targets. Unlike Dreyfus's parallel campaign, Fodor's has never been particularly concerned with the details of the models under attack (though he has been happy to endorse the particular criticisms developed by others), but has rather invoked and defended "principles" that, he claimed, were ineluctably violated by any and all versions of the heresy. For instance, he has argued that AI can be seen, when you look at it just right, to be just warmed-over "associationism" or "phenomenalism" or some other *ism* that philosophers decisively refuted ages ago. This has not set well with his targets, and it is interesting to compare their complaints, early and late. Johnson-Laird (1978) and Smolensky (1988c) have both charged that Fodor simply invented and demolished strawmen, and have amply defended their charges.

This "principled" turning of his back on AI has always baffled me. For someone who has claimed that *to believe is to be in a computational relation to a representation*, he has been remarkably uninterested in actual computational relations. Why, if one was sure that the road to the scientific salvation of mentalism was via a language of thought, would one be so unwilling to consider in detail the actual attempts to construct such languages of mental representation, by people working in what Haugeland (1985) calls GOFAI (Good Old Fashioned AI)? If their models were faulty, why not try to devise a better one? Because, Fodor apparently believed, the whole enterprise of GOFAI was ill-founded. What to put in its place? One might have supposed that Fodor would look with interest, if not outright enthusiasm, at the radical alternative now brewing: connectionism. The other arch-critic of GOFAI, Dreyfus, has done just that. But Fodor has declared that enterprise to be, if anything, even more severely benighted, in all possible versions.

That would not seem to leave much room to maneuver for the serious scientist of mental representations, and that hunch is confirmed by Fodor, in his most sweeping attack on AI, in Fodor (1983). Here we find an a priori argument from first principles that supposedly spells doom:

1　"The condition for successful science (in physics, by the way, as well as psychology), is that nature should have joints to carve it at: relatively simple sub-systems which can be artificially isolated and which behave, in isolation, in something like the way they behave *in situ*. Modules satisfy this condition ..." (Fodor, 1983:128).

2　But "belief-fixation," the basically analogical and holistic process that occurs in the "central system" inboard of the modules, lacks this condition for successful science (p. 128).

3　Therefore, there is no possibility of discovering psychological laws governing the processes of belief-fixation, no possibility of a science of the *central* mind at all.

So it is no wonder Fodor has no use for either connectionism or GOFAI; he has an argument to prove not only that AI, in all its forms, is impossible, but that no conceivable successor science could do any better! "I am suggesting that there is a good reason why nothing is known about [the neuropsychology of thought] – namely, that there is nothing *to* know about it" (Fodor, 1983:128).

Safe science is "classical" science, Fodor has always insisted, but with Granny urging him on, he admits that the safest science is *no science at all*. One can see signs of this underlying scientific nihilism in other passages in Fodor's work. Most striking, perhaps, is the gag with which he ends "Methodological Solipsism":

> My point, then, is *of course* not that solipsism is true; it's just that truth, reference and the rest of the semantic notions aren't psychological categories. What they are is: they're modes of *Dasein*. I don't know what *Dasein* is, but I'm sure that there's lots of it around, and I'm sure that you and I and Cincinnati have all got it."
> (Fodor, 1980c:71)

And in Fodor (1985b) he recognized what he calls the "idealization problem" – the principle of charity in disguise – as an unsolved problem and admitted he saw "no reason to assume that the problem can be solved" within his Realistic boundaries. That paper ends with the following observation. "But of the semanticity of mental representations, we have, as things now stand, no adequate account."

It was into this breach that Fodor launched Psychosemantics (1987d), in which he attempted to hang on to his realism by adopting a denotative semantics: "concepts are individuated by reference to the properties they express, thoughts by the states of affairs they correspond to, and so forth." Independently of any functional role that a concept or mental representation might play within an interanimated set of its fellows, it can, as a matter of brute metaphysical fact, denote (or express) a property, thanks to its causal (but not functional) link to that property.

So if Fodor's hope for a Realistic but still Naturalistic theory of content is to be fulfilled, it must be fulfilled by an account of content that meets some strict requirements: a theory of content has to be (1) "factive" – not a matter of interpretation; (2) "naturalistic" – but only in the sense that it is physicalistic and atomistic. It avoids "meaning holism'," and the reason it must avoid meaning holism is that meaning holism would prevent the existence of *psychological laws,* and without laws, there is no proper Science. But this means that at least the content part of the theory cannot be functionalistic, because holism reigns for functional attribution. That is the message from Darwin.

This means that Fodor cannot avail himself of any teleological formulations, and this threatens to put him in mysterious waters indeed – for it is going to be passing strange if biological creatures have come to rely on *Dasein* for their psychology.[3]

In Dennett (1987, p. 308) I offered a diagnosis of Fodor's puzzling antipathy to Darwin: he "sees that the most one can ever get from any such [Darwinian] story, however well buttressed by scrupulously gathered facts from the fossil record, etc., is a story with ... the potential for indeterminacy." He has subsequently confirmed this diagnosis, and gone on the attack, in Fodor (in press-f). What is particularly interesting about his attack is that it brings the conservatism of his Intentional Realism into even sharper focus than in Fodor (1987d). Here is what he says:

> contrary to advertisements you may have seen, the teleological story about intentionality does *not* solve the disjunction problem. The reason it doesn't is that teleological notions, insofar as they are themselves naturalistic, always have a problem about indeterminacy just where intentionality has its problem about disjunction.
>
> (Fodor, in press-f)

Let us consider, as so often before, the frog with its bug-detecting eyes and responsive tongue. Fodor, criticizing efforts by Israel (unpublished) and Millikan (1984) to explain the content of the frog's perceptual states, points out that while one evolutionary/optimality story explains that the frog's ON state is *about* flies, "there is nothing to stop you from telling the story quite a different way. On the alternative account, what the neural mechanism is designed to respond to is little ambient black things (or, *mutatis mutandis*, characteristic patterns of ocular irradiation *as of* little ambient black things)." And, Fodor claims, "*Darwin doesn't care which of these ways you tell the teleological story*" (in the press-f, p. 17).

He is almost right. A Darwinian story is quite capable of distinguishing, as advertised, between large and interesting classes of errors and the "proper" functioning of those detectors. One does it by considerations of cost-effectiveness, as I outline in Dennett (1987:290–305). Such considerations do indeed depend on a certain "interest-relative" tactic of interpretation – roughly, the decision to ignore nitpickers. Hence, such considerations will not serve to rule out heroically Pickwickian interpretations, e.g., the sort of phenomenalistic interpretation that insists that the frog lives its whole life caring only about "little ambient black things" or its ocular irradiation patterns and other states of its receptors. We human beings are ever so much more particular about the objects of our intentional states, but in the limit the same conclusion holds for us: Darwin doesn't care whether we grew up on Earth or Twin Earth.

That is to say, one *can* tell a purely phenomenalistic story (for instance) about the frog or about us; "there is nothing to stop you," as Fodor says, but also, there is nothing to recommend it. Ever since Descartes we have had to live with the startling but no doubt negligible fact that a human mind well-equipped to live in the real world is, by definition, equally well-equipped to live in the fantasy world conjured up by the evil demon. It would be a wonder if Darwin's vision gave us a scientific talisman with which to ward off the evil demon.

So in a way Fodor is right: the resources of the theory of natural selection cannot provide a foundational, interpretation-free criterion of *real content* – of what the frog's states are *really* about. Recall Fodor's early definitions of behaviorism and mentalism quoted above: a behaviorist believes the following is a necessary truth, and the mentalist denies it: for each mental predicate that can be employed in a psychological explanation, there must be at least one description of behavior to which it bears a logical connection. The theory of natural selection is, in Fodor's terms, *behavioristic* – beyond a certain point, as Fodor says, "Darwin doesn't care" which way we tell the story. So Fodor's attack on the teleological/ functional story convicts it of only what I have been insisting upon all along: there is no *determinacy of function* to be obtained from evolutionary considerations.

But so what? Only if you believe, with Granny, that there is an ultimate fact of the matter should this be an objection. That is, Granny believes that the following situation is (always?) logically possible:

> according to our canvassing of the frog and its lifeworld, all considerations of efficiency and cost-effectiveness (all teleological considerations, that is) weigh in favor of attributing to it the belief that *p*, but *in fact* the frog believes something else.

"Behavioristic" theories such as mine (or such as any properly naturalistic theory that bases content ascription on function rather than mysterious denotational power) simply deny this possibility.

I fear this will shock Granny right off her rocker, but I would try to break it to her gently by pointing out all the interesting scientific problems still around to solve once we give up the defense of Intentional Realism as a lost cause. Besides, I would add, there is something ludicrous about the spectacle of her grandson trying to dissuade – one might as well say prohibit – scientists from attempting empirical explorations of models on the grounds that he has an a priori proof that all such models are hopeless. This tactic has been tried before by philosophers, and it has never washed well. In the past, it has been philosophers' categories that have typically been shown not to carve (models of) nature at the joints, and one way or another, the banished models have been seen to leak back through the defenses of the censors. So on tactical grounds alone (if not because he has undergone a theoretical conversion), Granny should advise her hero to drop it.

Let me summarize the results of this survey of Fodor's campaigns over the years. He has, in fact, had a quite single and steady vision, which he has defended against all comers: the "mentalism" he defined in 1968 in opposition to "behaviorism." But as various inroads have been made in cognitive science, threatening to establish one "logical connection" or another between "behavior" (including internal, neural behavior) and mental predicates, Fodor's mentalism has been driven back, back, back, to the extremely conservative and well-nigh mystical position that he currently defends:

(i)   no science of the "central system" is possible;
(ii) content is real, and determinate, but strictly independent of both behavior and biological function (to the extent that that is determinable).

Granny is no doubt quite pleased with this development, but while she and Jerry wait around for the day that scientists give up trying to understand the mind (when they get to say "I told you so!"), the rest of us have our own retort to fling: if we're so wrong and you're so right, how come we're advancing and you're retreating?

NOTES

Many of the ideas herein were provoked/inspired/unearthed by Kathleen Akins (1988), and in discussions with me during the last three years.

1   Jerry's Granny is not to be confused with his Aunty, who "speaks with the voice of the Establishment" (1987d:135), and turns out to be a "New Connectionist Groupie" (1987d: 139).
2   Chomsky has often expressed the view that if scientific psychology can't be "like physics," we would do better to look to novels for our knowledge of human thinking. A relatively early expression of this view was in 1978, recounted by me in Dennett (1988a: 285). He has recently reiterated the view: "Thus it is quite possible – overwhelmingly probable, one might guess – that we will always learn more about human life and human personality from novels than from scientific psychology" (Chomsky, 1988: 159).
3   See Dennett (1988b:384-9) for further discussion of the difficulties with Fodor's denotative semantics.

6

Why Fodor Can't Have It Both Ways

MICHAEL DEVITT

Since I am very busy just now, please do not ask me what "inputs" and "outputs" are.

Fodor, *Psychosemantics*

Part I: Introduction

1 Stich's Puzzle

In his influential paper, "Methodological Solipsism," (1980c) Jerry Fodor urges "the computational theory of the mind" (CTM) according to which "mental states and processes are COMPUTATIONAL." Fodor explains CTM as follows:

> mental processes have access only to formal (nonsemantic) properties of the mental representations over which they are defined (p. 63).

Fodor calls this "the formality condition." He partly explains his use of "formal" as follows:

> computational processes ... are formal because they apply to representations in virtue of (roughly) the *syntax* of the representations.
> What makes syntactic operations a species of formal operations is that being syntactic is a way of *not* being semantic.
>
> (1980c:64)

For Fodor, the terms, "formal," "syntactic," and "nonsemantic" are rough synonyms (1982:100).

Consider next, Stephen Stich's "Syntactic Theory of the Mind" (STM):

> cognitive states ... can be systematically mapped to abstract syntactic objects in such a way that causal interactions among cognitive states, as well as causal links with stimuli and behavioral events, can be described in terms of the syntactic properties and relations of the abstract objects to which the cognitive states are mapped.
>
> (1983:149)[1]

What is the relation between CTM and STM? Stich is saying that mental processes can be described syntactically, which for Fodor is much the same as saying that they can be described formally and nonsemantically. And Stich thinks

95

that this is the only way they *are* described for the purposes of psychology (p. 154). So STM seems similar to CTM.

This leads to Stich's puzzle. For there is another aspect of Fodor's view that is inconsistent with STM. Fodor is a friend of the folk.

Time and again Fodor has claimed that cognitive psychology should endorse folk psychology. The following is a typical statement.

> Cognitivism lives in the expectation that folk materials, when subjected to experimental evaluation and theoretical elaboration, can provide the foundations of a science.
>
> (unpublished-b:2)

Folk psychology ascribes thoughts or propositional attitudes to people; beliefs, desires, and so on. These thoughts have *contents* or *semantic* properties. It is common to think that these contents are "wide" truth-conditional ones. Fodor thinks that cognitive psychology endorses contents through its commitment to "the representational theory of the mind" (RTM) according to which propositional attitudes "are relations that organisms bear to mental representations" (1980c:63). These representations have contents and the generalizations of psychology advert to those contents.

Contrast this view with STM. According to STM the generalizations of psychology advert not to contents but to syntactic structures. So how can Fodor subscribe to RTM *and* CTM, a doctrine that seems so like STM?

> How is it possible for Fodor to have it both ways, for him to urge *both* that cognitive generalizations apply to mental states in virtue of their content and that "only *non*semantic properties of mental representations can figure in determining which mental operations apply to them?" (Stich, 1983:188; the quotation is from Fodor, 1990:315)

How can we reconcile the Fodor who is an enthusiast for the intentional talk of folk psychology with the Fodor who believes in CTM and the formality condition? That is Stich's puzzle.[2]

I think that there is good reason to be puzzled by Fodor's position, yet Stich is almost alone in being so.[3] So far as I know, nobody posed the puzzle before Stich, and his posing of it has generated no discussion, except by Fodor himself.

2   Having It Both Ways (1)

In *Psychosemantics* Fodor responds to Stich's puzzle with a deal of impatience:

> The vocabulary required to articulate the characteristic laws of a special science is – almost invariably – different from the vocabulary required to articulate the mechanisms by which these laws are sustained, the theory of the mechanisms being pitched – to put it crudely – one level down. So the typical *laws* of psychology are intentional, and the typical operations of psychological mechanisms are computational, and everything's fine except that Stich has missed a distinction.
>
> (1987d:166n.)

In the text that this note accompanies (pp. 139–40), Fodor talks of the psychological mechanisms of mental causation as *implementing* psychological laws. He gives an analogy of the relation he has in mind:

it's a law, more or less, that tall parents have tall children. And there's a pretty neat story about the mechanisms that implement that law. But the property of *being tall* doesn't figure in the story about the implementation; all that figures in that story is *genetic* properties.

(p. 140)

So, the way to explain both Stich's puzzlement and Fodor's impatience seems clear. Stich takes the formality condition to be a theory of mental processes at one level whereas Fodor takes it to be a theory of them at a different level. The problem is finding the appropriate levels.

Fodor's analogy with tallness suggests that we should solve our problem of levels along the following lines. Stich takes the formality condition to be a theory of the *nature* of mental processes *qua mental* and so to be at the psychological level. In contrast, Fodor takes the condition to be a theory of the *realization* of mental processes in something more physically basic; it is at the level of the implementation of psychological properties. We need to be more precise about this.

On the Stich interpretation of the condition, it says something about what properties of representations are mental (rather than biological or physiological, say); about the ones used to taxonomize the representations for psychological purposes: the ones postulated by psychology; the ones adverted to in psychological laws; the ones that subsume the states containing the representations under those laws; the ones essential for those states to instantiate those laws. On the Fodor interpretation, in contrast, the condition says something about what properties implement or realize the properties of representations identified as mental in the above way; the ones the mental properties supervene on, in the way the tendency to tallness supervenes on genetic properties.

We might try to capture the two interpretations of CTM in a way that highlights this difference as follows:

PSYCHOLOGY. The laws of mental processes advert to properties of representations that are only formal (nonsemantic).

IMPLEMENTATION. The laws of mental processes advert to properties of representations that are implemented only by formal (nonsemantic) properties of representations.

If the formality condition is interpreted as PSYCHOLOGY then it may well seem to imply STM; hence Stich's puzzlement. If the condition is interpreted as IMPLEMENTATION then to infer STM from it would be gross; hence Fodor's impatience.

So far, our reconciliation of Stich and Fodor is going well. The difficulties start when we ask: what exactly is the implementational level? The analogy with the implementation of tallness suggests that the appropriate level is that of human brain descriptions and computer hardware descriptions; the level of "neurological (circuit-theoretic: generally 'hard-science') explanation" (Fodor, 1985b:82). The level is fairly "brute-physical." So, according to IMPLEMENTATION, CTM restricts psychology to properties that can be implemented in formal (nonsemantic) properties at that hardware level.

There are certainly signs of commitment to IMPLEMENTATION, understood in this way, in Fodor's discussion of CTM. However, the discussion is predominantly concerned with a psychological level not this implementational level. As a result, CTM has been taken as PSYCHOLOGY, or something similar, by friend and foe alike.[4] The very use of the term "Methodological Solipsism" suggests this interpretation, for that term was introduced by Putnam as a psychological assumption (1975b:220). So too does the name "the computational theory of the *mind*." We are left with Stich's original puzzle: insofar as CTM concerns a psychological level how can it not concern the level of psychological laws; how can it be implementational?

The answer is that Fodor, in urging CTM, mostly has in mind a different implementational level from the brute-physical hardware one mentioned above. It is a level "between commonsense belief/desire psychology, on the one hand, and [the above-mentioned one] on the other" (1985b:82). It is not the intentional level of psychological laws which advert to content, but it is nonetheless psychological. It is the level of the psychological theory of "mental processes," or "mental causation." Though this is not at the brute-physical level, it "worries about mechanism and implementation" (1987d:153–4). Fodor attempts to distinguish the two psychological levels in the following passage.

> Now the main point to be made about [psychological generalizations that quantify over the contents of mental states] . . . is that CTM does not imply – and I see no reason to believe – that they can themselves be stated in purely syntactic terms. CTM constrains *mental processes* to define their ranges and domains by reference to the syntactic properties of mental symbols. But CTM leaves it open that there may be true, counterfactual, supporting *generalizations about the mind* which specify *their* ranges and domains in terms of the contents of mental states. Moreover, precisely because psychological generalizations typically apply to mental states in virtue of their contents (and not in virtue of such nonsemantic properties as, according to CTM, mental processes engage) the mental states subsumed by a given psychological generalization may well be quite heterogenous in their syntactic/computational characteristics. One would expect this whenever – to put it roughly but intuitively – similar psychological effects are produced by a range of different computational means. This suggests that the generalizations that cognitive theory construction starts from are quite likely *irreducibly* semantic.
>
> (Fodor, unpublished-b:5–6)

For Fodor, "counterfactual supporting generalizations about the mind" concern one psychological level, and laws of mental processes concern another. So, for him, my discussion of PSYCHOLOGY and IMPLEMENTATION collapses three levels into two.

Fodor explained his attempt to have it both ways only recently in *Psychosemantics*, and then half in a note. His only other remarks clearly in support of the attempt are the unpublished ones just quoted. So his impatience with Stich indicates that he must think that the distinction of levels on which his attempt rests is obvious. I think that it is very far from obvious.

Appeals to levels can be too easy. Suppose that a good scientific theory makes no reference to the entities and properties posited by folk opinion in that area. So eliminativism threatens. What is to stop us always saving folk opinion by claiming that it is "at a different level"? At least two things. First, folk opinion must be performing an explanatory task that is not performed by that scientific theory so that it seems plausible that we could develop it into another scientific theory that was compatible with the first theory. Second, it must seem plausible that the folk entities and properties supervene on the entities and properties of the first theory in either of two ways: by reduction, the way water is reducible to H_2O; or by implementation, the way human pain is implemented by brain states.

Fodor's talk of the semantic being implemented in the syntactic is clearly an acknowledgment of the supervention requirement. His discussion of CTM does not address the explanation requirement. I shall argue that Fodor's view meets neither requirement: folk psychology cannot be reconciled with CTM in the way Fodor thinks it can; the "counterfactual supporting generalizations about the mind" – let us call these, briefly, "the laws of the mind" — simply *are* the laws of mental processes. Most important of all, perhaps, these laws are not implemented syntactically. Fodor can't have it both ways.

Which way should he have it? In my view, he should have it the folk way. However, I think that he can *partly* have it the CTM way too. So he can *partly* have it both ways. But differences of level, and syntactic implementation, have nothing to do with managing this.

There is more to life than interpreting Fodor, fascinating though that is. In the next part I shall be concerned with CTM and related views as they arise not only in Fodor but also in others. I will mostly set aside the folk aspect of Fodor's view and therefore any attempt to come to conclusions about the correct interpretation of Fodor. In discussing CTM, I shall distinguish and assess a number of doctrines which are interesting in their own right, quite aside from their relations to Fodor's view. Some of the distinctions I shall make have often not been observed, leading to considerable confusion in the debate.

In this discussion of CTM I shall presuppose what I have just claimed and what Fodor denies:

PRESUPPOSITION. The laws of the mind are the laws of mental processes.

This alone makes any rush to judgment on the interpretation of Fodor inappropriate. I shall examine PRESUPPOSITION when I focus again on the interpretative question, taking account of the folk aspect of Fodor's view and his attempt to have it both ways (part III).

Central to my approach is an emphasis on three distinctions: that between formal properties and syntactic properties; that between thought processes and mental processes in general; and that between syntactic properties and narrow semantic properties.

Part II: CTM

3 "Syntactic" and "Formal"

We must start by examining carefully some of the terminology used to state the formality condition. This terminology fails to distinguish two notions, one of which has its place at a psychological level, and so would be appropriate in PSYCHOLOGY; and the other of which has its place at a physical level, and so would be appropriate in IMPLEMENTATION. Furthermore, care about usage is necessary to sustain a central thesis of this paper: the mind is not purely syntactic at any level, even the implementational.

I have already noted that Fodor uses "formal," "syntactic," and "nonsemantic" as rough synonyms (section 1). This usage is common in cognitive science. It is confusing, even if not confused.

In this section I will discuss "formal" and "syntactic." I shall start with their "ordinary" meaning and then briefly consider a technical meaning of "formal" stemming from formal logic. I will discuss "nonsemantic" at the end of the next section.

Ordinarily, a form of an object is a "shape, arrangement of parts, visible aspect." A property of an object is formal if it concerns "the outward form, shape, appearance, arrangement, or external qualities." A form of a word is "one of the shapes [it takes] in spelling, pronunciation, or inflexion" (*Concise Oxford Dictionary*). So the formal properties of an object are some of its *intrinsic* and fairly brute-physical properties. And its formal relations to another object are ones that hold in virtue of the object's intrinsic brute-physical properties. A formal property of the inscription '*Fa*' is that of beginning with an inscription shaped such-and-such (replace 'such-and-such' with a description of the shape of '*F*'). A formal relation between '*Fa*' and '*Fb*' is that of both beginning with an inscription of the same shape. A formal property of a symbol in a computer is that of being a certain pattern of on-off switches. A formal property of a symbol in the brain is a certain array of neurons.[5]

Syntax is "sentence-construction, the grammatical arrangement of words in speech or writing, set of rules governing this" (*COD*). Linguists use the term "syntax" to refer also to the study of such matters. "Syntax is the study of the principles and processes by which sentences are constructed in particular languages" (Chomsky, 1957:11). Syntactic properties and relations are ones that bear on that construction and are talked about in that study. A syntactic property of 'Ron' is that of being a noun; of 'loves,' that of being a two-place predicate; of 'Ron loves Maggie,' that of being a sentence.[6] A syntactic relation between 'Ron loves Maggie' and 'Maggie is loved by Ron' is that of the latter being the passive of the former. Syntactic properties are ones that a representation has in virtue of its role in relation to other representations in the language; they are functional properties and *extrinsic* to the object.[7]

If the terms "formal" and "syntactic" are used in the way I have just explained, they refer to very different types of properties and relations. They have their places at different levels, the one physical, the other functional. It is not even the case that formal and syntactic properties of representations match up, so that whenever there is a difference in one there is a difference in the other.[8] Written and spoken tokens of the one sentence are syntactically alike but formally very different. Two tokens of "Dad is cooking" printed out by the same machine are formally alike but may be syntactically different.

Aside from this "ordinary" sense of "formal" there is a technical sense that arises out of the notions of a *formal language* and a *formal system*. Formal properties and relations, in this technical sense, are functional just like syntactic ones. Indeed, they are often called "syntactic," most notably by Carnap (1937). They are quite different from formal properties in the earlier "ordinary" sense.[9]

From now on I shall use the terms "formal" and "syntactic" in the "ordinary" senses explained first. And I shall take "syntactic" to cover functional properties of symbols referred to by "formal" in the technical sense just mentioned. I am thus going against the practice in cognitive science of using the two terms as rough synonyms. My point in so doing is not to make a fuss about usage but to mark an important distinction in a convenient way. This distinction is the first of the three that I wish to emphasize.

The most important thing about syntactic properties for the purposes of this paper is that they are ones that a representation has solely in virtue of its relations to other representations within a system of representations. Its relations to anything outside that system are irrelevant to these properties.

Return to the formality condition. We can now distinguish two versions of both PSYCHOLOGY and IMPLEMENTATION, one talking of formal properties and one of syntactic, in my senses of those terms. However, the version of PSYCHOLOGY that talks of formal properties is obviously false: formal properties are at the level of brute-physical implementation of mental properties and hence at the wrong level to be adverted to by psychological laws. Psychological laws about cognitive states will no more advert to the formal properties of representations than will psychological generalizations about pain advert to the firing of c-fibres. If you go formal, you stop doing psychology. So we are left with three versions of the formality condition.

SYNTACTIC PSYCHOLOGY. The laws of mental processes advert to properties of representations that are only syntactic.

SYNTACTIC IMPLEMENTATION. The laws of mental processes advert to properties of representations that are implemented only by syntactic properties of representations.

FORMAL IMPLEMENTATION. The laws of mental processes advert to properties of representations that are implemented only by formal properties of representations.

A problem in discussions of CTM and STM is that the uses of "syntactic" and "formal" do not clearly distinguish the syntactic from the formal. When the terms "syntactic" and "formal" seem to refer to formal properties, as they sometimes do,[10] it is reasonable to interpret statements of the doctrines as FORMAL IMPLEMENTATION. On the other hand, when the terms seem to refer to syntactic properties, which they usually do,[11] it is reasonable to interpret the statements as SYNTACTIC PSYCHOLOGY.[12] Yet these are very different doctrines.

I think that it is because doctrines like STM and CTM have been understood as SYNTACTIC PSYCHOLOGY that they have seemed so *excitingly* radical to their proponents and so *dangerously* radical to their opponents.

Of course, SYNTACTIC PSYCHOLOGY does not seem radical to Fodor because he does *not* presuppose, as others do, that the laws of mental processes are the same as the "counterfactual supporting generalizations about the mind"; he does not accept PRESUPPOSITION. So he does not, as others do, take SYNTACTIC PSYCHOLOGY to eliminate the need for content.

SYNTACTIC IMPLEMENTATION is of interest only because, *if we adopt* PRESUPPOSITION, it foreshadows Fodor's attempted solution to Stich's puzzle. If it were true, folk psychology, with its wide truth-conditional content, could be at one level, and yet CTM could be concerned with a different psychological level that implemented those contents syntactically. For syntactic properties are functional; they are above the brute-physical level of formal properties. So they could plausibly be seen as psychological. I shall return to Fodor's attempted solution later (part III).

4   What do the Arguments for CTM show?

In this section, I shall consider the bearing of the two main arguments for CTM on SYNTACTIC PSYCHOLOGY and FORMAL IMPLEMENTATION. This will lead to the introduction of further doctrines.

The Argument from the Computer Analogy. This argument has a dual aspect which is brought out nicely in the following passage from Zenon Pylyshyn:

> the most fundamental reason why cognition ought to be viewed as computation . . . rests on the fact that computation is the only worked-out view of *process* that is both compatible with a materialist view of how a process is realized and that attributes the behavior of the process to the operation of rules upon representations.
>
> (1980a:113)

The aspect about the "behavior of the process" bears on SYNTACTIC PSYCHOLOGY; the aspect about materialism or, as I would prefer to call it, physicalism, bears on FORMAL IMPLEMENTATION.

Consider, first, the aspect about the behavior of the process. It is argued that we should take the computer analogy seriously and so see thought processes as computational. Now computational processes are defined syntactically; they are "syntactic operations over symbolic expressions" (Pylyshyn, 1980a:113); they are "both *symbolic* and *formal*" (Fodor, 1980c:64). So we should see thought processes as defined syntactically. A typical example of a law that satisfies this requirement might be one for *modus ponens* inferences: "Whenever a person believes both a conditional and its antecedent, she tends to infer its consequent."

What we have learnt from formal logic is that all the properties of representations adverted to in such rules are syntactic. Examples like this lead Stich to STM (1983:154–6).

This may seem to be an argument for:

SYNTACTIC PSYCHOLOGY. The laws of mental processes advert to properties of representations that are only syntactic.

However, it is an argument only if we overlook a crucial distinction: the distinction between thought processes and mental processes in general. The mental processes that concern (cognitive) psychology come in three sorts, as our initial quote from Stich brought out (section 1):

T–T processes from thoughts to thoughts;
T–T processes from sensory inputs to thoughts;
T–O processes from thoughts to behavioral outputs.

What I have been calling "thought processes" are T–T processes: inferential processes. Computation is indeed a good analogy for those. In my view, the analogy provides a sufficient reason for taking T–T processes to be syntactic; it establishes:

SYNTACTIC THOUGHT PROCESSES. The laws of thought processes advert to properties of representations that are only syntactic.[13]

SYNTACTIC PSYCHOLOGY is much stronger than this doctrine. It requires that I–T and T–O processes also be syntactic. Since the literature provides no reason to believe that a computer's input and output processes are analogous to I–T and T–O nor, if they were, that such processes would be syntactic, the argument from the computer analogy gives no reason to believe the stronger doctrine. The argument has no bearing on whether the laws of mental processes in general have to advert to semantic properties or contents.

I have argued elsewhere that SYNTACTIC PSYCHOLOGY is false (1989a:381–7). In brief, it makes I–T and T–O laws impossible. I–T laws must explain the *distinctive* role of a certain input, in conjunction with certain thoughts, in forming other thoughts. T–O laws must explain the *distinctive* role of a certain thought, in conjunction with certain other thoughts, in causing output. Laws that advert only to the syntactic properties of representations cannot possibly account for these distinctive roles. For, syntactic properties are constituted solely by relations *among representations*. To explain the distinctive roles, we need to advert to properties of representations that are constituted partly by relations between representations *and other things*, for example perceptual causes.

The distinction between thought processes and mental processes in general is the second distinction that I wish to emphasize. Participants in the debate about the mind are strangely uninterested in this distinction. The problem is not that they are unaware of it: typically discussions will start with what amounts to an acknowledgment of the distinction – as, for example, in the initial quote from Stich. The problem is that from then on all processes except thought processes, T–T, tend to be ignored. T–T are treated as if they were representative of them all. Fodor is particularly striking in this respect. He begins his dicussion of CTM by distinguishing the three sorts of process, referring to T–T is the "most interesting" (1987d:12). Yet a few pages later, in a passage important enough to be displayed, he describes "the nature of mental processes" in a way that applies only to T–T:

Claim 2 (the nature of mental processes)
Mental processes are causal sequences of tokenings of mental representations.

(p. 17)

The most interesting ones have become the only ones.[14] Despite this, there is every sign that he takes CTM to cover all mental processes.[15]

Consider, next, the physicalist aspect of the argument from the computer analogy. Computers are undoubtedly physical things. So, by seeing the mind as like a computer, we can make our theory of the mind conform with the very plausible overarching principle of physicalism. However, the move from the computer analogy to the physicalistic doctrine:

FORMAL IMPLEMENTATION. The laws of mental processes advert to properties of representations that are implemented only by formal properties of representations,

is too swift. What the analogy shows is that syntactically defined processes are implemented formally, for that is how they are implemented in a computer. If SYNTACTIC PSYCHOLOGY *were* true then FORMAL IMPLEMENTATION *would be* true. But the computer analogy gives no reason to think that SYNTACTIC PSYCHOLOGY is true and I have argued that it is false.

If SYNTACTIC PSYCHOLOGY is indeed false (though SYNTACTIC THOUGHT PROCESSES is true), I–T and T–O laws involve *non*syntactic properties of representations. Such properties, unlike syntactic ones, cannot be implemented in the formal properties of representations. Syntactic properties, we have noted, are constituted solely by relations among representations. The computer analogy shows that these relations are implemented in formal relations that hold in virtue of the formal properties of the representations (shape, etc.). Nonsyntactic properties, in contrast, are constituted partly by relations between representations and other things. These relations cannot be implemented in formal relations that hold solely in virtue of the formal properties *of representations.* Of course, a physicalist (who is prepared to use "formal" generously) will think that these relations are implemented in formal relations that hold in virtue of the formal properties of representations *and of other things,* for example of perceptual causes. Strictly speaking, the, FORMAL IMPLEMENTATION is false. However, if its talk of the "formal properties of representations" is extended to cover their formal relations, *including their relations to other things,* a physicalist will think it true. But that is a lot to read out of the computer analogy. The analogy supports FORMAL IMPLEMENTATION only insofar as it concerns thought processes.

The Argument from Methodological Solipsism and Psychological Autonomy. The argument is familiar. It appeals, *inter alia,* to Twin-Earth considerations to argue that psychology should advert only to properties that supervene on what is "inside the skin."

The argument is open to question, as Burge has shown (1986). Nevertheless, I think that it is basically correct (1989a:387–94).[16] Assume that it is. Then it establishes that truth-conditional properties are irrelevant to psychology. These do not supervene on the brain. The point to be made now is that the argument does *not* establish SYNTACTIC PSYCHOLOGY. Let us take for granted that syntactic properties are relevant to psychology. The argument does not establish that *only* syntactic properties are relevant. To establish that we need the further premise that there are no other non-truth-conditional properties, supervenient on the brain, that are relevant; that a "narrow" meaning *that goes beyond syntax* is not relevant. To my knowledge, *no argument for this premise has ever been given.*

Further, the argument does not establish that only "nonsemantic" properties are relevant to psychology, nor that representations are "meaningless" (Field, 1978:101) or "uninterpreted" (Schiffer, 1981:214–15; Churchland and Churchland, 1983:10) so far as psychology is concerned, unless "nonsemantic," "meaningless," and "uninterpreted," simply *mean* non-truth-condition.[17] I am as enthusiastic as anyone about truth-conditional semantics, but surely the question whether it is the *right* semantics is an empirical one, not something to be settled by definition. Whether *truth* and *reference* are appropriate notions for explaining semantic phenomena is an open question to be answered by close attention to what semantics is *for*.[18]

A narrow non-truth-conditional semantics is not a mere possibility. Consider functional- (conceptual-) role semantics. Typically such a semantics ascribes a meaning that is determined by the *internal* functional role of the representation. This meaning supervenes on the brain and so is narrow.[19] Syntactic properties, determined by functional relations between representations, are part of narrow meaning but do not exhaust it. The narrow meaning of a sentence is determined not only by its syntactic structure but also be the narrow meanings of the words that go into that structure. These word meanings are determined by the functional relations between representations, inputs and, perhaps, outputs. For example, what makes a token mean *echidna* (narrowly) and not *platypus* is being linked to echidna-ish not platypus-ish inputs and, perhaps, outputs. Being an "echidna" token is mostly not a matter of syntax at all, for it is not a property a representation has in virtue of its relations to other representations.

Insofar as the argument from methodological solipsism is good, it establishes that psychology needs at most a narrow semantics, whether a functional-role semantics or some other sort. So the argument is compatible with

NARROW PSYCHOLOGY The laws of mental processes advert to properties of representations that are only narrow semantic.

This should be read as a commitment to laws that advert to properties that are not syntactic; for example, narrow word meanings. Hence it is inconsistent with SYNTACTIC PSYCHOLOGY. However, it should also be read as allowing that *some* laws of mental processes may advert only to syntactic properties; narrow semantic should be taken to *include* syntactic. So NARROW SEMANTIC is consistent with SYNTACTIC THOUGHT PROCESSES. This is as it should be because the argument from methodological solipsism does not count against SYNTACTIC THOUGHT PROCESSES.

The distinction between syntactic and narrow semantic properties, hence that between SYNTACTIC PSYCHOLOGY and NARROW PSYCHOLOGY, is the third distinction that I wish to emphasize. There is nothing in the argument from methodological solipsism to suggest that SYNTACTIC PSYCHOLOGY is correct.

The contrast between NARROW PSYCHOLOGY and what is alleged to be the folk view can be brought out neatly by the following statement of that view:

WIDE PSYCHOLOGY. The laws of mental processes advert to properties of representations that are wide semantic.

I have argued elsewhere that NARROW PSYCHOLOGY is the correct doctrine (1989a).[20]

If both SYNTACTIC THOUGHT PROCESSES and NARROW PSYCHOLOGY are right, as I think they are, the significance of the distinction between thought processes and mental processes in general is apparent. The laws of thought processes – T–T laws – advert only to syntactic properties, but the laws of mental processes in general must cover I–T and T–O and so must advert to meanings. It is only when we are concerned with these latter, largely ignored, processes that there is a need for semantics in psychology.

Though doctrines like CTM and STM are most frequently urged using "syntactic" and "formal," so that the doctrines seem to be SYNTACTIC PSYCHOLOGY, they are sometimes urged, often in the same breath, as if they were committed to narrow functional-role meaning; i.e., as if they were NARROW PSYCHOLOGY.[21] Yet, as we have seen, these two doctrines about psychology are very different. Perhaps when people talk of "syntactic" or "formal" properties, they mean to cover some sort of narrow meaning. If so, their talk shows a Humpty-Dumptyish contempt for the conventions of language (and even Humpty Dumpty *told us* what he meant by "glory"). Narrow word meanings are not syntactic, in any ordinary sense of that term. Nor are they like the formal properties of symbols in a formal system.[22]

Finally, FORMAL IMPLEMENTATION is unsupported by the argument from methodological solipsism just as it was by the argument from the computer analogy. The present argument is for mental supervention on the brain, but FORMAL IMPLEMENTATION requires something much more restrictive: supervention on the formal properties of mental representations. The narrow meanings required to explain I–T and T–O do not supervene on those properties (though a physicalist may think they supervene on the formal properties of representations *and other things*).

In sum, the arguments from the computer analogy and methodological solipsism establish neither SYNTACTIC PSYCHOLOGY nor FORMAL IMPLEMENTATION. The argument from the computer analogy establishes SYNTACTIC THOUGHT PROCESSES and the related more restricted version of IMPLEMENTATION. The argument from methodological solipsism may support NARROW PSYCHOLOGY and the irrelevance of truth-conditional properties to psychology, but it does not establish that only syntactic ones are relevant. I have argued elsewhere that SYNTACTIC PSYCHOLOGY is false. A consequence of this argument is that FORMAL IMPLEMENTATION (strictly construed) is also false.

I think that the failure to attend sufficiently to the three distinctions I have been emphasizing has led to considerable confusion in the discussion of doctrines like CTM and STM. Each failure confuses the false SYNTACTIC PSYCHOLOGY with a different plausible doctrine. (1) Failing to attend to the distinction between formal and syntactic properties confuses the doctrine with FORMAL IMPLEMENTATION. Though this doctrine is strictly false, it is close to one that a physicalist will find plausible. (2) Failing to attend to the distinction between thought processes and mental processes in general, a failure encouraged by the computer analogy, confuses the doctrine with SYNTACTIC THOUGHT PROCESSES, which is true. (3) Failing to attend to the distinction between syntactic properties and narrow semantic ones confuses the doctrine with NARROW PSYCHOLOGY, which is also true.

All of this matters to psychosemantics because the difference between the syntactic properties required for thought processes and the narrow semantic properties required for mental processes in general is great. One important consequence of this difference is its bearing on the future of folk psychology. Folk psychology is committed to much more than syntactic properties and so a psychology restricted to syntactic properties is radically revisionist. In contrast, a psychology committed to narrow semantic properties may not be revisionist at all.

It is time to draw some conclusions about the interpretation of Fodor. To do this we must return to his solution to Stich's puzzle: Fodor's attempt to have it both ways.

Part III: Interpreting Fodor

5   Having It Both Ways (2)

We have seen that there are various natural ways to understand CTM depending on how one understands "syntactic" and "formal" and on whether talk of "mental processes" is taken to be about mental processes in general or only thought processes. Taking acount of this, and the arguments offered for CTM, I think that there is a basis for attributing each of the following to Fodor: FORMAL IMPLEMEN- TATION and SYNTACTIC PSYCHOLOGY, which I have claimed are false; SYNTACTIC THOUGHT PROCESSES and NARROW PSYCHOLOGY, which I have claimed are true.

To complete the interpretation of Fodor, we must take account of the other aspect of his view: his enthusiasm for the intentional talk of folk psychology. Fodor attempts to combine this aspect with the CTM aspect by claiming that the semantic properties of folk psychology are *implemented in* the level that concerns CTM. That is how he hopes to solve Stich's puzzle and have it both ways.

There would be no puzzle if CTM were simply FORMAL IMPLEMENTATION. but that interpretation misses the predominantly psychological nature of CTM (section 2). There would be no puzzle either if the psychological nature of CTM were captured by SYNTACTIC THOUGHT PROCESSES, because a doctrine restricted to thought processes is quite consistent with the view that the theory of the mind *in general* must advert to contents. However, this restricted doctrine is inadequate as an interpretation because Fodor intends CTM to cover all mental processes.

To capture both the general and the psychological nature of Fodor's discussion of CTM, the doctrine must be taken to be, at least partly, either SYNTACTIC PSYCHOLOGY or NARROW PSYCHOLOGY. The puzzle, then, is how Fodor reconciles these doctrines with the folk aspect of his view.

What is the folk aspect? It may seem to amount to a commitment to WIDE PSYCHOLOGY. However, the latter talks of "the laws of mental processes." Central to Fodor's attempt to have it both ways is his rejection of PRESUPPOSITION: he does not think that the "counterfactual supporting generalizations about the mind" which, according to folk psychology, advert to content, *are* the laws of mental processes (section 2). Perhaps we can capture the folk aspect of Fodor's view by replacing WIDE PSYCHOLOGY's talk of laws of mental processes with talk of laws of the mind (for that is what the counterfactual supporting generalizations are):

WIDE PSYCHOLOGY (F) The laws of the mind advert to properties of representations that are wide semantic.

It has become clear recently that Fodor is not committed to quite this. He thinks that the difference between wide and narrow semantic properties is of little significance, because they both involve a commitment to intentional content. He thinks that narrow content is what we need for psychology (1987d:45–53). So his commitment is really to

NARROW PSYCHOLOGY (F) The laws of the mind advert to properties of represen- tations that are only narrow semantic.[23]

The properties mentioned by NARROW PSYCHOLOGY (F) are of the same sort as those mentioned by NARROW PSYCHOLOGY: both are narrow meanings. So one way to solve Stich's puzzle and reconcile the folk aspect of Fodor's view with the CTM aspect would be to interpret CTM as NARROW PSYCHOLOGY.[24] Indeed, I have argued (1989a) that this is the right way to combine the considerations that led to CTM and STM with a respect for intentional content. A problem with the interpretation is that it construes Fodor's talk of "syntactic" and "formal" as meaning *narrow semantic*. However, there is a more decisive objection to the interpretation. This solution cannot be Fodor's. He does not think that the properties adverted to by the laws of the mind *are* those adverted to by the laws of mental processes. He thinks that the former properties are *implemented by* the latter.

Only one possible interpretation of CTM remains:

SYNTACTIC PSYCHOLOGY The laws of mental processes advert to properties of representations that are only syntactic.

We must reconcile this with NARROW PSYCHOLOGY (F). This interpretation has the disadvantage that SYNTACTIC PSYCHOLOGY is false. Aside from that, I shall argue that the reconciliation fails.

My interpretation of Fodor's CTM has rested on the assumption that he rejects PRESUPPOSITION. It is easy to see that the reconciliation depends on his being right in this rejection. If he is not, the laws of the mind become the laws of mental processes. So NARROW PSYCHOLOGY (F) becomes NARROW PSYCHOLOGY, which is straightforwardly inconsistent with SYNTACTIC PSYCHOLOGY: if the laws advert only to syntactic properties they do not advert to the narrow semantic ones which go beyond syntax. So, given PRESUPPOSITION, if the CTM aspect of Fodor's view is SYNTACTIC PSYCHOLOGY, that aspect cannot be reconciled with the folk aspect; Fodor cannot have it both ways.

Fodor's solution depends not only on the falsity of PRESUPPOSITION but also on:

SYNTACTIC IMPLEMENTATION (F) The laws of the mind advert to properties of representations that are implemented only by syntactic properties of representations.

According to the folk aspect of Fodor's view – NARROW PSYCHOLOGY (F) – the laws of the mind advert to narrow meanings. According to the CTM aspect of his view – SYNTACTIC PSYCHOLOGY – the laws of mental processes advert to syntactic properties. According to SYNTACTIC IMPLEMENTATION (F), the former narrow meanings are implemented in the latter syntactic properties. (This solution was foreshadowed in the earlier discussion of SYNTACTIC IMPLEMENTATION; section 3.)

In rejecting PRESUPPOSITION, Fodor places the theory of the mind at a different level from the theory of mental processes. In this way he hopes to reconcile folk theory with CTM. I pointed out earlier that two requirements must be met to avoid spurious attempts to reconcile folk theory with science by appeals to levels: an explanation requirement and a supervention requirement (section 2). Fodor clearly aims to meet the supervention requirement with SYNTACTIC IMPLEMENTATION (F). So this doctrine is doubly important to Fodor.

In the next section, I shall start the defense of PRESUPPOSITION by considering the explanation requirement. In the following section I shall argue that

SYNTACTIC IMPLEMENTATIONS (F) is false, which completes my defense of PRESUPPOSI-TION.

My conclusion is that Stich is right in thinking that Fodor can't have it both ways. But where Stich thinks that Fodor should be influenced by the arguments for CTM to adopt SYNTACTIC PSYCHOLOGY and abandon content,[25] I think that he should be influenced by those arguments to adopt NARROW PSYCHOLOGY and abandon the view that the theory of the mind is purely syntactic at any level.

6 The Explanation Requirement

If the nonintentional theory of mental processes is to be reconciled with the intentional theory of the mind, the explanation requirement must be met:

> There must be some explanatory task performed by the theory of mental processes that is not performed by the theory of the mind.

In the next section, we shall see how this requirement could be met for thought processes. The problem is meeting it for the processes involving sensory inputs and behavioral outputs. Fodor has argued, persuasively in my view, that behavior must be described intentionally for the purposes of psychology[26] and that we need content to explain behavior so described (see, for example, 1982). What could the theory of mental processes explain if not behavior under that intentional description? Fodor says that "CTM leaves it open that there may be true, counterfactual supporting *generalizations about the mind*" which advert to contents (unpublished-b:5). For CTM to leave this open there must be a place for these generalizations *as well as* the ones covering mental processes, which are, of course, equally counterfactual supporting. Behavioral output, and sensory input, must be involved in mental processes under some nonintentional description.

Fodor's discussions of CTM, focused as they are on thought processes, give no indication of the appropriate form of description. And it is hard to see how there *could be* a suitable description which, though nonintentional, was nonetheless *psychological*. What description, then, does Fodor have in mind? A wider reading of Fodor's work, and that of his collaborator Pylyshyn, suggests an answer:[27] Fodor has in mind a description that is not psychological at all but *brute-physical*.

Fodor's picture of the explanatory task at the level of mental processes is as follows. I–T laws explain the formation of syntactically described thoughts as the results of physically described inputs. T–T laws explain the formation of syntactically described thoughts as the result of other syntactically described thoughts. T–O laws explain physically described outputs as the result of syntactically described thoughts. This whole level implements the laws of the mind, which are intentional throughout: intentionally described inputs lead to semantically described thoughts which lead to intentionally described output.

On this picture the theory of mental processes and the theory of the mind describe inputs and outputs differently and so the picture may seem to meet the explanation requirement. However, I do not think that it does. First, it is surely very misleading to call the processes from physically described inputs to thoughts, and from thoughts to physically described outputs, "mental" processes. They are psychophysical processes, not psychological ones. And the I–T and T–O laws that explain them are psychophysical and hence not appropriately placed in a theory of mental processes. More importantly, these laws, together with the syntactic T–T laws, do not form a "level," in the appropriate sense. Psychophysical laws are *between* levels; they are bridging laws. They hold in virtue of the fact that a totally psychological level, *including psychologically described inputs and outputs*, is implemented in a totally physical level, *including physically described thoughts*.[28]

We started our discussion of Stich's puzzle with an easy solution that distinguished the psychological level from the physical (section 2). Wherever there are two levels, it will be necessary to explain the relations between them. So if Fodor's proposal were simply that there were these two levels, and the relations between them, the puzzle could have been laid to rest. What kept it alive was the implication in Fodor that there was a further psychological level, the level of mental processes, between the intentional psychological level and the brute-physical. The present picture undermines the idea of this third level (so far as I–T and T–O laws are concerned); explaining the relation between the psychological and the physical level does not establish another psychological level.

If this is right, Fodor has failed to meet the explanation requirement and so has failed to show, contra PRESUPPOSITION, that there is a level of mental processes different from the level of the intentional laws of the mind. However, the strongest support for PRESUPPOSITION in the face of Fodor's discussion comes from a consideration of SYNTACTIC IMPLEMENTATION (F). For this is the doctrine by which Fodor relates his level of mental processes to the laws of the mind. So it is his way of meeting the supervention requirement. I shall argue that SYNTACTIC IMPLEMEN-TATION (F) is false.

7   Syntactic Implementation (F)

The arguments for CTM (section 4) do not establish SYNTACTIC IMPLEMENTATION (F): the argument from the computer analogy is for SYNTACTIC THOUGHT PROCESSES; the argument from methodological solipsism is for NARROW PSYCHOLOGY. Does Fodor offer anything in support of his claim that the semantic level of intentional psychology is implemented syntactically? The unpublished remarks quoted earlier (section 2) suggesting that the intentional is *multiply* implemented at the computational level are the only ones that seem clearly directed to this end. I shall discuss the suggestion at the end of this section. First, however, I shall discuss some other remarks, not clearly directed to this end, about the relation of the semantic to the syntactic. My case against SYNTACTIC IMPLEMENTATION (F) will emerge in these discussions.

Fodor has some important things to say about the connection between the contents of mental states and their causal roles:

1   the causal roles of mental states typically closely parallel the implicational structures of their propositional objects. (1985b:90; see also 1987d:18)
2   within certain famous limits, the semantic relation that holds between two symbols when the proposition expressed by the one is entailed by the proposition expressed by the other can be mimicked by syntactic relations in virtue of which one of the symbols is derivable from the other. (1987d:19;

see also 1985b:93)
3 You connect the causal properties of a symbol with its semantic properties *via its syntax*. (Fodor, 1987d:18; see also 1985b:93)

According to SYNTACTIC PSYCHOLOGY, the causal relations between mental states are determined by their syntactic properties. (1) says that these syntactically determined causal relations parallel semantic relations. (2) says that syntactic relations mimic semantic ones. (3) says that the mimicking explains the parallelism.

"Mimic" and "parallel" would be weasel words to use to talk about the robust relation of implementation. There is no clear evidence that Fodor intends (1) to (3) to support his view that the psychological laws which advert to content are implemented syntactically. However, (1) to (3) certainly relate the semantic to the syntactic and so might appear to support Fodor's view. And Fodor has said so little else in support. I shall examine the appearance.

First comment. At best, (1) to (3) are evidence for the syntactic implementation of T–T laws, laws of *thought processes*. They could provide no evidence on the implementation of the laws of *the mind in general*, which include I–T and T–O laws as well. So they could not justify SYNTACTIC IMPLEMENTATIONS (F).

The intentional I–T laws will talk of certain sorts of input, together with other factors, causing thoughts with a certain sort of content; a crude example of an application of such a law might be that the sight of Maggie, along with various background thoughts, causes thoughts about Maggie. The claim that causal relations between inputs and mental states parallel semantic relations between propositions would be absurd. The claim that the syntactic relations between inputs and mental states mimic semantic relations would be nonsensical: inputs are not representations and so stand in no syntactic relations.[29] Fodor does not make these claims: he talks only of the causal, semantic, and syntactic relations between states/symbols. So his remarks about syntax mimicking semantics could cast no light on how I–T laws are syntactically implemented. The same goes for T–O laws.

(1) to (3) provide no support for the view that the word meanings adverted to in intentional I–T and T–O laws could be implemented syntactically. Furthermore, the view is obviously false. This can be brought out using Fodor's own semantics (1987d:45–95). He urges a "denotational" semantics according to which wide meanings are simply extensions and narrow meanings are simply functions from contexts to extensions. So the wide meaning of 'Maggie' is its role of denoting Maggie, and its narrow meaning is a function that has the value Maggie on Earth, Twin Maggie on Twin Earth, and so on.[30] The property of *denoting Maggie* can no more be implemented syntactically than it can be implemented in the formal properties of representations; similarly the property that becomes that of *denoting Maggie* in the Earthly context (section 4). There is no level at which a representation has these properties simply in virtue of its relations to other representations; it has them partly in virtue of, for example, its relation to Maggie or Twin Maggie. So there is no level at which it has these properties simply in virtue of its syntactic properties. SYNTACTIC IMPLEMENTATIONS (F) is false.

Fodor's semantics raises a further problem, which warrants a short digression. It is unclear how his narrow meanings do, or could, have any bearing on mental causation. If narrow meanings were implemented syntactically, it would be clear how they played a causal role in the life of the mind. But we have just seen that they are not. If they were identified with functional-role meanings, as I think they should be,[31] their causal role would also be clear. But Fodor will have nothing to do with functional-role semantics.[32] He thinks that it leads to meaning holism, which threatens Life As We Know It. Why, then are his narrow meanings not mere epiphenomena?

At one point (1987d:89–91), Fodor confronts the objection that his theory breaks the internal connection between believing a certain thing and behaving in a certain way. Fodor accepts the break, blithely outSmarting the objector. He appeals to Duhem, pointing out that no behavioral predictions do follow from a belief on its own: ancillary hypotheses are needed. This is beside the point of the objection. The key thing about beliefs – what makes us posit them in the first place – is that each one has a distinctive causal role in producing behavior: if all the ancillary hypotheses are held constant, then believing such-and-such will have different behavioral consequences from believing so-and-so. A theory of content cannot break this causal connection.

Returning to the main theme, Fodor's discussion of the relation between the causal, semantic, and syntactic properties of representations exemplifies the usual lack of interest in the distinction between thought processes and mental processes in general. A theory of thought processes is being falsely packaged as a theory of the mind. This is especially important because it is the theory of processes other than thought processes that needs semantics.

Second comment. I shall now consider the bearing of (1) to (3) on the implementation of the laws of thought processes – T–T laws – only. So this comment is much less important than the first one. I have claimed that the argument from the computer analogy shows that T–T laws *are* syntactic: SYNTACTIC THOUGHT PROCESSES is true. I shall go on to allow that they are also *implemented* syntactically. So, I think that, *if restricted to T–T laws*, SYNTACTIC IMPLEMENTATIONS (F) is true. However, (1) to (3) are irrelevant to establishing this. Further, this implementation is not a case, *contra* Fodor, of the semantic being implemented in the syntactic.

Consider the earlier example of a T–T law:

> Whenever a person believes both a conditional and its antecedent, she tends to infer its consequent.

This law specifies a causal process that parallels the semantic relations between propositions in *modus ponens* inferences, as (1) requires. And these relations are indeed mimicked by the syntactic ones between symbols in those inferences, as (2) requires. Finally, that mimicking does explain the parallelism, as (3) requires.

This is important, but it has nothing to do with SYNTACTIC IMPLEMENTATION (F). That doctrine requires that the mechanisms underlying the law be syntactic. So, it requires that the properties adverted to by the laws be implemented syntactically, and that the causal process specified in the law hold because of that implementation. The law does not advert to any *semantic relation* – for example, *entailment* – between representations; it adverts to the *syntactic properties* of *being a conditional, being an antecedent,* and *being a consequent.* So the parallelism of the causal process it specifies to any semantic relation, and the mimicking of any semantic relation by a syntactic one, are irrelevant to the implementation of the law. What is relevant are the mechanisms underlying those syntactic properties – for example, being a conditional – in virtue of which the specified process holds.

The parallelism and the mimicry are indeed relevant to something, just not to SYNTACTIC IMPLEMENTATIONS (F).

The parallelism between the causal and the semantic is relevant to *the rationality of people.* If people were ideally rational, their thought processes would always be perfectly parallel to sound inductive and deductive semantic relations. Statements of (1) and (2) can often suggest that people are close to ideally rational, though this is certainly not Fodor's view (1987d:88). There is no *a priori* reason to think that people are close to ideally rational[33] and a good deal of empirical evidence to show that they are not.[34] Thus there is considerable evidence that people are very bad at *modus tollens.* The following might be a law:

Whenever a person believes both a conditional and the negation of its consequent, she tends not to infer the negation of its antecedent.

Here there is no parallelism between the causal and a sound semantic relation. The lack of parallelism is a failure of rationality.

Such failures have no significance at all to T–T laws. The causal role specified by the above law is no more, nor any less, problematic than that specified by the earlier law where there was a parallelism. To say this is not, of course, to say that the rationality reflected in parallelism is unimportant. Without some of it, "there wouldn't," as Fodor puts it, "be much profit in thinking" (1987d:14). But how much there is of it is beside the point of T–T laws. The causal relations between mental states have to be connected to the semantic and syntactic relations between representations, whether the causal relations parallel rational or irrational semantic and syntactic relations.

The mimicking of the semantic by the syntactic is relevant to *the explanation of semantic relations.* A syntactic relation of derivability holds between the representations mentioned in the *modus ponens* laws. This relation mimics the semantic relation of entailment between the representations. Why? Because the syntactic one *is* the semantic one. Or rather, it *would be* if we could overlook the famous limits. Entailment is (partially) *reduced* to derivability. (In saying this, I am not of course saying that, limits aside, 'derivable from' *means* 'entailed by.' Water is H_2O even though 'water' does not mean 'H_2O.') This reduction, achieved by logicians, is very significant for semantics but it has no significance for T–T laws, or their implementation, because those laws say nothing about entailment.

This is not to deny the significance of the reduction to the theory of the mind. Put the reduction together with the computer analogy of thought processes, and we can explain how people can be, at least partially, rational. That is what Fodor's (1) to (3) bring out. So (1) to (3) are certainly important. However, they are irrelevant to SYNTACTIC IMPLEMENTATION (F) even when the doctrine is restricted to T–T laws. (I repeat that there is no clear evidence that Fodor thinks otherwise.)

How true is the doctrine so restricted? The first thing to notice is that, whatever the facts are about the implementation of T–T laws, those laws themselves advert to syntactic properties; properties like *being a conditional* already are syntactic. That is what we learnt from formal logic and the computer analogy, which led us to embrace SYNTACTIC THOUGHT PROCESSES (section 4). Syntax gets into the psychological picture first at the level of the laws, not their implementation.

T–T laws are not semantic at any level. In saying this, I am not of course denying that the representations adverted to in the laws *have* semantic properties. It is essential to their role in explaining behavior that they do have. That is a conclusion of the argument against SYNTACTIC PSYCHOLOGY mentioned in section 4. The point is simply that the laws that explain the transitions from one thought to another do not need to advert to any semantic properties.

The computer analogy is apt for T–T processes only, and is primarily concerned with their nature, not their implementation. What the analogy with computation throws light on, primarily, is *the nature of part* of the mind, not *the implementation of the whole* of the mind.

Of course, the fact that thought processes are syntactic does not show that they are not also implemented syntactically. The computer analogy suggests that they are indeed so implemented.

This brings us to Fodor's unpublished remarks that are clearly offered in support of SYNTACTIC IMPLEMENTATION (F). Where there is implementation there is the possibility of *multiple* implementation. In a passage quoted before (section 2), Fodor suggests, somewhat tentatively, that there is multiple implementation of the semantic in the syntactic; "similar psychological effects are produced by a range of different computational means" (unpublished-b:5–6; also 1987d:52).

This claim, just like (1) to (3) above, must be restricted to thought processes if it is to be true. However, so restricted, it is true. There are many different ways of getting a computer to implement laws like the ones above. And many of these may be at levels above the brute-physical hardware level. Using Marr's distinction (1982:22–5), we can think of the law as at the computational level, and the various computational means as at the algorithmic level. The properties at the algorithmic level are indeed syntactic. So, if we continue to follow the computer analogy, the properties adverted to in T–T laws are implemented in syntactic properties at the algorithmic level. To this extent then, SYNTACTIC IMPLEMENTATION (F) is correct.

However, this is not a case of the *semantic* level being implemented in syntax, for the properties that are implemented – ones like *being a conditional* – are themselves syntactic. T–T laws advert to syntactic properties in one symbol system. These properties are implemented in syntactic properties in a different symbol system. Note further that SYNTACTIC IMPLEMENTATION (F) is true only for thought processes. The reasons for thinking that it is false in general, set out in my first comment, still stand.

Return to PRESUPPOSITION. In rejecting this, Fodor must meet two requirements. To meet the explanation requirement he must show that the laws of mental processes have a different explanatory task from that of the intentional laws of the mind. I argued that this requirement was not met so far as I–T and T–O laws were concerned (section 6). We can now see that it could be met for T–T laws: the explanatory task at the algorithmic level is different from that at the computational level. Fodor's way of meeting the supervention requirement is SYNTACTIC

IMPLEMENTATIONS (F). We have just seen that this also could be met for T–T laws but not for I–T and T–O laws. Given the failure to meet either requirement for the I–T and T–O laws, Fodor has not shown that we can distinguish a level that is the concern of the theory of mental processes from the level that concerns the laws of the mind.

Summary of Part III. For Fodor to have it both ways he must combine the CTM aspect of his view with the folk aspect, NARROW PSYCHOLOGY (F). Discussion of CTM suggests four distinct doctrines. FORMAL IMPLEMENTATION must be ruled out as an interpretation of Fodor because it misses the psychological nature of his discussion. SYNTACTIC THOUGHT PROCESSES must be ruled out because it is not general enought. NARROW PSYCHOLOGY must be ruled out because it is incompatible with Fodor's view that CTM concerns a level that implements the semantic properties at the folk level. One possible interpretation remains: SYNTACTIC PSYCHOLOGY. Combining this with NARROW PSYCHOLOGY (F) is impossible if PRESUPPOSITION is right and the laws of the mind are the same as the laws of mental processes; the laws cannot be only syntactic and yet also narrow semantic. I have argued that PRESUPPOSITION is right. Further, Fodor's way of combining the two aspects requires SYNTACTIC IMPLEMENTATION (F). I have argued that SYNTACTIC IMPLEMENTATION (F) is unsupported and wrong, except insofar as it concerns thought processes. Insofar as it concerns thought processes, it is right, but this implementation is not a matter of the semantic being implemented in the syntactic, as Fodor claims. It is a matter of the syntactic being implemented in the syntactic.

We have seen that I–T and T–O laws are not syntactic at any level. In contrast, T–T laws are syntactic at every level above the formal.

Part IV: Conclusion

8 Conclusion

Stich is puzzled: how can Fodor have it both ways? Fodor urges CTM, according to which the theory of mental processes adverts only to syntactic properties, and yet remains an enthusiast for intentional psychology, which adverts to meanings. Fodor thinks the answer is easy: intentional psychology is at one level; the theory of mental processes is at a different level that *implements* the first level. In brief, the syntactic implements the semantic.

I have argued that the theory of mental processes is not at a different level from intentional psychology. The theory does not have a separate explanatory task from that psychology, and the psychology is not, in general, implemented in the syntactic properties which, according to Fodor, are adverted to in the theory. The mind as a whole is not purely syntactic at any level (though part of it is). Fodor's attempt to have it both ways fails.

Along the way, I have accepted that the laws of thought processes advert only to the syntactic properties of representations – SYNTACTIC THOUGHT PROCESSES, whilst denying that the laws of mental processes in general to – SYNTACTIC PSYCHOLOGY. So Fodor can partly have it the CTM way. Elsewhere (1989a) I have argued that the laws of mental processes in general advert to narrow semantic properties – NARROW

PSYCHOLOGY. So he can have it the folk way. Implementation has nothing to do with this partial solution to Stich's puzzle.

Central to my approach has been an emphasis on three distinctions; that between formal properties, which are intrinsic to a representation and fairly "brute-physical," and syntactic properties, which are extrinsic and functional; that between processes that hold between thoughts, and processes that hold between inputs and thoughts and between thoughts and outputs; and that between syntactic properties, which a representation has solely in virtue of its relations to other representations, and narrow semantic properties (other than syntactic ones), which a representation has partly in virtue of its relations to inputs and, perhaps, outputs.[35]

NOTES

1 Similar views have been urged by others, including Hartry Field (1978:100–2) and Stephen Schiffer (1981:214–15).

2 Zenon Pylyshyn generates the same puzzle: on the one hand he endorses CTM and the formality condition (1980a:111–15; 1980b:158–61; 1984:xiii); on the other, folk psychology (1980b:159–61).

3 Patricia Kitcher is some company: she finds the combination of CTM with RTM "rather perverse" (1985:89).

4 E.g., Baker, (1986:41); Demopoulos, (1980); Kitcher, (1985:89); Lepore and Loewer, (1986:598–9); Lycan, (1984:91–2); McGinn, (1982:208); Schiffer (1981:214–15); Stich, (1980:97). Surprisingly, none of these philosphers, apart from Stich and Kitcher, seems worried by the fact that Fodor is *also* an enthusiast for folk psychology (cf. n. 24).

5 Note that a sentence or word can appear in indefinitely many forms. Similarly, a letter, if letters are taken to make up a word in all its forms. However, letters are often taken to be restricted to inscriptions, in which case a letter can appear in a more limited number of forms.

6 I do not mean to suggest that properties like *being a noun* may not *also* be semantic.

7 This is the deep truth in the structuralist tradition in linguistics. For the deep falsehood, particularly in the French version, see Devitt and Sterelny, (1987:ch. 13).

8 Formal and syntactic properties obviously don't match up if we remove the restriction to representations. Objects like the Harbour Bridge and the Opera House have a form but no syntax.

9 For more on this technical sense of formal, see my (1989:372–3), which draws on Haugeland, (1978:5–10, 21–2; 1985:4, 50–2, 58–63, 100–3).

10 E.g., Fodor, (1980c:64; 1980d:106; 1982:102). See also the following commentaries, with which Fodor largely agrees: Haugeland, (1980:81–2); Rey, (1980b:91). Stich (1983:44) also sometimes seems to have this interpretation in mind.

11 E.g., Fodor, (1985b:93; 1987d:18–19, 156n). In comments on Fodor (1980c), with which Fodor also agrees (1980d:105), Loar distinguishes the two senses and takes Fodor to intend the functional one (1980:90). See also Pylyshyn, (1980a:111–15) (but note that Pylyshyn takes syntactic properties to be intrinsic to a representation); Stich, (1983:152–3). Many show no interest in the distinction; e.g., Baker, (1986:27); Block, (1986:616). See also n. 21 and accompanying text.

12 See n. 4 for some examples of people who seem to interpret the formality condition in this way.

13 What about laws like, "If x believes that y is a bachelor, x will tend to believe that y is unmarried"? I think that the analogy shows that such lower level laws are derived

from an application of upper level laws like, "If x believes that all Fs are G and that y is an F then he will tend to believe that y is a G." Such upper level laws are the concern of the theory of thought processes and they advert only to syntactic properties of representations. The semantic content comes in only at the level of the application of the laws.

14 See also the transition in Fodor, (1985b) from a start in which thinkings is "the paradigm of mental process" (p. 78) to an ending in which it is as if thinking were the only such process. For an example of a swifter transition, see Block, (1986:628).

Note that the common view that the mind goes representational very soon after receiving a sensory input does not save Claim 2. Certainly all processes from then on until the formation of a thought are, on this view, causal sequences of representations. However, the total I–T process is not, for that process has a beginning – the sensory input – that is not representational. Whether or not I–T processes should be broken down into subsidiary processes involving representational states that are prior to thoughts is beside the point.

Claim 2 could be saved by taking the psychologically relevant inputs and outputs themselves to involve representations. However, this seems a very strange idea. It is plausible to think, as Fodor does, that the psychologically relevant nature of a piece of behavior is partly determined by the nature of the representational states – the thoughts – that caused it; the thoughts determine that the behavior has a certain intentional description (1975a:28–31). It is another thing to think that the intentional description applies because the behavior itself involves a representation. I take it that Fodor does not believe this (1981d:152–63).

15 Some evidence for this. (i) Fodor takes the formality condition to show that prima facie mental states involving semantic notions – like *knowledge* and *perception* – have no place in psychology (1980c:64). (ii) He argues that we need a psychology that accepts the formality condition and that this is all we can have (1980c:66). (iii) He takes CTM to tell "the whole story about mental causation" (1987d:139). (iv) He relates CTM to methodological solipsism (1980c:64–5; 1987d:43), which concerns psychology in general, not just thought processes.

16 After leaving my hands, the heading of this section changed from the correct, "The Sufficiency of Narrow Meaning," to the incorrect, "The Insufficiency of Narrow Meaning."

17 It is common to use "semantic," "meaning", and "content" as if they must involve truth and reference as Loar (1980:90) and Rey (1980b:91) note in their commentaries on Fodor, (1980c).

18 For more along these lines, see my (1989b).

19 Harman's conceptual-role meaning is an exception (1982, 1983).

20 The version of NARROW PSYCHOLOGY that I argue for posits a narrow functional-role meaning for an expression that is *part of* its wide truth-conditional meaning. The narrow part is obtained by abstracting from the reference-determining causal links that are "outside the skin." My theory differs, therefore, from "two-factor" theories which tend to treat the truth-conditional factor as if it were unrelated to the functional-role factor; see, e.g., McGinn, (1982:211, 230); Loar, (1982:280–2; 1983:629). On my theory, the first factor includes the second; (1989a:377–81). (After leaving my hands, a "not" was mistakenly added to the last sentence of this paper, which should read: "One semantic theory will do for psychology and linguistics"; p. 395).

21 For evidence of this in Fodor, see Loar's commentary (1980:90) and Fodor's response (1980d:105); and Fodor's response to Geach (1980d:102). Note further that Fodor takes the formality condition as "a sort of methodological solipsism" (1980c:65), and takes the ordinary opaque taxonomy of mental states as roughly the same as that according to the formality condition (pp 66–70). See also: Block and Bromberger's

commentary (1980:74) and Fodor's response (1980d:99); Rey's commentary (1980b:91) and Fodor's response (1980d:106). For evidence in some others, see Field, (1978:100–1); Stich, (1983:190–1); Baker, (1986) (a critic of CTM and STM):27.

22   A claim to have meant by "only syntactic properties," *only syntactic properties, or narrow semantic properties needed to explain behavior*, might be compared to a vegetable grower's claim to have meant by "only natural fertilizers," *only natural fertilizers, or artificial fertilizers needed to keep vegetables alive*. Stich's claim (this volume) to have meant *fat syntax* by "syntax" is of this sort. If the claim is correct, STM is NARROW PSYCHOLOGY not SYNTACTIC PSYCHOLOGY. The only radical part of his view is, then, the sadly fashionable commitment to meaning holism. Stich has been enjoying the rhetoric of a revolution without being prepared to put up with the revolution itself.

23   The only examples of narrow semantic properties that I gave were functional-role meanings (section 4). Fodor rejects functional-role semantics in favor of a "denotational" semantics to be described later (section 7).

24   Bill Lycan tells me that it is because people interpret CTM in this way that they are not worried by Fodor's attempt to have it both ways; cf. n. 4.

25   Taking Stich's STM to be the revolutionary view it purports to be, not the mildly revisionist view (holism aside) that allows "fat syntax" into psychology. See n. 22.

26   If NARROW PSYCHOLOGY is right, fully intentional descriptions of input and output are unsuitable for the laws of psychology. I have argued that the descriptions must be "proto-intentional" (1989a:393–4).

27   Fodor, (1975a:42–51; 1983:38–52; 1987d:112–22); Fodor and Pylyshyn, (1981b); Pylyshyn, (1984:147–91). It also helps enormously to talk to Fodor. That's how I found out.

28   To say this is not, of course, to cast any aspersions on the importance of seeking psychophysical I–T and T–O laws. The psychological must be related to the physical somehow and nothing can be settled a priori about the best way to do this. It will clearly be profitable to seek psychophysical I–T and T–O laws for any species which implements thoughts in many ways but has a uniform implementation of intentionally described inputs and outputs. If Fodor's modularity thesis (1983) is close to right, the human species is like this.

29   But see n. 14 and accompanying text.

30   This is, in effect, a direct-reference semantics. I have offered detailed arguments against such a semantics; (1989b).

31   I think that the narrow functional-role meaning of 'Maggie' *determines* the function that yields Maggie as value on Earth, but I avoid direct reference by not taking the meaning to be *identical to* that function (1989b).

32   This raises another puzzle. Fodor thinks that mental states are individuated by their causal powers (1987d:27–45). A mental state is a complex consisting of an attitude and a content. So contents must be individuated by their causal powers. How does this differ from individuation by functional roles?

33   Cf. Davidson (1980, 1984: *passim*) and Dennett (1978a: particularly, 3–22). See Levin, (1988) for a strong argument against principles of rationality. I have argued against them in (1981:115–18; 1984:172–9); Devitt and Sterelny, (1987:247–9).

34   See Stich (1985) for a nice summary of the evidence.

35   Earlier versions of this material were parts of seminars I gave at the University of Sydney in 1987 and the University of Maryland in 1988. I am indebted to the members of those seminars; also to at least the following for comments: John Bacon, Fiona Cowie, Hartry Field, Denise Gamble, Bill Lycan, Kim Sterelny, Stephen Stich, and especially Jerry Fodor and Georges Rey.

7

Can We Explain Intentionality?

BRIAN LOAR

I

Jerry Fodor's treatment of intentionality in chapter 4 of *Psychosemantics* (1987d) is wonderfully direct, so much so that the first time through you can hardly believe the effrontery of it. Even many causal theorists have come to think that what determines the reference of predicates cannot be simple. But Fodor puts aside holism, anti-individualism and all the rest to propose an exceedingly straightforward theory of meaning (some would say reference), one that is atomistic in the extreme, reductionist with no hedging at all, and completely unfazed by anti-individualism. Not that he explicitly undertakes to explain all intentionality, for he formally proposes a sufficient rather than a necessary or general condition for predicate reference, happy if he shows that intentionality can at least sometimes be secured by his naturalistic conditions. But you do get the impression that he is inclined to think the account points to a general solution. This stimulating and provocative theory, which Fodor so adeptly applies to difficult cases, is admirable in its not mincing about but striding boldly through the landmines – atomism, reductionism, individualism, bracing stuff.

The theory is a variant on the idea that meaning is information, that a predicate means the property to which its ascriptions are responsive. The question arises how falsity is possible on any such theory. Meaning, as Fodor puts it, is "robust"; a predicate F's meaning P can survive indefinitely many ascriptions of F to non-Ps[1], and thus F does not mean just any property to which it is responsive. His solution is this. If you falsely call some goats "sheep," the causal relation of those goats to your utterance depends in part on the semantic fact that the word "sheep" means sheep; had it meant anchovy, or bottle of beer, or nothing at all the goats would not have occasioned you to utter it. Now, Fodor says, keep that structure; but instead of saying that false ascriptions of "sheep" to goats depend on the independent semantic relation of "sheep" to sheep, say they depend on an independent *causal* relation of "sheep" to sheep. Then you have a sufficient condition of meaning: sheep cause ascriptions of "sheep," and if any non-sheep cause them, this latter relation depends on the former causal relation; and this does not also hold the other way around. So a predicate F means a property P if things that are P cause F and any such causal relation between some other property and F is asymmetrically dependent on the former relation. In a recent paper[2] Fodor modifies this to allow for F's meaning an uninstantiated property (cf. "unicorn"), by weakening the causal requirement: things that are P need not actually have caused F but there must be a "nomic relation" (some counterfactual causal relation) between P and F, on which false ascriptions would asymmetrically depend.[3]

Fodor is, I believe, right to hold that discriminative causal relations, socially unmediated, can determine meaning or reference. But this seems to me to obtain not for "sheep," "horse," and the like as they normally occur in our thoughts, but rather for predicative concepts of a distinctive and not widely acknowledged variety. Even for these, however, we will not find the fully naturalistic treatment Fodor seeks, for no causal condition can explicate reference except in conjunction with further intentional conditions. This leads me to reject the strict atomism Fodor aims at, although something more or less atomistic about the reference of such predicates will survive.

II

Begin with this sample question: which predicates or predicative concepts might Fodor's condition fit? Many predicates in my thoughts do not apparently have meaning or reference in Fodor's way. Their reference derives, not from my ascriptions of them, but rather from the language I speak, from the social semantic relations I draw on. This fact stems from my *semantic deference,* my accepting that thoughts that ascribe such a predicate can be false because I misconceived its meaning as that is determined socially. I mistook the meaning of "maple," often ascribing it to the sweet gums I saw, taking it to mean them. Those ascriptions in no way depended on cases in which maples caused me to judge "maple"; there were no such cases. Not that it was not in my power to use "maple" in my thoughts to refer to sweet gums. Social meanings do not deprive me of semantic autonomy when I insist on it. But for many predicates I waive autonomy for the sake of drawing on social reference, and thereby risk a certain kind of falsehood. I pass by the question why socially deferential concepts are desirable,[4] and simply take for granted that they are central in our thinking.[5]

Socially deferential concepts make vivid the need to be specific about which concepts are candidates for fitting Fodor's condition: they must acquire reference as a function of non-socially mediated discriminations of an individual's ascriptions. A natural idea is that they are a kind of demonstrative, of the form "thing of that sort" (which I see here and there). While Fodor speaks not of demonstratives but of common nouns like "horse" and even "proton" (which he takes on with admirable sang-froid), perhaps those words may sometimes serve to express demonstrative conceptions. But consider what he says about "proton." Suppose a person ascribes it in response to visible traces of protons, depending on theoretical beliefs to the effect that these traces are caused by protons in such-and -such physical ways. According to Fodor, "proton" can come to refer to protons by virtue of such a causal connection (he turns aside the objection that this presupposes the intentionality of the theoretical beliefs).[6] But as we described the case, "proton" does not express a demonstrative that acquires its reference from those discriminations, as becomes clear by comparing another case. You observe the same visible phenomenon and with no theory of protons in mind you form the conception "that sort of thing," the conception of that, whatever it is. If you succeed in referring to an underlying property or kind, the referential link is in a general way demonstrative.[7] But that is not what happens in Fodor's case, where "proton" is already embedded in a background physical theory and has a cognitive role independent of and presupposed by its employment in the current discrimination of traces, which apparently makes it not a demonstrative whose reference derives from that discrimination.[8] So to take Fodor as accounting just for demonstrative concepts does not fit what he says about this case. [9] But they may yet be the best candidates for his theory and he probably should not want it to explain reference for the "proton" in that case.[10] Indeed, comparing the two proton examples strongly suggests that it is demonstrative concepts that individualist information-based theories, Fodor's included, should focus on, a more modest objective than usual.

It is clear enough to me that most of the predicative concepts I express using common nouns, "water," "horse," and even "red," are not demonstratives whose reference in my thoughts to external kinds is determined by my discriminations.[11] But it also seems to me that we do have such demonstrative concepts, recognitional concepts as we might call them.[12] If you go to Mississippi for the first time, you may learn to discriminate new natural kinds, initially thinking of them as "this kind of bird, that sort of vine"; and you may invent names to express those demonstrative concepts. When you then learn a standard name, say for the kudzu vine, it could have a double role in your thoughts, in its marking your recognitional concept and in meaning kudzu properly so called, concepts you implicitly hold coextensive. And nothing prevents complete expropriation of "kudzu," so that it expresses only a personal recognitional concept ("vine of that sort") for you, regarding others' using it to refer to the same kind as merely incidental. This would not be the usual thing, but it is up to you.[13]

More will be said in characterizing personal recognitional concepts and answering doubts even that there are such things, but we perhaps have enough to go on (pro tem). If any of our concepts fit Fodor's account of reference, such recognitional concepts are prime candidates, and the question is whether Fodor's condition is sufficient for reference for them. And although he has not proposed a generally necessary condition of reference, if his condition were not satisfied by these concepts (because, e.g., the asymmetrical dependence condition is too strong) then, given no other plausible candidates, we might conclude that Fodor's theory does not explain intentionality for any concepts of ours.

III

Problems for Sufficiency: Deferential Concepts. The existence of socially deferential concepts raises the following difficulty for any information-based theory of reference that purports to give a sufficient condition free of intentional notions. Suppose my concept "horse" is deferential, that I implicitly take its reference to be determined by the language I speak, that I intend to refer in my thinking to whatever "horse" refers to in that language. But suppose I take "horse" to apply both to the usual creatures and to (what are in fact) gazelles, that is I take its extension to be, as others would say, horses or gazelles, so that my ascribing "horse" to gazelles does not asymmetrically depend on my ascribing it to horses. Then if Fodor's condition (or certain other information-theoretic conditions) were sufficient for reference it would follow that my concept "horse" in fact refers to both horses and gazelles. But given the deferential status of my concept that is not so.

The most straightforward strengthening would require that a concept be undeferential and demonstrative in the manner of recognitional concepts, that it have, as we might say, an undeferential conceptual role. The question is how to capture that. One might attempt it negatively: the concept is not deferential, not one whose ascriptions one would withdraw on the grounds that (i.e., because one believed that) one had mistaken its meaning. Or positively: the concept is of "things of that perceived or remembered type," i.e., has that intuitively indicated intentional property. In neither case is it obvious how to de-intentionalize these characterizations of undeferential concepts, and it seems we must require a concept to be undeferential if an individualist information-based condition is to determine its reference.[14]

Fodor has a general line of reply to any complaint that some intentional property is presupposed: look to the nomic relation (roughly the counterfactual) between predicate and referred-to property, the one that false ascriptions asymmetrically depend on, and do not worry about whether the language in which we are inclined to describe the connection between predicate and property happens to be intentional; what matters is the nomic relation. But to apply this to the present question requires showing that ascribing the deferential "horse" to gazelles asymmetrically depends on the concept's nomic relation to horses. Suppose it is said that were one's mistake corrected one would no longer call gazelles "horse" (except when mistaking them for horses), and hence that one's ascriptions are asymmetrically dependent on the nomic relation of "horse" to horses. But this would not be correct. Ascriptions of "horse" to gazelles *would* be asymmetrically dependent on the ascriptions of "horse" to horses, and this *given* the satisfaction of a certain condition, a condition that involves apparently ineliminable intentionality (accepting correction, etc.). It does not follow that ascribing "horse" to gazelles in fact asymmetrically depends on ascribing "horse" to horses. In the case described, ascriptions of "horse" to horses and to gazelles are symmetrically dependent, even though, because of semantic deference, "horse" is not true of gazelles.

Questions about Sufficiency: Guiding Conceptions.

Consider Armand, a novice bird watcher who learns that the birds he has been identifying under a certain recognitional concept are of two not especially closely related kinds. There are three potential upshots. (i) He would regard his past usage as having lacked a determinate reference ("I meant to be referring to a single kind of bird"). (ii) He would now regard his past usage as referring to what has turned out to be a disjunctive kind. (iii) He would regard the information as irrelevant to his reference, which was meant to be determined by a resemblance in configuration, one that further kinds may well share, and which we may suppose in fact to be objective even if superficial. (Of course it is also possible that he did not conceive his reference in any such specific way.)

A natural account of these cases is that, because Armand has in each conceived his reference differently – as a natural kind (a species or something on that order), as a kind with a principled but not necessarily monolithic basis, or as a configurational kind, his reference in each differs or may differ from the others. Given the facts, it seems reasonable to say that in case (i) Armand's conception has failed of reference, that it has picked out no property, that, as Armand would judge, there is no such thing as "that kind of bird"; that in (ii) it referred to the disjunctive kind; and that in (iii) it referred to the configurational kind. (The last two differ in reference if unobserved instances of the disjunctive kind differ in appearance from the observed ones or if other unobserved kinds have their appearance.)

Fodor's condition apparently does not distinguish these cases, but implies that reference in each is to the disjunctive kind (or to the configurational kind?), despite the difference in guiding conceptions. Suppose it is insisted that in case (i) Armand has simply misconceived his reference, which is, say, the disjunctive kind. To insist on this seems theory-driven, as compared with agreeing with Armand that there is no such thing as "that kind of bird." And why should one's general conception of the reference of a recognitional predicate *not* constrain it?[15] But then Fodor's condition requires an intentional supplement, the satisfaction of guiding conceptions. One virtually never refers demonstratively, whether singularly or predicatively, without some at least general conception that constrains one's reference, and this is a problem for any causal condition that purports to suffice for reference.

A possible reply to this objection is that the Fodor condition, understood properly, does not after all imply that Armand's predicative concept in case (i) refers to the disjunctive property, and that in fact it refers to no property, implying this entirely on causal grounds and without appeal to the intentional features of guiding conceptions. It was always counterfactually true that, were Armand to discover the real state of things, he would withdraw that recognitional concept from active predicative use; and so, it might be said, that relevant nomic relation does not relate it to any property. The problem of course is that this counterfactual depends on an intentional condition, viz. Armand's discovering the real state of things. To point beyond that intentional counterfactual to *the* relevant nomic relation is to rely on a fiction. There is no more reason to regard a counterfactual that depends on Armand's forming a *correct* belief than one that depends on his forming an *incorrect* belief (which is a quite ordinary possibility) as indicating the *real* nomic relation.

There is another problem. Suppose Armand would never have noticed rhododendrons had he seen only small ones, but that certain grand ones around the neighborhood catch his eye, so that he forms the conception "plant of that kind." Only then does he notice the occasional small one, and they bring him to judge "plant of that kind" only because the large ones do; still he would produce that concept in response to the large ones even were he not to notice the small ones. This is not a diachronic asymmetry; it is true of Armand at t that were large rhododendrons not causes of his concept at t then small rhododendrons would not be causes of it at t, while the converse does not hold. So if Fodor's condition were sufficient Armand's concept would refer to the property of being a large rhododendron. (The general idea of this comes from Steven Wagner.)[16]

It might be replied that the objection depends on an unsympathetic reading of the counterfactual, which should be understood as: "were it the case *in the circumstances* that small ones failed to elicit the concept then it would be the case that large ones did." Since that is true, the reply goes, the extension is the whole set of rhododendrons by Fodor's criterion. But this is not obvious. Were small ones not to have elicited the concept, this could "in the circumstances" have been because Armand failed to recognize them as of the same kind as the large ones that do elicit the concept. So the counterfactual asymmetry would obtain and Fodor's condition would incorrectly imply that Armand's concept refers only to large rhododendrons.

Now this dialogue could continue, but trading counterfactuals seems pointless. It is difficult to accept that the concept's referring to all rhododendrons rather than to large ones depends on a counterfactual or nomic relation that we have no clear rules for selecting, rather than on the fact that Armand conceives his references as "plant of that kind," knowing full well that they come in all sizes. The natural account of things makes Armand's reference depend in part on that further intentional fact.

Another case. Suppose Armand, never having seen pomegranates, is presented with papier mâché ones but told they are real. He forms the conception "fruit of that kind." Shown real pomegranates he then easily distinguishes them from the others; but he takes the real ones to be papier mâché. If Fodor's condition were sufficient for reference, Armand's concept "fruit of that kind" would be true of the papier mâché fakes, and that seems wrong, for the simple reason that the fakes do not satisfy his guiding conception.[17] Once again it is doubtful that this can be blocked by appeal to counterfactuals free of intentional provisos. The intentional properties of guiding conceptions play a role in determining the reference of recognitional concepts, a role that, I surmise, cannot be eliminated in armchair theorizing. (Which is not to belittle armchair theorizing; it takes us some distance in these matters.)

Questions about Sufficiency: References Outside the Head.

Fodor's condition appears to imply that some concepts refer to states of one's visual-cognitive system when in fact they refer to external objects. He considers this and denies it, but let me make the case. One is tempted to say that the fact that sheep trigger a recognitional conception of sheep depends asymmetrically on certain retinal states' triggering the concept, and that would imply that the concept refers to those states. Fodor would reply that no retinal-state-kind that is not open-endedly disjunctive will have this feature; for any concept of sheep may be sensitive to appearances that are far from models of sheepliness, e.g., when the bush shakes or when you glimpse a shepherd wielding his crook. No retinal state worth counting as a kind is common to all sheep detections.

I see three problems with this reply. For one thing, its presupposition that all sheep discriminations are equally reference-determining is questionable; the reference of an ordinary recognitional concept of sheep does not appear to be determined as much by shaking bushes as by paradigm sightings of sheep. As in the "proton" case, correct ascriptions can depend on a concept's background role, its reference determined independently of those ascriptions; this can be true just as much of demonstrative concepts as of theoretical concepts. If a demonstrative concept refers to so-and-sos, that stems, it seems to me, only from its sensitivity to so-and-sos in certain reference-determining elicitings. This is firmly denied by Fodor, and I will return to the point; but if correct it means that ascriptions of the concept to sheep may well asymmetrically depend on the concept's triggering by a fairly *unified* property of the visual system, one common to reference-determining sightings of sheep. Then the question is why the recognitional concept does not refer to that property.

A second point is this. It could happen that a person has a recognitional concept of, say, tennis balls, but lacks beliefs that enable him to detect tennis balls other than stationary ones in full view. (Suppose any attempts to do so turn out false.) Then, quite apart from the foregoing point, there may be a unified property of the visual system, one that typically arises from straight-on views of unmoving tennis balls, on which his ascription of the concept to tennis balls asymmetrically depends, and which Fodor's theory then counts as the reference.

Third, even if we were to grant that any true ascription of a recognitional concept is as relevant to its reference as any other, who is to say there is no unified neural property deep in the visual-cognitive processing system that is the immediate cause of all and only ascriptions by a particular person of a particular recognitional concept of sheep? But if there were such a property Fodor's condition would count it as the referent.

One suspects that any theory that takes reference to consist in a causal relation unconstrained by guiding conceptions is vulnerable to the objection. And this suggests that referring to external properties depends on, in some sense, *conceiving* them as external. It should be clear that this is no objection to the idea that the reference of a recognitional concept is determined causally, as long as that is constrained by the concept's guiding conception, which is an intentional property.[18]

The last claim may seem rebuttable, by a competing explanation of reference to external objects: the external property counts as the referent because the very point of ascribing reference to others is to mark their propensity to register features of the passing scene. Now this seems to me not to get to the heart of the matter. Even when an external property is being tracked it is not always the reference: nothing prevents me from having a recognitional conception of a kind of visual sensation, which happens to be caused, say, by stationary tennis balls. No point in replying that this responsiveness to tennis balls asymmetrically depends on responsiveness to tennis ball sensations, for that is true also when tennis balls are the reference. The difference in the two cases lies apparently in how the reference is conceived.

One's interest in how others track external properties, moreover, presumably depends on one's own interest in external objects. The claim that a non-intentional condition suffices for the reference of *one's own* concepts is hardly vindicated if one has to add "provided one's interest in external properties is taken into account." That seems just a backhanded way of admitting the ineliminable role of the guiding conception "external property."

IV

Simple Predicates and Atomic Reference. Keep in mind that Fodor's condition is not meant to explain reference for complex expressions, and it may appear that, by fixing on recognitional concepts that incorporate guiding conceptions which have independently determined reference, one has departed from the scope of this concern. But it has to be observed that, if such concepts lie outside the scope of an individualist information-based theory of predicate reference, it is doubtful that such a theory applies to concepts of *ours.* Perhaps there are odd cases,[19] but they will hardly be central. Moreover, a concept's incorporating a guiding conception is no bar to its having information-based reference. Consider singular demonstratives: they typically are qualified at least in a general way, so that the reference of "that moving object there" must be a physical thing (you are not referring to a glint of light on the lenses of your field glasses); but of course a causal condition determines which physical thing is referred to. So with the reference of recognitional concepts to properties.

It is natural to think that, however dependent one may be on concepts whose reference is socially determined, one's ability to think about the world requires at least having the capacity to form one's own recognitional concepts.[20] And it may be natural further to think that that capacity is in some way foundational for other referential capabilities. But this should not imply strong atomism, that the reference of foundational information-based predicates must depend on no further intentional backing. A recognitional concept is "atomic" in a weak sense; its reference is not determined by the reference of semantically independent constituents, and it does depend on the concept's distinctive external relations. To deny that causal theories of reference give us strongly atomic concepts of course contradicts their promise to provide a basis for reference in completely naturalistic terms.

V

Reference-Determining Circumstances. As noted, Fodor's considered view is that reference requires no causal relation to actual so-and-sos; it suffices that "unicorn" stands in a suitable nomic relation to the property unicornhood.[21] But qualifying the straight causal condition for this reason seems to me misguided. Is there such a property as unicornhood? There is the property of looking like a horse with a horn, but then if that is what "unicorn" means, presumably it expresses a description, and such descriptive concepts are not candidates for Fodor's theory. If "unicorn" is noncomposite and purports to refer as it were to a real essence, then (as my intuitions have it, at least) it lacks reference[22]; if composite, its reference is not determined directly by an information theoretic mechanism; and thus either way an information based theory should ignore it.

A natural view is that a recognitional concept picks out the kind of thing that in some way actually occasions its ascription.[23] But suppose certain ascriptions of *F* are occasioned by things of a certain kind only given a background belief that involves *F*. It seems the intuitive view, of the role of such a belief in those ascriptions, presupposes that F has independent reference (as appeared to be the case with "proton"). And then, of course, those ascriptions are not determinative of F's reference.[24] This is not to say that reference-determining ascriptions of a concept must not depend on background beliefs, but rather that the ascription must not be mediated by a belief in the manner mentioned. "The role of that belief in these ascriptions presupposes that the predicate has independent reference" does *not* mean merely that were these ascriptions not to have occurred the predicate would still have referred to whatever it refers to. That, presumably, holds of recognitional concepts for which later ascriptions can be as relevant to their reference as earlier ones, even though the earlier ones were sufficient to determine what is in fact their reference. This can happen because those later ascriptions are in some sense as stipulative as the earlier ones, because if they *had* been occasioned by a property different from the earlier ones (think of Armand's bird-watching) the concept might have, depending on the guiding conception, failed of reference, or referred to a disjunctive property. But on the natural understanding of how "proton" occurred in the background belief, had the particle traces and therefore those ascriptions of "proton" been caused by positrons, "proton" would still have referred to protons.

We already know that not all of a person's predicates refer to properties that cause his ascriptions of them and thus that not all predicates are recognitional concepts. The point aimed at here, though, is that what was true of "proton" can be true of recognitional concepts themselves. Suppose such a concept arises from my seeing crows ("those creatures"), and that subsequently I form the belief that cawings tend to be caused by those creatures. When later I hear cawings in the garden they cause me, given that belief, to judge "one of them." But these latter ascriptions need be *in no way* determinative of the reference of my conception; if, unknown to me, the caws had issued from my neighbor's mouth, that will not have undercut the reference of the recognitional concept ("one of them") to crows. Some ascriptions of a recognitional concept are naturally viewed as reference-determining or stipulative and others not.

But this conflicts with a primary motivation for Fodor's "asymmetrical dependence" explanation of falsity. Straight information theoretic accounts of reference must explain falsity, according to Fodor, by distinguishing "type 1" situations in which ascriptions of a predicate are determinative of its referent and "type 2" situations in which they are not and in which falsity can occur. Fodor rejects this, on the grounds that meaning can be robust throughout situations of all kinds; there is no kind of situation (specified non-question-beggingly) in which F's ascription to non-Ps *ipso facto* interferes with F's continuing straightforwardly to mean P.

One will be misled on this point if one ignores the difference between deferential and recognitional concepts. Doubtless deferential predicates are robust across situations in Fodor's sense; but then the reference of my deferential "sheep" is not determined by *my* ascriptions of it, and its general robustness in my ascriptions stems from that fact. [25] But as regards personal recognitional concepts, intuition seems to count against across the board robustness. If I see novel creatures up close, some llamas, say, and form a new demonstrative conception of "those creatures," that seems connected with a special *perspective* on them. For compare these cases. (i) I ascribe "one of those creatures" to all and only llamas in front of my nose, but then over-confidently ascribe it to creatures across the field that happen to be sheep. (ii) As in the first case, I ascribe it to all llamas in front of my nose but also start applying it to sheep seen in just those circumstances. In case (i) the across-the -field ascriptions seem perfectly consistent with taking the concept to refer to llamas and therefore with taking those ascriptions to be false. In case (ii), one is inclined not to say that the concept refers (just) to llamas. And this suggests that, for recognitional concepts, some perspectives are reference-determining, so that their reference is not robust through all situations.

Now Fodor may wish to say that his theory also accounts for the intuition, while explaining it differently: the across-the-field ascriptions asymmetrically depend on the up-close ascriptions, and the ascriptions to sheep and to llamas are neither asymmetrically dependent on the other. Let me note that I propose the example not as an objection to the asymmetric dependence condition but rather to show that the distinction between reference-determining and non-reference-determining perpectives is an intuitive one. But, of course, it is also of interest to consider whether the asymmetric dependence mechanism does in fact explain that intuition. The difficulties raised so far have concerned the sufficiency of Fodor's condition. And that leaves open the possibility that, while not sufficient, it plays a role in explaining falsity for recognitional concepts, in the following departure from an *echt* Fodorian formulation. Suppose Q captures the guiding conception of a recognitional concept F: then we might say that F refers to Ps provided that Ps are Q, Ps cause F, and if any other Qs cause F that is asymmetrically dependent on Ps causing F. (Then false ascriptions of F would be either to non-Qs or to non-Ps whose causing F is asymmetrically dependent on Ps causing F.)

Now I do not think this is the best explanation of falsity for recognitional concepts. The giant rhodondendron example was earlier used to raise a problem for sufficiency; but it raises one also for necessity. In that example Armand's concept referred to rhododendrons in general, while its ascription to non-giant ones was asymmetrically dependent on its ascription to giant ones. But then the condition is too strong to account for the reference of recognitional concepts in general, and that calls into question its explaining reference and falsity in any case.

Let us return to the main point, the viability of a perspectival constraint. In my view it is quite a good explanation of what is going on in the llama case to say that it is how one conceives "creatures of that kind" which makes the perspective in question determinative of its reference and makes its causal relations apart from that perspective not determinative of its reference. This is a somewhat weaker claim than the one Fodor rejected, which was that there is a certain kind of situation that for *all concepts is* reference-determining (although the weaker claim is doubtless no more palatable to him). On my view each recognitional concept has a sort of built-in perspective. Suppose that in Kenya you see animals with a distinctive distant appearance wandering across the valley, and you cannot tell how they would look up close. You form the conception "creatures of that kind." You also see nearby gazelles of a certain species, and form the conception "creatures of this kind." If you then come to think they are the same, it yet seems natural to say that the reference of the first conception is determined by the distant sightings and not by the proximal sightings, and vice versa for the reference of the second. This accords with cases that similarly involve pairs of singular perceptual demonstratives and/ or memory demonstratives.

The point has two interesting implications. First, it would undercut a motivation for the asymmetric dependence condition if that stems from the thought that one cannot explain falsity by distinguishing reference-determining and non-reference-determining circumstances. (A recognitional conception of those creatures seen across the valley is falsely ascribed to creatures seen up close if they are not of the same kind as the creatures seen across the valley. More on this shortly.) And second, it points to another way unanalyzed intentionality crops up. The perspectival slant of a recognitional concept seems part of the concept itself; it points to its reference from an at least implicitly conceived perpective. This suggests a somewhat Fregean view of demonstratives; for both singular demonstratives and recognitional concepts, a demonstrative mode of presentation is an intentional feature and it is perspectival. Some perspective is part of the sense of the concept, of how it conceives its reference.

VI

False Ascriptions of Recognitional Concepts. So far we have seen the following points about falsity. First, granted that deferential concepts such as one's ordinary concept "horse" are robust, that is, can be false through all situations, this may not apply to recognitional concepts. Second, the asymmetric dependence condition does not explain falsity for recognitional concepts. False ascriptions of the rhododendron concept in the above example are not identical with those that are asymmetrically dependent on ascriptions that determine the concept's reference; for its ascription to small rhododendrons can be asymmetrically dependent on ascriptions to giant ones without being false. Third, the perspectivalness of recognitional concepts allows for the falsity of certain ascriptions, to certain objects outside the relevant perspective. (In many cases false ascriptions are indeed asymmetrically dependent on reference-determining ascriptions. This I surmise accounts for what is intuitive in Fodor's condition, even though if I am right that condition is not the essential explanation.)

Consider again the question whether a recognitional concept can be robust even in situations I would count as reference-determining for it. A negative answer was suggested in connection with llama example above, but there is more to be said. Suppose a recognitional conception deriving from llama-sightings is subsequently ascribed to a few alpacas from the same perspective. It seems that these ascriptions could well count as false, that the recently observed creatures are not of the demonstrated kind. And does this not show that a recognitional concept is robust even through a situation that according to me is reference-determining for it?

Let us distinguish two closely related sorts of demonstrative predicative concepts: recognitional concepts, and what we may call "pure type-memory demonstratives." A concept of the former kind typically points backwards and forwards, by involving both the memory of a perceived kind and a stipulative disposition to include new things in its extension.[26] This happens when there is no reason to distinguish the role of current dispositions and past identifications in stipulatively fixing the concept's reference. (Of course this makes the reference-conditions of such concepts potentially unstable; for such a concept to make a contribution to truth conditions, things beyond the thinker's control have to be just right. As with singular demonstratives, nothing in the concept itself *guarantees* that it contributes anything to, as it were, the possible world truth conditions of the thoughts in which it occurs.) Here is an example of a pure type-memory demonstrative: you remember a kind of bird from childhood but count no current ascriptions of your conception as stipulative of what you mean by "that kind of bird," so that the demonstrative points exclusively in memory. This is a fossilized recognitional concept, and the possibility of a false current ascription of it requires no special explanation.

Now the question is whether a recognitional concept can be falsely ascribed from any perspective whatever. My answer is, despite what has been said so far, yes in a manner of speaking. Suppose you have a recognitional conception of a kind of bird, a stipulatively active concept and not a fossilized pure type-memory demonstrative, and suppose that from the relevant perspective you nod "one of those" at a bird of a different kind. It may yet be useful to *treat* this concept as a pure type-memory demonstrative and thus to count the present ascription as false. (Suppose you conceive your concept's intended reference as a unified kind. We might then say "false" in order to register that your current ascription deviates from a hitherto unified string of identifications. But this will make sense for only the odd exception; larger deviations lead to referential breakdowns of the sort already encountered in the first Armand case.) So we may have it both ways: a recognitional concept's ascription can be from a reference-determining perspective, and yet be treated for certain purposes as false, if we bracket the concept's ongoing stipulativeness and attend solely to what kind it memorializes. This gives the appearance of robustness throughout all perspectives, but it is compatible with a recognitional concept's being *perspectival*, that is, being such that only ascriptions made from a certain perspective are reference-determining.[27]

In calling attention to recognitional concepts as the most promising predicative candidate for an information-based account of reference, and in explaining falsity without asymmetric dependence, I have made essential use of a number of intentional notions. These I take to be ineliminable in any armchair explication of reference, and that seems in direct conflict with Jerry Fodor's objective of naturalizing intentionally, at least if naturalizing means philosophical explication.

But a lesson learned from concepts of phenomenal qualities is that it does not follow, from the unavailability of a naturalistic philosophical explication of a notion, that the notion does not fully have application by virtue of entirely natural features of its reference: nothing in the unanalyzability of phenomenal concepts implies that phenomenal qualities are not physical-functional properties.[28] Similarly with certain notions of intentionality, as I argue in another paper.[29] The intentional notions invoked in the present paper, of specific guiding conceptions, of conceiving a reference as an external object, and so on, should be taken as reflexive or subjective notions, arising not within an objective or impersonal framework of description and explanation, but from subjective reflection on how our own thoughts appear to us. The third-person use of such intentional notions can be regarded as a sort of projection. The lack of an explication, as I argue there, is compatible with such subjective intentional (second-order) conceptions' discriminating thoroughly physical-functional properties.[30]

The resulting idea of what determines the reference of recognitional concepts, as regards armchair explication, is: a mixture of subjective and objective factors. The former include "conceiving of those things as external objects," "conceiving of those things as viewed from this perspective," and so on. The latter include those specified causal/counterfactual relations that make a certain property the one being discriminated and hence referred to. This combination of subjective and objective factors is unsurprising, once one gives up the idea that naturalism requires that intentionality be explicated in objective and externalist terms. Intuitively, the reference of a demonstrative is determined both by one's conception and by an extrinsic relation; and how a demonstrative, whether singular or predicative, *conceives* its reference determines, at least from a subjective perspective, which objects or properties are candidates for reference, and which causal or discriminative relation selects the reference from the among them.

These abbreviated comments about subjective intentionality are hardly satisfactory in themselves. And they are not essential to the basic points of this paper. Suppose it is correct that no purely causal or counterfactual or nomic conditions can explain the reference of recognitional concepts, that is, without the help of intentional notions. And suppose those notions of intentional properties are not themselves explicable in naturalistic terms, and that no extrinsic naturalistic constraint secures that they pick out a determinate reference relation. Then we should have to conclude that the reference of recognitional concepts cannot be wholly a matter of objective naturalistic factors.

NOTES

1 Fodor rejects a certain natural class of solutions, to the effect that a term's meaning consists in what it discriminates in special meaning-determining situations, that meaning consists in information modulo such situations, while in other situations truth or falsity depends on meaning thus determined. Fodor objects that there are no such meaning-determining situations; in all situations it will be possible to assert "sheep" of a goat, and nevertheless mean sheep and not sheep-or-goat (or whatever). More on this below.

2 Fodor (In press-f).

3 If ordered to say "sheep" by a maniac holding a gun to my head, I would comply; but then Fodor's condition does not secure that "sheep" means sheep for me, for not every utterance of "sheep" by me would either be caused by a sheep or be asymmetrically dependent on such a causal connection (my complying would not hang on the meaning of "sheep"). Such a counterfactual may well be true of virtually every term of mine, so that Fodor's condition would be satisfied by none of them; but a sufficient condition of meaning that applies to none of my words is not very interesting.

There is this answer. It is in the spirit of the theory to require that F have the cognitive-functional role characteristic of assenting predication, assuming that that is accountable for in wholly non-semantic terms. More specifically, to require that the relevant nomic relation hold between P and ascriptions of F that have that functional role and that any ascriptions with that functional role should depend asymmetrically on that nomic relation. Perhaps we should not object to appealing to non-semantic functional conditions at this level of generality. But the more specific the functional role, the more dubious it is that a non-semantic or non-intentional specification of that role is waiting in the wings.

4   I suggest reasons in "Personal references", (forthcoming-a). I also argue there that the social determination of the reference of such concepts cannot be explained away by construing them as metalinguistic.

5   Given the agility with which Fodor adapts his theory to various cases (both in 1987d and in 1990b), it is worth asking whether it can also be made to accommodate semantic deference. Suppose it is said that, while "maple" has never in fact been caused by maples, there still is a suitable "nomic relation" between them on which my ascription of "maple" to sweet gums has depended. For had my usage been adjusted in response to correction, maples would have cause judgments of "maple", and had that socially mediated causal counterfactual not obtained (i.e., to the effect that had I corrected my usage maples would have caused "maple"), I would not have ascribed "maple" to sweet gums, for I would not have ascribed it to anything.

There are two problems with this. The first is that my false ascriptions did not in fact depend on such a nomic relation between me and maples. Even if we grant that were "maple" not to have meant maple it would not have meant anything and in consequence would not have been uttered by me at all, still my actual usage depended on the social fact and not on the irrelevant further matter of whether such a counterfactual causal relation also obtained between me and maples. Many contingencies could have broken that counterfactual connection, without disturbing the social facts or my actual ascriptions of "maple."

The second problem is that the relevant counterfactual, to the effect that maples would have prompted judgments of "maple" had I accepted correction, relies implicitly on the social meaning of "maple," for "accepting correction" means changing to a usage that conforms to the social meaning. It is hard to see how *that* counterfactual causal connection between maples and my uttering "maple" could be expressed without appealing in the antecedent to something semantic. There are many different causal counterfactuals that relate my utterance of "maple" to objects of all sorts, depending on what adjusting condition is envisaged in the antecedent. And it is difficult to see how one could say that only the socially mediated counterfactual corresponds to the *real* nomic relation between maples and "maple."

Fodor directly faces up to objections of this sort in other cases, maintaining that in pointing to such a nomic relation the semantic property is appealed to eliminably, and that the nomic relation is in itself nonsemantic. Now I do not doubt that in some sense the underlying causal mechanisms involved in adjusting one's usage in response to correction could ultimately be accounted for in nonsemantic terms. But it would not follow that the semantic property is there appealed to eliminably in the sense Fodor apparently requires. His project is not just to assert that semantic properties need not be mentioned in fundamental causal explanations, but rather to naturalize intentionality. And by this Fodor appears to mean something like providing an armchair condition that suffices for intentionality, or, better, providing an armchair condition that relies on further semantic notions only if (a) they are ancillary, that is , do not do the main explanatory work, and (b) it is not implausible to suppose that they are in turn susceptible of armchair explication. Now, given that we are taking the armchair naturalizing of semantic notions as the main point here, it is far from obvious that social semantic notions are in fact thus susceptible. But, more importantly in the current case, it seems that for socially deferential concepts the central referential mechanism is precisely social, so that the notion of "correction" in the above counterfactual is hardly ancillary. It presupposes what is essential to the reference of my socially deferential concepts. We cannot naturalize intentionality in the armchair by presupposing social semantic reference.

6   (1987d: 121–2).

7   Demonstratives can be indirect, as when you point towards a bulge in the curtain and say "that's Rover."

8   This does not rule it out that "proton" is a demonstrative that gets its reference independently, although of course that would be unusual.

9   Unless I misunderstand his discussion and he does mean the case to be taken in the straight demonstrative way.

10   Suppose your theory that those traces are caused by protons is false; they are caused by positrons. This is possible because, as mentioned in the text, the conceptual role of your "proton" presupposes that it has reference independent of your current discriminations. Then, if Fodor is successful in bending the example in the text to his condition, it would follow that in the present example "proton" refers to positrons.

11   I am puzzled by the facile verificationism that underlies so much "anti-realist" and "realist" discussion, and also many discussions of Kripke's Wittgenstein. My dispositions in verifying the applicability of a predicate can hardly determine reference for my socially deferential concepts, which is to say, the bulk of the concepts I express using English predicates.

12   I have given a somewhat detailed treatment of recognitional concepts in "Personal references," in Loar (forthcoming-a).

13   A sign of this would be your not being disposed to accept semantic correction.

14   Suppose there were undeferential concepts that were not recognitional concepts but theoretical concepts, i.e. they get their reference somehow from their role in a systematic personal theory of things. They could be ascribed on the basis of perception, but they would not get their reference from such ascriptions. (A personal analog of how I took "proton" to behave in Fodor's example.) But that means that such a concept could in an information theoretic or a Fodorian way discriminate a property P, even though P is not its reference. This generates a counterexample to sufficiency that does not depend on the existence of deferential concepts. This seems to show that a sufficient condition requires a positive characterization of recognitional concepts, and as I indicate in the text it is not easy to see how that can be done except in intentional terms, in armchair theorizing, that is.

15   If a singular memory demonstrative, "that person", derives equally from preceptions of two persons whom one has conflated, the natural call seems to be that the demonstrative fails of reference. On the other hand, if one lived in a world of twins and so had implicitly been aware that two people might be involved, one's guiding conception might implicitly have been "that person or persons," which in some ways would be analogous to the disjunctive-kind guiding conception. A proposed sufficient condition of reference for singular demonstratives that failed to take such guiding conceptions into account would be open to counterexample. The causal condition on its own is not enough.

But of course, not everything that looks like a guiding conception is a constraint on reference; some predicates associated with a demonstrative may well be better construed as registering judgments about its references rather than as constraints on it.

16   Letter to Jerry Fodor.

17   My point does not require the stronger claim that this concept refers to the real pomegranates; given the oddness of the case one may not know what to say about that. The point is that it does not refer to the fake ones.

18   Can there be reference without a guiding conception? Suppose I am strapped down and cannot move my head in a strange environment, not able to tell whether what appear to be spots fluttering before my eyes are specks of dust in the air, shadows on

the wall, *muscae volitantes*, or strange events deep in my brain. If I am, in fact, tracking specks of dust it seems my concept "things of that sort" refers to them; but if there are no suitable external things, then my concept perhaps refers to internal events. I am not sure that this example shows reference without a guiding conception. Perhaps one has implicitly a sort of conditional guiding conception: "fluttering things out there if there are any or otherwise internal occurrences." As regards what I say in the next paragraph in the text, it is true that in such a case, unless our interest focuses on internal states, we seem to want to choose the external property if there is one. But this may simply reflect the fact that we are most basically interested in external causes of our states if there are any (see the conclusion of the next paragraph). This would mean that "external object or property" is a sort of default guiding conception.

19   See 18 above.

20   The qualification is due to this. As I try to make clear in Loar (forthcoming-a) a recognitional ability attached to a socially deferential concept may not in itself have the role of a separate concept. But it presumably always *could*, and it is difficult to see how ordinary thinking about the world could go on without such a capacity.

21   Fodor (in press-f).

22   Consider this: "unicornhood is the genetic property responsible for such an appearance in a possible world closer to the actual world than any other world in which a genetic property is responsible for that appearance." But it might then follow (who knows) that unicornhood is the property of being a kind of mutant donkey. And it strikes me that there would be as little reason to count that as the reference of "unicorn" as there is to count a fat man in a red suit at the North Pole as Santa Claus.

23   A painter may imagine a shade of blue she has never seen, and then be sure when she encounters a new blue that it was the one she imagined. Perhaps in certain circumstances we would regard her as having genuinely conceived that shade, that property. But this may be a very special exception to the condition in the text; for perhaps it applies only to property concepts that fit phenomenally into a spectrum of concepts whose references are independently determined by causation by actual instances. "Unicorn" seems different.

24   Analogy: I see a man wearing a kilt and carrying a bagpipe, and then see him several times subsequently in trousers and without the bagpipe, and each time think "it's that guy," where the reference goes back to the earlier sighting and is in no way determined by the later ascriptions.

25   A qualification: if I think "sheep" (in both spoken and written forms) means "sound made by canaries and other small birds" then, even though it has a deferential conceptual role for me, "sheep" does not refer to sheep in my thoughts. This contrasts with what I said about the above case in which a person takes it to refer to sheep and gazelles (as we would say). If you accept my intuitions about both cases, they may suggest something like this rule: if x's concept F is deferential and F refers to Ps in the language to which x defers, then F refers to Ps in x's thoughts *unless* x has too radically misconceived the reference of F. From this we should expect broad borderline areas of unclarity as to whether a predicate has in x's thoughts the reference it has in the language to which x defers. Moreover, we might expect that what counts as too radical a misconception varies across types of concept. Thus a technical concept may refer in x's thoughts to its social reference despite a fairly substantial misconception of that reference by x, whereas less technical everday concepts may tolerate a lesser degree of misconception, that is without finding a difference in reference. If this is a fair intuition, I believe one can give a satisfactory account of it.

26   See Loar (forthcoming-a) for more on the distinction between pure type memory demonstratives and ordinary recognitional concepts.

27   A question remains. Suppose that, were I removed to a distant planet, I would ascribe

to some non-gazelles (same appearance, different genetics) a concept that apparently refers only to gazelles. Should we then say that the concept refers to a disjunctive kind, or even that it fails of reference, as in the first Armand case?

What Fodor says about Twin-Earth cases implies that his theory counts only gazelles as the reference, on the grounds that the nomic relation of that concept to any non-gazelles depends asymmetrically on its relation to gazelles, and this because of the discriminations one *would* make were one to discover how to tell those other creatures from gazelles. But as I indicated earlier, this is unsatisfactory, for, in determining these nomic relations, nothing that is not question-begging gives a privileged role to counterfactuals about how one would discriminate things given correct information, over related counterfactuals given incorrect information.

No point in invoking the perspectival condition, for my distant discriminations of those non-gazelles would be from the same psychological perspective. We need a contextual factor, and the question is whether we have to fall back on relativizing: "the reference of concept C is P relative to context K." There is a difference between that and holding that the concept's reference to gazelles is determined by its context. (Compare saying "the reference of my utterance of 'I' is relative to context" (false) with "the reference of my utterance of 'I' is determined by context" (true). My inclination is to say that the concept may well refer just to gazelles despite the counterfactual in question. And I suggest that this calls for yet a further intentional element: I *conceive* the reference of the recognitional concept as (say) a natural kind in my present context (vaguely drawn).

28 See Loar (forthcoming-b).
29 Loar (1987b).
30 As if our second-order conceptions of our first-order conceptions are recognitional concepts, the former discriminating those internal properties that constitute the latter. How this might account for the appearance of intentionality is discussed in Loar (1987b).

8

Is There Vindication Through Representationalism?

ROBERT J. MATTHEWS

Introduction: The Representational Theory of Mind

Many philosophers, including myself, envision the possibility of a developed scientific psychology whose ontology explicitly postulates states that exhibit the sorts of properties that commonsense takes to be essential to propositional attitudes. In particular, like Fodor (1987d), we envision a physicalistically respectable psychology that postulates states satisfying the following conditions: (i) they are semantically evaluable; (ii) they have causal powers; and (iii) the implicit generalizations of commonsense belief-desire psychology are largely true of them. The development of such a psychology would represent the long-awaited, and in many quarters unexpected, scientific vindication of commonsense belief/desire explanations of behavior.

Unlike many of us, Fodor claims to have an especially clear vision of this Godot of the psychological world: it will take the form of the Representational Theory of Mind (hereafter, the RTM). In its most recent formulation (Fodor, 1987d:17), the RTM is presented as the conjunction of two claims:

Claim 1 (the nature of propositional attitudes):
For any organism O, any attitude A, and any proposition P, there is a (computational/ functional) relation R and a mental representation MR such that MR means that P, and O has A [to P] iff O bears R to MR.

Thus, for example, to believe that it is sunny outside is to bear the appropriate computational/functional relation to a mental representation (i.e., symbol token or formula) that represents that state of affairs.

Claim 2 (the nature of mental processes):
Mental processes are causal sequences of tokenings of mental representations.

Thus, according to this second claim, a train of thought is "a causal sequence of tokenings of mental representations which express the propositions that are the objects of the thoughts" (Fodor, 1987d:17).

Fodor offers two sorts of reasons for believing that the RTM is more or less true. First, "some or other version of RTM underlies practically all current

137

psychological research on mentation, and our best science is *ipso facto* our best estimate of what there is and what it's made of" (ibid.). Second, only the RTM has been able to explain the "striking parallelism" between the causal relations among mental states, on the one hand, and the semantic relations that hold among their propositional objects, on the other; more specifically, only the RTM has been able to explain the fact that, as Fodor (1987d:13) puts it, "causal relations very often respect the semantic ones." The first sort of reason is discussed only in passing in Fodor's latest book; it was the focus of Fodor (1975a). The second, however, is developed in considerable detail.

In Matthews (1988), I criticized Fodor's claim that the RTM enjoys strong empirical support from the cognitive sciences. In the present paper I wish to examine Fodor's claim that the RTM is able to sketch the broad outlines of the long awaited scientific vindication of commonsense psychological explanation. I begin by considering Fodor's recent "polishing" of the RTM, which, as he himself admits, is necessary if the RTM is to survive certain well-known objections. I argue that Fodor's attempt to insulate the RTM from these objections is unsuccessful, and the failure of the RTM to circumvent these objections undermines the doctrine's claim to provide a vindication of commonsense psychological explanation.

Fodor's Polishing of the RTM: Does it Succeed?

According to claim 1, the RTM entails both that for each tokening of a propositional attitude, there is a tokening of a corresponding computational relation between an organism and a mental representation, and that for each tokening of such a relation, there is a tokening of a corresponding propositional attitude. Fodor concedes that the equivalence fails in both directions. There are cases of attitude tokenings without corresponding relation tokenings, and cases of relation tokenings without corresponding attitude tokenings.

Cases of the second sort, viz., relation tokenings without corresponding attitude tokenings, present little difficulty for the RTM. For as Fodor points out, there is no reason to suppose that the folk-psychological inventory of propositional attitudes is exhaustive. Faced with a case of this sort, proponents of the RTM can simply coin a corresponding attitude (cf., for example, Chomsky's "cognize," the propositional attitude that native speakers are said to bear to the grammatical rules of their language). Cases of the first sort, however, do present a challenge to the RTM. As an example of such a case, Fodor cites Dennett's (1981c) example of a chess-playing program that thinks "it should get its Queen out early." In the program that Dennett describes, there are many levels of explicit representation, but at none of these levels is there anything explicitly tokened that is even roughly synonymous with "I must get my Queen out early." Fodor takes the point of Dennett's example to be that "*none* of the principles in accordance with which a computational system operates need be explicitly represented by a formula tokened in the device; there is no guarantee that the program of the machine will be explicitly represented in the machine whose program it is" (1987d; 22–3). In fact, this was presumably not the point of Dennett's counterexample. Dennett was objecting to the very notion that propositional attitudes are to be construed as computational relations to token representations.

Fodor's way around such counterexamples is to argue that under its proper construal the RTM need hold only for what the RTM identifies as "core cases":

> According to claim 2, mental processes are causal sequences of transformations of mental representations. It follows that tokenings of attitudes *must* correspond to tokenings of mental representations when they – the attitude tokenings – are episodes in mental processes. If the intentional objects of such causally efficacious attitude tokenings are *not* explicitly represented, then RTM is simply false. I repeat for emphasis: If the occurrence of a thought is an episode in a mental process, then RTM is committed to the explicit representation of its content. The motto is therefore No Intentional Causation without Explicit Representation.
>
> Notice that this way of choosing core cases squares us with the alleged counterexamples. [. . .] Roughly: According to RTM, programs – corresponding to the "laws of thought" – *may* be explicitly represented; but "data structures" – corresponding to the contents of thoughts – *have to be.*
>
> (1987d:24–25)

Fodor thus proposes to circumvent Dennett's counterexample by arguing that the RTM does not require the explicit representation of the chess program's thought that it must get its Queen out early, since that thought is not an episode in the mental processes of the machine; rather it is one of the "laws of thought" – part of the program – that governs the program's chess-play. By contrast, says Fodor, "the representations of the board – of actual or possible states of play – over which the machine's computations are defined *must* be explicit, precisely *because* the machine's computations *are* defined over them" (ibid.). These successive representations of the board, says Fodor, "constitute the machine's 'mental processes,' so either they are causal sequences of explicit representations, or the representational theory of chess playing is simply false of the machine" (ibid.).

In attempting to circumvent Dennett's counterexample to the RTM, Fodor seemingly overlooks an obvious difficulty with his proposed way around. His defense of the RTM is purchased only at the price of having to concede that the RTM provides no account – and hence no "vindication" – of what he calls "derivative cases" of propositional attitude ascription. This is no small price! Dennett's chess program, for example, is said to play chess in the way that it does *because* it thinks that it must get its Queen out early; yet because that thought is not explicitly represented within the program, the RTM provides no account of the explanatory role of that thought ascription in an explanation of the program's chess play. In Shimon Ullman's (1979) theory of the visual system's recovery of shape from motion, the visual system is said to be able to effect this recovery *because* it assumes that objects are rigid under translation; yet because that assumption is not explicitly represented in Ullman's computational model of the visual system, the RTM provides no account of the explanatory role of that assumption ascription in an explanation of the visual system's recovery of shape from motion. Or, to take yet a third example, in current psycholinguistic theory, the native speaker's judgment that certain sentences are ungrammatical (e.g., *What did he ask where/whether Bill hid?*) is explained in terms of that speaker's knowledge of the so-called "*wh*-island constraint" (which states that no constituent can be moved out of any clause containing a *wh*-phrase in COMP). Yet, once again, the RTM provides no account of the explanatory role of the knowledge ascription, since in virtually all currently proposed parsings models, locality constraints such as *wh*-island constraints are implemented procedurally and thus not explicitly represented.[1]

Cases such as these are ubiquitous in computational psychology. Examine virtually any computational model of one or another cognitive process or human capacity; you will find that of the propositional attitudes that commonsense would ascribe to its possessor as part of an explanation of that subject's behavior, some will be implemented procedurally. The reason is clear: such models are responsive to considerations that in some cases militate against the explicit representation of the contents of these attitudes (e.g., efficiency, resource availability, preference for known algorithms).

Not only does Fodor's defense of the RTM leave him with no account of the seemingly ubiquitous "derivative cases," the very notion of a "core case" upon which that defense rests seems not to be well-defined independently of the RTM. Fodor proposes to identify as core cases those attitude tokenings that are "episodes in mental processes." But how are such tokenings to be identified, except by appeal to the RTM? Fodor, it will be recalled, argues that the chess program's thought that it should get its Queen out early is not an episode in the mental processes of the machine but is rather a "law of thought" that governs those processes, and hence need not be explicitly represented. By contrast, the program's thought about an actual or possible board configuration *is* such an episode and hence *must* be explicitly represented. But what is the difference between these two mental states that makes the one, but not the other, an episode in the mental processes of the machine? Surely it is not the presumably more transitory nature of the latter. States of mind do not become more episodic (more event-like) simply by virtue of being more transitory. If the tokening of the second of these states is to count as an episode in a mental process, so, too, will the tokening of the former, albeit not necessarily an episode in the same mental process as the former. The chess program's tokening of the thought that it should get its Queen out early (or indeed its tokening of any of its presumably many thoughts about how chess is best played) is presumably a datable event or episode in the mental life of that machine, even though this tokening predates the tokening of thoughts about board configurations that occurs in games that exhibit the chess program's thought that it should get its Queen out early. The point here is simply this: many of the propositional attitudes that Fodor proposes to treat as "derivative" are presumably acquired in the course of some mental process (e.g., through learning or perception) and hence according to Fodor's criterion would also be "core".

The only way in which there could fail to be a datable tokening of the chess program's thought that it should get its Queen out early would be if this thought were innate, i.e., inherent in the program's basic design. But perhaps this is just what Fodor has in mind. Perhaps Fodor's proposal is to identify as "core cases" all and only those attitudes that are actually *acquired* in the course of some mental process (e.g., through perception or learning). This might explain his surprising remark that perhaps none of the "laws of thought" is explicitly represented. Fodor would presumably not entertain such a possibility if the "laws of thought" included anything learned, since if the laws of thought did include anything learned, this fact would undercut the RTM's claim to provide both a vindication of commonsense pscyhological explanation and a foundational underpinning for current psychological research. Current research, like commonsense folk psychology, presumes that we behave as we do in part *because* of what we have learned, i.e., what is learned is presumed to play a causally efficacious role in the production of behavior. If the RTM can provide no account of this causal role then what many psychologists regard as the central domain of human psychology, viz., inquiry into the impact of learning upon behavior, would be beyond the purview of the RTM. Yet if Fodor does indeed propose to identify as "core cases" all and only acquired attitudes, then his proposal is untenable on empirical grounds, since it is common knowledge within computational psychology that acquired attitudes (e.g., grammatical knowledge) can be, and probably often are, implemented procedurally rather than explicitly represented.[2]

So here is where we stand: Ford's attempt to rescue the RTM from counterexamples of the sort raised by Dennett rests on a seemingly untenable distinction between core and derivative cases. There would seem to be no principled way of drawing the distinction so as to save the RTM from such counterexamples that does not *either* (i) undercut the RTM's claim to provide a general account, and hence vindication, of the explanatory role of propositional attitude ascriptions in both commonsense and scientific psychology *or* (ii) conflict with the persuasive empirical evidence (that Fodor accepts) regarding the procedural implementation of many acquired propositional attitudes.

Fodor's Parallelism Argument

Commonsense belief/desire psychology presumes that thought is a causal process in which one semantically evaluable mental state gives rise to another. Fodor points out that in such a propositional attitude psychology it's not just that causal powers and contents are attributed to states that are taken to be semantically evaluable, "it's also that causal relations among propositional attitudes somehow typically contrive to respect their relations of content, and typical belief/desire explanations often turn on this" (1987d:12). All this leads Fodor to ask (1987d:14), "what sort of mechanism could have states that are both semantically and causally connected, and such that the causal connections respect the semantic ones?" The answer, Fodor argues, is a mechanism of the sort postulated by the RTM, viz., one in which the mental representations postulated by the RTM interact causally in a way dictated by their syntactic structures that preserves the appropriate semantic relations between the contents of these representations. The mind, he argues, is a "syntax-driven machine" whose operations are proof-theoretic in character and thus satisfy both syntactic and semantic descriptions: under their syntactic description mental operations instantiate certain causal relations, while under their semantic description they instantiate certain inferential relations.

Fodor claims to find support for the RTM in the supposed fact that if the mind were a mechanism of the postulated sort, then that would explain the "striking parallelism" between the causal relations among mental states, on the one hand, and the semantic relations that hold among their propositional objects, on the other. The claimed support, however, is illusory. Proof-theoretic devices of the sort described by Fodor certainly exhibit a parallelism between syntactic relations and semantic relations, but they do not provide a model that explains the psychological parallelism that Fodor finds so striking. The reason, very simply, is that this parallelism is exhibited *both* by mental states that satisfy the RTM *and* by those that don't. Only in the former case can the parallelism be explained on Fodor's proof-theoretic model. According to current psycholinguistic theory, for example, an English speaker's knowledge that sentences are ungrammatical if they violate the *wh*-island constraint not only causes that speaker to judge that the sentence *What did he ask where/whether Bill hid?* is ungrammatical but also serves as a premise in a deductive argument that has this grammatically judgement as a conclusion. The semantic relation, as Fodor would put it, "parallels" the causal one. Yet the parallelism here cannot be explained by Fodor's proof-theoretic model since, as we noted, this knowledge is presumed not to be explicitly represented. Clearly Fodor's proposed explanation cannot be a general one, since there will be numerous cases, viz., those involving so-called derivative attitudes, that cannot be explained in this way.

Fodor claims that his proof-theoretic account of mental processes is the only available theory that isn't known to be false (see, e.g., 1987d;19–20). But this at once overestimates the RTM and underestimates its alternatives. The RTM is not a theory at all, but a theory-schema (or better: only the barest sketch of such a schema). The RTM, for example, is said to offer an account of the striking parallelism between causal relations and semantic relations among mental states, but what is the account? Very little is offered by way of a characterization of the semantic relations that the causal relations are said to respect; nothing is offered by way of a characterization of the syntax in virtue of which the symbol tokens postulated by the RTM are said to interact causally. All that we have by way of an account of this parallelism is the bare *possibility* that in the mind's design, just as in computer design, causal role is brought into phase with content by exploiting a potential parallelism between the syntax of a symbol and its semantics. If bare possibilities are the stuff of which accounts can be made, then alternatives to the RTM abound. In logic circuits, for example, causal role is also brought into phase with content, though without utilizing data structures that explicitly represent these contents. Some of these alternatives may have the added virtue that they, unlike the RTM, explain why derivative attitudes also exhibit this parallelism.

The question, then, is this: if, as I have argued elsewhere, the RTM does not enjoy the empirical support claimed for it, and if, as I have suggested above, the RTM offers no more than the bare possibility of a partial account of propositional attitudes, why does Fodor find the doctrine so compelling? Why does it seem to Fodor that only the likes of the RTM can provide the long awaited vindication of commonsense psychological explanation? Perhaps it is because he believes, as he says (1987d:25), that there can be no intentional causation without explicit representation.

Intentional Causation without Explicit Representation?

Fodor apparently intends the motto "No Intentional Causation without Explicit Representation" to be understood as the expression of a nomologically necessary condition on intentional causation, one that the RTM, when restricted to so-called "core cases," satisfies. Fodor offers no justification of the condition; however, some sort of argument is clearly in order, since if the condition is tenable, then we will be forced to conclude not only that those propositional attitudes that Fodor classes as "derivative cases" cannot be intentionally causally efficacious, but also that intentional realists are committed to the RTM – a consequence that many intentional realists would be loath to accept.

Fodor (1989b) understands the notion of intentional causation as follows: to say that mental events are *intentionally* causally efficacious is to say that such events are causally efficacious in virtue of their having certain intentional properties. The latter notion is explained as follows: there are causal laws according to which the occurrence of an event instantiating certain intentional properties is nomologically sufficient for the occurrence of an event instantiating certain other properties; to say that a mental event is causally efficacious in virtue of its having certain intentional properties is to say that this event is covered by an intentional causal law and furthermore has the intentional properties that the antecedent of this law specifies. Thus, for example, my desire to raise my arm is intentionally causally efficacious in bringing me to raise my arm if there is a causal law according to which the occurrence of an event instantiating the intentional property of being a desire to raise my arm is nomologically sufficient for the occurrence of an event instantiating the behavioral property of my raising my arm.

The point to be noted in the present context regarding Fodor's notion of intentional causation is that he proposes to explicate that notion in terms of the notion of intentional causal laws: mental events are causally efficacious in virtue of certain intentional properties if these events are subsumed by causal laws that mention these intentional properties in their antecedents. If, as Fodor claims, there is no intentional causation without explicit representation, then presumably this must be attributable in some way to the nature of intentional causal laws, but why should this be?

Fodor (1989b:8) holds that, as with the laws of all special sciences, the satisfaction of the antecedent of an intentional causal law necessitates the satisfaction of its consequent only via the operation of an intervening mechanism:

> If 'Fs cause Gs' is *non*basic, then there is always a story about what goes on when – and in virtue of which – Fs cause Gs.

Thus, if there is, as Fodor supposes, an intentional causal law that connects believing that P & (P → Q) to believing that Q, then "it follows that there must be a mechanism in virtue of which believing that P & (P → Q) *brings it about* that one believes that Q" (ibid).

Assume Fodor is right in thinking that the causal laws of intentional psychology hold in virtue of the existence of some intervening mechanism. There is nothing so far in any of this that would seem to require explicit representation. Any mechanism will do so as long as it is able to mediate the events (states, etc.) that intentional causal laws subsume; we have as yet no reason to suppose that mechanisms capable of effecting this mediation *must* explicitly represent the contents of the events (states, etc.) that these laws subsume. Indeed, the ubiquity of Fodor's "derivative cases" argues conclusively against this supposition. Mechanisms employing the resources of explicit representation can mediate the events that a causal intentional law subsumes *only if* the contents of these events are explicitly represented. In many cases, however, most notably in these "derivative cases," the contents of such events are *not* explicitly represented, so such mechanisms cannot, and do not, mediate some of the events that causal intentional laws subsume. What is not possible in some cases is certainly not necessary in all cases.

So it looks as if intentional causation does *not* require explicit representation after all. The only way to avoid this conclusion would be to argue that the laws that subsume derivative cases are not genuine causal intentional laws. Such a conclusion, however, would be difficult to establish. Lawlike generalizations that subsume derivative cases satisfy the usual criteria for being both causal and intentional just as well as do laws that subsume only core cases. Fodor might be tempted to appeal to the supposedly episodic character of core cases, arguing that only such episodic propositional attitudes can be causes. Such an argument would face challenges on two fronts. First, as suggested above, there would seem to be no reason to suppose that core cases are any more episodic (event-like) than derivative cases. Second, even of there were a sense in which core cases were more episodic, it is unclear what relevance such a distinction would have, since it would appear that it is propositional attitude *states*, whatever their temporal duration, that are causally efficacious in the production of behavior.

Vindication through Representationalism

If, as Fodor argues, mental events are causally efficacious in virtue of being subsumed by intentional causal laws, and if, as Fodor further argues, these laws hold in virtue of the existence of mechanisms that mediate the events that these laws subsume, then the claim to have vindicated commonsense folk psychological explanation would seem to depend crucially on the transparency of the implementation that these mechanisms effect. Consider, once again, Dennett's (1981c:107) description of the chess program that thinks that it should get its Queen out early:

> But for all the many levels of explicit representation to be found in that program, nowhere is anything roughly synonymous with "I should get my Queen out early" explicitly tokened. The level of analysis to which the designer's remark belongs describes features of the program that are, in an entirely innocent way, emergent properties of the computational processes that have "engineering reality." I see no reason to believe that the relation between belief-talk and psychological-process talk will be any more direct.

The prospect that Dennett describes will seem bleak to anyone who believes that commonsense psychological explanation requires scientific vindication. For what such a person would presumably demand by way of vindication is an account of the computational implementation of the ascribed propositional attitudes that would lay to rest *reasonable* doubts about their physicalistic respectability. That is to say, the required account would establish beyond reasonable doubt that the ascribed attitudes were physical states of the system to which they were ascribed. The prospect that Dennett describes would preclude just such an account: propositional attitudes turn out to be "emergent properties" of their computational implementation, which is to say that the implementation is so *diffuse* as to preclude any vindication of commonsense psychological explanation; there is simply no answer to the question of which computational structures and processes implement a given propositional attitude.

The RTM, by contrast, promises a *localist* implementation of propositional attitudes: it holds, we will recall, that for any organism O, and any attitude A towards a proposition P, there is a computational relation R and a mental representation ("data structure") MR such that MR means that P, and O has A [to P] if and only if O bears R to MR. Thus, to the question, "How are propositional attitudes implemented?" the RTM proposes a single, general answer, namely, that the propositional content of an attitude is explicitly represented by some specifiable data structure, while the attitude itself is implemented by some specifiable computational process defined over that data structure. Thus, for example, what makes it true that I believe that it is sunny outside today is that there is a data structure that represents this state of affairs, and this data structure plays the particular causal functional role in my psycho-functional processes that beliefs in fact play.

According to the RTM, then, the implementation of propositional attitudes instantiates a mapping of attitudes onto computational states and processes of a very specific sort: the attitudes themselves are mapped onto certain computational relations, the propositional contents of these attitudes onto certain data structures over which these relations are defined. More precisely, there is a *homomorphism* between propositional attitudes and computational states and processes that preserves, on the computational level, the type distinction drawn at the intentional level between attitudes and their contents. The hypothesized homomorphism falls shorts of an isomorphism inasmuch as the RTM does not require that tokens of a given type of attitude or content be mapped to tokens of a single type of computational relation or data structure, respectively; it is compatible with the RTM that tokens of the first sort be mapped to tokens of *different* types of computational relations and data structures. Thus, although two subjects who share a given propositional attitude will both implement that propositional attitude in the same general way, viz., in both subjects the content of the propositional attitude is implemented by a data structure, the attitude itself by a computational relation defined over that data structure, these subjects may implement the attitude and its content by means of different computational relations and data structures.

The RTM's claim about the nature of the mapping of propositional attitudes into computational states and processes is empirically significant, and not simply because it is a matter of empirical fact whether a given mapping instances such a homomorphism. The postulated homomorphism can be implemented only within a computational architecture in which one can draw the required distinction between data structures, on the one hand, and the computational processes defined over these structures, on the other. This implementational commitment precludes not only the possibility that propositional attitudes might be implemented within classical Turing/von Neumann architectures in ways not envisioned by the RTM (e.g., the sorts of cases described by Dennett (1981c) and Matthews (1984, 1988)), but also the possibility that propositional attitudes might be implemented within non-classical (e.g., connectionist) architectures that fail to preserve a principled distinction between data structures and computational processes. The RTM thus makes a significant empirical claim regarding human computational architecture.

A computational-theoretic vindication of commonsense psychological explanation would have to establish that there is a principled computational interpretation of the propositional attitude ascriptions that figure in such explanations. The interpretation would have to be principled in the sense that the mapping of propositional attitudes into computational states and processes would have to preserve the salient properties of propositional attitudes. In particular, the mapping would have to preserve (in large measure) the semantic evaluability of propositional attitudes, their causal powers, the implicit generalizations of commonsense psychology true of them, the criteria for their individuation, their seeming productivity and systematicity, and the apparent parallelism between their causal and semantic relations. Fodor's proposed computational-theoretic vindication of commonsense psychological explanation preserves these properties in a breath-takingly simple way: for every propositional attitude ascription-type, there is claimed to be a corresponding computational structure that exhibits the syntactic and semantic properties of the complement construction that figures in that ascription-type. The proposed vindication thus combines two distinct, but often conflated doctrines: the RTM, and the so-called Language of Thought hypothesis (the LOT), which holds that mental states have basically the same syntactic and semantic properties as sentences of a natural language.[3] The RTM promises a localist implementation of propositional attitudes that associates with each type-distinct propositional content a type-distinct computational structure (data structure), and with each type-distinct attitude a type-distinct computational relation. The LOT the reads back onto these computational structures the syntactic and semantic properties of the sentential complement constructions by which we ascribe the propositional contents of attitudes. (Thus, for example, the RTM associates with the belief that it is sunny today a computational counterpart, viz., a data structure, that according to the LOT has the syntactic and semantic properties of the sentence "it is sunny outside today.")

By fiat, then, Fodor's postulated implementation of propositional attitudes preserves the semantic evaluability, the productivity and systematicity, and the distinctive individuation criteria of propositional attitudes. These properties are captured syntactically and semantically by the sentences by which we ascribe propositional attitudes, and the postulated implementation maps each propositional attitude-type onto a computational counterpart having the syntactic and semantic properties of the sentence that ascribes tokens of that type. The role of the homomorphism postulated by the RTM should be clear: it guarantees the existence of a computational structure that can serve as the postulated counterpart. Given a computational description of an individual to whom certain propositional attitudes are truly ascribed, there is guaranteed to be an answer to the question "Which computational structure is the counterpart of this particular propositional attitude?"

The strategy of reading the linguistic properties of the ascription back onto a computational counterpart does not guarantee that the mapping will preserve the relevant causal powers of propositional attitudes. Nor, of course, does the strategy guarantee the existence of a computational counterpart of the postulated sort. Fodor's proposed vindication of commonsense psychological explanation can fail, either because the causal powers of the computational counterparts cannot be made to model the causal powers of propositional attitudes, or because counterparts of the postulated sort are not to be had. Fodor's critics (e.g., Dennett, 1981c; Matthews, 1988) have argued that not only is there no reason to suppose that there will always be such a counterpart, but also there is evidence that in many cases there is no such counterpart. Fodor's response to such criticisms has been to attempt to circumscribe the domain of the RTM in such a way as to circumvent these counterexamples. The problem, we have seen, is that there seems to be no tenable way of redefining this domain that does not undercut the project of vindicating commonsense psychological explanation.

Can There Be Vindication without Representationalism?

If, as would seem to be the case, the RTM cannot be salvaged, then commonsense psychological explanation will have to look for its vindication elsewhere. That vindication may eventually be found in the results of empirical research; however, in the interim there remains the philosophical project outlined by Fodor of determining whether there exist any non-Representationalist accounts of propositional attitudes that could in principle provide the required vindication. The project promises to be a difficult one, since with the abandonment of the RTM we give up the relatively straightforward account of the properties of propositional attitudes promised by the RTM/LOT. Specifically, we give up the mapping of propositional attitude contents into data structures that insures that every propositional attitude has a computational counterpart to which we can impute the syntactic and semantic properties of the sentence-type by which we ascribe that propositional attitude. The most obvious difficulty here is that of specifying an alternative mapping of propositional attitudes into computational states and processes that will preserve the apparent productivity and systematicity of propositional attitudes. There are no concrete proposals about how this is to be achieved, except along the lines proposed by the RTM/LOT, where propositional attitudes are mapped onto computational structures that have a recursively defined constituent structure. The counterexamples to the RTM discussed earlier in this chapter provide no guidance as to how to proceed in this matter. The procedural implementation of these particular propositional attitudes does not entail any particular account of the implementation of other propositional attitudes. Yet productivity and systematicity, as the terminology would suggest, are properties of *systems* of propositional attitudes, and hence will presumably be explained in terms of the implementation of such systems.

The philosophical project of providing a scientific vindication of common-sense psychological explanation has been frustrated by the lack of any clear understanding of the possibility space in which the required implementation of propositional attitudes would have to be articulated. Presumably our best strategy for developing such an understanding will be to examine proposed computational models of various cognitive processes with an eye to determining whether they afford a transparent account of the implementation of the propositional attitudes that we are antecedently inclined to ascribe to such processes (or their possessors). Such a strategy would not be very promising if, as Fodor has argued, computational models of cognitive processes presume the truth of the RTM. In fact, as the counterexamples mentioned earlier in the paper might suggest, computational theorists do not seem wedded to the RTM. The computational interpretations that these theorists devise for their intentional state descriptions of the cognitive processes that they are modelling often (indeed, typically) diverge significantly from the interpretation proposed by the RTM. Given this divergence, which is hardly surprising given the other considerations to which these computational models must be responsive (e.g., efficiency, resource availability, preference for known algorithms), the strategy of examining proposed models is actually quite promising. The task of understanding the implementation proposed in these models is often facilitated by the theorists themselves, who in explaining their proposed model will often sketch its interpretation of their own intentional description of the cognitive processes being modelled. Roughly speaking, they justify their proposed computational model by presenting it as an interpretation of an antecedently justified intentional theory.

A second strategy for exploring the possibility of a non-Representationalist vindication of commonsense psychological explanation involves exploring alternative computational architectures with an eye to determining whether these architectures can provide the required implementation of propositional attitudes (viz., one that preserves their salient properties in a transparent fashion). Fodor and Pylyshyn's (1988a) criticism of connectionist models of cognition illustrates this second strategy: they argue (unconvincingly, to my mind) that connectionist architectures cannot be construed as *cognitive* models, since such architectures are allegedly unable to model the systematicity of intentional states. Connectionist architectures are said to be unable to do this, because they lack the representational resources necessary to define the notion of a state that has a constituent structure. As Fodor and Pylyshyn formulate their criticism, it might seem as if they suppose that there are computational tasks that classical (von Neumann) architectures can accomplish that connectionist architectures cannot. But this cannot be so, since by all accounts, the architectures are Turing equivalent. What Fodor and Pylyshyn's criticism really seems to come to is the objection that there is no interpretation of propositional attitudes ascriptions in connectionist models that will preserve in a transparent fashion the systematicity of propositional attitudes: systematicity in such models will be one of Dennett's emergent properties. Such an eventuality would not necessarily disqualify such models as cognitive; however, if the best cognitive models turn out to be connectionist, then there would be no scientific vindication of commonsense psychological explanation.

The two strategies outlined above promise only to provide us with at least a sense of the possibility space in which a vindication would have to be articulated. They cannot provide the vindication itself; nor can they convince us that none is to be had. But, pursued sufficiently far, they might well convince us that a vindication of commonsense psychological explanation was no longer worth worrying about. For if we were to discover that a vindication seemed possible in principle (or that it seemed impossible), that would presumably empty the problem of its philosophical interest.

NOTES

I have profited from discussions of this chapter with Frances Egan, whose views are largely sympathetic with those expressed here. I would also like to thank Shaun Nichols and Alastair Tait for their helpful comments and criticisms.
1 See, for example, Marcus (1980); Berwick (1986).
2 See, for example, Stabler (1983); Matthews (1988).
3 See Fodor (1975a;1987d).

9

Speaking Up for Darwin

RUTH GARRETT MILLIKAN

Trying to arrest Jerry Fodor's views on naturalization of semantic content is rather like trying to arrest Mr Toad for traffic violations. You can take down the license number but before you have written the ticket he has smashed that motorcar, purchased a new and shinier one, and is off once again, loudly crying "Poop! Poop!" Still, it is heartening that Fodor now acknowledges that you can't win Uncle Wilifred's game of mental representations[1] without a theory of mental semantic content, that is, without a theory of what mental representations *are*. I also find it heartening that Fodor doesn't like, any better than I do, Uncle Wilifred's original strategy of using language of thought entry and exit transitions and inference rules – causal role – for the purpose of capturing content. But there is another feature of Uncle Wilifred's style of play that it really would be wise of Fodor to emulate.

Wilfrid Sellars taught us that truth and meaning and even "representing" (the last only, for Sellars, is a sort of correspondence relation) are all entangled in the "logical order," and that the logical order is part of the *normative* order. Meaning and truth cannot be naturalized without a theory that naturalizes norms generally. Sellars followed Wittgenstein, grounding his theory of norms in community. An alternative, some of us have argued, is to ground the needed norms in evolutionary biology – to let Darwinian natural purposes set the standards against which failures, untruths, incorrectnesses, etc. are measured. Fodor will have none of this. But it is exactly Fodor's inability to supply the needed normative dimension to meaning and truth that has kept tripping him up in his attempts to naturalize semantic content for the language of thought. And Fodor's rejection of Darwin's offer to provide the needed normativity has been based on misunderstandings. It is true that the Darwinian program cannot be carried through in the manner that Fodor once hoped. But Fodor's arguments against Fodor's own abandoned program should not be confused with arguments against Darwin.

I

I will begin with Fodor's *Psychosemantics* (Fodor, 1987d). Decorum requires, I suppose, that one acknowledge the published work, even though already half-orphaned, before considering the unpublished. (The chore does induce a

151

certain lassitude, however. My whispered advice is to skip directly to part II.) My purpose will not be serious criticism of the theory of content in *Psychosemantics*. Others have fairly swarmed to that task, guesses about what Fodor might have meant already well outnumber the interpreters, and Fodor is in the midst of clarifying and revising his theory in a manuscript called "A theory of content" (in press-f). My primary purpose will be to bring out the contrast between the sort of program that Fodor initiated in *Psychosemantics* and an approach that would tackle the normative dimension of meaning head-on. I will, however, introduce a few skeptical remarks, for whatever they are worth, as I proceed.

Fodor's strategy in *Psychosemantics* for locating the source of semantic content for mental representations is to begin with what he believes would be an ideal solution to the problem if it were only available, then hunt for a limited domain in which this solution actually is available. If only it were the case that occurrences of mental representations in one's "belief box" in fact covaried with what these representations were about, Fodor wistfully muses, this simple covariation could determine content. But of course there is in fact no such covariation. Numerous representations enter the belief box that do not correspond as they should to the world but instead are false. And a vanishingly small proportion of the infinite number of occurrences in the world that our systems of inner representation are capable of representing, actually get represented in the belief box: most truths we never know. But perhaps, Fodor thinks, we might narrow the focus, restrict the conditions, until just that narrow range of cases remains in which there *is* necessary covariation between the world and our beliefs. Perhaps that narrow range can be used to define content. That is, rather than treating reliability and completeness of the belief set as norms that define an *ideal* for one's cognitive systems and then attempting to naturalize the normative, Fodor will attempt to delimit conditions under which the relevant norms are facts. If we can delimit a domain in which cognition is, in fact, infallible and perfect, where the ideal equals the real, then we can define content without reference to the ideal.

Fodor's first move is to exclude every type of belief fixation except perceptual judgment, indeed, except indexical perceptual judgment: "That is red," "Here is a horse," etc. Then he divides the issue. First, how do we exclude cases of false perceptual judgment? Second, how do we account for failures to judge at all, for absences of judgments about existing items in the world?

At one time (1984a, 1985b) Fodor entertained the idea that there were special content-fixing circumstances, which he called "optimal circumstances," under which perceptual beliefs are invariably true. The reference to "optimal circumstances" was to be cashed by reference to biological norms. Soon I will take up Fodor's reasons for abandoning this project. In *Psychosemantics*, Fodor deals with the problem of false perceptual beliefs, beliefs "produced by the wrong causes," by claiming that there is an asymmetrical dependency of incorrect tokenings of a perceptual belief type upon the causal processes that lead to its correct tokenings. One way he explains this is to claim that, schematically, where 'A's are mental representations of A's, but B's sometimes cause (false or, as Fodor puts it, "wild") 'A' tokens, then it is so that:

1 A's cause 'A's.
2 'A' tokens are *not* caused by B's in nearby worlds in which A's *don't* cause 'A's.

3 A's cause 'A's in nearby worlds in which B's don't cause 'A's.

(Psychosemantics: 108–9)

As an example, Fodor suggests letting 'A' be a mental term 'horse,' letting A's be horses, and letting B's be cows that have been mistaken for horses. The problem to be solved is to tell why, if either horses or cows *can* cause 'horses,' it isn't the case that 'horse' means *horse or cow*. Hence he calls it "the disjunction problem."

In giving the above solution to the disjunction problem, Fodor doesn't tell us – and I, for one, find this very confusing – whether the "nearby worlds" to which he refers are to be worlds in which the A's and/or B's are different from those in this world (say, the cows are purple, or the horses nonexistent or zebra-striped) or whether they are worlds in which the perceptual-cognitive systems are different (say, there are slightly different filters on horse or cow perception), or worlds where mediation conditions are different (say, cow-smells travel with the speed of light). (Clearly *something* would have to vary to make the antecedents of the relevant conditionals true.) But in any event, the strategy seems to reduce more or less to this: 'A's represent A's iff the current head-world scene is closer to scenes in which 'A's are infallibly produced by A's than to scenes in which they are infallibly produced by B's – or by any other category of non-A's. Compare: if we wish to know whether that is really a heffalump trap or whether it is, rather, really a Pooh trap, we should check to see whether it would be easier to filter out just the heffalumps or to filter out just the Poohs from getting stuck there – check to see which of those worlds is the "nearer." Say, if Poohs don't get stuck in those nearby worlds where heffalumps don't, but heffalumps do get stuck in nearby worlds in which Poohs don't, then it is a heffalump trap. (Failing an asymmetrical result, the trap would be disjunctive – it would be a heffalump-or-Pooh trap.) Translating into terms of real vs. ideal, the ideal here appears not as what actually happens in some restricted set of cases, but as whatever form of perfection the real comes closest to.

The quickest reason this doesn't work, it seems to me, is this. There are cases in which the route from A's to 'A's is such that it traps B's in precisely the same manner, for precisely the same reasons, that it traps A's. For example, many people discriminate birch trees so poorly that they take poplars to be birches whenever encountered. (For most such people, the poplar encounters are correspondingly infrequent, but not for all.) For these people, the powers of birches and of poplars to produce mental 'birch' tokens are precisely the same powers; neither is more perfect than the other nor easier to eliminate than the other. Yet it is poplars these people mistake for birches (why *does* it nearly always go that way?) not birches for poplars – nor are these people's 'birch' thoughts disjunctive. Nor can Fodor fall back on the position that this asymmetry results from the meaning's being mediated by a prior intention to track the English word "birch." This route obviously would lead to a regress in the naturalistic definition of intentionality, and/or to holism, which Fodor is determined to avoid. The lesson seems perfectly clear: a perceptual recognition technique does not a determinate concept make; atomistic verificationism doesn't wash.

Fodor has a second way with the disjunction problem which goes a little differently. If 'A's mean A rather than A-or-B this will be because the fact that B's cause 'A's depends on the fact that A's cause 'A's but not the other way around. Compare: it's a heffalump trap if Poohs fall in it only because heffalumps do but it's not the case that heffalumps fall in it only because Poohs do. Here the ideal appears as the more fundamental, as that on which the merely real rides piggyback.

But if I may play the role of G. E. Moore here for a moment, what on earth can it *mean* to say that one causal relation "depends" on another? Fodor rules out that the dependency should be temporal. The idea is not supposed to be that Poohs now fall in the trap only because heffalumps did in the past. Rather, the causal dependency is to be "synchronic." I cannot think of anything this could mean, unless that the causal link or process corresponding to the first causal relation actually contains or *includes* the causal link corresponding to the second, either as part of itself, or as producing a necessary condition for its holding. Thus the heffalump trap might catch Poohs only by using heffalumps for bait, so that a heffalump's falling in is part of the process by which it catches Poohs. Similarly, if cows managed to produce 'horse's only by herding horses into view, then the route from cows to 'horse's would indeed depend on the route from horses to 'horse's. But that's not, of course, how it goes.

Nor will this suggestion do (which Cummins (1989), at least, takes to be the correct reading of Fodor here): cows cause 'horses' only by causing horsey looks, whereas horses don't need to cause cowy looks in order to cause 'horse's. Hence cows *poach* on the horse to 'horse' connection, but not vice versa. Compare: Poohs must travel some distance on a heffalump path before they fall in whereas heffalumps need not travel any Pooh paths to fall in. But how do you determine that the path that both Poohs and heffalumps must travel in order to fall in is indeed just a heffalump path and not a heffalump-or-Pooh path? Remember that the dependency is to be "synchronic," e.g., it cannot be a heffalump path in the relevant sense only because it was heffalumps that *made* it or because only heffalumps have traveled it in the past. Similarly, how is "horsey look" to be defined here? It cannot be defined as a look that only horses can cause, since by hypothesis cows can cause this kind of look too. (On that reading what gets caused would be horse-or-cow-y looks.) Nor can it be defined as a look that causes 'horse's, for unless we assume what we are trying to prove, namely that 'horse' means horse, this will not yield *any* connection, hence obviously will not yield the desired connection, with horses. And "horsey look" cannot be defined as a look that causes whatever-mental-term-stands-for-horses, for our problem is to determine which term that is; we cannot presuppose that we know that without regress. Any other suggestions?

Well, I have one. What I very strongly suspect is that the asymmetrical dependency relation that Fodor senses is not a causal dependency at all, but a teleological dependency. It is an accident of the design of the programs whose *function* is to provide a causal route from horses to 'horse's that they also sometimes provide a route from cows to 'horse's. In that sense and in that sense only, it is "only because" there is a route from horses to 'horse's that there is a route from cows to 'horse's and not vice versa. The "because" here is teleological.

The other side of Fodor's problem is to account for the fact that horses produce so few 'horses'. I had written a few paragraphs suggesting that *Psychosemantics* seems to be rather far from solving that problem. But it appears that in "A theory of content", which I have just received (it is a March 1989 version), Fodor opines that this second side of the content problem is a false problem. Good!

II

It is clear that Fodor's program in *Psychosemantics* for naturalizing mental semantic content falls short of the mark. A puzzling fact is that earlier (in 1984a and 1985b) Fodor clearly had it in mind to apply a more general strategy to the problem, using the notion of biological purpose or function to set a standard, a norm, in terms of which mental truth and meaning might be defined. Had he given us good clear reasons for abandoning this tack, the jury-rigged views in *Psychosemantics* might command our sympathy if not our allegiance. But *Psychosemantics* gives us only the most shaky of reasons for abandoning teleology. Let us take a look at them. There are three.

The teleological story that Fodor once had in mind, he tells us, interprets the content fixing conditions for symbols in the belief box as conditions under which "the mechanisms of belief fixation are functioning as they are supposed to" (p. 105). Fodor terms these conditions "optimal circumstances." "We could then hold that a [mental] symbol expresses its 'optimal' property; viz., the property that would causally control its tokening in optimal circumstances" (p. 104).

> The story has it that only A's cause 'A's in optimal circumstances; hence, that when the mechanisms of belief fixation are operating properly the beliefs they fix are true. But how do we know . . . that the mechanisms of belief fixation *are* designed always to deliver truths? Suppose some of these mechanisms are designed to *repress* truths; truths, for example, the acknowledgement of which would be unbearable. Clearly we can't define "optimal circumstances" in terms of the teleology of *those* mechanisms.
> . . . But there's no obvious way to weed mechanisms of repression out of the definition of optimality unless we can independently identify them *as* mechanisms of repression . . .
> . . . there is no guarantee that the kind of optimality that teleology constructs has much to do with the kind of optimality that the explication of 'truth' requires.
>
> (pp. 106–7)

That argument has the feel of sand thrown in the eyes, and like sand in the eyes, it needs a little care to remedy. Let us try the following comparison.

Suppose that you wish to know what constitute nutrients for a heffalump, what is nourishing for it to eat. (Pooh and Piglet, you recall, were uncertain about this.) You might try to begin by considering the heffalump's mechanisms for stomach-contents-fixation. Surely, you may think, *nutritious* stomach contents, for heffalumps, will be the same as what the heffalump's stomach-contents-fixers put in the stomach when operating properly under optimal conditions? But alas, the heffalump, besides having sense organs for detecting its food and paws (or was it a trunk?) for stuffing it in, also has (as do many modern mammal species but few others) specialized mechanisms for regurgitating the stomach's contents under certain conditions. Sadly, these mechanisms often must regurgitate even contents that are chock full of nutrition, should these contents contain poison as well. These mechanisms are obviously stomach-contents-fixers too: when they function properly they determine the stomach to be stark (Pooh says, "eleven o'clock-ishly") empty. And optimal conditions for *them* to function properly have nothing to do with whether the stomach contents are nutritious or not. These optimal conditions include only poison in the environment, then in the stomach, for only under these conditions is the operation of the vomiting reflex of any use to the biological system. "There is no guarantee," it seems, that the kind of optimality that teleology constructs has much to do with the kind of optimality that the explanation of [nutrition] requires" either.

It does look as though we had better start over.

Suppose we ask this: how did we know which *was* the heffalump's stomach? (After all, not every useful-place-to-put-things-in is a stomach. It might be a pouch.) That this is the stomach, we tell by knowing or guessing its *function*. Its function must be, minimally, to head a process that ends by fueling metabolic processes in the heffalump's cells. This doesn't mean, of course, that it *actually* heads such a process. It may *actually* head only processes of poisoning (hence the vomiting reflex). Rather, it is *supposed* to head such a process: that is its teleofunction, not necessarily its mechanofunction. Now by looking to the teleofunction of the stomach, we also see that only some of the mechanisms that control the stomach's contents help to produce (optimal conditions for) the stomach's proper operation, (optimal conditions for) its heading up a process that ends, in the normal way, with metabolism in the cells. The vomiting reflex is not one of these mechanisms. It has nothing to do with nutrition. Moreover, we see that what constitutes nutrition for the heffalump is *initially* determined not by looking to the stomach-contents-fixers but by looking to the stomach itself. It is determined by the *stomach's* function. Nutritious contents are contents that supply optimal conditions for the stomach's proper function of facilitating cell metabolism.

Similarly, let us press the question, how do we know which is the belief box? About this, Fodor says, "Remember that we're assuming a functional theory of *believing* (though not, of course, a functional theory of *believing that* p . . .). On this assumption, having a belief is just being in a state with a certain causal role" (p. 105). *Right There* Fodor has abandoned the teleological view that he claims he is putting to the test. For on a teleological analysis, the belief box will have to be defined by its teleofunction, not by its causal disposition, not by its mechanofunction. Or it will have to be defined by the teleofunction, not the mechanofunction, of its contents.

If, following Fodor, we look only to what all beliefs are *actually* disposed to do, we will find only things that both true *and false* beliefs do, hence nothing to distinguish between these. What true and false beliefs both do, assuming, of course, an intact organism, is to move one another about in the head, and to help produce efferent nerve firings, in accordance, perhaps, with certain specifiable internal patterns of arrangement. Coversely, the difference between true and false beliefs obviously is not to be found by inspecting any of these arrangements in the head. Being very accurate, participation in these specified internal arrangements *is*, actually, *one* teleofunction of beliefs. That is what the (clearly normative) reference to "intact organism" abbreviates. But the teleofunctions that mark off true from false beliefs are performed, *when* they are performed, not inside the organism, but within the wider (intact) organism-environment system.

Let us ask, then, about the wider teleofunction of the things that belong in the belief box. How are they used? Well, these items are supposed to combine with other beliefs and with desires to yield life sustaining and enhancing actions. That will do for a starter. True beliefs now appear as those that supply optimal belief-box contents, optimal conditions for the belief-using systems to perform these wider functions in a normal way (i.e., not just by accident, as when you mistakenly think "that's a dime on the sidewalk," pause to pick it up, hence avoid being run over by a sudden truck). These optimal conditions are that the beliefs should be mapping, so, onto the world, i.e., that there obtain a certain well defined correspondence between them and the world.

Fodor's mechanisms of belief repression now appear, of course, as interrupters of these wider teleofunctions, not as mechanisms that help to condition their proper performance. Similarly, the vomiting reflex serves to interrupt rather than to condition proper performance of digestion.

That was Fodor's first attempt to scotch teleology. Here is his second:

> ... there's no obvious reason why conditions that are optimal for the tokening of one sort of mental symbol need be optimal for the tokening of other sorts. Perhaps the optimal conditions for fixing beliefs about very large objects (you do best from the middle distance) are different from the optimal conditions for fixing beliefs about very small ones (you do best from quite close up) ... but this raises the possibility that if we're to say which conditions are optimal for the fixation of a belief, we'll have to know what the content of the belief is – what it's a belief *about*.
>
> (p. 106)

Similarly, conditions that are optimal for the vomiting reflex to perform its proper function of ridding the digestive system of poison include that there be poison in the stomach, but this is not an optimal condition for proper performance of the rest of the digestive system. Nor are optimal conditions for one's swimming programs to perform properly the same as for one's walking programs, etc. Optimal conditions are optimal relative to the function to be performed. So of course one must know what the function is before determing optimality. The function of the belief-fixing mechanisms – what they are supposed to do, not what they always do do – is to fix *true* beliefs. So we must know which are the true beliefs before knowing which are the optimal conditions for their fixation. It follows there is something wrong with Fodor's suggestion that the way to introduce teleology into mental semantics is to look for optimality conditions for belief fixation. Obviously that won't do the job. Rather, one needs to look at the functions of the systems that *use* beliefs, at what conditions *they* need to condition their proper operation.

Fodor's third objection to teleology goes this way:

> You can now see why Darwinian teleological apparatus does no good for the purposes at hand. Suppose you *could* get a teleological notion of optimal conditions as – e.g. – the ones that obtain when the cognitive mechanisms are behaving as the forces of selection intended them to. Even so, you still couldn't infer from (a) the presence of a horse and (b) the optimality of the conditions that (c) 'horse' will get tokened. For: there is no Darwinian guarantee that a properly functioning intentional system ipso facto has the concept HORSE (to say nothing of the concept PROTON). And what you don't have, you can't token.
>
> (pp. 116–17)

Crudely, Darwin didn't give us 'horse' concepts and 'electron' concepts, so obviously Darwin can't tell when 'horse' and 'electron' concepts are being properly vs. improperly tokened.

So who *did* give us our 'horse' concepts and our 'electron' concepts? Skinner, perhaps: learning rather than evolution? The results of learning are not Darwin's province. Darwin finished up when we were born – when we were conceived? Darwin oversees nature, Skinner oversees nurture. Darwin is heredity; Skinner is environment. Now Jerry Fodor may be Granny's boy (see Dennett, this volume) but surely his Granny is more sophisticated than that! No. That fact that we learn *what* we do *in the way* we do is as much programmed into us via evolution as the fact that we digest what we do in the way we do.

But, you may say, surely we are not living in the same sort of environment that Nature intended us to. How could Darwin be supervising what we are now learning about jet liners and quarks? Well, how could he be supervising the digestion of Fritos and Coke? Nature doesn't name trade names. Nature lays down *principles* of interaction between organism and environment. Apparently the principles that Nature laid down to govern human language learning, human concept formation and human thought were extremely general, all-purpose principles – a quite noteworthy invention, the mind. But to suppose that you are thinking as you now are about philosophy by accident, say, by genetic drift (though you may, of course, speak for yourself), and not because your brain was selected for thinking – or, being more accurate, *preserved* over the last many generations for thinking, would be more mad than to suppose you were digesting your TV dinner by genetic drift. (For considerably more defense along these lines, see Millikan (1989b, 1990b). For discussion of how processes of concept formation might yield *specific biological functions for specific concepts*, see Millikan (1984: chapters 2, 8, 18, 19) or, for the general plan, Millikan (1990a).

It is worth noting that these three objections that Fodor has raised to Darwin show a common pattern. In each case it is a failure to see that telefunctions must be described by reference to the functioning item's larger environment that trips him. The telos of belief has to do not merely with what happens prior to the belief box, or with what happens in the brain, but also with what transpires via the belief-consuming mechanisms, then via action in the outside world, the effects of which circle round to impinge on the organism again. Similarly, learning differs from other functions in that it more *obviously* loops through the world, more obviously takes place via the environment, than does the completion of other biological functions. In (Millikan, forthcoming a,b) I have argued that it is this same blindness to psychology as an *ecological* biological science that has produced Fodor's methodological solipsism and sent him in search of the grail of narrow content.

III

Fodor's most sustained and recent attacks on Darwin are in "Information and Representation" (in press-b) and in "On there not being an Evolutionary Theory Of Content" (unpublished). Fodor begins these essays with a barbed attack on my work and some shots at David Israel. (For my case, Fodor relies entirely upon an inventive (mis)reading of my (1986), a secondary paper sketching implications of some aspects of my (1984) Darwinian theory of content. On those of his misunderstandings that are understandable, see footnotes 7, 11 and 17 in Millikan (1989b). In his (unpublished) Fodor then settles down to give what he says will now be a "principled argument" against Darwin (private correspondence).[2] Fodor's principles are offended by what appear to him to be sloppy and misleading uses of the "Nature designed it" metaphor among contemporary Darwin admirers, e.g., "what Mother Nature has in mind" (taken from Dennett), "mechanisms that evolution designed with other things in mind" (taken from Millikan). (I have, of course, been merciless with these metaphors throughout.) Mother Nature, Fodor emphasizes, has nothing whatever in mind. In particular, she sorts, selects, so that some things are kept and other things thrown away, but she doesn't sort under any *labels*. When she is done there are things in her domain, and other things that have been excluded, but these have neither been included nor excluded under *descriptions*. At least not under descriptions that are fine-grained enough to yield determinate semantic contents. In particular (Fodor says he is guessing here) "appeals to mechanisms of selection won't decide between *reliably equivalent* content ascriptions; i.e., they won't decide between any pair of equivalent content ascriptions where the equivalence is counterfactual supporting" (unpublished, p. 11).

Fodor takes the familiar example of the frog catching flies. How shall we describe the function of the mechanisms in the frog that accomplish this task? For what were they selected? They catch flies. They also catch little ambient black things. And they catch things in the category FLIES OR BEE-BEES – Fodor says "flee-bees." In the environment in which frogs evolved, we can suppose, these three categories were coextensive, indeed, Fodor assumes, "reliably coextensive." (I honestly don't *understand* the supporting counterfactuals here, let alone know if they are true. But it won't matter.) Nature never had a chance to sort, then, between mechanisms that caught flies but not flee-bees and those that caught both, or between those that caught all little black ambient things and those that caught only flies. So Nature can't be said to have chosen any of these kinds over the others. Similarly, the little wichimacallit detector that fires in the frog's optic nerve to indicate the appearance of a wichimacallit is just as much a flee-bee detector or a little black ambient thing detector as a fly detector. And, we gather, it is only saved from being a what-Granny-hates-more-than-anything-in-her-kitchen detector by the fact that Granny's feelings aren't quite strong enough to support the relevant counterfactuals. After all, "if you always ["reliably"] get Fs when you get Gs then a mechanism that selects Fs [note italics] *thereby* selects Gs, so the utility of being F and that of being G always come out the same" (unpublished, fn. 4). Hence, "contrary to the many advertisements you may have seen – the teleological story about intentionality does not solve the disjunction problem" (unpublished, p. 8). Indeed, it appears to have exacerbated it considerably.

Now the first thing that we should lay on the table, for comparison at least, is the distinction between what is *selected* and what is *selected for*. Sober, in *The Nature of Selection* (1984), illustrates this distinction with a child's toy consisting of filters stacked one above the next, each having holes larger than the ones below. The toy sorts balls that are sealed inside it, only the smallest going through to the bottom layer, the largest remaining on top. Now the smallest balls, Sober tells us, are all green. So the toy selects green balls to go on the bottom layer. But obviously green is not what it selects *for*. It selects *for* size.

It selects for size, not greenness, even if there is a nomological connection between small size and greenness. For example, if the toy selects blueberries, the large blue ripe ones staying on top, the middle-sized red almost-mature ones sticking in the middle, the tiny completely immature green ones falling through to the bottom, it still selects for size, not for greenness. What a system selects *for* depends upon the causal *mechanisms* of selection, in particular, upon the properties one has to mention in giving a causal explanation of how some items got selected in while others were selected out. Many properties, such as the greenness of the balls (or the blueberries) in the bottom layer of Sober's toy, are not *causes* of the selection process. Their presence is merely an *effect* of the selection process.

Because Granny's distaste for flies developed after the evolution of the frog's fly-catching mechanisms, it obviously is not a candidate for a cause of the selection of these mechanisms. It is for *this* reason that catching what-annoys-Granny is not one of their functions. Similarly, there are certain other kinds of properties that are not even in the business of being causes or conditions upon which explanations can be based. For example, disjunctive properties are not. Disjunctive properties can enter into the premises of inferences from *knowledge* of earlier situations to *knowledge* of later ones, but this kind of deductive inference from past conditions to future ones often has nothing to do with causal explanation. That the frog's ancestors caught flies-or-bee-bees and there were no bee-bees, is no more part of a causal explanation for proliferation of frogs, than that I caught the measles or the flu and I didn't catch the flu, is part of the causal explanation of my red rash. Hence the frog's fly-catching mechanisms assuredly are not flee-bee catchers; that is not one of their functions.

It is not the disjunction problem, then, that Darwin fails to solve. He solves that problem quite neatly. But there *is* a problem left nonetheless – the very same indeterminacy problem to which Dretske has been calling our attention for several years (1986, 1988). Dretske's key example concerns what the pull of the magnetosomes represents in certain species of northern hemisphere bacteria. These bacteria orient themselves away from toxic oxygen-rich surface water by attending to their magnetosomes, tiny inner magnets, which pull toward the North Pole, hence pull down. (Southern hemisphere bacteria have their magnetosomes reversed.) The function of the magnetosome thus appears to be to effect that the bacterium moves into oxygen-free water. Correlatively, a function of the magnetotactic *system* is to produce signs, states, that accord with the whereabouts of oxygen-free water. But, of course, if one holds a suitably oriented bar magnet overhead, these bacteria will swim up, hence towards toxic water, hence will destory themselves. Dretske comments:

> It was said that it was the function of their magnetotactic system to indicate the whereabouts of oxygen-free environments. But why describe the function of this system in this way? Why not say that it is the function of this system to indicate the direction of geomagnetic north? Perhaps, to be even more modest, this sensor should be assigned the function of indicating the whereabouts (direction) of magnetic (not necessarily *geo magnetic*) north. This primitive sensory mechanism is, after all, functioning perfectly well when, under the bar magnet's influence, it leads its possessor into a toxic environment. *Something* is going wrong in this case, of course, but I see no reason to place the blame on the sensory mechanism, no reason to say it isn't performing *its* function.

Compare Fodor:

> It bears emphasis that *Darwin doesn't care which of these ways you tell the teleogical story.* You can have it that the neural mechanism Normally mediates fly snaps, in which case snaps at bee-bees are ipso facto errors. Or you can have it that the mechanism Normally mediates black dot snaps that are, as one says at Stanford, "situated" in an environment in which black dots are Normally flies. (On the latter reading, it is not the frog but the world that has gone wrong when a frog snaps at a bee-bee; what you've got is a Normal snap in an abNormal situation.)
>
> (unpublished, pp. 9–10)

We can put this problem in terms of what the magnetosome, or the frog's detecting mechanism, was selected *for*. It is clear that both being moved in the direction of the magnetic field and, consequently, under normal conditions, being moved to point towards the whereabouts of oxygen-free water, are equally parts of the explanatory causal mechanism that eventuated in the proliferation of magnetosome-equipped bacteria. And it is clear that both being fired by small opaque moving objects (it is the small-opaque-movingness that causes firing, not the flies *per se*) and being fired when flies are present (due to the normal coextensiveness of these two) are equally parts of the explanatory causal mechanisms that proliferated modern frogs. Hence these various activities *all* correspond to biological functions. Dretske's comment that the magnetosome is "functioning perfectly well when, under the bar magnet's influence, it leads its possessor into a toxic environment" trades on an irrelevant sense of "functioning perfectly well" – the sense in which that means, merely, not being *broken*, i.e., that the organism, not the organism–environment system as a whole, is intact. In that sense, one's digestive system may "function perfectly well" with nothing but barium paste in it, but it certainly is *not* functioning perfectly well in the sense of actually performing its biological functions. Fodor, too, is a bit off center if he thinks that there is an *indeterminacy* about function here. Is the heart's function to pump, or to pump blood? Both, I should think. Is the function of the eyeblink reflex to cause the eye to be covered or to keep out the sand? Well both, presumably; why not? And so with the magnetosome and with the frog's detecting mechanisms; they have multiple functions.

Before examining the effect upon the content question of the distressing discovery that items can have multiple biological functions, it is worth noting that this multiplicity has nothing to do with coextensiveness. The eyeblink reflex mechanism may produce coverings of the eyes dozens of times before it ever actually bars entrance to any grain of sand. Similarly, allow me to switch for a minute from frogs to goldfish. Goldfish, too, contain a mechanism whereby small specks of material, this time floating in the water, stimulate the eye and nervous system such that they are taken inside the mouth. I assume this, too, is a reflex, and that an appropriate detector fires signals inside the fish. But a very high proportion of what the goldfish sucks into the mouth turns out in fact to be inedible, and is accordingly blown out of the mouth again. What is the function of the taking-in reflex mechanism? Is it supposed to take in little specks? Or is it really supposed to take in food – as the eyeblink reflex is really supposed to keep out the sand? Both, presumably. Natural selection doesn't care about coextensiveness: so long as once in a while one of those specks is a bit of fish food, all is well by Darwin.

Nor should we suppose that there is no *content* problem in the case of the goldfish because of the relatively poor count on detector firings that coincide with food as opposed to those that coincide with specks – because of the lack of coextensivity between these. Consider: rabbit thumps signal rabbit dangers, but given how timid rabbits are, the count on actual correspondences of dangers to thumps is probably quite small. So why shouldn't the fish's detectors signal food, even though they, too, are mostly wrong? (Nor are selection processes interested in the results of such counts, except perhaps as *relative to* the counts on actual competing mechanisms. For considerably more on this, see Millikan (1990b, 1991).

Is there, then, a content problem that results from multiple functions? For Fodor, yes. Here, put somewhat differently this time, is his candidate Darwinian theory of content: "So there are these cognitive mechanisms, and there are these cognitive states; and the [sic] function of the former is to produce instances of the latter upon environmentally appropriate occasions." It is a function of the fly-catching mechanism to fire its detectors when little black ambient specks are about, and also a function of it to fire when flies are about – and also when shadows cross the retina. So Fodor certainly is in trouble.

But Darwin is not. This is not an appropriate place fully to spell out, once again, my own views on content. But at least three crucial departures from the simple Darwinian theory of content that Fodor has had in mind (and that he has been reading into the minds of others) are needed. These are exemplified in detail in Millikan (1984) and abbreviated in (1989b, 1991). First, and at least superficially most important, a shift of focus from the inner representation producers TO THE INNER REPRESENTATION CONSUMERS OR USERS is needed. (When we looked for a theory of nutrition, we found that we had to study *first* what the digestive system *did* with the offerings to the stomach.) Second, a shift from focus upon function to focus upon biologically optimal *conditions* for proper functioning of these consumers is needed. (We discovered heffalump nutrition when we looked to what *conditioned* proper performance on the part of the stomach contents users.) Third (lest nutrition become blurred with representation, nutritiousness with truth), a theory that remarks on the compositional structure of all representations is needed – yes, even the medium of the message of the frog's fly detectors is structured, I have argued, and the magnetosome signal too. Representations always "map" in at least a minimal way, onto what they are about Millikan (1984, 1991).

I tremble to put anything briefly, for the hurried man will snatch it and run – anything light to carry. But putting things VERY CRUDELY, inner representations are distinguished by the fact that (1) it is a proper function of some mechanism to produce them – true ones, (2) the true ones are those that map onto the world in accordance with such-and-such specifiable mapping rules, and (3) it is a condition for proper functioning, in accordance with an historically typical explanation for proper performance, of the mechanisms that use the representations, that the representations in fact are corresponding to the world by these rules – which is what it means to say that these rules define truth for the inner representational system.

Ignoring, for simplicity, what is in the end actually the most crucial of details – the mapping of representations, their essential membership in a *system* of representation – VERY CRUDELY the solution to the magnetosome and the fly detector problems is this. The mechanisms THAT USE the magnetosome's offerings don't care at all whether the magnet points to magnetic north, geomagnetic north or, say, to the North Star. The only one of the conditions Dretske mentioned that is necessary FOR THE USER'S PROPER FUNCTIONING is that the magnet point in the direction of lesser oxygen. So lesser oxygen is what it means. Similarly, the systems that use, that respond to, the frog's fly detector's signals, don't care at all whether these correspond to anything black or ambient or specklike, but only whether they correspond to frog food. In particular, they do not care at all *how it came about* that the firings correspond to frog food – a live electrode intruding in the nerve in the right place causing firing at the right time would be perfectly fine by these systems, so long as some food coincided. So the firing means frog food. (Similarly, even though the fish's food detectors are absurdly inefficient, even though they are wrong a large portion of the time, they still signal fish food, not floating specks.)

But in order to make any of this work, you have to be careful. You can't be sloppy and run everything so together. You need, among other things, a clear definition of "(proper) function" (teleofunction), another for "normal explanation for proper performance of function," a careful analysis of how things like beliefs can be said to have functions (concepts are indeed learned, so we must understand how the results of learning and its applications have biological functions), and a careful definition of "mapping" or of "compositional structure." For these, see Millikan (1984; chapters 1, 2, 6, 8, 9, 18, 19 – also 1989a, 1990, 1991, forthcoming b).

I would like to add a couple of final observations on determinacy of content for those who are still attracted to the idea of getting Darwin to determine it for us. If it is true that content falls out of normal conditions for *usefulness* of representations, then how determinate Darwin's content designations are will depend on how picky the representation users are. In (1984, 1986, 1989b) I have argued that human beliefs are probably distinguished from most other inner representations harbored by members of the animal kingdom, in part by the fact that they participate in inference processes. And I have argued (1984: ch. 15) that mediate inference involves the performance of acts of *identifying* the content of one's representations. Here, I suggest, is where Darwin starts to get very picky indeed. It is systems that need to perform numerous acts of identifying that are most capable of zeroing in on content.

A second suggestion follows from the view that representations are like maps. Maps can map the same area while being different in their projections and details. Content is a function of projection and detail, not merely of denotation. Thus, reliance on Darwin is perfectly compatible with a theory that handles coextensive but distinguishable contents.[3, 4]

NOTES

1   The allusion is to Fodor (1985b).

2   This principled argument seems to recur – along with now mildly watered-down Millikan misreadings – in Fodor (in press-f) of March 1989. My page references below are to Fodor (unpublished).

3   For a Darwin-inspired solution to the birch–poplar problem raised in section I above,

see Millikan (1984: ch. 9).

4 My gratitude to Peter Godfrey-Smith for prodding me to clarify the text in several places.

10

Fodor and Psychological Explanations

JOHN PERRY AND DAVID ISRAEL

1 Introduction

1.1 The Texts

We begin with some quotations from Fodor.

> [I]t is crucial to the whole program of explaining behavior by reference to mental states that the propositional attitudes belonging to these [causal] chains are typically non-arbitrarily related in respect to their content (taking "content" of a propositional attitude, informally, to be whatever it is that the complement of the corresponding PA-ascribing sentence expresses). One can imagine the occurrence of causal chains of mental states which are not otherwise related (as, e.g., a thought that two is a prime number, causing a desire for tea . . .) . . . Still if all our mental life were like this, it's hard to see what point ascriptions of contents to mental states would have . . . The paradigm situation – the grist for the cognitivist's mill – is the one where the propositional attitudes interact causally and do so in virtue of their content. And the paradigm of this paradigm is the practical syllogism . . . John believes that it will rain if he washes his car. John wants it to rain. So John acts in a manner intended to be a car-washing . . . Our common-sense psychological generalizations relate mental states in virtue of their content . . .
>
> (1981c: 182–4)

> I dearly wish that I could leave this topic here, because it would be very convenient to be able to say, without qualification, what I strongly implied above: the opaque readings of propositional attitude ascriptions tell us how people represent the objects of their propositional attitudes . . .
>
> (Fodor, 236)

> What I think is exactly right is that the construal of propositional attitudes which such a psychology renders is nontransparent . . . The trouble is that nontransparency isn't quite the same notion as opacity, as we shall now see.
>
> (ibid: 236)

> Having said all this, I now propose largely to ignore it . . .
>
> (ibid: 239)

2   The Contents and Causal Powers of Tokens of Mentalese

Fodor takes propositional attitudes to be relations to tokens of an internal language ("Mentalese") that have content. If Jerry believes that P, Jerry has a token of mentalese in his belief structure that has the content that P. These tokens have causal properties as well as content; they are related in law-like ways in virtue of their causal properties. But the laws must (in the paradigm cases that are grist for the cognitivist's mill) make sense in terms of the contents of the tokens. It is the contents that are related in commonsense psychological principles, and it is the meshing of content and causal properties that makes it conceivable that cognitive psychology might work.

What exactly is the relation between the contents and causal properties of tokens? The first quotation above, from "Propositional Attitudes", suggests a simple answer: tokens interact as they do in virtue of their content. But Fodor begins "Methodological solipsism" with a quotation from Hume that states a problem for this view.

> ... to form the idea of an object and to form an idea simply is the same thing; the reference of the idea to an object being an extraneous denomination, of which in itself it bears no mark or character.[1]

The fact that my idea of red is an idea of one color rather than another is an *external denomination* – a relation between the idea and a color – not something that can influence the way it interacts with other ideas. The view that emerges in "Methodological solipsism" is not that tokens interact in virtue of their contents, but that both the causal facts and the content facts about a token are settled by its *formal* properties. The formal properties are, roughly, those that a processor scanning the tokens can detect and by which its actions can be systematically determined. If both the contents and the causal powers of a token depend on its form, the two kinds of properties might mesh in the ways necessary to have the content-based principles of cognitive psychology (or commonsense psychology) backed by causal laws relating formally individuated states. One imagines a species-wide causal role for a given type of token and a species-wide interpretive function that assigns contents to types. The two mesh so that, for example, within the human species, if a belief and a desire cause a volition, then the contents of the belief, desire, and volition have some sensible, rational connection with one another.

One imagines the interpretive function fixing the reference of a certain formal type as the property of being red, once and for all – the same for each member of a cognizing species. But it seems that the reference of many of our ideas is not only external, but *circumstantial*. The interpretive function and the formal properties of a token do not fully determine the reference; particular circumstances that vary among formally identical tokens, also must be taken into account. Suppose, for example, that Jerry is looking at a cup. The cup that he is looking at will be the referent of the Mentalese phrases that are analogues to "the cup in front of me" or "that cup." Tokens of the same Mentalese phrases, in the head of someone else, looking at a different cup, will have different referents.[2]

How can causal and content properties of tokens mesh, if the content properties of a token depend both on its form and on such particular external circumstances, while the causal properties depend on form alone? If contents are sensitive to external circumstances, and so classify persons who are internally similar as different, and those who are internally different as similar, how can content-based principles of rationality mesh with causal laws?

If such circumstantially determined external references of phrases become part of the truth-conditions of the sentences in which they occur, then those truth conditions will also be infected with circumstantiality. It seems a causally coherent psychology should not individuate states in terms of such external denominations. But the contents that are ascribed to mental states by our practices of propositional attitude reporting are often based on just such circumstantially determined external denominations. The contents that a person believes and the people who are counted as believing the same thing, depend in part on external facts about reference and hence on nonformal properties of their tokens. As a result, people with formally identical tokens may believe different things; people with formally differing tokens may believe the same thing.

Fodor would have liked the following response to this worry to work.

> Transparent reports of attitudes do classify mental states in a circumstantial, nonformal way. But because this is so, we do not take transparent reports to tell us how the agent is thinking, and for this reason explanations using transparent reports are impotent. But opaque reports are explanatorily valuable, because they do tell us how agents think; they can do this because they don't classify mental states circumstantially, but in terms of contents that mesh with formal properties.

But in the remarks quoted above from "Methodological Solipsism," he indicates that this response is not quite right. Even opaque reports rely on circumstantial classification. In effect, he postulates a level of *fully opaque (nontransparent)* content that works the way he had hoped the opaque classification would. But he does not provide very many details.[3]

In this paper we sketch a theory, within a Fodorian conception of cognition, of how the formal properties and external circumstances of tokens relate to the contents of tokens, and of how commonsense explanations might work given this framework. We conclude that

- Circumstantially determined content properties can mesh with causal properties.
- Attitude reports in terms of circumstantially determined content can be explanatory, that is, can enter into adequate psychological explanations.
- It is scarcely conceivable that some content properties not be circumstantially determined.

Like Fodor, we believe cognitive psychology is possible, and that there are strong empirical arguments in favor, and only weak and avoidable arguments against, the thesis that a *component* of that psychology will be individualistic. We think of ourselves as providing a way of looking at content and content-based explanations that should be helpful to those, like Fodor and ourselves, who believe cognitive psychology can and should include such an individualistic component. There are, nevertheless, some points of disagreement between us and Fodor on the topics covered in this essay. We think transparent explanations can work well; Fodor does not. In our reconstruction, even fully opaque attitude reports will be somewhat circumstantial. We provide a completely noncircumstantial level of content, but claim that to understand the rationality of laws, one needs to bring in the (admittedly rather modest) circumstance that the relevant tokens of mentalese belong to the same agent.

2.1   A Broader Context of Disagreement

Given the amicable goal of this essay, perhaps we should indicate some broad areas of disagreement before plunging in. Like Fodor, we conceive of individualistic cognitive psychology as requiring structured internal states that have both content and causal role. And like him, we believe that the postulation of such states is empirically reasonable and that the success and structure of our ordinary psychological concepts provides important evidence for it. We are inclined, however, to think that Fodor's talk of the language of thought and mentalese may encourage the assumption that the internal structures are more language-like than there is any reason to believe. And we worry about whether the notion of *formality* coalesces conditions from a number of different areas that have less in common than Fodor thinks that they do.[4] But for the purposes of this paper we set aside these worries.

Other areas of disagreement concern questions of how the causal and content properties of internal states relate to one another. An important issue is the source of what we shall call the interpretive function, which assigns contents to formally individuated mental states. We sympathize with the aim and intent of approaches that see content properties as ultimately reducible (in some weak sense) to causal properties, with a role for information "Wisconsin style." But we do not think that any such reduction to causal/informational concepts can succeed. Our own view is a sort of naturalistic functionalism that stresses *functions* and *purposes* – hence, the results of actions measured in terms of degree of success in bringing about some specified condition – in the classification of mental states. We are inclined to think, with Dennett, that the distinction between merely attributed intentionality and real intentionality can be understood within this framework, rather than constituting a refutation of it. From this perspective, we try to practice an approach that is an amalgam of the design-oriented approach of work in artificial intelligence with H. P. Grice's conceptual creature construction.[5] This approach seeks to understand intentionality through understanding the reasons that intentionalistic theories are useful in dealing with (or designing) various systems, beginning with very subhuman systems. We think that cognitive psychology depends on naturalistic psychology and that Fodor's arguments against the possibility of the latter are not very convincing.[6]

From both our perspective and Fodor's, it is necessary to have an account of how the contents and causal powers of the structured states of individual intelligent beings can mesh in the way presupposed by common sense and by cognitive psychology. We try to provide such an account in this paper.

2.2 An Example

We shall look closely at an example that brings out the problems that concern us. Suppose Jerry wants to drink some decaffeinated coffee. He sees before him a brown cup, c; just a few seconds before, he had seen a brown cup being filled with what he believed was decaffeinated coffee. He moves his arm and hand in a complicated manner, grasping the cup, lifting it to his lips at an angle as he tilts his head a bit, and opens his mouth. Call this type of movement M for later reference. In Jerry's circumstances, this movement constitutes picking up the cup and bringing it to his lips. Gravity and his digestive system take over, and he gets what he wants. The explanation of Jerry's doings might go like this:

Why did Jerry decide to pick up the cup and bring it to his lips?

He wanted to drink some decaffeinated coffee, and he believed that the cup in front of him was filled with decaffeinated coffee.

This example can be used to illustrate the problems engendered by the fact that common sense psychology classifies mental states in terms of external, circumstantial denominations. We explain Jerry's action by citing a belief and a desire. The belief and the desire make sense of the action. The action will promote the satisfaction of the desire if the belief is true. But the way the belief, desire, and action are individuated appears to depend on factors external to the formal properties of the mental tokens involved. One way to see this is by focusing on what we count as having *the same belief*. Construed transparently, the belief attributed to Jerry is individuated in terms of a certain cup c, rather than the way Jerry thinks of it. Someone would agree with Jerry – would have the same belief – who believed that c contained decaffeinated coffee, no matter how the other person thought of c. Yet only the ways of thinking, not the external reference, could conceivably be correlated with the formal properties of belief tokens.

Construed opaquely, things are a bit better. But the belief still seems to be individuated in terms of Jerry.[7] As Fodor points out, opaque attributions still allow some slack as to how the agent is thinking. Someone else, who is looking both at Jerry and at c but thinking "The cup in front of him contains decaffeinated coffee," would be said to believe the same thing that Jerry does. But then it is at least possible that Jerry could believe just what he does, opaquely construed, while being in a different state.[8] Perhaps, sitting in a restaurant, gazing in a mirror while waiting impatiently for his cup of decaf, Jerry sees a waitress fill a customer's cup from the pot with the characteristic decaf indicator – the pot has an orange neck. He thinks, "Now the cup in front of him contains decaffeinated coffee . . . I wonder when the cup in front of me will do so." In such a circumstance, it would be misleading to report that Jerry believes the cup in front of him contains decaffeinated coffee; but would it be incorrect, would what the reporter said be false? It seems not, for as we noted, someone else, who thinks "The cup in front of that man contains decaffeinated coffee," with reference to Jerry, would be counted as believing just what Jerry believes when Jerry thinks "The cup in front of me contains decaffeinated coffee."[9] So it seems that opaque attitude reports also do not focus exclusively on the sorts of intrinsic (formal) properties needed by a causal theory of mind.[10]

3   The Need for Circumstantial Content

Fodor uses the phrase "object of an attitude" to refer to the mentalese tokens that are involved in cognition according to his theory. We try to avoid this phrase, which is often used instead for what we shall call *the contents of the propositional attitudes*. We assume that the tokens have contents, and that these contents are referred to by the complements of attitude reports. So "*A* believes that *P*" means, roughly, that *A* has in his head a belief token, whose content is that *P*. We take these contents, the *designata* of phrases of the form "that *P*," to be propositions. Propositions are truth-evaluable; that is, not true or false as spoken by one person, or at one time, but simply true or false.[11] We use "believes that . . . ," "desires that . . . ," and "intends that . . ." as canonical forms for reporting beliefs, desires, and volitions.[12]

Sentences in ordinary language may be separated into those that are *eternal* and those that are *context-sensitive*. Different utterances of an eternal sentence express the same proposition. The class of eternal sentences is arguably empty, but sentences such as "$7 + 5 = 12$" and "The first person born in the twenty-first century was, is, or will be a philosopher" are at least candidates.[13] Different utterances of context-sensitive sentences express different propositions, depending on such factors of the utterance as the agent, the time, the persons the agent is addressing, the objects the agent is attending to, and other wider circumstances. The class of context-sensitive sentences includes those with indexicals, demonstratives, tense markers, and, arguably, proper names. Thus if Jerry and Zenon each say, "The cup in front of me contains coffee," they express different propositions that may be true and false independently. Context-sensitive sentences in mentalese will work the same way; if Jerry and Zenon each have "The cup in front of me contains coffee" (= *S*) written in their belief structure, they will believe different things. But is there any reason to suppose that there are context-sensitive sentences in mentalese? What reasons would a psychological theory that adopted Fodor's language of thought hypothesis have to include such sentences in the language postulated?

Suppose Jerry and Zenon are each thirsty, and each has a cup of coffee in front of him. They each execute movement *M*, and each satisfies his desire. Both the similarities and differences are easy to conceive, if we suppose that the beliefs Jerry and Zenon have are context-sensitive – in particular, if what they believe, in virtue of the occurrence of a token of *S* in their heads, is systematically related to the same simple fact about that token, namely in whose head it does occur. For instance, we can imagine that Jerry and Zenon have different instances of a certain type *V* of visual impression;[14] that because of these impressions a token of *S* is written in the belief structure of each; and that this, given the presence of "I drink coffee" in the desire structure of each, causes a token of "I pick up the cup in front of me and drink from it," to be written in their volitional structure, which causes each of them to execute *M*. Jerry and Zenon thus go through the same succession of states, and these processes are instances of the same psychological law. But Jerry and Zenon see, believe, desire, intend, and do different things. In particular, what Jerry believes could be true, while what Zenon believes is false, and vice versa. What Jerry believes (that there is a cup in front of Jerry) would not be a good reason for Zenon to execute *M*. It might be true that there is a cup in front of Jerry, while there is an irritable gorilla in front of Zenon. Executing *M* in these circumstances would not be a good idea.

We want to emphasize that it is also important to have beliefs that are less sensitive to context. Consider the case with which we began. Jerry doesn't just want coffee; he wants decaffeinated coffee. A moment or two ago he saw that a certain cup contained decaffeinated coffee. Now suppose that since that time he has left the room; the cup became perceptually inaccessible to him. He needs to be able to store the relevant information about the cup, in a way that retains the same content through the change in context, as he diverts his attention from the cup and leaves the room, and throughout the (short) interval of his absence. And he needs to retain it in a form that will allow him to reidentify the cup upon his return and make use of his knowledge. This requires a way of thinking of the cup that continues to pick out that particular cup through the changes of context. This way of thinking will probably be context-sensitive, but not as context-sensitive as the way of thinking of the cup that is associated with a contemporaneous visual perception of it. For example, he might think of it as "the cup I saw at my table a moment ago." This way of thinking does not shift its reference as Jerry moves about or shifts his attention to other objects.

A (relatively) basic physical action, like the execution of *M*, has different results depending on who does it, when, and in what circumstances. A system of beliefs should lead to the actions that will be successful, relative to one's desires, in the circumstances that make the beliefs true. But humans do not just depend on their perceptions at the time of action to provide them with the beliefs needed for decision and volition, but earlier perceptions, inferences, and the perceptions and inferences of others. In all of these cases in which the pragmatic effect of information is delayed or distanced, ways of preserving content through change of context are needed. It would be very misguided to take the simple and relatively automatic case of picking up a cup of coffee when thirsty as a complete guide to the role of the attitudes. Still, the need for context-sensitive representation never goes away. If he wants to drink the coffee, Jerry still has to pick up the cup in front of him.

Consider, for a different example, Jerry's making a phone call to Zenon. Here the belief, say "Zenon's phone number is 555-5555," is relatively context insensitive. There is the present tense marker, but phone numbers are relatively stable properties of persons, so we can ignore that. When Jerry calls Zenon, the perceptions that originally gave rise to the belief may be remote in time, and the effect of the action that fulfills the goal – the ringing of Zenon's telephone and his answering it – are remote in space. Neither the number nor Zenon needs to be thought of demonstratively or indexically to understand the transaction. But, like all human action – except perhaps pure ratiocination – the crux of the matter involves physical interactions with a physical object. The practical reasoning involved will terminate with some context-sensitive way of thinking about the telephone. The Fodorian version of half of Kant's maxim about concepts and intuitions should be "Eternal tokens of mentalese without context-sensitive tokens of mentalese are blind."

4   The Basic Concepts

4.1   A Fodorian Model of Cognition

We have so far been supposing a Fodorian model; we shall now sketch an extremely simple version of a mentalese account of the structure of cognitive states. We note that states are repeatable types; we shall speak of instances of such. Instances are concrete, nonrepeatable episodes. We shall assume that there are three functionally specified components of the mental states of our agent: the belief component, the appetitive component, and the volitional component. These three components are realized in three distinct, but connected, concrete structures. Conceived of abstractly, that is, functionally, each of these is like a file, into which tokens of sentences are written, in which they can be stored and manipulated in various ways, and from which they can be read. We shall further assume that Mentalese is a lot like English; indeed, we shall assume that it is English.[15] With reference to the first example, we might expect to find the following in Jerry's mind:

- In the belief structure, a token of "The cup in front of me has decaffeinated coffee in it."
- In the appetitive structure, a token of "I drink some decaffeinated coffee."
- In the volitional structure, a token of "I pick up the cup and bring it to my lips."

These tokens are concrete structures, characterizable in many different ways. We have classified them by their syntactic type, given that they are tokens of English. This leaves open many difficult questions about the relations between type and token; we shall ignore these here. We can classify agents in many different ways, too, of course. We introduce three relational symbols, $thinks_B$, $thinks_D$, and $thinks_V$ for the relations that hold of an agent A, a time t, and a type T, just in case there is a token of type T in A's belief (appetitive, volitional) structure at t. We shall usually ignore the temporal *relatum*. We shall also treat these symbols as if they were transitive verbs. Thus $thinking_D$ "I drink some decaffeinated coffee" is an appetitive state and is also a (partial) mental state. Many different agents, at different times and locations, can be in that mental state, with or without being in the $thinks_B$ state we supposed Jerry to be in. Of course, no two instances of these states are identical; we leave open the possibility that a single agent, at a single time, can have two distinct tokens of the same type in one of its mental structures.

Following Fodor, we shall assume that there is a single central processor, which can read the tokens in the various structures and can perform various operations on them. The processor is a deterministic device. In this respect, then, the agent's psychology is lawlike. We further assume that every agent of a given kind or species has the same kind of central processor, and indeed this is partly definitive of what we mean by a kind or species of agent. Of course, different experiences will have led to quite different sentences being written in the structures of various agents of the same species.

As noted, the psychologies of our agents are lawlike. There are laws relating the various states. Here is a candidate law, implausibly simple, that we will assume to hold:

> (*L*): If an agent *thinks$_B$* "The cup in front of me has decaffeinated coffee in it," and *thinks$_D$* "I drink some decaffeinated coffee," it will (normally or ceteris paribus) come to *think$_V$* "I pick up the cup and bring it to my lips."

The above statement of the law conceals reference to tokens of the displayed types, but for there to be laws like *L*, or like *L* except for being much more complex, the syntactic type of a mentalese token must be a property of tokens that the processor can detect. We assume that the processor can only detect local, physical properties of the tokens. It is not quite clear what this includes, but there are a number of things that are clearly not included. For example, the processor cannot detect anything about the cup or the coffee. This is not to say that the agent's sensors can't detect such things; nor is it to say that the agent can't. In any event the law, as stated, is quite independent of the meaningfulness of the tokens and of whatever particular contents they have.

We need to make three points about *L* and the extremely simple psychology it reflects. First, we are ignoring background beliefs and a number of interesting questions they raise. The use of the phrase "normally or *ceteris paribus*" is simply an indication that we are aware of these issues, not an attempt to treat them.[16] Second, we are making no allowance whatsoever for weighing the pros and cons of various alternative courses of action or for deliberation to resolve conflicts among appetites. Finally, we are using the volitional structure to model central motor control functions. Belief states and appetitive states lead to volitional states; these, in turn, cause bodily movements. A given volitional structure could be wired up to the wrong kind of body, one that had nothing like hands with opposable digits, or to a body with arms that were too short, etc. It could also be ill-wired to the right kind of body. We ignore all such unhappy possibilities.

4.2   A Semantics for Mentalese

We assume that a cognitive psychology assigns contents to tokens of mentalese in virtue of (i) the basic meanings associated with the types of the tokens and (ii) other facts. These other facts we gather into the following basic categories.

(a) Facts about the tokens themselves, specifically whose head they occur in (or, as we shall say, who owns them), and when; these facts determine the reference of such indexicals as "I," "me," and "now."

(b) Facts about the owners of the tokens, such as which objects they are attending to, talking to, and the like. These facts, together with facts of category (a), determine the reference of indexicals and demonstratives such as "you," "he," "her," and the like.

(c) Other facts that may be relevant, together with facts of categories (a) and (b), in determining the reference of definite descriptions and perhaps names.[17] This may include facts that are not in any clear and intuitive sense about either the token itself or its owner.

We take the meanings associated with the types to be functions from circumstances to contents, where contents may have as constituents individuals external to the mind of the agent. In these respects, our semantics follows the semantics for "schemata" in chapter 10 of Barwise and Perry (1983). But we differ with that approach in two related ways. First, we do not assign a single content to a token. Each token will have three contents: a fully opaque content, an opaque content, and a transparent content. Second, we do not take the function from context to content(s) to be the basic fact about meaning, but to result from a basic assignment of *token reflexive conditions of truth*. Thus our semantics will assign (up to) three contents to each expression: truth conditions – which we will take to be the fully opaque content – opaque, and transparent content. All are assigned circumstantially.

The following is an attempt to indicate the form of our semantic account by treating the sentence "The cup in front of me contains decaffeinated coffee" in some detail. We start with the content of the terms "me" and "the cup in front of me":

$$T = \text{"me"}$$

1 Basic condition of reference for a token t of T = *being the owner of t*.
2 Opaque content of t (condition of reference, given that Jerry owns t) = *being [identical to] Jerry*.
3 Transparent content of t (condition of reference given that Jerry owns t and any other facts) is the same as the opaque condition = *being Jerry*.

$$T = \text{"the cup in front of me"}$$

1 Basic condition of reference for a token t of T = *being the unique cup in front of the owner of t*.
2 Opaque content of t (condition of reference, given that Jerry owns t) = *being the unique cup in front of Jerry*.
3 Transparent content of t (condition of reference, given that Jerry owns t and that c is the cup in front of Jerry) = *being c*.

$$T = \text{"The cup in front of me contains decaffeinated coffee."}$$

1 Basic condition of truth for a token t of T = *Someone x is the owner of t, something y is the unique cup in front of x, and y contains decaffeinated coffee.*
2 Opaque content of t (condition of truth, given that Jerry is the owner of t) = *Something y is the unique cup in front of Jerry, and y contains decaffeinated coffee.*
3 Transparent content of t (condition of truth, given that c is the cup in front of Jerry) = *c contains decaffeinated coffee.*

To get at the level 1 and 2 contents (fully opaque and opaque), we shall use the sentences "The cup in front of the owner of t contains decaffeinated coffee" and "The cup in front of Jerry contains decaffeinated coffee." When we do this we will be using the descriptions *attributively*. Thus in the first sentence, t is referred to, but the owner of t and the cup are not referred to. In the second, Jerry is referred to, but the cup is not.

We use the notions of *loading* and *unloading* to get at relations between the fully opaque and the opaque, and the opaque and the transparent contents of a token of T. Loading is an operation that takes us from a proposition that contains a complex property, like being the owner of t, to a proposition that contains an object that uniquely instantiates the property, like Jerry. More precisely, we load a proposition with respect to a complex property and a set of circumstances. In going from the level 1 to level 2, we are loading the proposition with respect to the property of being the unique owner of t and the circumstance that Jerry is that owner. In going from the level 2 to level 3, we are loading the 2-level proposition with respect to the property of being the unique cup in front of Jerry, and the circumstance that c is that cup. Unloading is just the opposite of loading. The proposition that the cup in front of Jerry contains coffee is the result of unloading the proposition that c contains coffee with the circumstance that c is the cup in front of Jerry.[18]

We take the truth conditions of a mentalese token to be its fully opaque content. This is the only content it has that depends only on the form of the token and the interpretive function.

We said at the beginning of this that "Fodor takes propositional attitudes to be relations to tokens of an internal language . . . that have content. If Jerry believes that S, Jerry has a token of mentalese in his belief structure that has the content that S." The picture we have arrived at requires an account that is a bit more complicated, however. First, we should note that when the context of the attitude reporter and the agent differ, different sentences will be required to get at the same content. Thus to report what Jerry believes in virtue of his having a token of "I am sitting" in his belief structure, I'll have to say something like "Jerry believes that he is sitting" or "The author of 'Methodological solipsism' believes that he is sitting." If I use a token of the same sentence, and say "Jerry believes that I am sitting," I do not convey the right message.

Second, we now have three levels of content. We shall introduce subscripts and say things like

Jerry *believes$_{FO}$* (*desires$_{FO}$*) that . . .

Jerry *believes$_O$* (*intends$_O$*) that . . .

Jerry *believes$_T$* (*desires$_T$*) that . . .

This notation is not really adequate, since there are cases in which one term in a content sentence should be taken opaquely and another transparently. For the purposes of this essay, however, this notation will suffice.

We should emphasize that *believes$_{FO}$* is *not* one of our ordinary belief concepts. In the ordinary senses (opaque and transparent) of "believes," people don't usually believe the fully opaque content of their beliefs, since most people do not have beliefs about tokens of mentalese in their heads. And note further, that even for people who do have such beliefs, the belief in the fully opaque content of a belief token *b* will not be the belief one has in virtue of having *b*. To see this, note that Jerry and Georges might both believe, of Jerry's belief token *b*, that the cup in front of the owner of it contains decaffeinated coffee. Imagine Jerry and Georges are talking about mentalese, using one of Jerry's beliefs as an example, while Jerry drinks decaffeinated coffee. This belief about Jerry's token is not the same belief that Jerry has in virtue of having the token. This may seem a bit puzzling. But suppose that Jerry uttered "The cup in front of me contains decaffeinated coffee." Call the utterance *u*. The belief about *u*, that the cup in front of the person who made it contains decaffeinated coffee, has to be distinguished from what Jerry said (the proposition he expressed) with *u*. What Jerry said could be true, even if he never spoke, and *u* never existed. This is analogous to the belief case, and perhaps will make it seem less puzzling. Our ordinary propositional attitude reports simply do not focus on fully opaque content.

So we have to be careful with *believes$_{FO}$* and remember that its meaning derives from the theory, not from common usage. Saying that Jerry *believes$_{FO}$* that the cup in front of the owner of *b* contains decaffeinated coffee is just saying that *b* is a token in Jerry's head, whose fully opaque content is that the cup in front of its owner contains decaffeinated coffee. Jerry doesn't believe this in the ordinary sense. That is he doesn't *believe$_O$* it. Georges does *believe$_O$* it, but doesn't *believe$_{FO}$* it. So, of Georges, but not of Jerry, it can be said that he believes that the cup in front of the owner of b contains decaf.

5 Rational Laws and Adequate Explanations

The basic idea of a rational law is this. Suppose a belief and a desire cause an action. Then the action should promote the satisfaction of the desire, given the truth of the belief. This is a version of Fodor's point in the initial quotation, which we have made before with respect to our example. Jerry's belief that the cup in front of him contains decaffeinated coffee and his desire to have decaffeinated coffee lead him to will to move in a way that results, if the belief is true, in his desire being satisfied. There is surely something quite appropriate about this. Suppose Jerry's belief and desire led him instead to a movement that results in splashing the coffee onto his forehead. That would in some sense be inappropriate. As Fodor points out, it is perfectly conceivable that beliefs and desires, conceived as internal states, should have such inappropriate effects, but such effects of beliefs and desires are not what cognitive psychology is all about – they are not grist for the cognitivist's mill.

It will help discussion to define a relation among four propositions *P*, *R*, *Q*, and *C*, thought of as the contents of a belief, a volition, and a desire, and background conditions: (the belief that) *P rationalizes* (bringing it about that) *R*, relative to (the desire that) *Q*, given (the condition that) *C*. We'll write this

Rationalizes$_Q$ (P, R | C)

We think of this relation as one of *incremental rationality*.

If *C* is given, then if *P* is true also, bringing it about that *R* will guarantee (or at least promote) bringing it about that Q.[19]

To see one source of the need for, and role of, the background condition, consider the fully opaque contents of the tokens in our basic example. Let P = the proposition that the cup in front of the owner of b contains decaffeinated coffee, Q = that the owner of d (a token of "I drink decaffeinated coffee") drinks decaffeinated coffee, and R = that the owner of v picks up the cup in front of him and brings it to his lips. Then it is not the case that bringing it about that R is true will bring it about that Q is true, if P is true – *without the further condition that b, d, and v belong to the same agent*. This is our reason for saying that without some appeal to circumstances, the rationality of laws of cognitive psychology cannot be understood.[20]

Now consider a law, like our L, to the effect that a belief token b of type B and a desire d of type D, in the same agent, will cause that agent to have a volition v of type V. Such a law is *rational* if for every b, d, and v that instantiate it,

$$Rationalizes_{Con_{FO}(d)} \; (Con_{FO}(b), \; Con_{FO}(v) \mid C)$$

where $Con_{FO}(b)$ is the fully opaque content of b, and where C is the condition that b, d, and v belong to the same agent (and conditions are normal). When beliefs and desires cause volitions in accord with such laws, we can say that they motivate in two senses. The belief and desire cause the volition, and they rationalize it.

We should say a word about *normal conditions*. In our conception of cognitive psychology, the specification of an environment, which includes specification of a range of normal conditions, will be an important part of the psychological theory for a kind or species of agent. In our conception, agents are attuned to certain environments, and the apparatus of perception and belief is used to pick up and store information about factors that vary within those limits. We see the circumstantial nature of thought as one aspect of this attunement. The way visual information is used to guide our hands, for example, involves attunement to the normal relations between the orientation of limbs and the orientation of eyes. Such attunement only goes so far, however, and that is where the function of systems of storable, manipulable, relatively context-insensitive representations comes to the fore – for instance, as they are involved in belief. These points are rather tangential to our main aim in this essay, however.

The conception of a rational law explained a few paragraphs earlier makes it clear that fully opaque explanations, involving rational laws, would be fine. By subsuming behavior under causal laws, they would also subsume it under rational laws. But as we mentioned, we don't ordinarily use attitude reports to attribute fully opaque belief – what we say when we say "Jerry believes that . . ." is not understood on the model "Jerry *believes_{FO}* that . . ." We want then to consider how explanations using ordinary opaque and transparent attitude attributions could be adequate, and how they can go wrong.

The basic idea is as follows. When we explain an action in terms of a belief and a desire, we are basically explaining the occurrence of a volition of a sort for which the action is a more or less basic mode of execution.[21] The explanation will be correct only if it can be unloaded down to an instance of a rational law where the consequent volition is thus executable. To see what this means, let's work through our example.

Consider this explanation of Jerry's executing movement M, thereby picking up c and bringing it to his lips:

Jerry believes c contains decaffeinated coffee and desires that he drink some decaffeinated coffee.

What does this come to? Here's what:

- Jerry *believes$_T$* that c contains decaffeinated coffee in virtue of *believing$_O$* that the cup in front of him contains decaffeinated coffee together with the external circumstance that c is the cup in front of him. He *believes$_O$* this in virtue of owning a belief b whose fully opaque content is that the cup in front of the owner of b contains decaffeinated coffee.
- Jerry *desires$_O$* that he drink some decaffeinated coffee in virtue of owning a desire d whose fully opaque content is that the owner of d drink some decaffeinated coffee.
- Movement M is a basic way of executing a volition v whose fully opaque content is that the owner of v pick up the cup of coffee in front of him.
- Given the assumption that there is a rational law like L above, the belief and desire cited explain the action.

Now consider the case in which Jerry looks in the mirror. Here he doesn't actually perform any action. But we want to understand why, knowing about his belief and desire, we shouldn't expect an action such as his reaching for the cup by executing movement M.

The type of the volition and the desire are just as before. Further, Jerry again *believes$_T$* that c contains decaffeinated coffee in virtue of *believing$_O$* that the cup in front of him contains decaffeinated coffee, in the circumstance in which c is the cup in front of him. He *believes$_O$* this, however, in virtue of owning a token b' with the fully opaque content that the cup in front of the man whom the owner of b' is watching contains decaffeinated coffee. The belief b', the desire d, and a volition v of which the (missing) action would be an execution are not instances of a rational law. They are not instances of L, because the fully opaque content of the belief is not right. Moreover, if there were a law linking beliefs of this type, with this fully opaque content, with desires and volitions of the types of d and v, it would not be rational. Lucky folks like Jerry would get a drink of coffee, but in most cases the agent would be knocking over things, pawing empty space, or irritating irritable gorillas.

NOTES

The research reported in this paper has been made possible by a gift from the System Development Foundation.
1   Fodor (1979a: 225), quoting from Book I of Hume's *Treatise of Human Nature*.
2   See section 3 below, where we argue for such analogs, and section 4.2, where we sketch a semantics for Mentalese in which the relation between English sentences and sentences of mentalese is taken to be identity.
3   The present essay is the result of years of arguing about essays in Fodor (1979a),

particularly "Methodological Solipsism Considered as a Research Strategy in Cognitive Psychology." Many of the most fruitful of these arguments have involved Lisa Hall and Brian Smith, whom we thank. Special thanks to Georges Rey for a thoughtful and illuminating critique of an early draft. We intend the present piece as an outward and visible symbol of the inner cycles of inspiration and frustration we owe to that essay. We have not been able to pay as much attention to Fodor's later work (1987d) as would have been optimal.

4   Our thinking on this point has been much influenced by conversations with Brian Smith. He addresses the issues concerning formality in Smith, (in preparation).

5   H. P. Grice, (1975).

6   Some of these ideas are developed, or at least hinted at, in Perry and Israel (1990).

7   Here, we follow Fodor's discussion of *transparent* and *opaque* classifications, in Fodor (1980c). Note in particular his treatment of the "I'm sick"/"He's sick" and the "I'm ill" examples.

8   Following Fodor and many others, we have allowed ourselves use of locutions of the form *A thinks (believes)* "...." We regard this as an alternative notation for fully opaque belief attributions, which means that there is a token of the quoted type in the agent's belief structure. See below, section 4.2. It is interesting to note that this odd way of speaking is often accepted without any explanation.

9   On this, compare Fodor's treatment of the "That's edible"/"This is edible" example in Fodor (1980c).

10   On the view of belief reports developed in Barwise and Perry (1983), this report would be misleading but literally true. On the view developed in Crimmins and Perry (1989), there is a reading, indeed the natural reading, on which the report would be literally false. But even on that reading, the proposition that Jerry is reported to believe is the same as that he expresses with his use of "The cup in front of me contains decaffeinated coffee" – even though the *beliefs* are different. The present authors subscribe to the latter approach. Here, however, we are dealing with the propositional attitudes themselves, not the semantics of attitude reports. It is crucial for the strategy in Crimmins and Perry (1989) that beliefs be concrete cognitive structures. It therefore fits well with Fodor's token-oriented approach. Crimmins (1989) discusses a variety of ways in which attitudes could be concrete cognitive structures that are less language-like than mentalese is often taken to be.

11   Relativity to a possible world is a different matter.

12   For present purposes, we are simply identifying volitions and *intentions in action*.

13   But the first seems relative to a base – it's true base 10, false base 12 – while the second depends on a frame of reference for fixing dates, which seems to smuggle in some noneternality.

14   We are supposing then that they are similarly situated with respect to their respective cups, insofar as their perceptual apparatus is concerned.

15   We hope it is clear that this assumption is for the sake of simplicity, not chauvinism.

16   Also, see below section 5. We basically agree with Fodor (1987d: 4ff) that the laws of psychology will be *ceteris paribus* laws. But we suspect that physical laws are as dependent on *ceteris paribus* clauses as any others. See Cartwright (1983).

17   Fodor's remarks on transparency, opacity, and full opacity are not too definitive with respect to names, and we steer clear of them in this essay.

18   In Perry and Israel (1989), we sketch a theory of propositions, within a version of situation theory, in which these notions can be given precise, formal embodiments. Notice that the operation of unloading is *not* analogous to the allegedly impossible operation of going from a denotation (or reference) to a sense. The circumstantial fact, together with the object, determines the complex, typically relational, property.

19   Since *P, Q*, etc. are propositions, and since we assume that the whole clause "that *S*"

(where S is a sentence) refers to a proposition, consistency would dictate saying "the belief S" rather than "the belief that S." But it sounds better the inconsistent way.

20   This should not be taken to exclude the necessity of other background conditions as well, such as that the movement is taking place in the earth's gravitational field. Some background conditions might themselves be the contents of the agent's background beliefs; the condition just noted is not likely to be one of those. See below.

21   The route from action to volition will be more complex when the context of explanation includes background about other beliefs and desires of the agent that could be involved in more complex strategies of execution.

11

Does Mentalese have a Compositional Semantics?

STEPHEN SCHIFFER

Suppose we think in a language of thought. Should we then also suppose that it has a compositional semantics? Yes, Jerry Fodor argues,[1] but I am unconvinced, and therein lies this paper's central topic. I shall, however, be slow to get directly on this central topic, one which goes to the heart of important issues in the philosophical theory of propositional attitudes.

Propositional attitudes have been in this century a source of philosophical interest as a result of two different concerns. One begins with Frege and is about the "logical form" of sentences that ascribe propositional attitudes. A discussion of this, in section I, will reveal both a deep connection with compositional semantics and part of my interest in the question that gives this paper its title. The other concern is the mind–body problem in its post-Cartesian guise; it is about the need to reduce, and the prospects for reducing, propositional-attitude properties to properties whose naturalistic integrity is transparent. I take a familiar line on the question of reduction in section II, and later apply it to Fodor's argument that Mentalese, the neural language of thought, has a compositional semantics.

Section III is essentially a bridge between its flanking sections, and in it the general discussion of reduction is rehashed in connection with the language-of-thought proposal. Section IV, the *dénouement*, reconstructs Fodor's reasons for supposing Mentalese to have a compositional semantics and gives my response to them.

I   Logical Form, Compositional Semantics, and Believing as a Relation to Propositions

Many philosophers, influenced by Frege, suppose that each natural language has a correct compositional truth-theoretic semantics: a true, finitely axiomatizable theory whose axioms assign semantic values to the language's words and state recursive conditions on those values, and whose theorems assign to each of the language's truth-evaluable sentences the conditions under which it would be true. When a philosopher who shares this supposition wonders about the "logical form" of a sentence, his question is about how that sentence's truth condition is

181

determined by a correct compositional truth-theoretic semantics for the language to which the sentence belongs. Among the sentences such philosophers have worried about are those that ascribe propositional attitudes; and they have worried about them, we know, because it isn't clear what kinds of semantic values a compositional semantics must assign to words for their occurrences in the 'that'-clauses distinctive of propositional-attitude sentences.

The sentence

[*] Lester believes that Fido is a dog

looks as though it's saying that Lester stands in the belief relation to something referred to by the singular term 'that Fido is a dog.' For we may infer

Lester believes something

from [*], and from it together with

That Fido is a dog is pure speculation

we may infer

Lester believes something that is pure speculation.

But what is this thing, *that Fido is a dog*, which is the referent of the 'that'-clause singular term? Evidently, it's abstract, in that it has no spatial location; it's mind- and language-independent, in that it exists and has properties in possible worlds in which there are neither thinkers nor speakers; and it has essentially the truth condition it has, in that, necessarily, that Fido is a dog is true just in case Fido is a dog. So it would seem that referents of 'that'-clauses, and *a fortiori* the objects in the ranges of propositional-attitude relations, are *propositions*: abstract, mind- and language-independent objects that have essentially the truth conditions they have.

This is useful for ruling out other candidates for propositional-attitude objects, such as sentences of inner or outer languages,[2] but it doesn't resolve the basic puzzle about logical form, as it doesn't tell us what semantic values words take when they occur in 'that'-clauses. The problem may be posed in the following way. If English has a compositional semantics, then the reference of the singular term 'that Fido is a dog' is determined by its syntax and, perhaps *inter alia*, the references of 'Fido' and 'dog.' But what are these references? Knowing that the 'that'-clause refers to the proposition that Fido is a dog, where that is understood in the way just glossed, helps somewhat, in that it rules out certain possible answers, but it doesn't answer the question. A compositional semantics that hoped to assign just a single semantic value to each of 'Fido' and 'dog' adequate to all their appearances might try to get by with Fido for 'Fido' and doghood for 'dog,' yet there are famous good reasons for doubting that you can necessarily substitute *salva veritate* terms in [*]'s 'that'-clause which aren't synonymous for Lester but are co-referential by the proposal. For example, Lester may use 'Mickey' to refer to the creature, which he takes to be a mouse, that eats the cheese left out for Fido, in which case, it would seem, it's false that Lester believes that Mickey is a dog, even though, as it happens, Mickey is Fido. Or it may be that Lester came upon some strange creatures which he took to constitute a newly discovered zoological species, and introduced 'shmog' as a predicate to apply to any creature of the same zoological species as those creatures, even though, as it happens, what he stumbled upon wasn't a new species but rather a new race of dogs. In the event, it would seem that 'shmog' expresses the same property as 'dog,' but it would also seem that we still can't conclude that Lester believes that Fido is a shmog.

Two solutions find favor among those who hold both that English enjoys a correct compositional semantics and that 'that'-clauses refer to propositions, and they are importantly similar. The first, in its application to our example, claims that the references of 'Fido' and 'dog' in the 'that'-clause aren't Fido and doghood; rather they are "modes of presentation" of Fido and doghood. The second solution keeps Fido and doghood as the references but, in order to defuse the formidable evidence against that position, claims that believing is, or is to be analyzed in terms of, a three-place relation which, if [*] is true, holds among Lester, the proposition that Fido is a dog, and a mode of presentation of that proposition, which mode of presentation is itself determined, at least in part, by modes of presentation of Fido and doghood. Now 'mode of presentation' is here a term of art, short in the theorist's mouth for 'whatever it is that can do the job which, by my lights, needs to be done,' and as such the theorist owes us a non-question-begging account of what things do the job, an account of what modes of presentation are. But, as I've argued elsewhere,[3] it's doubtful this can be done, doubtful, that is, that there exists anything capable of playing the mode-of-presentation role.

Yet I also believe that if English has a correct compositional truth-theoretic semantics, then (i) 'that'-clauses refer to propositions, (ii) the reference of a 'that'-clause is determined (roughly speaking) by its syntax and the references of its component words, and (iii) "modes of presentation" are needed either as those references or, less plausibly in my opinion, in the other way just indicated. Since I doubt the availability of modes of presentation, I doubt that propositional-attitude sentences can be accommodated within a compositional semantics. Since I don't doubt that there are true propositional-attitude sentences, I am motivated to doubt that natural languages have correct compositional truth-theoretic semantics, and in *Remnants of Meaning* (1987a) I tried to defeat the reasons for thinking that they must have them. I did, however, acknowledge that if we think in Mentalese, then English has a compositional semantics if and only if Mentalese has, but I tried to show that there was no good route to a compositional semantics for Mentalese that was independent of already defeated public-language considerations. Fodor thinks I may have overlooked something, and this will occupy us presently.

There is still a question of sorts about "logical form" for the theorist, such as myself, who thinks no compositional semantics is needed to account for anything about belief sentences (or anything else). Roughly speaking, this theorist has two options. The first is to deny that 'that'-clauses are genuine singular terms having objectual reference; to deny, in other words (nearly enough), that 'y' in 'x believes y' is an *objectual* variable. The second is to allow that 'that'-clauses are genuine singular terms having objectual reference to propositions but to deny that their references are a function of the references of their component words. This allows one to say that [*] and 'Lester believes that Mickey is a shmog' may have different truth-values because their 'that'-clauses refer to different propositions (that Fido is a dog $\neq$ that Mickey is a shmog) while, at the same time, it lets one off the hook of having to find four different "modes of presentation" to be the referents of ‚'Fido,' 'Mickey,' 'dog,' and 'shmog.' The second option helps with the denial of a compositional semantics because it enables the theorist to deny that there is any way of accommodating 'that'-clauses within a compositional semantics, and the first option helps even more because it *also* enables the theorist to deny that there is any way of accommodating 'believes' within a compositional semantics. I took the first option in *Remnants of Meaning*, but now wonder whether the second might not be more attractive.[4] None of this, though, matters here; my purpose is to expedite the discussion below by pointing out that there is a motivated position wherein one both denies that propositional-attitude sentences can be accommodated within a compositional semantics and allows that believing *et al.* are relations to propositions. In fact, for the rest of this paper I shall assume, as a working hypothesis, that propositional attitudes *are* relations to propositions (that 'y' in 'x believes y' is an objectual variable whose values are propositions). I make this assumption because, first, I don't think there's a chance that propositional-attitude sentences can be accommodated within a compositional semantics unless the assumption is true; second, Fodor accepts the assumption; and third, my response to Fodor's reasons for supposing Mentalese to need a compositional semantics doesn't require me to deny the relational hypothesis.

II   Naturalizing the Belief Relation

Lester, as I said, believes that Fido is a dog, and we are entitled to this pleonastic restatement: Lester has the property of believing that Fido is a dog. Many philosophers feel that the legitimacy of propositional-attitude properties – properties like believing that Fido is a dog – demands that they be somehow *reducible* to physicalistic or at least topic-neutral properties, properties that enjoy intrinsic specifications in nonintentional, nonmentalistic terms. The most popular motivation for reduction is the need to account for the role of propositional-attitude properties in correct explanations of behavior, but at least one philosopher, Jerry Fodor,[5] thinks that the crucial motivation is simply to account for how a physical object like Lester can have such a property as believing that Fido is a dog.

Now we are supposing that believing is a relation to propositions, and this means that belief properties of the form *believing that such-and-such* are composite properties, made up of *the belief relation* and *the proposition that such-and-such*, just as the property of kissing the Pope's ring is made up of the kiss relation and the Pope's ring.[6] Since propositions are already physicalistically (which isn't to say *nominalistically*) kosher, one achieves a naturalistically acceptable reduction of each of the infinitely many belief properties simply by identifying the belief relation with a relation that is intrinsically specifiable in physicalistic or topic-neutral terms. Yet there are weaker notions of reduction, and, to get directly to what will ultimately matter to us, a theorist may feel that the considerations which motivate talk of "reduction" will be satisfied if, but only if, the following *Reduction Principle* is true:

There is a relation R between persons and propositions such that (1) R is intrinsically and finitely specifiable in physicalistic or topic-neutral terms, (2) bearing R to a proposition is metaphysically sufficient for believing it, and (3) if anyone actually believes a proposition, then he bears R to it.

Condition (2) means that x believes p in every possible world in which x bears R to p. And (3), designed to relieve one of the responsibility of stating a metaphysically necessary condition for believing a proposition, expresses the sentiment that we shouldn't care about faraway possible worlds; it's enough to account for why anyone in this world has the beliefs she has.

It's condition (1) that will come to matter most for the issue of compositional semantics, but nothing fancy is intended by it. It simply means that there is a two-place open sentence that expresses R, contains only physicalistic or topic-neutral predicates, and is of finite length. It's simply the sort of thing philosophers hope to achieve when they try to write down a naturalistically acceptable completion of 'Necessarily, (x)(p)(x believes p if . . .).'

I don't think the Reduction Principle is true, and I don't think its falsity prevents us from having beliefs. I've offered support for this hardly renegade view elsewhere,[7] and while I recognize that the final word hasn't been said on these difficult questions, I don't propose to argue against the Reduction Principle here. I shall be content to have shown, when this paper ends, that Mentalese needs a compositional semantics only if the Reduction Principle is true.

While I reject the Reduction Principle, I don't reject the following supervenience claim:

[S] We have the propositional attitudes we actually have in every possible world that's physically indistinguishable from the actual world.

Perhaps it's arguable that we can't make good sense of our thoughts having physical realizations unless we assume [S]; but I admit that I accept it mainly because I can't conceive what a counterexample to it would look like. Still, I'm happy to accept it for this paper, because, as will emerge, the language-of-thought hypothesis may not be able to do without it.

It follows from [S] that if x believes p, then there's a physical state of affairs which obtains and which is metaphysically sufficient for x's believing p; but [S] doesn't imply the Reduction Principle. For suppose that Lester believes both that Shirely's soul has been incarnated exactly 47 times and that God, being omnipotent, can create a weight too heavy for Him to lift. Then there are physical states of affairs α and β such that Lester's having his Shirley belief supervenes on α while his having his God belief supervenes on β, and it seems harmless enough to restate this thus: there are physicalistic properties Φ and Θ such that Lester's believing that Shirley's soul . . . supervenes on his having Φ and his believing that God . . . supervenes on his having Θ. It's quite consistent with this that there is no relation R such that (i) Φ = bearing R to the proposition that Shirley's soul has been incarnated exactly 47 times and (ii) Θ = bearing R to the proposition that God, being omnipotent, can create a weight too heavy for Him to lift, and the same goes for whatever other physicalistic properties might realize these beliefs. But if [S] doesn't entail the existence of a physicalistic relation that satisfies the Reduction Principle, then it's pretty hard to see how it could entail the existence of a topic-neutral relation that satisfies the principle.

So [S], we may assume, is consistent with the negation of the Reduction Principle, and it will be important for what comes later that we notice that it follows from [S] and the negation of the Reduction Principle that there is no finitely and nonintentionally specifiable way of correlating the physicalistic supervenience properties with the propositions whose being believed they secure.[8] For suppose we could finitely define, in wholly physicalistic or topic-neutral terms, a function f from these physicalistic supervenience properties to propositions such that

Necessarily, if $f(\Phi)$ = p and one has Φ, then one believes p.

Then we would have a physicalistic or topic-neutral relation R such that

Rxp iff $(E\Phi)$ $(\Phi x \,\&\, f(\Phi)$ = p$)$,

and, as this specification is finite and the properties in the domain of f explain why we believe what we believe, the Reduction Principle would be true.

Is there anything especially problematic with the conjunction of [S] and the denial of the Reduction Principle which isn't merely a problem with one of the conjuncts? Some may feel that it is illegitimate to invoke supervenience unless it can be shown to be a species of some familiar kind of entailment, which, in the case at hand, would require the Reduction Principle. This isn't my feeling, but I don't think I can do anything to allay the worry, and I'm not sure what it would take to allay it. Perhaps this could be done if one could derive the conjunction from antecedently recognized features of the concept of belief, but I see no reason to think that's possible. In any case, a theorist who accepts the Reduction Principle can't press this stricture about supervenience unless he's prepared to *identify* the belief relation with the relation R the principle describes. For suppose Φ is the physicalistic property on which Lester's believing that Shirley's soul ... supervenes. The worry in play is about how we're to *explain* the fact that Lester's having Φ is metaphysically sufficient for his having his belief about Shirley's soul. But exactly the same worry can be aired about how we're to explain the fact that Lester's bearing R to the proposition that Shirley's soul ... is metaphysically sufficient for his believing it, when it's not claimed that R *is* the belief relation. The Reduction Principle is required by the demand that supervenience be shown to be a species of a more familiar kind of entailment just because that demand would necessitate *identifying* the belief relation with a physicalistic or topic-neutral relation. This is pertinent to Fodor, for he is wont to insist both that the Reduction Principle is true and that you can't give necessary and sufficient conditions for believing a proposition.

So I accept [S] and reject the Reduction Principle, and I'll close this section by saying what little more I can about the physical realization of thoughts.

Suppose that belief state tokens are neural state tokens.[9] Then there is some state token n of Lester's that is both a token of a neural state type and a belief that Shirley's soul has been incarnated exactly 47 times. Philosophers who are happy with this assumption are apt also to suppose that there is some physicalistic property of n, however complex, that *realizes* the belief about Shirley, in that n's having that physicalistic property is nomologically sufficient for its also having the property of being a belief that Shirley's soul ... If one accepts the Reduction Principle, then one will say that the physicalistic property in question is the property of standing in such-and-such physicalistic relation to the proposition that Shirley's soul has been incarnated exactly 47 times;[10] but the question is what can I, who reject that principle but accept [S], say. Well, if [S] is true, then n has some physicalistic property whose possession is metaphysically sufficient for n's being a belief that Shirley's soul ...; so the question is, what can be said about this property?

It's convenient to think of the supervenience property as having an inner and an outer "part." The inner part is what stays the same in all nomologically identical worlds in which Lester's central nervous system is in its present total state but the external world in which he's located, as well as his history in it, varies arbitrarily; and the outer part is whatever is undetermined by the inner part. The inner part will determine that n is a token of a certain neural state type that has two crucial functional roles.[11] The first functional role will secure that n is a belief, and it will be a functional role that accounts for why each belief state token is a belief. Actually, this is highly speculative, as it assumes that the property of being a belief is a functional property,[12] and no one has come close to telling us what functional property it is, or even how to determine what it is. At the same time, it seems plausible, there is no known good objection to it, and my making the assumption is concessive to the position I shall eventually be criticizing.

But it isn't plausible that the property of being a belief that Shirley's soul ... is a functional property, for it would be easy to construct Twin Earth and Burgean counterexamples to the claim that it was. Nevertheless, it is plausible that the neural state type already alluded to, the one having the belief-making functional role, will have another functional role that is a necessary part of the supervenience property's being a supervenience property for the belief that Shirley's soul ... This functional role, to be sure, will be a very complex affair, relating the neural state type having it to sensory inputs, to other neural state types (which realize other propositional attitudes), and to bodily movements in various intricate ways.

Turning to the outer part of the supervenience property, I find myself with little to say. Must the supervenience property involve some causal relation to Shirley? Not obviously, for Lester's reference-determining knowledge of her may be by description, and even if it were obvious we wouldn't know how to characterize the causal relation. I won't even guess at what needs to be said about the other conceptual components of Lester's belief – *soul, incarnation, exactly, 47*. If Burge is right,[13] and I think he is, the content of Lester's belief may be partly determined by the meanings of words in his linguistic community, and when we also notice the myriad essential connections of the concepts involved in Lester's belief with other concepts, it's clear that the outer part of the supervenience property will take in a huge amount of territory.

I'm not surprised by my inability to say much about the supervenience property, for I think the following is a fair gloss of what's going on. I have noninferential knowledge that 'Shirley's soul has been incarnated exactly 47 times' means, in my mouth, that Shirley's soul has been incarnated exactly 47 times. By virtue of this, I can identify the content of the belief that would be expressed by my sincere utterance of the sentence – namely, that Shirley's soul has been incarnated exactly forty-seven times. On reflection, and as a philosopher, I can't see how the world could be physically just as it is while the sentence 'Shirley's soul ...' has a different meaning for me than it actually has, and the generalization to the supervenience of my beliefs is obvious, from which point I extend the courtesy to Lester of assuming he's relevantly like me. But none of these steps throws any light at all on the nature of the supervenience property. Yet it will later be important that we can notice that nothing prevents the supervenience property from being a finitely specifiable property that is determined by properties of components of the neural state type whose tokening would instance the belief about Shirley's soul.

III The Language-of-Thought Hypothesis

This is the hypothesis that we think in a formally specifiable neural code, and the issue, not yet joined, will be whether the hypothesis requires that the neural code, Mentalese, has a compositional semantics.

Let M be a formally specifiable neural language. To say that it's a neural language is to say that it's a language whose expression types are sequences of neural state types. To say that it's formally specifiable is to say that recursive conditions can be formulated that (a) will determine whether any given sequence of neural state types is a well-formed expression of M but (b) won't tell us what any expression means, or refers to, or has as a truth condition.

To say that we think in M is to say that for any propositional attitude we might have, there's some sentence of M whose being tokened in a certain way would realize our having that propositional attitude. Let me elaborate.

First, I shall assume, with Fodor, that there is some computational (and hence functional) relation that holds between thinkers in M and sentence tokens of M such that to bear that relation to a sentence token entails being in a belief state. Other computational relations will help to realize other kinds of propositional-attitude states, and the assumption that these relations exist is for the language-of-thought theorist tantamount to the assumption, discussed above, that properties like being a belief and being a desire are functional properties. A vivid way to keep the assumption in mind is to pretend that in each person's head there is a box for each kind of basic propositional attitude: to have a belief is to have an M sentence tokened in the belief-box; to have a desire is to have one tokened in the desire-box; and so on.

It's next required that having an M sentence tokened in the belief-box will realize a *particular* belief, say, a belief that lobsters make lousy pets. This means that the sentence has some property such that its both having that property and being tokened in the belief-box is nomologically sufficient for believing that lobsters make lousy pets. Thus, if we let 'σ' range over sentences of M, and 'Φ' over properties of those sentences, then we can express the hypothesis that we think in M thus:

(σ) (EΦ) (Ep) ($\Phi\sigma$ & it's nomologically sufficient for believing p that ($\Phi\sigma$ & σ is tokened in the belief-box)).

When in this way σ realizes the belief p, then we may say that σ "means" p, and we may express the language-of-thought hypothesis in Fodor's favorite way:

x believes p iff x has in his belief-box some sentence of his *lingua mentis* which means p

(and likewise, *mutatis mutandis*, for the other propositional-attitude relations). But do bear in mind that this simply *abbreviates*

> x believes p iff (Eσ) (EΦ) (Φσ & σ is a sentence of x's *lingua mentis* & σ is in x's belief-box & it's nomologically sufficient for x's believing p that (Φσ & σ is in x's belief-box)),

or else (among other things) you're apt to get the impression that the language-of-thought hypothesis virtually requires a gloss of the "meaning" relation that would secure the Reduction Principle.

So the question arises: what can be said about these content-determining properties, the values of 'Φ' in the displayed formulas? One who accepts the Reduction Principle will suppose that there is some relation R holding between neural sentences and propositions, which relation is finitely and intrinsically specifiable in physicalistic or topic-neutral terms, and that each content-determining Φ is of the form *bearing R to the proposition that such and such*. But no one has succeeded in saying what R is, and, as I've said, I very much doubt that anyone can.

There are two other possible answers worth mentioning; the first only because it has relevance to the next section and might, in any case, already have crossed the mind of an anti-reductionist language-of-thought theorist. This is the idea that there is some relation R′ between neural sentences and propositions such that (a) R′ doesn't presuppose the belief relation and can thus be used in a reductive explication of it, (b) R′ can't be intrinsically specified in physicalistic or topic-neutral terms, and (c) one believes p just in case some sentence of one's *lingua mentis* bears R′ to p and is in one's belief-box. In other words, each content-determining Φ is of the form *bearing R′ to the proposition that such-and-such*.

I find this proposal very unappealing. First, it entails that the mysterious relation R′ is one that can't be specified in *any* terms. The relation isn't definable in nonsemantic terms, and there is no existing semantic predicate that expresses it. Certainly, the predicate 'σ means p' can't express it: in its already-displayed Fodorian use it serves as the indicated abbreviation, and there seems not to be any literal use of the verb 'to mean' that has a correct application to one's neural states. In its *literal* use, the verb applies only to public-language items, and for a thing to have meaning it must be capable of being used to perform speech acts, and its having its meaning would supervene on the intentions and practices of those apt to produce it. We are reduced, on the present proposal, to saying that there is some magical *je-ne-sais-quoi* relation that secures meaning for sentences in the language of thought. No doubt one making the mysterious proposal envisages the relation that obtains between neural sentences and propositions as being definable in terms of relations between neural words and propositional constituents, but what was just said applies to those relations too. It's one thing to say that the belief relation is indefinable; it's quite another thing to say that it's definable in terms of indefinable relations that no terms express. Second, it's hard to see how the proposal can comport with physicalistic supervenience, thereby making it a mystery what the brain has to do with the mind.

The other possible account of the content-determining Φs is the one I favor; the one you get when you reject the Reduction Principle but accept the supervenience thesis [S]. On this account, each M sentence σ has a physicalistic property Φ such that, for some p, it's metaphysically sufficient for one's believing p that σ both have Φ and be in one's belief-box. The supervenience property will have, in the way already indicated, an inner and an outer part. I'll have to forgo any further discussion about the nature of these content-determining supervenience properties, but we can observe that nothing precludes the possibility of a finitely statable theory that generates each of the content-determining supervenience properties. However, as we'll presently see, it won't be possible, if the Reduction Principle is false, to have a finite theory that *both* generates those infinitely many properties *and* correlates them with the propositions providing the contents of the beliefs those properties determine.[14] The stage is now set for the eponymous issue.

IV   Compositional Semantics and the Language of Thought

Suppose we think in the neural language M. Must M have a compositional semantics? Earlier I discussed a compositional *truth-theoretic* semantics (I needed that to make the point about the logical form of belief sentences), but the issues stay relevantly the same if we now follow Fodor in understanding a compositional semantics for M as being a compositional meaning theory for M; that is, a finitely axiomatizable theory of M which makes assignments to the words and syntactic structures of M in such a way as to yield, for each sentence of M, a theorem of the form 'σ means p.'[15] Fodor says yes, M must have a compositional semantics, and offers the following *productivity argument.*[16]

1   Each of infinitely many M sentences means its uniquely own proposition (one means that lobsters make lousy pets, another that only *Parsifal* is more boring than sailing, and so on).
2   If (1), then M has a compositional semantics.
3   Ergo, M has a compositional semantics.

Fodor is aware that some would deny (1), drawing the meaningful-sentence line at those sequences of M words whose complexity prohibits entry into the belief-box, and for them he is prepared to replace (1)'s appeal to the productivity of M with an appeal to the "systematicity" of M.[17] The systematicity argument is worth considering for its own sake, and I shall consider it later. But I am prepared to grant Fodor the idealizations needed for (1), the productivity of M, making the other premise of this little valid argument the point at which issue is taken.

So why does Fodor assert (2)? Because, he says laconically, "nobody has the slightest idea how M could be semantically productive unless it has a compositional semantics."[18] I think the intended expansion would go as follows. We have infinitely many facts of the form σ *means* p. What *explains* this infinity of meaning facts? Broadly speaking, there are two types of answer one might offer. One says there is some finite basis from which the infinity of meaning facts emanates; some complex but finitely statable state of affairs whose obtaining somehow determines that each Mentalese sentence has the meaning it has. The other type of answer says it's turtles – I mean meaning facts – all the way down. There is no finite state of affairs that generates them all; *nothing* generates the infinitely many distinct meaning facts, unless it's some separate infinity of generating facts, one for each meaning fact. It may be that each meaning fact has an explanation, but then we'll have infinitely many distinct explanations, with nothing to unify them into a single, finitely statable explanation of the whole infinite lot. But surely the second answer is kind of crazy; it's too incredible that the infinity of meaning facts is all there is, unsustained by a finite foundation. The only sensible thing to think, at least at this stage of the game, is that the infinity of meaning facts is somehow secured by some large but finitely describable state of affairs, some nonendless way the world is. But if, as the first answer entails, there is some finitely statable proposition whose truth determines each of the infinitely many meaning facts, then how can M fail to have a compositional semantics? The finite basis must certainly determine properties for M's words, and it must determine recursive conditions which use those properties to generate meaning-determing properties for M's sentences, and it looks as though in having all that one would have a finitely axiomatizable theory of M whose theorems told us what each sentence of M means, a compositional semantics for M.

Let's call this argument for premise (2) of the productivity argument the *explanatory argument*, since it holds that a compositional semantics is needed to *explain* the productivity of M. I have two things to say in response to the argument. The first is in the nature of a relevant comment on the explanatory argument, only indirectly a ground for questioning it. The second, which questions a crucial step in the argument, is directly an objection to it. Let's take these in turn.

1 My comment is that *the explanatory argument requires the Reduction Principle*, for there couldn't be an explanatory compositional semantics – that is, a compositional semantics which explained the infinity of meaning facts – unless that principle were true. This, if right, is of interest for at least two reasons. First, there are philosophers who reject the Reduction Principle but accept the language-of-thought hypothesis and suppose that something which needs to be explained will go unexplained unless Mentalese has a compositional semantics. Second, if the explanatory argument isn't sound unless the Reduction Principle is true, then all the evidence against the principle, which is formidable, is evidence against the soundness of the argument. Of course, this cuts both ways, as someone might argue that the explanatory argument has the unexpected but welcome consequence of establishing the Reduction Principle. In any event, why think the explanatory argument does require the Reduction Principle?

The explanatory argument is that semantic productivity (i.e., premise (1)) requires a compositional semantics because a compositional semantics is needed to *explain* semantic productivity, to explain the fact that each sentence of M has the meaning it has. Let's suppose this is so and ask about the shape of such an *explanatory* compositional semantics for M. The question is important because not just any correct compositional semantics would *explain* semantic productivity. After all, a correct compositional semantics for M, if it has one, might simply be a theory that (i) baldly pairs, in a listlike way, each word of M with a propositional constituent, (ii) uses the listlike pairings to specify a recursive function f from the sentences of M onto those propositions which happen to be their meanings, and (iii) contains the axiom that for any M sentence σ and proposition p, σ means p if f(σ) = p. But while this true theory would yield a correct meaning-ascribing theorem for each sentence of M, it wouldn't *explain* why any sentence has the meaning it has; it wouldn't answer the worry of how a finite way the world is could give rise to the infinity of meaning facts. For to say that σ means p is to say that σ has a property Φ such that it's nomologically sufficient for believing p that σ both have Φ and be in the belief-box, and, clearly, you don't explain the fact that a neural sentence has such a belief-realizing property merely by deriving a theorem which says that it does from a finite number of axioms. Someone who wants to know how the infinity of meaning facts is possible wants to know where the infinitely many belief-realizing Φs come from, *but nothing in the trivial theory even entails that the infinitely many Φs are generated from a finite basis.*

An explanation of the productivity of M ought to explain why each sentence of M means the proposition it means; and an explanation of the fact that σ means p – i.e., the fact that σ has some property Φ such that it's nomologically sufficient for believing p that σ both have Φ and be in the belief-box – ought at least to identify the belief-realizing Φ and show how σ's having it is determined by properties of its words and syntax. If we want to explain, all at once, why each of the infinitely many sentences of M means the particular proposition it means, then it's not unreasonable to suppose that this big explanation will incorporate a compositional semantics for M. The question, to repeat it, is what shape this *explanatory* compositional semantics must take.

A compositional semantics for M that explains productivity must be a finitely axiomatizable theory that does two things. First, it assigns a belief-realizing property to each sentence of M; that is to say, for each sentence of M the theory entails a theorem of the form 'σ has Φ,' where 'Φ' holds the place of a property such that, for some p, a sentence's having it and being in the belief-box is nomologically sufficient for one's believing p. Second, the theory enables one to move from each such theorem to a further theorem of the form 'σ means p.' The theory must do the second thing if it's to be a compositional semantics, and it must do the first if it's to be suitably explanatory of M's productivity. Notice that a theory that does the first thing is not thereby one that does the second thing too; a true, finitely axiomatizable theory that assigns a belief-realizing property to each sentence of M is not thereby a compositional semantics for M. To say that σ means p is to say that σ has some property Φ such that σ's both having Φ and being in the belief-box is nomologically sufficient for one's believing p; but a theory can tell you that σ has Φ without, for some p, its also telling you, what may in fact be the case, that σ's both having Φ and being in the belief-box is nomologically sufficient for one's believing p. (Presently I shall dwell on the possibility that M has no correct compositional semantics but does have a correct, finitely axiomatizable theory that assigns a belief-realizing property to each sentence of M.)

So let us suppose that M has an explanatory compositional semantics: it takes us to theorems of the form 'σ has Φ,' and from there to theorems of the form 'σ means p.' How the theory achieves these transitions will depend on the nature of the belief-realizing properties, the values of 'Φ.' Suppose that each Φ is a composite property of the form *bearing* R *to* p, with constant R and changing p.[19] Then the explanatory compositional semantics for M will have the following shape. First, it will contain the axiom that, for any σ and any p, it's nomologically sufficient for one's believing p that σ both bears R to p and is in one's belief-box. Second, it will have an axiom for each word and primitive syntactical construction of M which assigns to the word or construction some substantive property. And third, it will state finitely many compositional rules which show how the aforementioned properties of M's words and constructions determine, for each sentence of M, that it bears R to some particular proposition. Since 'σ means p' abbreviates 'σ has some property Φ such that its both having Φ and being in the belief-box is nomologically sufficient for one's believing p,' this theory will issue in theorems of the form 'σ means p.'

Now there are two possibilities as regards the relation R: either it is specifiable in physicalistic or topic-neutral terms, or it isn't. If it isn't, then we have the intentionally irreducible mystery relation disparaged on p. 199, which option I am assuming not to be acceptable. But if R is specifiable in physicalistic or topic-neutral terms, then, by virtue of its incorporation in a compositional semantics, we know that it's finitely specifiable in those terms, and we virtually have the Reduction Principle. I say "virtually" because the Reduction Principle requires metaphysical sufficiency whereas the belief-realizing properties have been glossed in the weaker terms of nomological sufficiency. Yet I shall ignore this difference and suppose that in the present context the nomological sufficiency of belief-realizing properties carries with it their metaphysical sufficiency; for we are entitled to this if we accept the supervenience thesis [S] in conjunction with the language-of-thought hypothesis, and the only theorist who would oppose supervenience in this context is the already dismissed advocate of the intentionally irreducible *je-ne-sais-quoi* mystery relation. In this way, we see that an explanatory compositional semantics for M presupposes the Reduction Principle if its belief-realizing properties are composite properties of the form *bearing* R *to* p, with constant R and changing p.

Now suppose that the theory's belief-realizing properties aren't of this form, so that the theory can't secure the move from 'σ has Φ' to 'σ means p' via an axiom of the form '(σ) (p) (it's nomologically sufficient for believing p that Rσp & σ is in the belief-box).' Since supervenience is being presupposed, we may take these belief-realizing Φs to be physicalistic or topic-neutral properties. The question is, how will the finite theory enable us to move from each theorem of the form 'σ has Φ' to a further theorem of the form 'σ means p'? I can think of but one way. The theory will recursively define a function f that maps each belief-realizing property furnished by the theory onto the proposition that is the content of the belief the property helps to realize, and then it will state the axiom that

(σ) (Φ) (p) (if Φσ & f(Φ) = p, then it's nomologically sufficient for believing p that (Φσ & σ is tokened in the belief-box)).

And it is clear how the function f would have to work. Each belief-realizing property the theory assigns to a sentence would itself have to be a function of other properties the theory assigns to the sentence's words, and each proposition in the range of f would have to be a function of items ("semantic values") correlated with the word-sized properties of which the belief-realizing properties are a function. The definition of f would then simply exploit these correlations and matching functions in familiar ways. The details don't matter; what is important is the evident fact that f would be specifiable in perfectly kosher topic-neutral terms; there would be no place in its definition where irreducibly intentional notions would find employment.

The trouble is, if there were such a function then there would be a reduction relation and the Reduction Principle would be correct. For let f continue to be the naturalistically accredited, recursively definable function in question. Then – to repeat, in effect, the point made on p. 196 – we could define a relation R,

Rσp iff (EΦ) (Φσ & f(Φ) = p),

and then have it that

(σ) (Ep) (Rσp & it's nomologically sufficient for believing p that (Rσp & σ is tokened in the belief-box)).

But since in this context nomological sufficiency goes with metaphysical sufficiency, we also have

(σ) (Ep) (Rσp & it's metaphysically sufficient for believing p that (Rσp & σ is tokened in the belief-box)),

thereby yielding the Reduction Principle. A correct, finitely axiomatizable theory that yields theorems of the form 'σ has Φ' is consistent with the rejection of the Reduction Principle. But it won't also yield theorems of the form 'σ means p,' and so won't be a compositional semantics, unless the Reduction Principle is true.

So I conclude that no compositional semantics can *explain* the semantic productivity of M unless the Reduction Principle is true. For, to recapitulate: To say that σ means p is to say that it has some property which would make an occurrence of σ in the belief-box a realization of the belief p. Given this, we know that if a compositional semantics is to explain why each of the infinitely many sentences of M means what it does, then it must do two things. First, it must entail for each sentence a theorem of the form 'σ has Φ,' where 'Φ' holds the place of a term designating a belief-realizing property. Second, it must enable one to move from each such theorem to a further theorem of the form 'σ means p.' But there are only two real possibilities as to how this might go, and both imply the Reduction Principle: either the belief-realizing properties are composite properties of the form *bearing* R *to* p, where R is a finitely specifiable physicalistic or topic-neutral relation; or else the theory must use physicalistic belief-realizing properties in conjunction with a certain topic-neutral function in a way that entails a reduction relation, and with it the Reduction Principle.

2   My second response to the explanatory argument is that it has a fallacious step and that, when this is appreciated, we'll see that it's false that productivity can be explained only on the assumption that M has a compositional semantics. We *can* explain the productivity of M even on the assumption that M has no compositional semantics.

Fodor's explanatory argument first concludes that the infinitely many meaning facts must emanate from a finite basis, and then moves from *this* to the further conclusion that M must have a correct compositional semantics. But this simply doesn't follow. There might be a finite *supervenience basis* for the infinitely many meaning facts even though M has no compositional semantics. Moreover, this finite supervenience basis may yield a true, finitely axiomatizable theory that explains M's productivity but isn't a compositional semantics.

Before I try to spell this out, it is important that we be clear as to what's at issue. Fodor has argued that a compositional semantics is required to explain productivity. To refute this, therefore, I needn't show that M doesn't have a compositional semantics. My task is merely to show how productivity can be explained on the assumption that M doesn't have a compositional semantics. My own personal case against compositional semantics does indeed have two parts: positive reasons, of the sort adumbrated in section I, for doubting that languages have compositional semantics, and attempts to defeat the reasons for thinking that languages must have compositional semantics. Only the second part is now in play, and my argument that productivity may be explained even on the assumption that M has no compositional semantics doesn't presuppose that there are any good positive reasons for denying compositional semantics.

So let's assume that M doesn't have a compositional semantics. We have already seen that the supervenience thesis [S] doesn't entail the Reduction Principle, and that, consequently, there is the possibility of a correct, finitely axiomatizable theory of M that assigns a belief-realizing property to each sentence of M (issues in theorems of the form 'σ has Φ') but is incapable of saying what any M sentence means (can't issue in theorems of the form 'σ means p'), because there is no finite way of specifying the propositional contents that supervene on the infinity of physicalistic supervenience properties generated by the theory. Such a theory may be suitably explanatory of productivity, and I think it will be if it has the properties I shall ascribe to the supervenience theory $T^\star$ of M.

$T^\star$ is a true, finitely axiomatizable theory that assigns to each word and primitive structure of M its uniquely own physicalistic property and states compositional rules that operate on these properties to assign to each sentence σ a physicalistic property Φ such that: (i) σ's having Φ is logically equivalent to the parts and structure of σ having the properties $T^\star$ assigns to them, (ii) for some p, σ's having Φ is minimally metaphysically sufficient for σ's meaning p, in that σ's meaning p supervenes on σ's having Φ but doesn't so supervene on any property entailed by, but not logically equivalent to, Φ, and (iii) no proposition which thus supervenes on σ's having Φ also thus supervenes on any other sentence's having any other property $T^\star$ assigns to it. (Condition (ii) secures that $T^\star$ assigns a meaning-determining property to each sentence, and (iii) secures that infinitely many distinct meanings are thus generated.) Of course, the existence of $T^\star$ isn't secured by the mere supervenience thesis [S], but the point is that $T^\star$ is consistent with [S] and the denial of compositional semantics, and $T^\star$ would explain M's productivity.

$T^\star$ would not explain productivity by entailing meaning-ascribing theorems for the sentences of M, as it entails no such theorems. But it certainly shows how the infinity of meaning facts is determined by a finitely specifiable state of affairs, a nonendless way the world is. Moreover, that M is productive is further explained in that, necessarily, M *is* productive if $T^\star$ is true, and $T^\star$ may be known to assign to each sentence that specific property which fully accounts for the sentence's having the particular meaning it has. That we can have a finite theory that assigns to each sentence the property on which its meaning supervenes but can't assign to any sentence its meaning is merely the result of having supervenience without the Reduction Principle. But the explanation of productivity such a theory affords is, I submit, explanation enough. After all, what that obviously needs explanation, as regards productivity, is now going unexplained? Certainly it's not how the infinitely many meaning facts emanate from a finite state of affairs.

I have heard the objection that it's impossible to see how M could fail to have a compositional semantics if T* were true. Well, here's how. The challenge, remember, is to show how productivity can be explained *on the assumption that M has no compositional semantics.* Now if M has no compositional semantics, then, as I indicated in section I,[20] that will be because it's impossible to assign appropriate *semantic values* to all the words of M, for the semantic values required for words in a compositional meaning theory (as opposed to a mere truth theory) are precisely the referents of words in 'that'-clauses, and if compositional semantics are impossible it's because the referent of a 'that'-clause isn't a function of the referents of its component words. Yet a word may have a physicalistic property that plays its part in a sentence-size meaning-determining physicalistic supervenience property even if the word can be assigned no appropriate "semantic value"; that is to say, it's consistent with a word's having the physicalistic property T* assigns to it that no *propositional constituent* can be correlated with it to play its required role in a correct compositional meaning theory for M.[21]

I conclude that Fodor's productivity argument fails to establish that M has a compositional semantics, and now-familiar points can be redeployed to reach a similarly skeptical conclusion about Fodor's systematicity argument for compositional semantics.

The systematicity argument says that a compositional semantics is needed to explain the *systematicity* of M, and Fodor is pleased to have this second argument because a language can be systematic without being productive. A language is *systematic* if "the ability to produce/understand some of the sentences is *intrinsically* connected to the ability to produce/understand many of the others."[22] Suppose we think in English; then its systematicity is revealed in the fact that a tokening of 'John loves Mary' wouldn't realize the thought that John loves Mary unless a tokening of 'Mary loves John' realized the thought that Mary loves John. Systematicity really boils down to the platitude that syntactic structures and words help to determine the meanings of the sentences in which they occur in uniform ways. Systematicity, when you pursue it, comes even to this: that the meaning of each sentence is determined by properties of its words and syntax, and that those properties (roughly speaking) play the same meaning-determining roles in each sentence in which words or syntactic structures having them occur.

I have no quarrel with the claim that M is systematic. My reply is that no compositional semantics is required to account for it. For it is consistent with M's having no compositional semantics that T* is true, and T* can be used to explain the systematicity of M. Necessarily, if T* is true, then each sentence has some physicalistic property on which its meaning supervenes, and this property, and so the meaning of the sentence, is determined by properties of the words and syntactic structures that compose the sentence, properties which play the same meaning-determining roles in each sentence in which words or syntactic structures having them occur. Thus, even though T* assigns no propositional constituents, no semantic values, to M's words, and even though it has no meaning-ascribing theorems, it does explain systematicity in that, necessarily, M *is* systematic if T* is true, and T* reveals the mechansims by which M's systematicity is achieved. Let me elaborate this a little by showing how, armed with T* but without a compositional semantics, I might meet a challenge posed by Christopher Peacocke.[23]

Suppose, merely for simplicity, that M is English. Then it's a fact that if a sentence of the form '. . . water . . .' is in one's belief-box, then one believes something of the form *that . . . water . . .* (in other words, every sentence containing 'water' means a proposition that's about water), and likewise for every other word of M. This fact ought to be a bona fide explanandum, and the question is whether a uniform explanation can be given of it. We know how this explanation would go if M had a certain kind of compositional semantics: it would show how the compositional semantics assigned a certain entity to 'water' (water itself or a mode of presentation of water) that, by the further machinery of the semantics, was a constituent of every proposition assigned as a meaning to every sentence containing 'water'. But what sort of uniform explanation can I provide? Quite simply, the following, on the assumption that T* is true. If a sentence means a proposition of the form *that . . . water . . .*, then that's because its having that meaning supervenes on its having the physicalistic property T* assigns to it. Now the physicalistic property T* assigns to a sentence containing 'water' will be partly determined by the single physicalistic property that T*, in its base axioms, assigns to 'water,' and this single property will help to determine, in ways T* reveals, the infinitely many physicalistic properties T* assigns to the infinitely many sentences containing 'water.' It's precisely because 'water' has this physicalistic property that any sentence of the form '. . . water . . .' means a proposition of the form *that . . . water . . . . Voila!* But surely to have the capacity to provide such uniform explanations just is to have the capacity to explain systematicity.[24] So I conclude that Fodor's systematicity argument fails to establish that M has a compositional semantics.

Jerry Fodor has argued that we should accept that Mentalese has a compositional semantics because it's only on that assumption that we can explain its productivity and systematicity. I have urged two things in response: first, that a compositional semantics can explain productivity (and systematicity, too, although this wasn't addressed) only if the Reduction Principle is true, and second, that it's possible to explain productivity and systematicity even on the assumption that M has no compositional semantics. Perhaps Fodor won't be too disturbed by the first point, since he accepts the Reduction Principle. And perhaps he needn't be all that disturbed by the second point. I can see him saying in response: "Big deal, so it's CONCEIVABLE that productivity and systematicity can be explained without a compositional semantics. But what Granny is really and ultimately interested in is what's in fact the best explanation of these features, and, since the Reduction Principle is correct, that best explanation, we should suppose, is a suitably explanatory compositional semantics."

Well, OK, fair enough. But does Jerry really want to pin the case for compositional semantics on his theory of asymmetric dependence, and how, in any case, can he answer the positive reasons for doubting that Mentalese has a correct compositional semantics?[25]

NOTES

1   This is explicitly argued in Fodor, 1989b, but the arguments are also implicitly contained in the Appendix to Fodor, 1987.
2   In his 1981c Fodor argues that believing is a relation to neural sentences, in the sense that they are the referents of 'that'-clauses and the values of 'y' in 'x believes y'; but his present view, more sensibly, is that believing is a relation to propositions – which relation, to be sure, must be explicated in terms of relations to Mentalese sentences. See Fodor, 1987d:17 *and passim*, and forthcoming-a.
3   See Schiffer, 1987a: ch. 3, 1987b, and forthcoming-a.
4   See Johnston, 1988 and Schiffer, 1988. Part of the idea is to allow that propositions exist but to combine this with what might be called the *pleonastic conception of propositions*, the view, certain qualifications apart, that every meaningful 'that'-clause *ipso facto* determines a proposition, just as, on a similarly pleonastic conception of properties, every meaningful predicate, certain qualifications apart, determines a property.
5   See Fodor, 1989a.
6   Talk of such properties' being composite may be merely a harmless *façon de parler*, as it would be, say, for a theorist who thinks that properties are functions from possible worlds to sets of things in those worlds.
7   See Schiffer, 1987a and 1989.
8   It's easy to have a finite, intentional specification of such a correlation: $f(\Phi) = p$ iff p is the propositional content of the belief which supervenes on having Φ. Of course, this gives no way of determining the propositional content of the belief which supervenes on having Φ, and for this reason such a correlation can't do the work a finitely specifiable correlation might be needed for.
9   Actually, I have doubts about the token-token identity thesis, but my supposition is harmlessly concessive to the Fodorian view and simplifies the discussion of physical realization.
10   This would be the view even of someone who thought that only a topic-neutral relation satisfied the Reduction Principle; for this theorist holds that the topic-neutral relation must always, in any particular instantiation, be *realized* by a physicalistic relation.
11   A *functional role* is a second-level property of first-level state types (i.e., state types whose tokens are particulars) which entails that the state type possessing it is counterfactually related to inputs, to other state types, or to outputs in a certain way. See Schiffer 1987a:21–3.
12   A *functional property* is a property of the form *being a token of a state type that has such-and-such functional role*. If F is a functional role, then it determines the functional property of being a token of a type having F. See Schiffer, 1987a:21–3.
13   See Burge, 1979, and forthcoming.
14   A fourth proposal worth mentioning is like mine only it denies that the physicalistic basis is anything more than nomologically sufficient: a neural sentence's having Φ in fact makes it capable of realizing the belief p, but there are possible worlds in which it doesn't. The problem with this is that it seems to require a contingent, *causal* relation between a neural sentence's having Φ and its helping to realize the belief p. What story could one possibly tell about the nature of the causal mechanisms? That it works without any? This suggests that the language-of-thought hypothesis may

require [S].

15 In one way, this is no big switch, for on the continuing assumption that meanings are propositions, a correct compositional meaning theory would determine a correct compositional truth-theoretic semantics, and a language wouldn't have a correct compositional truth-theoretic semantics unless it had a correct compositional meaning theory. In another way, however, the switch to a propositional meaning theory, as opposed to a merely extensional truth theory, hugely exacerbates the problem mentioned in section I. When only compositional truth-theoretic semantics was at issue, the objection was (nearly enough) that no semantic values could be assigned to words to accommodate their occurrences in 'that'-clauses. But if what's at issue is a propositional meaning theory – a finite theory issuing in theorems of the form 'σ means p' – then the objection is that no semantic values can be assigned to words, period; for the semantic value such a theory assigns to a word is precisely its referent in a 'that'-clause, since the assignments to words must determine the *propositions* meant by the sentences containing those words.

16 The displayed argument is my restatement. Fodor, following Chomsky, understands a language to be "semantically productive" if it has infinitely many meaningful sentences.

17 Fodor is also aware that his productivity and systematicity arguments equally apply to public languages. The restriction to Mentalese is due to the assumption, which I am not challenging, that public-language meaning is inherited from meaning in Mentalese. I especially welcome the move to Mentalese, since it prescinds from arguments that hope to establish compositional semantics on the basic of considerations pertaining to public-language understanding. See my (1987a: chs 7 and 8).

18 Fodor, 1989b:422.

19 Constant R may, of course, be a disjunctive relation.

20 For the full treatment see my (1987a: especially chs 1, 7, and 8).

21 For example, in my 1987a I argued that no base axiom could be written for 'believes' in a correct compositional semantics because (a) if 'believes' had an appropriate semantic value, it would have to be a relation between believers and things believed, and (b) there was no such relation. But I certainly never intended to deny that, say, 'Ralph believes that flounders snore' has some physicalistic property on which its meaning supervenes and that this property is itself determined by physicalistic properties of its syntax and component words, including 'believes.'

22 Fodor, 1987d:149.

23 In Peacocke, 1986.

24 Now it's true that we may not be able to say very much about *why* the relevant meaning facts supervene on the relevant physicalistic facts, but that's the price of having supervenience without the strongest possible application of the Reduction Principle (see pp. 196–198 below), and it's a price we must frequently pay quite apart from the present issues: How, for example, is one to explain the fact that the gracefulness of a dancer supervenes on such-and-such physicalistic properties?

25 Thanks to Paul Boghossian, John Carroll, Jennifer Church, Marian David, Hartry Field, Jerry Fodor, Dick Grandy, Jean Kazez, Brian Loar, Barry Loewer, Colin McGinn, Brent Mundy, Christopher Peacocke, and Georges Rey for recent helpful conversations on these topics.

12

Connectionism, Constituency, and the Language of Thought

PAUL SMOLENSKY

I'm the only President you've got.

Lyndon Johnson[1]

In their paper, "Connectionism and cognitive architecture," Fodor and Pylyshyn (1988a) argue that connectionism cannot offer a cognitive architecture that is both viable and different from the Classical language of thought architecture: if it differs from the Classical architecture it is because it reinstantiates simple associationism, and is therefore not a viable candidate; if it is viable, it is because it implements the Classical view and therefore does not offer a new cognitive architecture – just a new implementation of the old one. It is my purpose here to expose the false dichotomy in this argument, to show that the space of connectionist cognitive architectures is much richer than this simple dichotomy presumes, and that in this space is a large region of architectures that are implementations neither of a Classical architecture nor of a simple associationist architecture; these architectures provide structured mental representations and structure-sensitive processes in a truly non-Classical way.

In section 1, I make a number of general remarks about connectionism, Fodor and Pylyshyn's argumentation, and the abuse of the term "implementation." In section 2, I focus on the crux of their argument, which turns on the compositional structure of mental states. I develop in some detail the argument that, unlike simple associationist models, connectionist models using *distributed representations* can embody compositionality at the same time as providing a new cognitive architecture that is not an implementation of a Classical language of thought. In section 3, I bring together the more technical discussion of section 2 back in contact with the more general issues raised in section 1. I argue that the debate surrounding compositionality illustrates the general point that by finding new formal instantiations of basic computational notions in the category of continuous mathematics, connectionism can open up genuinely new and powerful accounts of computation and cognition that go well beyond the limited progress that can be afforded by the kind of implementationalist strategy that Fodor and Pylyshyn advocate.

1   General Remarks

1.1   The True Commitment of Connectionism: PTC Version

In this paper I adopt a view of connectionism that was presented and discussed at some length in Smolensky (1988a,b), a view I call PTC (for the Proper Treatment of Connectionism). Oversimplifying a bit, according to PTC, the true commitment of connectionism is to a very general formalism for describing mental representations and mental processes. The Classical view is, of course, committed to the hypothesis that mental representations are elements of a *symbol system*, and that mental processes consist of symbol manipulation operations. PTC is committed to the hypothesis that mental representations are *vectors* partially specifying the state of a dynamical system (the activities of units in a connectionist network), and that mental processes are specified by the differential equations governing the evolution of that dynamical system.

The main point is this: under the influence of the Classical view, computation and cognition have been studied almost exclusively under the umbrella of discrete mathematics; the connectionist approach, on the other hand, brings the study of computation and cognition squarely in contact with the other half of mathematics – continuous mathematics. The true commitment, according to PTC, is to uncovering the insights this other half of mathematics can provide us into the nature of computation and cognition.

On the PTC account, simple associationism is a particularly impoverished and impotent corner of the connectionist universe. It may well be that the attraction a number of people feel to connectionism is an attraction to neo-associationism; but it is nonetheless a serious mistake to presume connectionism to be committed to simple associationist principles. To equate connectionism with simple associationism is no more appropriate than equating Classical symbolic theory with Aristotelean logic. (The temptation Fodor may provide his readers notwithstanding, I don't recommend the second identification any more than the first.)

In fact, the comparison with Aristotle is not wholly inappropriate. Our current understanding of the power of connectionist computation might well be compared with Aristotle's understanding of symbolic computation; before connectionists can take really serious shots at cognitive modeling, we probably have at least as far to go in developing connectionist computation as symbolic computation had to go between Aristotle and Turing. In giving up symbolic computation to undertake connectionist modeling, we connectionists have taken out an enormous loan, on which we are still paying nearly all interest: solving the basic problems we have created for ourselves rather than solving the problems of cognition. In my view, the loan is worth taking out for the goal of understanding how symbolic computation, or approximations to it, can emerge from numerical computation in a class of dynamical systems sharing the most general characteristics of neural computation.

Because cognitive modeling demands so much further progress in the development of connectionist computational techniques, I will argue here not for the superiority (nor even the plausibility) of a connectionist approach to cognitive modeling. Rather, I will argue that connectionism should be given a chance to progress unhampered by the misconception, fueled in significant part by Fodor and Pylyshyn (1988a; henceforth, F&P), that there is little point in pursuing the connectionist approach since it is doomed at the outset on fundamental grounds.

Given this characterization of the commitments of the Classical and connectionist approach, to claim, as F&P explicitly do, that any cognitive architecture that incorporates structured mental representations and processes sensitive to that structure is a Classical architecture, is to bloat the notion of "Classical architecture" well beyond reasonable bounds.

1.2   Implementation vs. Refinement

The bottom line of F&P can be paraphrased as follows. "*Standard* connectionism is just simple associationism wrapped in new jargon, and as such, is fatally flawed. Connectionists should pursue instead a *nonstandard* connectionism, embracing the principles of compositionality and structure-sensitive processing: they should accept the Classical view and should design their nets to be implementations of Classical architectures." Behind this moral is the assumption that connectionist models with compositionally structured representations must necessarily be implementations of a Classical architecture; it will be my major purpose to show that this is false. The connectionist systems I will advocate hypothesize models that are not an *implementation* but rather a *refinement* of the Classical symbolic approach; these connectionist models hypothesize a truly different cognitive architecture, to which the Classical architecture is a scientifically important approximation. The reader may suspect that I will be splitting hairs and that the difference between "implementation" and "refinement" will be of no philosophical significance. But in fact the new cognitive architecture I will hypothesize lacks the most crucial property of Fodor and Pylyshyn's Classical architecture: mental representations and mental processes are *not* supported by the same formal entities – there are no "symbols" that can do both jobs.[2] The new cognitive architecture is fundamentally two-level: formal, algorithmic specification of processing mechanisms, on the one hand, and semantic interpretation, on the other, must be done at two different levels of description.

There is a sense of "implementation" that cognitive science has inherited from computer science, and I propose that we use it. If there is an account of a computational system at one level and an account at a lower level, then the lower one is an *implementation* of the higher one if and only if the higher description is a complete, precise, algorithmic account of the behavior of that system. It is *not* sufficient that the higher-level account provide some sort of rough summary of the interactions at the lower level. It is *not* sufficient that the lower-level account involve some of the same basic ideas of how the problem is to be solved (for example, a decomposition of the problem into subproblems). Such weak usages of "implementation" abound in the literature, particularly in the numerous attempts to dismiss connectionism as "mere implementation." But in its correct usage, *implementation* requires that the higher-level account provide an exact, precise, algorithmic account of the system's behavior.

It's important to see that, unless this definition of implementation is adopted, it is impossible to legitimately argue to F&P's ultimate conclusion: as long as connectionists are doing implementation, they're not going to provide a new cognitive architecture. If it is shown only that connectionism "implements" the Classical architecture under a looser definition of the term, then the conclusion that follows is that the Classical account provides a rough, higher-level approximation to the connectionist account, or involves some of the same basic ideas about how information is represented and processed. This is a *much weaker* conclusion that what F&P are after. They want the conclusion that only true implementation will license: since the Classical account provides a complete, precise, algorithmic account of the cognitive system, there is nothing to be gained by going to the lower level account, as long as the phenomena of interest can be seen at the higher level; and, of course, it is exactly those phenomena that the Classicist will count as "truly cognitive." To account for intrinsically lower-level phenomena – in which category the Classicist will certainly include neural phenomena and may also include certain perceptual/motor phenomena – the Classicist will acknowledge the need to condescend to a lower level account; but within the domain of "pure cognition," Classicists won't need to get their hands so dirty. These are the sorts of conclusions that Classicists have pushed for decades on the basis of analogies to higher- and lower-level computer languages. But of course these languages, *by design*, satisfy the *correct* definition of implementation; none of these conclusions follows from weaker definitions, and none follows from the connectionist position I defend here. Far from the conclusion that "*nothing* can be gained from going to the lower level account," there is *plenty* to be gained: completeness, precision, and algorithmic accounts of processing, none of which is in general available at the higher level, according to PTC.

To see how the distributed connectionist architecture differs fundamentally from the Classical one – fails to provide an "implementation" using the correct definition of the term – I will now sketch how the connectionist architecture is intrinsically split over two levels of description. We'll consider the purest case: distributed connectionist models having the following two properties:

1 a Interpretation can be assigned to large-scale activity patterns but not to individual units;
   b The dynamics governing the interaction of individual units is sufficiently complex that the algorithm defining the interactions of individual units cannot be translated into a tractably-specified algorithm for the interaction of whole patterns.[3]

As a result of these two properties, we can see that there are two levels of analysis with very different characteristics. At the lower level, where the state variables are the activities of individual units, the processing is described by a complete, precise, and formal algorithm, but semantic interpretation cannot be done. At the higher level, where the system's state is described in terms of the presence of certain large-scale patterns, semantic interpretation can be done, but now complete, precise algorithms for the processing cannot be stated. As I have characterized this in Smolensky (1988a), the *syntax* or processing algorithm strictly resides at the lower level, while the *semantics* strictly resides at the upper level. Since both the syntax and the semantics are essential to the cognitive architecture, we have an intrinsically split-level cognitive architecture here: There is no account of the architecture in which the same elements carry both the syntax and the semantics. Thus we have a fundamentally new candidate for the cognitive architecture which is simply *not* an implementation of the Classical one.

Note that the conclusions of this section depend crucially on the assumption (1a) that connectionist representations are *distributed* (when viewed at the level of individual units, the level at which processing algorithms can be identified (1b)). Thus, while F&P attempt to give the impression that the issue of local vs. distributed representations is a little technical squabble between connectionists of no philosophical consequence, I believe this to be a profound mistake. Distributed representations, when combined with (1b), entail that in the connectionist cognitive architecture, mental representations bear a fundamentally different relation to mental processes than is true in the Classical account. I will return to this crucial point in section 3.

2 Compositionality and Distributed Connectionist Representations

I shall not seek, and I will not accept, the nomination of my party for another term as your President.

Lyndon Johnson

In this section I consider the crux of F&P's argument, and argue that distributed connectionist architectures, without implementing the Classical architecture, can nonetheless provide structured mental representations and mental processes sensitive to that structure.

2.1 The Ultralocal Case

Here is a quick summary of what I take to be the central argument of F&P.

2 a Thoughts have composite structure.

By this they mean things like: the thought that *John loves the girl* is not atomic; it's a composite mental state built out of thoughts about *John, loves* and *the girl*.

2 b Mental processes are sensitive to this composite structure.

For example, from any thought of the form $p \ \& \ q$ – regardless of what p and q are – we can deduce p.

F&P elevate (2) to the status of defining the Classical View of Cognition, and claim that this is what is being challenged by connectionism. I am arguing that this is wrong, but for now we continue with F&P's argument.

Having identified claims (2) as definitive of the Classical View, F&P go on to argue that there are compelling arguments for these claims.[4] According to these arguments, mental states have the properties of productivity, systematicity, compositionality, and inferential coherence. Without going into all these arguments, let me simply state that for present purposes I'm willing to accept that they are convincing enough to justify the conclusion that (2) must be taken quite seriously.

Now for F&P's analysis of connectionism. They assert that in (standard) connectionism, all representations are atomic; mental states have no composite structure, violating (2a). Furthermore, they assert, (standard) connectionist processing is association which is sensitive only to *statistics*, not to *structure* – in violation of (2b). Therefore, they conclude, (standard) connectionism is maximally non-Classical: it violates both the defining principles. Therefore connectionism is defeated by the compelling arguments in favor of the Classical view.

What makes F&P say that connectionist representations are atomic? The second figure of their paper (p. 16) says it all – it is rendered here as figure 1. This

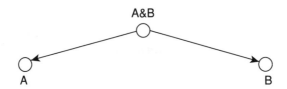

Figure 1: Fodor & Pylyshyn's network

network is supposed to illustrate the standard connectionist account of the inference from *A & B* to *A* and to *B*. It is true that Ballard and Hayes wrote a paper (Ballard and Hayes, 1984; also Ballard, 1986) about using connectionist networks to do automated resolution theorem proving in which networks like this appear. However it is a serious mistake to view this as the paradigmatic connectionist account for anything like human inferences of this sort. The kind of *ultralocal* connectionist representation, in which entire propositions are represented by individual nodes, is far from typical of connectionist models, and certainly not to be taken as *definitive* of the connectionist approach.[5]

A central claim in my response to F&P is that any critique of the connectionist approach must consider the consequences of using distributed representations, in which the representations of high level conceptual entities such as propositions are distributed over many nodes, and the same nodes simultaneously participate in the representation of many entities. Their response, in section 2.13 (p. 19), is as follows. The distributed/local representation issue concerns (they assume) whether each of the nodes in figure 1 refers to something complicated and lower level (the distributed case) or not (the local case). But, they claim, this issue is irrelevant, because it pertains to a *between-level* issue, and the compositionality of mental states is a *within level* issue.

My response is that they are correct that compositionality is a within-level issue, and correct that the distributed/local distinction is a between-level issue. Their argument presumes that because of this difference, one issue cannot influence the other. But that is a fallacy. It assumes that the between-level relation in distributed representations cannot have any consequences on the *within-level* structure of the relationships between the representations of *A & B* and the representation of *A*. And that's simply false. There are profound implications of distributed representations for compositionality; these are the subject of all of section 2 of this paper. In particular, it will turn out that figure 1 is exactly as relevant to a distributed connectionist account of inference as it is to a symbolic account. In the ultralocal case, figure 1 is relevant and their critique stands; in the distributed case, figure 1 is a bogus characterization of the connectionist account and their critique completely misses its target. It will further turn out that a valid analysis of the actual distributed case, based on suggestions of Pylyshyn himself, leads to quite the opposite conclusion: connectionist models using distributed representations describe mental states with a relevant kind of (within-level) constituent structure. The rather weak sense of constituent structure in generic distributed representations, identified in section 2.2, will be made much stronger in explicitly designed distributed representations, discussed in section 2.3, in which constituents can fill varying structural roles.

2.2   The Distributed (Weakly Compositional) Case

For now, the goal is to show that generic connectionist models using distributed representations ascribe to mental states the kind of compositional structure demanded by (2a), contrary to F&P's conclusion based on the ultralocal network of figure 1.

2.2.1   The Coffee Story

My argument consists primarily in carrying out an analysis that was suggested by Zenon Pylyshyn himself at the 1984 Cognitive Science Meeting in Boulder.[6]

We'll take a *distributed* representation of *cup with coffee* and subtract from it a distributed representation of *cup without coffee* and call what's left, following Pylyshyn, "the connectionist representation of *coffee.*"

To generate these distributed representations I will use a set of "microfeatures" (Hinton, McClelland, and Rumelhart, 1986) that are not very micro – but that's always what happens in examples that are cooked up to be intuitively understandable in a nontechnical exposition. These microfeatures are shown in figure 2.

Figure 2 shows a distributed representation of *cup with coffee*: a pattern of activity in which those units that are active (black) are those that correspond to microfeatures present in the description of a cup containing coffee. Obviously, this is a crude, nearly sensory-level representation, but, again, that helps make the example more intuitive – it's not essential.

Given the representation of *cup with coffee* displayed in figure 2, Pylyshyn suggests we subtract the representation of *cup without coffee*. The representation of *cup without coffee* is shown in figure 3, and figure 4 shows the result of subtracting it from the representation of *cup with coffee*.

So what does this procedure produce as "the connectionist representation of *coffee*"? Reading off from figure 4, we have a burnt odor and hot brown liquid with curved sides and bottom surfaces contacting porcelain. This is indeed a representation of *coffee*, but in a very particular context: the context provided by *cup*.

Units	Microfeatures
●	upright container
●	hot liquid
○	glass contacting wood
●	porcelain curved surface
●	burnt odor
●	brown liquid contacting porcelain
○	oblong silver object
●	finger-sized handle
●	brown liquid with curved sides and bottom

Figure 2 Representation of cup with coffee.

What does this mean for Pylyshyn's conclusion that "the connectionist representation of *cup with coffee* is just the representation of *cup without coffee* combined with the representation of *coffee*"? What is involved in combining the representations of figures 3 & 4 back together to form that of figure 2? We

Units	Microfeatures
●	upright container
○	hot liquid
○	glass contacting wood
●	porcelain curved surface
○	burnt odor
○	brown liquid contacting porcelain
○	oblong silver object
●	finger-sized handle
○	brown liquid with curved sides and bottom

Figure 3 Representation of cup without coffee.

assemble the representation of *cup with coffee* from a representation of a *cup*, and a representation of *coffee*, but it's a rather strange combination. There's also the representation of the *interaction* of the cup with coffee – like *brown liquid contacting porcelain*. Thus the composite representation is built from coffee *extracted* from the situation *cup with coffee*, together with *cup* extracted from the situation *cup with coffee*, together with their interaction.

So the compositional structure is there, but it's there is an *approximate* sense. It's *not* equivalent to taking a context-independent representation of *coffee* and a context-independent representation of *cup* – and certainly not equivalent to taking a context-independent representation of the relationship *in* or *with* – and sticking them all together in a symbolic structure, concatenating them together to form the kind of syntactic compositional structures like with (cup, coffee) that F&P want connectionist nets to implement.

Units	Microfeatures
○	upright container
●	hot liquid
○	glass contacting wood
○	porcelain curved surface
●	burnt odor
●	brown liquid contacting porcelain
○	oblong silver object
○	finger-sized handle
●	brown liquid with curved sides and bottom

Figure 4 "Representation of coffee"

To draw this point out further, let's reconsider the representation of *coffee* once the cup has been subtracted off. This, suggests Pylyshyn, is the connectionist representation of *coffee*. But as we have already observed, this is really a representation of *coffee* in the particular context of being inside a cup. According to Pylyshyn's formula, to get the connectionist representation of *coffee* it should have been in principle possible to take the connectionist representation of *can with coffee* and subtract from it the connectionist representation of *can without coffee*. What would happen if we actually did this? We would get a representation of ground brown burnt smelling granules stacked in a cylindrical shape, together with granules contacting tin. This is the connectionist representation of *coffee* we get by starting with *can with coffee* instead of *cup with coffee*. Or we could start with the representation of *tree with coffee* and subtract off *tree without coffee*. We would get a connectionist representation for *coffee* which would be a representation of brown beans in a funny shape hanging suspended in mid-air. Or again we could start with *man with coffee* and get still another connectionist representation of *coffee*: one quite similar to the entire representation of *cup with coffee* from which we extracted our first representation of *coffee*.

The point is that the representation of *coffee* that we get out of the construction starting with *cup with coffee* leads to a different representation of *coffee* than we get out of other constructions that have equivalent a priori status. That means that if you want to talk about the connectionist representation of *coffee* in this distributed scheme, you have to talk about a *family of distributed activity patterns*. What knits together all these particular representations of *coffee* is nothing other than a type of family resemblance.

2.2.2 Morals of the Coffee Story

The first moral I want to draw out of this *coffee* story is this: unlike the ultralocal case of figure 1, with distributed representations, complex representations *are* composed of representations of constituents. The constituency relation here is a *within-level* relation, as F&P require: the pattern or *vector* representing *cup with coffee* is composed of a *vector* that can be identified as a distributed representation of *cup without coffee* together with a *vector* that can be identified as a particular distributed representation of *coffee*. In characterizing the constituent vectors of the vector representing the composite, we are *not* concerned with the fact that the vector representing *cup with coffee* is a vector comprised of the activity of individual microfeature units. The *between-level* relation between the vector and its individual numerical elements is *not* the constituency relation, and so section 2.1.4 (pp. 19–28) of F&P is irrelevant – it addresses a mistake that is not being made.

The second moral is that the constituency relation among distributed representations is one that is important for the analysis of connectionist models, and for explaining their behavior, but it is *not* a part of the information processing mechanism within the connectionist model. In order to process the vector representing *cup with coffee*, the network does not have to decompose it into constituents. For processing, it is the *between-level* relation, not the within-level relation, that matters. The processing of the vector representing *cup with coffee* is determined by the individual numerical activities that make up the vector: it is over these lower-level activities that the processes are defined. Thus the fact that there is considerable arbitrariness in the way the constituents of *cup with coffee* are defined introduced no ambiguities in the way the network processes that representation – the ambiguities exist only for us who analyze the model and try to explain its behavior. Any particular definition of constituency that gives us explanatory leverage is a valid definition of constituency; lack of uniqueness is not a problem.

This leads directly to the third moral: the decomposition of composite states into their constituents is not precise and uniquely defined. The notion of constituency is important but attempts to formalize it are likely to crucially involve *approximation*. As discussed at some length in Smolensky (1988a), this is the typical case: notions from symbolic computation provide important tools for constructing higher-level accounts of the behavior of connectionist models using distributed representation – but these notions provide approximate, not precise, accounts.

Which leads to the fourth moral: while connectionist networks using distributed representations *do* describe mental states with the type of constituency required by (2a), they do *not* provide an implementation – correctly defined – of a symbolic language of thought. The context-dependency of the constituents, the interactions that must be accommodated when they are combined, the inability to uniquely and precisely identify constituents, the imperative to take seriously the notion that the representation of *coffee* is a collection of vectors knit together by family resemblance – all these entail that the relation between connectionist constituency and syntactic symbolic constituency is *not* one of implementation. In particular, it would be absurd to claim that even if the connectionist story is correct then that would have no implications for the cognitive architecture, that it would merely fill in lower-level details without important implications for the higher-level account.

These conclusions all address compositional representation (2a) without explicitly addressing structure-sensitive processing (2b). Addressing structure -sensitivity to the depth necessary to grapple with real cognitive modeling is far beyond the scope of this paper; to a considerable extent, it is beyond the scope of current connectionism. However, let me simply state the fundamental hypothesis of PTC that weaves the statistical sensitivity characteristic of connectionist processing together with the notion of structure sensitivity: *the mind is a statistics-sensitive engine operating on structure-sensitive (numerical) representations.* The previous arguments have shown that distributed representations do possess constituency relations, and that, properly analyzed, these representations can be seen to encode structure. Extending this is to grapple with the complexity of the kinds of rich structures implicated in complex cognitive processes which is the topic of the next section. Here it suffices to observe that once we have complex structured information represented in distributed numerical patterns, statistics-sensitive processes can proceed to analyze the statistical regularities in a fully structure-sensitive way. Whether such processes can provide structure-sensitivity that is adequate to cope with the demands of linguistic and inferential processing is sure to be unknown for some time yet.

The conclusion, then, is that distributed models *can* satisfy (2). Whether (2) can be satisfied to the depth required by the full demands of cognitive modeling is of course an open empirical question – just as it is for the symbolic approach to satisfying (2). At the same time, distributed connectionist models do *not* amount to an implementation of the symbolic instantiations of (2) that F&P are committed to.

Before summing up, I'd like to return to figure 1. In what sense can figure 1 be said to describe the relation between the distributed representation of *A&B* and the distributed representations of *A* and *B*? It was the intent of the *coffee* story to show that the distributed representations of the constituents are, in an approximate but explanation-relevant sense, part of the representation of the composite. Thus, in the distributed case, the relation between the node of figure 1 labeled *A&B* and the others is one kind of whole/part relation. An inference mechanism that takes as input the vector representing *A&B* and produces as output the vector representing *A* is a mechanism that extracts a part from a whole. And in this sense it is no different from a symbolic inference mechanism that takes the syntactic structure A & B and extracts from it the syntactic constituent A. The connectionist mechanisms for doing this are of course quite different than the symbolic mechanisms, and the approximate nature of the whole/part relation gives the connectionist computation different overall characteristics: we don't have simply a new implementation of the old computation.

It is clear that, just as figure 1 offers a crude summary of the symbolic process of passing from A & B to A, a summary that uses the labels to encode hidden internal structures within the nodes, *exactly the same is true of the distributed connectionist case.* In the distributed connectionist case – *just as in the symbolic case* – the links in figure 1 are crude summaries of complex processes and not simple-minded causal channels that pass activity from the top node to the lower nodes. Such a simple causal story applies only to the ultralocal connectionist case, which is the only legitimate target of F&P's attack.

Let me be clear: there is no serious distributed connectionist model, as far as I know, of the kind of formal inference F&P have in mind here. Many proponents of connectionism would be content to claim that formal inference is a specially trained, poorly practiced skill that is far from central to cognition, and that therefore we can afford to put off worrying about providing a connectionist model of it for a long time. I prefer to say that, at root, the F&P argument concerns an important and central issue: the constituent structure of mental states; formal inference is just one setting in which to see the importance of that constituent structure. So the preceding discussion of the constituent structure of distributed representations does address the heart of their critique, even if a well-developed connectionist account of formal inference remains unavailable.

2.3   The Distributed (Strongly Compositional) Case

But, one might well argue, the sense in which the vector encoding the distributed representation of *cup with coffee* has constituent vectors representing *cup* and *coffee* is too weak to serve all the uses of constituent structure – in particular, too weak to support formal inference – because the vector representing *cup* cannot fill multiple structural roles. A true constituent can move around and fill any of a number of different roles in different structures. Can *this* be done with vectors encoding distributed representations, and be done in a way that doesn't amount to simply implementing symbolic syntactic constituency? The purpose of this section is to describe research showing that the answer is affirmative.

A large class of connectionist representations, which I call *tensor product representations*, is defined and analyzed in Smolensky (1987a), and applied in Dolan and Smolensky (1988). We generate various members of this class by variously specifying several parameters in a highly general method for creating connectionist representations of structured information. The resulting parametric variation in the representations is very broad, encompassing very simple representations such as the case of figure 1, as well as representations that are close to true implementations of a syntactic language of thought. This class of representations covers the spectrum from fully distributed representations to ultralocal ones, and includes representations with a full sense of constituency, where role-independent constituents are assigned to roles in a structure and the representation of the structure is built up systematically from the representation of the constituents.

The problem that motivates this work is mapping complex structure such as parse trees into vectors of activity in connectionist networks, in such a way that the constituent structure is available for connectionist processing. A general formal framework for stating this problem is to assume that there is a set of discrete structures S (like parse trees) and a vector space V – a space of activity states of a connectionist network. A connectionist representation is a mapping from S to V; the theorist's job is to identify such mappings having various desirable properties. Tensor product representations can provide many of these properties.

A particular tensor product representation is constructed in two steps.

3   a   Specify a decompositional process whereby the discrete structures are explicitly broken down as a set of constituents, each filling a particular role in the structure as a whole. This step has nothing to do with connectionism *per se*; it just amounts to being specific about the kind of constituent structure we want to represent.

  b   Specify two connectionist representations: one for the structural roles and another for their fillers (the constituents). Thus, for every filler, we assign a vector in the state space of some network for representing fillers; similarly, we assign to every role a vector in the state space of some network for representing roles.

These two steps indicate the "parameters" in the general tensor product representational scheme that must be specified to individuate a particular representation. Once these parameters are specified, two very simple operations from the theory of vector spaces are used to generate the representation of a particular discrete structure. The representation of the whole is built from the representation of its constituent parts by the operation of *superposition* which is simply *vector addition*: the vector representing the whole is the sum of the vectors representing the parts. Step (3a) above specifies exactly what constituents are involved in this process. The vector representing a given constituent is actually a role-sensitive representation: a representation of that constituent *in the role it plays in the whole*. This vector is built by taking a particular vector product of the vector that represents the constituent independent of any role, and the vector representing the role in the structure that is filled by the constituent. Step (3b) specifies a set of vectors that represent individual structural roles and another set of vectors that represent individual fillers for those roles (constituents) independently of any role. The product operation here is a vector operation called the *tensor product* that takes two vectors and products a new vector; if the two vectors consist of n and m activity values, then their tensor product is a vector of nm activity values, each one being a different product (using ordinary numerical multiplication) of two activity values, one from each of the original vectors.[7]

The tensor product provides a general solution to a problem that his been nagging the distributed connectionist representational world for a long time, the so-called *variable binding problem*. How can we take an activity pattern representing a variable and another pattern representing a value and generate a connectionist representation of their binding that has the right computational properties? The simplicity of the tensor product makes it possible to show it does in fact satisfy the computational demands of (distributed) connectionist variable binding. The tensor product technique is a generalization of specific tricks (especially, *conjunctive coding*: Hinton, McClelland, and Rumelhart, 1986; McClelland and Kawamoto, 1986; Smolensky, forthcoming) that have been used to solve this problem in particular instances in the past.

The tensor product representation of constituent structure considerably strengthens the notion of constituency brought out in the previous section through the *coffee* story. There we saw that the whole/part relation between *cup with coffee* and *coffee* is mirrored in a whole/part relation between their respective representations: the latter relation was not the whole/part relation between molecular symbolic structures and their atomic constituents, as in a symbolic language of thought, but rather the relation between a sum vector $\mathbf{w}$ and the component vectors that add up to it: $\mathbf{w} = \mathbf{c}_1 + \mathbf{c}_2 + \ldots$ The same is true here generally with respect to tensor product representations, but now in addition we can identify the representations of each constituent as a role-*dependent* representation built in a systematic way (through tensor product variable binding) from a role-*independent* representation of the filler and a filler-independent representation of its role.

Among the computational properties required of the variable binding mechanism is the possibility of *unbinding*: from the role-dependent representation of some constituent we must be able to extract the role-independent representation of that constituent. Similarly, given the vector representing a symbolic structure as a whole, it should be possible to extract the role-independent representation of the filler of any given role in the structure. Under a wide variety of conditions this is possible with the tensor product representation, although when so many roles are simultaneously filled that the capacity of the representing network is exceeded, corruptions, confusions, and errors can be introduced during unbinding. The conditions under which error-free unbinding can be performed, and characterization of the errors occurring when these conditions are violated, can be computed (Smolensky, 1987a). Thus, for example, if we have a tensor product representation for *P&Q*, and we wish to extract the first element *P* as part of a deductive process, then as long as the representing network is not trivially small, we can easily do so without error, using very simple (linear) connectionist processes.

So, returning to F&P's critique, let's see what the tensor product representational scheme can do for us in terms of the simple inference problems they talk about.

Using the tensor product technique, it is possible to define a family of representations of tree structures. We can consider a simple tree for *P&Q* consisting of *&* at the top, *P* as its left child, and *Q* as its right child; and we can view the roles as positions in the tree, the simplest kind of role decomposition. The tensor product representation of that tree structure is a vector $\mathbf{F}(P\&Q)$ which is related to the vectors representing the constituents, $\mathbf{F}(P)$ and $\mathbf{F}(Q)$, by a function $\mathbf{B}_\&$ that is particular to constructing conjunctions:

$$\mathbf{F}(P\&Q) = \mathbf{B}_\& [\mathbf{F}(P), \mathbf{F}(Q)]$$

The function $B_\&$ is defined by

$$\mathbf{B}_\&(\mathbf{u}, \mathbf{v}) = \mathbf{c}_\& + \tau_0\mathbf{u} + \tau_1\mathbf{v}$$

where $\mathbf{c}_\&$ is a constant vector and τ_0 and τ_1 are linear operators (the most natural vector operators) that vary depending on how the parameters individuating the tensor product representation are chosen.

I have descended to this level of detail and used this notation because in footnote 9 (p. 14) of F&P, exactly this property is chosen to define $\mathbf{F}$ as a "physical instantiation mapping of combinatorial structure." In this sense the tensor product representation meets F&P's formal requirements for a representation of combinatorial structure.

But have we merely provided an implementation then of a symbolic language of thought? In general, the answer is "no." Depending on how we have chosen to set the parameters in specifying the tensor product representation (which determines the properties of τ_0 and τ_1), we can fail to have any of the following properties holding (Smolensky, 1987a):

4   a   *Uniqueness with respect to roles or fillers.* If we're not careful, even though the above equation is satisfied, we can end up with *P&Q* having the same representation as *Q&P*, or other more subtle ambiguities about what fills various roles in the structure.

b *Unbounded depth.* We may avoid the first problem (4a) for sufficiently small structures, but when representing sufficiently large or deep structures, these problems may appear. Unless the vector space in which we do our representation is infinite-dimensional (corresponding to a network with infinitely many units), we cannot solve (4a) for unbounded depth. (Of course, the same is true of Turing/von Neumann machines if they are only allowed bounded resources; but whereas the capacity limit in the symbolic case is a hard one, the tensor product representation allows for graceful degradation as resources are saturated.)

c *Nonconfusability in memory.* Even when problem (4a) is avoided, when we have representations with uniquely determined filler/role bindings, it can easily happen that we cannot simultaneously store many such structures in a connectionist memory without getting intrusions of undesired memories during the retrieval of a given memory.

d *Processing independence.* This is in a sense a generalization of the preceding point, concerning processing constraints that may arise even when problem (4a) is avoided. In simple associative processing, for example, we may find that we can associate two vectors representing symbolic structures with what we like, but then find ourselves unable to associate the representation of a third structure with what we like, because its associate is constrained by the other two.

With all these properties potentially failing to hold, it doesn't sound to me like we're dealing with an implementation of a symbolic language of thought. But at this point somebody's going to want to say, "Well, you've just got a *lousy* implementation of a symbolic language of thought." But it's not that simple. We may have lost some (superficially desirable, at least) features of a symbolic language of thought, but we've gained some (superficially desirable, at least) features of connectionist processing in return.

5 a *Massive parallelism.* Since we have a vector that represents an entire tree at once, we can feed it into the usual connectionist massively parallel processes. Unlike traditional AI programs, we don't have to spend all our time painfully traversing step-by-step long descending chains into the bowels of complex symbolic data structures: it's all there at once, all accessible in parallel.[8]

b *Content-addressable memory.* This is the usual distributed connectionist story, but now it applies to *structural information*.

c *Statistical inference.* F&P are among the first to attack connectionism for basing its processing mechanisms on statistical inference. One more reason for them to deny that the connectionist framework I am discussing truly constitutes an implementation of their preferred architecture. Yet their arguments *against* statistical processing are much less compelling than their arguments *for* structure-sensitive processing. We are now in a position to go after *both*, in a unified framework, dissolving a long-standing tension arising from a failure to see how to formally unify structure-sensitive and statistical processing. Rather than having to model the mind as *either* a structure cruncher *or* a number cruncher, we can now see it as a number cruncher in which the numbers crunched are in fact representing complex structures.[9]

d   *Statistical learning.* Since structure can now be brought fully into the world of connectionist learning research, we can move from declarations of dogma to actual empirical results about what structurally-rich representations and processes can and cannot be acquired from experience through statistically based learning. We can now foresee a time when it will be too late to put your money down on the fate of the "poverty of the stimulus" dogma.

The point is that the parametric variation in tensor product representations covers a rich territory, and an important item on the connectionist cognitive modeling agenda is to determine whether in that territory there is a set of representations that has the right mixture of the power of (5) and the limitations of (4) to capture real human behavior. This large space of tensor product representations extends from simple ultralocal representations of the sort F&P correctly dismiss towards – I hesitate to say all the way up to, but quite close to – a true implementation of a symbolic language of thought. If you want such an implementation, you have to go to a limit that includes the following characteristics:

6   a   *Orthogonality.* The angle between the vectors representing different roles needs to go to 90 degrees, and similarly for vectors representing the fillers, to eliminate non-uniqueness and minimize interference in memory.

b   *Infinite-dimensional representations.* Otherwise, we can't represent unboundedly deep structures without confusion.

c   *Simple operations.* If we happen to want an implementation of sequential algorithms, then in processing these representations we insist that the vector equivalent of the primitive symbolic operations (like Lisp's car, cdr, and cons) are all that can be done in one time step: We don't avail ourselves of the massively parallel operations that otherwise would be available to us.

I have talked so far mostly about representations and little about processing. If we are interested, as F&P are, in inferences such as that from *P&Q* to *P*, it turns out that with tensor product representations, this operation can be achieved by a simple linear transformation upon these representational vectors, the kind of transformation most natural in this category of representations.[10] Not only can this structure-sensitive process be achieved by connectionist mechanisms on connectionist representations, but it can be achieved through the simplest of all connectionist operations: linear mapping. All in an architecture that differs fundamentally from the Classical one; we have not implemented a symbolic language of thought.

3   Connectionism, Implementationalism, and Limitivism

I am not a crook.

Richard Nixon

Let me now bring the arguments of section 2 to bear on the general issues raised in section 1.

3.1 The methodological Implications of Implementationalism and Limitivism

It seems to me most likely that symbolic descriptions *will* provide scientifically important *approximate* higher level accounts of how the ultimate connectionist cognitive models compute – but that these distributed connectionist models will not implement a symbolic language of thought, under the relevant (and correct) definition of the word. The approximations involved demand a willingness to accept context-sensitive symbols and interactional components present in compositional structures, and the other funny business that came out in the *coffee* example. If we're willing to live with all those degrees of approximation, then we can usefully view these symbolic level descriptions as approximate higher level accounts of the processing in a connectionist network.

An important overall conclusion in the constituency issue, then, is that the Classical and connectionist approaches differ *not* in whether they accept principles (2), *but in how they formally instantiate them.* To really confront the Classical/connectionist dispute, one has to be willing to descend to the level of the particular formal instantiations they give to the nonformal principles (2). To fail to descend to this level of detail is to miss much of the issue. In the Classical approach, principles (2) are formalized using syntactic structures for mental representations and symbol manipulation for mental processes. In the distributed connectionist approach (2) are formalized using vectorial representations for mental representations, and the corresponding notion of compositionality, together with numerical mental processes that derive their structure sensitivity from the differential way that they treat the parts of vectors corresponding to different structural roles.

In terms of research methodology, this means that the agenda for connectionism should not be to develop a connectionist implementation of the symbolic language of thought, but rather to develop formal analysis of vectorial representations of complex structures and operations on those structures that are sufficiently structure-sensitive to do the required work. This is exactly the kind of research that, for example, tensor product representations are being used to support.

Thus the PTC position is that distributed representations provide a description of mental states with semantically interpretable constituents, but that there is no complete, precise formal account of the construction of composites or of mental processes in general that can be stated solely in terms of context-independent semantically interpretable constituents. On this account, there *is* a language of thought – but only approximately; the language of thought by itself does not provide a basis for an exact formal account of mental structure or processes – it cannot by itself support a precise formal account of the cognitive architecture.

Constituency is one illustration of a central component of the general PTC approach to connectionism: the relation hypothesized between connectionist models based on continuous mathematics and Classical models based on discrete, symbolic computation. That relationship might be called the *cognitive correspondence principle*: when powerful connectionist computational systems are appropriately analyzed at higher levels, elements of symbolic computation appear as emergent properties.

Figure 5 schematically illustrates the cognitive correspondence principle. At the top are nonformal notions: the central hypotheses that the principles of cognition consist in principles of memory, of inference, of compositionality and constituent structure, etc. In the F&P argument, the relevant nonformal principles are their compositionality principles (2).

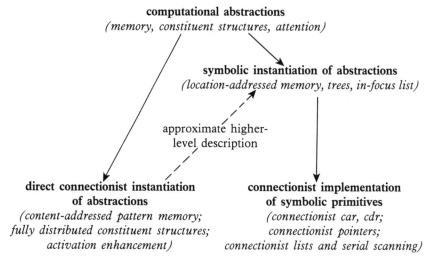

computational abstractions
(memory, constituent structures, attention)

symbolic instantiation of abstractions
(location-addressed memory, trees, in-focus list)

approximate higher-
level description

**direct connectionist instantiation
of abstractions**
*(content-addressed pattern memory;
fully distributed constituent structures;
activation enhancement)*

**connectionist implementation
of symbolic primitives**
*(connectionist car, cdr;
connectionist pointers;
connectionist lists and serial scanning)*

Figure 5 PTC vs. implementationalism (Reprinted with permission of *The Behavioral and Brain Sciences.*)

The nonformal principles at the top of figure 5 have certain formalizations in the discrete mathematical category, which are shown one level down on the right branch. For example, memory is formalized as standard location-addressed memory or some appropriately more sophisticated related notion. Inference gets formalized in the discrete category as logical inference, a particular form of symbol manipulation. And so on.

The PTC research agenda consists in taking these kinds of cognitive principles and finding new ways to instantiate them in formal principles based on the continuous mathematics of dynamical systems; these are shown in figure 5 at the lowest level on the left branch. The concept of memory retrieval is reformalized in terms of the continuous evolution of a dynamical system towards a point attractor whose position in the state space is the memory; we naturally get content-addressed memory instead of location-addressed memory. (Memory storage becomes modification of the dynamics of the system so that its attractors are located where the memories are supposed to be; thus the principles of memory storage are even more unlike their symbolic counterparts than those of memory retrieval.) When reformalizing inference principles, the continuous formalism leads naturally to principles of statistical inference rather than logical inference. And so on.

The cognitive correspondence principle states that the general relationship between the connectionist formal principles and the symbolic formal principles – given that they are both instantiations of common nonformal notions, and to the extent that ultimately they are both scientifically valid descriptions of the same cognitive system – is that if we take a higher level analysis of what's going on in the connectionist systems we find that it matches, to some kind of approximation, what's going on in the symbolic formalism. This relation is indicated in figure 5 by the dotted arrow.

This is to be contrasted with an implementational view of connectionism such as that which F&P advocate. As portrayed in figure 5, the implementational methodology is to proceed from the top to the bottom not directly, via the left branch, but indirectly, via the right branch: connectionists should take the symbolic instantiations of the nonformal principles and should find ways of implementing *them* in connectionist networks.

The PTC methodology is to be contrasted not just with the implementational approach, but also with the eliminativist one. In terms of these methodological considerations, eliminativism has a strong and a weak form. The weak form advocates taking the left branch of figure 5 but ignoring altogether the symbolic formalizations, on the belief that the symbolic notions will confuse rather than enlighten us in our attempts to understand connectionist computation. The strong eliminativist position states that even viewing the nonformal principles at the top of figure 5 as a starting point for thinking about cognition is a mistake – that it is better, for example, to pursue a blind bottom-up strategy in which we take low-level connectionist principles from neuroscience and see where they lead us, without being prejudiced by archaic prescientifc notions such as those at the top of figure 5.

In rejecting both the implementationalist and eliminativist positions, PTC views connectionist accounts in significant part as reducing and explaining symbolic accounts. Connectionist accounts serve to refine symbolic accounts, to reduce the degree of approximation required, to enrich the computational notions from the symbolic and discrete world, to fill them out with notions of continuous computation. Primarily that's done by descending to a lower level of analysis, by exposing the hidden microstructure in these kinds of large-scale, discrete symbolic operations.

I have dubbed the PTC position *limitivism* because it views connectionism as delimiting the domain D of validity of symbolic accounts, and explaining the validity of the symbolic approximation through passage to the "Classical limit," a general theoretical limit incorporating, e.g., the specifics described in (6), in which connectionist accounts admit, more and more exactly, higher-level symbolic accounts – at least in the limited domain D. This limitivist position on the relation between connectionism and symbolic theory is obviously modeled after a relation frequently observed in the refinement of physical theories, e.g., the relation between quantum and Newtonian mechanics.

The cognitive correspondence principle is so named because I believe that it has a role to play in the developing microtheory of cognition that's analogous to the role that the quantum correspondence principle played in the development of microtheory in physics. This case from physics instantiates the structure of figure 5 quite directly. There are certain fundamental physical principles that arch over both the classical and quantum formalisms: the notions of space and time and associated invariance principles, the principles of energy and momentum conservation, force laws, and so on. These principles at the top of figure 5 are instantiated in particular ways in the classical formalism, corresponding to the point one level down on the right branch. To go to a lower level of physical analysis requires the development of a new formalism. In this quantum formalism the fundamental principles are reinstantiated: they occupy the bottom of the left branch. The classical formalism can be looked at as a higher level description of the same principles operating at the lower quantum level: the dotted line of figure 5. Of course quantum mechanics does not *implement* classical mechanics: the accounts are intimately related, but classical mechanics provides an approximate, not an exact, higher-level account.[11] In a fundamental sense, the quantum and classical theories are quite incompatible: according to the ontology of quantum mechanics, the ontology of classical mechanics is quite impossible to realize in this world. But there is no denying that the classical ontology and the accompanying principles are theoretically essential, for at least two reasons: (a) to provide explanations (literally, perhaps, approximate ones) of an enormous range of classical phenomena for which direct explanation from quantum principles is hopelessly infeasible, and (b) historically, to provide the guidance necessary to discover the quantum principles in the first place. To try to develop lower-level principles without looking at the higher-level principles for guidance, given the insights we have gained from those principles, would seem – to put it mildly – inadvisable. It is basically this pragmatic consideration that motivates the cognitive correspondence principle and the PTC position it leads to.

3.2   Constituency via Vector Decomposition, Explanatory Relevance, and Causal Efficacy

As a final topic I would like to show how the previous methodological considerations relate specifically to the technical heart of this paper. I want to show that, if we take the general position advocated above that the research agenda of distributed connectionism is to find formal means within the continuous mathematics of dynamical systems for naturally and powerfully embodying central nonformal principles of computation and cognition, then the connectionist analysis of constituent structure I have described here is, if not inevitable, then at least perfectly natural. I take up this topic because it has been suggested that in my analysis, perhaps in order to cook up a refutation of F&P, I have seriously contorted the notion of constituency; that superposition of vectors, and tensor product binding, are just not appropriate means of instantiating constituency.

At the same time, I will consider the central question: "Is the sense in which vector decomposition constitutes a constituency relation adequate to make constituency *explanatorily relevant* to or *causally efficacious* in the account of the systematicity of thought, the basic problem motivating F&P's critique?"

Let me begin with a few words about the idea of decomposing a vector into a sum or superposition of component vectors: $\mathbf{w} = \mathbf{c}_1 + \mathbf{c}_2 + \ldots$. This technique is very commonly used to explain the behavior of dynamical systems; it works best for simple linear systems, where the equations governing the interaction between state variables are linear (such as the very simplest connectionist models). In that case – and the technique gets more complicated from there – the story is as follows.

We want to know, if we start the system off in some initial state described by the vector $\mathbf{w}$, what will the system's subsequent behavior be? (In the connectionist case, $\mathbf{w}$ characterizes the input, and we want to know what states the system will then go through; especially, what the later state that determines the output will be.) First we ask, how can the vector $\mathbf{w}$ be decomposed: $\mathbf{w} = \mathbf{c}_1 + \mathbf{c}_2 + \ldots$, so that the component vectors $\mathbf{c}_i$ are along certain special directions, determined by the linear interaction equations of the system; these directions $\mathbf{e}_i$ are called the "normal modes" of the system, and each $\mathbf{c}_i = c_i \mathbf{e}_i$, where the coefficient c_i tells how strongly represented in this particular input $\mathbf{w}$ the tth normal mode is. Once we have decomposed the vector into components in the directions of the normal modes, we can write down in a closed form expression the state of the system at any later time: it is just the superposition of the states arising from each of the normal modes independently, and those normal modes are defined exactly so that it is possible to write down how they evolve in time.[12] Thus, knowing the interaction equations of the system, we can compute the normal modes and how they evolve in time, and then we can explain how *any* state evolves in time, simply be decomposing that state into components in the directions of the normal modes. To see an example of this technique applied to actual connectionist networks, see the general analysis of Smolensky (1986) and the specific analysis in Anderson and Mozer (1981) of the categorization performed in J. A. Anderson's "Brain-State-in-a-Box" model. (Both these analyses deal with what I call *quasi-linear* networks, a class covering many actual connectionist systems, in which the heart of the computation is linear, but a certain degree of non-linearity is also important.)

Thus, to explain the behavior of the system, we usually choose to decompose the state vector into components in the directions of the normal modes, which are conveniently related to the particular dynamics of this system. If there is change in how the system interacts with itself (as in connectionist networks that learn), over time we'll change the way we choose to break up the state in order to explain the behavior. There's no unique way to decompose a vector. That is to say, there are lots of ways that this input vector could be viewed as composed of constituents, but normal mode decomposition happens to enable a good explanation for behavior over time. In general, there may well be other compositions that are explanatorily relevant.

So, far from being an unnatural way to break up the part of a connectionist state vector that represents an input, decomposing the vector into components is exactly what we'd expect to need to do to explain the processing of that input.[13] If the connections that mediate processing of the vectors representing composite structures have the effect of sensible processing of the vector in terms of the task demands, it is very likely that in order to *understand and explain* the regularities in the network's behavior we will need to break the vector for the structure into the vectors for the constituents, and relate the processing of the whole to the processing of the parts. That this decomposition, and not arbitrary decompositions into meaningless component vectors, is useful for explaining the processing is a consequence of the connections that embody the process. Those particular components are useful for those particular connections. In general, what distinguishes one decomposition of a state vector that is useful for predicting behavior from other decompositions that are not is that the useful decomposition bears some special relation to the dynamics of the system. It may well turn out that to explain various aspects of the system's behavior (for example, various cognitive processes acting on a given input), we will want to exploit various decompositions.

Are the vector constituents in physical and connectionist systems causally efficacious? It would appear not, since the real mechanism driving the behavior of the system operates oblivious to our descriptive predilection to vector decomposition. It is the numerical values comprising the vector (in the connectionist case, the individual activity values) that really drive the machine.

As Fodor and Pylyshyn will, I believe, agree, caution in treating "causal efficacy" is required even for the Classical case. When we write a Lisp program, are the symbolic structures we think in terms of causally efficacious in the operation of the computer that runs the program? There is a sense in which they are: even though we normally think of the "real" causes as physical and far below the symbolic level, there is nonetheless a complete and precise algorithmic (temporal) story to tell about the states of the machine described at the level of symbols. Traditional computers (the hardware and especially the software) are designed to make that true, and it is the main source of their power.

The hypothesis I have attributed to distributed connectionism is that there is no comparable story at the symbolic level in the human cognitive architecture: no algorithm in terms of semantically interpretable elements that gives a precise formal algorithmic account of the system's behavior over time. That is a difference with the Classical view that I have made much of. It may be that a good way to characterize the difference is in terms of whether the constituents in mental structures are causally efficacious in mental processing.

Such causal efficacy was not my goal in developing the tensor product representation; rather, the goal was and is the design of connectionist systems that display the kinds of complex systematic behavior seen, for example, in language processing – and the mathematical explanation of that systematicity. As the examples from physics show, it is not only wrong to claim that to explain systematicity by reference to constituent structures requires that those constituents be causally efficacious: it is also wrong (but more honest) to claim (as Fodor often does) that such an explanatory strategy, while not provably unique, constitutes "the only game in town." There is an alternative explanatory strategy that has been practiced very effectively in physics for centuries, and that strategy can be applied in cognitive science as well. There are now at least two games in town, and rather than pretending otherwise, we should get on with the business of playing those games for all we can. Odds are, given how hard cognitive science is, we'll need to be playing other games before too long.

The Classical strategy for explaining the systematicity of thought is to hypothesize that there is a precise formal account of the cognitive architecture in which the constituents of mental representations have causally efficacious roles in the mental processes acting on them. The PTC view denies that such an account of the cognitive architecture exists,[14] and hypothesizes instead that, like the constituents of structures in quantum mechanics, the systematic effects observed in the processing of mental representations arises because the evolution of vectors can be (at least partially and approximately) explained in terms of the evolution of their components, even though the precise dynamical equations apply at the lower level of the individual numbers comprising the vectors and cannot be pulled up to provide a precise temporal account of the processing at the level of entire constituents – i.e., even though the constituents are not causally efficacious.[15]

4 Summary

Therefore, I shall resign the presidency effective at noon tomorrow.

Richard Nixon

Shifting attention away from the refutation of F&P's argument, let me summarize what I take to be the positive contributions of this paper.

7 a As F&P plead, it *is* crucial for connectionism to separate itself from simplistic associationist psychology, and to accept the importance of a number of computational principles fundamental to traditional cognitive science, such as those relating to structure that F&P emphasize, which go beyond the computational repertoire of simple traditional connectionist networks.

   b The computational repertoire of connectionism should be extended by finding ways of directly, naturally, and powerfully realizing these computational principles within the continuous mathematics of dynamical systems.

   c Just as a set of symbolic structures offers a domain for modeling structured mental representation and processing, so do sets of vectors, once the appropriate notions (such as variable binding via tensor products) are recognized in the new mathematical category. Thus distributed connectionist representations provide a computational arena for structure processing.

   d The resulting connectionist model of mental processing is characterized by context-sensitive constituents, approximately (but not exactly) compositional semantics, massively parallel structure-sensitive processing, statistical inference and statistical learning with structured representations.

   e This connectionist cognitive architecture is intrinsically two-level: semantic interpretation is carried out at the level of patterns of activity while the complete, precise, and formal account of mental processing must be carried out at the level of individual activity values and connections. Mental processes reside at a lower level of analysis than mental representations.

   f Thus, not only is the connectionist cognitive architecture fundamentally different from the Classical one, so is the basic strategy for explaining the systematicity of thought. The systematic behavior of the cognitive system is to be explained by appealing to the systematic constituent structure of the representational vectors, and the connectivity patterns that give rise to and manipulate these vectors: but the mechanism responsible for that behavior does not (unlike in the Classical account) operate through laws or rules that are expressible formally at the level of the constituents.

The wind is changing

Mary Poppins

Only connect

E. M. Forster[16]

Acknowledgments

I have benefited greatly from personal conversations with Jerry Fodor and Zenon Pylyshyn, conversations extending from February 1986, when Fodor presented an early version of the argument ("Against connectionism") at the Workshop on the Foundations of AI in Las Cruces, New Mexico, through a (surprisingly enjoyable) public debate held at MIT in March 1988. The concerns that drove my research to tensor product representations were kindled through that interaction. I have learned a tremendous amount from Georges Rey, thanks to his wonderful insight, open-mindedness, and patience; I would also like to thank him for the invitation to contribute to this volume and for his most helpful suggestions for this paper. Thanks, too, to Terry Horgan for very helpful discussions, as well as to the other participants of the Spindel Conference on Connectionism and the Philosophy of Mind (which resulted in the collection of papers in which Smolensky (1987b) appears). I thank Terry Horgan, John Tienson, and the *Southern Journal of Philosophy* for permission to include a portion of Smolensky (1987b) here. Rob Cummins and Georg Schwarz have helped me enormously in sorting out a number of the issues discussed here, and I refer the reader to their papers for a number of important insights that have not been given their due here. Kevin Markey gets the credit for the crucial Presidential quotes. Finally I would like to thank Geoff Hinton, Jay McClelland, Dave Rumelhart, David Touretzky, and more recently, Alan Prince, for many helpful discussions on issues relating to connectionism and structure processing.

This work has been supported by NSF grants IRI-8609599 and ECE-8617947 to the author, by a grant to the author from the Sloan Foundation's computational neuroscience program, and by the Optical Connectionist Machine Program of the NSF Engineering Research Center for Optoelectronic Computing Systems at the University of Colorado at Boulder.

NOTES

1 Quoted in Fodor, 1975a, p. 27.
2 This point is brought out nicely in Cummins and Schwarz (1987), Schwarz (1987), and Cummins (1989).
3 The complexity criterion here is very low: the interactions should be more complex than purely linear. A lengthy and hopefully accessible discussion may be found in Smolensky, (1986).
4 They admit up front that these arguments are a rerun updated for the 80's, a colorized version of a film that was shown in black and white some time ago – where the color comes mainly from replacing everywhere the word "behaviorism" by "connectionism."
5 The conception of connectionist representation and processing embodied in figure 1 is at the center of this entire argument, so it is important to properly locate this network and the Ballard and Hayes paper in the connectionist landscape; for those not well familiar with the territory, this may be facilitated by a sociogeographical digression. Hayes is a leading figure in the logic-based approach to symbolic AI, and (to my knowledge) this collaborative exercise is his only foray onto connectionist turf. Ballard is a leading connectionist of the "Rochester school," which tends to favor local representations over distributed ones, and which as a result represents a radically different set of foundational commitments (see Feldman and Ballard, 1982) from those of the "San Diego" or "PDP" school, as articulated for example in the PDP books (Rumelhart, McClelland, and the PDP Research Group, 1986; McClelland, Rumelhart, and the PDP Research Group, 1986); my version of the PDP framework is articulated as PTC in Smolensky (1988a, b), which explicitly addresses the contrast with Feldman and Ballard (1982). (Incidentally, the name "PDP" was coined to differentiate the approach from the "connectionist" approach already defined by Feldman and Ballard, 1982; the referent of "connectionist" subsequently expanded to engulf the PDP approach (e.g., *Cognitive Science*, 1985). This left what I have referred to as the "Rochester" approach without a distinctive name; the term "structured connectionist networks" is now sometimes used, but it is potentially quite misleading.) As already evidenced in section 1, it turns out that on foundational issues generally, the local vs. distributed issues forces the two schools of connectionism to take quite different positions; a response to F&P from the Feldman and Ballard (1982) perspective would have to differ completely from the one I offer here. While F&P argue that distributed representations make no difference, I now proceed to identify a crucial fallacy in that argument, which this paper as a whole shows to be quite inadequate.
6 A sort of debate about connectionism was held between Geoffrey Hinton and David Rumelhart on the one hand, and Zenon Pylyshyn and Kurt VanLehn on the other. While pursuing the nature of connectionist representations, Pylyshyn asked Rumelhart: "Look, can you guys represent a cup of coffee in these networks?" Rumelhart's reply was "Sure" so Pylyshyn continued: "And can you represent a cup without coffee in it?" Waiting for the trap to close, Rumelhart said "Yes," at which point Pylyshyn pounced: "Ah-hah, well, the difference between the two is just the representation of *coffee* – you've just built a representation of *cup with coffee* by combining a representation of *cup* with a representation of *coffee*."
7 As suggested to me by Georges Rey, the tensor product representation scheme can be understood by analogy to Gödel number encodings. In the Gödel encoding, the representation of a string ab ... x ... is the number $v = p_1{}^a p_2{}^b ... p_i{}^x ...$ where x is the ith symbol in the string. Each of the symbols in the alphabet, a, b, ..., x, ... is assigned a unique whole number code, $a, b, ..., x, ...$ To each possible position i in the string corresponds a certain prime number p_i. Given v, it is possible to recover

the string it represents, provided we know both the set of primes used to code positions, $\{p_i\}$, and the encoding of the alphabet; this is because v has a unique decomposition into powers of primes. In the tensor product scheme, this string would be represented by a vector $\mathbf{v} = \mathbf{p}_1 \otimes \mathbf{a} + \mathbf{p}_2 \otimes \mathbf{b} + \ldots + \mathbf{p}_i \otimes \mathbf{x} + \ldots$ Instead of numbers, each symbol is now encoded by a vector of activity values ($\mathbf{x}$ is represented by $\mathbf{x}$, etc.); instead of primes, each position i is represented by an activity vector $\mathbf{p}_i$. In going from the Gödel scheme to the tensor product representation, numbers become vectors, the exponentiation used to bind symbols to their positions becomes the tensor product, and the multiplication used to combine the symbol/position bindings becomes vector addition. From $\mathbf{v}$ we can exactly recover the string if the vectors $\{\mathbf{p}_i\}$ are all linearly independent: if none can be expressed as a weighted sum of the others. This is the property that guarantees we can undo the vector addition operation, just as using primes ensures in the Gödel scheme that we can undo the multiplication operation (none of the p_i can be expressed as a product of the others). Gödel numbering can be done recursively, so that the exponents representing consecutive objects (e.g. lines in a proof) can themselves be the Gödel numbers of strings; likewise, tensor product representations can be built recursively, so that the vector representing a filler (or role) can itself be the tensor product representation of a structure. This is possible because the tensor product takes two vectors and creates a new vector which can then be used in a subsequent tensor product. (This is the reason that tensor algebra is natural here; in matrix algebra, which is to some degree a subset of tensor algebra, the outer product of two vectors, which is the same set of numbers as the tensor product of those vectors, is treated as a new type object: a matrix – this blocks recursion.)

8   It's all well and good to say, as F&P do, that the Classical view has no commitment to serial processing. "We like parallel computation too." Fine, give me a massively parallel symbolic model that processes tree structures and I'll be happy to compare it to this. But I don't see it out there.

See Dolan & Smolensky (1988) for an actual distributed connectionist model, TPPS, that uses the tensor product to represent a symbolic structure and operate on it with massive parallelism. The system is an exercise in applying the tensor product representation to put on a somewhat more general and simple mathematical footing Touretzky & Hinton's (1985) Boltzmann machine implementation of a distributed connectionist production system, DCPS. Each production in TPPS does pattern matching against the whole symbolic structure in working memory in parallel, and does all parts of its action in parallel. Since it is an implementation of a traditional production system, however, productions are fired one at a time, although conflict resolution is done in parallel.

9   Like connectionist networks, traditional computers were originally viewed exclusively as number processors. Newell and Simon are credited with teaching us that traditional computers could also be used as powerful structure processors. I am essentially trying to make the same point about connectionist networks.

10 This is true provided the parameter values defining the representation satisfy the very weak constraint that the simplest possible confusions are avoided (such as confusing *P&Q* with *Q&P* or with *P or Q*).

11 Many cases analogous to "implementation" *are* found in physics: Newton's laws provide an "implementation" of Kepler's laws; Maxwell's theory "implements" Coulomb's law; the quantum principles of the hydrogen atom "implement" Balmer's formula.

12 For example, in a dynamical system that oscillates, the evolution of the normal modes in time is given by: $\mathbf{e}_n(t) = e^{i\omega_n t} \mathbf{e_n}$. Each particular normal mode e_n consists of an oscillation with a particular frequency ω_n.

13 How reasonable is it to view this decomposition process as a formalization of the notion of decomposing a "structure" into its "constituents"? (I am indebted to Tim van Gelder, personal communication, for very useful discussion of this issue; see also van Gelder, 1989.) I take it that it is a reasonable use of the term "constituent" to say that "electrons are constituents of atoms." In modern physics, what is the relation between the representation of the electron and the representation of the atom?

The state of the atom, like the states of all systems in quantum theory, is represented by a vector in an abstract vector space. Each electron has an internal state (its "spin"); it also has a role it plays in the atom as a whole: it occupies some "orbital," essentially a cloud of probability for finding it at particular places in the atom. The internal state of an electron is represented by a "spin vector"; the orbital or role of the electron (part) in the atom (whole) is represented by another vector, which describes the probability cloud. The vector representing the electron as situated in the atom is the tensor product of the vector representing the internal state of the electron and the vector representing its orbital. The atom as a whole is represented by a vector that is the sum or superposition of vectors, each of which represents a particular electron situated in its orbital. (There are also contributions of the same sort from nucleons.)

Thus the vector representing the whole is the sum of tensor products of pairs of vectors; in each pair, one vector represents the part independent of its role in the whole, and the other represents the role in the whole independent of the part that fills the role. This is exactly the way I have used tensor products to construct distributed connectionist representations for wholes from distributed connectionist representations of their parts (and from distributed representations of the roles of parts in the whole) – and this is exactly where the idea came from.

So someone who claims that the tensor product representational scheme distorts the notion of constituency has some explaining to do.

So does someone who claims that the sense in which the whole has parts is not explanatorily relevant. We explain the properties of atoms by invoking properties of their electronic configuration all the time. Quantum theory aside, physical systems whose states are described by vectors have for centuries had their behavior explained by viewing the state vector as a superposition of component vectors, and explaining the evolution of the total state in terms of the evolution of its component vectors – as I have indicated in the preceding discussion of normal modes.

Are the constituents of mental representations as I have characterized them in distributed connectionist systems causally efficacious in mental processing?

The term "causally efficacious" must be used with some caution. The equations that drive the atom do not work by first figuring out what the component particles are, and then working on each of them separately. The equations take the elements comprising the vector for the whole atom and change them in time. We can *analyze* the system by breaking up the vector for the whole into the vectors for the parts, and in general that's a good way to do the analysis; but nature doesn't do that in updating the state of the system from one moment to the next. So, in this case, are the constituents causally efficacious or not? The same question arises in the connectionist case.

14 Except for that limited part of the architecture I have called the "conscious rule interpreter"; see Smolensky, 1988a.

15 I use this characterization rather tentatively because I am not yet convinced that the notion of causal efficacy it presupposes is less problematic than what it is being invoked to elucidate.

16 Quoted in Fodor, 1975a; p. vi.

13

How to Do Semantics for the Language of Thought

ROBERT STALNAKER

Okay, suppose there *is* a language of thought. More specifically, suppose that what makes mental states intentional is that they consist of the presence in the mind or the brain of the person in the states tokens of sentences of a mental language – tokens that play some appropriate functional or causal role (the role determining what *kind* of intentional state – belief, intention, hope, etc. – it is that the presence of the token constitutes). I do not claim that it is clear exactly what I am supposing, and I am not convinced that there is a way to understand this hypothesis so that it is both substantive and correct. But even without further explanation, the supposition does suggest the following agenda for those who want an account of intentionality: if we want to explain how mental states can have content, and to say for particular cases what content they have, we should do semantics for the mental language to which the tokens that constitute the mental states belong. But how do we do that? There is little agreement about how to do semantics, or even about the questions that define the subject of semantics, so even after we sign on to the agenda, we have some work to do before we know how to carry it out. For those who see the problem this way, Jerry Fodor, in his *Psychosemantics*,[1] has lots of advice to offer about how such a project should go, both constructive suggestions about the shape that a semantic theory for a mental language should take, and criticisms of approaches that he thinks are on the wrong track. As always, the suggestions and criticisms are interesting and provocative, but I am not convinced that the various things Fodor has to say all point in the same direction. My main aim in this paper is to try to bring out some tensions between different parts of Fodor's semantic project.

Here is a sketch of some of the pieces of advice that Fodor offers and argues for.

First, semantics for the language of thought should be *narrow* in the following sense: the semantic values that the semantics assigns to mental expressions should be determined by the intrinsic properties of the persons in whose minds those tokens reside. Thinkers who are intrinsically indistinguishable must have thoughts with the same meaning, whatever the facts about their external environments. Fodor accepts the conclusion of the Twin-Earth thought experiments that the thoughts of intrinsically indistinguishable thinkers can have different truth-conditional content, but takes this to show that a semantics for the language of thought should not by itself determine truth-conditional content. Instead, the semantic values of mental sentences should be functions taking external contexts into truth-conditional contents – functions that are determined by internal states.

Second, the semantics for the mental language must avoid that threat of *meaning holism* – the doctrine that "the identity – specifically the intentional content – of a propositional attitude is determined by the *totality* of its epistemic liaisons," (p. 56) where epistemic liaisons are the relations between the attitude and other potential items of information that are taken by the thinker to be relevant to the truth or falsity of the attitude. The problem with meaning holism is that it implies that meaning is extremely unstable and idiosyncratic. Any changes in my overall system of beliefs will force a change in the meanings of all the mental sentence tokens that constitute those beliefs; and even minor differences between my system of beliefs and yours will imply that your beliefs have different meaning and content from mine, even when we express them the same way. It is hard to see how a theory of meaning with such consequences could contribute to the explanation of action and communication in terms of beliefs and intentions. In fact, Fodor says, "Meaning Holism looks to be entirely destructive of the hope for a propositional attitude psychology" (p. 56). Fodor thinks that one popular approach to mental semantics – functional or conceptual role semantics – is committed to meaning holism, and so he is critical of that semantical strategy.

Third, the semantics for the mental language should be a good old-fashioned *denotational* semantics, where the relation between words and their denotations is explained in causal terms. Fodor defends denotational semantics against a number of criticisms, both technical criticisms based on the way denotational theories individuate semantic values, and some more elusive philosophical objections. Then, in his discussion of causal theories of representation, Fodor is critical of some attempts at developing such a theory, mainly because he thinks they cannot give an adequate account of misrepresentation, but he makes some suggestions about the kind of causal theory that he thinks can avoid the limitations of others that have been proposed.

Some of this seems right to me, but I have questions, first about what some of Fodor's suggestions mean, and second about how they fit together into a single approach. I will begin by trying to get clear about the thesis that the semantics for the language of thought must be narrow.

Tyler Burge has argued that the contents of both our words and our thoughts are determined, in part, by the external environment in which we talk and think.[2] Content, as ordinarily conceived, is *wide*. Two intrinsically indistinguishable thinkers might be thinking different thoughts if the kinds of things that exist or the causal conditions that obtain in their environments are different, or if the social norms and practices of the communities with which the thinkers identify are different. Some people seem to think that Burge's conclusions raise a problem for a realistic, explanatory theory of propositional attitudes, and Fodor seems to agree that there is at least a prima facie problem. But he thinks we can reconcile Burge's conclusion that content, in the ordinary sense, is wide with a narrow semantics by distinguishing the semantic values that an appropriate semantics will associate with mental sentences from the truth-conditional contents of those sentences. Narrow and wide content are not, on Fodor's account, two independent aspects of meaning or content – he argues forcefully against two factor theories of content. Wide content, according to Fodor, is determined by narrow content, together with the contextual or environmental facts that Burge's arguments and examples show to be relevant to the determination of content. What a narrow content is, according to Fodor, is a function taking possible environmental contexts into truth-conditional, or wide, contents. The model is David Kaplan's semantics for demonstratives. A semantic theory for sentences containing demonstratives, pronouns, and tenses will not by itself tell you what is said by the sentences – what propositional content their tokens have, since that will depend on who is speaking to whom, when, and what the speaker is pointing at. What Kaplan's semantics gives you as semantic values for the sentences are functions from context into propositional contents, where context is a specification of the relevant parameters: a speaker, time of utterance, addressee, and whatever else is necessary to determine content. This kind of semantic value might be determined by the intrinsic properties of a speaker or thinker even if the resulting propositional content is not.[3]

It is, I take it, essential to the narrow semantics thesis not only that somehow the facts determine functions of the appropriate kind, but also that these functions play a role in the explanation of why the mental sentences have the content they have. Once we identify a mental sentence, it is easy enough to define a function that has the right properties, whatever it is that determines the meaning or content of the sentence. Just consider the function whose argument is any actual or possible total environment in which a token of the sentence might occur, and whose value is the propositional content that the sentence would have in that total environment. This will be a partial function, since in some possible environments the sentence won't have any content, but it is a perfectly well defined partial function. But what won't necessarily be true is that a plausible semantics will appeal to functions of this kind in explaining why the sentence has the content that it in fact has in some particular context.

Let me use a simple example to try to clarify the distinction I am trying to make. Consider a certain type of acoustical event, say the type of sound made by an ordinary American uttering the word "water." (I use this description just to point to the sound pattern – I mean to be talking about a type of event individuated by its physical properties.) There are all kinds of possible contexts in which an event of this kind might occur – it might, for example, be a noise emitted by a reptile, or the sound of a tree falling in the forest. But some possible occurrences of such a sound will be meaningful utterances. One might be a token of a mass noun naming H_2O, or XYZ; or it might be a proper name of a cat, or a subordinate conjunction, or a personal pronoun. There are, of course, no limits on the imaginable meanings that an utterance with this acoustical shape might have. Now consider the function that takes as its arguments all the possible environments in which this type of event might occur and whose value is the meaning (if any) that the sound would have if uttered in that environment. This function has the right formal properties to be the narrow meaning of a word, but of course it is not. A semantics that appealed to such a function would get things backwards. The word "water" does not (in English) mean what it does *because* it expresses this function (and is being used in this environment). The function is derivative from the actual and possible facts (whatever they are) that determine the semantics of the different actual and possible words that have that sound. The semantics is not something internal that determines the function; rather, the semantics is a part of the environment that the function takes as its argument.

The contrived function I have defined is narrow in the appropriate sense. The same function will be associated with two utterances made by internally indistinguishable speakers; whatever the facts about the external environment. In fact, my function will be narrow in a stronger sense than Fodor requires. Being associated with this function will, by defintion, be intrinsic not only to the utterer of the sound, but to the sound itself. Not only is the external environment irrelevant to determining the function; so is the internal environment, including the internal facts about the mental life of the speaker. Fodor's narrow content, presumably, is not *this* narrow. His notion will surely permit the same mental token (individuated by its intrinsic physical properties) to have different narrow contents in different situations. And it will presumably also be possible for physically different tokens to have the same narrow content. But what is it that determines the identity conditions for the semantic values in a narrow semantics for the language of thought? What kinds of changes in a person's overall mental state will constitute a change in the narrow content of some mental token? What kinds of similarities and differences between the mental lives of two different individuals will imply that tokens in each of their minds have the same or different semantic values, or narrow contents? Except in a brief remark at the end of his discussion of meaning holism, Fodor does not address this question, but the requirement that the semantics be narrow does put some constraints on permissible answers. The narrow content of a token must be determined by the internal mental properties of the individual. External environment can't be relevant; and presumably internal *physical* differences that are not reflected in any difference in functional organization will not be relevant either. So the identity of narrow contents must be *wholly* determined in some way or other by the functional relationships between the tokens that have the content and other mental events, states, and objects, including, possibly, other tokens. But isn't a semantic theory that explains semantic values in this way a conceptual or functional role semantics, and doesn't this kind of semantics lead us, according to Fodor, into the swamp of meaning holism? Before considering how Fodor thinks the kind of semantics he advocates can escape this swamp, let me look at his exposition of the general argument for meaning holism – an argument some version of which he thinks conceptual role theorists are committed to.

Arguments for meaning holism, Fodor suggests, generally go something like this: the first premise is that *some* of the epistemic liaisons holding between a mental token and other tokens are determinants of content. The second premise is that there is no principled way of distinguishing between the epistemic liaisons with respect to their role in the determination of content, so either all are semantically relevant, or else none is. The conclusion is that they all are, and so any change or difference in epistemic liaisons will imply a change or difference in content.[4] One might think that the most promising way to attack this argument would be to find a principled basis for discriminating between epistemic or conceptual connections, but Fodor directs most of his fire at the first premise. He seems to assume that if one were to grant that functional role is the main determinant of meaning and content, then one would have to concede the case to the meaning holist. Fodor's response to the functional role theorist is to defend an alternative kind of semantics. My question will be whether there is an alternative that is compatible with the requirement that semantics be narrow.

Fodor grants that functional role will play *some* part in an adequate semantics. "What I hold," he says, "(to put it very roughly) is that functional role is a marginal – a not very important – determinant of meaning" (p. 72). But what else is available to determine meaning – what are the other more important determinants? Fodor's alternative to functional role semantics is denotational semantics. Here I am puzzled for two reasons. First, I am not sure just what Fodor means by denotational semantics, but it seems, on the face of it, that a denotational semantics must be a wide semantics. If the semantic value of a mental expression is just its denotation, and if "the denotation of a concept is," as Fodor says, "whatever it is about the world that the concept does – or would – apply to" (p. 72) then, assuming that expressions of a mental language do sometimes apply to things outside of the head, semantic values of mental expressions will have to be in part a function of facts about the external environment. In a narrow semantics of the kind Fodor advocates, semantic values are supposed to be, not denotations, but functions from possible external environments into denotations. If a denotational semantics, as Fodor is using the term, is one that contrasts with a Fregean sense theory, then such a narrow semantics will have to be more like a sense theory than like a simple denotational semantics, since the relation between a term and its denotation will be mediated by an abstract semantic value, a value that might determine different denotations in different contexts, and that might be distinct from semantic values that determined the same value in some contexts.

Suppose Fodor is really advocating, not a simple denotational semantics, but a semantics in which semantic values are abstract objects that determine denotations. There still remains a problem, which is the second reason I am puzzled by Fodor's advocacy of denotational semantics in this context: I don't see how any kind of truth-conditional semantics, whether extensional, Fregean, or Kaplanesque, is an *alternative* to conceptual role semantics. A truth-conditional semantic theory does not even address the question that conceptual role semantics is trying to answer: the question of what the determinants of meaning are. Truth-conditional semantic theories, whether extensional or intensional, say what the semantic values of expressions of different categories are, and how the semantic values of complex expressions are determined by the values of their parts. For example, an extensional semantics for a fragment of English might say that the extension of the common noun "bachelor" is the set of unmarried men, and that if x is a name and F a common noun, then *x is an F* will be true if and only if the referent of x is in the set that is the extension of F. But statements of this kind make no claim at all about what features of the mental states and behavior of the users of the expressions make it true that words have the extensions (or intensions) that they have; they say nothing about what makes it true that the values of complex expressions are determined by the rules they are determined by. But *this* is the kind of question that conceptual role semantics is trying to answer. So I don't see that Fodor's defense of denotational semantics is a defense of an alternative solution to the problem that conceptual role semantics seeks to solve.[5]

A causal theory of reference or meaning would be an alternative answer: such a theory tries to say, not just what the semantic value is, but also what facts make it the case that something has a certain semantic value. But the usual kind of causal theory is an externalist, wide semantics, and so is not compatible with Fodor's project. Causation might play a role in a narrow semantic theory. The narrow semantic value of an expression might be a function that takes as its value whatever it is that plays a certain causal role in producing, or producing in a certain way, tokens of the expression. But we still need an answer to the question, what makes it true that expressions have, as their values, the particular functions of this kind that they have. If semantics is to be narrow, there does not seem to be anything else around except the internal functional or conceptual role, to provide the answer.

Suppose we say that the semantic values of mental expressions are functions taking possible environments into denotations, functions that are determined by the conceptual role of the mental expressions (their internal inferential relations with other mental expressions). Will our semantic values be vulnerable to the kind of holistic instability that Fodor thinks threaten the viability of conceptual role semantics? In a brief discussion of some examples at the end of his chapter on meaning holism, Fodor seems to concede that *narrow* meaning and content of concepts and thoughts will be unstable, changing with changes in the status of the concepts and thoughts. Specifically, he argues that when a person comes to believe that water is H_2O, the narrow content of the mental token expressing that belief, and the narrow content of his concept of water, change. There is thus no one narrow content that the person previously disbelieved, and subsequently believes. But Fodor suggests that this is really no problem since *wide* content and denotation will remain constant. After granting that "learning what *anything* really is changes one's narrow concept of that thing," he says that nothing much turns on this. "Changing the narrow content of the concept WATER doesn't in and of itself 'change the topic' of water-conversations ... the topic of water-conversations always was, and always will be, H_2O. It is not *narrow* content that fixes topics, it's *broad* content that does" (p. 95).

I have two comments on this: first, I am not sure that Fodor need have made this concession – at least the argument he gives seems to me much less decisive than he suggests; but second, the response to the concession – that it does not matter that narrow content varies across times and persons so long as the topic remains the same – seems to me inadequate. First, here is the argument: "Consider somebody who learns that water is H_2O and thus comes to distinguish between water and XYZ ... this person has *no* concept which denotes water in my context and water2 in my Twin's, for the narrow WATER concept that he applied to H_2O he *ipso facto* withholds from XYZ, and vice versa. So he's not the same function from contexts to truth conditions that my Twin and I are. So learning what water really is changed his narrow concept of water" (p. 95). Now unless we opt for an extreme holism of narrow content according to which only cognitively indistinguishable persons can have thoughts with the same narrow contents, it can't be that a difference in what two people apply a concept to, in a given context, implies a difference in the narrow content of the concept applied. Suppose I think there is gin in the bottle, while you know that someone polished off the gin and replaced it with water. I withhold my water concept from the stuff in the bottle, while you apply your water concept to it. This, surely, does not imply that our water concepts differ in narrow content. Similarly, one could grant that learning what water is changes what one would apply it to in some contexts, even though the narrow content remains the same. But anyway, the fact that one learns what water is does not necessarily imply that one won't misapply the concept, in some contexts, and it won't imply that there is any difference at all between one on earth who knows what water is and one on Twin-Earth who *thinks* he does. Suppose that as I learn what water really is, my twin on Twin-Earth forms the false belief that the stuff he calls 'water' is H_2O. If my water concept changes with this change in my beliefs, so does my twin's; but the narrow content of his water concept will still be the same as mine, and we will apply it to the same things in the same contexts. What will my twin do when he finally learns that the stuff in the lakes is really XYZ? He will do exactly what I would do if I learned that: say that it turned out that "water" wasn't H_2O after all.

So I think Fodor need not have conceded that learning what something really is always changes one's narrow concept, but if he does concede it for the reasons he gives, I think he will have to follow the path into the swamp of meaning holism, and the appeal to the stability of denotation and wide content will not offer an escape. I agree that the topic of a conversation depends on denotation and wide content, and thus does not necessarily shift with a shift in meaning or narrow content. But if this is an adequate response to the problem of meaning holism, then it seems to me that there was not much of a problem to start with. Conceptual role theorists do not deny that names and words have denotation, and do not claim that denotation varies with every variation in conceptual role. Can they render the holistic consequences of their theory harmless just by pointing out that even though meanings shift wholesale with every shift in epistemic liaisons, this doesn't matter, since the topic of conversation and thought – the world we are talking and thinking about – remains the same? It is not just some notion of conversational topic that meaning holism threatens; it is the role of meaning and content in intentional explanations of behavior. But according to Fodor, such intentional explanations, if we are to understand them realistically, must appeal to narrow, not wide, contents. If wide content is stable only because very different and constantly changing narrow contents happen, by fortuitous cooperation of the environment, to keep getting hold of the same referents and topics, then the stability of content, and the continuity of intentional states will be psychologically irrelevant, at least if psychology is confined to what is in the head. We will have the following peculiar situation: on the one hand, there will be physical and *syntactic* stability within the head (the same mental token "there is water in the bathtub" sits quietly in the belief box in my mind even as I learn that water is H_2O), and on the other hand there will be stability of *wide* content (that mental token in my belief box will have the same truth-conditions – it will be true if and only if the stuff in the bathtub is H_2O – both before and after I learn what water really is). But the semantics that mediates between the inner states – the tokens – and their wide contents – the truth-conditions of the tokens – will be infected by meaning holism. One narrow content will explain why that token has those truth-conditions before I learn what water really is; a different one will explain it afterwards. Surely this cannot be the right way to do semantics for the language of thought.

My arguments have been *ad hominem*, trying to bring out some tensions between different parts of Fodor's program for doing semantics for the language of thought. One who was persuaded by my arguments might respond in various ways, depending on which parts of Fodor one found most plausible. A skeptic about intentional realism such as Stephen Stich might take the arguments as grist for his mill. He will agree with Fodor that psychology must be narrow, and that a holistic semantics is incompatible with intentional realism. So much the worse for intentional realism – psychology can get along with a purely syntactic account of the language of thought. One who was attached both to narrow psychology and to intentional realism might try to avoid meaning holism within the context of a conceptual role semantics by discriminating between epistemic liaisons. But my advice would be to give up the demand for a narrow semantics. It seems to me that Fodor's discussion of meaning holism and denotational semantics provides support for this advice, and points toward an explanation of the role of an externalist notion of content in intentional explanation. Regularities in the external environment and in the relations between thinkers and their environments help to provide the stability that makes semantics work – the stability that points the way around the problem of meaning holism. Is there a problem for the intentional realist if he concedes that there is no narrow semantics for the language of thought – no abstract object that is determined by purely internal properties, and that explains why internal states have the truth-conditional content they have? I don't see why a semantics can't be realistic, providing more or less determinate contents for mental states and using those contents to explain how people interact with their environments, even if it individuates internal states in terms of general features of their environments. A full story may have to give a purely internal characterization of mental states – an account of the mechanisms by which certain informational content is represented – but there is no reason to believe that there must be purely internal characterizations of states that are also semantic characterizations, and it is no threat to intentional realism if there are not.[6]

NOTES

1   Fodor (1987d). All page references in the text are to this book.
2   See Burge (1979a).
3   It is worth noting that it is no part of Kaplan's (1979) project to distinguish a purely internal determinant of content. Kaplan's meanings, or *characters* as he calls them, are not narrow in the sense required. It is not only that the referents of my uses of demonstratives depend on social and environmental facts, it is also true that it is a social fact that the demonstratives and other words I use have the meanings they have.
4   Fodor calls this "The Ur-argument for meaning holism." See *Psychosemantics*, p. 61.
5   I do not want to suggest that I think conceptual role theorists are always clear about the distinction I am trying to make between the two kinds of questions that different kinds of semantic theories try to answer. Ned Block, in a defense of conceptual role semantics, lists the following kinds of semantic theories, which he contrasts with conceptual role semantics: situation semantics, Davidsonian semantics, possible-worlds semantics, indicator semantics, Gricean semantics, Katzian semantics. Indicator semantics and Gricean semantics are attempts to say what gives expressions their

semantic properties, while possible-worlds semantics and Davidsonian truth-conditional semantics are attempts to say what kinds of objects semantic values are and what relationships hold between them. Davidson defends answers to both kinds of questions, but the answers are separable. On the one hand he has defended claims about the logical form of sentences of various kinds (for example about actions and events) and more generally has defended extensional truth-conditional theories for natural language. On the other hand, his theory of radical interpretation, appealing to the principle of charity, is a response to the problem of explaining what it is about a language user and his community that makes a certain semantic theory a correct theory of the language being used. See Block (1986).

6 In another paper discusssing Fodor, among others, on narrow content, I tried to argue in more detail that a theory that individuates mental states in terms of wide content is less mysterious and suspicious than is usually supposed. See Stalnaker (1989).

14

Narrow Content meets Fat Syntax

STEPHEN P. STICH

SSV: [Still Small Voice – could it be the voice of conscience?] I do believe
you've gone over to Steve Stich. Have you no conscience?
Answer: There, there; don't fret! What is emerging here is, in a certain
sense, a "no content" account of narrow content; but it is nevertheless also
a fully intentionalist account ... In effect I'm prepared to give Stich
everything except what he wants.

Fodor, *Psychosemantics*

1 Introduction

A bit over a decade ago I published a paper in which I argued that Putnam's much
discussed Twin Earth thought experiments posed a problem for the view that a
psychological theory aimed at explaining human behavior will invoke commonsense intentional concepts like belief and desire.[1] That argument relied on a pair
of premises. The first, which I (perhaps infelicitously) called the *principle of
psychological autonomy* maintains that any state or property properly invoked in
a psychological explanation should supervene on the current, internal, physical
state of the organism. Thus, a pair of Putnamian doppelgangers, being molecule
for molecule replicas of one another, must share all the same explanatory
psychological states and properties. The second premise was that commonsense
intentional properties, properties like *believing that Eisenhower played golf* (or
having a belief with the content that Eisenhower played golf) and *believing that
water is wet* (or *having a belief with the content that water is wet*) do not supervene
on a person's current, internal, physical state. For want of a better label, I'll call
this the *Autonomy* argument.

The first premise of the Autonomy argument was one that I took to be
intuitively obvious and widely shared. Thus I offered little by way of support. The
second premise seemed to be a straightforward consequence of the usual
intuitions about Twin-Earth style thought experiments. According to those
intuitions, the belief that my doppelganger expresses when he says "Eisenhower
played golf" is not *about* Eisenhower, the man whose hand I almost got to shake
during the 1956 presidential election; it is about some other statesman in a far off
corner of the universe. Thus the truth conditions of my belief and my

239

doppelganger's are different. But it is plausible to suppose that on the conception of content implicit in commonsense psychology, belief tokens that are about different people and that have different truth conditions must have different contents. So my doppelganger and I do not both have beliefs with the content that Eisenhower played golf.

This argument was part of a larger project. Influenced by Quine, I have long been suspicious about the integrity and scientific utility of the commonsense notions of meaning and intentional content. This is not, of course, to deny that the intentional idioms of ordinary discourse have their uses, nor that these uses are important. But, like Quine, I view ordinary intentional locutions as projective, context sensitive, observer relative, and essentially dramatic.[2] They are not the sorts of locutions we should welcome in serious scientific discourse. For those who share this Quinean skepticism, the sudden flourishing of cognitive psychology in the 1970s posed something of a problem. On the account offered by Fodor and other observers, the cognitive psychology of that period was exploiting both the ontology and the explanatory strategy of commonsense psychology. It proposed to explain cognition and certain aspects of behavior by positing beliefs, desires, and other psychological states with intentional content, and by couching generalizations about the interactions among those states in terms of their intentional content.[3] If this was right, then those of us who would banish talk of content in scientific settings would be throwing out the cognitive psychological baby with the intentional bath water. On my view, however, this account of cognitive psychology was seriously mistaken. The cognitive psychology of the 1970s and early 1980s was not positing contentful intentional states, nor was it adverting to content in its generalizations. Rather, I maintained, the cognitive psychology of the day was "really a kind of logical syntax (only psychologized)."[4] Moreover, it seemed to me that there were good reasons why cognitive psychology not only did not but *should* not traffic in intentional states. One of these reasons was provided by the Autonomy argument.

During the last decade, that argument and similar arguments offered by other writers have attracted a fair amount of attention, very little of it favorable.[5] Some critics have focused on the first premise, and have argued that explanatory psychology need not, and does not, restrict itself to states and properties that organisms and their doppelgangers share.[6] Others have focused on the second premise, with some arguing that commonsense psychology does not insist that beliefs with different truth conditions differ in content, or at least that it does not do so consistently, while others challenged the intuition that the beliefs of doppelgangers on Earth and Twin-Earth differ in truth conditions.[7] I think each of these objections raises serious issues, and each merits a detailed reply. But in the present paper I'll say very little about them. My focus here will be on quite a different reaction to the Autonomy argument – a reaction which grants both premises of the argument. This reaction concedes that the *commonsense* notion of intentional content will not play a role in scientific psychology. But it insists that *another* notion of intentional content will be central to psychology. For this second, more technical, and less commonsensical notion of content, it is not the case that if a pair of belief tokens differ in truth conditions, or in what they are about, then they also differ in content. Thus Twin Earth cases and others of their ilk will not show that *this* sort of content does not supervene on the current internal state of the organism. Though my doppelganger and I have beliefs that are about different people (or stuff) and thus have different truth conditions, those beliefs may still have the same content, when content is construed in this new way. Since the ordinary notion of content determines truth conditions – typically conditions in the world beyond the head – while the new technical notion does not, the new notion has been dubbed *narrow content*; the old commonsense notion is often said to be *broad* or *wide*. There are various lines along which the narrow content response to the Autonomy argument can be developed.[8] But, as is appropriate in a volume focused on Fodor, the line I propose to explore is the one that Fodor follows. In section 3.1, I'll give a quick overview of Fodor's account of narrow content.

An objection often urged against the notion of narrow content is that it is not really a species of content at all.[9] One reason for this suspicion is that while it is generally easy to *say* what the (ordinary, broad) content of a belief is, there often seems no way at all to say what the narrow content of a belief is. Narrow content appears to be "radically inexpressible." However, I will argue that this suspicion is mistaken. Indeed, in section 3.2 I will sketch a straightforward way in which readily available resources can be used to construct a vocabulary for attributing narrow content. Of course, this alone is not enough to show that narrow content really is a kind of content, properly so-called. And I must confess that I'm not at all sure what it *would* take to show that narrow content is, or isn't, really a kind of content. So I propose to leave that question to be debated by those who think they understand it. As I see it, the major objection to narrow content, as Fodor develops the notion, is that it is very unlikely to be of any more use to psychology than the commonsense notion of broad content. If we taxonomize mental states by their narrow content, there are going to be lots of psychological generalizations that we are not going to be able to state. My argument for this claim is set out in section 3.3.

That argument presupposes a certain conception of the cognitive mind – a conception that portrays the mind as analogous to a kind of computer. Though very familiar, this picture of the mind has never been without its critics, and with the recent flowering of connectionism it has become particularly controversial. However, in the present paper I don't propose to challenge the picture. Since Fodor himself has long been one of its most eloquent advocates, I will simply accept it, if only for argument's sake. In order to launch my argument against narrow content, it will be necessary to sketch in parts of the picture with somewhat more detail than is usually provided. This is the project I'll pursue in section 2.

Before getting on to any of this, however, we would do well to get a bit clearer about the issue that is in dispute. In the article in which I first set out the Autonomy argument, and in various subsequent publications, my "official" thesis was that serious scientific psychology should not invoke commonsense intentional notions like belief and desire. The official thesis certainly does not entail that beliefs, desires, and other propositional attitudes do not exist,[10] nor even that commonsense psychology is not "pretty close to being true"[11] – though it is, of course, consistent with these claims. But it is these claims that are at the heart of Fodor's concern. On his view, "if commonsense intentional psychology really were to collapse, that would be, beyond comparison, the greatest intellectual catastrophe in the history of our species . . . ." (*PS*:xii). This leaves us with a rather delicate question. Just what would it take to show that commonsense intentional psychology had collapsed? Nobody thinks that *all* of commonsense psychology is going to turn out to be correct. Indeed, Fodor cheerfully concedes that "a lot of what common sense believes about the attitudes must surely be false (a lot of what common sense believes about *anything* must surely be false)" (*PS*:15). He also concedes that "you can't make respectable science out of the attitudes as commonsensically individuated" (*PS*:30). The "identity conditions for mental states" that "we need, when doing psychology" are not going to be "those that common sense prefers" (*PS*:30). If all of this is not enough to undermine commonsense psychology and its intentional ontology, one might well wonder how much more it will take. Fortunately, Fodor tells us. He stipulates that a psychological theory will count as "endorsing" commonsense propositional attitudes "just in case it postulates states (entities, events, whatever) satisfying the following conditions:

(i)   They are semantically evaluable.
(ii) They have causal powers.
(iii) The implicit generalizations of commonsense belief/desire psychology are largely true of them.

In effect," Fodor tells us, "I am assuming that (i)–(iii) are the essential properties of the attitudes. This seems to me intuitively plausible; if it doesn't seem intuitively plausible to you, so be it. Squabbling about intuitions strikes me as vulgar" (*PS*:10)

I am not at all sure whether my intuitions agree with Fodor's here; indeed, I'm not even sure I *have* any intuitions about the essential properties of the attitudes. But no matter. This book is for Fodor; I'll play by his rules. What I propose to argue is that most of the implicit generalizations of commonsense psychology are not likely to turn out to be true of the states posited by psychological theories that cleave to the computational paradigm. So Fodor loses on (iii). Moreover, on at least one plausible reading of what it is to be "semantically evaluable," these states are not semantically evaluable either. Thus Fodor loses on (i) too. Whether or not we accept Fodor's intuitions about what is essential to the attitudes, this should be enough to show that propositional attitude psychology is in trouble.

2   The Computational Paradigm

My goal in this section is to provide a brief sketch of a familiar story about the cognitive mind. Since the basic outline is so well known, I will devote most of my attention to clarifying the ontological underpinnings of this account and the taxonomic strategies it exploits. Much of what I say in this section is based on the rather more detailed account I developed in *From Folk Psychology to Cognitive Science*. Since talk of *states* and the various ways in which they get taxonomized or individuated is going to be of some importance in what follows, I'll begin by making a few proposals about how this talk should be construed. So far as I can see, nothing in the arguments to follow depends on the details. We just need *some* systematic way of talking about states. Most any sensible proposal would do.

As I propose we view them, states are the instantiation of a *property* by an *object* during a *time interval*.[12] There are, of course, venerable disputes about what sorts of things properties are.[13] But for present purposes I propose to be quite permissive. Near enough, I'll count any open sentence with a reasonably clear extension as specifying a property. That raises the notorious question of when two open sentences specify the same property. Fortunately, this is not a question for which we will need any fully general answer. All we'll need is the weak principle that open sentences with different extensions specify different properties.

On the view I'm recommending, states count as *particulars* with a more or less definite location in space and time. States also admit of what might be called an *essential* classification into types. A pair of states are of the same *essential type* if and only if they are instantiations of the same property. Although each state has only one essential type, states, like other particulars, can be grouped into nonessential types in an endless variety of ways. A type of state is simply a category of particulars, and we have specified a type when we have set out conditions for membership in the category. Though we are conceiving of states as particulars, it will sometimes be convenient to use the word "state" to talk about a type or category of states, or the property that members of a category have in common. When ambiguity threatens, I'll use "state token" to refer to particulars and "state type" to refer to categories or types.

So much for states. Let me turn, now, to the story about the mind that I have been calling the *computational paradigm*. The central assumption of the story is that the cognitive mind can be viewed as a particular kind of computer – that the mind is, in Fodor's phrase, "a syntax-driven machine" (*PS*:20). On this view, each cognitive state token is a brain state token – its essential type is determined by some neurophysiological property or other. However, these neurophysiological state tokens can also be viewed as having syntactic structure in something like the same way that sentence tokens in a natural or formal language have a syntactic structure. That is, each cognitive state token can be viewed as belonging to a syntactic type (or having a "syntactic form"), just as each inscription of a sentence in English or in first order predicate calculus can be viewed as having a syntactic form. Cognitive processes consist of temporal sequences of these syntactically structured states. The reason that the cognitive mind can be thought of as a kind of computer is that the mechanism that controls these cognitive processes is "sensitive solely to syntactic properties" (*PS*:19).

This account of the cognitive mind as a computer or a "syntactic engine" has become very familiar in recent years. But, as Michael Devitt notes in a recent article,[14] the account is very easy to misconstrue. Often, when offering quick sketches of the mind-as-computer story, writers will conjure the image of a "belief box" and a "desire box" inside the head in which syntactically structured sentence-like entities are stored. For vividness, it may even be suggested that the sentences be thought of as well formed formulas of some familiar formalized language.[15] But, as Devitt notes, this image invites us to think of the syntactic properties of cognitive state tokens (the properties in virtue of which they fall into one or another syntactic category) as *intrinsic* or "brute physical" properties – properties that we could detect if we looked at the appropriate bits of the brain in isolation, much as we could see whether an inscription in a "belief box" had the shape: (x) Fx → Gx. If we think of the syntactic properties of mental states in this way, then it would make perfectly good sense to suppose that in certain brains syntactically structured states might be stored in the "belief box," though the mechanisms which control cognitive processes are *not* sensitive to the syntax. But, along with Devitt, I would urge that this is just the wrong way to conceive of things. Mental state tokens are brain state tokens. But the properties in virtue of which mental state tokens are classified into syntactic categories are not intrinsic features of those brain states; they are not features which depend exclusively on the shape or form or "brute physical" properties of the states. Rather, the syntactic properties of mental states are relational or functional properties – they are properties that certain states of the brain have in virtue of the way in which they causally interact with various other states of the system. To put the point in a slightly different way, we would have no reason to view brain states as syntactically structured unless that structure can be exploited in capturing generalizations about the workings of mind/brain's mechanisms. Attributing syntactic structure to brain state tokens – assigning them to syntactic types – is justified only if some interesting set of causal interactions among those tokens is isomorphic to formal relations among abstract syntactic objects. Here is how I elaborated on this theme in *From Folk Psychology to Cognitive Science*:

> The basic idea ... is that the cognitive states whose interaction is (in part) responsible for behavior can be systematically mapped to abstract syntactic objects in such a way that causal interactions among cognitive states, as well as causal links with stimuli and behavioral events, can be described in terms of the syntactic properties and relations of the abstract objects to which the cognitive states are mapped. More briefly, the idea is that causal relations among cognitive states mirror formal relations among syntactic objects. If this is right, then it will be natural to view cognitive state tokens as tokens of abstract syntactic objects ...
>
> The theorist's job in setting out [this sort of] cognitive theory can be viewed as having three parts. First, he must specify a class of [abstract] syntactic objects ... and do so in a way which assigns a formal or syntactic structure to each of these objects ...
>
> Second, the theorist hypothesizes that for each organism covered by the theory, there exists a set of state types whose tokens are causally implicated in the production of behavior. He also hypothesizes that there is a mapping from these state types to syntactic objects in the specified class. Several observations about these hypotheses are in order. First, the theorist need say very little about the essential nature of the state tokens which are causally implicated in the production of behavior. Presumably they are physical states of the brain, and thus the properties which constitute their essential types are neurological properties ... Second, in asserting the existence of the mapping, the order of the quantifiers is of some importance. The theorist is not claiming that the mapping is the same for each subject, but only that for each subject there is a mapping. So in different subjects, quite different neurological state types may be mapped to a given syntactic object. These ... two points ... are in the spirit of functionalism, which stresses the possibility of multiple realizations of mental states ...
>
> The third part of [this kind of] cognitive theory ... is a specification of the theory's generalizations. The core idea ... is that generalizations detailing causal relations among the hypothesized neurological states are to be specified indirectly via the formal relations among the syntactic objects to which the neurological states are

mapped. Similarly, generalizations specifying causal relations between stimuli and neurological states will identify the neurological states not by adverting to their essential neurological types but, rather, by adverting to the syntactic objects to which the neurological types are mapped. Ditto for generalizations specifying causal relations between neurological states and behavior.[16]

As Devitt rightly points out, there is a certain tension in this passage that emerges when we ask how we would go about determining whether a pair of brain state tokens in two different people (or in one person at two different times) are tokens of the same syntactic type. One criterion for the syntactic type identity of tokens would require only that the tokens' patterns of causal interactions *with other tokens* be pretty much the same, so both patterns could be captured by the same formal relations among the appropriate system of syntactic objects. A more stringent criterion would require not only that the tokens' patterns of causal interactions with each other be the same, but also that their patterns of causal interaction with *stimuli* and *behavior* be pretty much the same as well. Since the terms "broad" and "narrow" have been appropriated for distinguishing kinds of content, I will call these two standards for determining the syntactic type of a hypothesized brain state token *skinny* and *fat* respectively. Though my writing has sometimes been less than clear on the point, it has always been my intention to invoke *fat syntax* in typing mental state tokens. When Fodor describes the mind as a "syntax-driven machine" it is not clear whether the standard of syntactic type individuation he has in mind is fat or skinny. In what follows, I'll assume that the syntactic types exploited in computational theories of the mind are fat, not skinny, though most of my argument will work either way.

3   Narrow Content

So much for the computational paradigm. Let's now return to the Autonomy argument, and Fodor's strategy for dealing with it. Since the notion of "narrow" content plays a central role in that strategy, I'll start with a sketch of how Fodor proposes to construct the notion. Once that's been done, I'll set out a pair of reasons for doubting that Fodor's notion of narrow content will do what he wants. One of these, I'll argue, is pretty easy to handle. The other is not.

3.1   Mental states, we are supposing, are states of the brain. And, while their essential type is neurophysiological, they can also be classified into all sorts of other categories. One such categorization, provided by commonsense psychology, is to type mental state tokens by their content. The problem posed by the Autonomy argument is that the taxonomy imposed by ordinary, "broad" content does not supervene on a person's current, internal, physical properties. So while those states in Fodor's brain which count as beliefs and those in Twin-Fodor's brain which count as beliefs are neurophysiologially the same, they may well differ in content. This difference in content, Fodor notes, must be due to differences in the world around them and their relations to that world.

Presumably ... there's something about the relation between Twin-Earth and Twin-Me in virtue of which his "water"-thoughts are about XYZ even though my water-thoughts are not. Call this condition that's satisfied by (Twin-Me, Twin-Earth) condition C (because it determines the *Context* of his "water"-thoughts).

(*PS*:48)

Fodor's proposal for constructing a notion of narrow content is to start with the taxonomy provided by the ordinary, broad, truth-condition determining notion of content, and subtract out the contribution of the contextual conditions, like condition C, that "anchor" it.[17] One way of thinking of the narrow content of a thought is that it is what remains of the broad content when we "take away the anchoring conditions" (*PS*: 51). But Fodor cautions against taking this subtraction picture too literally. A better way of thinking of narrow content, he suggests, is to view the narrow content of a thought as a function (in the mathematical sense – a mapping) from contexts to broad contents. Since broad contents determine truth conditions, narrow contents will determine mappings from contexts to truth conditions. "Two [narrow] thought contents are identical only if they effect the same mapping of thoughts and contexts onto truth conditions" (*PS*:48). Thus the thought tokens that lead both Fodor and Twin-Fodor to say "Water is wet" have the same narrow content, since they would have the same broad content if they were embedded in the same context.

> [S]hort of a miracle the following counterfactual must be true: Given the neurological identity between us, in a world where I am in my Twin's context, my "water"-thoughts are about XYZ iff his are. (And, of course, vice versa: in a world in which my Twin is in my context . . . it must be that his water-thoughts are about H_2O iff mine are.)
>
> (*PS*:48)

3.2   One complaint about this notion of narrow content, the one that Fodor suspects "*really* bugs people," (*PS*:50), is that it seems impossible to say what the narrow content of a thought is. Fodor and Twin-Fodor have thought tokens with the same narrow content. But what is it that they both think? What is the narrow content of those thoughts? It can't be *that water is wet*, since Twin-Fodor doesn't think that. Nor can it be *that XYZ is wet*, since Fodor doesn't think that. It seems that "narrow content is radically inexpressible" (*PC*:50). If this is right, however, it is hard to see how narrow content could serve the purpose for which it is intended. Recall that narrow content was supposed to provide a species of content-based taxonomy that would be useful in scientific psychology. If we insist, as Fodor does, that the states and properties invoked in scientific psychology must supervene on physiological states and properties, then psychological generalizations cannot invoke broad content. An alternative strategy is to couch those generalizations in terms of narrow content. But if narrow content is "radically inexpressible" it would appear that psychology's generalizations could never be stated.[18]

Fodor's response to this problem is to suggest that while we can't *express* the narrow content of the thought that he and his Twin share, we can "sneak up on the shared content by *mentioning*" an appropriate English expression – in this case presumably the sentence: 'Water is wet.' But in offering this response I think Fodor seriously understates the case to be made for his notion of narrow content. We can do more than "sneak up" on the narrow content of a mental state; we can explicitly introduce a way of talking about it. The central idea is very simple. Expressions of the form: "—— believes that p" are predicates whose extension in any possible world is the class of people who believe that p in that world. Given these predicates along with the notion of a doppelganger, we can introduce expressions of the form "—— believes that [p]" (think of it as "bracketed" belief) whose extensions in any possible world include everyone in that world who believes that p, along with all of their doppelgangers. Similarly, expressions of the form "—— has the (broad) content that p" are predicates whose extension in any possible world included the class of brain state tokens whose broad content is p. Here we can introduce expressions of the form "—— has the (narrow) content that [p]" whose extension in any possible world includes the class of brain state tokens whose (broad) content is p, along with the physically identical tokens in all doppelgangers of people who harbor tokens whose broad content is p.[19] These "bracketed" predicates are no less clear and no less systematic than the broad-content predicates on which they are based.

This strategy for talking about narrow content has what might at first seem to be a curious feature. In some cases the extension of "—— has the (narrow) content that [p]" and the extension of "—— has the (narrow) content that [q]" are going to be the same even though 'p' and 'q' are replaced by sentences that differ in reference and truth value. Consider, for example, a version of Putnam's aluminum/molybdenum story. In the southern province of a certain English-speaking country, pots are typically made of aluminum, and this fact is known to a southerner, (Southern)Sam, who knows very little else about aluminum. In the northern province, pots are typically made of molybdenum. But in the north, molybdenum is called "aluminum." (Northern)Sam, who is (Southern)Sam's doppelganger, has a belief which he expresses with the words "Pots are typically made of aluminum." Though of course given the standard intuitions in these cases, the belief token he is expressing has the (broad) content that pots are typically made of molybdenum. Now what about the narrow content of the belief (Northern)Sam expresses? Since that belief has the (broad) content that pots are typically made of molybdenum, it has the (narrow) content that [pots are typically made of molybdenum]. But since it is neurophysiologically identical to (Southern)Sam's belief whose (broad) content is that pots are typically made of alumimum, it also has the (narrow) content that [pots are typically made of aluminum]. Similarly, the belief token that (Southern)Sam expresses when he says "Pots are typically made of aluminum" has both narrow (or bracketed) contents. There is nothing particularly surprising about any of this. The device we've introduced for attributing narrow contents exploits the expressions we would use in attributing broad contents and expands their extensions in a systematic way. It is to be expected that in some cases two of these enlarged extensions will coincide.[20]

The conclusion I would draw here is that the putative "radical inexpressibility" of narrow content is not a problem that Fodor need worry much about. It is easy enough to devise locutions for attributing narrow content to cognitive states, and these locutions can be used to state psychological generalizations in much the same way that locutions attributing broad content can.

3.3 As I see it, the real problem with narrow content does not derive from our inability to talk about it, and thus state generalizations in terms of it. Rather, the problem is that if the computational paradigm sketched in section 2 is on the right track, then many of the true generalizations – many of those that actually describe mental processes – are not going to be stable in terms of narrow content. The taxonomy of mental states imposed by narrow content is going to be both too coarse and too ill behaved to exploit in a serious scientific psychology. Perhaps the best way to see why a narrow content taxonomy is too coarse is to compare three taxonomic schemes: the one imposed by fat syntax, the one imposed by broad content, and the one imposed by narrow content.

Each mental state token is a brain state token; its "essential" type will be specified neurophysiologically. But a pair of brain state tokens in a pair of people may be very different neurophysiologically, and still count as tokens of the same fat syntactic type, provided that they have basically the same pattern of causal connections with stimuli, with behavior, and with other appropriate brain states. It's also worth noting that if there is a pair of neurophysiologically identical states embedded in a pair of neurophysiologically identical organisms, and if one of these states is in a fat syntactic category, the other will always be in the same fat syntactic category. Fat syntax supervenes on physiology. Our commonsense intuitions about broad content provide another scheme for classifying brain state tokens. The lesson to be learned from Twin-Earth, and from Burge's thought experiments, is that classification by broad content turns on physical, historical and linguistic *context*. Thus broad content does not supervene on physiology, and in this respect its taxonomic categories slice too finely; it sometimes puts an organism and its doppelganger in different categories. Narrow content provides a third strategy for classifying brain state tokens, one which starts with broad content but ignores context. Thus, despite the terminological oddness, the categories of narrow content are larger than those imposed by a broad content taxonomy. Moreover, like fat syntax, narrow content supervenes on physiology.

All of this might lead one to suppose that the taxonomies imposed by narrow content and fat syntax *coincide*. That is, it might lead one to think that a pair of brain state tokens in a pair of individuals will be of the same fat syntactic type if and only if they have the same narrow content. However, this is all but certain to be a mistake. If we ignore the vagueness of the narrow content taxonomy, a theme to which I'll return shortly, then it may be the case that sameness of fat syntax guarantees sameness of narrow content ("plus or minus a bit," as Fodor might say).[21] But on almost any plausible reading, the categories imposed by a narrow content taxonomy are much larger than those imposed by fat syntax. Thus sameness of narrow content does not guarantee sameness of fat syntax.

The literature is full of examples that illustrate this mismatch. Perhaps the most obvious examples involve people with unusual or defective perceptual systems. To take an extreme case, consider Helen Keller. If Ms Keller were to be told by a trusted informant that there is a fat cat in the room, she would come to believe that there is a fat cat in the room. That is, she would acquire a brain state which functions like a belief and which has the (broad) content that there is a fat cat in the room. Similarly, if I were told by a trusted informant that there is a fat cat in the room, I would acquire a brain state which functions like a belief and which has the (broad) content that there is a fat cat in the room. Thus both Ms Keller's brain state and mine would have the (narrow) content that [there is a fat cat in the room]. But surely those two states differ radically in their fat syntax. There are all sorts of perceptual stimuli (both visual and auditory) that would cause me, but not

Ms Keller, to acquire the belief that [there is a fat cat in the room]. And states whose patterns of causal interaction with stimuli differ substantially do not share the same fat syntax. Much the same point could be made, though perhaps less dramatically, with examples of people with other perceptual anomalies, both real, like color blindness, and imagined.[22]

In the Helen Keller example, differences in fat syntax are due to differences in the way stimuli affect mental states. But there are also cases in which differences in syntactic type are engendered by differences in the way mental states interact with *each other*. Some people are logically acute; it is plausible to suppose that the mechanism underlying their reasoning makes many valid inferences and few invalid ones. Other people are significantly less acute; their mental mechanism makes many fewer valid inferences and many more invalid ones. On a syntactic taxonomy – *even a skinny syntactic taxonomy* – the states being manipulated by these mechanisms are of different syntactic types. But in many such cases the intuitive commonsense taxonomy of broad content classifies the states being manipulated as having the same (broad) content. And, of course, states with the same broad content have the same narrow content. In addition to these normal interpersonal differences in inferential capacities, there are also lots of pathological cases, some real and some imagined, in which people reason in ways very different from the way I reason, but where commonsense psychology is still comfortable in attributing the same broad content.[23] Here too, syntax and narrow content will diverge.

What I have been arguing is that there are major differences between a taxonomy based on narrow content and one based on fat syntax (or skinny syntax, for that matter). In many cases the syntactic taxonomy will be substantially more fine grained, and will draw substantially more distinctions, than the narrow content taxonomy. There are lots of examples in which a pair of belief state tokens will differ in their fat syntax though not in their narrow content. The reason this is important is that, along with Fodor, I have been assuming that the cognitive mind is a "syntactic engine" and that the mechanism controlling cognitive processes is "sensitive solely to syntactic properties." But if this is right, then the generalizations that describe cognitive processes will be statable in syntactic terms, and these will typically be more fine grained than generalizations statable in terms of narrow content. The generalizations of a computational theory will describe different patterns of causal interaction for cognitive states with different fat syntax, even though in many cases those states will have the same narrow content. So if the computational paradigm is the right one, then many of the generalizations that describe the mind's workings are simply not going to be statable in terms of narrow content.

Throughout this section I have been writing as though the broad content taxonomy provided by commonsense psychology is reasonably clear and stable, and thus that predicates of the form "— has the (broad) content that p" have a reasonably well defined extension. However, there is good reason to doubt that this is so. Following Quine's lead, a number of writers have assembled cases which seem to show that commonsense intuitions about the extensions of such predicates are highly context sensitive. Whether or not a state can be comfortably classified as having the content that p depends, to a significant degree, on the context in which the question arises.[24] I have developed an account of the tacit principle underlying commonsense content attribution which views them as a sort of similarity judgment. This account explains their context sensitivity, and various other phenomena as well. But whether or not my explanation of the phenomena is correct, I am inclined to think that the data speak for themselves. By varying the context in which the question is asked, we can get competent users of commonsense psychology to judge that a particular cognitive state token clearly has the content that p, or that it clearly does not. If this is right, it provides yet another reason for thinking that the generalizations of a serious scientific psychology will not be stable in the taxonomic categories provided by narrow content. For the categories of a narrow content taxonomy are simply the categories of a broad content taxonomy extended to meet the demands of the principle of autonomy. But the broad content taxonomy of commonsense psychology is too vague, too context-sensitive and too unstable to use in a serious scientific theory. *Narrow* content inherits all of these deficits.

4   Keeping Score

Toward the end of section 1, I quoted the three conditions that, on Fodor's view, would have to be met by the states a psychological theory postulates, if that theory is to count as "endorsing" the propositional attitudes, and thus avoiding the "catastrophe" that would ensue "if commonsense intentional psychology really were to collapse." It's time to ask which of those conditions are likely to be met. Along with Fodor, I'll assume, as I have been all along, that the computational paradigm is correct, and that the mind is "a syntax driven machine" whose operations are "sensitive solely to syntactic properties."

The third condition on Fodor's list is that "the implicit generalizations of commonsense belief/desire psychology" must be "largely true" of the states postulated by the psychological theory in question. Presumably, Fodor's hope went something like this:

> The generalizations of commonsense psychology are couched in terms of (broad) content. But the Twin Earth examples show that "you can't make respectable science out of the attitudes as commonsensically individuated" (*PS*:30). Very well, then, we'll move to narrow content, since, unlike broad content, narrow content supervenes on physiology. Given any commonsense generalization about tokens of the belief that p, there will be a parallel narrow generalization – a generalization about the tokens of the belief that [p]. And that latter generalization will be scientifically respectable.

To satisfy Fodor's third condition, however, it is not sufficient that the narrow analogues of broad content generalizations be scientifically respectable. Most of them must also be true. Now if the mind really is a syntax driven machine, and if syntactic categories can be matched up, near enough, with the categories of narrow content, then it looks like we're home free. But the burden of my argument in 3.3 was that syntactic and narrow content taxonomies will not match up, because the latter is both too coarse and too ill-behaved. If the computational paradigm is correct, I argued, then many of the generalizations that describe the mind's workings are not going to be stable in terms of narrow content. If that's right, then Fodor's third condition will not be satisfied.

Let's turn, now, to Fodor's first condition: that the states a psychological theory postulates must be "semantically evaluable." How well do we fare on this one if the computational paradigm is correct? I am inclined to think that here again the ill behaved context sensitivity of semantic taxonomies poses real problems. If it is indeed the case that by varying the context of the question we can get competent users of commonsense psychology to judge that a particular cognitive state token clearly has the content that p, or that it clearly does not, then it's hard to see how even the tokens, let alone the types posited by a serious, computational, scientific psychology will be "semantically evaluable."

One final point. Suppose I am wrong about the mismatch between syntactic and narrow content taxonomies; suppose that the generalizations of a scientifically solid psychology really can be stated in terms of narrow content. Would it then follow that the states postulated by such a theory are "semantically evaluable"? Fodor himself seems ambivalent. Consider the following:

> [I]f you mean by content what can be semantically evaluated, then what my water-thoughts share with Twin "water"-thoughts *isn't* content . . . We can't say . . . what Twin thoughts have in common. This is because what can be said is ipso facto semantically evaluable; and what Twin-thoughts have in common is ipso facto not.
>
> (*PS*:50; the emphasis is Fodor's.)

But, of course, what Fodor's water-thoughts share with Twin 'water'-thoughts, what "Twin-thoughts have in common," *is* narrow content. So in this passage Fodor seems to admit – indeed insist – that narrow content is *not* semantically evaluable. Elsewhere he is even more explicit:

> You can have narrow content without functional-role semantics because *narrow contents aren't semantically evaluable*; only wide contents have conditions of satisfaction.
>
> (*PS*:83; the emphasis is Fodor's.)

Still, perhaps this is just a debater's point. For in several other passages Fodor notes that narrow content "is semantically evaluable relative to a context" (*PS*:51). And perhaps this is all that is required to satisfy his first condition. There's no need to decide the point since, as I see it, the real problem with narrow content is not that it fails to be "semantically evaluable" (whatever that might come to) but that it fails to match up with the syntactic taxonomy of a computational psychology.

The remaining item on Fodor's list of conditions is that the states posited by a psychological theory must "have causal powers." On this one Fodor wins easily. If the computational paradigm is on the right track, then the syntactically taxonomized states posited by a correct computational theory are sure to have causal powers.

By my count, the score against Fodor – and against intentional psychology – is two to one.[25]

NOTES

1 Stich (1978). For the details of Putnam's thought experiment, see Putnam (1975a).
2 Quine has urged this view of the propositional attitudes in many places. See, for example Quine (1960:219). For some elaboration on these themes, see Stich (1982); Stich (1983:chs 4–6); Gordon (1986); and Levin (1988).
3 See, for example, Fodor, (1975a:ch. 1); Fodor (1987d); Fodor (1980c); Fodor (1981d: "Introduction"); and Fodor (1987d:ch. 1).
4 The quote is from Fodor (1978b). For my account of the explanatory strategy of cognitive psychology, *circa* 1980, see Stich (1983:chs 7–9). Perhaps this is the place to say that when I talk of the cognitive psychology of the 1970s and early 1980s, what I have in mind is pre-connectionist cognitive psychology. The qualification is important since, on my view, neither Fodor's account of cognitive theorizing nor my syntactic account will mesh comfortably with the connectionist paradigm. For some elaboration of this point, see Ramsey, Stich, and Garon (1990).
5 For similar arguments, see Stack (unpublished); Putnam (1978); and Putnam (1983).
6 See, for example, Burge (1979); Burge (1986); Kitcher (1985); Owens (1987); Baker (1987a).
7 Loar (1987a); Lycan (1988: 76–9); Dow (in preparation).
8 See, for example, Block (1986); Dennett (1982); Devitt (1989a); Dow (in preparation); Loar (1987a).
9 See, for example, Owens (1987) and Baker (1987b).
10 On this point see Stich (1983:ch. 11 sec. 1).
11 Fodor, (1987d:x). Subsequent references to Fodor's *Psychosemantics* will be referred to as *PS* in the text.
12 My account of states is modeled on Kim's account of events. See Kim (1969) and Kim (1976).
13 See, for example, Armstrong (1978).
14 Devitt (1989a).
15 For a particularly vivid and influential example of the Belief-Box metaphor, see Schiffer (1981).
16 Stich (1983:149–51).
17 "I learned 'anchors' at Stanford," Fodor tells us. "[I]t is a very useful term despite – or maybe because of – not being very well defined" (*PS*:49).
18 I owe this way of making the point to Warren Dow. See Dow (in preparation). A similar point is made by Baker (1987a).
19 Something rather like this was suggested very briefly in Stich (1983:192, fn.). More recently, similar ideas have been developed by Valerie Walker (in press), and Michael Devitt (1989a). Perhaps I should add that I do not take my suggestion to be in competition with Fodor's strategy for "sneaking up on" narrow content; mine is just a bit more explicit. Indeed, were I to develop my definition more carefully, and without riding roughshod over the fine distinction between use and mention, it would be obvious that my story, like Fodor's, enables us to talk about narrow content by *mentioning* sentences.
20 This note is for afficionados only. I have argued that (Northern)Sam's belief falls within the extension of both

(i) "— has the (narrow) content that [pots are typically made of molybdenum]",

and

(ii) "— has the (narrow) content that [pots are typically made of aluminum]."

But it does not follow that (i) and (ii) are co-extensive. For consider the case of an expert in the North, someone who knows a great deal about how to distinguish aluminum from molybdenum and who also (broadly) believes that pots are typically made of molybdenum. Plainly, his belief is in the extension of (i). Is it also in the extension of (ii)? Not unless he has a doppelganger whose belief has the (broad) content that pots are typically made of aluminum. But if he has a doppelganger in the South, it is not at all clear that his doppelganger would (broadly) believe that pots are typically made of aluminum. More likely, the relevant mental state of the expert's Southern doppelganger would be so anomalous that it would have no broad content at all. For unless the story is told in a pretty strange way, you *can't*

(a)   be the doppelganger of an expert on aluminum and molybdenum who broadly believes that pots are typically made of molybdenum,

(b)   live in a world in which pots are typically made of aluminum,

(c)   (broadly) believe that pots are typically made of aluminum.

To see the point, imagine that the Northern expert can distinguish the two metals by touch and sight, and ask what his Southern doppelganger would say when confronting the aluminum pots that are typical in his environment.

21   Fodor (1980c:240).

22   For detailed examples along these lines, see Stich (1983:66–8) and Stich (1982:185–8).
      Kenneth Taylor has suggested that the objection I am urging against Fodor dissolves if we focus more steadfastly on Fodor's "official" account of narrow content which takes the narrow content of a thought to be a *function* from contexts to broad contents. On my account of narrow content, any two thoughts with the same broad content must have the same narrow content. But, Taylor urges, if we view the narrow content of a thought as a function from contexts to broad contents, then it is entirely possible that Ms Keller's thought and mine do not have the same narrow content. For there might be some contexts in which Ms Keller's thought and mine did not have the same broad content, and if this is possible, then on the function account of narrow content our thoughts do not have the same narrow content.
      I am inclined to think that the function account of narrow content is more than a bit obscure. For I am not at all clear about what a *context* is; nor am I sure how we are supposed to play the game of imagining people and their thoughts embedded in other contexts. Consider the example in the text. Is Ms Keller's context different from mine? If so, what would it be for me to be in her context? Would I have to have her handicaps? Would I have to have had the same biography? The mind boggles.
      But even if we suppose these questions can be answered in some coherent and principled way, I doubt the answers will do Fodor much good. To avoid the objection I am urging, it will have to be the case that the taxonomy generated by the function account of narrow content coincides with the taxonomy generated by fat syntax. And I see no reason to think this will be the case. Certainly, Fodor has offered no argument for this claim. Moreover, if as Taylor suggests, Ms Keller's belief and mine have different narrow contents on the function account, it is hard to see why the same will not be true of the beliefs of other people who broadly believe that there is a fat cat in the room, but who differ from me less radically than Ms Keller does. However, if this is the case, then the function account of narrow content runs the risk of individuating much too finely. Only doppelgangers will have thoughts with the same narrow content.

23   For some examples, see Stich (1983:68–72). For examples of a rather different sort, see Cherniak (1986). For another example, see Dennett (1981b:54–5).

24   See, for example, Stich (1982:180–203), where I describe the phenomenon as the "pragmatic sensitivity" of belief attributions. See also Stich (1983:90–110). Much the

same moral can be drawn from Dennett's examples of the use of intentional notions to describe trees and his example of the young child who asserts that Daddy is a doctor. For the first, see Dennett (1981a:22); for the second, see Dennett (1969:183).

25 I am indebted to many people for much useful conversation on these matters. Those I can recall are Daniel Dennett, Michael Devitt, Warren Dow, Jerry Fodor, Gary Hardcastle, Patricia Kitcher, Kenneth Taylor and Valerie Walker. I hope the others will accept my thanks anonymously. Special thanks are due to Warren Dow for his helpful comments on an earlier version of this paper.

15

Replies

JERRY A. FODOR

"Come on, it's easy!" squeaked Roo. And suddenly Tigger found how easy it was . . .
There was a crash, and a tearing noise, and a confused heap of everybody on the ground.
Christopher Robin and Pooh and Piglet picked themselves up first, and then they picked Tigger up, and underneath everybody else was Eeyore.
"Oh Eeyore!" cried Christopher Robin, "Are you hurt?" . . .
Eeyore said nothing for a long time. And then he said: "Is Tigger there?"
"Yes," said Christopher Robin . . ."
"Well, just thank him for me," said Eeyore.*

In like wise, I want to thank my commentators, who thought up Useful Things to say about my work; and Barry Loewer and Georges Rey, who organized this Useful Place to put the Useful Things in and wrote the Very Fine Introduction. (I'm specially indebted to Professor Rey for detailed and characteristically illuminating comments on earlier versions of these replies.) Further gratitude is due to the Series Editor, Ernie Lepore, without whose efforts this might all have been averted.

And so to work.

Antony and Levine

Premature burial is unpleasant and unhealthy. It is therefore courteous to postpone the obsequies until the corpse is dead. I'm prepared to argue that I am *not* dead, merely tenured.

A&L say – rightly, I think – that there is an internal "tension" between the following two ideas, both of which I'm attracted to: (a) the idea, deriving from informational semantics, that representation depends on lawful connections between, roughly, instances of what gets represented and tokens of what does the representing; and (b) the idea that the difference between us and paramecia is that they can't represent "anomic" properties – ones that don't enter into lawful relations – and we can.

255

If it were just a matter of choosing between two doctrines that it turns out I can't have both of, I would stick with the informational semantics and not worry about the paramecia. After all, there being a slippery slope between us and them doesn't seriously argue that intentionality isn't real; slippery slopes are notorious for leading from true premises to false conclusions. And, anyhow, it wouldn't matter if paramecia have intentional (viz. semantically evaluable) states, as long as they don't turn out to have beliefs and desires. And I take it that everyone is now clear that having the first does not entail having the second.

However, as A&L point out, I need the story about anomic properties if I'm going to argue (as I'm inclined to) that the Mentalese expression "horse" doesn't mean P(INF) (which is A&L's name for the disjunction of all the proximal stimuli which can cause "horse" to be tokened.)[1] I wanted to say that this is an open disjunction and that properties that are expressed by open disjunctions don't enter into laws. (In fact, given that tokenings of "horse" are often theory mediated, P(INF) probably includes *every* proximal stimulus since, as I remarked in *TOC* (*A Theory of Content* (1990b)), the merest ripple in horse infested waters can produce proximal stimuli which cause "horse" tokenings in the mind of a properly informed observer.)

Here, then, is the shopping list so far: If I'm to have an informational semantics, I need it that in typical cases where there is representation there are the corresponding nomic properties. If I'm to avoid "horse" meaning P(INF), I need it that not every property is nomic. Finally – and this needs to be taken seriously too – there are all sorts of concepts which either don't express properties ("round cube" and the like) or don't express properties whose instantiation is nomologically possible ("phlogiston" and the like;[2] and maybe "unicorn" depending on your metaphysical views about unicorns). One thus simply can't take the line that *all* concepts have the satisfaction conditions that they do because the properties they express enter into the nomic relations that they do. Given all this, I'm tentatively inclined to a two-tiered story: There are primitive predicates (like "horse") – about whose semanticity the information-plus-asymmetric-dependence story tells the whole and unvarnished truth – ; and there are defined predicates (like "crumpled shirt") which are introduced by definitions ("crumpled shirt" = df *crumpled and shirt*, just as you'd expect).

But what, then, about the paramecia? I don't mind there being a property of shirtness; I don't even mind there being laws about that property if that's what's required for 'shirt' tokens to carry information about shirts. But the intuition stands (*contra* Dennett) that SHIRT is the kind of concept that paramecia can't have *in principle*; and (contra Gibson) that shirtness is not the kind of property whose instantiation can be un-question-beggingly said to be directly and noninferentially picked up. A&L's question is: how can these intuitions be saved consonant with the requirements of informational semantics?

I now think the point to stress about SHIRT is that you can't build a shirt-transducer. In fact, as A&L remark, I've always thought this. But my thinking it didn't use to do me any good because I also thought that "the only difference between a transducer and anything else that responds selectively . . . is that transducers are devices whose outputs . . . are lawfully related to corresponding properties of their inputs . . ." (quoted by A&L, p. 11). So the transduced/ untransduced story seemed to add nothing to the nomic/anomic story. In particular, if there are laws about shirts (as the semantics of "shirt" requires) then shirtness is allowed to be transduced, which is what I wanted to avoid giving to Gibson.

I now think that was wrong. The polemically relevant point about transduction is not that it's nomic but that it's *non-inferential*. This is a point that a Gibsonian might take to be on the queston-begging side, since a Gibsonian is somebody who takes *all* perception to be non-inferential; indeed, it's a way of putting the Gibson point that whole organisms *are*, precisely, transducers for properties like shirtness (and crumpled shirtness . . . etc.),[3] and that there are indeed laws that involve these properties; viz. ecological laws.

But, on second thought, no question is begged. Remember we are assuming that we have a story about representation along the lines of representation-is-information-plus-asymmetric-dependence. Given such a story, we can say what it is for perceptual pickup to be nontransductive (i.e. inferentially mediated): even if Xness is a nomic property, the perception of Xs is inferential if the causal route from Xs to "X" tokenings runs via states which themselves satisfy the conditions for representation. (Whereas, if the detection of Xs is transductive, then none of the states which mediate the causation of "X" tokens by Xs satisfies the conditions for representation except, of course, the "X" tokenings.)

So, now, what to say to Gibsonians is: "It's not germane whether "shirt $-->$ 'shirt' " is a law (ecological or otherwise); what matters is that there is no noninferential way of detecting shirtness. *De facto*, all causal chains that run from shirts to the tokenings of (the Mentalese term) "shirt" contain tokenings of "shirt shaped" and the like among their links. *De facto*, you can't build a shirt detector that doesn't have a shirt-shape detector as one of its parts.

What to say about paramecia is not that they haven't got *intentional states*; there is nothing to stop them having transduced representations, and transduced representations are representations, hence semantically evaluable. The thing to say about paramecia is that they haven't got *inferred representations*. (*A fortiori*, since shirt detectors have to be inferential, they don't have "shirt".) Since, according to the present assumptions, there is a fact of the matter about representation, and since the notion of inference is principled if the notion of representation is, this gives us what intuition demands: a principled distinction between the paramecium's sort of mind and ours.

What to say about "horse" is that it can't be a primitive expression meaning P(INF) because P(INF) is anomic. (And it can't be a defined expression meaning P(INF) because, roughly, it's got the wrong functional role (I take it that "X" defines "Y" for intentional system S only if, *ceteris paribus*, S is disposed to have . . . X . . . in the belief-box iff S is disposed to have . . . Y . . . in the belief-box. And, of course, a disposition to token "horse" doesn't imply a disposition to token P(INF)). So "horse" doesn't mean P(INF).[4]

I am, nevertheless, not very happy about all this. If I could get away with weaker metaphysical assumptions I should be glad to do so. In particular, I don't like having to rest so much on the metaphysical assumption that P(INF) is anomic and shirtness and horseness aren't. On the other hand, it has yet to be demonstrated that the metaphysical assumptions that I require are false. I wish not only not to be buried before I am dead; I wish not to be buried before I am *demonstrably* dead.

Baker

I'm at a bit of a loss to know how to proceed with the Baker paper. It raises a lot of detailed worries about the theory of content in "A theory of content" and, though I don't think her objections actually cut ice, this stuff does get a little complicated; points need to be made that only a devotee of informational semantics could conceivably care about. Other readers are likely to go berserk and do themselves a harm, and I do not wish to have their blood on my hands.

So here's what I propose to do. I shall remark on just a few of the problems Baker raises, and I shall do so very briefly. My comments will probably seem intolerably cryptic: those who want more should take Baker in one hand and *TOC* in the other and decide for themselves how much damage the former does to the latter. The reader is thus invited to go berserk on his own time or not at all.

1   Shunicorns

I could live without shunicorns. In effect, they pile and H_2O/XYZ example on top of an uninstantiated-property example. This makes the case extremely confusing but, so far as I can tell, the examples don't interact; the problems the two raise together are just the sum of the problems raised by each alone.

So then:

I claim that "unicorn" means *unicorn* (and not *shunicorn*) if (i) unicorns cause "unicorns" in the nearby worlds where there are any, and (ii) the nearest world in which unicorns cause "unicorns" and shunicorns don't is closer to us than the nearest world in which shunicorns cause "unicorns" and unicorns don't.[5] Baker replies that this won't do because "worlds in which a person's shunicorn/ ["]U[nicorn"] connection remains intact are the same distance from the actual world as worlds in which her unicorn/U connection is broken, but her shunicorn/U connection remains intact. At least, we have no principled way to distinguish the two" (p. 20). This hasn't however, got the right form to be a counterexample to a putative sufficient condition. As I tried (very hard, really) to make clear in TOC, for purposes of stating a sufficient condition, I get to *stipulate* the nomic[6] relations, and Baker has then got to show that the relations I've stipulated don't suffice for content.

Now, of course, Baker has a lot of options as to how to show this. For example, she could argue that there isn't an ontological[7] distinction between the situation where *being a unicon* is nomically connected to *being a cause of "unicorn"s* and the situation where *being a shunicorn* is nomically connected to *being a cause of "unicorn"s*; or she can argue that the sufficient conditions I propose can't, in the nature of the case, be *uniquely* satisfied, so that the theory has to claim that *all* predicates are disjunctive (see Boghossian, where this strategy is attempted; not, in my view, successfully); or she can argue that my sufficient condition is incoherent and could thus *never* be satisfied . . . etc. But unless Baker has some such argument, I am not in trouble. And if she has one, she hasn't said what it is.

"Oh, sure, sure," you might reply, "anybody can win on points. But suppose somebody could show that the asymmetric dependence story doesn't work for "unicorn" (e.g. because the shunicorn-causing worlds turn out to be as close as the unicorn-causing worlds). What *would* you say about why "unicorn" means '*unicorn.*' For reasons that I hope are clear by now, *I don't have to answer this question.* But if I did answer it, I suppose I'd say "because it satisfies some sufficient condition for meaning other than the one I've been selling. Probably 'unicorn' is nonprimitive."

Baker anticipates this reply to the question I don't have to answer. She thinks that it's not plausible, but none of her objections strikes me as very compelling.

Against her objection (a):

It doesn't seem to me at all peculiar that the concepts that some people get by acquaintance others may get by description. Come to think of it, that view is venerable.

As to her objection that making "unicorn" nonprimitive would sever the connection between semantical and syntactic primitiveness, I find this unsurprising too. The *point* of introducing concepts by definition is that it allows for syntactically primitive expressions that are semantically equivalent to descriptions. (This is remarked upon in *TOC.*) Notice, however, that it presumably can't go the other way: a syntactically complex concept can't be semantically primitive (barring the Mentalese analog of idioms). So, *pace* Baker, what I said in *TOC* still goes; the asymmetric dependence theory "explicates the semantical relation between a *syntactically* primitive expression and the property it expresses", though not the relation between *every* syntactically primitive expression and the property it expresses.

Against her objection (b):

Phlogiston was (supposed to be) the X such that for stuff to burn is for it to give off X. What's the problem?

Against her objection (c):

A term for an artifact can be primitive for anyone to whom it is introduced (e.g.) ostensively, nonprimitive for anyone to whom it is introduced (e.g.) by description. Nonprimitiveness is not an enduring trait (as, indeed, seems independently plausible from cases like proper names. Compare our relation to "Homer" to Mrs Homer's).

2   Sally's Cats

None of what Baker says here strikes me as a reason for changing my mind about the analysis I gave in *TOC*. So I'll do this very fast.

If I opt for Sally's first "cat" meaning *cat or robot*, then I have to show that there is *some* sense in which Sally is right in now thinking that there was something wrong with what she said when she used to call robots "cat"s. But it's just question begging of Baker to require me to show that what was wrong was that Sally used to use "cat" about things that it didn't apply to. Baker says "It seems inconsistent to say both that the first 'cat' token means *cat or robot . . . and* that its tokening involves a mistake" (fo. 47). But, of course, its not inconsistent unless you also say that the mistake it involves is that of applying a term to something that's not in its extension. I went rather out of my way to show how Sally could have been making *a* mistake without making *that* one.

Baker also says that "the asymmetric dependence account leaves a large hole." Suppose Sally's initial cat-inspired "cat" is true because "cat" means *cat or robot.* Suppose, later, Sally learns about the difference between cats and robots and "cat" comes to mean *cat.* How do we describe, "in nonintentional and nonsemantic terms, the change from scene I (with no misrepresentation) to scene 2 (with misrepresentation . . .)." Answer, in scene 2, but not in scene 1, robot-inspired "cat" responses are asymmetrically dependent on cat-inspired "cat" responses; viz. Sally's dispositions change.[8]

Baker seems to want an answer that adverts to patterns of discriminations that Sally would, or could, perform. But, the condition for content is given in terms of nomic relations between Mentalese symbols and causal properties (see above), and I would not expect claims about what Sally means by "X" to translate into counterfactuals about how she would, or could, sort Xs. *A fortiori*, I'm at a loss to see why Baker thinks it's relevant that ". . . if she is presented with two small cats and a large cat, Sally can classify the two small cats as more like each other than either is to the large cat, but that does not count against their all being cats" (fo. 48). Having a response that's specific to a category is quite compatible with having *other* responses that distinguish among members of the category. It is, for example, possible to have the concept COLOR even if you are not color blind. All that's required is that you have one Mentalese symbol that is nomically connected to *being colored* and another one that's nomically connected to, say, *being red.*

Finally, Baker says that the difference between the two situations Sally might be in "bears an uncanny resemblance to the distinction . . ." (p. 25) between type 1 and type 2 situations. But it doesn't. According to theories that allow type 1 situations, whether "X" means *X* or *X or Y* depends only on what counterfactuals are true of Sally *in the type 1 situation.* So, if you take a timeslice of Sally, then there is one bundle of counterfactuals true of her at *t* that determine what happens when she's in a type 1 situation, and another batch of counterfactuals *also true of her at t* that determine what happens when she's *not* in a type 1 situation. (Roughly, in type 2 situations she would respond "X" to some non-Xs but in type 1 situations she wouldn't.) My story about Sally isn't anything like that. My story is that there's one batch of counterfactuals true of Sally at *t*1 and another, different batch true of her at *t*2; as remarked above, her dispositions change.

3   "cow" vs. #^"'c''^''o''^''w''^#

Baker keeps telling me that I'm confused about semantic typing as opposed to formal/"shape" typing; and I keep assuring her that I'm not. We may have to leave this to the reader to adjudicate. Anyhow, I hereby promise, Honest-Injun, cross my heart, that (whenever it matters) when I say things like: It's a law that Xs cause

"X"'s, the property of being and "X"-token is taken to be a nonsemantic property; e.g. it's an orthographic property. (Cf. the long, long discussion of this point in connection with "Block's objection" in *TOC*.)

Baker thinks, however, that I have the following problem. If I keep my promise about formal typing, robustness ceases to be a serious constraint on content. "For example, a token of nonsemantic type C, which is usually caused by cows, say, may be produced by an electric probe ... Since, presumably, tokens of (almost?) any nonsemantic type can be produced by appropriate electrical probes ... tokens typed nonsemantically are always robust" (p. 27). But this is a fallacy of subtraction: what's required for content is not just that there be some (nomologically possible) noncow-caused Cs, but also that these noncow-caused Cs should be asymmetrically dependent on the cow-caused Cs. In the present case, robustness requires not just that you can produce "cow"s with a probe, but that your being able to do so depends (synchronically, by the way) on your being able to produce them with a cow. Baker is right that if you can produce "cow"s with a cow then it's trivial that you can produce them with a probe. But it's not trivial that if you can produce them with a cow then your being able to produce them with a probe is nomically dependent on your being able to produce them with a cow; viz. that the probe $-->$ "cow" relations satisfy asymmetric dependence.

This sort of move also allows me to distinguish, non-question-beggingly, between really robust tokenings of "cow" (as in, say, metaphorical, or false tokenings, or tokenings in the course of cogitation) and the case where "cow" happens to be a vocable which, in some language (other than Mentalese) means, as it might be, *popcorn*. On my story, the existence of a popcorn $-->$ "cow" law would make (the phonetic/orthographic sequence) "cow" ambiguous *but it wouldn't make the cow* $-->$ "cow" relation robust. The situation would be that there are two "cow" laws, one which connects "cow"s to cows, and one which connects it to popcorn, *and neither of which is dependent on the other*. If robustness is, as I claim, a requirement for content, then so far we haven't got "cow" meaning either *cow* or *popcorn*. It would be further required that the cow $-->$ "cow" connection, and/or the popcorn $-->$ "cow" connection, each have other X $-->$ "cow" relations that are dependent on *them*.

So the possibility that "cow" might mean *popcorn* in some mouth/head or other doesn't trivialize the requirement that "cow" only means *cow* in my mouth/head if cow $-->$ "cow" is robust for me.[9]

Maybe a little further expatiation on these examples might be forgivable; they are sort of tricky.

There are three kinds of 'probe' worries one might think to have:

i   Suppose cows cause 'cows.' This relation is sure to be robust because probes will cause 'cows' too. So robustness is not a substantive constraint on content. I take it that this is Baker's worry. However, as we've seen, it's not serious. Robustness requires not just that something other than cows be "cow" causes but that this something other's being so is synchronically dependent on cows causing them. And that requirement is *not* trivially satisfied.

ii   "But if cows cause "cow" and probes cause "cows," then why doesn't "cow" mean *cow or probe*?" Well: if the probe's causing the "cow"s is asymmetrically dependent on the cows causing the "cow"s, then there's no problem; it's just the sort of case that robustness is designed to cope with. But suppose the probe's causing the "cow"s is *not* asymmetrically dependent on the cows causing them. (And suppose something-or-other's causing 'cow's is asymmetrically dependent on the probes causing them and not on the cow's causing them, so probes cause 'cow's robustly.) Doesn't the theory *then* have to say that "cow"s means *cow or probe*? And doesn't intuition boggle at saying that? (Georges Rey tells me I have to say something about this because Civilization As We Know It hasn't been able to sleep nights for wondering.)

Actually, I'm not clear that intuition *does* boggle at "cow" meaning *cow or probe* in the circumstances imagined. If it does, however, we can do a little better. We can have it that 'cow' means *cow* and 'cow' means *probe*; i.e., that 'cow' is ambiguous rather than disjunctive. Here's how you run the distinction. The disjunctive expression 'red or green' is nomically connected to red things and nomically connected to green things, and nomic connection to the one is *symmetrically* dependent on the nomic connection to the other. (i.e., we say 'red or green' of red things only because we say it of green things and vice versa.) Whereas the expression 'bat' is nomically connected to wooden sticks and nomically connected to flying mammals, and neither of these connections depends on the other. So 'bat' is (not disjunctive but) ambiguous.

I have consulted my intuitions about the case where "cow" is connected to cows and to probes and neither of the connections is dependent on the other, and my intuitions tell me that it's OK to say, in that case, that 'cow' is ambiguous between cows and probes. If your intuitions do not tell you that it is OK to say that, please have them fixed at your earliest convenience.

iii   Actually, I think the serious worry about probes is that it might be argued that cows causing 'cow's would be asymmetrically dependent on probes causing them (i.e., because cows cause 'cow's by stimulating the same neural mechanism that the probe does when it causes 'cow's). In which case 'cow' would mean *probe*, an outcome at which even my intuitions protest. It was exactly this kind of "causal chain" case that suggested making robustness a positive requirement for content; about which, see the discussion near the end of *TOC*.

It occurs to me that you may be getting a little tired of cows and probes. Let's proceed to other matters.

4   The "Outright Counterexample"

For what's wrong with Baker's "outright counterexample" see the discussion of RED/COLOR above (and the discussion of the Maudlin/Wienstein objection in *TOC*). Baker has apparently forgotten that asymmetric dependence is a relation among nomic relations among *properties*; not a relation among causal relations among *events*. Thus, fruit and apples and tomatoes all cause "fruit" *qua fruit*, so asymmetric dependences amongst them aren't germane to the case.[10] All that's relevant is asymmetric dependences between fruit causes of "fruit" and nonfruit causes of "fruit." If Baker says "who says apples and tomatoes cause 'fruit' *qua* fruit" the answer is "I do"; as remarked above, that's the way you play the sufficient conditions game.

Baker says that "there are no clear examples in which the allegedly sufficient conditions do hold" and that her "intuitions . . . boggle at comparing nomologically impossible worlds, as the asymmetric dependence condition requires" (p. 29). As to the first, there are plenty of examples in which the allegedly sufficient conditions hold *for all that we know*; and that should be of some interest to the sort of philosophical skeptic who just can't imagine how intentionality could be part of the natural order. As to the second, the worlds at issue are *nomically* impossible (you have to break laws to get to them) but not (as for as anybody knows) *physically impossible* (you don't have to break any laws of basic physics to get to them); so many of them may be quite nearby. Is it really more than Baker can bear, to think about a world in which, say, water at sealevel boils at 213°F rather than 212?

And anyhow, Baker doesn't have to worry about deciding whether the distance relations I need really hold because (all together now): *I get to stipulate that they do.*

Anybody who wants to know more about how the asymmetric dependence story about content fares in face of Baker's objections is now entirely on his own.

Block

Block's paper is very complicated and very detailed, and I wouldn't bet a lot that I've got the argument right. But if I have got it right, then I think that it commits quite a simple fallacy. At the risk of doing Block an injustice and causing the angels to weep, I'm going to propose a very schematic version of what I take to be his story and discuss it in that form.[11]

Now, as Block says, Fodor says that narrow contents are mappings from contexts to truth conditions. However "this formulation specifies only a pathetic version of the Mapping Theory". A nonpathetic version should answer questions like "How would we use the Mapping Theory to determine the narrow content of my utterance right now of 'Mud makes a good shampoo' "(ibid.). But there's a dilemma. Consider the Mentalese (or English) expression "dog," *i.e. the Mentalese expression such that every orthographic sequence #"d"ˆ"o"ˆ"g"# is ipso facto a token of that expression.* Well, "the Mapping Theory says that the narrow content of this utterance is a matter of the [broad] contents it would have in various total environments . . . ."[12] However, ". . . this [form of] utterance could mean *anything at all* depending on the language that the utterer has learned. In one context of acquisition it will mean that Thatcher is a duck [etc.] . . . Nothing will be constant across all these contexts except that an utterance of this physical shape occurs."

That's one horn of the dilemma . What exactly does it show? The "pathetic Mapping Theory" tells us what the narrow content of a thought is (viz. it's a certain function from contexts to broad contents.) Block never does say exactly what a nonpathetic Mapping Theory would have to do; but presumably it enumerates the internal (i.e. nonrelational; or, anyhow, non head-world relational) constraints on having a thought with a certain narrow content. If so, then the right nonpathetic theory can't be that having a thought with the narrow content *mud makes a good shampoo* is having in your belief-box a Mentalese expression with a certain orthographic form (e.g. with the form #″m″ˆ″u″ˆ″d″ˆ . . .) because, to put it crudely, the narrow content of a Mentalese expression has to constrain its broad content (it has to constrain broad content uniquely given a context) and the orthographic form of a Mentalese expression constrains its content not at all.

OK so far.

Here's the other horn of the dilemma: what *would* constrain the broad content of a Mentalese expression is its (internal) causal/conceptual role. Suppose that entertaining the narrow concept DOG involves tokening a Mentalese expression (of whatever orthographic shape) whose tokens play a certain actual and counterfactual role in your mental life. Then, of course, it won't be true that just any orthographically individuated Mentalese expression can have the narrow content DOG; on the contrary, only a Mentalese expression that plays the right inferential role can have that narrow content. (Maybe, for example, only a Mentalese expression whose tokening causes one to think *animal* can.)[13]

The trouble with this option is that it leads to holism. In fact, it does so by several routes. Here's the one that Block prefers. Suppose you think dogs can bark soprano and I think they can't. Then consider a world in which there are some animals that are just like what I think dogs are like (so these animals can't bark soprano) and other animals that are just like what you think dogs are like (so those animals can).[14] Then, in that world, your (Mentalese) "dog" tokens and mine have different extensions. So, in virtue of our disagreement about whether dogs can bark soprano, our "dog" thoughts express different mappings from contexts to extensions. So the Mapping Theory requires that we have different narrow contents associated with "dog."[15] But if this difference of internal role matters, then all differences of internal role matter, and there is no hope for the Mapping Theory.

Now, I'm not really sure how Block wants this part of the argument to run (though it may not matter since, as will presently be seen, I'm prepared to grant the conclusion). Maybe it's like this. To individuate by conceptual role is to identify having a concept with having a disposition to make certain inferences. Suppose having the concept X is identified with a disposition to infer X --> A, B, C. Now, it may be that in *this* world, being A, being B and being C always go together as properties of Xs. But, so long as being A, B, and C are logically (and metaphysically) independent properties, there will always be possible worlds (Block seems to think that there will always be NOMOLOGICALLY possible worlds; but I don't see why that follows) in which there are things that are A, B, and C, and things that are, say, A and B but not C. So, in those worlds, things that are A, B, and C will be in the extension of X, but things that are A, B, but not C won't be in the extension of X. So, whatever C is, it makes a difference of the extension of X in some world or other. So, if narrow content is a function from concepts to worlds, any difference in belief makes a difference in narrow content.

But this can't be right, quite aside from questions about holism (and, I should make clear, I'm far from certain that it's the argument Block intends). Suppose that I think all birds can fly (so I'm committed to the inferences Bird x --> Ax, Bx, . . . flies x . . . etc.). And then I come across ostriches; it turns out that there are things just like the things that satisfy my ʙɪʀᴅ concept except for not flying. It surely doesn't *follow* that ostrich isn't in the extension of ʙɪʀᴅ for me; the alternative is that I admit two kinds of birds: the ones that fly and the ones that don't. The long and the short is that Block's kind of argument only works for those properties of birds that I take to be essential to their birdhood.

But that's bad enough since we have no workable way of distinguishing inferences that involve essential properties from the rest; which is to say that we have no way of individuating conceptual roles; which is to say that if conceptual roles are constitutive of concepts, we have no principled alternative to "difference of roles --> difference of concepts." Which is precisely the holistic conclusion that a serious semantics has to avoid.

So: here's the dilemma. Either our nonpathetic theory says that orthography constitutes narrow content, in which case it slices narrow content much too thick; or it says that conceptual role constitutes narrow content, in which case it slices narrow content much too thin. Either way, we have no nonpathetic Mapping Theory. So there must be something wrong with the idea that narrow contents are Mappings.

As I said, I think this argument commits a simple fallacy (simple, but practically universal in the literature): it assumes that a theory that articulates the "internal" constraints on having a concept (a "nonpathetic" theory) is *ipso facto* a theory of concept individuation. In particular, Block takes if for granted that if the conditions for having a concept advert to internal "descriptions" ("conceptions," causal/inferential roles and the like), then it must be that these descriptions function to define satisfaction conditions for the concept.[16] But this is not argued, and it is not obvious, and it begs the question against the informational approach to semantics.

What *constitutes* the narrow content of 'dog' is that (partial) function that picks out the dogs in the context Earth, the twin-dogs in the context Twin-Earth, and so on for every context for which the function is defined. For present purposes, that's all we need to say about the question of *narrow concept identity*. But, of course, not every kind of creature can meet the conditions for having the narrow concept ᴅᴏɢ as so defined. Rocks can't for example. So you might reasonably ask what kind of creatures *can* meet them; what has to be in your head – in case you are the kind of creature that has a head – in order that you should be able to think the narrow thought ᴅᴏɢ. A natural answer to this question might appeal to internal constraints: you have to have certain "conceptions." You have to be a creature whose thoughts play a certain causal/inferential role.

How might this work out? Suppose, in the spirit of informational semantics, that there is some nomological relation N such that your "X" tokens refer to Xs in a certain world iff[17] they bear N to Xs in that world. Think of your brain as affording mechanism whose operations bring it about that tokens of Mentalese are N-related to their extensions. These mechanisms would plausibly include thoughts with appropriate causal/inferential roles:[18] you hear a woofish sort of noise, your brain does some churning and chuncking, and a token of "dog" appears in your belief-box. And so forth. Since a brain state has the narrow content ᴅᴏɢ only if it would be N-related to dogs on earth, twin-dogs on Twin-Earth, etc. . . ., it follows that nobody's 'dog' tokens express that concept unless his brain affords mechanisms that would coordinate them with the right extensions in each world for which the function DOG is defined. Presumably there is a (very large) disjunctive bundle of such mechanisms, any of which would serve to mediate this coordination. So the internal conditions for having the concept DOG include having a mental representation whose causal role satisfies one or another of the disjuncts of this disjunction.

So, to answer the question that Block starts out by raising, if you want to use the nonpathetic Mapping Theory to determine "right here and now" whether Jones has the narrow concept DOG, what you have to do is find out whether his internal state is such that, in virtue of his being in it, his 'dog' tokens would bear N to dogs if he were on earth, to twin dogs if he were on Twin-Earth, to things-just-like-our-dogs-except-for-having-longer-ears on Cousin-Earth . . . and so forth. The claim is that being in this sort of internal state is a necessary – and (unlike the putative orthographic requirements) a highly substantive – constraint on having the narrow concept DOG; and that (part of) being in such states surely involves having appropriate "conceptions." Externalist arguments that conceptions don't determine reference *do not constitute rebuttals of this claim*; and, *pace* what I take to be Block's main strategy, they oughtn't to be offered as such.

To have the narrow concept DOG, you have to have Mentalese tokens whose internal behavior is appropriate to mediate semantically relevant head-world correlations. Hence Mentalese tokens with the right causal roles. So there's the possibility of a nonpathetic Mapping Theory which says what these causal roles are. But holism doesn't follow since we have no reason to doubt that very many (possibly quite different) belief systems can mediate the same mapping from worlds to extensions. The N-relation is, I suppose *robust*;[19] many theories, including, by the way, many systems of false beliefs, might succeed in sustaining the N-relation between 'dogs' and dogs in this world, 'dogs' and twin-dogs in Twin-world, 'dogs' and things-just-like-our-dogs-except-for-the-ears in Cousin-world . . . and so forth. So, many different belief systems might implement the narrow content DOG. Or, if this is not right, Block needs an argument to show that it isn't. And, so far, I don't see that he's got one.

The general point is this: Problems about holism arise not from the assumption that there is an *empirical* connection between having a certain concept and having a certain inferential apparatus, but only from the assumption that there is a *constitutive* connection between them. It is thus open to the nonpathetic Mapping Theorist to allow that there are all sorts of substantive internal constraints that have to be satisfied if one is to have the narrow concept X, including all sorts of inferential role conditions, and still to argue that narrow concepts are individuated by mappings; hence that it's *logically* possible to have the concepts without having the inferential roles; hence that the *individuation* conditions on concepts are not holistic even if inferential roles are. Nonpathetic theories enumerate *internal* constraints on satisfying a relation (viz. the relation N) that is, however, defined in *external* terms (to put the point in a way that I snitched from Georges Rey).

Philosophers used to make the following mistake. Theories and telescopes, they argued, mediate the causal relations between stars and our "star" tokens. So what we mean by "star" depends on our theories and our telescopes. It is now widely recognized (well, *fairly* widely recognized; well, recognized) that it was a mistake for them to argue this *even assuming that a causal relation between stars and "star" tokens determines what "star" tokens mean and that telescopes are essential to mediate this causal relation.* I think that Block makes the same mistake, though in a subtler form. In effect, he argues that we can only get thin enough conditions for having narrow contents if the nonpathetic Mapping Theory adverts to conceptual roles. But then, if conceptual roles constitute content, holism notoriously ensues. The fallacy lies in supposing that the nonpathetic theory can't advert to conceptual roles unless they constitute content. It is, to put it in a nutshell, perfectly alright for a (pathetic) theory to say what *constitutes* content relations by quantifying over the mechanisms that a (nonpathetic) theory says are the ones required to *implement* content relations (and which must, therefore, be instantiated inside anyone who *has* the concept in any nomologically possible world).

To be a star-word (a word that means STAR) is to be a word whose tokens are reliably connected to stars. That's the informational version of the pathetic story about the broad content of star-words. To have a word whose tokens are reliably connected to stars requires having any of a disjunction of mechanisms to mediate the connection: visual systems, telescopes, brains, and so forth. That's the nonpathetic theory about star-words. It is not true that the constraints that this pathetic theory places on being a star-word are vacuous, nor is it true that the constraints that this nonpathetic theory places on having a star-word imply meaning holism.

It's implicit in the preceding couple of paragraphs that what Block really has is a problem about externalism, not about narrow content *per se.* The right formulation of Block's Worry is that an externalist just can't have a reasonable theory of what's required to have a concept (narrow *or* broad). For: either the externalist says that there are *no* internal constraints on having a concept – which is clearly mad; rocks can't have concepts in *any* context, and that is surely because they have the wrong sorts of insides – or he identifies the internal constraints with inferential roles, in which case he ceases to be an extenalist and holism ensues.

This is a real worry. Its solution is to recognize that, from the semantical point of view, the function of conceptual roles is not constitutive but *instrumental;* all they do that matters semantically is mediate the relation N.

A smattering of points to close.

1   Block imagines someone who is introduced to "tiger" by ostensions of tigers that are disguised to satisfy the panda stereotype. He argues that such a person has the concept TIGER, and that his doing so depends hardly at all on his conception of tigers (on "what's in his head"). But Block's treatment of this case is contaminated by his assumption that it is the learning context that determines broad content. On my view, the introducing ostension bestows the (broad) content *tiger* on the (Mentalese) term "tiger" only if it brings about a nomic relation between being a tiger and being a cause of "tiger" tokenings. Which, I suppose, it wouldn't do in the case that Block describes.

Block correctly remarks that "Fodor favors an 'indicator' theory of the nonsocial aspect of wide content . . . "; but he seems to forget this when he sets out his examples. In the present case, ostensive introductions to tigers disguised as pandas – assuming that they have any semantically relevant effect at all – would presumably set up a state whose tokening is a reliable indicator of pandas (not tigers). It does no good to say that one's "tiger" tokens nevertheless mean *tiger* because that's what "tiger" means in the language community. However persuasive this may be for English (about − 4 on a scale from 0 to 100, I should think) it pretty clearly cuts no ice for Mentalese. A theory that has the consequence that thoughts that reliably track pandas (and for the right reasons, mind you, since, after all, pandas do satisfy the panda stereotype and tigers don't) nevertheless have *de dicto* tiger contents is, I put it to you, in deep trouble.

2   Block sometimes worries that if conceptions don't constitute content, then content will be irrelevant to explaining behavior. Notice, however, that this is a worry about (externalist) theories of *broad* content and is thus not strictly relevant to the present discussion. But, for what it's worth: I think that externalism will make it turn out that the intentional generalizations that connect mental states with actions are characteristically contingent. Contingent generalizations can be reliable, intelligible, explicable, explanatory . . . etc., so why isn't that good enough? To deny that one's "conceptions" are constitutive of the content of one's concepts is *of course* not to deny "a major role for our conceptions of things in psychological explanation." It's just to say that it isn't a *necessary* truth that someone who has the concepts he does also has the conceptions he does.

3   Towards the end of his paper, Block wonders whether there is really anything psychological for narrow contents (*qua* characters) to do. I find his arguments puzzling. For example: "I feel cold, and so I turn up the thermostat. A detailed explanation of my action will appeal to my conception of myself as a person who is both a subject of experience (in this case, feeling cold), and capable of acting. . . . The rule that 'I' always refers to the utterer does not index anything that can do this explanatory job". This seems to confuse the question whether character is the appropriate construct for explaining behavior, which it may be, with the question whether the character of the world "I" provides a suitable explication of my concept of myself; which, of course, it doesn't. Any more than you would expect the character of the word "that" to provide a suitable explication of one's concept of the things one uses "that" to demonstrate.

Addendum

As the reader will have gathered, the canonical procedures for this sort of exchange have somehow come unstuck, and what you've just read is a reply to an earlier, and distinctly different, version of Block's paper than the one that appears in this volume. Not my fault, and certainly not my preference, but apparently not avoidable. To revise my reply in face of Block's revision would invite indefinite regress. Instead, I'll stick with what I've written with just the following addendum.

Revision and all, I'm still not clear what it is about narrow content individuation that is bugging Block. Here, in any event, is my story in a nutshell. Narrow contents are constructs out of broad contents; broad contents are defined by laws that connect environmental properties (being a dog, say) with mental properties (being a token of a Mentalese symbol, syntactically defined; 'dog' as it might be). The kinds of lawful covariances that mental symbols can enter into are constrained, not by their syntax, of course, but by the kinds of (e.g. computational, transductive, etc.) mechanisms available for mediating their mind/world covariances. Such constraints do *not* determine reference (that was the point I stressed in reply to Block's original paper), but they do determine, nomologically, what properties a given syntactically defined mental symbol can covary with; hence what broad content it can express; hence what narrow content it can express.

So, then: a mental symbol of mine has the broad content DOG if its tokenings are causally correlated, in the right ways (see *TOC*), with *dogness*. And the symbol that is, in fact, correlated in the right way with *dogness* depends for this correlation on a certain set of mechanisms which, in effect, fix its semantics insofar as its semantics depends on intrinsic properties of my mind.

Notoriously, however, its semantics doesn't depend *only* on intrinsic properties of my mind; in particular, broad content varies from world to world. Take my (syntactically individuated) 'dog' concept *together with its associated covariation-causing mechanisms* to Twin-Earth, and what you get is 'dog'/twin-dog covariation, instead of the 'dog'/dog covariation that you get around here. In effect, as you carry the 'dog'-and-mechanism pair from world to world, it picks out a set of properties; one for each world in which the narrow content of 'dog' is defined. This set of worlds-and-properties (including *Earth/dogness; Twin-Earth/twin-dogness*, etc.) is the narrow content of my mental symbol 'dog'. People share this narrow concept if they have a symbol-and-mechanism pair which picks out this same set of properties in this same set of worlds. The range of mechanisms that will do so is presumably large, so identity of covariance-causing mechanisms is sufficient but not necessary for identity of narrow content. And, of course, mere syntactical identity of mental symbols is *neither* necessary *nor* sufficient.

The crucial point in all this is that what *has* narrow content is not a syntactical object as such, but a syntactical object *together with the bundle of mechanisms that mediates its mind/world relations.* Block actually does discuss something sort of like this account. (Once. Briefly.) "There are all sorts of 'laws of thought' that link our 'mud' to recognitional capacities, related visual images . . . and so on. The input contexts for the narrow content of 'mud' are those in which language learners *end up* [sic] with these 'laws of thought', regardless of what is innate." Block says that this has " a plausible sound" but objects that it is "none other than our old friend functionalism." But that is quite wrong.

The functionalist idea is that identity of content is somehow defined by reference to an independently specified criterion for functional equivalence of psychological mechanisms (i.e. by reference to a criterion for identity of "functional role"). Whereas, my idea is that functional equivalence of psycholog-ical mechanisms is defined by reference to an independently specified criterion for identity of content. This goes in two steps; first broad content, then narrow. So far as fixing the broad concept DOG is concerned, all that's required of a mechanism is that it effect connectedness to *dogness*. So any mechanisms that connect a mental symbol to *dogness* are equivalent in respect of their broad semantic functions. Similarly for narrow content. Looked at one way, the mechanisms that connect me to *dogness* in this world imply a partial function from worlds to properties (see above). Looked at the other way, anybody who instantiates this function *ipso facto* shares my narrow concept DOG, whatever mechanisms he happens to use to mediate the mapping. So each narrow concept implies a criterion of functional equivalence for the implementing mechanisms.

To repeat: if you want to, you can think of narrow content externalism as just like functionalism, *only the order of analysis goes the other way round*. Instead of taking functional equivalence as basic and defining content identity in terms of it, you start with content identity and use it to define equivalence of function. What makes this way of proceeding attractive is that, whereas we have no notion of equivalence of functional roles except holistic ones, the Mapping Theory tells us what equivalence of content is; and the Mapping Theory isn't holistic.

We can now turn to Block's main worry, which is clear in this summary passage: " . . . the individuative demands of causal covariation between words and the world are in tension with the individuative demands of psychological explanation. The former require a vast disjunction of intervening states of mind *whose only constraint is that they mediate the causal covariation* [my emphasis]; the latter requires enough unity to be of use in psychological explanation."

This is a nonproblem. (Or it's a problem about externalism, not narrow content; see below.) The mechanisms that can mediate the covariances that define a narrow content are, as Block says, typically quite heterogeneous; whatever it is that organisms that share narrow contents have in common, it's presumably not these mediating mechanisms. So, what *else* might they share? The answer is, of course, that they satisfy *the same* (or much the same) *psychological laws*; i.e., my twins (and my cousins and my other near relations) *think and behave* in similar ways when provoked by similar stimuli (stimuli, thoughts, and behaviors all being individuated narrowly). Were this not so, the search for ways of carving things up so that our narrow mental states count as type identical would be simply unmotivated.

Type identity for narrow states is defined by the covariance test. It is not a *necessary* truth that there are psychological laws that subsume organisms insofar as their mental states are identical by this test; and if there are no such laws, then even if the notion of narrow content is well defined, it's useless. It is, however, perfectly OK to hold both that it's *necessarily* true that creatures are in much the same narrow states iff they realize much the same mind/world mappings, and that it's *contingently* true that when creatures are in much the same narrow states they obey much the same psychological laws. It is, indeed, the contingent truth that makes the necessary truth worth mentioning.

Block thinks there's the following dilemma: either we define type identity for narrow mental states by reference to their computational roles – in which case we've got the usual holism problems – or we define it by reference to mind/world covariance – in which case there's no guaranty that type identical mental states will have anything except the defining pattern of mind/world covariance in common. Well, we do type identify narrow mental states by mind/world covariance; and, there isn't a *guaranty* that mental states that are type identical by the covariance test will have anything else of interest in common. Which is to say that there didn't have to be laws about narrow mental states externally defined; it's contingent that you get natural kinds when you group cognitive mechanisms by the mapping functions they mediate. Oh well, there didn't *have* to be laws about mountains either; it's contingent that you get natural kinds when you distinguish big rock piles from little ones. It just turns out that God made the world so that you do get natural kinds that way; in both cases.

Not that it's particularly *surprising* that there should be laws about creatures that share narrow concepts. After all, the mental states of such creatures are sufficiently similar that – to put it as a Gibsonian might – they reasonate to the same properties in every (nearby) world. Indeed, assuming externalism, there is much less reason why there should be laws about creatures that share *broad* contents, since all that *they* are guaranteed to have in common is mental states that resonate to the same property in (as it might be) *this* world. Here as elsewhere, I suspect that it really is externalism, rather that narrow content *per se*, that is making Block unhappy. What was so nice about semantic functionalism was that it identified the mechanisms that generate behavior with the supervenience base for content, thereby guaranteeing a priori that psychology and semantics would never, never come unstuck. Clearly, Block is nostalgic for that sort of metaphysics. But from functionalism you get holism, and from holism you get nihilism. (Or worse, you get that paradigm of oxymorons, "cognitive neuroscience.") We've been down that road; alas, it leads to San Diego.

Boghossian[20]

Boghossian's paper consists of a number of loosely related arguments against the informational account of content that I set out in Fodor (1987d) and *TOC*. I propose to make a couple of brief preliminary remarks, and then I'll deal with these objections seriatim.

Preliminaries

First, quite a lot of the paper is about problems that arise when one attempts to capture the asymmetric dependence version of informational semantics in an ontology of possible worlds. I am quite capable of not taking such problems very seriously; I see no reason to believe that metric or set theoretic relations among possibilia are more fundamental, either metaphysically or epistemologically, than relations of nomic dependence among properties. There is, no doubt, some technical interest in the question how to translate informational theories into possible worlds vocabulary. For those that like that sort of thing. But I certainly don't suppose that the evaluation of informational semantics ought to depend on how – or, indeed, whether – such translations go through. If Boghossian does suppose this, he owes an argument for the supposition.

Second, Boghossian asks whether we really need a naturalizing theory? (Or – what comes to much the same, as Boghossian points out – whether we really need the supervenience of the intentional on the physical.) I suppose my view is that if there's a naturalizing theory of intentionality to be had, then we might as well have it. But I agree that it's an interesting question what the situation would be if no such theory is possible, and I think Boghossian is right to wonder "Why . . . must we think that no property can be real unless it is identical with, or supervenient upon, the properties that appear in the catalogue provided by physics?" (p. 65). But, whatever the answer to this may be, there is good reason to think that supervenience on physics is required of all the properties that can appear in special science laws. (The good reason for thinking this is that it's apparently true in all the untendentious cases.) If there is indeed this architectural constraint on special science laws, then if there is no naturalization of intentional properties it follows that there is no intentional science. (And I'm inclined to think it would also follow that there is no intentional causation; see my "Making mind matter more" in *TOC*.) For my money, the question whether intentional properties are "real" is hardly worth arguing about unless an affirmative answer implies that intentional science is possible. But I do understand that there are philosophers of the "interpretivist" persuasion who would like the intentional properties to hang around even if they don't do any scientific work. Presumably for the atomosphere of *Gemütlichkeit* that that they exude.

OK. Now for the objections.

Type 1 Situations

A type 1 situation is one in which the tokening of a symbol can be caused only by things that are in its extension. In particular, it's supposed to follow from the characterization of a type 1 situation that no tokening of a symbol can be *false* in a situation that is type 1 for that symbol.

Some naturalization theories require that there be *actual* situations that are type 1 for each intentional state. (For example, historical versions of Darwinian/teleological theories require this; see my discussion of Millikan in this volume.) Boghossian thinks that my asymmetric dependence story requires at least that type 1 situations be *physically possible*. He thinks this because he reads the possible-world translation of the theory as holding that "S means whatever properties are possible causes of S-tokens in the closest world with the smallest subset of S-token causes in the actual world" (p. 72). The argument he gives for accepting this translation is that he thinks he can show that the only plausible alternative doesn't work. But, as it turns out, the argument that the only plausible alternative doesn't work doesn't work. I propose to show this rather than take up the burden of defending the physical possibility of type 1 situations (a question on which I stand mute).

The proposal is something like this.[21] The nomic relation X $--\!\!\!\gg$ S is asymmetrically dependent on the nomic relation P $--\!\!\!\gg$ S iff P is the unique property that is nomologically connected to S in every (nearby) world in which any property is nomologically connected to S. Boghossian thinks he can show that there never *will* be a unique such property, which is to say that you can't get univocal content attributions out of the asymmetric dependence theory if it is set up in this way.

Here's how the argument goes. Suppose that cows, cats, and mice cause "cows" in the actual world, and suppose the situation with respect to "cow" tokens in nearby worlds is the following.

W1	W2
cows cause 'cows' (P $--\!\!\!\gg$ S)	cows cause 'cows'
cats cause 'cows' (Q $--\!\!\!\gg$ S)	cats don't cause 'cows'
mice don't cause 'cow'	mice cause 'cow' (R $--\!\!\!\gg$ S)

So, real-world 'cow's carry the information *cow or cat or mouse*, W1 'cow's carry the information cow or cat, and W2 'cow's carry the information *cow or mouse*. We want it to come out that cow means 'cow' because *cowhood* is the only property whose instances cause 'cow's in every world where anything does. But Boghossian objects that the present assumptions don't suffice to defeat the hypothesis that S means *(cow and cat) or (cow and mouse)* (call this disjunctive formula C). Boghossian remarks that "it is enough that there should be even *one* case where P & Q are compossible for this to go through."

But there is really a lot wrong with this. Notice, to begin with, that for S to mean P in this world, $P \dashrightarrow S$ has to be (not just true but) lawful in (relevant) worlds where other $X \dashrightarrow S$ laws fail. The argument for this is straightforward. The intuition that underlies the asymmetric dependence story is that S's meaning P depends on $P \dashrightarrow S$ but not on any other $X \dashrightarrow S$ connections. But this implies that any other $X \dashrightarrow S$ can fail consonant with whatever is required for S to mean P. But for S to mean P, Ss must carry information about P; and for Ss to carry information about P, $S \dashrightarrow P$ has to be a law. So X isn't a candidate for what S means in W_i unless $X \dashrightarrow S$ is a law in W_i.

So, then, the question arises whether we're guaranteed that C is a law in W1 and W2; and the answer is that we aren't. For one thing, as Boghossian is himself eager to emphasize (in a different context), "... the holistic character of belief fixation suggests that anything can cause the thought 'Lo, a [cow]' in just about *any* situation ...."[28]. But if this is so, then it's clear that the disjunctive antecedents of formulas like C will be *open*; and Boghossian agrees, at least for the sake of arguments, that hypotheticals whose antecedents are open disjunctions are *ipso facto* not nomic.

Second, Boghossian must be assuming that where $X \dashrightarrow S$ and $Y \dashrightarrow S$ are nomic, it follows that so too is $X\&Y \dashrightarrow S$. But *ceteris paribus* laws are notorious for not satisfying this pattern of inference. Boghossian himself notes that there's some doubt about such cases when X and Y aren't nomically compossible; and the doubts deepen, one might suppose, when X and Y aren't metaphysically compatible. And, even where X and Y are nomically compossible, their respective side-effects may interact to cancel S. Medicine offers a plethora of such cases. "And too many cooks spoil the broth" cackles Granny, dangerously overexcited.

Perhaps Boghossian's argument is that one case where X and Y are compossible *and* the inference goes through would do to defeat the theory. But that overlooks the point that what's on offer is a sufficient – not a necessary and sufficient – condition for content. We have, so far at least, no reason to doubt that the sufficiency condition would be satisfied for any triple of properties which fails the inference.[22] (These, on reflection, might well include most of the cases. I regularly think 'frog's of frogs and I occasionally think 'frog's of elephants; but Lord only knows what I would think of frelephants.)

I conclude that Boghossian has given us no reason to believe that C will be a candidate for determining the meaning of S whenever $P \dashrightarrow S$ is a candidate for determining the meaning of S. From which I further conclude that Boghossian has given us no reason for supposing that the asymmetric dependence story is committed to type 1 situations. From now on, I will largely ignore such of Boghossian's arguments as presuppose that it is.

The Verificationism Argument

This objection is directed (not against the asymmetric counterfactual story but) against informantional semantics *per se*. It says that informational theories are *ipso facto* unacceptably vertificationistic. What I probably ought to do is just refuse to play this game since it turns out that all the examples involve symbols (kind terms) about whose range of application speakers are assumed to have specific intentions; and of course that isn't the case for mental representations, which are the only symbols whose semantics I actually care about. Still, here's Boghossian's line:

> Suppose there were stuff – ABC – which is exactly like water except for its behavior in circumstances that are "physically inaccessible to humans . . . in all the physically possible worlds *that we can get to* . . . Lets suppose that this is because ABC would exhibit its distinctive characteristics only in gravitational fields of such intensity . . . that nothing as complex as a human body could survive them long enough to perform even the fleetest measurement; we needn't be too fussy about the physical details" (p. 75). Well, "standard intuition would have it, I submit, that ABC is no more in the extension of 'water' than XYZ is" (p. 76). After all, "physics doesn't taxonomize molecules with reference to our biological and medical limitations" (pp. 75–6).

Now this is an argument against any semantics which says that if 'water' means H_2O (and doesn't mean ABC) then there must be some physically possible world in which H_2O would cause 'water' tokens and ABC wouldn't. Boghossian's example postulates that there is no such world. So it is incumbent on an informational semanticist to argue that, in Boghossian's case, "water" means H_2O or ABC. So, what does intuition tell us about this case?

Well, to begin with, it's important not to confuse Boghossian's ABC with Putnam's XYZ. Putnam assumes that XYZ and H_2O are straightforwardly different chemicals, hence that there are nearby worlds in which we can tell them apart. ABC is *much* more outré. How much more? Boghossian needs to assume not only that it is physically impossible for us to be where the reaction that distinguishes H_2O from ABC occurs, but that it is a matter of physical law there is no effect of the interaction that our instruments could in principle detect. (We don't need to be able to get to Pluto to determine that it isn't made of green cheese.) Moreover, if ABC is to be indistinguishable from H_2O, then it must be that ABC obeys all the water laws (as far as we can tell) and is made out of constituents that obey all the hydrogen and oxygen laws (as far as we can tell). And similarly the rest of the way down. The constituents of the constituents of ABC must obey all the proton, gluon, quark . . . and so forth, laws and be made out of parts that are (as far as we can tell) indistinguishable from the constituents of the constituents . . . of water.

Digression: Boghossian seems to think that these sorts of issues are especially transparent in (of all places!) the case of terms for the ultimate particles themselves (see his n. 18). But that's only because, when he discusses such cases, he does the hard part by postulation. Boghossian just assumes that " 'T' is a name for a certain kind of elementary particle . . ." and then goes on to intuit, plausibly enough, that if T* particles are distinct from T-particles "according to the basic principles of elementary particle taxonomy" then they would, *ipso facto*, not be in "T"'s extension. However, this does rather beg the question whether "T" *could* somehow get to be a kind term in the sort of circumstances imagined. What would the scenario be like?

Maybe we introduce 'T-particle' by reference to a track on a photographic plate; " 'T-particles' are ones of the same kind as the one that made *that*."[23] But it turns out that there are other (T*) particles, different in kind from this one, but such that the difference is not detectable by us in any physically possible worlds. Now the crucial question is whether the ostensive introduction actually succeeded in establishing 'T' as a (nondisjunctive) kind term. Remember, it's assumed that there are actually T* particles around, and that the tracks they make, not just *would*, but actually *will*, in the course of time, get called 'T-particle' tracks by expert members of the scientific community. The text books will display T*-particle tracks as paradigms of T-particle tracks. The first high-energy synthesis of a T*-particle will be acclaimed as the first high-energy synthesis of a T-particle, and will receive a Nobel Prize under that description . . . and so forth. If, as Boghossian insists, these are misapplications of 'T-particle,' they are ones which, in point of physical law, will never be corrected.

Notice, too, that if the present track *had been* made by a T*-particle instead of a T-particle, that wouldn't have made *the slightest difference* to anything that happens in any scientific community that is a physically possible successor of ours; in particular, it doesn't make the slightest difference to what gets called a T-particle whether it's T-particles or T*-particles in connection with which the term is introduced. But Boghossian's intuition is that none of this matters to what "T-particle" means; all that matters is what kind of particle made the track that got baptized. Quine was wrong after all: some stipulations, it turns out, *are* enduring traits. All you have to do is just have the intention that your word should denote a kind and, *Voila!* It does. Come what may or come what might have.

Anybody who has clear intuitions about such cases is welcome to them, but that sounds to me like magic.[24]

So, to return to the main thread, the story has to be that ABC is just like H_2O *all the way down*, so far as we (where 'we' means us and our actual and possible experiments and our actual and possible theories) can tell. And the question is whether, given all this, it's a consequence *simply of our intention to use 'water' as a kind term* that ABC is excluded from its extension.

Well, for starters, you don't, in the present case, gain much by insisting that it is. After all, we don't (and, by assumption, can't) know anything about what, over and above the postulated difference of their behavior in black holes, the putative typological distinctness of ABC and H_2O consists in. Or, indeed, whether there *is* anything other than the postulated difference of their behavior in black holes that their putative typological distinctness consists in. In particular, there's no substantive sense in which their putative typological distinctness *explains* the difference between their behaviors. But if the notion of a difference in kind has come unstuck from its role in explaining differences in behavior, isn't the claim that we've *got* a difference in kind just posturing? Perhaps the right thing to say about Boghossian's case is that sometimes water behaves one way in black holes and sometimes it behaves another way. That would be an odd thing to have to say, but the insides of black holes are notorious for being odd places. All kinds tolerate variation in their instances; some kinds (like *mountain*, for example) tolerate quite a lot. What shows that *water* doesn't tolerate the difference between H_2O and ABC?

Boghossian has to show not just that "water" would denote a kind in the circumstances he imagines, but also that a kind couldn't be disjunctive in those sorts of circumstances. I don't think he's shown either of these things.

The Belief Holism Argument

The belief holism argument purports to show that, even if there are situations in which nothing but Ps cause Ss, still we would never be able to say, in non-question-begging terms, which circumstances they are. Since, however, we are not committed to situations in which nothing but Ps cause Ss, we aren't obliged to worry about this.

The Distance Metric Argument

Consider H_2O and XYZ. It's assumed that there are nearby worlds in which H_2O and XYZ are distinguishable, and that in some of these worlds XYZ rules (viz. XYZ causes 'water' tokens and H_2O doesn't); in other of these worlds, water rules (viz. H_2O causes 'water' tokens and XYZ doesn't). Now (putting it roughly), the asymmetric dependence story requires that, in order for 'water' to mean H_2O and not XYZ in the actual world every world in which water rules has to be closer to us than any world in which XYZ does. The reasoning that it's OK to require this might be that, if 'water' does mean H_2O and not XYZ in the actual world, then you'd have to *change more* to get to a world in which only XYZ causes 'water' tokens than you would to get to a world where only H_2O does. So (still putting it roughly) to get to the latter kind of world, you'd only have to make XYZ and H_2O distinguishable; to get to the former kind you'd have to both do that *and* alter the mechanisms that underlie our intentions to use 'water' only of stuff that's of the same kind as our local samples.

Boghossian objects, in effect, that if it turns out that you have to make a VERY BIG change to make a reliable H_2O detector, and only a rather small change to make a reliable XYZ detector, then the nearest world in which you have an H_2O detector could be further away than some world in which you have both an XYZ detector and some altered linguistic dispositions. So we can't after all, safely require that all the closest worlds where water is distinguishable from XYZ be ones where water rules.

But that's not hard to fix. What's needed is that each world in which H_2O and XYZ are distinguishable and we apply 'water' to H_2O but not to XYZ is closer to us than the world *that is closest to it* in which H_2O and XYZ are distinguishable and we apply 'water' to XYZ but not to H_2O. (This is a way of saying that *ceteris paribus* worlds in which water rules are closer to us than corresponding worlds in which XYZ does.) Any adequate distance measure should have this property because, as we've seen, you have to change more things to get to XYZ-but-not-H_2O worlds than you do to get to H_2O-but-not-XYZ worlds. And though, as Boghossian very properly reminds us, it is not required that the more things you have to change to get to a world, the further away that world has to be, it *is* required that the more things you have to change to get to a world, the further away that world has to be *ceteris paribus*.

Boghossian says "everything depends on whether the relevant similarity relation can be specified non-question-beggingly ... (p. 81)." But it doesn't, really. What everything depends on is the reliability of the intuition that I've been stressing; viz. that, *ceteris paribus*, you have to change fewer things to make water and XYZ distinguishable than you do to both make water and XYZ distinguishable and alter our linguistic dispositions.[25] If the intuition is right, somebody will cobble up a distance measure that captures it; and if the distance measure that somebody cobbles up *doesn't* capture it, so much the worse for the distance measure. Technique is one thing, philosophy another.

Two methodological morals: (a) Do not allow the tail to wag the dog; (b) If you should come across a tail that is wagging a dog, do not attempt to remedy the situation by cutting off the dog.

Dennett

"The cat is out of the bag. Jerry Fodor ... is a romantic conservative whose slogan might well be: What is good enough for Granny is good enough for science" (p. 87). Now, where did Dan Dennett *ever* get the idea that I keep my cat in a bag? I told Greycat and he fainted dead away. He's all nerves, poor thing.

Actually, I thought I'd made it pretty clear, over the years, that it was my view that the enormous practical success of belief/desire psychology makes a prima facie case for its approximate truth; that the major scientific successes in psychology tend to confirm this; and that anyway, from a methodological point of view, we haven't much choice but to try and make science out of Granny-Psychology because there aren't any other ideas around that it is possible to take seriously.

However, since Dennett has raised the point, this is as good a place as any for me to announce my pantheon. It seems to me, really, that only three things of lasting importance have happened in the history of cognitive science, and that all three suggest the essential rightness of Granny's view. There are:

1 Turing's proposal for a computational theory of rationality. Turing showed how machine processes might be truth preserving. So for the first time there were substantial – as opposed to merely metaphysical – grounds for supposing that the mind might be some sort of machine. (Associationism had been the only other attempt to characterize a truth-preserving mechanism. It was a disaster; and still is.) Precisely because he showed how *mechanical* processes can preserve *truth*, Turing's achievement went quite a long way towards vindicating Granny's understanding of mental processes as causal relations among semantically evaluable mental states.

2 Freud's demonstration that postulating unconscious beliefs and desires

allows a vast range of anomalous behavioral (and mental) phenomena to be brought within the purview of familiar forms of belief/desire explanation (of practical rationality). Freud thus anticipated by a hundred years or so, and roundly refuted, the charge that Granny-Psychology is stagnant science.

3   Two of Chomsky's insights: first, that if we assume that a grammar expresses what speaker/hearers know (believe/"cognize") about their language (and that structural descriptions express what they know about its sentences), the methods and results of linguistics can be brought wholesale into Granny's camp, And second, that there are serious grounds for supposing that a substantial amount of cognitive structure might be innate. (Granny had been worrying a lot about how anything could possibly *learn* to be a belief/desire machine.)

It seems to me, to put the matter in a nutshell, that things have been going pretty well for Granny, and nowhere at all for anybody else.

By the way, though it's true that I don't think much of connectionism, Dennett has the wrong story about why this is so. In particular, it is *quite* wrong to say that "connectionists . . . don't accept the facticity of the 'Classical' mental types and processes." On the contrary, as Pylyshyn and I were at some pains to point out, connectionists are intentional psychologists of the old school. Together with practically everybody since Descartes, (excepting, of course, behaviorists) connectionists assume that the main business of psychology is theorizing about inference, the fixation of perceptual belief, learning, and the like. What *is* true about connectionists, and what makes Granny *so annoyed* with them, is that they want to throw out Turing's picture of how such processes are to be mechanized. Granny thinks that Turing's was one of the precious few good ideas about the mind that anybody has had so far (see 1 above). As far as I can make out, the connectionists are in the process of providing an inadvertent demonstration of how right she is to think this. (It's also true about connectionists that they hold – wrongly in my view – that they can square their Intentional Realism with a holist view of the individuation of mental states. But they are hardly the first Intentional Realists to be muddled on this point.)

As to the issues about content, we are of course committed to taking them seriously just in proportion as we take Granny-Psychology seriously. And it is quite true that (unlike the rest of the philosophical community; *ça va sans dire*) I have found these issues very difficult and very confusing. When last heard from, I was still trying to work out a coherent view. It has, for example, only slowly grown upon me that you can't be Quinean about the analytic/synthetic distinction and functionalist about content; in effect, that a naturalized version of Granny-Psychology has to be atomistic. So – just as Dennett says – I dithered for a long while about content functionalism and then got off the wagon.

Dennett asks, in effect, why I don't buy a Darwinian theory of content at the price of allowing a bit of indeterminacy, the suggestion being that all that Darwin fails to rule out is "phenomenalistic interpretations" of the attitudes. But this misreads *TOC*. What I argue there is that a selection history story can't distinguish between organisms that represent the world as F and organisms that represent it as G in any case where "F iff G" is counterfactual supporting in the organism's world. In effect, Darwinian functionalism captures everything that's important about intentionality except its intensionality. (Unlike Dennett, Millikan sees that she has to find a way out of this, or the game is over. (see her paper in this volume.))

In fact, *TOC* offers a causal theory (not, however, Darwinian) which does provide a unique resolution of the disjunction problem for all the cases thus far proposed. So what's the fuss about? If " 'behavioristic' theories such as [Dennett's] ... simply deny this possibility" (p. 93) so much the worse for behaviorism. Again.

Can such a thing as an atomistic and naturalistic theory of content really be brought off? I don't know; but what does *not* impress me is an alleged philosophical consensus to the contrary. When I was a boy in graduate school, the consensus in the philosophy of mind was Ryle and Skinner. Then Chomsky blew and they were scattered. Consensus my Granny; the history of philosophy is the history of smart people saying things that mostly aren't true.

By the way, still speaking of content, I think the quotation on p. 90 is a little misleading. When I said that function is "a marginal – a not very important – determinant of meaning" I wasn't issuing a blank check. I think you need functional considerations to distinguish between (for example) the concept WATER and the concept H_2O (roughly, you can have the former but not the latter even if you don't have the concept HYDROGEN). But this is just the kind of functional relation that compositional semantics gives you anyway; it's just the decomposition of the semantics of syntactically complex formulas into the semantics of their syntactic parts. So it's (as Dennett would say I would say) egregiously untendentious.

About whether my attacks on AI, connectionism and the like "simply invented and demolished strawmen" (p. 91), that depends quite a lot on whether you think that the attacks have been answered. Procedural semantics seems to have disappeared; would that I could claim the credit. As for Smolensky's "tensor product" defense of connectionism, see Fodor and McLaughlin (1990). As far as I can tell, the argument has gone like this: Fodor and Pylyshyn claimed that you can't produce a connectionist theory of systematicity. Smolensky then replied by not producing a connectionist theory of systematicity. Who could have foreseen so cunning a rejoinder?

It is, nevertheless, true that the objections I've had to AI views have not, generally, "been particularly concerned with the details of the models under attack" (p. 90). That was because what was wrong with the models was so, well, egregious, that not much concern with the details seemed to be required. I do think it's been characteristic of AI to spend a lot of effort elaborating some pretty silly theories. Too much programming too soon, is my diagnosis.

In a sense, I do believe that the "whole enterprise of GOFAI was ill-founded" (p. 91). Not because it's got the wrong picture of the mind, however, but because it has a bad methodology for turning that picture into science. I don't think you do the science of complex phenomena by attempting to model gross observable variance. Physics, for example, is not the attempt to construct a machine that would be indistinguishable from the real world for the length of a conversation. We do not think of Disneyland as a major *scientific* achievement. I think you do the science of complex surface phenomena by trying to pick the complexity to pieces, setting up artificial (i.e. experimental) environments in which the underlying causes can be studied one at a time. This suggests that the science of the mind is Psychology, not AI. If Dennett's been reading my stuff, he will have noticed that I take psychology pretty seriously. I even try to do some from time to time.

Last topic: My view about the psychology of central processes is not that it's impossible in principle, and of course it's not that "scientists should be [prohibited] from attempting empirical explorations . . ." (pp. 93–4). My view is this: there are some problems you can't solve because key ideas are missing. Blustering doesn't help, throwing money at the problems doesn't help, arguments of the form "some theory must work, this is some theory, therefore this theory must work" don't help (although that's often quite a good form of argument); nothing helps until somebody gets some key ideas. If this picture is Romantic, blame it on Tom Kuhn.

It seems to me that if you look at what passes for the psychology/AI/neuroscience of central processes, it is just *obvious* that there's been asymptotically close to no progress; and that there isn't likely to be any until somebody has some key ideas that nobody has had so far. If, moreover, you consider the current research armamentarium, and how badly it fits what appear to be the main features of central processing, it's reasonable to suppose that when somebody does come up with a reasonable story about belief-fixation and the like, it will be quite a different kind of story than what's so far been successful in the treatment of relatively modular cognition. None of this strikes me as surprising, or tendentious, or even very worrying. Why are people so upset to be told that there are deep, unsolved problems about the mind? I thought *everybody's* Granny knew that.

As for "how come we're advancing and you're retreating," I suppose Napoleon might have described himself as advancing from Moscow to Paris. Well, it was *almost* an advance. Except for the direction.

Devitt

"Having it both ways" is having it turn out both that the laws of psychology are typically intentional (so Folk Psychology is true) and that mental processes are computational/formal/syntactic (so the Computational Theory of Mind is true too). I have supposed that there is no conflict between these doctrines because I have supposed that they apply at different levels of analysis: roughly, syntactical processes at the computational level implement causal laws at the intentional level.

Embracing the two-level story requires denying what Devitt calls PRESUPPOSITION (viz. the claim that "the laws of the mind – simply *are* the laws of mental processes" (p. 99). Now Devitt has it absolutely right; I do reject PRESUPPOSITION, and doing so is essential to the whole picture that I've been constructing. However, I don't regard rejecting PRESUPPOSITION as tendentious; on the contrary, PRESUPPOSITION is *Preposterous*. Here is a typical folk-psychological intentional law: *ceteris paribus*, the moon seems to be larger when it's on the horizon. How on *earth* could this be mistaken for a "law of mental processes"?[26] Nobody knows *what* mental process accounts for the moon illusion. Somewhere, at this very moment, some psychologist is spending your tax money trying to find out.

Devitt covers a lot of ground, and I haven't the space, or the time, or the spirit to go back over all of it. But I think what's at the heart of his paper is a suggestion of two ways in which the two-level story could break down (two ways in which the rejection of PRESUPPOSITION might prove to be unwarranted).

1 If there were a conceptual role notion of content (content constructed out of input specifications, output specifications, and syntax) then there would be no argument for the Computational Theory of Mind. As Devitt says, if CTM is the view that mental operations have access to formal/syntactic properties of mental representations *as opposed to* semantical properties of mental representations, then CTM is plausible only where "semantical" is read as something like "truth conditional." There would be no obvious basis for contrasting formal/syntactic mental processes with intentional mental laws if there were some kind of intentional content that can be reduced to formal/syntactic relations.

However, I do not think that there is any such kind of content. And, even if there were, I don't believe that it could be the kind of content that's required to explicate the intentionality of psychological states. Functional content is inherently holistic; and semantic holism undermines Realism about intentional laws. (As, indeed, Quine has taught us.)

2 Devitt thinks that the levels distinction can be sustained only for those mental processes that involve T–T (thought to thought) causal relations; as soon as one widens the view to include I–T (input to thought) and T–O (thought to output) causation, the distinction between the levels breaks down. At one point Devitt remarks, presumably with I–T and T–O laws in mind, that "the mind is not purely syntactic at any level, even the implementational" (p. 100).

Here's what I think: the intentional laws of folk psychology are implemented at a level of causal processes which are exhaustively syntactic and psychophysical, the T–T laws being the syntactic ones and the I–T and T–O laws being the psychophysical ones (what it is for them to be psychophysical will emerge momentarily). Since it's the I–T and T–O laws that Devitt's argument against the two-level picture turns on, I propose now to look at them in the light of PRESUPPOSITION.

What I have to argue to show that PRESUPPOSITION is plausibly false, is that neither I–T nor T–O generalizations provide access to the vocabulary required to state intentional psychological laws. (Devitt grants that T–T generalizations don't; they're agreed to be just syntactic.) So, then, here's the story: I–T and T–O generalizations are psychophysical. This means: they specify nomic relations between, on the one hand, proximal stimuli under physical description,[27] and, on the other hand, a certain (perhaps proprietary) class of mental representations under syntactic descriptions. In the psycholinguistic case, for example a psychophysical generalization might associate an utterance token described as an incident acoustic waveform with a spectrographic representation.[28] A spectrographic representation of a waveform counts as (*inter alia*) a syntactic object (you can think of it as a set of numerals if you like).[29] It is therefore potentially in the domain of syntactic transformations including, specifically, mental processes that extract phonetic features, assign parsing trees, and so forth. Parsing theory is the explication of these processes.

What about T–O laws? The general idea is that they correlate a (possibly proprietary) set of mental representations (under, as usual, syntactic description) with a proprietary set of motor gestures for which tokenings of the representation are causally sufficient *ceteris paribus*. In the psycholinguistic case, one perhaps thinks of the speech mechanisms as transducers that accept tokens of the Mentalese names for phones as inputs and produce tokens of the phones as outputs. (So, the little man who lives in your head says to your speech mechanisms (in Mentalese) "gimme a [d]". And in causal consequence, the tongue positions itself against the velum, the lungs puff air, the vocal chords vibrate, . . . *et voila!* a [d].)[30]

Up to this point I've been rehearsing received doctrine; every computational psychologist (in effect, everybody who's not a Gibsonian or a behaviorist or a fruitcake) takes it for granted. So much so that I've assumed it without much discussion in most of my philosophical writing about cognitive science (see, however, Fodor and Pylyshyn, 1981b, where some of this is unpacked). But now for a concession. It's probably going to turn out, given my view of how semantical relations work, that I–T and T–O generalizations specify content-making properties of head/world relations; they specify sufficient conditions for certain mental representations meaning what they do. This is a way in which I–T and T–O laws are really *quite* different from T–T laws. The latter hold simply in virtue of the syntactic relations among mental representations, and only the most benighted causal role semanticist could suppose that syntactic relations are, all by themselves, sufficient for content. (I assume that no causal role semanticist *that* benighted is party to this discussion.)

Because the conditions for *representation* are satisfied by the lawful psychophysical relations, the spectrographic representations that waveforms evoke mean that the input utterance has certain acoustic properties; the phonetic instruction that occasions the utterance of [d] means that the intended motor gesture is to be apt for the production of a token of [d]. And so forth. Psychophysical laws thus determine the contents of the mental representations they pair with Is and Os.

This concedes a point to Devitt; I–T and T–O laws *do* provide access to a vocabulary of content; specifically, to a vocabulary of psychophysical content. I–T and T–O laws specify properties of (certain) mental representations in virtue of which they represent the things they do. To put it another way, since the vocabulary of the computational level is syntactic *and* psychophysical, Devitt is right to say that "the mind is not purely syntactic at any level, even the implementational." So doesn't that show that my story about there being intentional laws at one level, and syntactic processes at a different level has now collapsed? Sure, if you like; but nothing follows.

The important point is this: I–T laws provide access *only* to representations of the physical properties of proximal stimuli; and T–O laws provide access *only* to representations of basic motor gestures. I take it to be simply obvious that this vocabulary is not remotely rich enough to state the full range of intentional psychological laws (try rewriting "the moon looks bigger on the horizon" with "the moon" and "the horizon" replaced by physical descriptions of proximal stimuli). So, what you end up with is: one level at which the available vocabularly is whatever you need to state whatever intentional laws there turn out to be; and another level at which the available vocabulary is exhaustively psychophysical and syntactical; and The Computational Theory of The Mind is the idea that the (mental)[31] processes specifiable at the second level implement the intentional laws specified at the first.

I'm afraid Devitt gets this picture wrong, and for a frustrating sort of reason. Devitt has snagged his foot on a terminological misunderstanding of the kind that convinces one that serious conversation between psychologists and philosophers is both urgent and impossible. Devitt understands psychophysical laws in such fashion that "together with the syntactic T–T laws [they] do *not* [my emphasis] form a 'level' in the appropriate sense. Psychophysical laws are *between* levels; they are bridging laws. They hold in virtue of the fact that a totally psychological level, *including psychologically described inputs and outputs*, is implemented in a totally physical level, *including physically described thoughts*" (p. 110; Devitt's emphasis). Now that *is* what philosophers often mean by "psychophysical law." For example, it's what Davidson appears to mean when he asserts that the anomalousness of the mental entails that there aren't any. For a philosopher, a psychophysical law is, as Devitt says, a species of bridge law: one which has intentional language on one end and nonintentional (e.g. neurological; anyhow physicalistic) language on the other.

But a moment's reflection will show that that is *not* (I repeat at a higher volume) that it is *NOT*, what "psychophysical" means in the preceding paragraphs. In the preceding paragraphs, psychophysical laws relate stimuli (or responses) under physicalistic description to mental representations under the descriptions under which mental representations enter into mental processes; hence, under syntactic descriptions if CTM is true. The point is, of course, that from the fact that psychophysical laws in Devitt's sense don't constitute a level with T–T laws, it doesn't follow that psychophysical laws in *my* sense don't constitute a level with T–T laws. On the contrary: since T–T processes are defined over the outputs of I–T laws, and since T–T laws define the inputs of T–O laws, the natural assumption would be that the three kinds of laws govern the same level of processing.[32] The moral is that if you assume, as all computational psychologists do, that I–T and T–O laws are psychophysical in the sense just discussed, then:

1   It's arguable (anyhow, I'm conceding) that I–T and T–O laws both establish head/world relations that are sufficient to determine content (so they differ from T–T laws).
2   But neither I–T laws nor T–O laws provide access to anything like a nonsyntactic vocabulary rich enough to state the laws of intentional psychology.
3   That's why adding such laws to a syntactical theory of T–T laws does not satisfy the demand for a vocabulary which allows the statement of intentional generalizations.
4   So, if you believe standard computational psychology *and* you believe folk psychology, then either your views are inconsistent (as Stich and Devitt think that mine are) or you think that computational psychology and intentional psychology specify mental processes at different levels of description.

To summarize: "Having it both ways" depends on there being distinct intentional and computational levels of psychological theory. Devitt suggests two ways in which the two-level picture could break down: if the intentional level were somehow a construction out of the computational level; or if the computational level itself had access to an intentional vocabulary via inputs and outputs that are "psychologically" described. But the former story won't wash because even if there is narrow content (in the sense of PSYCHOSEMANTICS) there is no functional role content; and the second won't wash because it partly defines the computational level that I–T and O–T laws are constrained to be psychophysical.

Interspersed among the many interesting and important observations that Devitt makes, there are some curious misreadings which I want to remark briefly upon.

Implementation:

I hold that intentional mental processes are typically implemented by computational processes. Devitt sometimes expresses this as "the semantic [is] implemented in the syntactic," from which he infers, on my behalf, the really bizarre view that denotation is somehow a syntactic relation. He can then proceed to beat me over the head with this presumed consequence of my presumed commitments: "The property of denoting Maggie can no more be implemented syntactically than it can be implemented in the formal properties of representations . . ." (p. 111), and so forth.

Sigh! Here's what "semantics is implemented syntactically" must mean, insofar as it means anything I believe: consider a psychological causal law of the form *A-states cause B-states* where "A" and "B" expresses intentional properties. For present purposes, the implementation principle says: for each individual that falls under the antecedent of this law there will be some syntactic property AS, such that for each individual that falls under the consequent of the law there will be some syntactic property BS such that *AS-states cause BS-states* is a law. I take it to be pretty obviously not a consequence of this claim that the expression "Maggie" bears a syntactical relation to the lady it denotes. (In fact, I do have a theory about what relation "Maggie" bears to Maggie in virtue of which the former denotes the latter; and this theory is, to put it mildly, not syntactic. Cf. my (1987d) and *TOC*.)

Parallelism:

On p. 113 Devitt says, rightly, that the syntax/semantics parallelism I keep harping on is "irrelevant to the implementation of the [intentional] law[s]," i.e., the theory of implementation *per se* doesn't mention the parallelism. Of course it doesn't. Parallelism is a *relation between* the implementation and the intentional processes that it implements. The theory of a relation is *ipso facto* not part of the theory of either of the *relata*. But, then, where *does* the parallelism come in? What's the point of going on about it?

To miss the point of going on about syntax/semantics parallelism is to miss what seems to me to be the main philosophical interest of the computational approach to psychology. There are, I think, three great metaphysical puzzles about the mind. How could anything material have conscious states? How could anything material have semantical properties? How could anything material be rational? (Where this means something like: how could the state transitions of a physical system preserve semantical properties?) The parallelism story – if, indeed, it can be made to work – answers question three.

The general point is: not only can one have it both ways (Folk Psychology is right about intentionality; CTM is right about mental processes) but it is only *by* having it both ways that we make progress on the one metaphysical problem about the mind that we've had any luck with so far. What we want to know is how the causal relations among mental states preserve their intentional/semantic properties. Having it both ways allows us to assume that mental processes are syntactically implemented, and then to invoke syntax/semantics parallelism to explain why mental processes are coherent under intentional description. Whereas, if you have it Devitt's way and ". . . implementation is not a matter of the semantic being implemented in the syntactic . . . It is a matter of the syntactic being implemented in the syntactic" (p. 115) the computational story about the mind becomes irrelevant to explaining its semantic integrity. We want philosophers to dissolve our failures, please; not our successes.

Turing said, in effect,: "When the states of a mechanism have both syntactic and semantic properties, then it is often possible to define causal processes over the syntactic properties in such fashion that the semantic properties are preserved." And then there was light.[33]

Loar

Loar's paper is characteristically subtle and deep and perceptive and I guess I don't believe a word of it. Really thrashing out the issues he raises would take a monograph; I don't begin to hope to do them justice here.[34]

However: Loar suggests two main kinds of worries for the sort of semantics I endorse. One is that it doesn't cover "deferential" concepts; and the other is that it fails to recognize the indispensability of "guiding conceptions," "perspectives" and the like in determining reference. I propose to say practically nothing about the first objection and only a little more than that about the second.

'Deferential Concepts'.

The idea (familiar, of course, from recent discussions of individualism) is that the extension of some of my concepts is determined by my intention that ". . . I implicitly take [their] reference to be determined by the language I speak, that I intend [them] to refer in my thinking to whatever [they refer] to in that language" (pp. 121–2).

Now, here's what I really think: The application of mental representations can't be deferential in this sense for at least two reasons: first, we have no policies with respect to our concepts (only with respect to our words); and, second, we think in a *de facto* private language, a policy of deference to other speakers of which would verge on incoherence. As for the reference of (e.g. English) words, it's parasitic on the reference of the concepts they are conventionally used to express. Deference "determines" their reference only in the sense that it's one of the conventions that determines which words express which concepts.

I defer to the language community as to whether "elm" expresses the concept ELM or the concept BEECH, so if I apply "elm" to a beech, what I've said is false. It's false even though I may be convinced that beeches are the kind of trees that "elm" is said of; even though I have always applied "elm" to beeches; even though I am disposed to apply "elm" to beeches in future . . . and so forth. (In fact, as Loar notes, this overstates the case; but it will do for the purposes at hand.) But it wouldn't follow from any of this that ELM or BEECH are themselves deferential in *any* sense. My thoughts have the contents they do for whatever reason they do; but I defer to the language community as to which thoughts my utterances are to be taken to express when it comes to judging the truth values of my utterances. The theory of meaning for words is "Gricean" and nonindividualistic, to put it in a nutshell. But the theory of meaning for concepts[35] is something quite other.

I'm aware that this sort of line is not currently fashionable; fortunately, I don't have to defend it here. For Loar is prepared to admit that "it is natural to think that, however dependent one may be on concepts whose reference is socially determined, one's ability to think about the world requires at least having the capacity to form one's own recognitional concepts" (p. 126). In fact it is natural to think something a good deal stronger: namely, that only a creature with an antecedently highly organized mental life *could* comply with a convention of deference. In short we're agreed that deferentiality isn't a *necessary* condition for mental content. Since *TOC* purports only to provide a *sufficient* condition for mental content, we can also agree to postpone the discussion of deferentiality till some other time. To put this point in a nutshell: *It's one thing to have a theory of intentionality; it's another thing to have a theory of language.* Not all the properties of a language follow just from the fact that it's formulas are semantically evaluable; some of them (deferentiality presumably included) follow from its conventional and social status; and still others follow from the psychological peculiarities of its speakers. And so forth. Try to capture all of this at once and you will end up getting none of it at all.[36]

'Guiding Conceptions'.

Loar has, pretty clearly, a certain picture of the semantics of paradigmatic nondeferential terms. Here, very much desubtlefied, is the picture: for such terms, there are typically introducing occasions which (partially) determine their extensions. In effect, these are occasions on which the terms are ostensively defined by reference to samples *conceived in a certain way.* How the samples are conceived on the introducing occasions enters decisively into determining the extension of the term so introduced.[37] For example:

> Armand . . . learns that the birds he has been identifying under a certain recognitional concept are of two not especially closely related kinds. There are three potential upshots. (i) He regards his past usage as having lacked a determinate reference . . . (ii) He would now regard his past usage as referring to what turned out to be a disjunctive kind. (iii) He would regard the information as irrelevant to his

reference, which was meant to be determined by a resemblance in configuration . . . [It's] because Armand has . . . [in each of the three cases]. . . conceived his reference differently . . . [that] . . . his reference in each [case] differs or may differ from the others (p. 123). . . . Fodor's condition [for content] requires an intentional supplement, the satisfaction of guiding conceptions. One virtually never refers demonstratively, whether singularly or predicatively, without some . . . general conception that constrains one's reference . . . (p. 123)

So, then, the difference between having a concept whose extension is the birds of a certain species and having a concept whose extension is (say) all the doppelgangers of the birds in a certain sample is something about the "guiding conceptions" with which the concept is formed or used; something about the intentions of the guy who has the concept. Here there can be no compromise. If entertaining "guiding conceptions" and the like is *constituitive* of the relations between one's concepts and their extensions, then there are intentional conditions on having a concept and we're back in the intentional circle.

Now, the first thing to say about all this is that – naturalism and reduction to one side – Loar's story about reference being fixed by demonstration and "guiding conceptions" is very different from the picture that we informational semanticists have in mind; and, much as we're fond of Brian, we would prefer that the question not be simply begged in his favor. On the informational view, *the only thing that counts for content is nomic relations among properties.* Ostensive definitions, "guiding conceptions," and the like may be among the mechanisms that occasion or sustain such nomic relations; but they aren't *constitutive* of semanticity; only the nomic relations themselves are. Loar has it that it's "because Armand has . . . [in each of the three cases]. . . " conceived his reference differently . . . [that] ". . . his reference in each [case] differs or may differ from the others" (p. 123). But, on an informational theory, the connection between how you conceive your reference and what your reference actually is has got to be contingent. What is *constitutive* of the difference between Armand's concepts in the three cases is *which property of the birds actually acquired the property of being a cause of the tokening of the concept*; viz. the property of being a bird of a certain kind (in case i); the property of looking like a certain kind of bird (in case iii); or the property of being that kind of bird or some other kind (in case ii).

You can see the dialectic of Loar's position very clearly from this sort of example. For, if you forget that it's nomic relations among properties that make or are supposed to make content, you might reasonably wish to ask yourself: "What, after all, could be the difference between the guy who introduces "ostrich" to mean *bird of that kind* and the guy who introduces "ostrich" to mean *looks like a bird of that kind?*" The only thing around to fill the gap is a "guiding conception" so it must be that guiding conceptions determine reference. Whereas, for better or for worse, informational semanticists want to externalize all that: What determines reference isn't guiding conceptions, it's what property of the birds in the sample your "ostrich" tokens actually latch on to.

Let's not worry, for the moment, who's right about this. For the moment, I just want to stress the difference between the two kinds of theories. Consider the rhododendrons: small rhododendrons causing "rhododendron"'s is asymmetrically dependent on the rest of the rhododendrons causing "rhododendron"'s (let's suppose); so "rhododendron" means *rhododendrons except for the small ones*. So the objection goes. This is a kind of case that is discussed in *Psychosemantics* (and again in *TOC*); but it keeps coming up, and the reason why it does is clear. You get the example to work only by taking it that the causal relations that count for content run between things and terms (between rhododendrons and "rhododendron"'s as it might be). Whereas, according to informational semanticists, content-making relations run between properties (between the property of being a rhododendron *of whatever size*) and the property of being a cause of "rhododendron"'s). Correspondingly, what determines that "rhododendron"'s refers to rhododendrons (and not to all the rhododendrons except the small ones) is not the speaker's having a "guiding conception" of the term as referring to a kind of flower; it's that, big and small, rhododendrons cause rhododendrons *qua rhododendrons*. Since, in particular, big rhododendrons cause 'rhododendrons' *qua* rhododendrons, and not *qua* big rhododendrons, the *TOC* condition for "rhododendron" meaning 'big rhododendron' isn't satisfied and the counterexample fails. (It may be thought that this begs the question; who says that big and small rhododendrons cause "rhododendron"'s *qua* rhododendrons? Answer: the counterfactuals say so. This small rhododendron would have been a cause of "rhododendron"'s even if it had been larger; this big rhododendron would have been a cause of "rhododendron"'s even if it had been smaller.)

It is, however, one thing to say that the informational story can cope with rhododendrons and the like. It's another to say that the informational story is true. So, then, who is right about what fixes meanings? Is it ostensive occasions with "guiding conceptions" or is it the nomological relations among properties that such ostensive occasions (may) engender? I remark in passing that it would be nice if the informational semanticists were right because their conception of meaning is atomistic and naturalistic and the opposed conception is neither of these. But being nice is one thing and being right is another; what about some arguments?

Here's one line of argument that seems to me worth trying. Not just my words, but also my mental states have extensions. But it won't do to argue that I must have intentions with respect to the satisfaction conditions of my mental states because, of course, having intentions is itself a mental state with satisfaction conditions, and the implied regress must somewhere come to an end. This seems to show that there must be some intentional states that you can have without having "guiding conceptions" about them; i.e. having guiding conceptions can't be a *necessary* condition for mental representation. But if that's right, then it's still open that purely informational conditions should prove to be *sufficient* for mental representation. Loar's worry (n. 14) about whether there could, even in principle, be reference without guiding conceptions seems patently misplaced for the reference of mental states.

Here, as in the discussion of deference, it seems to me that quite a lot of what Loar says depends on taking it for granted that intentional properties inhere in public language expressions in the first instance; hence in expressions whose use is typically introduced and sustained by the more or less explicit intentions of their users. I know that Wittgenstein (or somebody) is supposed to have given a transcendental argument that public languages must be the font and origin of semantic evaluability; but nobody seems to be able to remember how this argument goes, and I'm not inclined to buy it on credit. The *TOC* story, at any event, is set up to be the semantics of mental representations.

Suppose, however, that we don't insist on the difference between mental representation and representation in English. Then the residual considerations depend a lot on intuitions, and I'm not sure that Loar and I are in agreement about these. Consider: "On my [Loar's] view each recognitional concept has a sort of built-in perspective. Suppose that in Kenya you see animals with a distinctive distant appearance . . . and you cannot tell how they would look up close. You form the concept 'creatures of that kind.' You also see nearby gazelles . . . and form the conception 'creatures of this kind." I[f] you then come to think that they are still [sic; 'all'(?)] the same, still the reference of the first, it seems natural to say, is determined by the distant sightings and not by the proximal sightings, and vice versa for the reference of the second" (pp. 128–9).

Now, I'm not sure just what Loar wants to pack into claims about the reference being "determined by the distant sightings" in one case but not the other; but my intuition is that the difference between the sightings is just simply *semantically irrelevant*. Perspectives (and general conceptions) fix reference only in the Kripke sense, where conceptions can fix the reference of a term without providing semantically necessary conditions for being in its extension.

To put it slightly differently, fixing reference is not an enduring trait. I haven't the foggiest idea from what perspective, or with what general conceptions I learned "gazelle," but I'm pretty sure that, if the question is what I mean by "gazelle," none of that matters. This is, of course, just what an informational semantics predicts. Ostensive occasions are (among the) mechanisms whereby states of mind can come under the control of instantiated gazellehood. Having done this job, they *drop out*, taking with them general conceptions, perspectives and the like detritus of ostensive reference fixing. The Greeks thought stars were holes in the fabric of heaven; their "general conceptions" couldn't have been further off base. But they succeeded in referring to stars very nicely for all that, thank you.

I think the general point is this: concepts are typically remarkably robust with respect to their own causal history; including their *intentional* causal history. You may intend that your term refer to stars only if stars are holes in the fabric of heaven, and they will go and refer to stars in spite of your intentions. You may intend that you term refer to whales only if whales are a kind of fish, and they will go and refer to whales in spite of your intentions. This isn't because "star" and "whale" are "theoretical terms." On the contrary, it's for exactly the opposite reason; it's because the theories you have (and your general conceptions and your perspectives) don't matter to what you're referring to. It's not what's in your head that matters; it's how your head is connected to the world.[38]

Or rather, what's in your head matters only insofar as it *affects* how your head is connected to the world. And this leads me to something I find very perplexing about Loar's sort of view (though I'm having a little trouble making clear what my worry is, so maybe there's nothing to it). Suppose the program of naturalistic semantics really is hopeless and you decide to just live with the idea that intentional clauses are ineliminable from a definition of "extension" and other semantical notions. Well then, so be it. Even so, one doesn't want the connection between, on the one hand, somebody's having a certain intention with respect to the extension of a word and, on the other hand, the word's actually having that extension, to be *magical*. I'm worried that it's going to turn out to be magical on Loar's sort of story.

In the general case, we're prepared to recognize that, to put it crudely, mental states *make no difference* to their intentional objects. You may want like stink that Martha should turn into a fish, and yet Martha doesn't; you may believe till you're blue in the face that Napoleon was tall, and yet Napoleon wasn't; you may Propositional Attitude Verb as much as you like that (a is F) and yet the question whether a is F is *wide open*. Certainly it doesn't *account for* a's being F that you Propositional Attitude Verb that it should be so.[39]

Except, however, that according to the present view, if you intend that the extension of your word be such-and-such, then, *voila!* It *is* such-and-such. (Armand wanted his concept to be disjunctive, *so it was!*) How could this be so? What is this magical relation between intentions and extensions?

There is, of course, a classical answer to this sort of question, but it's one that Loar clearly isn't buying into: viz. that your intentions causally determine your dispositions to token words, and your dispositions to token words are constitutive of their content. Informational semantics is a special case of this sort of view, and, as I say, it's clear that Loar won't have it since it makes the relation between intentions and contents extrinsic, not constitutive. The question is, however, *what's the alternative?*

I think there's a general moral: Only naturalistic theories can explain *what makes things happen*; and this applies, *inter alia*, to semantical things like words having the extensions that they do. It is thus more than a craving for ontological tidiness (or worse, ontological respectability) that leads one to suppose that, really naturalism and eliminativism exhaust the options: it's the fear that, unless there is a naturalistic account of the semantic properties, it will be *unintelligible* how anything could have them. I think that Loar might wish to concede this; he seems to want to grant the naturalists their ontology but not their ideology. Thus, Loar emphasizes that "lack of a conceptual explication" is "quite compatible with . . . intentional . . . conceptions referring to . . . thoroughly physical-functional properties" (p. 131). This is correct but not to the point. Bother conceptual explications; the question is how intentions could be thoroughly physical-functional properties if there aren't physical-functional *sufficient conditions* for their instantiation.

Matthews

Almost all of Matthew's paper is constructed around the claim that a certain sort of intentional explanation provides a principled worry for RTM. The kind of case is familiar from Dennett: you can explain why the machine (or person; for these purposes the difference doesn't matter) plays chess the way it does by saying that it thinks that it ought to get its Queen out early. But ". . . nowhere [in the machine] is anything roughly synonymous with 'I should get my Queen out early' explicitly tokened. The level of analysis to which the . . . remark belongs describes features that are, in an entirely innocent way, emergent properties of the computational processes that have 'engineering reality' " (Dennett, 1981a:107).

Now, I had thought that my reply to this was rather neat; viz. that, while it's true (in the sort of case imagined) that no representation of "get the Queen out early" (hereafter the Q-sentence) is to be found in the machine, it's also true (in the sort of case imagined) that no tokening of the *thought* that one should get one's Queen out early (hereafter the Q-thought) occurs in the causal sequence of thoughts that eventuates in the machine's behavior. So, I suggested, one should refine crude RTM as follows: when a tokening of a thought *does* play such a causal role, then the propositional object of the thought must be explicitly represented. "No intentional causation without explicit representation."[40] I was, as I say, quite pleased with this; but Matthews thinks it won't do. Frankly, however, I don't see why not.

1   Matthews says that my treatment of the core cases is purchased only at the price of having no treatment of the derivative cases; so I have "to concede that the RTM provides no account – and hence no 'vindication' of [cases like Dennett's]." But just why do I have to concede this? The RTM treatment I outlined surely *constrains* our understanding of noncore explanations; for example, in Dennett's case it's ruled out that an episode of thinking the Q-thought plays a causal role in producing the machine's behavior. Further, this treatment suggests (though perhaps it doesn't demand) that one might construe noncore explanations as accounting for behavior by reference to dispositions that it manifests. (This machine is disposed to get its Queen out early; and is now doing so.) These dispositions, in turn, arise from (they are, as Dennett says, innocent emergents out of) occurrent processes of intentional causation: the very "core cases" for which the unelaborated RTM account holds literally.

The same sort of point applies at the level of laws. Matthews says: "So it looks as if intentional causation does *not* require explicit representation after all. The only way to avoid this conclusion would be to argue that the laws that subsume derivative cases are not genuine causal intentional laws" (p. 144). But why not argue, instead, that they are laws that subsume (e.g. behavioral) dispositions that organisms have in virtue of the occurrent causal processes that their minds undergo. These count as genuine causal intentional laws if you like and don't count as genuine causal intentional laws if you don't like. In either case, nothing of substance seems to be at issue.

According to this tarted-up version, then, RTM sometimes reads commonsense propositional attitude explanations as true in virtue of occurrent causal processes involving tokens of explicit representations; and sometimes it reads them as true in virtue of dispositions to instantiate these occurrent causal processes. (Even Ryle doesn't lose *all* of the time.) This seems to me to be pretty plausible. And it doesn't seem to me to be a *serious* objection to RTM that it fails to provide a *single* format to which all commonsense propositional attitude explanations correspond. Truth to tell, it doesn't seem to me to be an objection at all.

2   The argument just scouted was that RTM provides no account of "derivative" cases of commonsense propositional attitude explanation. Matthews also has an argument that's supposed to show that, given plausible empirical assumptions, the "core" cases cannot be identified with the ones where mental

representations have occurrent tokens. Matthews says that "the point here is . . . [that] many of the propositional attitudes that Fodor purposes to treat as 'derivative' are presumably acquired in the course of some mental processes (e.g. through learning or perception) and hence according to Fodor's criterion would also be 'core'" (p. 140).

But this is surely wrong. Why shouldn't a thought be a core case at t and purely dispositional at $t + n$? (For example, explicitly tokened Q-thoughts might produce structural changes that support being disposed to a Queen-early style of play and then be erased.) In which case, my way of distinguishing the core cases would work if construed synchronically (which is, anyhow, how it was intended to be construed): a thought is core at t if some of the machine's behaviors at t are causally dependent on tokening the thought.

3   Matthews asks, at one point, "how the core cases are to be identified." But my account of core cases was supposed to be ontic, not epistemic. Different ways of organizing a machine will trade off dispositions against explicit representations in different ways. To tell in a given case: do the science. ("How do you get to Carnegie Hall?" "Practice, practice.")

4   Matthews says that all the RTM gives us is the *"bare possibility"* of coordinating content with causal role. And he adds that "in logic circuits, for example, causal role is also brought into phase with contents, though without utilizing data structures that explicitly represent these contents" (p. 142). But one has to be careful about what "bare possibility" means here. Matthews makes it sound as though the most you can say for RTM is that it's a consistent theory. In fact you can say what's a good deal stronger: that *for all we know* the mind could work that way. (By contrast, it's *not* true that, for all we know, the mind could work by exploiting "logic circuits" since that wouldn't account for its systematicity and productivity.) I stick to what I said in the passage that Matthews refers to. RTM is the only way of coordinating causality with content that isn't ruled out on independent grounds; the only one that isn't "known to be false."

5   Suppose we take the dispositional line for the derivative cases. Matthews is concerned that unless the cases are all treated as core, "the computational implementation [of the attitudes] . . . is so *diffuse* as to preclude any vindication of commonsense psychological explanation" (p. 145). This is like the worry that unless the solubility is, as it were, *part of the salt*, whether the salt is soluble is "too diffuse" to be epistemically accessible.

6   In the very last section, Matthews argues that connectionist models offer an alternative to RTM. The idea is that there must be something wrong with Pylyshyn's and my claim that such models cannot account for productivity and systematicity because "by all accounts, the [connectionist] architectures are Turing equivalent" (p. 148). This is, in fact, a mistake, and one that Pylyshyn and I were careful to caution against.

From the point of view of the issues about mental representation, the relevant question is whether the architecture of the mind is connectionist *at the level of description at which mental states are represented as having intentional content.* By contrast, what the "Turing equivalence" considerations show is just that you can realize a "virtual" Turing machine on a causal substructure that has connectionist architecture. When you do this, however, what you get is *Turing* architecture at the intentional level and connectionist architecture (only) at subintentional (e.g. neuronal) levels. If, by contrast, the mind you construct has connectionist architecture at the intentional level, it won't be so much as productive (as, indeed, connectionists standardly admit) so fancy questions about Turing equivalence don't arise.

You can see exactly where Matthews went wrong on this. He says "Fodor and Pylyshyn's (1988a) criticism of connectionist models ... argue[s] ... that connectionist architectures cannot be construed as cognitive [*sic*] models, since such architectures are allegedly unable to model the systematicity of intentional states" (p. 148). But to the contrary: we argued that it is just insofar as connectionist models *are* construed as cognitive (specifically, it's just insofar as they are construed as exhibiting causal relations among *intentional* states) that they fail to account for systematicity. Construe them *non*cognitively (e.g. as exhibiting the causal architecture of some subintentional level) and then you *can* get them to be systematic; you can do so, for example, by using them to implement a virtual Turing machine. This is a little complicated, but unless you get your head around it you can't appreciate the deep, deep trouble that connectionists are in.

Could there be vindication of belief/desire psychology without representationalism? Could Intentional Realism be true even if RTM is false? Of course it could. But there aren't any serious candidates for *how* it could; and, as Chomsky likes to say in these sorts of circumstances, I am not holding my breath.

Millikan

I'm not going to discuss at all Millikan's objections to the asymmetric dependence story; just the part of her paper that is a defense of a Darwinian/historical theory about content. Even here, I'm going to be selective and concentrate more on Millikan's response to arguments in *TOC* than to arguments in *Psychosemantics*. Because, whereas the latter struck (and strike) me as providing a prima facie case, the former seem to me to suggest principled grounds for rejecting the evolutionary story.

It was a worry expressed in *Psychosemantics* that teleological theories might beg essential questions by unwarranted assumptions about the individuation of psychological mechanisms. It's all very well to say that the content of a belief is determined by the teleology (the Normal functioning) of the "belief-box"; but you get a different relation between Normalcy and content depending on whether you assume that the belief-box contains, for example, mechanisms of belief *repression*. Roughly, if you do assume this, then it will turn out that some Normally fixed beliefs are *false*; so you can't then identify the truth conditions of such beliefs with anything like their Normal causes.

So I asked "how do we know which [psychological mechanism] is the belief-box?" And, since I wanted the answer to be not question-begging, I added the reminder "that we're assuming a functional theory of *believing* ... on this assumption, having a belief is just being in a a state with a certain causal role." Millikan comments: "*right there* Fodor has already abandoned the teleological view that he claims he is putting to the test. For on a teleological analysis, the belief-box will have to be defined by its teleofunction ... " (p. 156). So be it: but then, how shall we decide what its teleofunction *is?* Is it to token true beliefs (so repression is a kind of malfunction) or is it to token true beliefs *excepting those true beliefs which it is supposed to repress*, in which case, repressing those true beliefs isn't a kind of malfunction after all. "Fodor's mechanisms of belief repression now appear, of course, as interrupters of these wider teleofunctions, not as mechanisms that help to condition their proper performance" (p. 157). But this is *utterly* arbitrary; at least it's utterly unargued. (And it would, by the way, have profoundly irritated Freud, whose emphasis was always on the *functionality* of repression, neurosis, dreams, and the like.)

The moral is: you can have your teleological underdetermination as a problem about the content of mental states; or you can have it as a problem about the individuation of cognitive mechanisms. Millikan sweeps it first under one rug, then under the other, hoping, apparently, that if she pushes it around enough it will eventually go away. But it won't.

By the way, the analogic appeal to "the teleofunction of the stomach" buys nothing here, the trouble with analogies being that they tend to run both ways. Millikan says that ". . . we . . . see that only some of the mechanisms that control the stomach's contents help to produce (optimal conditions for) the stomach's proper operation, (optimal conditions for) its heading up a process that ends, in the normal way, with metabolism in the cells. The vomiting reflex is not one of these mechanisms. It has nothing to do with nutrition" (p. 156). But this settles nothing, even about the stomach. Consider the process of shmutrician; it facilitates cell metabolism, on the one hand, by digesting food when food has been ingested, and, on the other hand, by regurgitating toxins when toxins have been ingested. (Regurgitating toxins is a Good Thing since digesting them tends to eventuate in death, which is known to inhibit Normal cell metabolism.) So now, what is the function of the stomach? Is it nutrition or shmutrician? *Mutatis mutandis*, is the function of the belief-forming mechanism to token true beliefs; or is it to token true beliefs when they're bearable and repress them when they're not? You can tell the historical/Darwinian story either way; I think Millikan hasn't begun to see how exiguous, how *undisciplined* a notion of function the historical/Darwinian story provides.

OK, now for the general worry raised in *TOC* which is that an evolutionary theory of content can't solve the disjunction problem because selectional processes can't distinguish an organism that represents things as F from one that represents things as G in a world where it's nomologically necessary (specifically counterfactual supporting) that F iff G.

It looks, for a while, as though Millikan's reply is going to come down heavy on the distinction between "selected" and "selected for." (The distinction is illustrated by an example of Sober's; see Millikan, pp. 159–60.) And well it might, because "selected for" has a higher order of intensionality than "selected." The question, however, is whether Millikan has a right to this distinction, given the sort of theory that she maintains.

In Sober's example, we know that what's selected for is shape rather than color because we know that the following counterfactuals are true: a red ball of the same shape would have have gone through; a green ball of a different shape would not have. So what makes the difference between being selected and being selected for is not *history* but *counterfactuals*. (Millikan says that it's the mechanism of selection that matters; but again, it's not facts about the *history* of the mechanism – about what balls it has actually let through – it's what counterfactuals the laws that govern the mechanism support.) Thus, in Sober's example, there's the historical fact that a green ball got through and there's also the historical fact that a round ball got through. So what happened (as opposed to what would have happened if . . .) doesn't distinguish between the story that there was a sort for green balls and the story that there was a sort for round ones. And, as Millikan is always rightly reminding us, on her theory the determinants of content are historical and *not* counterfactual.

In passing: the fact that the question about distinguishing "selection" from "selection for" can be raised and resolved for Sober's gadget shows just how little any appeal to selectional *advantage* has to do with drawing the distinction. When intensionality is the issue, the counterfactuals do all the work and Darwin goes out the window.

So, then, if it's not going to depend on "selection for," what *is* Millikan's solution to the disjunction problem in, say, the frog/fly case? There seem to be three suggestions, two of which are on the underdeveloped side.

(a) Appeal to inferential role. Millikan doesn't tell us how this will help in the frog case; or how content is determined by inferential role; or, most important in my view, how to avoid the debilitating holistic consequences of such appeals (see *Psychosemantics* (1987d)).

(b) "A second suggestion follows from the view that representations are like maps" (p. 163). Yeah, well. The last time I looked, the consensus was pretty general that picture theories of meaning had hopeless semantic indeterminacy problems of their own. (The relevant considerations have been common currency at least since Wittgenstein's *Investigations*; for discussion, see *Language of Thought* (1975a:ch. 4).) And also: you don't want the solution to the frog's disjunction problem to be a theory of mental representations that entails that there are *no* disjunctive concepts. But, how do you draw a picture of *P or Q*? (To say nothing of *not-P, if P then Q* and the like.)

(c) The third solution is, apparently, the one that Millikan takes seriously. It depends on emphasizing ". . . a shift of focus from inner representation producers to the inner representation consumers or users . . . " (p. 162). The key idea is that ". . . the systems that use, that respond to, the frog's fly detector's signals, don't care at all whether these correspond to anything black or ambient or specklike, but only whether they correspond to frog food . . . So the [detector] firing means frog food" (p. 163).

But this is just *simply* question-begging. After all, there's a way of describing the mechanisms that use the frog's fly detector's signals as caring *precisely* about whether the signals "correspond to something black or ambient or specklike," viz. they are mechanism designed to perform certain chemical (specifically digestive) processes on ambient black specklike things *in a world where the ambient black specklike things are largely food*. So, what Millikan needs, but doesn't have, is a Darwinian story that shows why we should describe the signal-using mechanisms her way instead of describing them that way. As far as I can see, Millikan's strategy is to solve the disjunction problem for the signals by describing the "consumers" of the signals *in intentional terms* (in terms of what they "care about") and then to beg the disjunction problem for the consumers. This yields a total gain of no yardage; less if time and effort are included.

A word about philosophical style. Millikan pretty clearly thinks that the reason I have made so little headway on these hard problems is my chronic untidiness: ". . . to make anything of this work, you have to be careful. You can't be sloppy and run everything together. You need, among other things, a clear definition of '(proper) function' . . ." (p. 163). And so forth. *Chacun à son métier*, of course; but I really do wonder if this is the best way to proceed. An alternative tactic would be: before one invests a lot in laying out the technical apparatus for the theory – defining the terms and so on – one might try asking oneself whether there is any reason to suppose that this *kind* of theory ought to work (or, worse, whether there's any reason to suppose that it oughtn't). In the present case, a root question seems to be whether it's plausible that intensional distinctions – like the distinction between *selection* and *selection for*, for example – can be reconstructed within a purely historical account of function. If there is reason to think that they can't, then polishing the definitions isn't going to help; the theory needs a general overhaul. And there *is*, after all, reason to think that they can't: The context "– happened" is transparent for the "–" position, so it would be sort of surprising if contexts defined in terms of it weren't transparent too.

Paul Postal once described one of his victims as being "in the position of a man who has inherited a spaghetti factory which will not, *in principle*, produce spaghetti." Quite so; tidy is nice, but it's the spaghetti that matters.

Perry and Israel

I liked a lot of what Perry and Israel say, so I don't propose to argue with much of it.[41] The story I told in "Methodological solipsism" (1980c) wanted to insist on the close connection between intentional explanations (hence, presumably, intentional laws) and the *opaque* readings of intentional ascriptions. The intuition was that if it's his wanting to meet the girl who lives next door that explains Sam's going calling, that must be because the expression "the girl next door" is somehow close to the way that Sam represents the girl next door. If Sam's way of representing the girl next door is something close to "the girl who languishes in Latvia," then his wanting to meet the girl next door *doesn't* explain his going calling after all; unless he goes calling in Lativia. "Methodological solipsism" supposed (as Perry and Israel now seem to be prepared to do) a language of thought unpacking of "the way Sam represents . . . " My story was, on the one hand, that the opaque reading of a propositional attitude (PA) ascription expresses the content of the mental representation that causes the ascribee's behavior; and, on the other hand, that the ascribee's behavior falls under the intentional laws that it does because the mental representations that cause his behavior have the content that they do.

But, clearly, that's not better than a first approximation and the right story is going to be complicated. For example, when I tell you whom Sam wants to meet, I refer to the girl next door to "him"; whereas, presumably, when Sam thinks about the girl he wants to meet, what goes through his head is (some Mentalese equivalent of) "the girl next door to *me*." (Emphasis mine, not Sam's.) "Meth sol" was aware of this sort of worry, and caveats were accordingly strewn about. So far as I can tell, Perry and Israel have now gone some way towards telling the story right: in particular, their way of telling the story secures what I took to be the essential connection between rationalizing explanations and opaque construals of propositional attitude contexts. This is helpful of Perry and Israel; good on them.[42]

Perry and Israel think that "without some appeal to circumstances, the rationality of laws of cognitive psychology cannot be understood" (p. 177). I think they're right. Suppose I want "I drink coffee" to be true, I believe "There is coffee in front of me" to be true, and I believe "Reaching for the coffee in front of me will bring about that I drink coffee" to be true . . . etc. Then my believing and wanting all that explains my reaching for the coffee. But it is, of course, part of the explanation that *it's the same guy throughout* who does the wanting and believing; as Perry and Israel say, it's required that all these attitudes belong to the same agent. There is, notoriously, no reason to think this requirement can be imposed by fooling with the way that the objects of the attitudes are represented. It wouldn't help to replace the "I" with "JAF," for example.

Another way to make much the same point: it's often natural to read intentional laws as quantifying into attitude clauses. Something like: (x) (if x believes Fx, and x wants Gx, then x acts to bring it about that Hx). Here the F, G, and H may be "fully opaque" and thus constrain the way that the agent represents the objects of his attitudes. But what's required of the bound variables is that they all instantiate *to the same guy*. That it *is* the same guy is a question not of how things are represented, of course, but of how they *actually are*. At a minimum, the moral is that there's a rather complicated relation between what someone has in his head (including the content of the representations that he has in his head) and the descriptions of his psychological states (including the opaque intentional descriptions of his psychological states) that rationalize/explain his behavior. It follows that the theory of rationality isn't purely solipsistic (/formal/syntactic): "is rational," like "knows," is a predicate that belongs partly to psychology and partly to semantics. Nothing, of course, follows about the solipsistic (or otherwise) character of mental *processes*; contextualism about rationality is thus quite compatible with a computational theory of the mind. I take it that this is now all common ground.

I am so happy about the apparent convergence of Perry and Israel's views with some that I hold dear – it's so nice to be *agreeing* with someone for a change – that I'm loath even to mention a point where I'm afraid they've got me wrong. In fact, I *wouldn't* mention it except that the complaint is recurrent: people at Stanford keep accusing me of holding that "the content facts about a token are settled by its *formal* properties" (p. 166); in effect, that "dog" means *dog* because it is spelled dˆoˆg. And I keep telling them that, Honest Injun, I hold no such thing. (See, for example, Barwise (1986) and Fodor (1987a).) I don't know what to do about this, I wonder if they'd accept a notarized disclaimer?

Perry and Israel would read me as disagreeing with the very passage from Hume that "Meth sol" had as its epigraph. Hume says that "the reference of [an] idea to an object [is] an extraneous denomination, of which in itself it bears no mark . . ." Perry and Israel kindly explain that this means that "the fact that my idea of red is an idea of one color rather than another is an *external denomination* – a relation between the idea and a color – [hence on my "syntactical" view of mental processes] not something that can influence the way it interacts with other ideas." Quite so. That's why I chose the passage for an epigraph. But I don't need this lecture; because I don't think that the content facts about a token are settled by its formal properties (see above) though I do think its role in mental processes is (see below).[43]

So, what you've got in your head doesn't, in and of itself, determine (fully opaque or any other) content; and the relation between the content of what you've got in your head and the intentional explanation of your behavior is, anyhow, fairly indirect. So, where does what you've got in your head come into the story? What's so solipsistic about methodological solipsism?

As far as I can tell, Perry and Israel think it comes in in the specification of psychological laws. Notice that their law L specifies a relation defined on the syntactical structure of Mentalese expression (according to their n. 8, the "believes '...,'" notation means "that there is token of the quoted type in the agent's belief structure (p. 179)." So the view is apparently that psychological laws are Stichesque (they're syntactic) even though psychological explanations appeal to the contents of mental states. This is already a little puzzling since, if the vocabulary of the laws is syntactic, you'd expect the vocabulary of the explanations of the events that the laws subsume to be syntactic too; yet Perry and Israel clearly think that typical psychological explanations are fully intentional. And, anyhow, it just isn't true that psychological laws are syntactic; they too are intentional through and through.

Here's what I think (for further discussion, see the replies to Devitt and to Stich): mental representations can differ in content without differing in their intrinsic, formal, nonrelational, nonsemantic properties. But they can't differ in respect of the mental processes that subsume them except as they differ in their intrinsic, formal, nonrelational, nonsemantical properties. If two mental representations are identical in respect of such properties, then they play the same role in mental processes, even if their semantical properties (their truth conditions, for example) are different (because of, for example, differences in the embedding circumstances). This is a constraint – albeit a negative constraint – on "how ... causal and content properties of tokens mesh" (p. 166) and it holds even if the determination of the intentional properties in virtue of which mental states are subsumed by intentional laws are ineliminably situational.

It is, I think, very, very important to keep clear on the difference between the following two questions. "What's the story about the properties of mental states in virtue of which they are subsumed by psychological laws?" and "What's the story about the properties of mental states in virtue of which they are engaged by mental processes?" If the computational theory of the mind is true; then the properties of mental states in virtue of which they are engaged by mental processes are intrinsic/syntactic. If informational theories of content are right, then the properties of mental states in virtue of which they are subsumed by psychological laws are extrinsic/relational. I *think* – though I wouldn't swear to it – that Perry and Israel have failed to take it to heart that these two questions can get quite different answers.

Stalnaker

I want to start by clearing up some quasi-terminological issues.

I have this story that goes: "truth-conditional semantics is fine, conceptual role semantics is not." Stalnaker remarks: "Truth-conditional semantic theories . . . say what the semantic values of expressions of different categories are, and how the semantic values of complex expressions are determined by the values of their parts. . . . But statements of this kind make no claim at all about what features of the mental states and behavior of the users of the expressions make it true that words have the extensions (or intensions) that they have . . . *this* is the kind of question that conceptual role semantics is trying to answer" (p. 233).

That is, in my understanding, exactly right; I am depressed that I have written things which seemed to Stalnaker to deny it. For the record, here's my view. The basic semantic relations are denotational (hence "wide" in the sense that they hold between mental representations and things in the world). So, a semantic theory for Mentalese specifies (let's say) a satisfaction condition for each semantically evaluable expression of Mentalese. Stalnaker is, to repeat, exactly right to say that this kind of theory tells you nothing at all about what makes something the meaning of a Mentalese (or any other) expression; it just says *what the meaning is* (assuming, as denotational theories do, that meanings are satisfaction conditions).

Now, I have also used "sementic theory" for the kind of theory that *does* (or, anyhow, does purport to) tell you what makes something the meaning of an expression. I take it that the main contenders here are: functional role theories and causal theories. I prefer the latter, because the former seem to me to be intrinsically and hopelessly holistic and I hate holism. (Because holism always leads to relativism, and I *really* hate relativism.) In my view, a causal semantics completes a denotational semantics by telling you *in virtue of what facts about the (causal) relations* between a symbol and things in the world the symbol has the satisfaction conditions it does.

Now, Stalnaker sees the possibility of holding that a causal theory completes a denotational theory in this way. He remarks: "a causal theory . . . tries to say, not just what the semantic value is, but also what makes it the case that something has a certain semantic value" (p. 234). But, he thinks that can't be my picture because "the usual kind of causal theory is an externalist, wide semantics, and so is not compatible with Fodor's project" (p. 234). However, I'm unclear where the incompatibility is supposed to reside. On the one hand:

A causal theory tells you what it is about a certain environment that determines the satisfaction condition that (actual or possible) tokens of a symbol (would) have in that environment. So, for example, it answers questions like: "What is it about Earth tokens of 'water' in virtue of which they mean *water*?" (Rough answer: causal connections to water); and "What is it about Twin-Earth tokens of 'water' in virtue of which they mean *XYX*?" (Rough answer: causal connections to XYZ). And, on the other hand:

Narrow content is a (partial) function from environments to satisfaction conditions; you can think of it as a set of ordered pairs. The narrow content for "water" would include the ordered pairs . . . {Earth; water}, {Twin-Earth; XYZ} . . . etc.

So then: a denotational theory specifies the satisfaction condition of a certain expression (in a certain environment); a causal theory tells you *what makes* something the satisfaction condition of that expression in that environment; and narrow content provides a notion of *same mental state* that generalizes over the environments relative to which mental states are semantically evaluable. Everything looks compatible so far.[44]

However, none of this terminological sorting out answers the question that is really (and properly) bugging Stalnaker, which is: ". . . what makes it true that expressions have, as their [narrow] values, the particular functions of this kind they have. If semantics is to be narrow, there doesn't seem to be anything else around except the internal functional or conceptual role, to provide the answer" (p. 234). So, here are two mental states, M and M' one of whose narrow content is C, and the other of whose narrow content is C'. The definition of narrow content says that C and C' are sets of ordered pairs; but that doesn't, all by itself, say what it is about M and M' that *makes*, for example, C the narrow content of M and C' the narrow content of M' rather than the other way round. Stalnaker is right to say that a theory which postulates narrow content of the kind I've been pushing for had better have some sort of answer in hand. (Block makes the same sort of point, and what I say here is amplified in my discussion of his paper.)

Now, I regard my views on this issue as labile even by my standards, and my standards for lability are high. Here, however, are some remarks; for whatever good they may do.

1   It's plausible that a notion of narrow content will have scientific work to do; hence that there are facts of the matter about narrow content. For example, the intuition that Twins should belong to the same natural kind for purposes of psychological explanation is very strong. So I assume motivation; we should construct a notion of narrow content if we can.[45] Anyhow, I think I have an argument that shows that a taxonomy of psychological states by their causal powers cannot respect differences of broad content per se (see my 1987d: chapter 2, and in press-d). If this is right it ups the ante; it means that either (scientific) psychological taxonomy is narrow or it is not intentional at all.

2   We know *some* conditions for identity and difference of narrow content. For example, physical identity is sufficient (Twins have the same narrow thoughts). Presumably *functional* identity would be sufficient too, so physical identity isn't *necessary.*

And certain sorts of physical (/functional) differences are sufficient for *non*identity of narrow content. For example, having the physical/ functional structure of a rock is sufficient for not having the narrow concept *water.* This observation about rocks is actually not uninteresting. A necessary condition for a state having *narrow* content is that there be some environment in which it would have broad content (some context relative to which it is semantically evaluable). If you believe informational theories, what makes a mental state semantically evaluable relative to a context is some sort of control relation between tokenings of the state and tokenings of certain features of the environment. To be in this kind of control relation, you have to have the right kind of internal organization;

the kind that can be controlled by environmental variables in the right kind of way. Rocks don't have internal organizations of that kind; so the states of rocks aren't semantically evaluable; so rocks don't have narrow contents.

The moral of these observations is that, if there *is* something that determines when states have narrow content, it seems to be something about the internal structure of the creature whose states they are. But what could that be if it isn't the functional role of the states? (And it would appear that it musn't be the functional role, on pain of holism.)

3 I remark, in passing, that if somebody could show how to draw a substantive analytic/synthetic distinction, then we could appeal to functional role to be what determines narrow content after all, and everything would be fine. (I take it that Stalnaker agrees with this.) However, nobody is going to show how to draw a substantive analytic/synthetic distinction. Quine was right; there is no analytic/synthetic distinction. Not even a small one.

4 But be of good cheer. Functional role doesn't have to *be* content in order to *determine* content. It is, to put it another way, very important to distinguish between determining content and constituting it.

The present question is: "What is it that me and my Twin have in common with one another, but not with rocks, such that the narrow contents of our mental states are the same in virtue of our having that in common?" And this means: "What is it in virtue of which, when you put me or my Twin in the sort of environment that I'm now actually in, you get the sort of causal relation between our mental state tokens and the local water tokens that the informational theory says is required for our mental state tokens to denote water? (And such that, if you put a rock in that environment, you don't get that sort of causal relation?)" Well, if you put the question *that* way, the answer is *surely*: "it's the actual and counterfactual functional structure of our nervous systems; it's our nervous systems being the kinds of mechanism whose states *can* come to be controlled by water in the way that is required for the state tokens to denote water. Whatever that way is."

5 Notice that appealing to functional organization to answer the question, "What determines narrow content?" is quite different from appealing to functional organization to *individuate* narrow content. The individuation condition for narrow contents is given by the principle that they are identical iff they are the same function from contexts to satisfaction conditions. It is, prima facie, the use of functional role to *individuate* content that raises the holism problems which I propose to keep locked up if I possibily can. (See my reply to Block.)

6 Functional organization is, as it were, the mechanism that sustains the causal relations on which broad semantic evaluability depends. Since narrow content is a construct out of broad content, functional organization is the mechanism that sustains narrow content too; functional organization is *what it is about an organism* in virtue of which the organism instantiates a certain function from context to satisfaction conditions. But – and this is a point I push very hard in *TOC*; it does seem to me a very important point – the sufficient conditions for a semantic relation to obtain can, as it were, quantify over the mechanisms whose operation is empirically necessary for meeting those conditions. In the present case: functional organization may be what sustains narrow content; it does *not*

follow that the narrow content of a state is constituted by (or individuated by reference to) its functional role.

So then: narrow contents are functions, hence extensionally individuated. The functional (/causal) roles of their mental states are the properties of organisms in virtue of which they instantiate the narrow-content-function that they do. But identity of functional role need not be required for identity of narrow-content-function-instantiated; it's wide open that functional roles might map many to one onto narrow contents. So, prima facie, my story resists the sort of holism to which functional semantics is prone since it lets thoughts with different functional roles have the same narrow contents.

For all of which, I want to concede that there is the tension that Stalnaker notes between two projects, both of which I favor: going externalist on content (so as to avoid functional role semantics and the holism problems it brings) and going individualist on psychological generalizations (so as to allow intentional laws to subsume Twins *inter alia*). Maybe there's no room to sail between this particular Scylla and Charybdis; clearly I shall have to tack a lot to pull it off. But it seems to me to be worth trying. If it can't be done, then I'm no worse off than I started: I'll have to give up on either semantic atomism or intentional individualism. But if it can, then that's a real discovery, and we should revise the charts.

I close with some thoughts about the cases that Stalnaker discusses towards the end of his paper.

If narrow content is a function from contexts to satisfaction conditions, then my Twin and I have the same narrow *water* concept only if a certain counterfactual is true: he has a concept which *would* denote water (if he were in my context) and I have a concept which *would* denote XYZ (if I were in his context). Now, consider the following (slight) difference between me and my almost-Twin; he thinks, "You never find water in Pepsi bottles"[46] and I don't think this. So then there are likely to be environments (ones where there are Pepsi bottles) in which he would have 'water' thoughts where I would not. So don't we have different narrow contents? In which case, isn't there a holism problem about narrow content after all?

This is, of course, a real problem for a naturalistic semantics; maybe it's the ultimate problem for a naturalistic semantics. So it's important to be *quite* clear that it has *nothing to do with narrow content per se*. The way to see this is to notice that you still have this problem even if you just give up on narrow content and assume that all intentional relations are broad.

After all, you still need identity conditions for *broad* content. And if, as per the current assumptions, you are running a causal/informational semantics, then the identity conditions for broad content will have something to do with the covariance between water in the world and 'water' tokens in the head. But, prima facie, these covariances will be *different* for the guy who thinks you never get water in Pepsi bottles and the guy who thinks you sometimes do. Viz. the former will sometimes think 'water' of liquid in Pepsi bottles and the latter won't.

I don't want to consider how an informational theory might hope to cope with this problem; suffice it that you get *some* room to wiggle if you think of denotation in terms of nomic relations among properties (instead of covariances among their instantiations) since you might then argue that the Pepsi guy and the non-Pepsi guy are *both* subsumed by a water $-->$ 'water' law despite the postulated differences between them. (Remember these are *ceteris paribus* laws, and what actual and counterfactual causal claims they license depends a very great deal on interaction effects. See the discussion in *TOC*.) And you maybe get more room still if you distinguish the idea that 'water' meaning *water* depends on water causing 'water' to be tokened from the idea that it depends on water causing 'water' to be tokened *in the belief-box*. (That the conditions for belief-fixation are holistic does not, in and of itself, imply that the conditions for entertaining a concept are.) This gives you some wiggle room because, though the "no water in Pepsi bottles" guy believes the stuff in this Pepsi bottle not to be water, still the route by which he arrives at this belief may well involve the tokening of (the Mentalese for) 'water.' Perhaps he thinks: "By Gosh, this looks like water; I would have been taken in but that water doesn't come in Pepsi bottles." This might be enough for him to count as instantiating a *water* $-->$ *'water' ceteris paribus* law.

Whether these sorts of considerations give you all the wiggle-room you need is, of course, up for argument.

Anyhow, if you want *necessary and* sufficient conditions for identity of *broad* content in the context of an informational semantics, you are going to have to face up to the question of just exactly what is required for there to be a nomic connection between *being water* and *being a cause of 'water'* tokening; and if the same nomic connection can't hold for the guy who has the Pepsi-belief and the guy who doesn't, then informational semantics is in deep trouble. All I want to argue here is that you have to face this question as soon as you take the naturalization of *broad* content seriously. *Narrow* content is *not* the culprit.

Now, consider another case (one I discussed in *Psychosemantics* (1987d)). Suppose I have found out what water is (I know it's H_2O, hence *not* XYZ) and my erstwhile-Twin hasn't. It seems reasonable to suppose (though I don't claim it's apodictic) that, however you construe "nomically connected," there would then be possible environments in which my erstwhile Twin's 'water' thoughts would be nomically connected to XYZ and mine would not. (One of the things that learning what water is buys me is that I'm no longer inclined to confuse it with XYZ.) But it is stipulated that narrow contents can't be identical if there is an environment in which they yield different broad contents. So it looks plausible, given the criterion for narrow content identity that I favor, that learning what water is would change my narrow concept of water. I had thought that accepting this was *concessive*; I was allowing that, even assuming my extensionalist account of how contents are individuated, some "internal" changes would be tantamount to meaning changes (though, with luck, not all such would be).[47]

Suppose, then, just for the sake of argument, that learning what something is does change head/world relations in a way that is sufficient to change broad content in some context. (And hence, derivatively, to change narrow content too.) Then there's a sense in which I don't mean by "water" what Homer did since I know what water is and he didn't. If this is right, then it turns out that theory change sometimes is meaning change after all: not for the usual reason (viz. that theory determines functional role and functional role constitutes meaning) but rather because the theories you hold can affect the actual and counterfactual head/world causal relations on which (I'm supposing) broad and narrow content both depend. But, I suggested in *Psychosemantics*, one might be prepared to live with some of this as long as you don't get too much of it (as long as not every theory change turns out to be a meaning change). For example, theory change could change meaning in this sense without implying that changing the theory changes the topic of theorizing.

Stalnaker replies: "I agree that the topic of a conversation depends on denotation and wide content.... But if this is an adequate response to the problem of meaning holism, then it seems to me that there was not much of a problem to start with" (p. 235). Absolutely. But it *wasn't intended* as a response to the problem of meaning holism. My response to the problem of meaning holism is guarded and programmatic. I claim that (a) the standard arguments for holism depend on assuming functional role semantics; (b) informational theories suggest that you can provide metaphysically sufficient conditions for content that are atomistic; hence that the connection between content and functional role is not internal. So (c) there is no convincing argument for meaning holism as things now stand.[48] As *Psychosemantics* remarked, for polemical purposes I'll settle for a Scotch verdict on holism since that's all that's needed to stop philosophers using it in arguments against Intentional Realism.

What I had in mind in the discussion of "what fixes the topic" was responding to worries about *incommensurability*. The idea was: it's *OK* to admit meaning change as a consequence of theory change so long as it comes out that we know something about water that Homer didn't. But that's in jeopardy only if changing theory changes meaning *and* changing meaning changes topic. I wanted not to admit the second conjunct even if it turns out that there are cases where I have to admit the first.

Here's the moral: if you're a holist, then any difference in belief is a difference in content, and there is no such thing as psychological explanation by appeal to intentional generalizations. If you're (my kind of) atomistic externalist, then changes in belief eventuate in changes in meaning only if they affect the head/world relations by which content is constituted. The less that happens, the more content laws can generalize over heterogeneous believers; so it would be best if it weren't to happen at all. It may nevertheless be that it happens *sometimes*; even atomistic externalism doesn't guaranty that changes of theory *never* constitute changes of meaning. My point was, however, that conceding this isn't conceding incommensurability; whereas, conceding holism is.

Schiffer

It's important to Stephen Schiffer's skepticism about what he calls "Intention Based Semantics" for him to maintain that you can't give a compositional semantics for a language with the expressive power of English. Well, Mentalese has to have the expressive power of English, and, in my review of Schiffer's *Remnants of Meaning* (1987a) I argued that Mentalese must have a compositional semantics. The point was that language of thought stories trace the productivity and systematicity of the propositional attitudes to the productivity of Mentalese and "nobody has the slightest idea how M[entalese] could be semantically productive [or systematic] unless" its semantics is compositional. This was supposed to be (and Schiffer correctly reads it as intended to be) some sort of argument to the best explanation. The claim wasn't that productivity *entails* compositionality, but just that there is a pervasive lack of an alternative story. Schiffer's current essay is intended to remedy this lack.

Now, *not having the slightest idea how it could fail to be the case that P* is a delicate, and largely undefined epistemic condition; rational agents can reasonably disagree about when they're in it. I have taken Schiffer's story to heart and I find his sense of the philosophical geography impeccable as usual. But the bottom line is: we *still* don't have the slightest idea how Mentalese could be productive and fail to have a compositional semantics. Or so it seems to me.

Here, without the niceties, is how I take Schiffer's story to go. Suppose that, for each Mentalese formula, there is some (physicalistic) *belief-making* property such that an agent's having a formula with that property in his belief-box is a *supervenience base* for his believing such-and-such. Suppose further that, whatever the belief-making property is, it's not identical to any semantical property; for example, it's not identical to a formula's meaning what it does or its having the truth condition that it does.

Now, it's not in dispute that Mentalese has a compositional *something*; for example, it's not in dispute that it has a compositional *syntax*. This means, close enough, that each of the infinitely many Mentalese sentences has a syntactic structure that is determined in some finitely specifiable way by the Mentalese words it contains, together with their syntactic values. So now, I take it that Schiffer's idea is something like this: each Mentalese word contributes to each Mentalese sentence it occurs in "its uniquely own physicalistic property" (p. 195) such that the belief-making property of a Mentalese sentence is uniquely determined by its syntax, together with what its constituent words contribute. The function that assigns belief-making properties to Mentalese formulas is presumably finitely specifiable since the syntactic theory of Mentalese is presumably finite and each word makes a finite contribution to the sentences it appears in. So we can see how you could get a finite theory that assigns a supervenience base to each of indefinitely many belief states and thereby explains the productivity of the attitudes.

But yet such a theory needn't be a combinatorial semantics for Mentalese. For, since the belief-making properties are, by assumption, not semantic properties, the "uniquely own physicalistic property" that each word contributes to determining the belief-making property assigned to a Mentalese formula needn't be a semantic value. But a compositional semantics for Mentalese is, sort of by definition, a theory which explains how the meaning (or truth condition) of a Mentalese formula is determined by the semantic values that its constituent words contribute. The long and short is: a theory of the productivity of the attitudes could rest on a productive theory of the belief-making properties of Mentalese formulas. Such a theory would not imply a compositional semantics for Mentalese so long as attitude instantiations are supervenient on – rather than identical to – tokenings of Mentalese formulas with attitude-making properties.

On this reconstruction, Schiffer's rejection of the reduction thesis is part of a defensive strategy: as long as the reduction thesis is assumed false, the existence of a theory that assigns belief-making supervenience bases to Mentalese sentences would not *ipso facto* imply the existence of a compositional semantics for Mentalese. However, Schiffer also apparently holds that a compositional semantics – or, anyhow, an "explanatory" compositional semantics – would actually *entail* the reduction thesis, so that anyone who is committed to the semantical story is thereby committed to the metaphysical one.

In fact, I find this a little puzzling (though perhaps it doesn't matter to the main issues). On the one hand, I would have thought that if the reduction thesis would license the inference from a productive theory of the supervenience bases to a compositional semantics for Mentalese, then so, too, would any other thesis that identifies intentional states with their supervenience bases *whether or not the putative identifications were reductionistic*. For, if semantic properties are identified with their supervenience bases, then if what words contribute to sentences constitutes the latter, it must thereby constitute the former. So, then, why does Schiffer think that *reduction* is the crucial issue? It looks like what he wants is the entirely general claim that the properties that constitute the supervenience base for beliefs are nonsemantical. *Punkt.*

And, on the other hand, I would have thought that specifying a compositional semantics for a language might explain its productivity even if one's theory stands mute on the metaphysical questions that reduction raises. Doesn't its having a compositional semantics explain the productivity of propositional calculus? I expect I must have missed something.

Anyhow, I do think that Schiffer's line of argument suggests something that a best explanation argument for the compositionality of Mentalese semantics should grant: namely, that there is logical space for an alternative account of the productivity of the attitudes. It is, however, less clear that it shows there is metaphysical or epistemological space for an alternative account. The point here is familiar, and I won't dwell upon it: supervenience without identity is mysterious, especially when you are dealing with causally efficacious properties. Professor Schiffer, do permit me to introduce Professor Boghossian: "... a naturalized theory of meaning is needed ... to render the supervenience thesis intelligible. In its absence, a supervenience thesis linking the intentional and the physical must be regarded as hopelessly mysterious and cannot be accepted" (p. 66). Quite so. So, one worry one might have about Schiffer's argument is that if you did have a productivity theory of the sort that Schiffer imagines, the temptation might be overwhelming to simply *identify* the semantic values of words with "the uniquely own physicalistic properties" that they contribute to determining the belief-making properties of Mentalese formulas.

Of course, Schiffer's point is that, in principle, we might have a perfectly OK productivity theory even if there were some or other consideration that blocked such identifications. And, no doubt, that's true *in principle*. What's less obviously true is that such a situation could come about *in practice*; and, "in practice" is what best explanation arguments are about. It might well be that, in practice, productivity theories that provide only supervenience bases are epistemologically unstable; that, if we had such a theory, we would always be pushed to the corresponding identity theory, and hence to a compositional semantics. (Perhaps supervenience theories about causally efficacious properties are *always* epistemologically unstable; perhaps we're always pushed either towards identification or towards elimination.)

And what is still less obvious is that we can actually now imagine an epistemologically/metaphysically stable supervenience theory that would account for the productivity of the attitudes. Equivalently, we can't, as things stand, imagine *what* would block the move to identification if we had a supervenience theory.[49] At one point Schiffer remarks that he "has heard the objection that it's impossible to see how M[entalese] could fail to have a compositional semantics if [the productivity thesis] were true. Well, here's how . . . if M has no compositional semantics, then . . . that will be because it's impossible to assign appropriate *semantic values* to all the words of M" (p. 196). Which is to say: "I'll tell you what's the alternative to compositional semantics being true of M; it's compositional semantics *not* being true of M." Well, yes; but that's not exactly what I imagine the objector had in mind. What he had in mind was: show us some reason to suppose that we could actually have a productivity theory that resists the move from supervenience to identity; show us what an epistemically stable situation of that sort would be like. The "best explanation" argument is that – as things stand – nobody *can* shows us that.

So, there's the metaphysical worry that supervenience bases would represent semantical/intentional properties as ontolgical danglers and hence be epistemologically unstable. But there are internal worries too. Consider: for purposes of the present argument, everybody agrees that, for any B, tokening a Mentalese formula with the appropriate belief-making property is sufficient for believing B. That is, for each of x's beliefs, the productivity theory will entail a theorem of the form "x believes B if x tokens Mi and Mi is P" (where P is a belief-making property). Nor, I take it, does anybody really doubt that such a theorem can be true only if it's also true that Mi *means that* B. So, for example, if (x believes that water gurgles if x tokens of Mi and Mi is P), then it must be that Mi means that *water gurgles*.

As I say, Schiffer really does agree with this, but he thinks that it's harmless because he thinks that this way of talking "simply abbreviates . . ." Actually, I don't have enough symbols on my machine to quote what he says it simply abbreviates; you can look it up for yourself. But the rough idea is that "Mi means that B" is just a way of saying that Mi is indeed the formula such that if it's tokened with the appropriate belief-making property, then that tokening constitutes an instance of believing that B. What shows that "it can only serve as the indicated abbreviation [is that] there is no literal use of the verb 'to mean' that has a correct application to one's neural states. In its *literal* use, the verb applies only to public-language items . . . " (p. 189).

Now I do think this is on the tendentious side. Whether neural states can literally have semantical properties depends on what semantical properties *literally are*. And, for us essentialists anyway, that question is not to be answered by appealing to, for Pete's sake, a *paradigm case* argument. It might well be a consequence of informational semantic theories, for example, that Mentalese expressions and English ones are meaningful in *exactly* the same sense; viz., both are involved in the symbol-world covariances in terms of which semantical properties are defined. (For discussion, see *TOC*, p. 100.) So, then: it's common ground that whatever Mentalese words contribute to Mentalese sentences determines their belief-making properties (perhaps by determining supervenience bases for these properties). But, prima facie, what a word contributes determines the belief-making property of a Mentalese sentence only if what it contributes determines the meaning (/truth condition) of that sentence; and we have, so far, no reason for talking this condition (as Schiffer would put it) "pleonastically."

And now you can appreciate the force of the best explanation argument for compositional semantics. Because it is, to put it mildly, sort of hard to imagine what an expression *could* contribute to a sentence that would determine the meaning of the sentence unless what an expression contributes to a sentence is its semantic value. What, if not a reference to flounders,[50] could 'flounders' conceivably contribute that would determine the meaning of 'flounders snore'? What, if not their truth conditions, could P and Q conceivably contribute that would determine the truth conditions of P&Q?

I do understand, of course, that Schiffer thinks that there's an independent argument why there can't be a theory of what words contribute to determining sentence meanings; viz., that no such theories work. *Remnants of Meaning* (1987a) consists largely of Schiffer's setting out grounds for that claim. My present concern is just to emphasize how much Schiffer needs this independent argument. For, if it begs the question one way to assume that Mentalese formulas have literally got truth conditions and the like, it begs the question the other way to assume that they literally don't. Schiffer warns that if you assume that they literally do, then "you're apt to get the impression that the language-of-thought hypothesis virtually requires a gloss of the 'meaning' relation that would secure [a compositional semantics]" (p. 189). Well, if you assume that they literally don't, then you're apt to get the impression that you can take seriously the question of what words contribute to the determination of belief-making properties without taking seriously the question of what they contribute to the determination of meanings. This looks to me like a stand-off unless you're convinced, as I guess I'm not, that *Remnants* actually *showed* that the compositional semantics program can't be carried out. Compositional semanticists can't, of course, run a best explanation defense if what they've got is a demonstrably bankrupt theory.

But if you're prepared to believe, *pace Remnants*, that compositional semantics is at least in the running, then what's really at issue between Schiffer and me is what, exactly, you're required to do to defeat a best explanation argument. I think you're required to sketch an alternative explanation, not just to show that there is logical space for such an alternative. Perhaps I can make this plausible by transferring the case to an area where philosophers are less invested than they are likely to be in semantics. Here's a fable.

Once upon a time there was a linguist – call him Larry for the sake of the alliteration – who got tired of syntax. "Syntax," Larry said, "is supposed to be the theory of how the *structural descriptions* of sentences are determined by the *syntactic values* of their constituent words (together with general principles). (So, for example, it's supposed to tell you how, by contributing the syntactic values *plural noun* and *verb* respectively, the worlds "flounders" and "snore" determine that the structural description of "Flounders snore" is, say:

$$(((\text{flounders})_N)_{NP} \ ((\text{snore})_V)_{VP})_S$$

"Well, I'm fed up. I mean: hundreds of us have been trying for more person-hours than I can bear to think about[51] to figure out how the structural descriptions of sentences are determined by the syntactic values of their constituent words, and *nobody can do it*. And nobody in his right mind thinks we're going to do it in the foreseeable future.

"To say nothing of there being no general account of *what it is* for a word to have a syntactic value. To say nothing of saying nothing of there being no *physicalistic* general account of what it is for a word to have a syntactic value.

"So I quit," said Larry.

Now, when linguists get into this mood, there is an 800 number they can call to get a soothing, pre-recorded argument to the best explanation. "There, there," the recording says, "it's *true* that we don't know what it is for a word to have a syntactic value, and it's true that we don't know how the syntactic values of words determine the structural descriptions of the sentences that contain them. But the theory that words have syntactic values and that there is a finitely specifiable function that yields the structural description of a sentence, given the syntactic values of its constituents, is the *only* idea anybody has had about how natural languages could be productive and systematic. So words must have syntactic values which they contribute to the determination of structural descriptions; and everything is going to be alright."

It's because they have this argument, and for no other reason really, that linguists believe that words have syntactic values which they contribute to determining the structural descriptions of sentences. I suppose it to be clearly rational of linguists to assume this posture. What with one thing and another – including paying the mortgage and securing domestic tranquillity – I can hardly afford to suppose otherwise.

But now, imagine that Larry were to argue as follows. "This best explanation argument is not, after all, any damned good. For, look: there might be, for each sentence S and each structural description SD, some (physicalistic, though, in fact, that doesn't really matter) property of its tokens such that:

(i) such properties are not themselves syntactic (in particular, none of them is the property of *having the structural description* . . .).

(ii) instantiations of these properties are supervenience bases for structural descriptions (each sentence satisfies the antecedent of something of the form "if the tokens of a sentence have the property . . ., then the sentence has SD").

(iii) Each word in a sentence contributes something – specifically something *other than a syntactic value* – which partially determines which such property the sentence has.

(iv) There is a finitely specifiable function that determines which such property a sentence has given a specification of its lexical constituents.

"Linguists have no argument that shows that there could not be nonsyntactic supervenience bases that satisfy (i)–(iv). So linguists have no reason to believe," Larry concluded, running nearly out of breath, "that English has a compositional syntax. *Nur eines will ich noch: das Ende.*" [*Linguistics obligingly stops.*]

Now, I take it that the intuition is very clear that Larry has not, thus far, got a good objection to the standard best explanation argument that words have syntactic values. And I take it that it's also clear *why* he doesn't. Here is what I think one should say to Larry. "Look, Larry" I think one should say, "you are certainly right that there *could be* some nonsyntactic properties that are supervenience bases for structural descriptions; and you are also right that, if there were such properties, then it could be their determination, rather than the determination of structural descriptions *per se*, that words contribute to; and that what words contribute to determining the supervenience bases of structural descriptions could then be something other than their syntactic values. But though, as I say, you are certainly right *that* this could be the case, still nobody has the slightest idea *how* it could be the case. In particular, *nobody has the slightest idea what this nonsyntactic property that having a structural description supervenes on could be.* And as long as nobody has any idea what this nonsyntactic property could be, it's reasonable to believe that there is no such property. *Possible* theories don't defeat best-explanation arguments; only *actual* theories do."

The thing is: if it's right to say that to Larry, I don't see why one shouldn't say it to Schiffer, too.

Smolensky

Smolensky's paper has been floating around, in one version or other, for the past couple of years. It is, to my knowledge, the only serious attempt by a Connectionist to face up to the problems that systematicity and productivity pose for their research program. As such, it deserves a more detailed and technical analysis than I could provide here. Brian McLaughlin and I have, however, given it a full-dress treatment in a *Cognition* article which responds to an earlier version of the present paper. Suffice it, then, to record my conviction that – advertisements to the contrary notwithstanding – Smolensky doesn't have what he and I agree that a Connectionist explanation of systematicity would require: mental representations with constituent structure. The reader who wishes to see this claim made good is referred to Fodor and McLaughlin (1990), "Connectionism and the problem of systematicity: why Smolensky's solution doesn't work."

Stich

Stich offers two reasons for preferring fat syntax as he conceives it to narrow content as I conceive it. They are these:

Narrow content is a construct out of wide content; since the latter is "highly context sensitive," so is the former. "Whether or not a state can be comfortably classified as having the content that p depends, to a significant degree, on the context in which the question arises" (p. 249), and that, clearly, is a property that we do not wish the categories of a scientific psychology to have.

However, I simply don't believe this context sensitivity stuff. Doubtless the commonsense intuitions about beliefs and desires will prove no more reliable, under theoretical pressure, than commonsense intuitions about whether whales are fish or planets are stars or glass is a solid. But, on my view, there is a matter of fact about the content of intentional states in light of which commonsense can be refined and reconstructed. And this matter of fact depends not at all upon "the context in which the question arises" but only on how God made the world: in particular, on what nomic relations a mental state and things in the world enter into (see *Psychosemantics; A Theory of Content* (1990b)). I am, as the reader will no doubt have surmised, a Realist and an Essentialist on these matters.

Stich's second point is that narrow content slices mental states thicker than fat syntax; hence, thicker than a respectable computational view of the mind allows.

> ... consider Helen Keller. If Ms Keller were to be told ... that there is a fat cat in the room ... she would acquire a brain state which ... has the (broad) content that there is a fat cat in the room.... [And so would Stich under comparable circumstances] Thus both Ms Keller's brain state and [Stich's] would have the (narrow) content that *there is a fat cat in the room*. But surely those two states differ radically in their fat syntax (p. 248).

So Stich takes the Helen Keller case to show that narrow content slices mental states too thick, assuming that the computational theory of the mind is true and that its taxonomy is the one which slices things just right.

I think this argument rests on a mistake; but there may be an underlying disagreement of intuition as well.

The mistake involves the issue I discuss in my reply to Devitt. Stich thinks that to accept the computational picture of mental *processes* requires one to hold that psychological *laws* must be articulated in computational vocabulary. Since, for example, the computational processes that underlie the fixation of fat-cat-in-the-room beliefs must be very different in Helen Keller's case than they are in Stich's ("there are all sorts of perceptual stimuli ... that would cause me, but not Ms Keller, to acquire the belief that [there is a fat cat in the room] ..." (pp. 248–249). Stich concludes that, if the computational account of the mind is right, then he and Helen Keller must belong to different psychological kinds.

But that simply doesn't follow. On the contrary, there is just nothing at all wrong with a psychology where, on the one hand, the laws are intentional (and subsume Stich, Helen Keller and everybody else who has fat cat beliefs) and, on the other hand, the processes by which the intentional laws are implemented are syntactical/computational through and through. So we can "have it both ways"; for more of this than it is likely that you want to hear, see my reply to Devitt.

Now we come to where it may be that Stich's intuitions differ from mine. In my view, if the price of a computational psychology really were a taxonomy that assigns Keller and Stich to different natural kinds, that would be a convincing *reductio* of the computational picture. *Pace* Stich, what I take the Keller case to show is precisely that we *need* an intentional taxonomy because the computational one slices mental states to thin. I say that this seems to be a clash of intuition; but fortunately it's quite clear whose intuitions are right. Namely, mine.

Consider: just what is the achievement of Helen Keller's that we all admire so much? Why is it that we think of her as a hero? These questions are rhetorical. The answer is: it's her having arrived, under conditions of what might have seemed insuperable disadvantage, at the very same view of the world that informs the rest of our common humanity. Like us, she came to know about the fat cat in the room. Only, what we were given on a platter, she attained against all odds.

And, for that very reason, by the most arduous and eccentric means. We need a taxonomy that slices things thick enough to recognize Keller's having achieved the normal human cognitive condition; and this the intentional vocabulary provides. But we also need a taxonomy that recognizes the circuitous route by which she achieved it; and that's what the computational story provides. If we couldn't coherently deploy both taxonomies together, we would be unable to say what the Keller case pretty clearly requires us to: viz., that she got to where we did, but not by the same route.[52]

Thus common sense; and so too, science, I suppose. What's scientifically striking about the Helen Keller case is the emergence of normal intentional psychology under conditions of the extremest perceptual deprivation. (See also Landau and Gleitman (1985), where similar though less drastic cases are studied and this moral is drawn explicitly.) In every respect that matters taxonomically, Helen Keller's mind was *just like ours*. So, a good psychology should have access to a vocabulary that generalizes over our mental states and hers; hence to a vocabulary that abstracts from many distinctions that fat syntax insists that we observe. Broad content provides such a vocabulary. So, too, does narrow content as I conceive it. Since fat syntax doesn't, so much the worse for fat syntax.

The deepest question – maybe, in the long run, the *only* question – of cognitive psychology is this: how, on the basis of such fragmentary and idiosyncratic experience, does everybody manage to converge on virtually the same inventory of beliefs and desires; on the fat cat in the room, to put it in a nutshell. (There are anthropological relativists, who deny that everybody does converge on virtually the same inventory of beliefs and desires; but they are not to be taken seriously. There are also direct realists, who deny that the experiential basis of cognition is fragmentary and idiosyncratic; but they are not to be taken seriously either.) The problem about how Helen Keller could have come to believe and desire much the same things that the rest of us do is a special case of this question. So, too, is Chomsky's problem about how language learning is achieved in face of the "poverty of the stimulus." So, too, is the problem of explaining perceptual and behavioral constancy. And so, too, is Kant's problem about how empirical science could be objective (where an "empirical" science is one for which the evidence is typically nondemonstrative and an "objective" science is one which, given the evidence, commends itself to *any* rational observer).

Content taxonomies don't answer this question, of course; but it is their decisive importance that they provide a vocabulary that is apt for its formulation. So we can't do without them.

NOTES

*From A. A. Milne's *The House at Pooh Corner*, of course.

Antony and Levine

1   Actually, it's uncertain that I do need to appeal to P(INF) being anomic to rule out "'horse' means P(INF)." The alternative is to appeal to the robustness condition, a

solution that A&L "originally thought ... would save the day." They rejected this strategy on second thought because ". . . any candidate for the mental representation of horse that meets [the robustness] condition is unfortunately going to meet the following condition: non-P(INF)-caused H[orse]-tokenings are asymmetrically dependent upon P(INF)-caused H-tokenings, because horses have to effect H-tokenings *through* P(INF)s" (p. 13). The idea is presumably that we wouldn't have "detached" H-tokens except that we have P(INF)-caused H-tokens.

However, it's not clear that this is true in the way that A&L require. What's the case (I suppose) is that detached H-tokens are *diachronically* dependent on P(INF)-caused H-tokens; no intellectual career that hasn't included any of the latter will include any of the former. However, what robustness requires is *synchronic* asymmetric dependence: it requires that if you *now* break the P(INF) --> "horse" connection, you lose the detached "horse"s. And it's by no means clear that this is so. Presumably I can figure out that there must be a horse behind the bush, thereby achieving a detached tokening of "horse," without tokening any proximal stimulus belonging to P(INF). Close your eyes and think *horse*. See? Easy.

But, for fun, let's see how the argument goes on the assumption that A&L accept; viz. that what rules out "P(INF) --> "horse" is just that P(INF) is anomic."

2 I take it that the case about phlogiston is not just that there doesn't happen to be any, but that, given the facts about burning, it's nomologically impossible that anything *could* have the properties that phlogiston was supposed to.

3 I don't know what Gibsonians think about roundsquareness and unicornicity; presumably nothing transduces ("resonates" to) properties about which there aren't laws. Maybe the theory is supposed to cover only concepts that express perceptual properties (though Gibson's texts often resist this interpretation).

4 Notice, however, that to say that horseness, shirtness, and the like aren't transduced is *not* to say that 'horse,' 'shirt,' and the like are defined. It's easy to think that concepts must be defined in terms of the transduced properties that mediate their tokening. (Empiricists were notorious for thinking this.) But in fact there's no such requirement and there is nothing to stop the concept 'horse' from being both untransduced and primitive. Roughly, in this usage, 'primitive' is a linguistic notion, 'transduced' is psychological.

Baker

5 This formulation is *not* adjusted to meet the worry about distance measures raised by Boghossian (q.v.); but it's good enough for the present purposes.

6 Baker remarks that what conception of law is at issue here needs a good deal of spelling out. Sure, but that is *not my fault* and it's also *not my problem*. That lawful relations can asymmetrically depend on one another seems hard to doubt; see, for example, causal chain cases. Since this is so, we are going to have to find *some* philosophically respectable way of saying that it is so; and whatever way that is, the semantics can co-opt it.

7 NB ontological; epistemological won't do.

8 It is, I think, perfectly OK to help oneself to Sally's dispositions, policies etc. in the course of naturalization, so long as one treats them simply as mechanisms that mediate the symbol/world relations in terms of which content is defined. (Cf. Skinner (1957): semantical relations are *purely* functional; naturalization quantifies over the mecha-

nisms – intentional, neurological, hydrodynamic, or whatever – that sustain these functional relations. I go on about this at length in *TOC*.) Baker is darkly suspicious that this way of proceeding is circular because "If you, the theorist, don't have access to the content of the intentions [viz. of the intentions that support the counterfactuals in terms of which asymmetric dependence is defined] how do you know over which mechanisms to quantify?" (n. 15, p. 31). Answer: you quantify over *all* of the mechanisms; *only* the nomic relations between Mentalese symbols and the properties whose instantiations (would) cause their tokening count for content.

9   Note that this is offered as a necessary condition for satisfying a certain sufficient condition for "cow" to mean *cow, not as a necessary condition for "cow" to mean cow*. I told you that you weren't going to like this.

10   In passing: the structure of Baker's example suggests she thinks that the application of "X" to unprototypical Xs depends asymmetrically on its application to the X-prototype. But that is untrue. *Ceteris paribus*, swallows would still be in the extension of 'bird' even if it were to turn out – against all expectation – that sparrows are a kind of vegetable.

Block

11   For the purposes of this discussion I shall assume, as Block does, that some version of the standard Language of Thought story is true: token thoughts are relations to token mental representations; mental representations are sentences of Mentalese; Mentalese is morphosyntactically indistinguishable from English . . . etc. Also, I won't distinguish the semantical issues about concepts from the corresponding ones about linguistic expressions in Mentalese (or in English) except where the distinction matters to the argument.

12   Block adds ". . . in which the appropriate bits of language are learned." But, unlike Stephen White, I don't hold a "context of acquisition" account of broad content; indeed, I don't think that being acquired can be an essential condition for having content. This actually makes a difference in evaluating some of Block's arguments. See, in particular, the discussion of pandas and tigers below; and, generally, *caveat emptor*.

13   If the theory of narrow content is supposed to be reductive then "roles" will have to be individuated by their *non*intentional properties; but, for present purposes, I propose to ignore this, as does Block.

14   Actually, Block stipulates that these are different kinds of animals (different species); but, as far as I can see, that doesn't alter the case. What's crucial to his argument is the assumption that, insofar as our conception of Xs does any work at all *vis-à-vis* our X-concept, the work it does must be to determine the extension of the concept (in some worlds or other).

15   At this point in the argument, Block is heuristically assuming a description theory, according to which your "conception" of Xs determines the extension of your X-concept. But even when he relaxes this assumption, he takes it for granted that if "descriptions" are to provide internal constraints on having a concept, they must determine (perhaps partial) satisfaction conditions for the concept. So "any description will make a referential difference in *some* possible world, so holism follows."

16   Block is, in fact, pretty explicit about taking this for granted. Consider "[for the usual externalist reasons] . . . the burden of proof is on anyone who claims that the difference between your tiger conception and your panda conception has much to do with determining that your 'tiger' and your tiger conception applies to tigers, whereas your 'panda' applies to pandas. . . . *For this reason* [my emphasis] the narrow contents

specified by these mappings seem unsuitable for psychological explanation: they are too coarse grained" That is: if your nonpathetic theory wants to appeal to "conceptions" to make the internal conditions for having concepts fine grained, it is also required to buy the semantical theory that these conceptions determine what your concepts apply to. Just who instituted this requirement, I wonder; and on just what authority?

17 In fact, the informational semantics that I favor offers only a sufficient condition for content. But that doesn't matter for present purposes.

18 At least they would in the fancier sorts of minds. See my discussion of Levine and Antony's comments.

19 In a somewhat different sense of the notion than the one that figured in *TOC*.

Boghossian

20 I'm very much indebted to Brian McLaughlin and Ernie Lepore for discussions of this material.

21 This is a first approximation; more presently.

22 The proposal isn't, of course, that we should add the requirement that the inference fails to the naturalization theory; we can't do that since valid inference and the like are semantical notions. Rather, the theory is just that it's sufficient for S to mean P that S --> P be the unique law that holds for S-tokens in every world where any law holds for them. The fact that the disjunctive formula can fail to be lawful in worlds like W1 and W2 shows that we have, so far, no reason to doubt that this condition is sometimes satisfied.

23 It's common ground that the present discussion concerns *only* the semantics of "primitive" expressions, hence ones whose extensions are determined by ostensions rather than (e.g.) explicit definitions. It's important to keep this in mind, since it may well affect your intuitions about the cases.

24 What seems to matter to Boghossian's intuitions is that only a *small number* of the things we call T-particles are T*. Oh well, so be it. Let's revise the semantical story to say that when a term carries information about As and Bs in every physically possible world, then the term means *A or B* except where As and Bs are both natural kinds and almost all the things that are As or Bs in the actual world are As. In which case, the term means *A*. As far as I can see, nothing central to informational semantics turns on this.

25 Cf. the discussion of 'Block's objection' in *TOC* (pt. II).

Devitt

26 Except, of course, in the trivial sense that there must be some mental process or other that accounts for the illusion.

27 It could be distal stimuli under physical description for all that the present discussion cares. It's the "under physical description" bit that does the work.

28 Or maybe with a zero-crossing analysis; or whatever. It's hard to give real-life examples here because psychophysics is one of the areas of psychology in which there is actually some developed theory; so disputes about empirical details tend to be ferocious. For extensive discussion, see any standard text on the psychoacoustics of speech. There is a vast literature on the corresponding issues in vision; Marr offers some well-known speculations.

29 The *"inter alia"* is because it counts as a semantical object too; it's a token of a Mentalese type that represents the spectrographic properties of a certain proximal stimulus. See below.

30　In fact, this is much too simple; for example, you'd probably tell the story in terms of subphonetic features if you were doing it seriously. But the morals would be the same.

31　For some reason, it seems to be important to Devitt that psychophysical relations not be mental. Would mental2 be OK? If so, could we just abbreviate 'mental2' to 'mental'?

32　Two other conceptions of psychophysical law have been historically influential. According to one, they connect stimuli under physical description with mental states under neurological description (e.g. with states of neural activation); according to the other, they connect stimuli under physical description with sensations. Neither of these conceptions serves the purpose of a computational psychology; even so, it's worth noticing that neither makes psychophysical laws *bridge* laws. On the first view they aren't bridge laws because they are physical-physical and hence not inter-level; on the second view, though they're inter-level (viz., physical-mental), they're also *causal*, which bridge laws aren't allowed to be. Being H_2O doesn't *cause* stuff to be water.

33　I suspect that Devitt and I really do disagree about issues in the philosophy of logic that are too broad for discussion here. Devitt thinks that the moral of proof theory is that "entailment is (partially) *reduced* to derivability ..." (p. 113). Insofar as parallelism holds, it's because "the syntactic [relation] is the semantic one" (*ibid.*). I note without argument that this seems to me utterly wrong. Entailment and the like are relations among (roughly) propositions; derivability and the like are relations among (roughly) sentences. In consequence the second, but not the first, is language relative.

However, even if Devitt is right, the two-level picture still doesn't collapse since the vocabulary of syntactically reducible semantic properties would clearly be inadequate to state the full range of intentional laws.

Loar

34　In particular, I won't discuss Loar's putative counterexamples to the asymmetric dependence treatment of content except where they raise systematic issues. In many cases it seems fairly obvious how they should be handled. For example, Loar is worried that I would comply "if ordered to say 'sheep' by a maniac holding a gun to my head ... [since] such a counterfactual may well be true of virtually every term of mine ... Fodor's condition would be satisfied by none of them ..." (n. 3). However, precisely *because* I'll say *whatever* an armed maniac tells me to, it's easy to exclude the case: a causal condition that constrains the tokening of all "X"s doesn't count for the content of any of them.

35　This is, of course, the psychologist's usage, in which concepts are mental representations, rather than the philosopher's usage in which they are what mental representations express.

36　Loar is worried that we can't even pick out the nondeferential concepts without relying on intentional notions; but, at least in principle, this isn't a serious worry. The content of X is nondeferential if X's having content doesn't depend on anything else's having content. This is noncircular if the conditions for content are independently defined.

On anybody's story, there must *be* content that is nondeferential in this sense. The content of my thoughts may depend on the contents of the expert's thoughts. Upon whose thoughts' contents does the content of the expert's thoughts depend?

37　Which is not to deny that extension fixing by later uses may override extension fixing by earlier ones, thus limiting robustness. See Armand below and also Lore's llamas.

38　Compare what Loar says about protons and in n. 14; he seems simply to take it for granted that theories (partly) determine the meaning of theoretical terms. When you consider how much trouble that assumption has made for us in the philosophy of science, you'd think people would ask themselves whether, perhaps we can't get along without it. (Or at least whether there is actually any reason to believe it; I have yet to hear of one.) See *Psychosemantics:, ch. 3.*

39   I suppose your intending that your arm should rise accounts for its rising; but here the relation between the intention and the motion is plausibly causal and, anyhow, it works only for basic actions. So it provides no precedent that explains how your intending that 'F' should have the Fs as its extension makes it the case that 'F' does have the Fs as its extension.

Matthews

40   For the sake of the argument, and because I am an obliging chap, I'm going along with the assumption that there is a fact of the matter about what beliefs a machine (or a person) has in the sort of case that Dennett imagines; in particular, that it might be literally true, in such circumstances, that the machine plays the way it does because it has the Q-belief. But, in fact, the question that one ought to say about Dennett's machine is of a piece with the question whether someone who believes Peano's axioms *ipso facto* believes that there is no largest prime; or the question which grammar of one's language one "cognizes" given the assumption that parsers but *not* grammars are internally represented. As Bill Lycan has pointed out, it is OK for an Intentional Realist to hold that there isn't, in general, a matter of fact about such cases, hence that there's nothing for Realism to reconstruct. That is, even Intentional Realists can take an instrumental view of beliefs and desires which, by assumption, aren't occurrent causes. It's only mental states that are episodes in mental processes that Realism requires Realists to be Realistic about.

Perry and Israel

41   Some of the things that they say that I disagree with don't matter to the main issue, so I won't insist upon them here. For example, I think that a reductive account of intentionality is mandatory for any theory that proposes to take intentional explanation seriously, and that appeals to "naturalistic functionalism" can neither provide nor dispense with the reduction. See *TOC* (pt. I) for discussion.

42   This isn't to say that I want to sign on for all the details. For me, the "fully opaque" reading of a sentence is what a compositional semantics says about it, so that "he's drinking coffee" and "I'm drinking coffee" have different fully opaque readings even if they are both thought about me. Fully opaque content, for Perry and Israel, is closer to truth conditional content; in particular these two sentences do have the same fully opaque content if they are both thought about me.

It is, of course, just terminological whether we reserve "full opacity" for the thinner way of slicing things; the point of substance is that the thinner slices will be required if the theory of mental content is to connect properly with the theory of mental processes. Does the thought that *it's time for us to leave* have the same content as the thought that *it's time for him and her and me to leave* when both are thought of him and her and me? But you can imagine a situation in which one arrives at the second thought *by an inference from the first.*

43   Actually, even if I did think that intrinsic properties determine content I'd still be OK with Hume. Hume held that Ideas *resemble* their referents; the idea of red is an idea

of red in virtue of being a red thing. When Hume says that the reference of an idea to an object is an extraneous denomination, "the reference of an idea" means *whether the idea refers,* not (as Perry and Israel parse it) *what the idea refers to.* Hume is denying that you can tell whether there are unicorns by inspecting your mental representations. But he doesn't deny that you can tell, just by inspecting it, that your mental representation of unicorns refers to unicorns if it refers to anything.

Stalnaker

44 I'm not wanting to suggest, however, that decisions among semantic theories *qua* theories-that-say-what-meanings-formulas-have and semantic theories *qua* theories-that-say-what-makes-formulas-have-the-meanings-they-do are entirely orthogonal. For example: if I'm right about the holistic consequences of conceptual role theories, then the choice of conceptual roles as the meaning-makers implies that only whole languages (/theories) get interpreted by the denotational theory.

45 What the Putnam/Burge examples show is that the broad, folk-theoretic notions of semantic property exhibit a previously unnoticed relativization to context. Narrow content wants to generalize over the contexts to which broad content relativizes, hence permitting psychological laws which hold without respect to context.

  Abstracting from context sensitivity is a standard way of achieving scientific generalization. We could have done physics with *weight,* but the price would be context sensitivity in the laws of mechanics. *Mass* generalizes over the contexts to which weight relativizes and is the preferred parameter for precisely that reason. Such precedents would motivate narrow content even if metaphysical arguments for supervenience didn't.

46 Viz., he is disposed to token that Mentalese sentence in his belief-box.

47 Stalnaker says: ". . . the fact that one learns what water is does not necessarily imply that one won't misapply the concept, in some contexts . . ." (p. 235). I take his point to be that it wouldn't *follow* from the assumption that there are worlds in which my almost-Twin confuses water and XYZ and I don't, that our thoughts have different broad contents in those worlds. And, of course, it's common ground that, whatever the causal conditions for the denotation of a concept are, they clearly can't require that the concept never be misapplied. I was assuming, however, that these conditions for 'water' to denote XYZ would very plausibly fail to be satisfied by someone who systematically declines to apply 'water' to XYZ; as, presumably, someone who knew water not to be XYZ might well be expected to do.

48 An argument that *necessary and* sufficient conditions for content couldn't be atomistic would do the trick; but, so far as I know, there are no such arguments on offer. The key question is whether an atomistic theory can allow almost-Twins to share concepts. As we've seen, if you're an informational semanticist, a lot will probably depend on how the notion of nomic head/world connection is construed.

Schiffer

49 The case we're trying to imagine can't, for example, just be one in which semantical/intentional properties are physically "multiply realized." For then there would be *functional* properties on which the semantical/intentional ones supervene; and the question would arise why the semantical/intentional properties should not be construed as identical to *them.*

50 Or to flounderhood if you prefer; that's not what's at issue here.
51 Thirty-five years since *Syntactic Structures*. And counting.

Stich

52 A mixed taxonomy, in which level L provides the vocabulary to state the generaliza-tions and level L-minus-one-or-more provides the vocabulary to account for their implementation, is the standard tactic of the special sciences. That this tactic works so well is presumably *why* the sciences are organized hierarchically.

Bibliography

The Works of Jerry Fodor

Fodor, J. A. (1960) "What do you mean?," *Journal of Philosophy*, 57, 499–506.
—— (1961a) "Projection and paraphrase in semantics," *Analysis*, 21, 73–7.
—— (1961b) "Of words and uses," *Inquiry*, 4, 190–208.
—— (1964a) "On knowing what we would say," *Philosophical Review*, 73, 198–212.
—— (1965a) "Explanation in psychology" in *Philosophy in America*, ed. Max Black, Muirhead Library of Philosophy.
—— (1965b) "Could meaning be an rm?," *Journal of Verbal Learning and Verbal Behavior*, 4, 414–4.
—— (1965g) "Some remarks on the philosophy of language," in *Aspects of Contemporary American Philosophy*, F. Donnell, ed. Physica-verlag.
—— (1966a) "Could there be a theory of perception?," *Journal of Philosophy*, 63.
—— (1966b) "More about mediators: a reply to Berlyne and Osgood," *Journal of Verbal Learning and Verbal Behavior*, 5, 412–15.
—— (1967b) "How to learn to talk, some simple ways," in *The Genesis of Language*, ed. C. Reed, Appleton-Century-Crofts.
—— (1968c) "The appeal to tacit knowledge in psychological explanation," *Journal of Philosophy*, 65, 627–40.
—— (1968d) *Psychological Explanation*, Random House.
—— (1969) "Meaning and convention in *The Blue Book*," in *The Business of Reason*, eds J. Macintosh and S. Coval, Routledge and Kegan Paul.
—— (1970a) "Three reasons for not deriving 'kill' from 'cause to die,' " *Linguistic Inquiry*, 1, 429–38.
—— (1970b) "Troubles about actions," *Synthèse*, 21, 298–319.
—— (1971) "Current approaches to syntax recognition" in *The Perception of Language*, eds D. Horton and J. Jenkins, Chales E. Merrill Co.
—— (1972a) "Some reflections on L. S. Vygotsky's *Thought and Language*," *Congnition*, 1, 83–95.
—— (1974b) "Special sciences," *Synthèse*, 28, 97–115.
—— (1975a) *The Language of Thought*, Thomas Y. Crowell. (Paperback, Harvard University Press).
—— (1977a) "The philosophy of psychology," in *Collier's Encyclopedia*.
—— (1977b) "Mind," in *Encyclopedia Einaudi*, Torino, Italy.
—— (1978a) "Computation and reduction," in *Minnesota Studies in the Philosophy of Science*, Vol. 9, ed. W. Savage, University of Minnesota Press.
—— (1978b) "Tom Swift and his procedural grandmother," *Cognition*, 6, 229–47.
—— (1978c) "Three cheers for propositional attitudes," in *Sentence Processing* eds E. Cooper and E. Walker, Erlbaum.
—— (1978d) "Propositional attitudes, " *The Monist*, 61 (4) 501–23.

—— (1980b) "In reply to Philip Johnson-Laird," *Cognition*, 7, 93–5.

—— (1980c) "Methodological solipsism considered as a research strategy in cognitive science," *Behavioral and Brain Sciences*, 3, 63–109.

—— (1980d), Replies to Commentators [on 1980c], *Behavioral and Brain Sciences*, 3, 99–109.

—— (1981a) "The mind-body problem," *Scientific American*, January, 114–23.

—— (1981c) "Propositional Attitudes," in (1981d), pp. 177–203.

—— (1981d) *RePresentations: Philosophical Essays on the Foundations of Cognitive Science*, MIT Press/Bradford Books.

—— (1982) "Cognitive science and the twin-earth problem," *Notre Dame Journal of Formal Logic*, 23, 98–119.

—— (1983) *The Modularity of Mind: An Essay on Faculty Psychology*, MIT Press/Bradford Books.

—— (1984a) "Semantics, Wisconsin style," *Synthèse*, 59, 231–50.

—— (1984b) "Observation reconsidered," *Philosophy of Science*, 51, 23–43.

—— (1985a) "Précis of 'Modularity of Mind,' " *The Behavioral and Brain Sciences*, 8, 1–42.

—— (1985b) "Fodor's guide to mental representation," *Mind*, Spring, 66–100.

—— (1985c) "Banish disContent" in *Language, Mind and Logic*, ed. J. Butterfield, Cambridge Uiversity Press.

—— (1986a) "Information and association," *Notre Dame Journal of Formal Logic*, 27 (3) 307–23.

—— (1986b) "Why paramecia don't have mental representations," in *Midwest Studies in Philosophy*, vol. 10, eds P. French, T. Uehling, Jr, and H. Wettstein, University of Minnesota Press.

—— (1987a) "A situated grandmother?," *Mind and Language*, 2, (1) 64–81.

—— (1987b) "Mental representation: an introduction" in *Scientific Inquiry in Philosophical Perspective*, ed. N. Rescher, University Press of America.

—— (1987c) "Frames, Fridgeons, Sleeping Dogs and The Music of The Spheres," in *The Robot's Dilemma; the Frame Problem in Artificial Intelligence*, ed. Z. Pylyshin, Ablex, NJ.

—— (1987d) *Psychosemantics: the Problem of Meaning in the Philosophy of Mind*, MIT Press/Bradford Books.

—— (1988b) "A reply to Churchland's 'Perceptual plasticity and theoretical neutrality,' " *Philosophy of Science*, 55, 188–98.

—— (1989a) "Why should mind be modular?," in *Reflections on Chomsky*, ed. A. George, Blackwell.

—— (1989b) "Making mind matter more," *Philosophical Topics*, 67, (1) 59–79.

—— (1989c) "Review Essay: *Remnants of Meaning*, by Stephen Schiffer," *Philosophy and Phenomenological Research*, 50 (2) 409–23.

—— (1990) "Psychosemantics, or Where do truth conditions come from" in *Mind and Cognition*, ed. W. Lycan Blackwell, pp. 312–38.

—— (1990b) *A Theory of Content and Other Essays*, MIT Press/Bradford Books. (forthcoming) *Mind*.

—— (in press-a) "Substitution arguments and the individuation of beliefs," in *Essays for Hilary Putnam*, ed. G. Boolos, Blackwell.

—— (in press-b) "Information and representation," in *Information, Language, and Cognition*, ed. P. Hanson, Vancouver Studies in Cognitive Science, Vol. 1, University of British Columbia Press.

—— (in press-d) "A modal argument for narrow content," forthcoming in *Journal of Philosophy*.

——(in press-e) "The dogma that didn't bark, a fragment of a naturalized epistemology."

—— (unpublished-a), "On there not being an Evolutionary Theory of Content, or Why if you've been waiting around for Darwin to pull Brentano's chestnuts out of the fire, my advice to you is: forget it," unpublished, delivered at Conference on Mind and Meaning at Columbia University, December 1989.

—— (unpublished-b), "Narrow Content and Meaning Holism."

—— (unpublished-c), reply to Baker, American Philosophical Association, Eastern Meeting, Washington DC, December 1988.

Co-authored Works

Fodor, J. A. and Jerrold Katz (1964b), "A reply to Dixon's 'A trend in semantics,'" *Linguistics*, 1, 19–29.

—— and Jerrold Katz (eds) (1964c), *The Structure of Language*, Prentice Hall.

—— and Bever, T. (1965c), "The psychological reality of linguistic segments," *Journal of Verbal Learning and Verbal Behavior*, 4, 414–20.

——, Bever, T. and Weksel, W. (1965d), "On the acquisition of syntax: a critique of contextual generalization," *Psychological Review*, 72, 467–82.

——, Bever, T. and Weksel, W. (1965e), "Is linguistics empirical?," *Psychological Review*, 72, 493–500.

——, Bever, T. and Garrett, M. (1968b), "A formal limitation of associationism," in *Verbal Behavior and General Behavior Theory*, eds T. Dixon and D. Horton, Prentice Hall.

——, Bever, T. and Garrett, M. (1974a), *The Psychology of Language*, McGraw Hill.

—— and Block, N. (1972b), "What psychological states are not," *Philosophical Review*, 81, 159–81.

—— and Chihara, C. (1965f), "Operationalism and ordinary language," *American Philosophical Quarterly*, 2, 281–95.

—— and Cutler, A. (1975b), "Semantic focus and sentence comprehension" *Cognition* 7, 49–59.

——, Fodor, J. D. and Garrett, M. (1975c), "The psychological unreality of semantic representatons," *Linguistic Inquiry*, 6, 515–31.

—— and Fodor, J. D., (1980a), "Functional structure, quantifiers and meaning postulates," *Linguistic Inquiry*, 11, 4.

—— and Freed, R. (1961c), "Pains, puns, persons and pronouns," *Analysis*, 22.

—— and Freed, R. (1963c), "Some types of ambiguous tokens," *Analysis*, 24.

—— and Garrett, M. (1966c), "Some reflections on competence and performance," in *Psycholinguistic Papers*, eds D. Lyons and R. Wales, Edinburgh University Press.

—— and Garrett, M. (1967a), "Some syntactic determinants of sentential complexity," *Perception and Psychophysics*, 2, 289–96.

—— and Garrett, M. (1968a), "Psychological theories and linguistic constructs," in *Verbal Behavior and General Behavior Theory*, eds T. Dixon and T. Horton, Prentice Hall.

——, Garrett, M., and Bever, T. (1966d), "The active use of grammar in speech perception," *Perception and Psychophysics*, 1, 30–2.

——, Garrett, M. and Brill, S. (1975b), "Pi ka pu: the perception of speech sounds by prelinguistic infants," *Perception and Psychophysics*, 18, 74–8.

——, Garrett, M., Walker, E., and Parkes, C. (1980e), "Against defintions," *Cognition*, 8, 263–367.

——, Jenkins, J., and Saporta, S. (1967c), "Psycholinguistics and communication theory," in *Human Communication Theory*, ed. F. Dance, Holt Reinhart and Winston.

—— and Katz, J. (1962), "What's wrong with the philosophy of language?," *Inquiry*, 39, 197–237.

—— and Katz, J. (1963a), "The structure of a semantic theory," *Language*, 170–210.

—— and Katz, J. (1963b), "The availability of what we say," *Philosophical Review*, 73,

51–71.

—— and Lepore, E. (in preparation-a), *Holism, A Shopper's Guide.*

—— and McLaughlin, B. (1990), "Connectionism and the problem of systematicity; why Smolensky's solution doesn't work," *Cognition*, Vol. 35 (2), 183–204.

—— and Pylyshyn, Z. (1981b), "How direct is visual perception? Some reflections on Gibson's 'ecological approach,' " *Cognition*, 9, 139–96.

—— and Pylyshyn, Z. (1988a), "Connectionism and cognitive architecture: a critical analysis," *Cognition*, Vol. 28, (1–2) 3–71.

—— and Pylyshyn, Z. (in preparation-b), *Studies in Cognitive Architecture.*

General Bibliography

Akins, K. (1988), doctoral dissertation, University of Michigan.

Anderson, J. A. and Mozer, M. C. (1981), "Categorization and selective neurons," in *Parallel models of associative memory*, eds G. E. Hinton and J. A. Anderson, Erlbaum.

Antony, L. (1989), "Anomalous monism and the problem of explanatory force," *Philosophical Review* (2), 153–87.

Armstrong, D. (1978), *A Theory of Universals*, Cambridge University Press.

Asquith, P. D., and Nickles, T., eds, (1983), *PSA 1982*, Vol. 2, Philosophy of Science Association.

Baker, L. (1986), "Just what do we have in mind?," in *Midwest Studies in Philosophy*, eds P. French, T. Uehling, Jr and H. Wettstein, University of Minnesota Press, pp. 25–48.

Baker, L. (1987a), *Saving Belief: a Critique of Physicalism*, Princeton University Press.

Baker, L. (1987b), "Content by courtesy," *Journal of Philosophy*, 84, 197–213.

Baker, L. (1988), "What is a mental representation?," paper presented at American Philosophical Association Eastern Meeting 1988, Washington DC.

Baker, L. (1989), "On a causal theory of content," in *Philosophical Perspectives 3: Philosophy of Mind and Action Theory 1989*, ed. J. E. Tomberlin, Ridgeview Publishing Co., pp. 165–86.

Ballard, D. (1986), *Parallel Logical Inference and Energy Minimization*, Technical Report TR142, Computer Science Department, University of Rochester.

Ballard, D., and Hayes, P. J. (1984), "Parallel logical inference," *Proceedings of the Sixth Annual Conference of the Cognitive Science Society*, Rochester, NY.

Barwise, J. (1986), "Information and circumstance," *Notre Dame Journal of Formal Logic*, 27, 324–38.

Barwise, J., and Perry J. (1983), *Situations and Attitudes*, MIT Press/Bradford Books.

Bealer, G. (1982), *Quality and Concept*, Clarendon Press.

Bealer, G. (1984), "Mind and anti-mind," in *Midwest Studies in Philosophy*, Vol. 9, University of Minnesota Press, 283–328.

Berwick, R. (1986), *The Acquisition of Syntactic Knowledge*, MIT Press/Bradford Books.

Block, N. (1978), "Troubles with Functionalism," in Block (1980), 268–306.

Block, N., ed., (1980), *Readings in the Philosophy of Psychology*, 2 vols., Harvard University Press.

Block, N., ed., (1981), *Imagery*, MIT Press/Bradford Books.

Block, N. (1986), "Advertisement for a semantics for psychology," in *Studies in the Philososphy of Mind*, eds P. French, T. Uehling, Jr, and H. Wettstein, Vol. 10 of *Midwest Studies in Philosophy*, University of Minnesota Press.

Block, N. (1990), "The computer model of the mind," in *Thinking*, eds D. Osherson and E. Smith, MIT Press.

Block, N., and Bromberger, S. (1980), "States' Rights," *Behavioral and Brain Sciences* 3, 73–4.

Boghossian, P. (1986), *Essays on Meaning and Belief*, Ph. D. Thesis, Princeton University.

Boghossian, P. (1989), "The rule following considerations," *Mind*, October, 507–49.

Burge, T. (1977), "Belief De Re," *Journal of Philosophy*, 74 (6), 338–62.

Burge, T. (1978), "Belief and synonymy," *Journal of Philosophy*, 75, 119–38.

Burge, T. (1979), "Individualism and the mental," *Midwest Studies in Philosophy*, 4, 73–121.

Burge, T. (1982), "Two thought experiments reviewed," *Notre Dame Journal of Formal Logic*, 23, 284–93.

Burge, T. (1986), "Individualism and psychology," *Philosophical Review*, 95 (1) 3–46.

Burge, T. (forthcoming), "The social character of language," *Journal of Philosophy*.

Burge, T. (in preparation), "Individualism and causation in psychology."

Carnap, R. (1937), *The Logical Syntax of Language*, Harcourt, Brace.

Cartwright, N. (1983), *How the Laws of Physics Lie*, Clarendon Press.

Casteneda, H. (1966), " 'He': a study in the logic of self consciousness," *Ratio*, 8, 130–57.

Cherniak, C. (1986), *Minimal Rationality*, MIT Press/Bradford Books.

Chisholm, R. (1957), *Perceiving: a Philosophical Study*, Cornell University Press.

Chisholm, R. (1981), *The First Person*, University of Minnesota Press.

Chomsky, N. (1959), "Review of Skinner's *Verbal Behavior*," *Language* 35 (1), 26–58.

Chomsky, N. (1965), *Aspects of the Theory of Syntax*, MIT Press.

Chomsky, N. (1968), *Language and Mind*, Harcourt, Brace and World.

Chomsky, N. (1980), *Rules and Representations*, Columbia University Press.

Chomsky, N. (1988), *Language and Problems of Knowledge*, MIT Press.

Church, A. (1946), Review of Morton White's "A note on the 'Paradox of Analysis,' " Max Black's "The 'Paradox of Analysis' again: a reply"; Morton White's "Analysis and identity: a rejoinder," and Max Black's "How can analysis be informative?"; in *Journal of Symbolic Logic*, 11, 132–33.

Churchland, P. M. (1979), *Scientific Realism and the Plasticity of Mind*, Cambridge University Press.

Churchland, P. M. (1981), "Eliminative materialism and propositional attitudes," *Journal of Philosophy*, 78 (2), 67–89.

Churchland, P. M. (1984), *Matter and Consciousness*, MIT Press.

Churchland, P. S. (1986), *Neurophilosophy: Toward a Unified Science of the Mind-Brain*, MIT Press/Bradford Books.

Churchland, P. S. and Churchland, P. M. (1983) "Stalking the wild epistemic engine," *Nous*, 17, 5–20.

Cognitive Science. (1985), Special issue on connectionist models and their applications, 9(1).

Collins, A., (1979), "Why beliefs can't be sentences in the head," *Journal of Philosophy*, 76 (5), 225–42.

Crimmins, M. (1989), *Talk about Beliefs*, dissertation, Stanford University.

Crimmins, M, and Perry, C. (1989), "The prince and the phone booth: reporting puzzling beliefs," *Journal of Philosophy*, 86 (December), 685–711.

Cummins, R. (1986), "Inexplicit information," in *Problems in the Representation of Knowledge and Belief*, eds M. Brand and M. Harnish, University of Arizona Press.

Cummins, R. (1989), *Meaning and Mental Representation*, MIT Press/Bradford Books.

Cummins R., and Schwarz, G. (1987), "Radical connectionism," *Southern Journal of Philosophy*, 26 (Supplement), 43–61.

Davidson, D. (1970a/1980), "Mental events," in Davidson (1980), 207–228.

Davidson, D. (1980), *Essays on Actions and Events*, Clarendon Press.

Davidson, D. (1984), *Inquiries into Truth and Interpretion*, Clarendon Press.

Davidson, D. (1987), "Knowing one's own mind," in *Proceedings and Addresses of the American Philosophical Association*, Lancaster Press, pp. 441–58.

Davidson, D. and Hintikka, J. (1969), *Words and Objections*, Reidel.

Demopoulos, William (1980), "A remark on the completeness of the computational model of mind," *Behavioral and Brain Sciences*, 3, 135.

Dennett, D. (1969), *Content and Consciousness*, Routledge and Kegan Paul.

Dennett, D. (1971), "Intentional systems," in Dennett (1978a).

Dennett, D. (1976), "Conditions of personhood," in Dennett (1978a) pp. 267–285.

Dennett, D. (1978a), *Brainstorms*, MIT Press/Bradford Books.

Dennett, D. (1978b), "Skinner skinned," in Dennett (1978a) 53–70.

Dennett, D. (1978c), "Why the law of effect won't go away," in Dennett (1978a) pp. 71–89.

Dennett, D. (1978d), "Towards a cognitive theory of consciousness," in Dennett (1978a) pp. 149–173.

Dennett, D. (1981a), "True believers: the intentional strategy and why it works," in *Scientific Explanation*, ed. A. Heath, Oxford University Press.

Dennett D. (1981b), "Three kinds of intentional psychology," in *Reduction, Time and Reality*, ed. R. Healy, Cambridge University Press.

Dennett, D. (1981c), "A cure for the common code," in *Brainstorms*, MIT Press/Bradford Books.

Dennett, D. (1982) "Beyond belief," in *Thought and Object*, ed. A. Woodfield, Oxford University Press, pp. 207–58.

Dennett, D. (1984), "Cognitive wheels: the frame problem of AI," in Hookway (1984), pp. 129–51.

Dennett, D. (1987), *The Intentional Stance*, MIT Press/Bradford Books.

Dennett, D. (1988a), "When philosophers encounter AI," *Daedalus*, Winter, p. 285

Dennett, D. (1988b), "Review of *Psychosemantics*," *Journal of Philosophy*, 85 384–89.

Dennett, D. (unpublished), "Quining Qualia."

Descartes, R. (1673/1973), "Discourse on the method," in *The Philosophical Works of Descartes*, trans. E. S. Haldane and G. R. T. Ross, Cambridge University Press.

Descartes, R. (1649/1892), "Letter to Henry More," in *The Philosophy of Descartes*, trans. H A. P. Torrey, Henry Holt.

Devitt, M. (1981), *Designation*, Columbia University Press.

Devitt, M. (1981), *Realism and Truth*, Blackwell.

Devitt, M., (1985), "Critical notice of the varieties of reference," *Australasian Journal of Philosophy*, 63, 216–32.

Devitt, M. (1989a), "A narrow representational theory of the mind," in *Representations: Readings in the Philiosophy of Mental Representation*, ed. S. Silvers, Kluwer.

Devitt, M. (1989b), "Against direct reference," in *Midwest Studies in Philosophy, Vol. 13: Contemporary Perspectives in the Philosophy of Language II*, ed. P. French, T. Uehling Jr, and H. Wettstein, University of Notre Dame Press, pp. 205–40.

Devitt, M. and Sterelny, K. (1987), *Language and Reality*, MIT Press/Bradford Books.

Dolan, C. and Smolensky, P. (1988), "Implementing a connectionist production system using tensor products," in *Proceedings of the Connectionist Models Summer School, 1988*, eds D. Touretzky, G. E. Hinton, and T. J. Sejnowski, Morgan Kaufmann.

Donnellan, K. (1962), "Necessity and criteria," *Journal of Philosophy*, 59(22), 647–58.

Donnellan, K. (1966), "Reference and definite descrioptions," *Philosophical Review*, 75(3), 281–304.

Dow, W. (in preparation), *Content and Psychology*, Ph.D. dissertation, UCSD.

Dretske, F. I. (1981), *Knowledge and the Flow of Information*, MIT Press/Bradford Books.

Dretske, F. I. (1986), "Misrepresentation," in *Belief: Form, Content, and Function*, ed. Radu Bogdan, Clarendon Press, pp. 17–36.

Dretske, F. I. (1988), *Explaining Behavior: Reasons in a World of Causes*, MIT Press/Bradford Books.

Dreyfus, H. (1972/1979), *What Computers Can't Do*, 2nd (revised) ed, Harper and Row.

Dreyfus, H. and Dreyfus S. (1986), *Mind Over Machine*, New York: Free Press.

Enc, Berent (1983), "In defense of the identity theory," Journal of Philosophy, 80, 279–98.

Ericsson, K. and Simon, H. (1984), *Protocol Analysis, Verbal Report as Data*, MIT Press/Bradford Books.

Evans, G. (1977), "The causal theory of names," in *Naming, Necessity, and Natural Kinds*, ed. S. P. Schwartz, Cornell University Press. First published 1973 in *Aristotelian Society Supplementary Volume* 47.

Evans, G. (1982), *The Varieties of Reference*, Oxford University Press.

Feldman, J. A. and Ballard, D. H. (1982), "Connectionist models and their properties," *Cognitive Science*, 6, 205–54.

Festinger, N. (1957), *Cognitive Dissonance*, Stanford University Press.

Field, H. (1977), "Logic meaning, and conceptual role," *Journal of Philosophy*, 74 (July), 379–408.

Field, H. (1978), "Mental representation," in *Readings in Philosophy of Psychology*, Vol. 2, ed. N. Block, Harvard University Press, pp. 78–114.

French, P., Uehling, T., and Wettstein, H. (1979), *Contemporary Perspectives in the Philosophy of Language*, University of Minnesota Press.

Garfield, J. ed. (1987), *Modularity in Knowledge Representation and Natural Language Understanding*, MIT Press/Bradford Books.

Gergely, G. and Bever, T. (1986), "Related intuitions and mental representations of causative verbs in adults and children," *Cognition*, 23, 211–77.

Gibson, J. J. (1979), *The Ecological Approach to Visual Perception*, Houghton Mifflin.

Gleitman, H. (1986), *Psychology*, 2nd ed., Norton and Co.

Goldman, A. (1986), *Epistemology and Cognition*, Harvard University Press.

Goodman, N. (1956), *Fact, Fiction, and Forecast*, Bobbs-Merrill.

Goodman, N. (1978), *Ways of Worldmaking*, Hackett.

Gordon, R. (1986), "Folk psychology as simulation," *Mind and Language*, 1, 158–71.

Gould, S. and Lewontin, R. (1979), "The spandrels of San Marco and the Panglossian paradigm: a critique of the adaptionist paradigm," in *Proceedings of the Royal Society*, B205, 581–98.

Gregory, R. (1970), *The Intelligent Eye*, McGraw-Hill.

Grice, H. P. (1957), "Meaning," *Philosophical Review*, 66, 377–88.

Grice, H. P. (1975), "Method in philosophical psychology (from the banal to the bizarre)," *Proceedings and Addresses of the American Philosophical Association*, pp. 23–53.

Grice, H. P. and Strawson, P. (1956), "In defense of a dogma," *Philosophical Review*, 65, 141–58.

Hanson, N. (1961), *Patterns of Discovery*, Cambridge University Press.

Harman, G. (1972), *Thought*, Princeton University Press.

Harman, G. (1982), "Conceptual role semantics," *Notre Dame Journal of Formal Logic*, 23, 242–56.

Harman, G. (1983), "Beliefs and concepts: comments on Brian Loar," in *PSA 1982*, Vol. 2, ed. P. D. Asquith and T. Nickles, Philosophy of Science Association.

Haugeland, J. (1978), "The nature and plausibility of cognitivism," *Behavioral and Brain Sciences*, 1, 215–26.

Haugeland, J. (1981), *Mind Design*, MIT Press/Bradford Books.

Haugeland, J. (1985), *Artificial Intelligence: the Very Idea*, MIT Press/Bradford Books.

Hempel, C. (1965), *Aspects of Scientific Explanation*, New York: Free Press.

Hinton, G. E., McClelland, J. L., and Rumelhart, D. E. (1986), "Distributed representations," in *Parallel Distributed Processing: Explorations in the Microstructure of Cognition, Vol. 2: Psychological and Biological Models*, eds J. L. McClelland, D. E. Rumelhart, and the PDP Research Group MIT Press/Bradford Books.

Hookway, C., ed. (1984), *Minds, Machines and Evolution*, Cambridge University Press.

Horgan, T. and Woodward, J. (1985), "Folk psychology is here to stay," *Philosophical*

Review, 94; 197–226.

Israel, D. (1987), "The role of propositional objects of belief in action," CSLI Report, Stanford University.

Israel, D. and Perry, J. (1990), "What is information?," in *Information, Language and Cognition*, Vancouver Studies in Cognitive Science, Vol. 1, ed. P. Hanson, University of British Columbia Press, pp. 1–19.

Jackendoff, R. (1987), *Consciousness and Computational Mind*, MIT Press.

Jackendoff, R. (1989), "What is a concept that a person may grasp it?," *Mind and Language*, Vol. 4, 1 and 2, 68–102.

Johnson-Laird, P. (1978), "What's wrong with Grandma's guide to procedural semantics: a reply to Fodor," *Cognition*, 6, 249–61.

Johnson-Laird, P. (1983), *Mental Models*, Harvard University Press.

Johnson, M. (1988), "The end of Theory of Meaning," *Mind and Language*, 3, 28–42.

Kahneman, D., Slovic, P. and Tversky, A. (1982), *Judgment Under Uncertainty: Heuristics and Biases*, Cambridge University Press.

Kant, I. (1781/1968), *Critique of Pure Reason*, trans. N. K. Smith, St Martin's Press.

Kaplan, D. (1969), "Quantifying in," in Davidson and Hintikka (1968).

Kaplan, D. (1979a), "On the logic of demonstratives," in *Contemporary Perspectives in the Philosophy of Language*, University of Minnesota Press.

Kaplan, D., (1979b), "Dthat," in *Contemporary Perspectives in the Philosophy of Language*, University of Minnesota Press.

Kaplan, D. (1989), "Demonstratives: an essay on semantics, logic, metaphysics, and epistemology of demonstratives and other indexicals," in *Themes from Kaplan*, ed. J. Allmog, J. Perry, and H. Wettstein, Oxford University Press, pp. 481–563.

Katz, J. (1971), *The Underlying Reality of Language and Its Philosophical Import*, Harper and Row.

Katz, J. (1972), *Semantic Theory*, Harper and Row.

Kim, J. (1969), "Events and Their Descriptions: Some Considerations," in *Essays in Honor of C. G. Hempel*, eds N. Rescher et. al., Reidel.

Kim, J. (1976), "Events and property exemplifications," in *Action Theory*, eds M. Brand and D. Walton, Reidel.

Kim, J. (1984), "Concepts of supervenience," *Philosophy and Phenomenological Research*, 45(2), 153–76.

Kitcher, Patricia (1985), "Narrow taxonomy and wide functionalism," *Philosophy of Science*, 52, 1.

Kosslyn, S. (1980), *Image and Mind*, Harvard University Press.

Kripke, S. (1972/1980), *Naming and Necessity*, Harvard University Press.

Kripke, S. (1979), "A puzzle about belief," in *Meaning and Use*, ed. A. Margalit, Reidel.

Kripke, S. (1982), *Wittgenstein on Rules and Private Language*, Harvard University Press.

Kuhn, T. (1962), *The Structure of Scientific Revolutions*, University of Chicago Press.

Kuhn, T. (1989), "Possible worlds in humanities, arts and sciences," in *Possible Worlds in Humanities, Arts and Sciences*, Proceedings of The Nobel Symposium 65, ed. Sture Allen de Gruyter pp. 9–32. A slightly condensed form of the same paper is in press in Minnesota Studies under the title "Dubbing and redubbing: the vulnerability of rigid designation."

Landau, B. and Gleitman, L. (1985), *Language and Experience*, Harvard University Press.

Lepore, E. and Loewer, B. (1980), "Solipsistic semantics," *Midwest Studies in Philosophy*, 10, 595–614.

Lepore, E. and Loewer, B. (1987), "Dual aspect semantics," in ed. Lepore, E., *New Directions in Semantics*, Kluwer Academic Press.

Lettvin, J., Maturana, H., McCulloch, W., and Pitts, W. (1951), "What the frog's eye tells the frog's brain," *Proceedings of the IRE*, Vol. 47.

Levin, J. (1988), "Must reasons be rational?'" *Philosophy of Science*, 55.

Lewis, D. (1969), *Convention A Philosophical Study*, Harvard University Press.

Lewis, D. (1974), "Radical interpretation," *Synthèse*, 23, 331–44.

Lewis, D. (1974/1980), "Psychophysical and theoretical identifications," *Australasian Journal of Philosophy*, 50(3), 249–58; also in Block (1980), pp. 207–15.

Loar, B. (1980), "Syntax, functional semantics, and referential semantics," *Behavioral and Brain Sicences*, 3, 89–90.

Loar, B. (1981), *Mind and Meaning*, Cambridge University Press, UK.

Loar, B. (1982), "Conceptual role and truth conditions," *Notre Dame Journal of Formal Logic*, 23; 272–83.

Loar, B. (1983), "Syntax, functional semantics, and referential semantics," *Behavioral and Brain Sciences*, 3; 89–90.

Loar, B. (1987a), "Social content and psychological content," in *Contents of Thought: Proceedings of the 1985 Oberlin Colloquium in Philososphy*, eds R. Grimm and D. Merrill, University of Arizona Press.

Loar, B. (1987b), "Subjective intentionality," *Philosophical Topics*, Spring, 89–124.

Loar, B. (forthcoming-a), "Personal references," in *Information, Semantics, and Epistemology*, ed. E. Villanueva, Blackwell.

Loar, B. (forthcoming-b), "Phenomenal states," in *Philosophical Perspectives*, vol. 4, ed. J. Toberlin, Ridgeview, pp. 81–108.

Loar, B. (unpublished), published as Loar (1987a).

Loewer, B. (1987), "From information to intentionality," *Synthèse*, 70, 287–317.

Loewer, B. and Lepore, E. (1987), "Making mind matter more," *The Journal of Philiosophy*, 93, 630–42.

Loewer, B. and Lepore, E. (1989), "More on making mind matter," *Philosophical Topics*, 17 (1), 175–91.

Lycan, W. (1981), "Form, function, and feel," *Journal of Philosphy*, 78, 24–50.

Lycan, W. (1984), "The paradox of naming," in *Analytical Philosophy in Comparative Perspective*, ed. B. K. Matilal and J. L. Shaw, Reidel, pp. 81–102.

Lycan, W. (1987), *Consciousness*, MIT Press/Bradford Books.

Lycan, W. (1988), *Judgment and Justification*, Cambridge University Press.

Lycan, W. (1990), *Mind and Cognition*, Blackwell.

Lyons, W. (1986), *The Disappearance of Introspection*, MIT Press/Bradford Books.

McClelland, J. L. and Kawamoto, A. H. (1986), "Mechanisms of sentence processing: assigning roles to constituents," in *Parallel distributed Processing: Explorations in the Microstructure of Cognition, Vol. 2: Psychological and Biological Models*, eds J. L. McClelland, D. E. Rumelhart, and the PDP Research Group, MIT Press/Bradford Books.

McClelland, J. L., Rumelhart, D. E., and the PDP Research Group (1986), *Parallel Distributed Processing: Explorations in the Microstructure of Cognition, Vol. 2: Psychological and Biological Models*, MIT Press/Bradford Books.

McGinn, C. (1982), "The structure of content," in *Thought and Object*, ed. A. Woodfield, Oxford University Press, pp. 207–58.

McLaughlin, Brian P., (1989), "Type epiphenomenalism, type dualism, and the causal priority of the physical," in *Philosophical Perspectives*, 3, Ridgeview.

Marcus, Mitchell (1980), *A Theory of Syntactic Recognition for Natural Language*, MIT Press/Bradford Books.

Marr, D. (1982), *Vision*, Freeman and Co.

Mates, B. (1951), "Synonymity," *University of California Publications in Philosophy*, 25, 201–26. Reprinted in *Semantics and the Philosophy of Language*, ed. B. Linsky, University of Chicago Press, 1952.

Matthews, R. (1984), "Troubles with representationalism," *Social Research* 51, 1065–97.

Matthews, R. (1988), "The alleged evidence for representationalism." in *Rerepresentations*, ed. S. Silvers, Kluwer.

Millikan, R. (1984), *Language, Thought, and Other Biological Categories*, MIT Press/ Bradford Books.

Millikan, R. (1986), "Thoughts without laws; cognitive science with content," *The Philosophical Review*, 95, 47–80.

Millikan, R. (1989a), "In defense of proper functions," *Philosophy of Science*, 56(2), 288–302.

Millikan, R. (1989b), "Biosemantics," *Journal of Philosophy*, 86, 281–97.

Millikan, R. (1990a), "Truth rules, hoverflies, and the Kripke–Wittgenstein paradox," *Philosophical Review*, 99, 232–53.

Millikan, R. (1990b), "Seismographic readings for Explaining Behavior," *Philosophy and Phenomenological Research*, 50 (June).

Millikan 1991 "Compare and contrast Dretske, Fodor and Millikan on teleosemantics" *Philosophical Topics* 18.2

Millikan, R. (forthcoming-a), "The green grass growing all around," in *White Queen Psychology and Other Essays for Alice*, MIT Press/Bradford Books.

Millikan (forthcoming-b), "Explanation in biopsychology", ed., J. Heil and A. Mele, *Mental Causation*, Oxford University Press.

Morris, C. (1946), *Signs, Language, and Behavior*, Prentice-Hall.

Nagel, T. (1986), *The View from Nowhere*, Oxford University Press.

Nagel, T. (1965), "Physicalism," in Rosenthal (1971).

Nagel, T. (1974), "What is it like to be a bat?," *Philosophical Review*, 83, 435–50.

Newell, A. and Simon, H. (1981), "Computer science as an empirical inquiry," in *Mind Design*, ed. J. Haugeland, MIT Press/Bradford Books.

Newport, E. (forthcoming), "The critical periods for language acquisition," in *Biology and Knowledge: Structural Constraints on Development*, eds S. Carey and R. Gelman, Erlbaum.

Nisbett, R. and Wilson, T. (1977), "On saying more than we can know," *Psychological Review*, 84(3), 231–59.

Owens, J. (1987), "In defense of a different doppelganger," *Philosophical Review*, 96.

Papineau, D. (1987), *Reality and Representation*, Blackwell.

Peacocke, C. (1981), "Demonstrative thought and psychological explanation," *Synthèse*, 49, 187–217.

Peacocke, C. (1986), "Reply to Stephen Schiffer," *Mind and Language*, 1, 393–5.

Perry, J. (1977), "Frege on demonstratives," Philosophical Review, 86, 474–97.

Perry, J. (1979), "The problem of the essential indexical," *Nous*, 13, 3–12.

Pettit, P. and McDowell, J. (1986), *Subject, Thought and Context*, Oxford University Press.

Pierce, C. S. (1931), *Collected Papers*, Vol. 2; Harvard University Press.

Putnam, H. (1960), "Minds and machines," in *Mind, Language, and Reality* (Philosophical Papers, Vol. 2, 1975), Cambridge University Press, UK, pp. 362–85.

Putnam, H. (1962a), "It ain't necessarily so," *Journal of Philosophy*, 59(22), 658–71.

Putnam, H. (1962b), "Dreaming and 'depth grammar,' " in *Mind, Language, and Reality* (Philosophical Papers, Vol. 2 1975), Cambridge University Press, UK, pp. 304–24.

Putnam, H. (1975a), "The Meaning of 'Meaning' " in *Mind, Language, and Reality* (Philosophical Papers, Vol. 2, 1975), Cambridge University Press, UK pp. 215–71.

Putnam, H. (1975b), *Mind, Language and Reality*, Cambridge University Press, UK.

Putnam, H. (1978), *Meaning and Moral Sciences*, Routledge & Kegan Paul.

Putnam, H. (1983), "Computational psychology and interpretation theory," in *Realism and Reason*, Philosoplical Papers, (Vol. 3) Cambridge University Press.

Putnam, H. (1988), *Representation and Reality*, MIT Press.

Pylyshyn, Z. (1980a), "Computation and cognition: issues in the foundations of cognitive science," *Behavioral and Brain Sciences*, 3, 111–32.

Pylyshyn, Z. (1980b), "Cognitive representation and the process-architecture distinction," *Behavioral and Brain Sciences*, 3, 154–69.

Pylyshyn, Z. (1981), "The imagery debate: analog media vs. tacit knowledge," in Block (1981).

Pylyshyn, Z. (1984), *Computation and Cognition*, MIT Press/Bradford Books.

Quine, W. V. (1953), *From a Logical Point of View and Other Essays*, Harper & Row.

Quine, W. V. (1956a), "Quantifiers and propositional attitudes," in *Ways of Paradox and other Essays*, (2nd edn, 1976), Harvard University Press, pp. 185–96.

Quine, W. V. (1956b), "Carnap and logical truth," in *Ways of Paradox and other Essays*, (2nd edn, 1976), Harvard University Press, pp. 107–32.

Quine, W. V. (1960), *Word and Object*, MIT Press.

Quine, W. V. (1968), "Replies," *Synthèse*, 19(1), 264–322.

Quine, W. V. (1969), *Ontological Relativity and Other Essays*, Columbia University Press.

Quine, W. V. (1970), "On the Reasons for the Indeterminacy of Translation," *Journal of Philosophy*, 67, 178–83.

Ramsey, W., Stich, S., and Garon, J. (1990), "Connectionism, eliminativism and the future of folk psychology," *Philosophical Perspectives*, 4, in *Philosophy and Connectionist Theory*, ed. W. Ramsey, S. Stich, and D. Rumelhart, Erlbaum.

Rey, G. (1980a), "What are mental images?," in *Readings in the Philosophy of Psychology*, Vol. 2 (1981) ed. N. Block, Harvard University Press, pp. 117–27.

Rey, G. (1980b), "The formal and the opaque," commentary on Fodor, J. A., "Methodological solipsism as a research strategy in cognitive psychology," *Behavioral and Brain Sciences*, 3, 290–92.

Rey, G. (1980c), "Functionalism and the emotions," in *Explaining Emotions*, ed. A. Rorty, University of California Press, pp. 163–95.

Rey, G. (1983a), "A reason for doubting the existence of consciousness," in *Consciousness and Self-Regulation*, Vol. 3, eds R. Davidson, G. Schwartz, and D. Shapiro, Plenum, pp. 1–39.

Rey, G. (1983b), "Concepts and stereotypes," *Cognition*, 15, 237–62.

Rey, G. (1985), "Concepts and conceptions," *Cognition*, 19, 297–303.

Rey, G. (1986), "What's really going on in Searle's 'Chinese Room'," *Philosophical Studies*, 50, 169–85.

Rey, G. (1988a), "Towards a computational theory of akrasia and self-deception," in *Perspectives on Self-Deception*, eds B. McLaughlin and A. Rorty, University of California Press.

Rey, G. (1988b), "A question about consciousness," in *Perspectives on Mind*, ed. H. Otto and J. Tuedio, Reidel.

Richardson, R. (1979), "Functionalism and reductionism," *Philosophy of Science*, 46, 533–58.

Rorty, R. (1979), *Philosophy and the Mirror of Nature*, Princeton University Press.

Rosenthal, D. (1971), *Materialism and the Mind/Body Problem*, Prentice-Hall.

Rosenthal, D. (1990), *The Nature of Mind*, Oxford University Press.

Rumelhart, D. E., McClelland, J. L., and the PDP Rescarch Group (1986), *Parallel Distributed Processing: Explorations in the Microstructure of Cognition. Vol. 1: Foundations*, MIT Press/Bradford Books.

Ryle, G. (1949), *The Concept of Mind*, Hutchinson's University Library.

Salmon, N. (1986), *Frege's Puzzle*, MIT Press/Bradford Books.

Salmon, N. (1989), "Reference and information content: names and descriptions," in *Handbook of Philosophical Logic* Vol. 4, eds D. Gabbay and F. Guenther, Reidel, pp. 409–61.

Samet, J. (in preparation), *Nativism*, MIT Press/Bradford Books.

Schiffer, S. (1972), *Meaning*, Oxford University Press.

Schiffer, S. (1981), "Truth and the theory of content," in *Meaning and Understanding*, ed. H. Parret and P. Bouverese, de Gruyter.

Schiffer, S. (1986). "Peacocke on explanation in psychology," *Mind and Language*, 362–71.

Schiffer, S. (1987a), *Remnants of Meaning*, MIT Press/Bradford Books.

Schiffer, S. (1987b), "The 'Fido'-Fido theory of belief," in *Philosophical Perspectives, 1, Metaphysics*, ed. J. Tomberlin, Ridgeview.

Schiffer, S. (1988), "Reply to Mark Johnston," *Mind and Language*, 3, 58–62.

Schiffer, S. (1989), "Physicalism," in *Philososphical Perspectives, 3, Philosophy of Mind*, ed. J. Tomberlin.

Schiffer, S. (forthcoming-a), "The mode-of-presentation problem," in *Propositional Attitudes: the Role of Content in Logic, Language, and Mond*, eds C. Anderson and J. Owen, CSLI, Stanford University (distributed by University of Chicago Press).

Schiffer, S. (forthcoming-b), "Reduction and the explanatory role of content."

Schwarz, G. (1987), "Explaining cognition as computation," Master's thesis, department of philosophy, University of Colorado at Boulder.

Schwarz, S. (1978), "Putnam on artifacts," *Philososphical Review*, 88, 566–74.

Searle, J. (1980), "Minds, brains, and programs," *Behavioral and Brain Sciences*, 3, 417–24.

Searle, J. (1984), *Minds, Brains and Science*, Harvard University Press.

Searle, J. (in press), "Consciousness, Explanatory Inversion, and Cognitive Science," *Behavioral and Brain Sciences*.

Sellars, W. (1956), "Empiricism and the philosophy of mind," in *Minnesota Studies in the Philosophy of Science*, vol. 1, ed. M. Scriven, P. Feyerabend, and G. Maxwell, University of Minnesota Press, pp. 253–329.

Shoemaker, S. (1984), *Identity, Cause and Mind*, Cambridge University Press.

Skinner, B. (1957), *Verbal Behavior*, Appleton-Century-Crofts.

Smith, E., Medin, D., and Rips, L. (1984), "A psychological approach to concepts: comments on Rey's 'Concepts and Stereotypes,' " *Cognition*, 17, 265–74.

Smith, B. (in preparation), *A View from Somewhere: Foundations of Computation and Intentionality*.

Smith, E. and Medin, D. (1981), *Categories and Concepts*, Harvard University Press.

Smolensky, P. (1986). "Neural and conceptual interpretations of parallel distributed processing models," in *Parallel Distributed Processing: Explorations in the Microstructure of Cognition. Vol. 2: Psychological and Biological Models*, ed. J. L. McClelland, D. E. Rumelhart, and the PDP Research Group, MIT Press/Bradford Books.

Smolensky, P. (1987a), "On variable binding and the representation of symbolic structures in connectionist systems," Technical Report CU-CS-355-87, Department of Computer Science, University of Colorado at Boulder. (Revised version to appear in *Artificial Intelligence*.)

Smolensky, P. (1987b), "The constituent structure of connectionist mental states: a reply to Fodor and Pylyshyn," *Southern Journal of Philosophy*, 26 (Supplement), 137–63.

Smolensky, P. (1988a), "On the proper treatment of connectionism," *The Behavioral and Brain Sciences*, 11, 1–23.

Smolensky, P. (1988b), "Putting together connectionism – again," *The Behavioral and Brain Sciences*, 11, 59–74.

Smolensky, P. (1988c), "Commentary on Fodor and Pylyshyn," MIT Cognitive Science Colloquium, March, p. 29.

Smolensky, P. (forthcoming), *Lectures on Connectionist Cognitive Modeling*, Erlbaum.

Sober, E. (1984), *The Nature of Selection*, MIT Press/Bradford Books.

Stabler, E. (1983) "How are grammars represented?," *Behavioral and Brain Sciences*, 6, 391–421.

Stack, M. (unpublished), "Why I don't believe in beliefs and you shouldn't," paper delivered at annual meeting of Society for Philosophy and Psychology, 1980.

Stalnaker, R. (1984), *Inquiry*, MIT Press/Bradford Books.

Stalnaker, R. (1989), "On what's in the head," in *Philosophical Perspectives, Vol. 3, Philosophy of Mind and Action Theory*, ed. J. E. Tomberlin, Ridgeview, pp. 287–316.

Stampe, D. (1977), "Towards a causal theory of linguistic representation," in *Midwest Studies in Philosophy*, eds P. French, T. Uehling, and H. Wettstein, University of Minnesota Press, pp. 42–63.

Stich, S. (1978), "Autonomous psychology and the belief-desire thesis," *The Monist*, 61, 4. Reprinted in Lycan (1990) and Rosenthal (1990).

Stich, S. (1980), "Paying the price for methodological solipsism," *Behavioral and Brain Sciences*, 3, 97–8.

Stich, S. (1982), "On the ascription of content," in *Thought and Object*, ed. A Woodfield, Oxford University Press.

Stich, S. (1983), *From Folk Psychology to Cognitive Science: The Case Against Belief*, MIT Press/Bradford Books.

Stich, S. (1985), "Could man be an irrational animal? Some notes on the epistemology of rationality," in *Naturalizing Epistemology*, ed. H. Kornblith, MIT Press/Bradford Books, pp. 249–67.

Stich, S. (1986), "Are belief predicates systematically ambiguous?," in *Belief: Form, Content and Function*, ed. R. Bogdan, Oxford University Press.

Taylor, C. (1967), "Mind-body identity, a side issue?,", *Philosophical Review*, 76, 201–13.

Teller, P. (1984), "A poor man's guide to supervenience and determination," *Southern Journal of Philosophy*, 22 (Supplement), 137–62.

Tomberlin, J., ed. (1989), *Philosophical Perspectives 3: philosophy of mind and action theory 1989*, Ridgeview.

Touretzky, D. S. and Hinton, G. E. (1985), "Symbols among the neurons: details of a connectionist inference architecture," *Proceedings of the International Joint Conference on Artificial Intelligence*, pp. 238–43.

Turvey, M. T., Shaw, R. E., Reed, E. S., and Mace, W. M. (1981), "Ecological laws of perceiving and acting: in reply to Fodor and Pylyshyn", *Cognition*, 9.

Ullman, Shimon (1979), *The Interpretation of Visual Motion*, MIT Press.

van Gulick, R. (1989) "Metaphysical arguments for individualism, and why they don't work," in *Re-Representations*, ed. Philosophical Studies 40, Kluwer Academic.

van Gelder, T. (1989), "Compositionality: variation on a classical theme" (manuscript).

Walker, V. (in press), "In defense of a different taxonomy," forthcoming in *Philosophical Review*.

White, S. (1982), "Partial character and the language of thought," *Pacific Philosophical Quarterly*, 63, 347–65.

Wittgenstein, L. (1953/1968), *Philosophical Investigations*, 3rd edn, trans. G. E. M. Anscombe, Macmillan.

Yablo, Stephen (forthcoming), "Mental causation."

Index